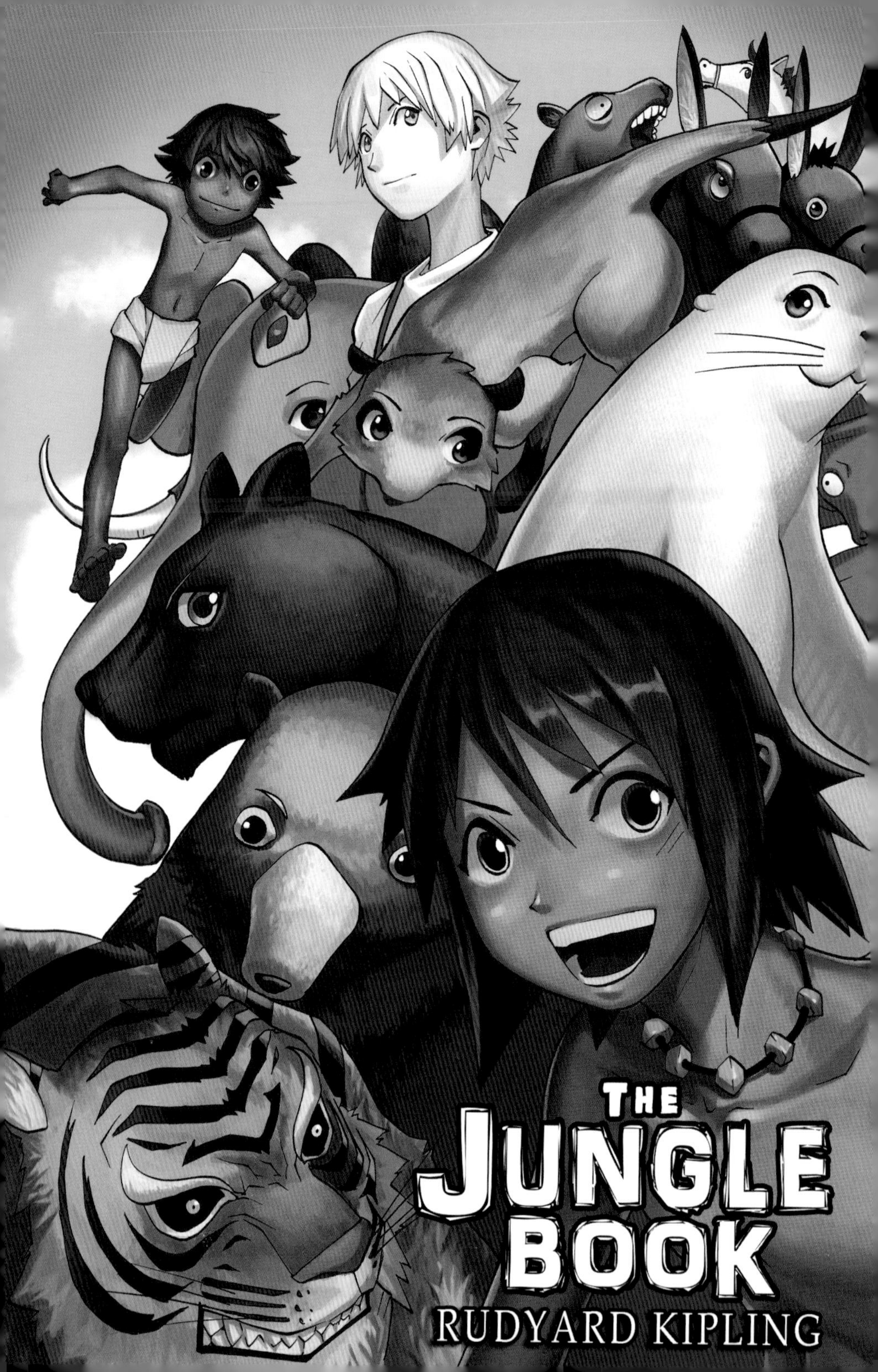
THE
JUNGLE
BOOK
RUDYARD KIPLING

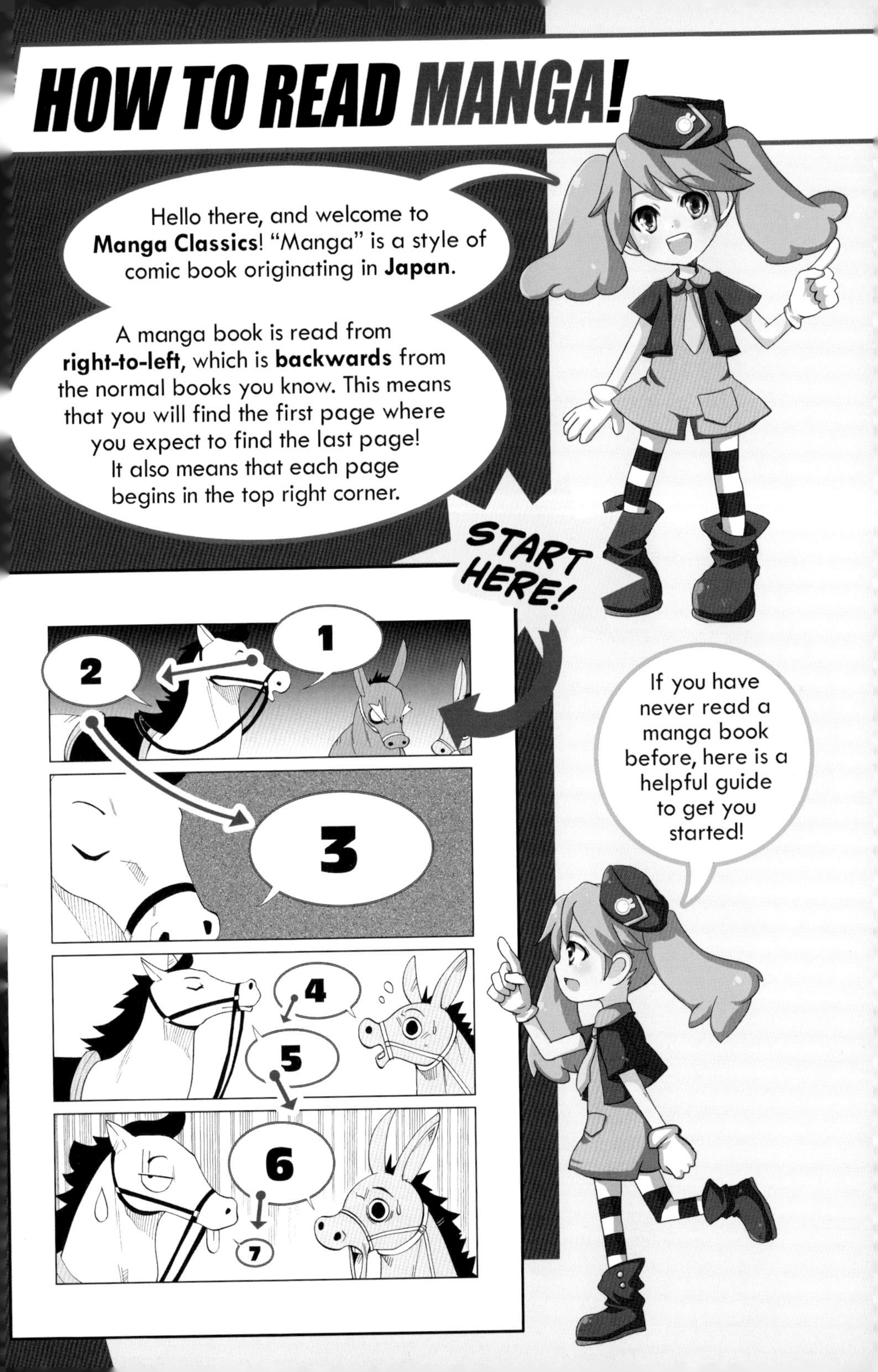
HOW TO READ MANGA!
Hello there, and welcome to Manga Classics! "Manga" is a style of comic book originating in Japan.
A manga book is read from right-to-left, which is backwards from the normal books you know. This means that you will find the first page where you expect to find the last page! It also means that each page begins in the top right corner.
START HERE!
If you have never read a manga book before, here is a helpful guide to get you started!
1
2
3
4
5
6
7

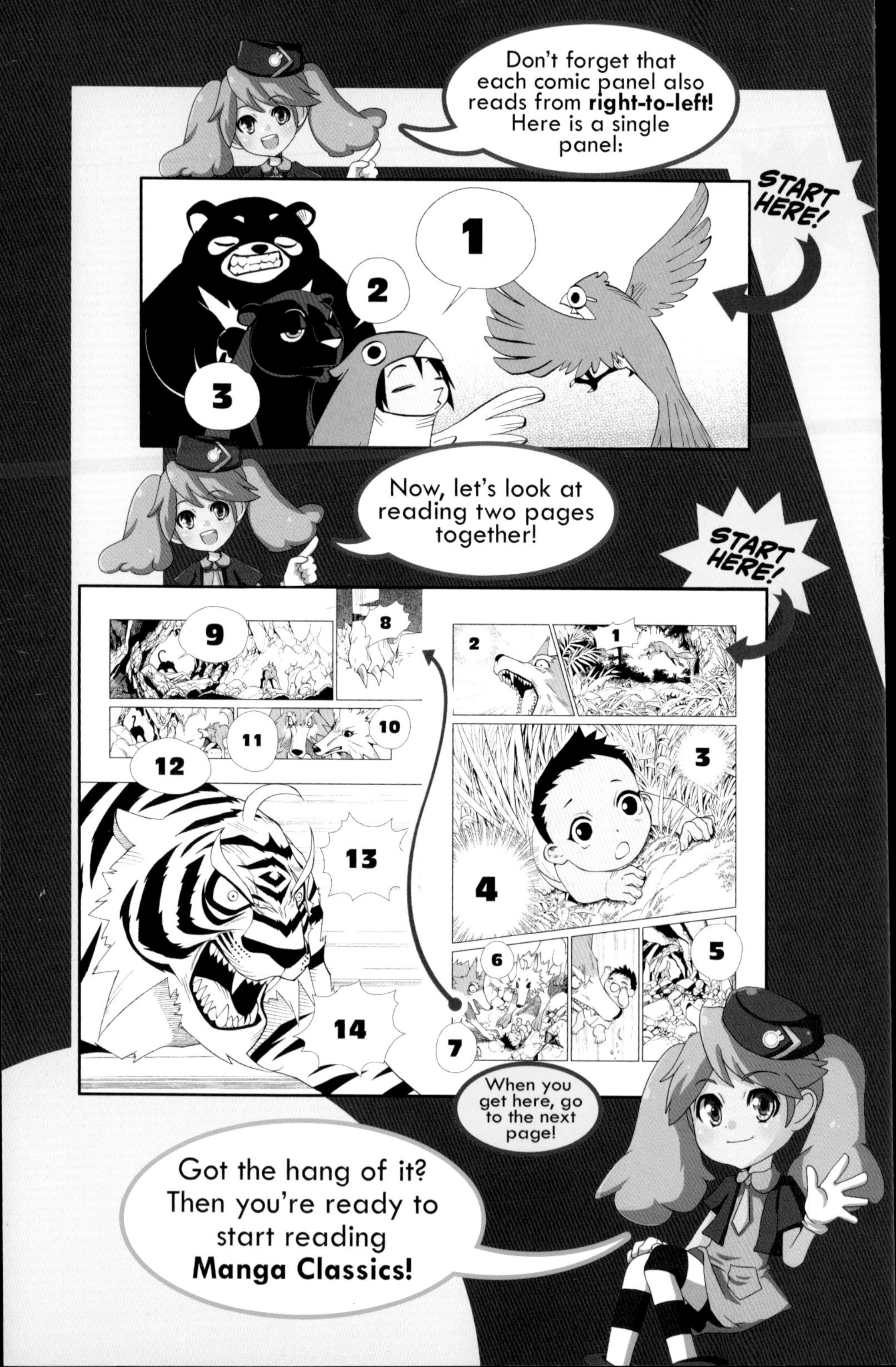
Don't forget that each comic panel also reads from **right-to-left!** Here is a single panel:
START HERE!
1
2
3
Now, let's look at reading two pages together!
START HERE!
1
2
3
4
5
6
7
8
9
10
11
12
13
14
When you get here, go to the next page!
Got the hang of it? Then you're ready to start reading **Manga Classics!**

CONTENTS:

STORIES -

POEMS -

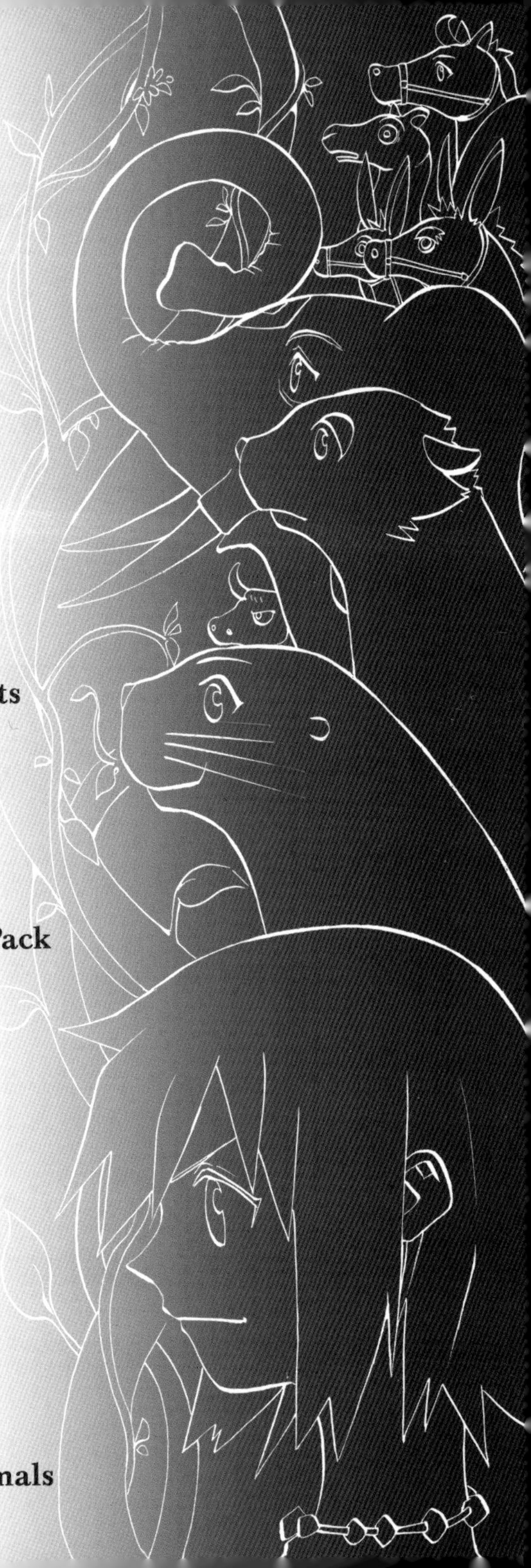

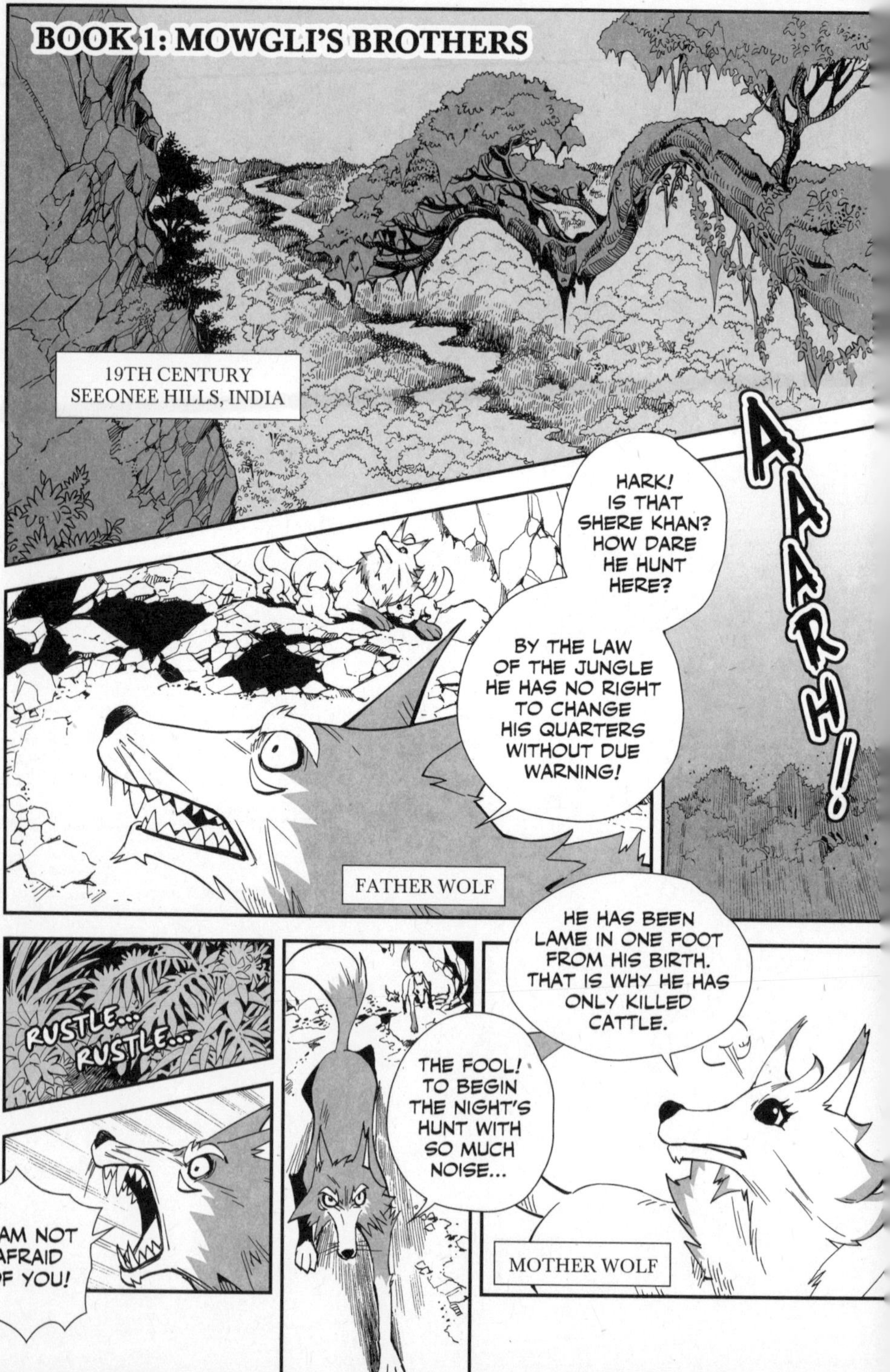
BOOK 1: MOWGLI'S BROTHERS
19TH CENTURY
SEEONEE HILLS, INDIA
AAARH!
HARK! IS THAT SHERE KHAN? HOW DARE HE HUNT HERE?
BY THE LAW OF THE JUNGLE HE HAS NO RIGHT TO CHANGE HIS QUARTERS WITHOUT DUE WARNING!
FATHER WOLF
HE HAS BEEN LAME IN ONE FOOT FROM HIS BIRTH. THAT IS WHY HE HAS ONLY KILLED CATTLE.
MOTHER WOLF
THE FOOL! TO BEGIN THE NIGHT'S HUNT WITH SO MUCH NOISE...
RUSTLE... RUSTLE...
I AM NOT AFRAID OF YOU!

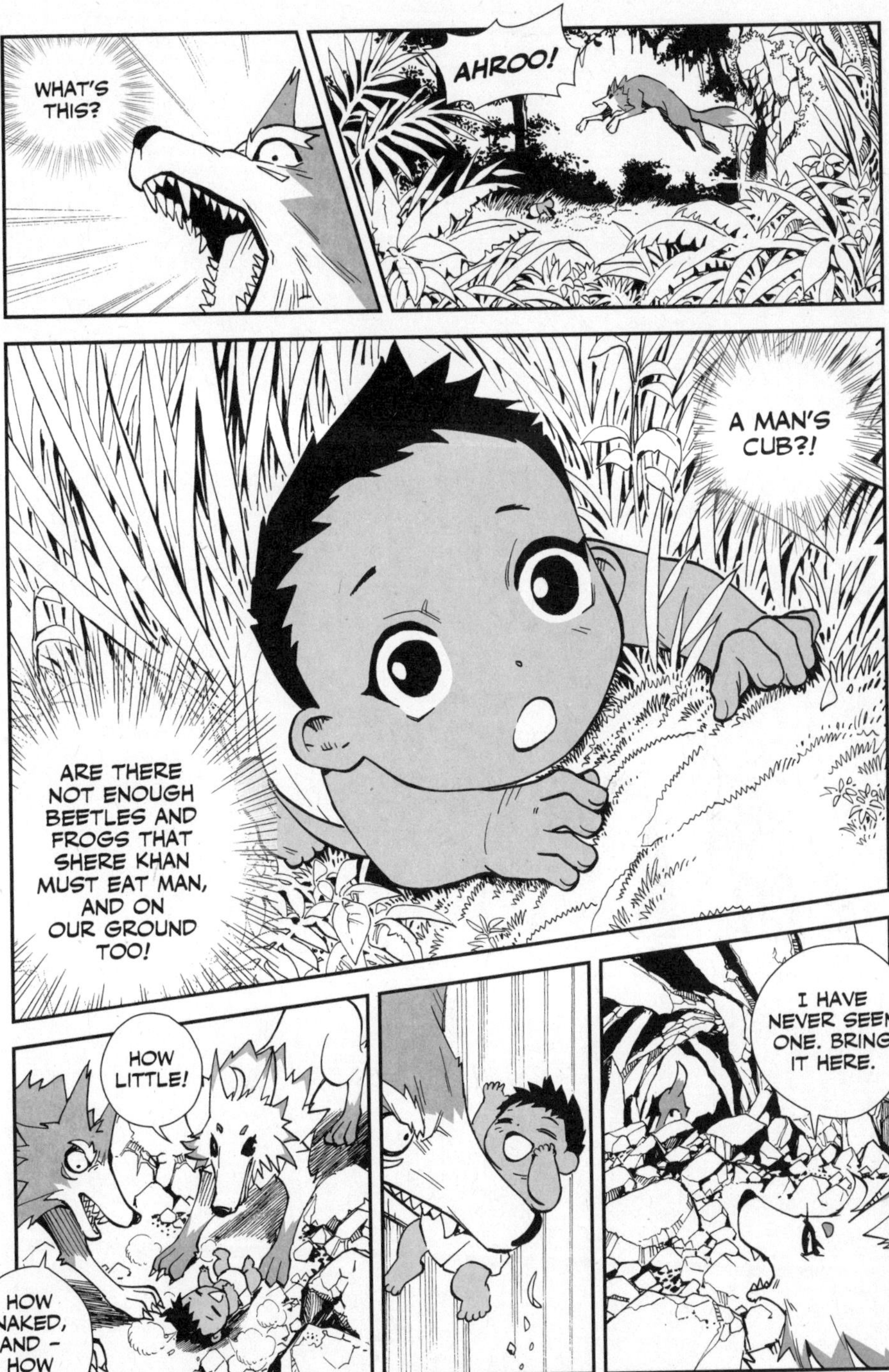
AHROO!
WHAT'S THIS?
A MAN'S CUB?!
ARE THERE NOT ENOUGH BEETLES AND FROGS THAT SHERE KHAN MUST EAT MAN, AND ON OUR GROUND TOO!
I HAVE NEVER SEEN ONE. BRING IT HERE.
HOW LITTLE!
HOW NAKED, AND - HOW BOLD!

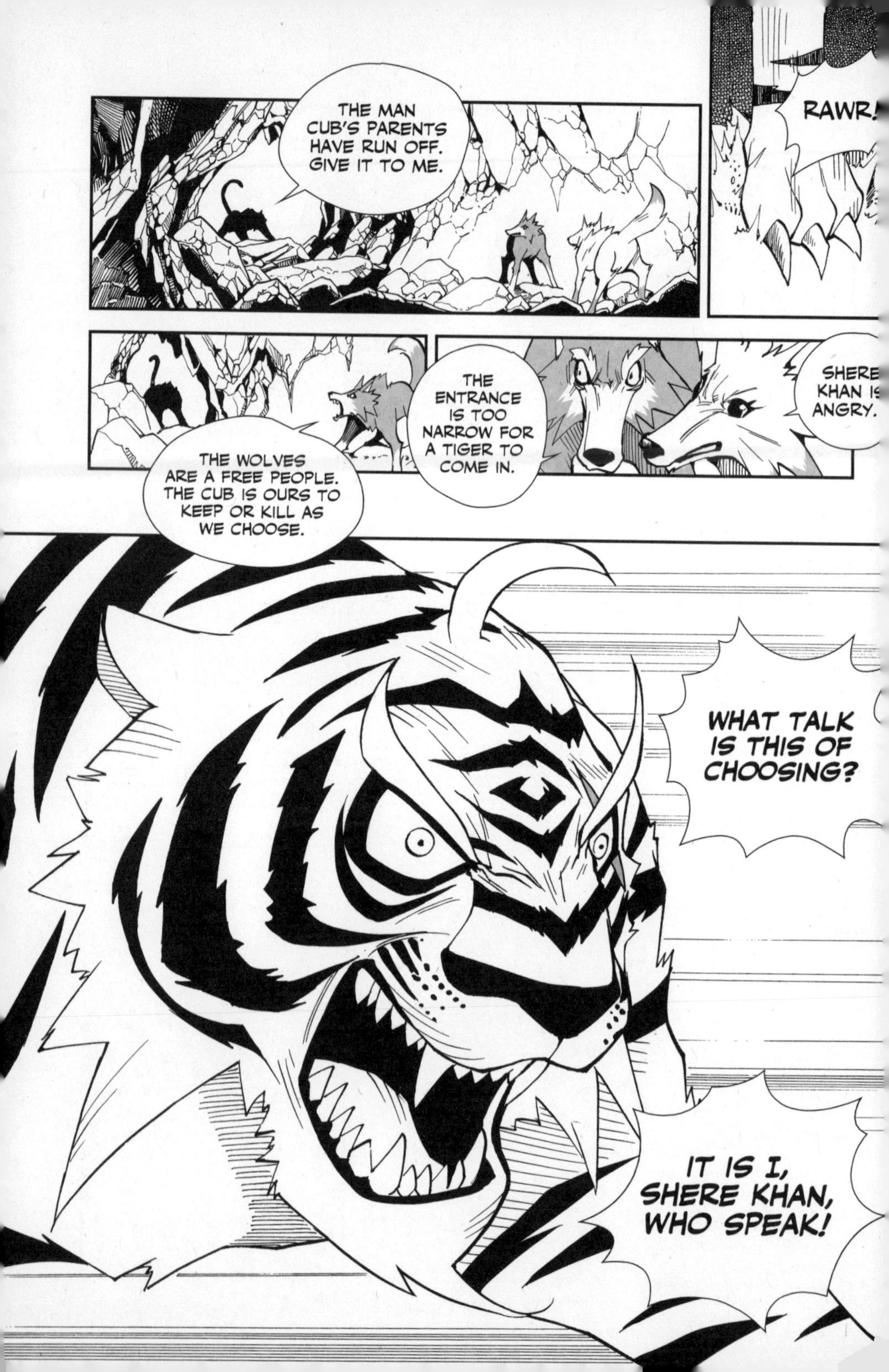
RAWR!
THE MAN CUB'S PARENTS HAVE RUN OFF. GIVE IT TO ME.
SHERE KHAN IS ANGRY.
THE ENTRANCE IS TOO NARROW FOR A TIGER TO COME IN.
THE WOLVES ARE A FREE PEOPLE. THE CUB IS OURS TO KEEP OR KILL AS WE CHOOSE.
WHAT TALK IS THIS OF CHOOSING?
IT IS I, SHERE KHAN, WHO SPEAK!

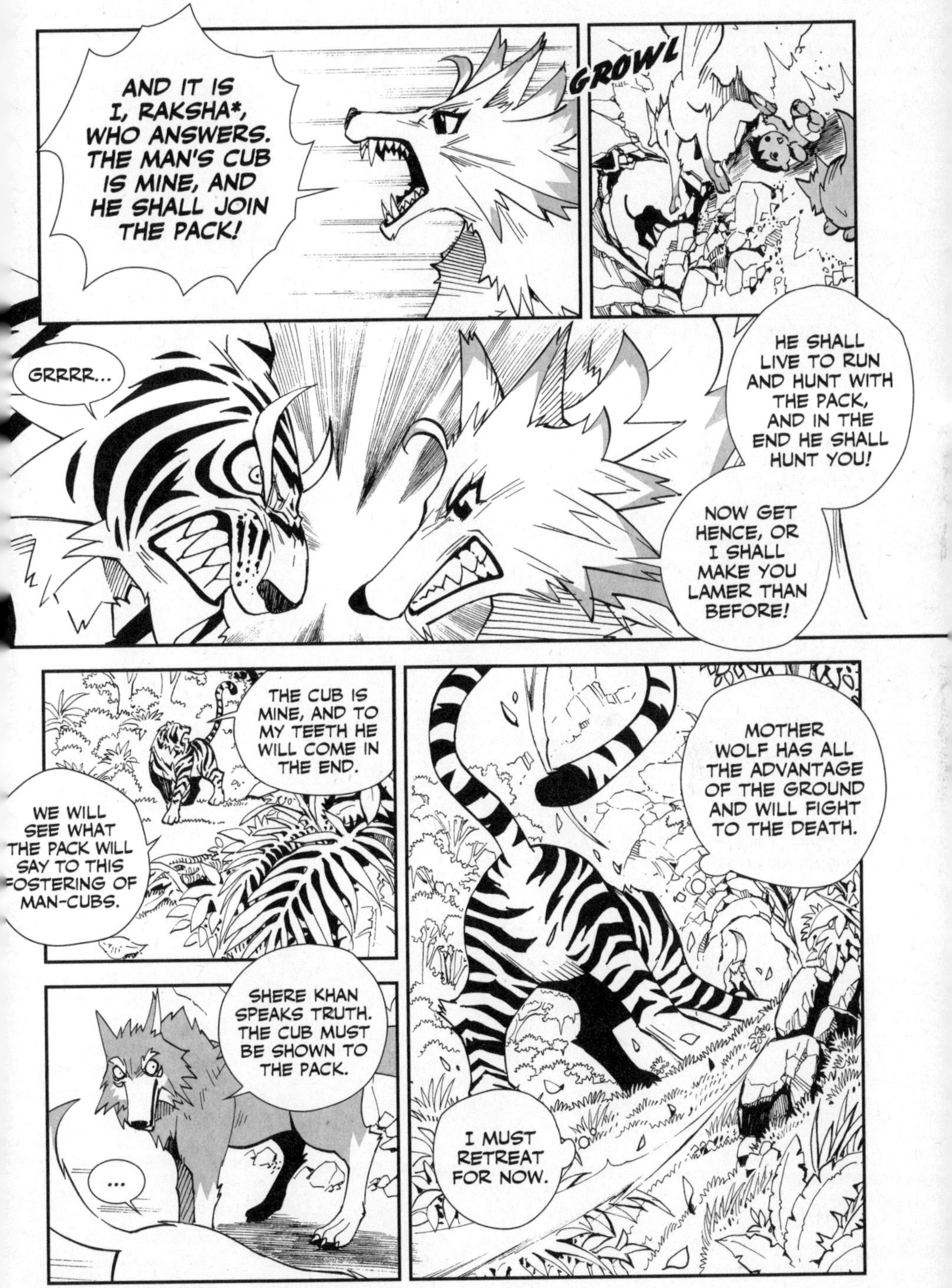
GROWL
AND IT IS I, RAKSHA*, WHO ANSWERS. THE MAN'S CUB IS MINE, AND HE SHALL JOIN THE PACK!
HE SHALL LIVE TO RUN AND HUNT WITH THE PACK, AND IN THE END HE SHALL HUNT YOU!
NOW GET HENCE, OR I SHALL MAKE YOU LAMER THAN BEFORE!
GRRRR...
MOTHER WOLF HAS ALL THE ADVANTAGE OF THE GROUND AND WILL FIGHT TO THE DEATH.
I MUST RETREAT FOR NOW.
THE CUB IS MINE, AND TO MY TEETH HE WILL COME IN THE END.
WE WILL SEE WHAT THE PACK WILL SAY TO THIS FOSTERING OF MAN-CUBS.
SHERE KHAN SPEAKS TRUTH. THE CUB MUST BE SHOWN TO THE PACK.
...

*RAKSHA: THE DEMON

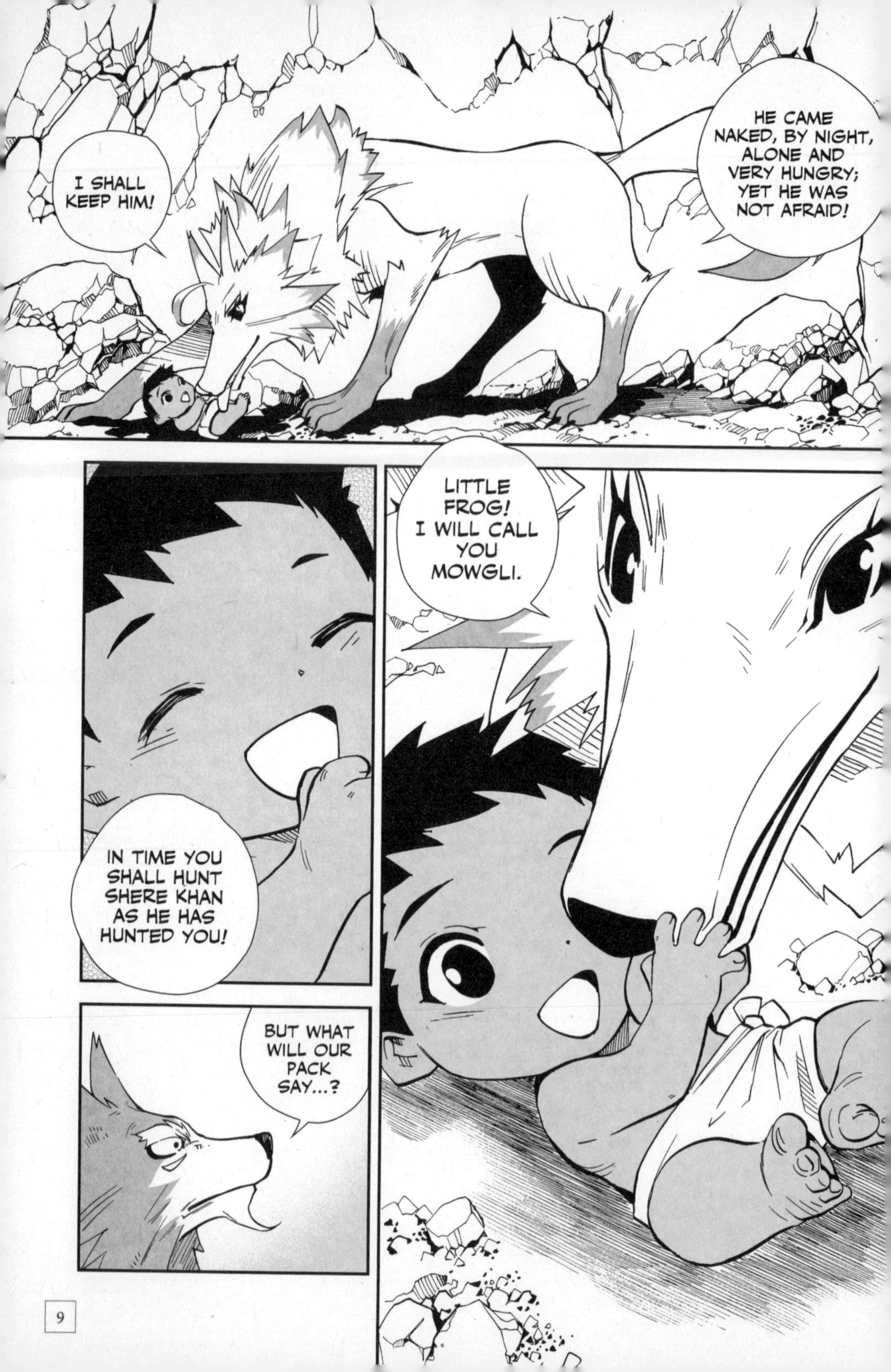
HE CAME NAKED, BY NIGHT, ALONE AND VERY HUNGRY; YET HE WAS NOT AFRAID!
I SHALL KEEP HIM!
LITTLE FROG! I WILL CALL YOU MOWGLI.
IN TIME YOU SHALL HUNT SHERE KHAN AS HE HAS HUNTED YOU!
BUT WHAT WILL OUR PACK SAY...?

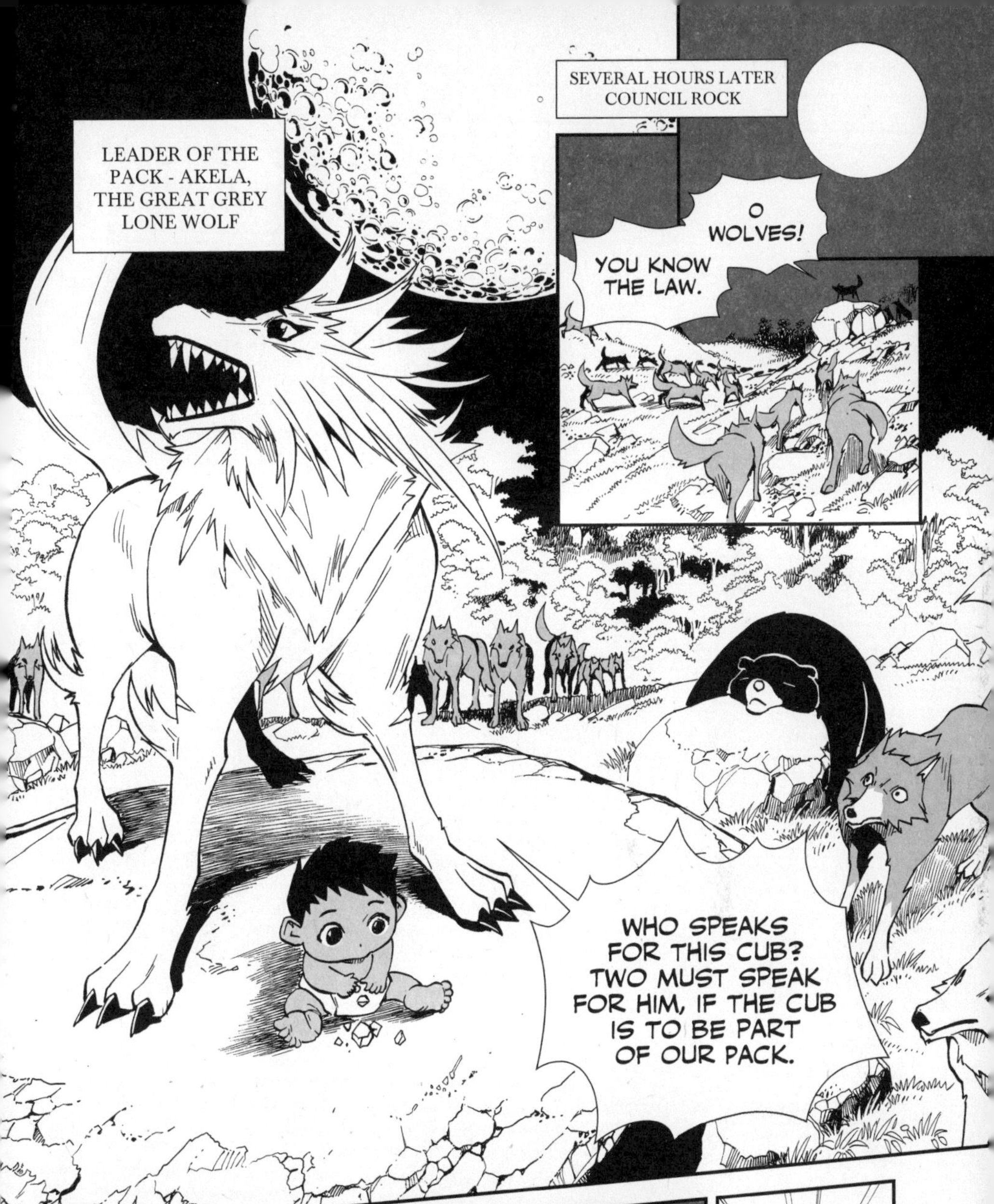
SEVERAL HOURS LATER COUNCIL ROCK
O WOLVES!
YOU KNOW THE LAW.
LEADER OF THE PACK - AKELA, THE GREAT GREY LONE WOLF
WHO SPEAKS FOR THIS CUB? TWO MUST SPEAK FOR HIM, IF THE CUB IS TO BE PART OF OUR PACK.
THAT CUB IS MINE!
GIVE IT TO ME!

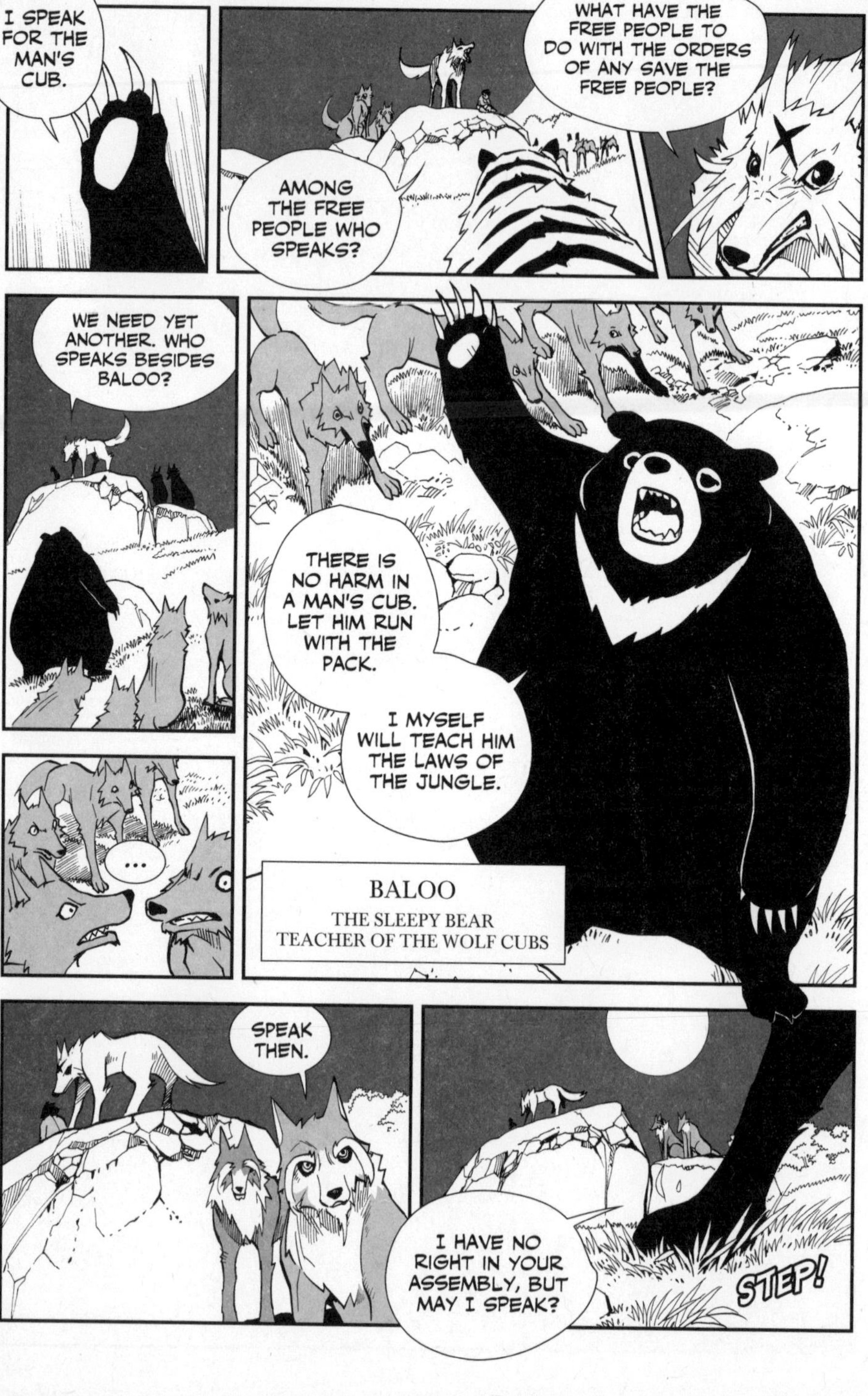
WHAT HAVE THE FREE PEOPLE TO DO WITH THE ORDERS OF ANY SAVE THE FREE PEOPLE?
AMONG THE FREE PEOPLE WHO SPEAKS?
I SPEAK FOR THE MAN'S CUB.
THERE IS NO HARM IN A MAN'S CUB. LET HIM RUN WITH THE PACK.
I MYSELF WILL TEACH HIM THE LAWS OF THE JUNGLE.
BALOO
THE SLEEPY BEAR
TEACHER OF THE WOLF CUBS
WE NEED YET ANOTHER. WHO SPEAKS BESIDES BALOO?
...
STEP!
I HAVE NO RIGHT IN YOUR ASSEMBLY, BUT MAY I SPEAK?
SPEAK THEN.

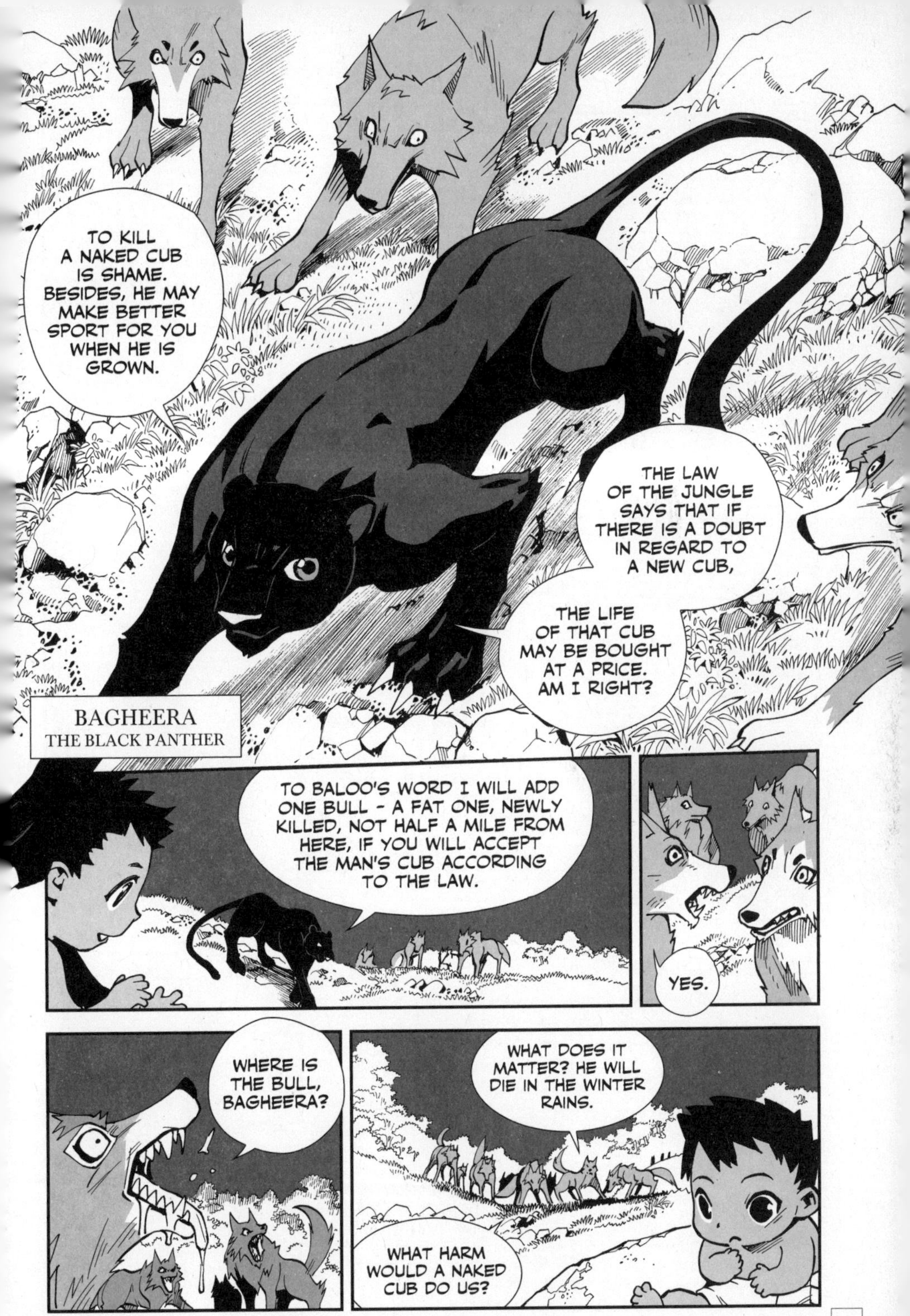
THE LAW OF THE JUNGLE SAYS THAT IF THERE IS A DOUBT IN REGARD TO A NEW CUB,
THE LIFE OF THAT CUB MAY BE BOUGHT AT A PRICE. AM I RIGHT?
TO KILL A NAKED CUB IS SHAME. BESIDES, HE MAY MAKE BETTER SPORT FOR YOU WHEN HE IS GROWN.
BAGHEERA THE BLACK PANTHER
YES.
TO BALOO'S WORD I WILL ADD ONE BULL - A FAT ONE, NEWLY KILLED, NOT HALF A MILE FROM HERE, IF YOU WILL ACCEPT THE MAN'S CUB ACCORDING TO THE LAW.
WHAT DOES IT MATTER? HE WILL DIE IN THE WINTER RAINS.
WHAT HARM WOULD A NAKED CUB DO US?
WHERE IS THE BULL, BAGHEERA?

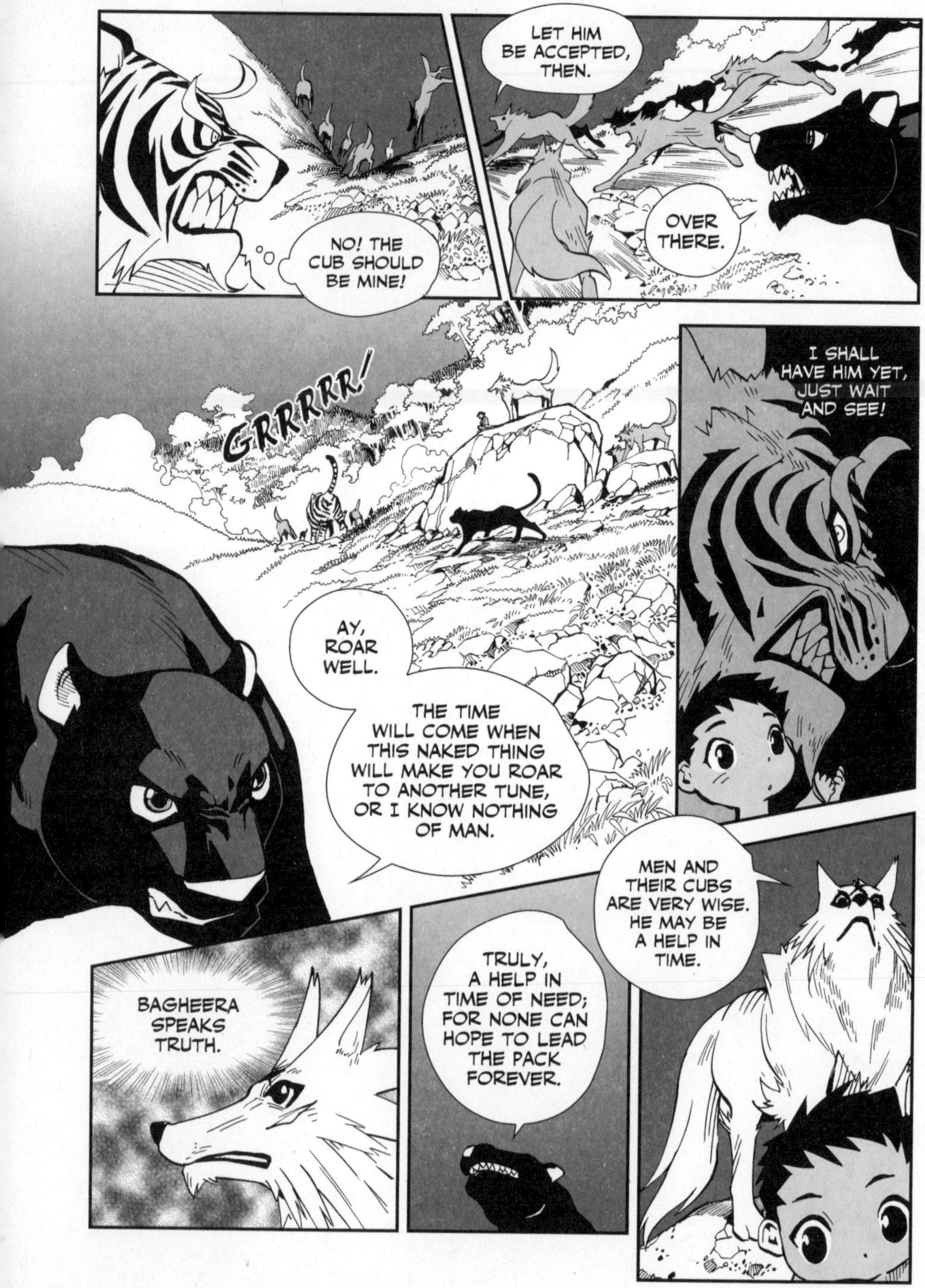
LET HIM BE ACCEPTED, THEN.
OVER THERE.
NO! THE CUB SHOULD BE MINE!
I SHALL HAVE HIM YET, JUST WAIT AND SEE!
GRRRRR!
AY, ROAR WELL.
THE TIME WILL COME WHEN THIS NAKED THING WILL MAKE YOU ROAR TO ANOTHER TUNE, OR I KNOW NOTHING OF MAN.
MEN AND THEIR CUBS ARE VERY WISE. HE MAY BE A HELP IN TIME.
TRULY, A HELP IN TIME OF NEED; FOR NONE CAN HOPE TO LEAD THE PACK FOREVER.
BAGHEERA SPEAKS TRUTH.

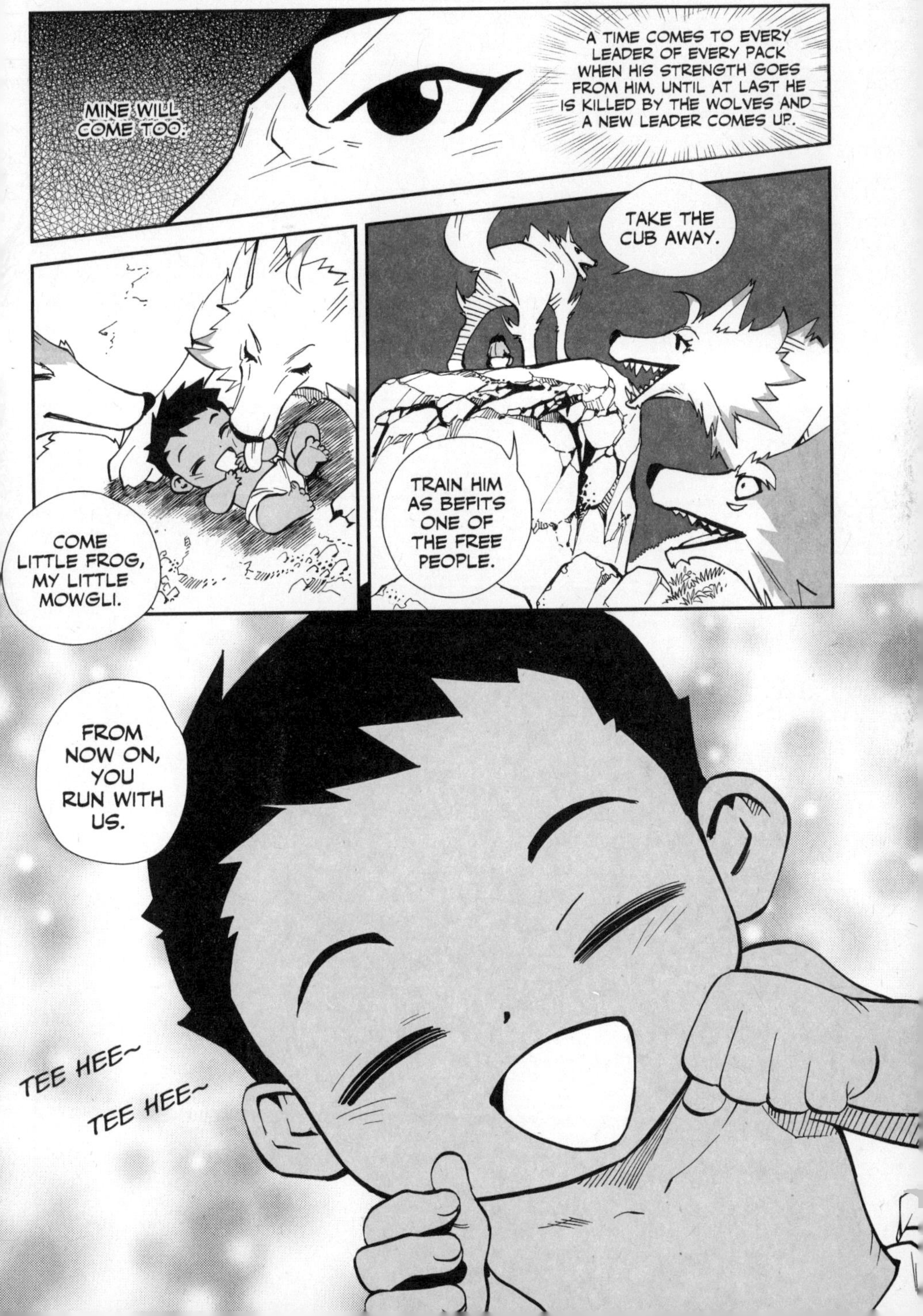
A TIME COMES TO EVERY LEADER OF EVERY PACK WHEN HIS STRENGTH GOES FROM HIM, UNTIL AT LAST HE IS KILLED BY THE WOLVES AND A NEW LEADER COMES UP.
MINE WILL COME TOO.
TAKE THE CUB AWAY.
TRAIN HIM AS BEFITS ONE OF THE FREE PEOPLE.
COME LITTLE FROG, MY LITTLE MOWGLI.
FROM NOW ON, YOU RUN WITH US.
TEE HEE~
TEE HEE~

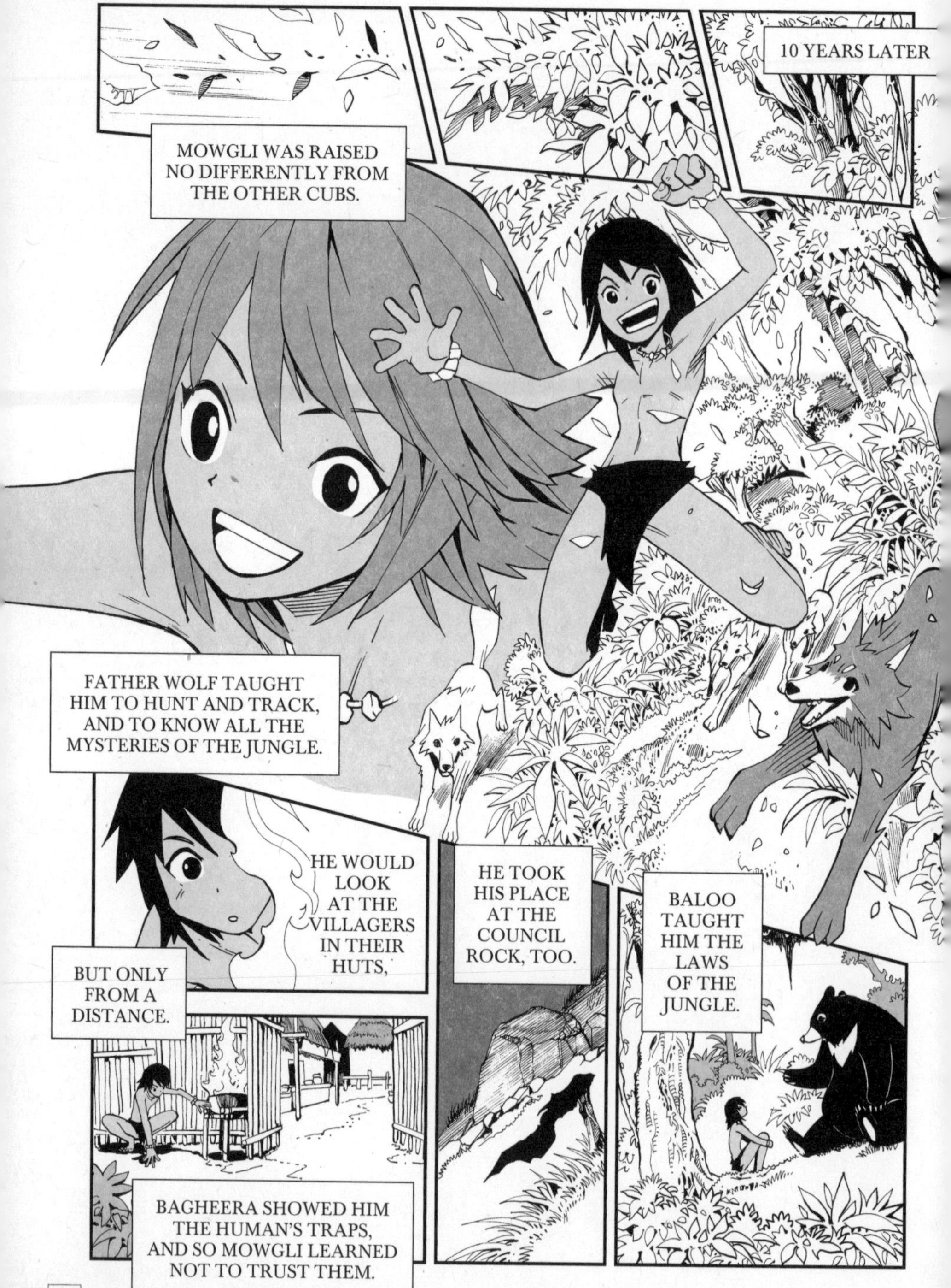
10 YEARS LATER
MOWGLI WAS RAISED NO DIFFERENTLY FROM THE OTHER CUBS.
FATHER WOLF TAUGHT HIM TO HUNT AND TRACK, AND TO KNOW ALL THE MYSTERIES OF THE JUNGLE.
BALOO TAUGHT HIM THE LAWS OF THE JUNGLE.
HE TOOK HIS PLACE AT THE COUNCIL ROCK, TOO.
HE WOULD LOOK AT THE VILLAGERS IN THEIR HUTS,
BUT ONLY FROM A DISTANCE.
BAGHEERA SHOWED HIM THE HUMAN'S TRAPS, AND SO MOWGLI LEARNED NOT TO TRUST THEM.

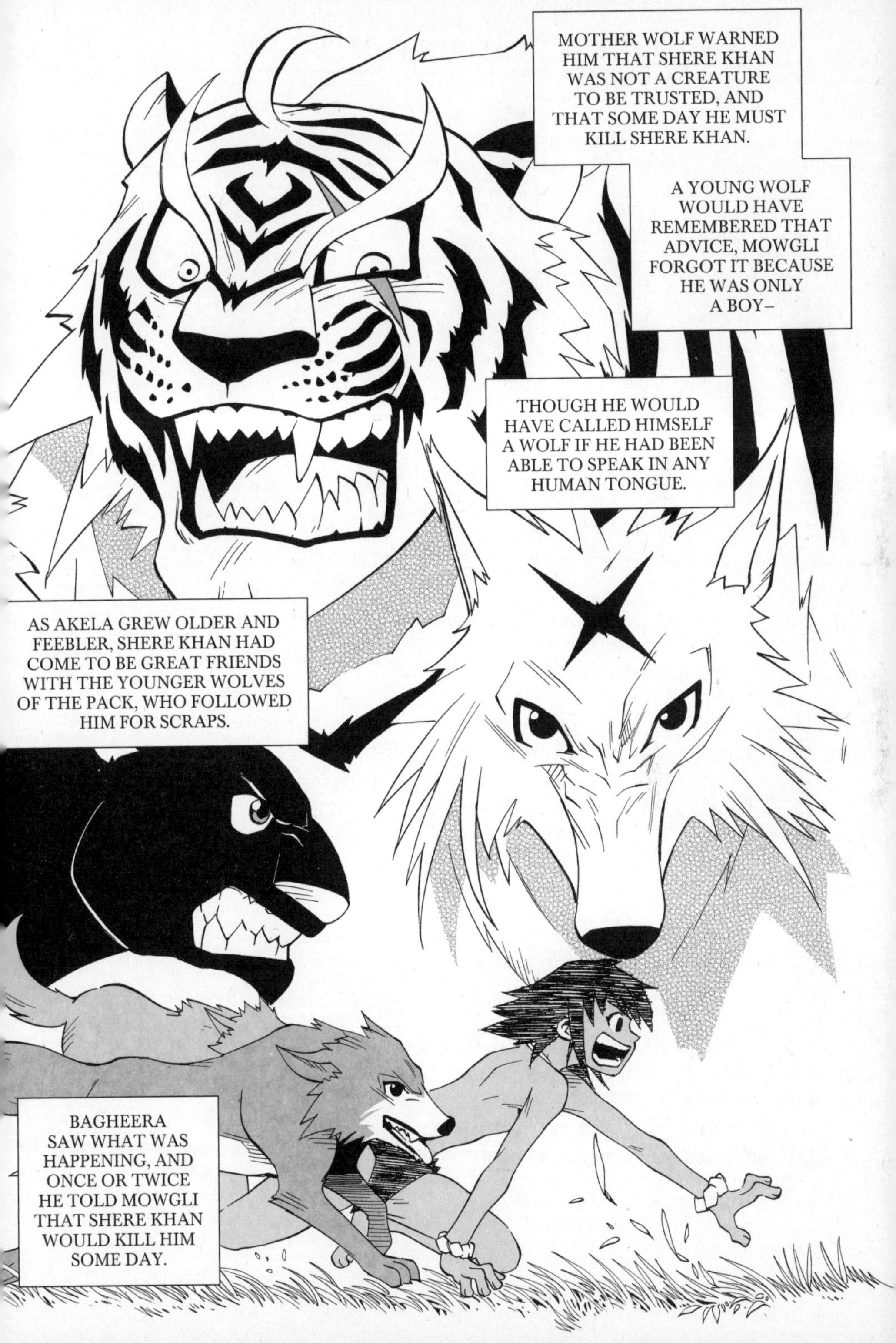
MOTHER WOLF WARNED HIM THAT SHERE KHAN WAS NOT A CREATURE TO BE TRUSTED, AND THAT SOME DAY HE MUST KILL SHERE KHAN.
A YOUNG WOLF WOULD HAVE REMEMBERED THAT ADVICE, MOWGLI FORGOT IT BECAUSE HE WAS ONLY A BOY–
THOUGH HE WOULD HAVE CALLED HIMSELF A WOLF IF HE HAD BEEN ABLE TO SPEAK IN ANY HUMAN TONGUE.
AS AKELA GREW OLDER AND FEEBLER, SHERE KHAN HAD COME TO BE GREAT FRIENDS WITH THE YOUNGER WOLVES OF THE PACK, WHO FOLLOWED HIM FOR SCRAPS.
BAGHEERA SAW WHAT WAS HAPPENING, AND ONCE OR TWICE HE TOLD MOWGLI THAT SHERE KHAN WOULD KILL HIM SOME DAY.

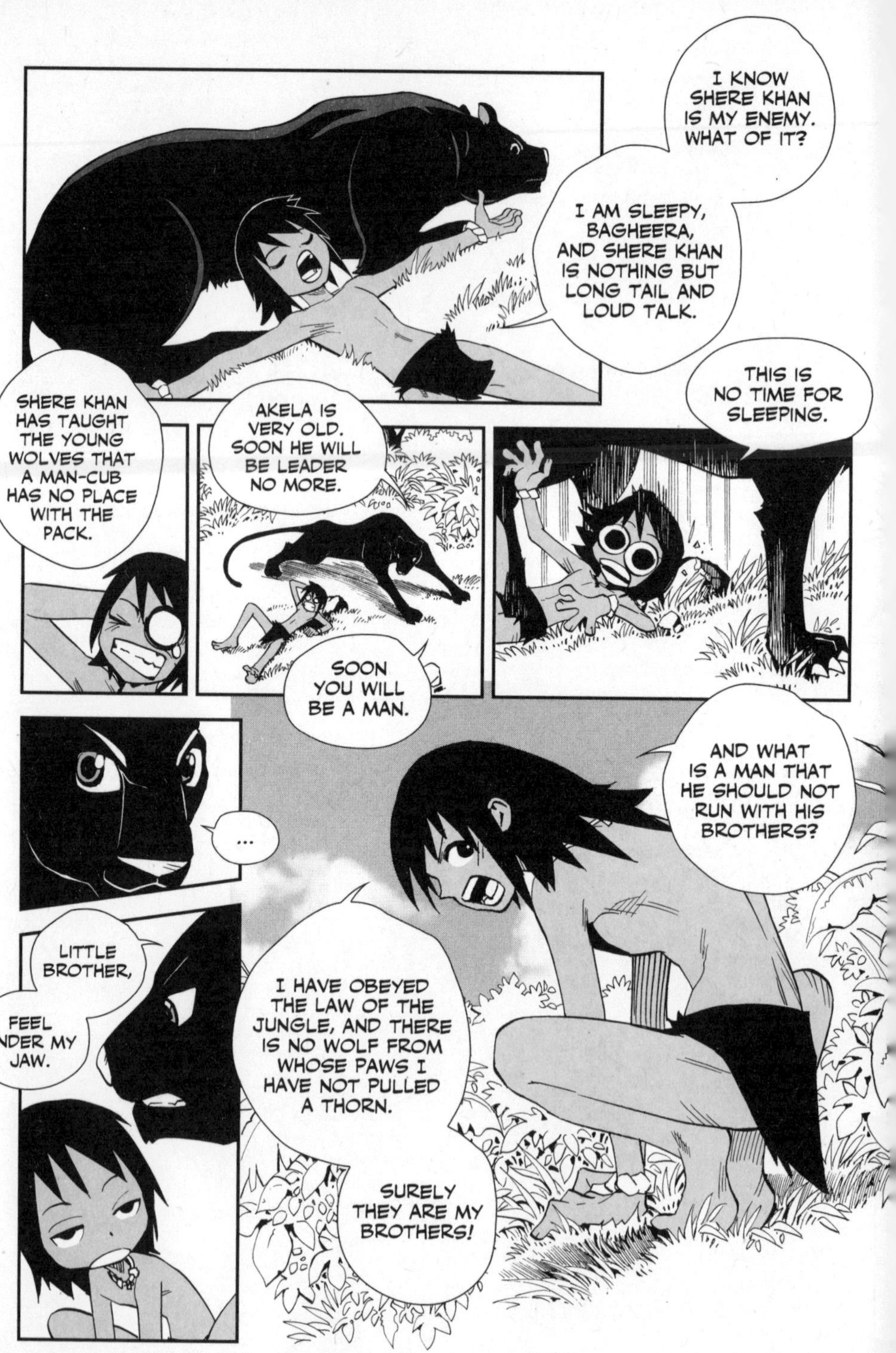
I KNOW SHERE KHAN IS MY ENEMY. WHAT OF IT?
I AM SLEEPY, BAGHEERA, AND SHERE KHAN IS NOTHING BUT LONG TAIL AND LOUD TALK.
THIS IS NO TIME FOR SLEEPING.
AKELA IS VERY OLD. SOON HE WILL BE LEADER NO MORE.
SOON YOU WILL BE A MAN.
SHERE KHAN HAS TAUGHT THE YOUNG WOLVES THAT A MAN-CUB HAS NO PLACE WITH THE PACK.
AND WHAT IS A MAN THAT HE SHOULD NOT RUN WITH HIS BROTHERS?
I HAVE OBEYED THE LAW OF THE JUNGLE, AND THERE IS NO WOLF FROM WHOSE PAWS I HAVE NOT PULLED A THORN.
SURELY THEY ARE MY BROTHERS!
...
LITTLE BROTHER,
FEEL UNDER MY JAW.

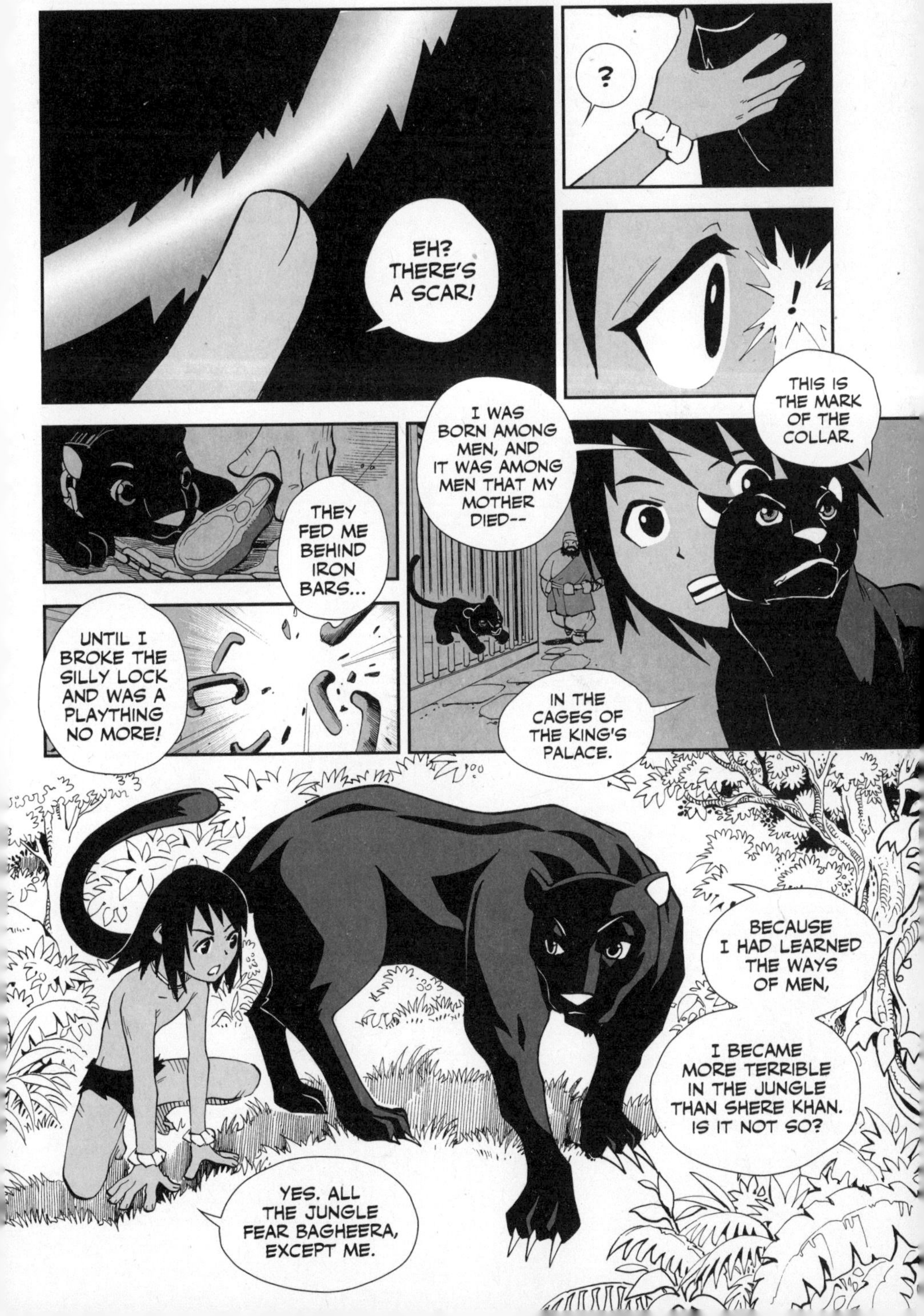
?
!
EH? THERE'S A SCAR!
THIS IS THE MARK OF THE COLLAR.
I WAS BORN AMONG MEN, AND IT WAS AMONG MEN THAT MY MOTHER DIED--
IN THE CAGES OF THE KING'S PALACE.
THEY FED ME BEHIND IRON BARS...
UNTIL I BROKE THE SILLY LOCK AND WAS A PLAYTHING NO MORE!
BECAUSE I HAD LEARNED THE WAYS OF MEN,
I BECAME MORE TERRIBLE IN THE JUNGLE THAN SHERE KHAN. IS IT NOT SO?
YES. ALL THE JUNGLE FEAR BAGHEERA, EXCEPT ME.

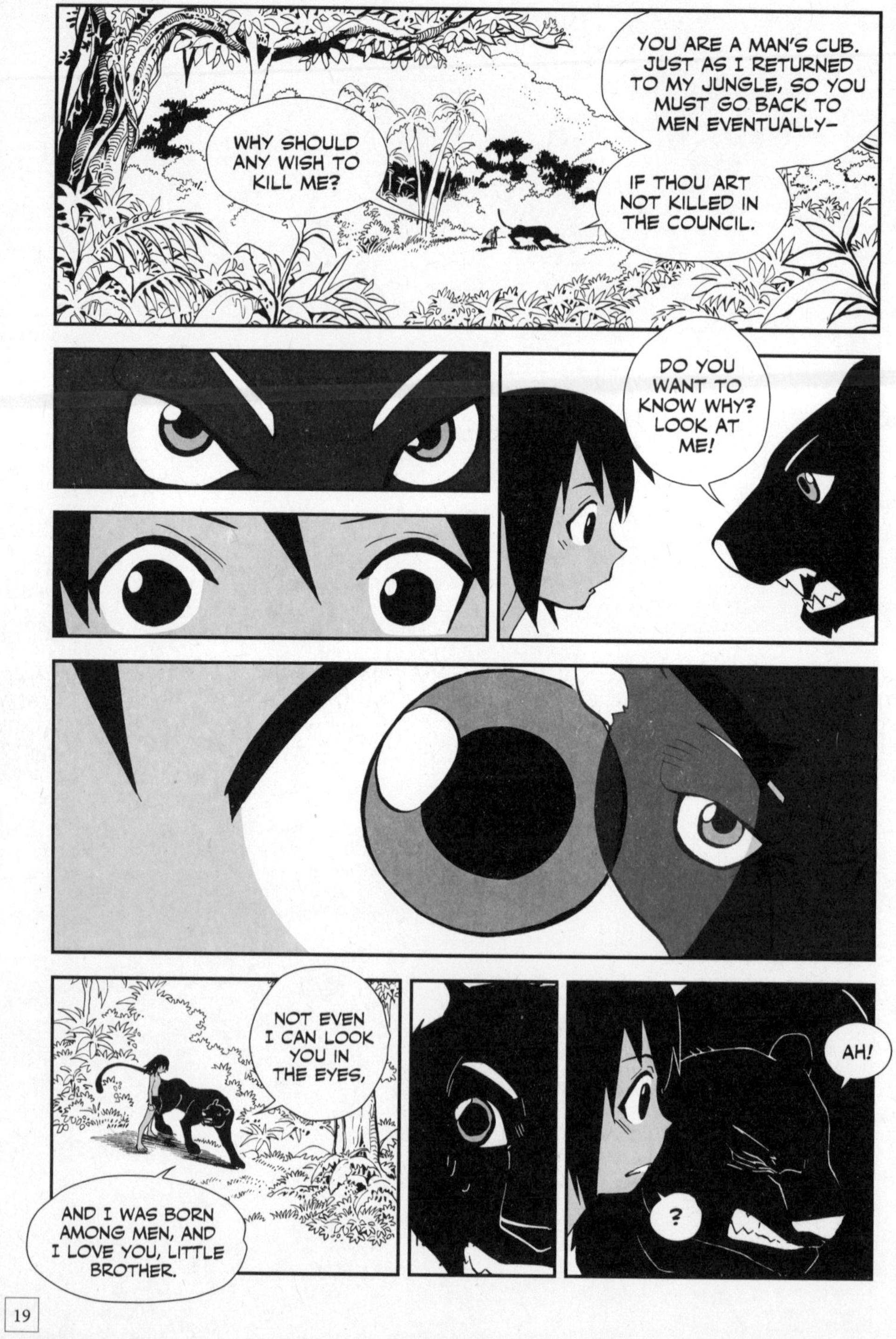
YOU ARE A MAN'S CUB. JUST AS I RETURNED TO MY JUNGLE, SO YOU MUST GO BACK TO MEN EVENTUALLY–
IF THOU ART NOT KILLED IN THE COUNCIL.
WHY SHOULD ANY WISH TO KILL ME?
DO YOU WANT TO KNOW WHY? LOOK AT ME!
AH!
?
NOT EVEN I CAN LOOK YOU IN THE EYES,
AND I WAS BORN AMONG MEN, AND I LOVE YOU, LITTLE BROTHER.

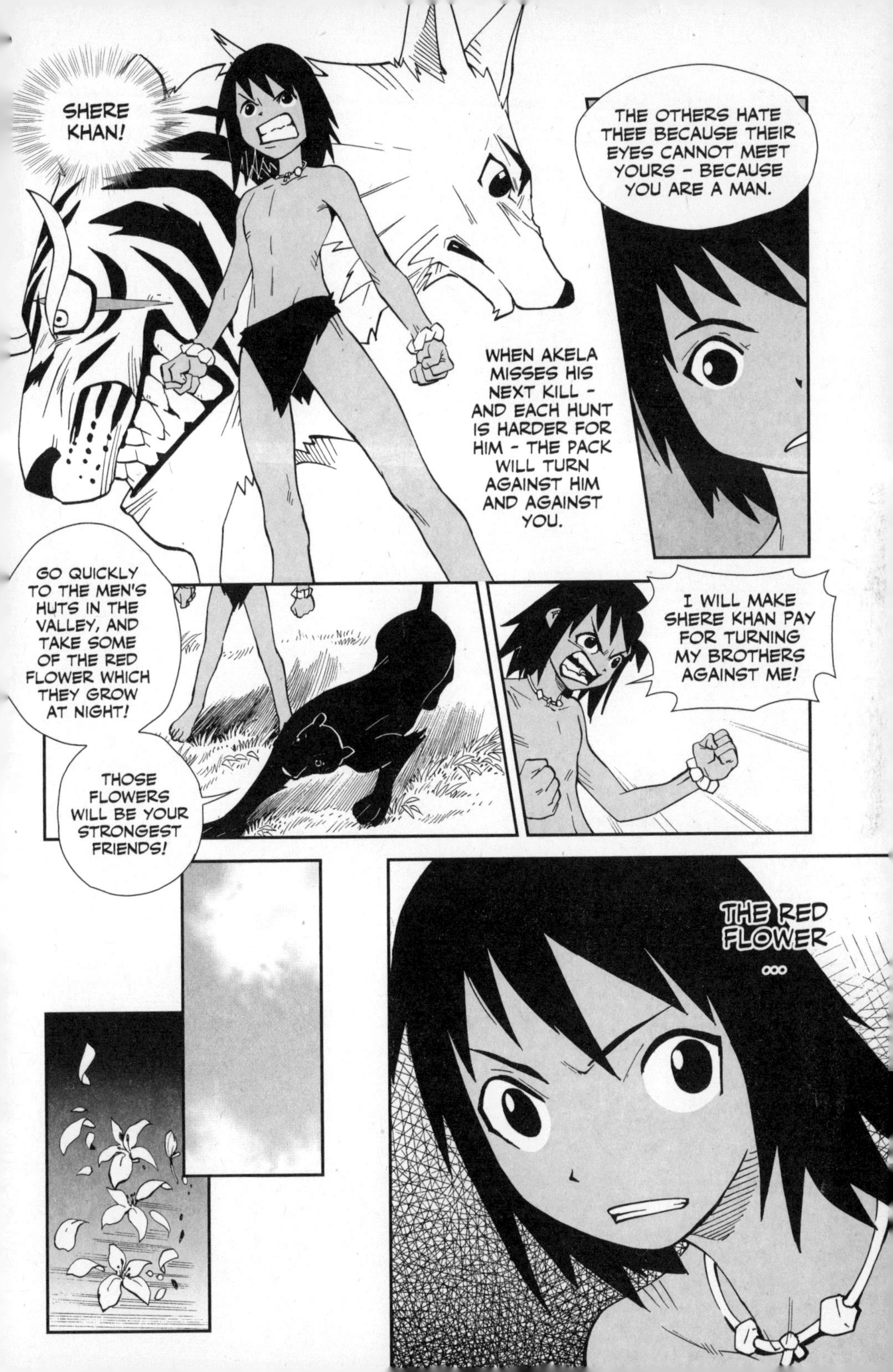
THE OTHERS HATE THEE BECAUSE THEIR EYES CANNOT MEET YOURS - BECAUSE YOU ARE A MAN.
SHERE KHAN!
WHEN AKELA MISSES HIS NEXT KILL - AND EACH HUNT IS HARDER FOR HIM - THE PACK WILL TURN AGAINST HIM AND AGAINST YOU.
I WILL MAKE SHERE KHAN PAY FOR TURNING MY BROTHERS AGAINST ME!
GO QUICKLY TO THE MEN'S HUTS IN THE VALLEY, AND TAKE SOME OF THE RED FLOWER WHICH THEY GROW AT NIGHT!
THOSE FLOWERS WILL BE YOUR STRONGEST FRIENDS!
THE RED FLOWER ...

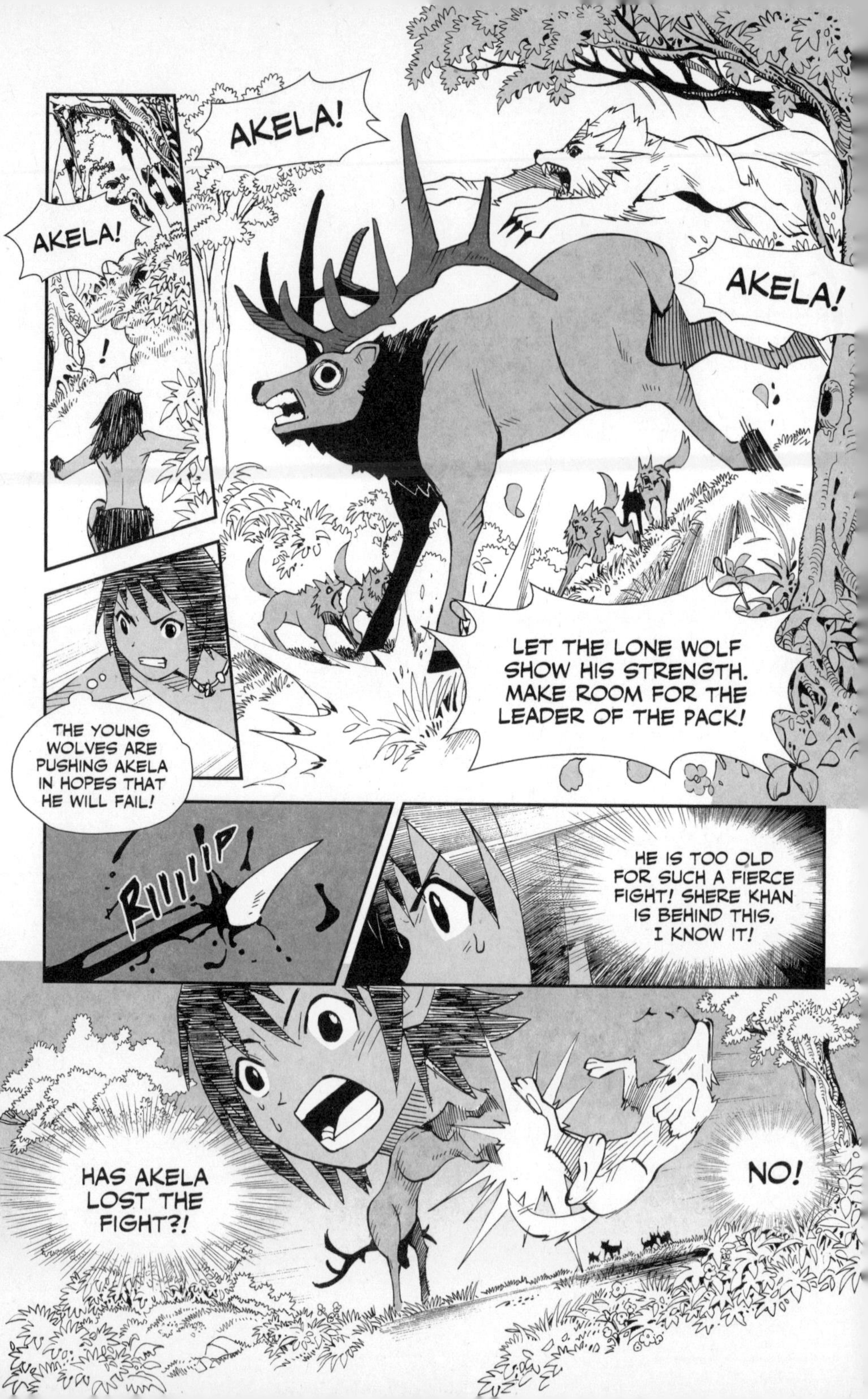
AKELA!
AKELA!
LET THE LONE WOLF SHOW HIS STRENGTH. MAKE ROOM FOR THE LEADER OF THE PACK!
AKELA!
!
THE YOUNG WOLVES ARE PUSHING AKELA IN HOPES THAT HE WILL FAIL!
HE IS TOO OLD FOR SUCH A FIERCE FIGHT! SHERE KHAN IS BEHIND THIS, I KNOW IT!
RIIIIIP!
NO!
HAS AKELA LOST THE FIGHT?!

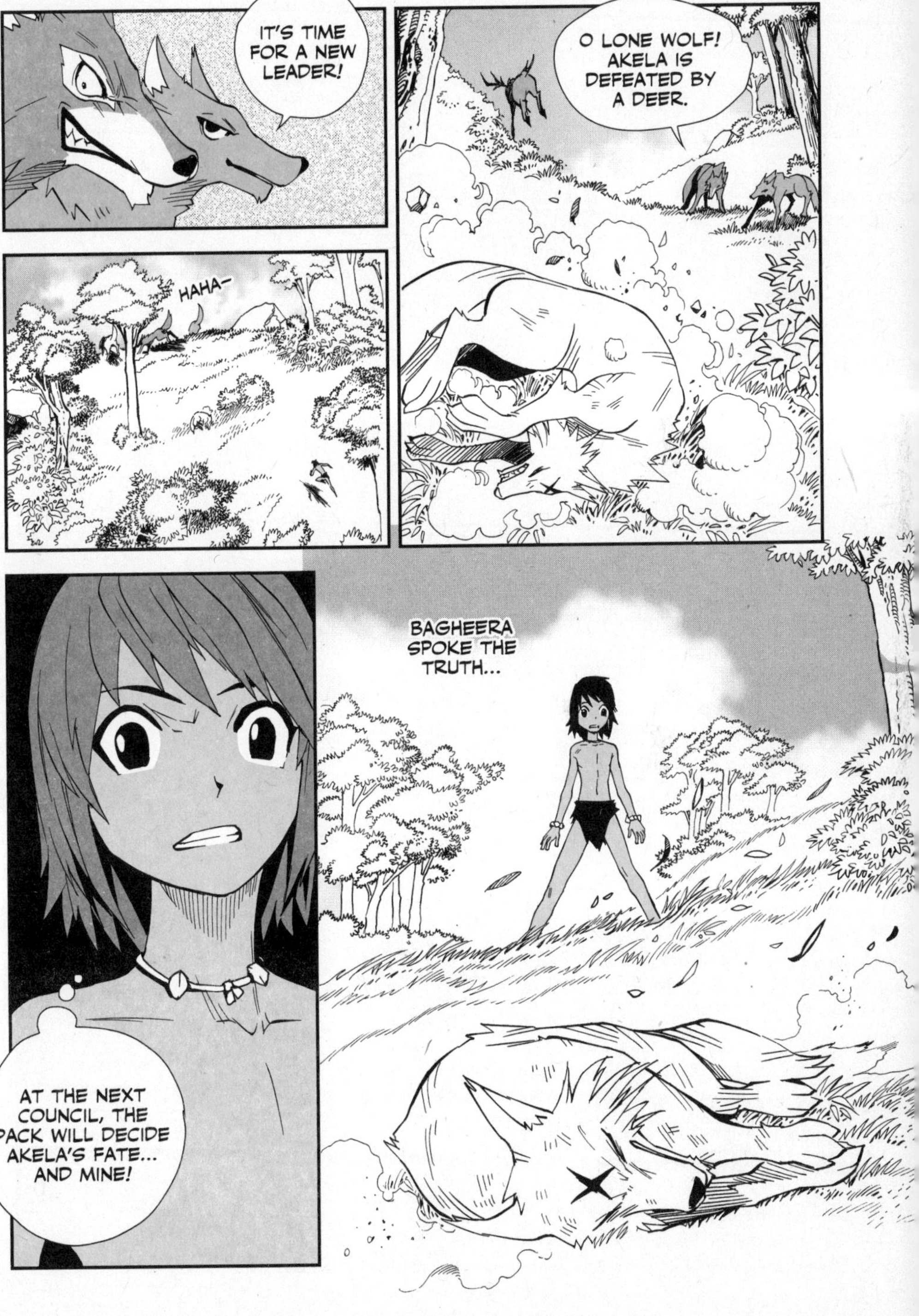
O LONE WOLF! AKELA IS DEFEATED BY A DEER.
IT'S TIME FOR A NEW LEADER!
HAHA-
BAGHEERA SPOKE THE TRUTH...
AT THE NEXT COUNCIL, THE PACK WILL DECIDE AKELA'S FATE... AND MINE!

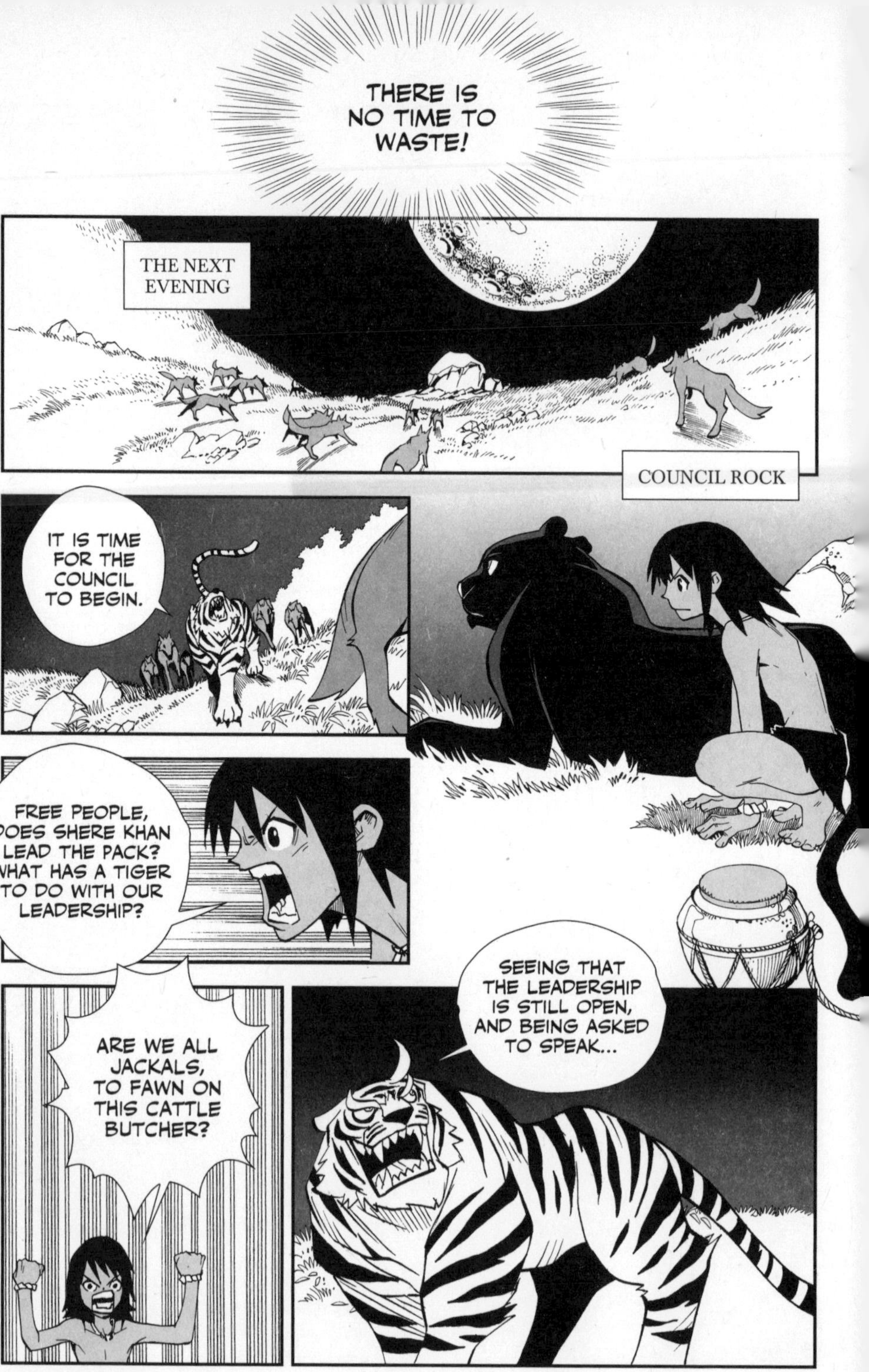
THERE IS NO TIME TO WASTE!
THE NEXT EVENING
COUNCIL ROCK
IT IS TIME FOR THE COUNCIL TO BEGIN.
FREE PEOPLE, DOES SHERE KHAN LEAD THE PACK? WHAT HAS A TIGER TO DO WITH OUR LEADERSHIP?
SEEING THAT THE LEADERSHIP IS STILL OPEN, AND BEING ASKED TO SPEAK...
ARE WE ALL JACKALS, TO FAWN ON THIS CATTLE BUTCHER?

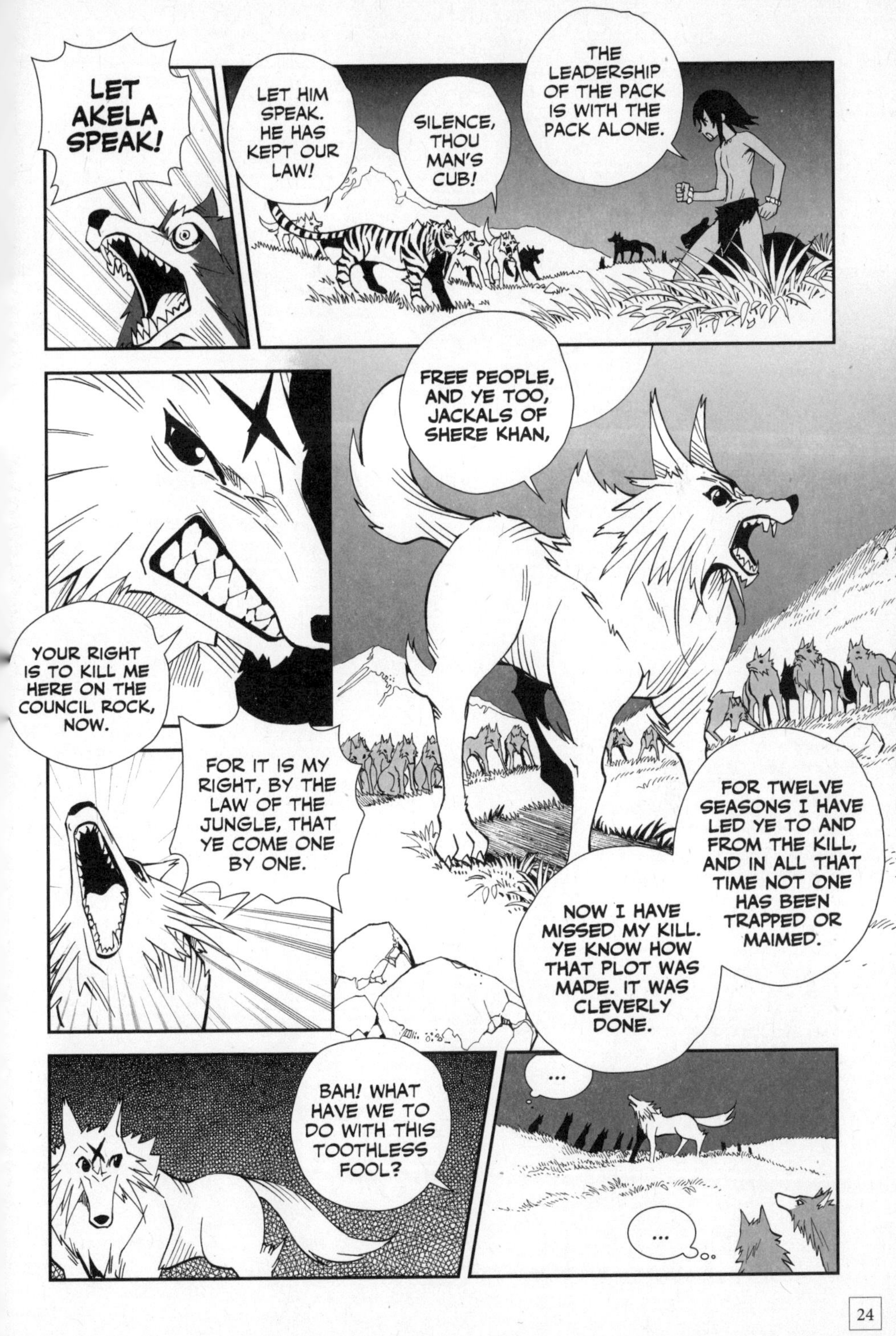
THE LEADERSHIP OF THE PACK IS WITH THE PACK ALONE.
SILENCE, THOU MAN'S CUB!
LET HIM SPEAK. HE HAS KEPT OUR LAW!
LET AKELA SPEAK!
FREE PEOPLE, AND YE TOO, JACKALS OF SHERE KHAN,
FOR TWELVE SEASONS I HAVE LED YE TO AND FROM THE KILL, AND IN ALL THAT TIME NOT ONE HAS BEEN TRAPPED OR MAIMED.
NOW I HAVE MISSED MY KILL. YE KNOW HOW THAT PLOT WAS MADE. IT WAS CLEVERLY DONE.
YOUR RIGHT IS TO KILL ME HERE ON THE COUNCIL ROCK, NOW.
FOR IT IS MY RIGHT, BY THE LAW OF THE JUNGLE, THAT YE COME ONE BY ONE.
...
...
BAH! WHAT HAVE WE TO DO WITH THIS TOOTHLESS FOOL?

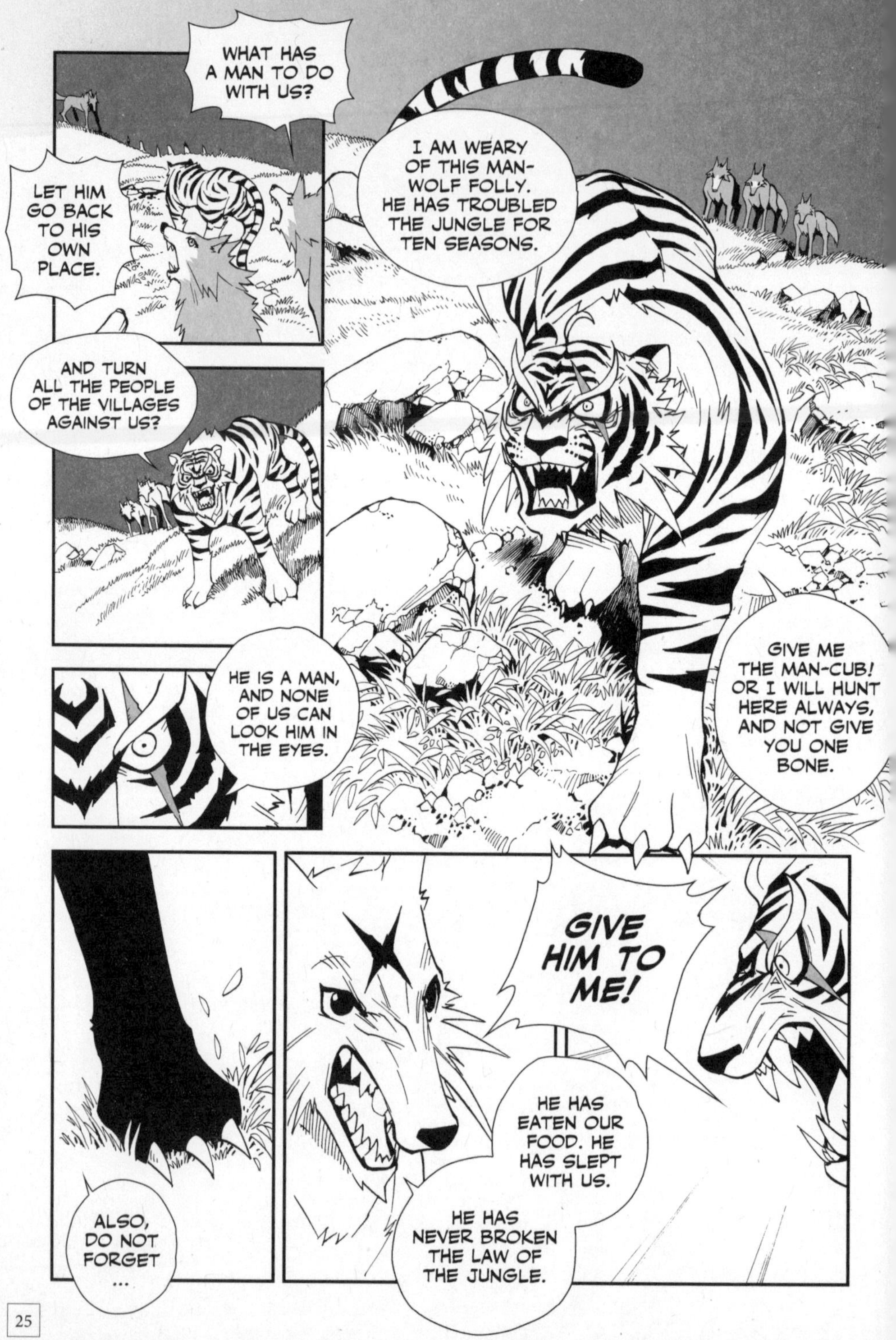
I AM WEARY OF THIS MAN-WOLF FOLLY. HE HAS TROUBLED THE JUNGLE FOR TEN SEASONS.
GIVE ME THE MAN-CUB! OR I WILL HUNT HERE ALWAYS, AND NOT GIVE YOU ONE BONE.
WHAT HAS A MAN TO DO WITH US?
LET HIM GO BACK TO HIS OWN PLACE.
AND TURN ALL THE PEOPLE OF THE VILLAGES AGAINST US?
HE IS A MAN, AND NONE OF US CAN LOOK HIM IN THE EYES.
GIVE HIM TO ME!
HE HAS EATEN OUR FOOD. HE HAS SLEPT WITH US.
HE HAS NEVER BROKEN THE LAW OF THE JUNGLE.
ALSO, DO NOT FORGET ...

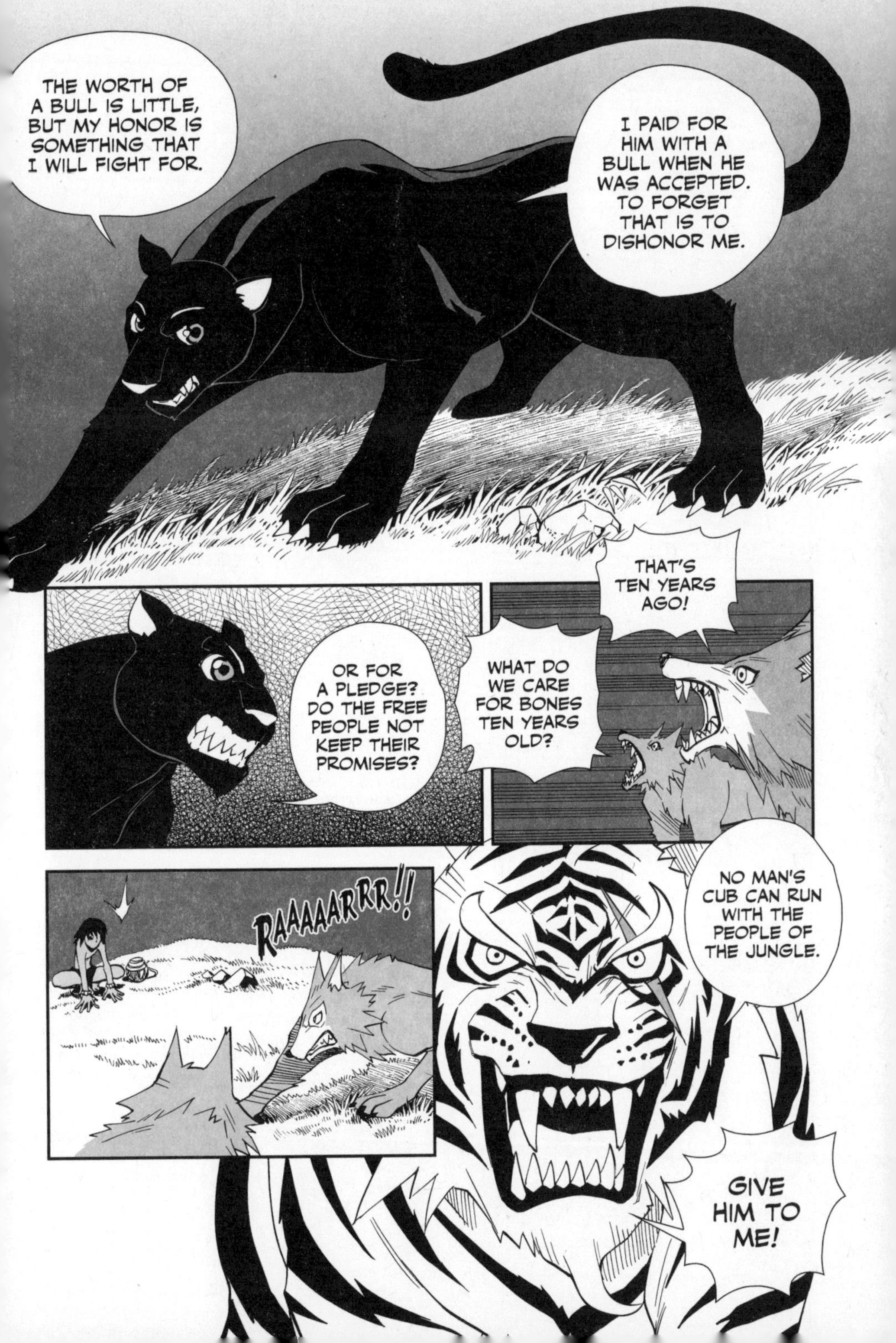
I PAID FOR HIM WITH A BULL WHEN HE WAS ACCEPTED. TO FORGET THAT IS TO DISHONOR ME.
THE WORTH OF A BULL IS LITTLE, BUT MY HONOR IS SOMETHING THAT I WILL FIGHT FOR.
THAT'S TEN YEARS AGO!
WHAT DO WE CARE FOR BONES TEN YEARS OLD?
OR FOR A PLEDGE? DO THE FREE PEOPLE NOT KEEP THEIR PROMISES?
NO MAN'S CUB CAN RUN WITH THE PEOPLE OF THE JUNGLE.
GIVE HIM TO ME!
RAAAAARRR!!

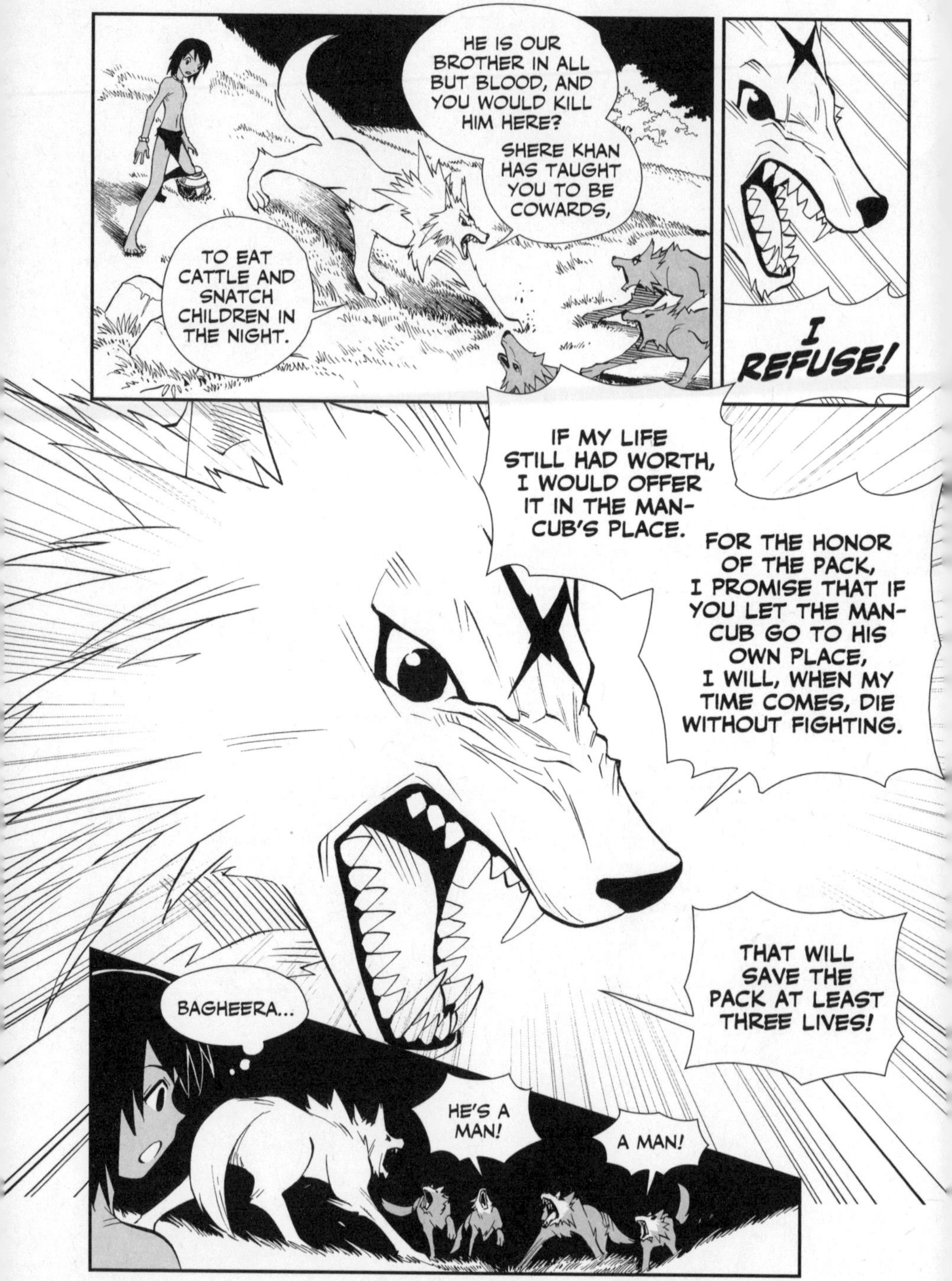
I REFUSE!
HE IS OUR BROTHER IN ALL BUT BLOOD, AND YOU WOULD KILL HIM HERE?
SHERE KHAN HAS TAUGHT YOU TO BE COWARDS,
TO EAT CATTLE AND SNATCH CHILDREN IN THE NIGHT.
IF MY LIFE STILL HAD WORTH, I WOULD OFFER IT IN THE MAN-CUB'S PLACE.
FOR THE HONOR OF THE PACK, I PROMISE THAT IF YOU LET THE MAN-CUB GO TO HIS OWN PLACE, I WILL, WHEN MY TIME COMES, DIE WITHOUT FIGHTING.
THAT WILL SAVE THE PACK AT LEAST THREE LIVES!
A MAN!
HE'S A MAN!
BAGHEERA...

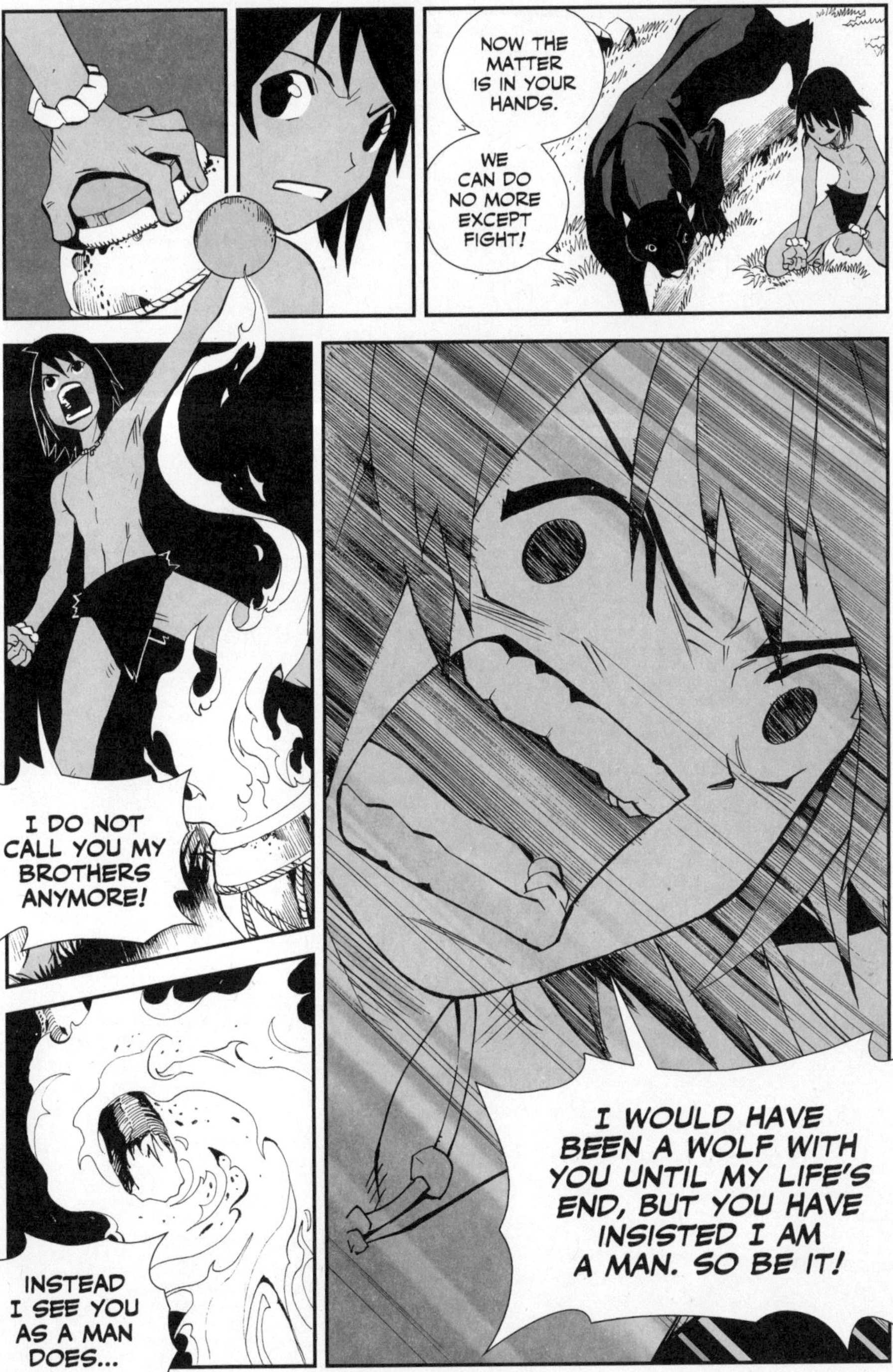
NOW THE MATTER IS IN YOUR HANDS.
WE CAN DO NO MORE EXCEPT FIGHT!
I WOULD HAVE BEEN A WOLF WITH YOU UNTIL MY LIFE'S END, BUT YOU HAVE INSISTED I AM A MAN. SO BE IT!
I DO NOT CALL YOU MY BROTHERS ANYMORE!
INSTEAD I SEE YOU AS A MAN DOES...

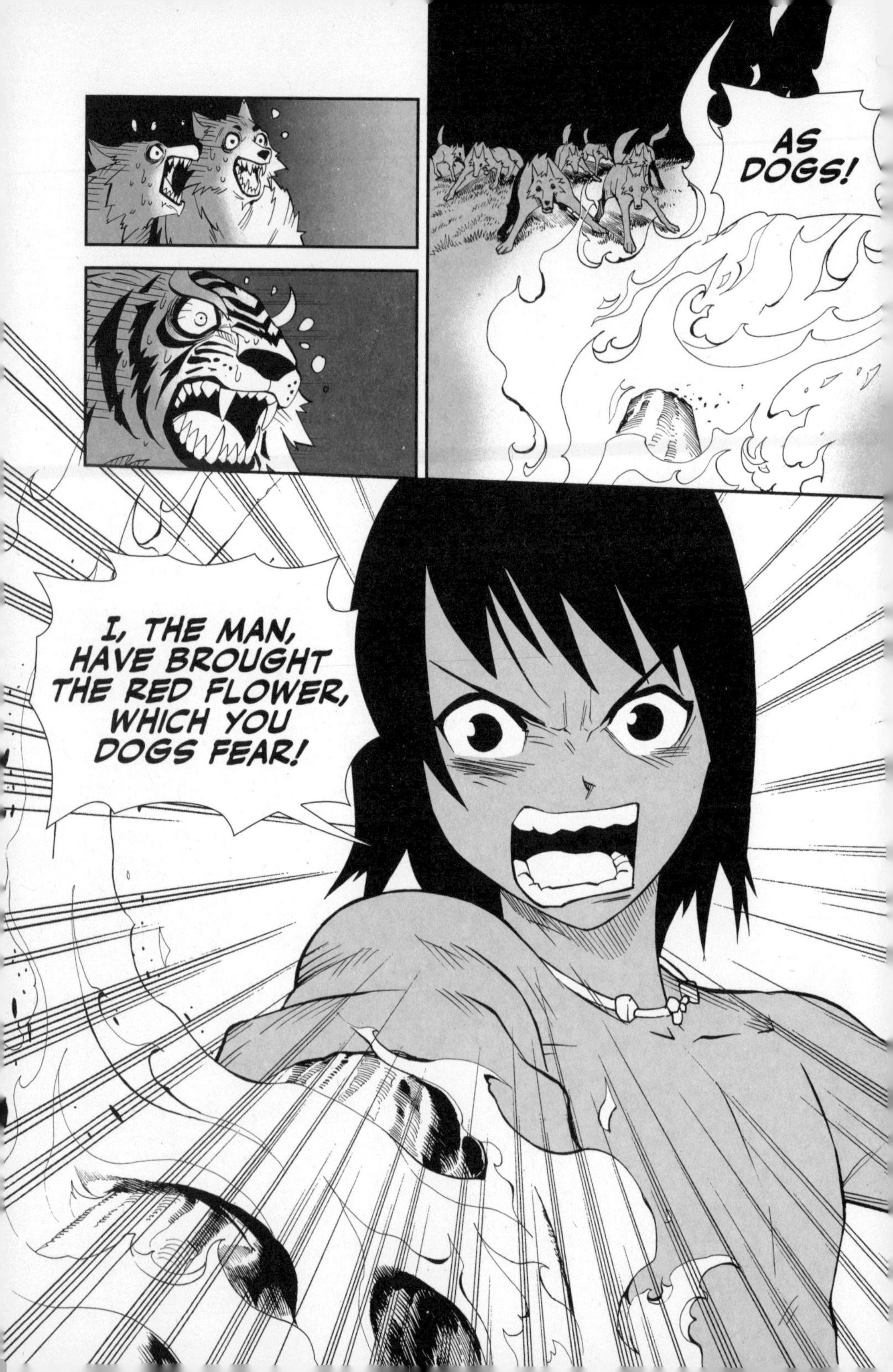
AS DOGS!
I, THE MAN, HAVE BROUGHT THE RED FLOWER, WHICH YOU DOGS FEAR!

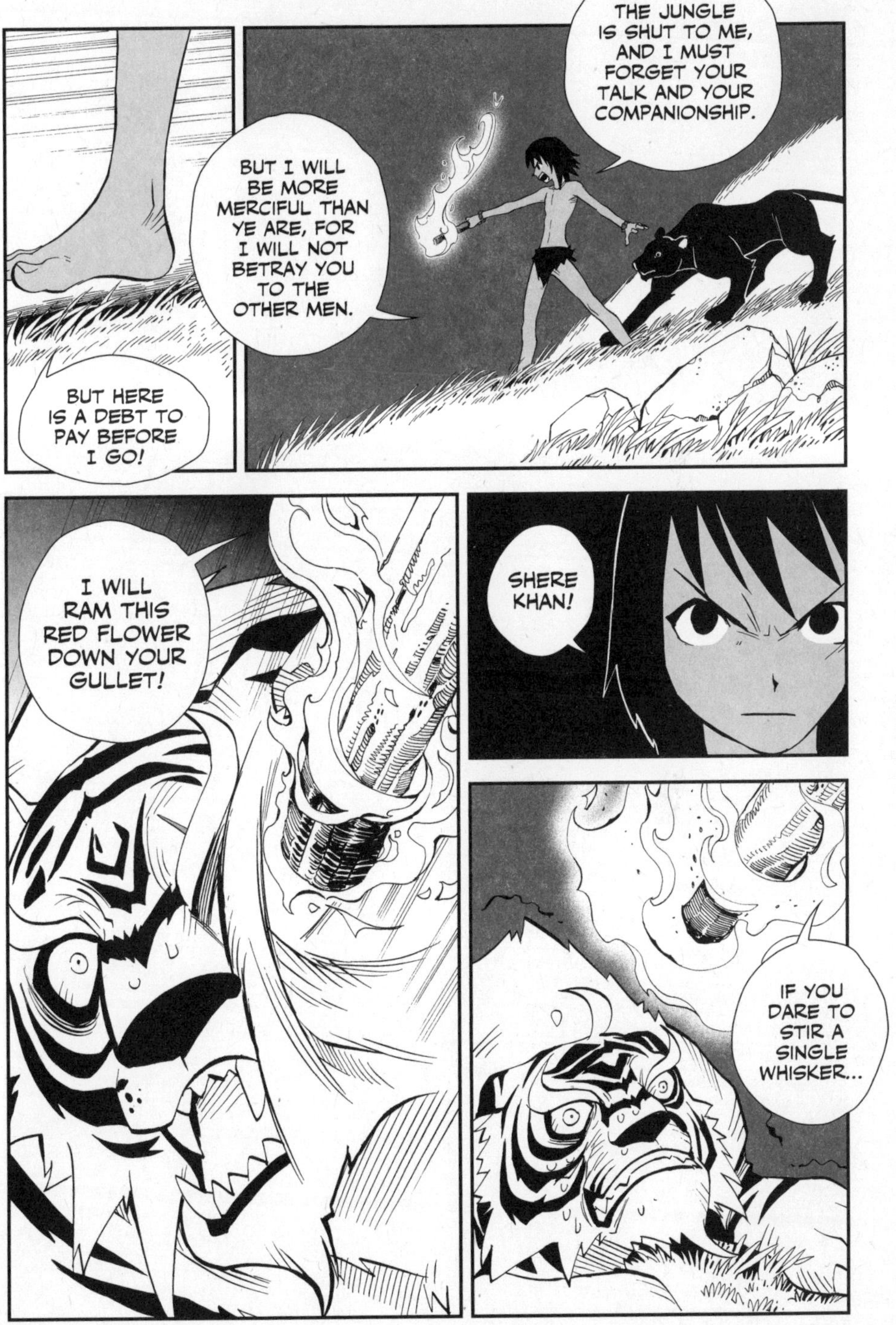
THE JUNGLE IS SHUT TO ME, AND I MUST FORGET YOUR TALK AND YOUR COMPANIONSHIP.
BUT I WILL BE MORE MERCIFUL THAN YE ARE, FOR I WILL NOT BETRAY YOU TO THE OTHER MEN.
BUT HERE IS A DEBT TO PAY BEFORE I GO!
SHERE KHAN!
IF YOU DARE TO STIR A SINGLE WHISKER...
I WILL RAM THIS RED FLOWER DOWN YOUR GULLET!

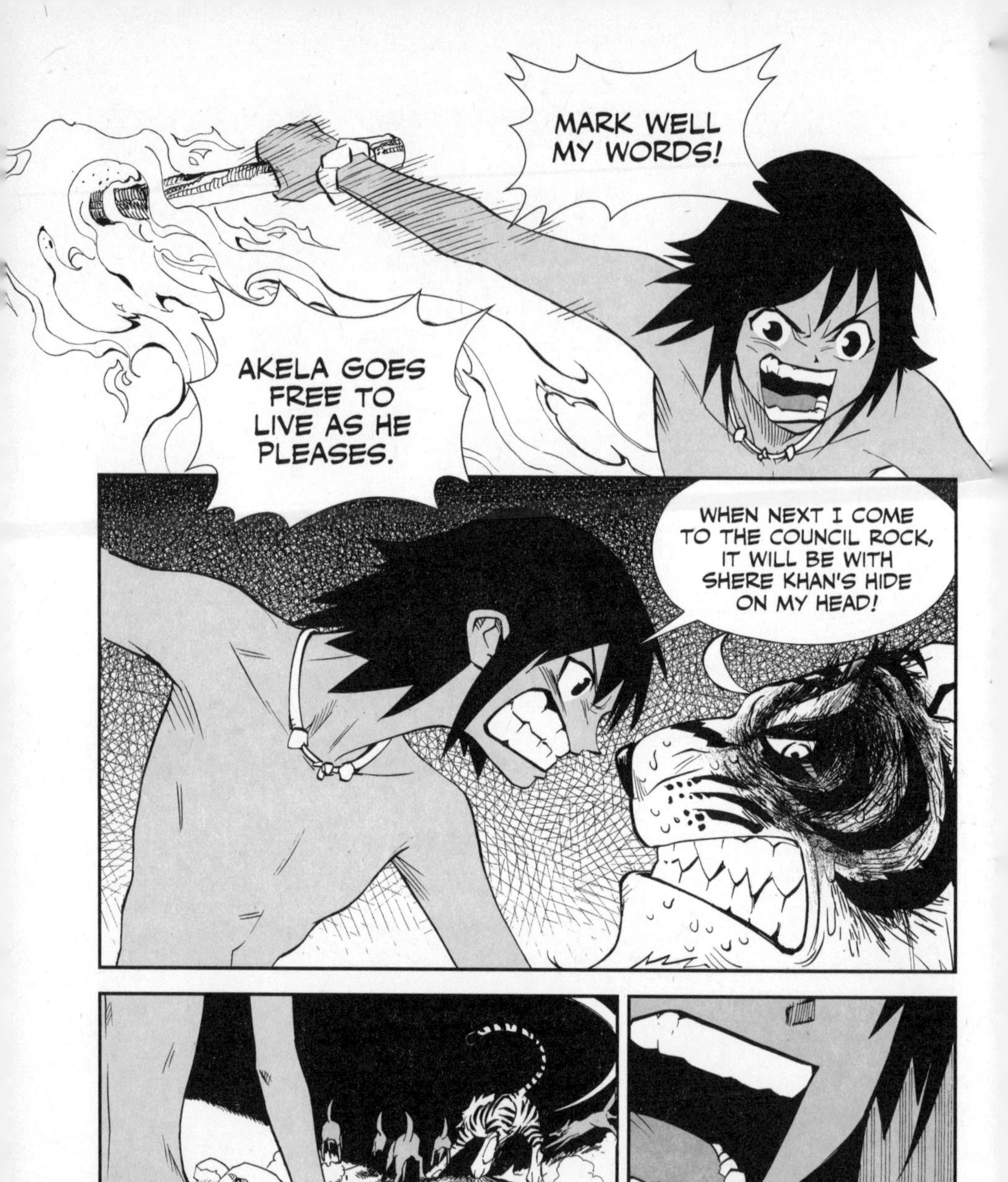
MARK WELL MY WORDS!
AKELA GOES FREE TO LIVE AS HE PLEASES.
WHEN NEXT I COME TO THE COUNCIL ROCK, IT WILL BE WITH SHERE KHAN'S HIDE ON MY HEAD!
GO! GO AWAY NOW!

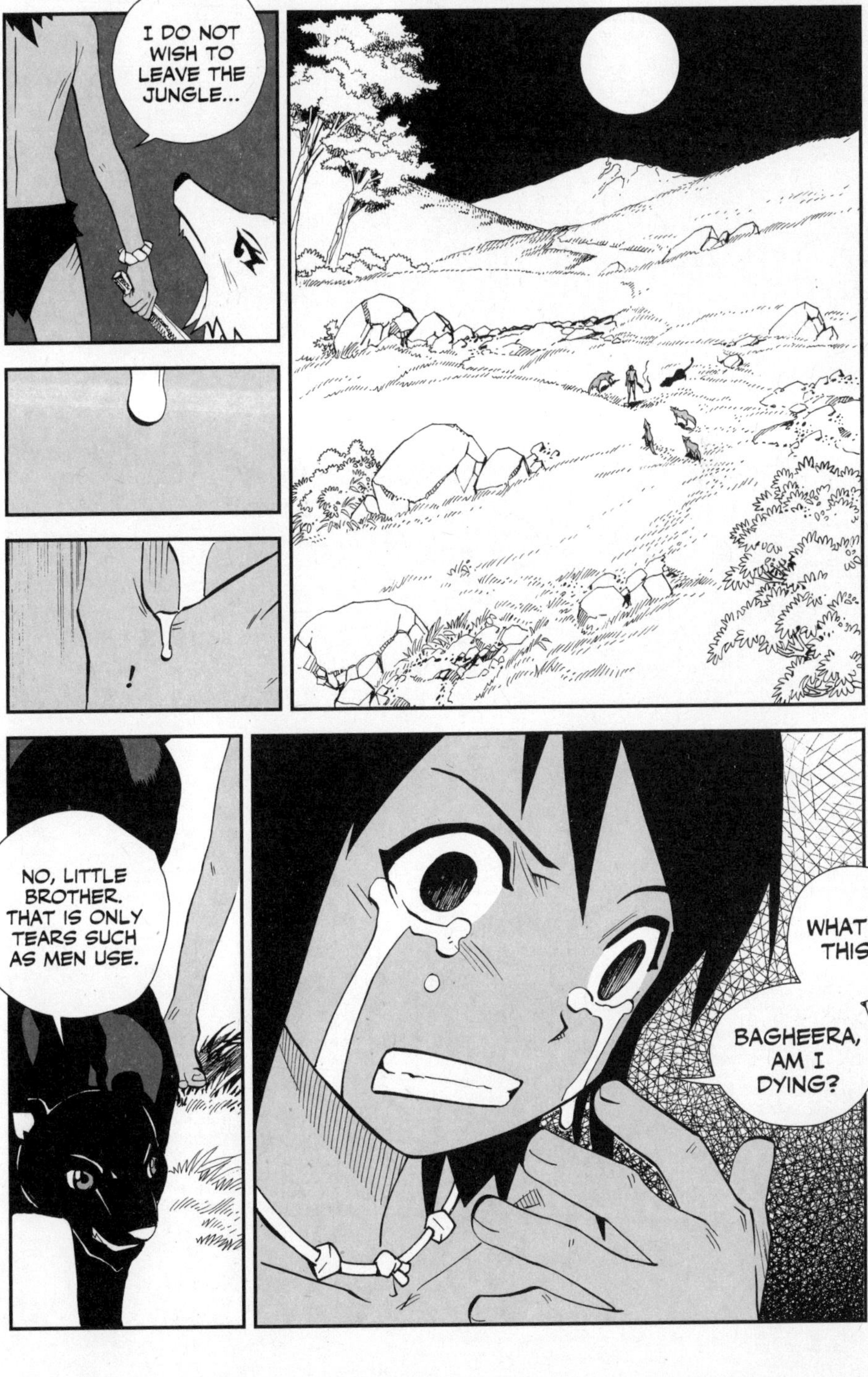
I DO NOT WISH TO LEAVE THE JUNGLE...
!
WHAT IS THIS?
BAGHEERA, AM I DYING?
NO, LITTLE BROTHER. THAT IS ONLY TEARS SUCH AS MEN USE.

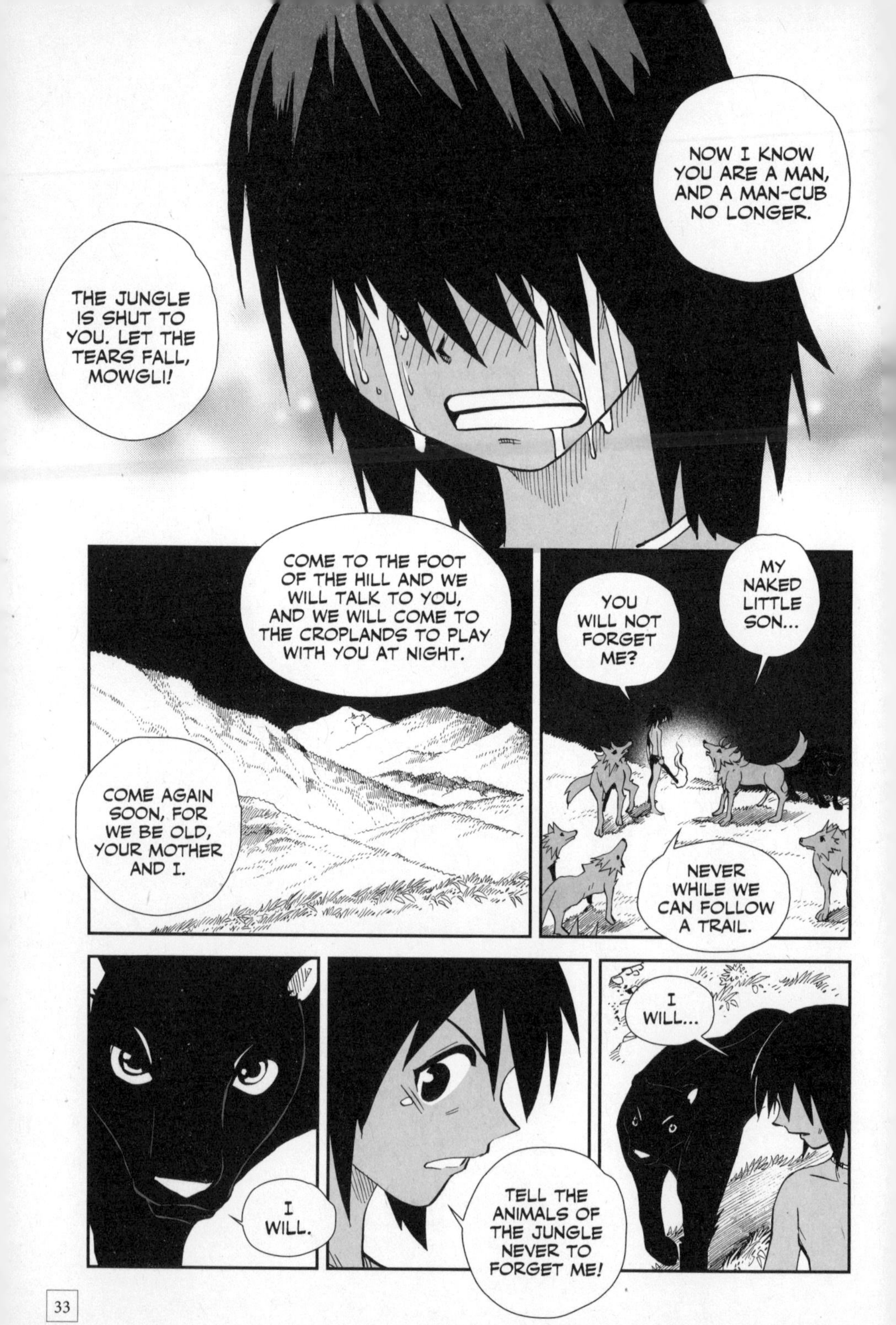
NOW I KNOW YOU ARE A MAN, AND A MAN-CUB NO LONGER.
THE JUNGLE IS SHUT TO YOU. LET THE TEARS FALL, MOWGLI!
MY NAKED LITTLE SON...
YOU WILL NOT FORGET ME?
NEVER WHILE WE CAN FOLLOW A TRAIL.
COME TO THE FOOT OF THE HILL AND WE WILL TALK TO YOU, AND WE WILL COME TO THE CROPLANDS TO PLAY WITH YOU AT NIGHT.
COME AGAIN SOON, FOR WE BE OLD, YOUR MOTHER AND I.
I WILL...
TELL THE ANIMALS OF THE JUNGLE NEVER TO FORGET ME!
I WILL.

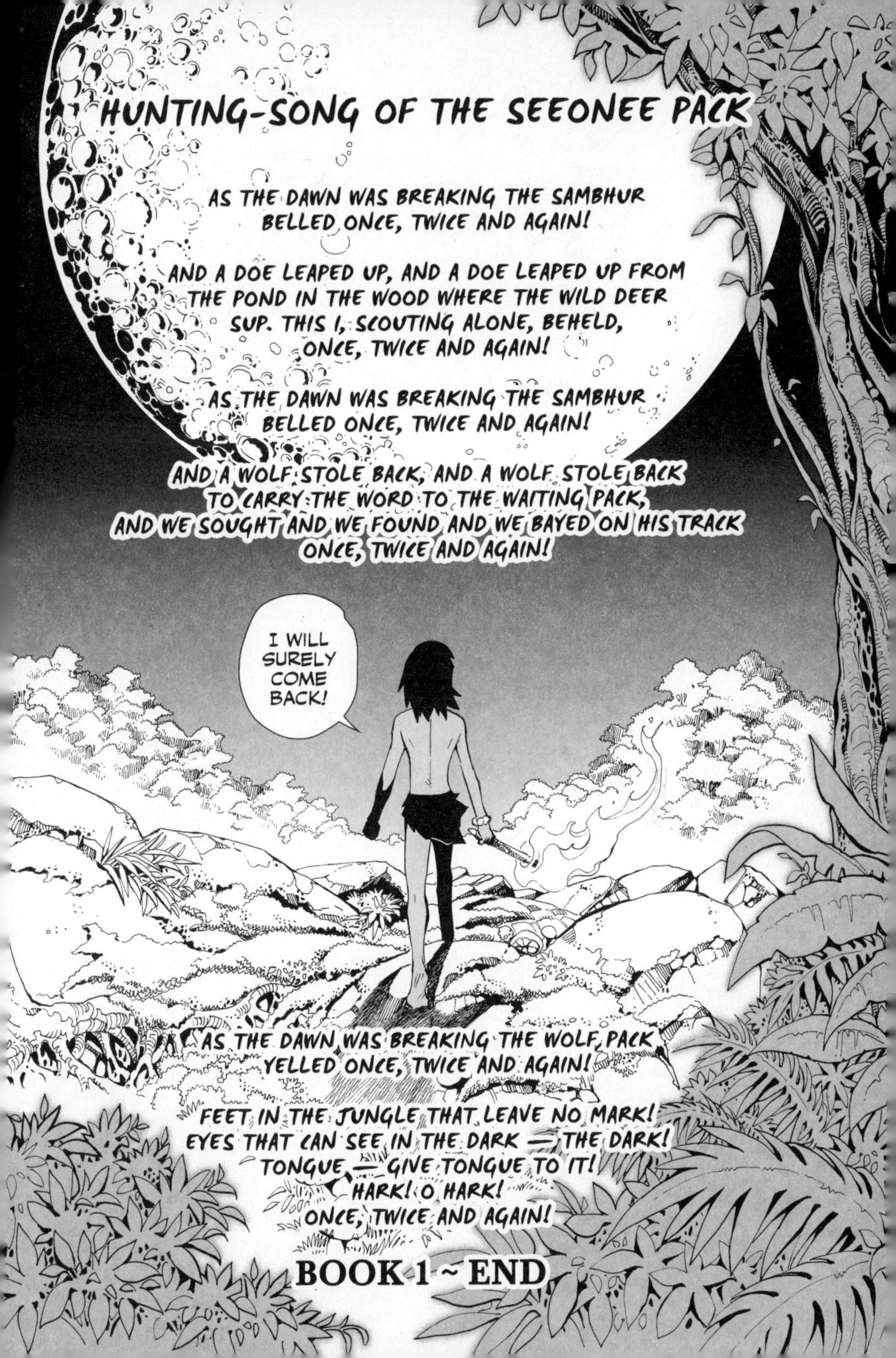
HUNTING-SONG OF THE SEEONEE PACK
AS THE DAWN WAS BREAKING THE SAMBHUR BELLED ONCE, TWICE AND AGAIN!
AND A DOE LEAPED UP, AND A DOE LEAPED UP FROM THE POND IN THE WOOD WHERE THE WILD DEER SUP. THIS I, SCOUTING ALONE, BEHELD, ONCE, TWICE AND AGAIN!
AS THE DAWN WAS BREAKING THE SAMBHUR BELLED ONCE, TWICE AND AGAIN!
AND A WOLF STOLE BACK, AND A WOLF STOLE BACK TO CARRY THE WORD TO THE WAITING PACK, AND WE SOUGHT AND WE FOUND AND WE BAYED ON HIS TRACK ONCE, TWICE AND AGAIN!
I WILL SURELY COME BACK!
AS THE DAWN WAS BREAKING THE WOLF PACK YELLED ONCE, TWICE AND AGAIN!
FEET IN THE JUNGLE THAT LEAVE NO MARK! EYES THAT CAN SEE IN THE DARK — THE DARK! TONGUE — GIVE TONGUE TO IT! HARK! O HARK! ONCE, TWICE AND AGAIN!
BOOK 1 ~ END

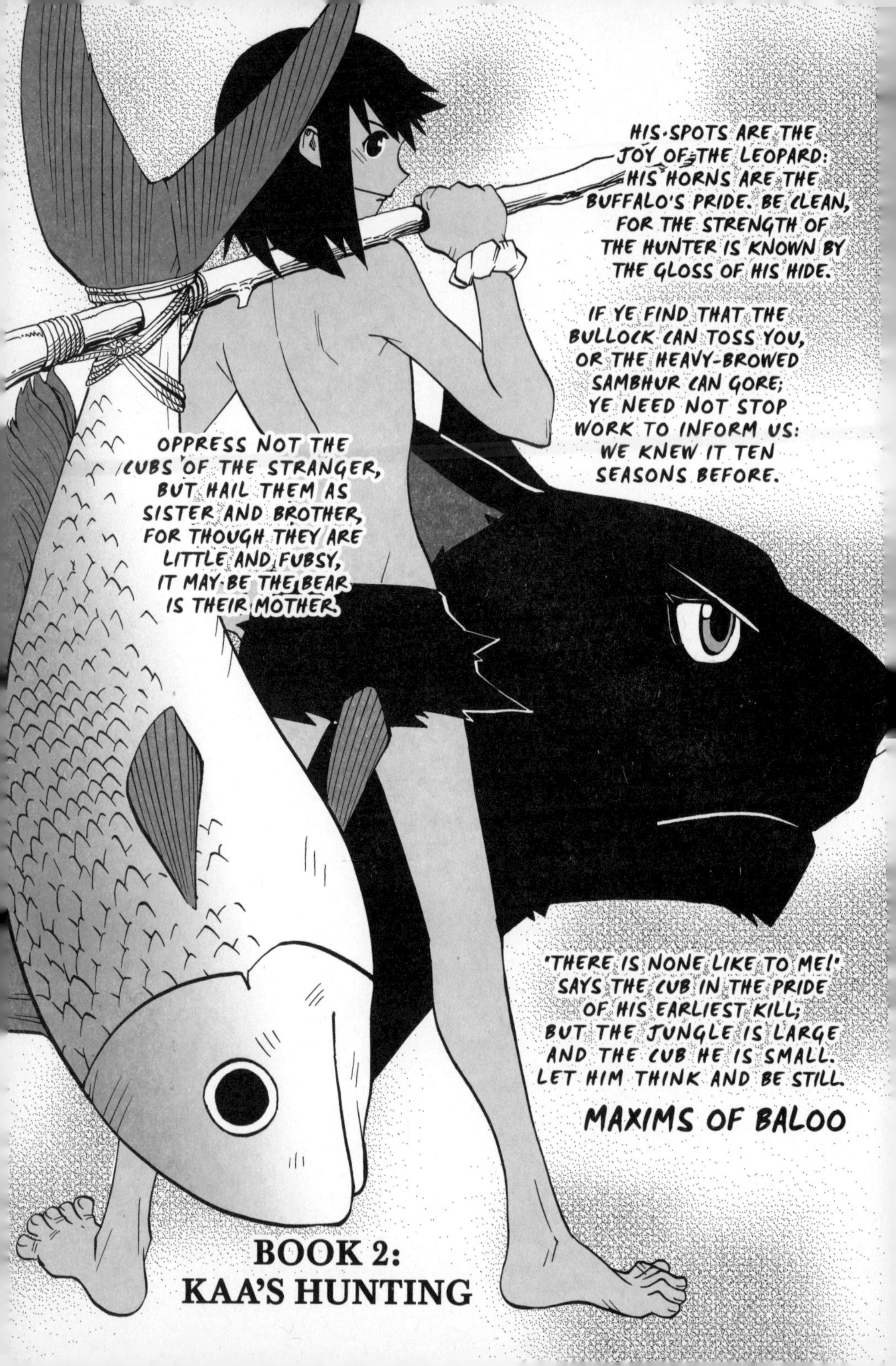
HIS SPOTS ARE THE JOY OF THE LEOPARD: HIS HORNS ARE THE BUFFALO'S PRIDE. BE CLEAN, FOR THE STRENGTH OF THE HUNTER IS KNOWN BY THE GLOSS OF HIS HIDE.
IF YE FIND THAT THE BULLOCK CAN TOSS YOU, OR THE HEAVY-BROWED SAMBHUR CAN GORE; YE NEED NOT STOP WORK TO INFORM US: WE KNEW IT TEN SEASONS BEFORE.
OPPRESS NOT THE CUBS OF THE STRANGER, BUT HAIL THEM AS SISTER AND BROTHER, FOR THOUGH THEY ARE LITTLE AND FUBSY, IT MAY BE THE BEAR IS THEIR MOTHER.
'THERE IS NONE LIKE TO ME!' SAYS THE CUB IN THE PRIDE OF HIS EARLIEST KILL; BUT THE JUNGLE IS LARGE AND THE CUB HE IS SMALL. LET HIM THINK AND BE STILL.
MAXIMS OF BALOO
BOOK 2:
KAA'S HUNTING

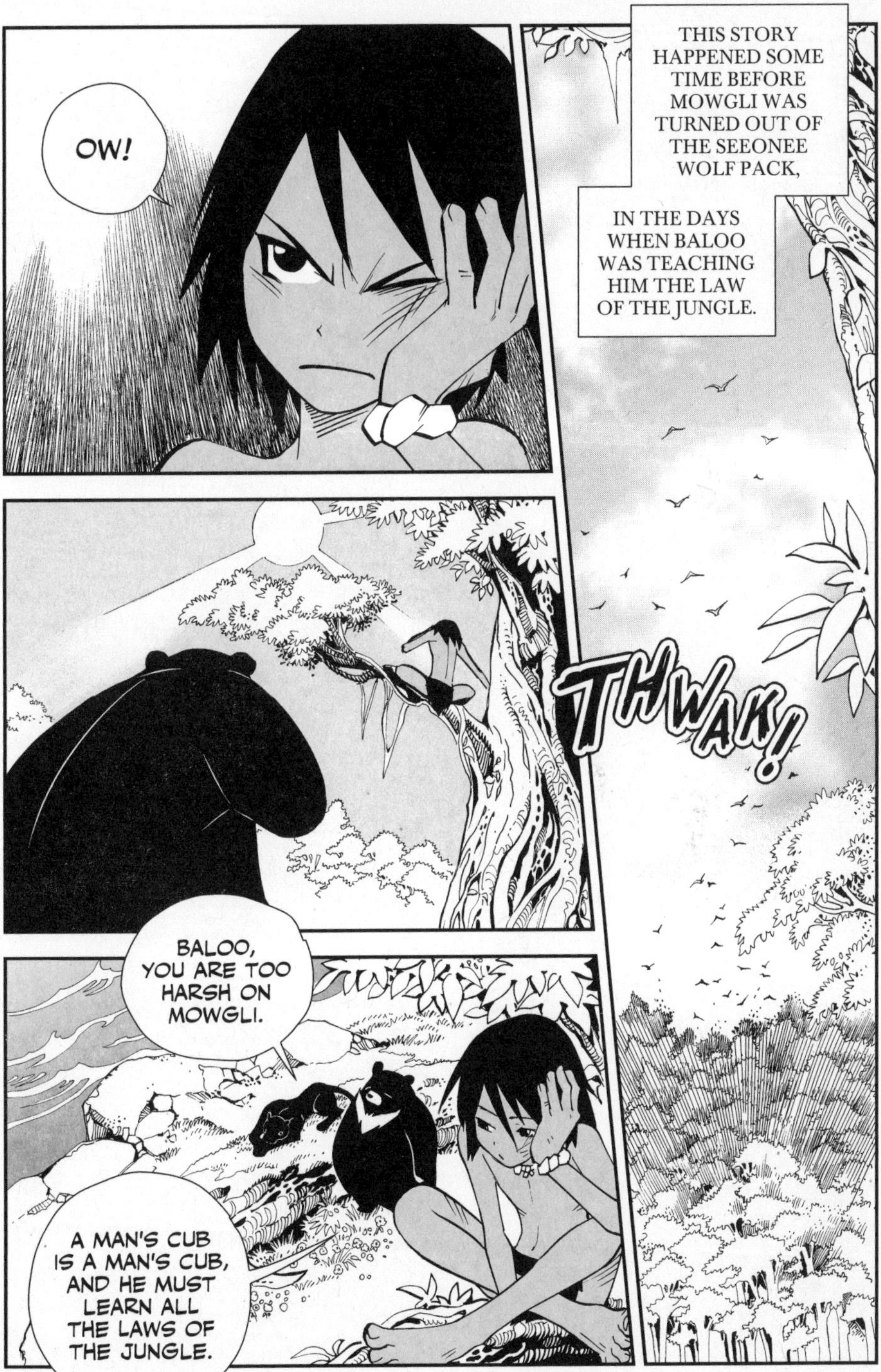
THIS STORY HAPPENED SOME TIME BEFORE MOWGLI WAS TURNED OUT OF THE SEEONEE WOLF PACK,
IN THE DAYS WHEN BALOO WAS TEACHING HIM THE LAW OF THE JUNGLE.
THWAK!
OW!
BALOO, YOU ARE TOO HARSH ON MOWGLI.
A MAN'S CUB IS A MAN'S CUB, AND HE MUST LEARN ALL THE LAWS OF THE JUNGLE.

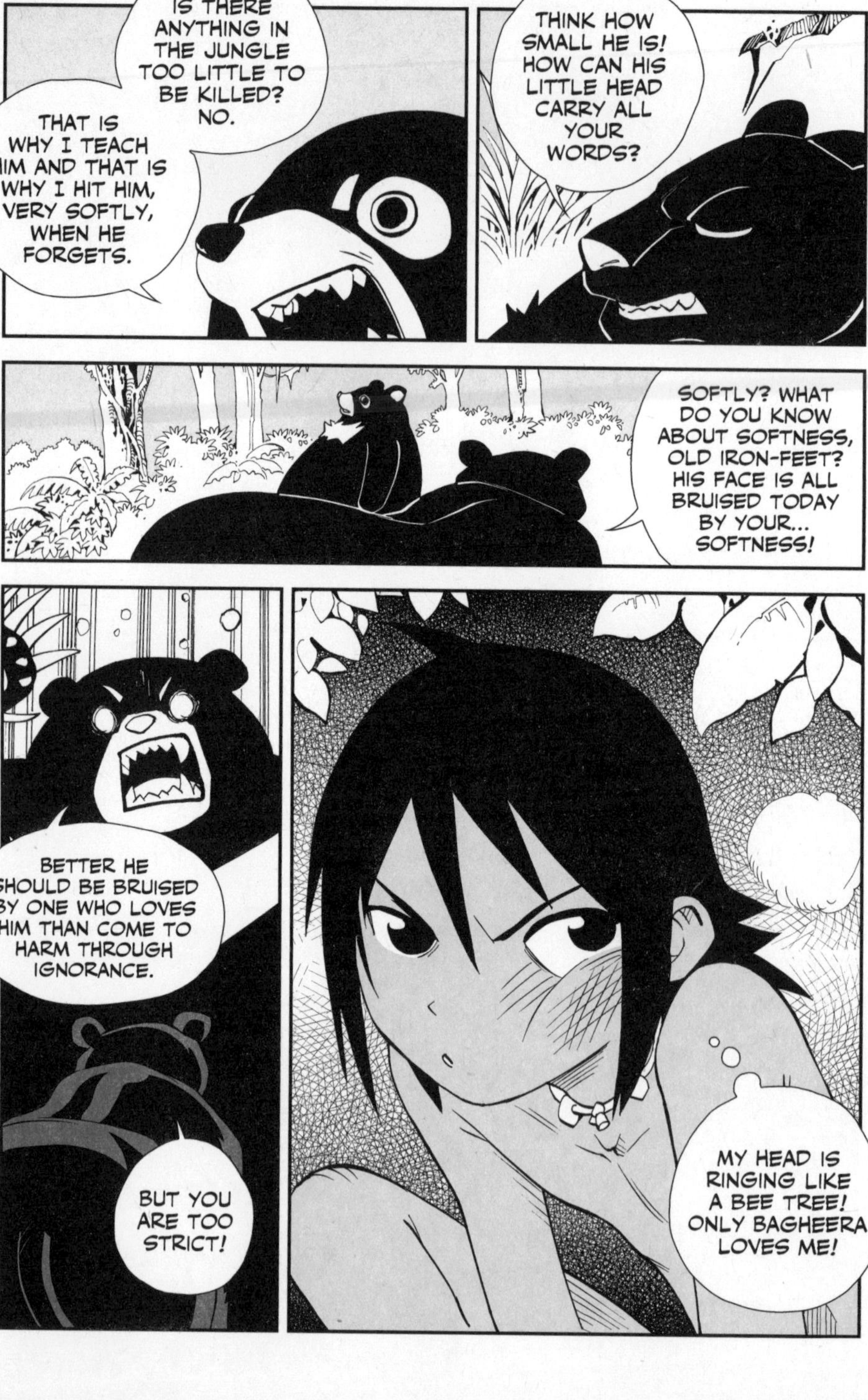
THINK HOW SMALL HE IS! HOW CAN HIS LITTLE HEAD CARRY ALL YOUR WORDS?
IS THERE ANYTHING IN THE JUNGLE TOO LITTLE TO BE KILLED? NO.
THAT IS WHY I TEACH HIM AND THAT IS WHY I HIT HIM, VERY SOFTLY, WHEN HE FORGETS.
SOFTLY? WHAT DO YOU KNOW ABOUT SOFTNESS, OLD IRON-FEET? HIS FACE IS ALL BRUISED TODAY BY YOUR... SOFTNESS!
MY HEAD IS RINGING LIKE A BEE TREE! ONLY BAGHEERA LOVES ME!
BETTER HE SHOULD BE BRUISED BY ONE WHO LOVES HIM THAN COME TO HARM THROUGH IGNORANCE.
BUT YOU ARE TOO STRICT!

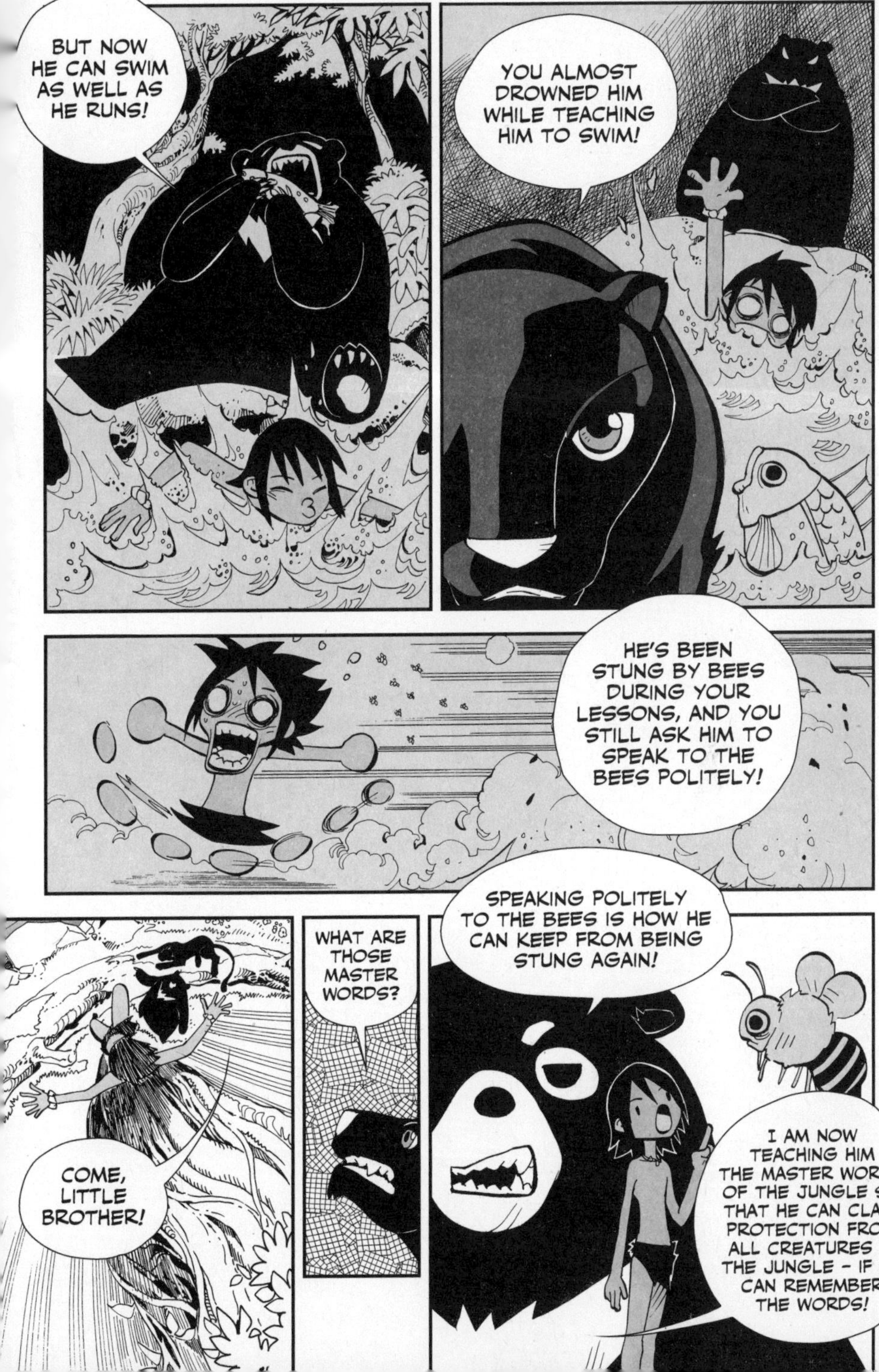
YOU ALMOST DROWNED HIM WHILE TEACHING HIM TO SWIM!
BUT NOW HE CAN SWIM AS WELL AS HE RUNS!
HE'S BEEN STUNG BY BEES DURING YOUR LESSONS, AND YOU STILL ASK HIM TO SPEAK TO THE BEES POLITELY!
SPEAKING POLITELY TO THE BEES IS HOW HE CAN KEEP FROM BEING STUNG AGAIN!
I AM NOW TEACHING HIM THE MASTER WORDS OF THE JUNGLE SO THAT HE CAN CLAIM PROTECTION FROM ALL CREATURES IN THE JUNGLE - IF HE CAN REMEMBER THE WORDS!
WHAT ARE THOSE MASTER WORDS?
COME, LITTLE BROTHER!

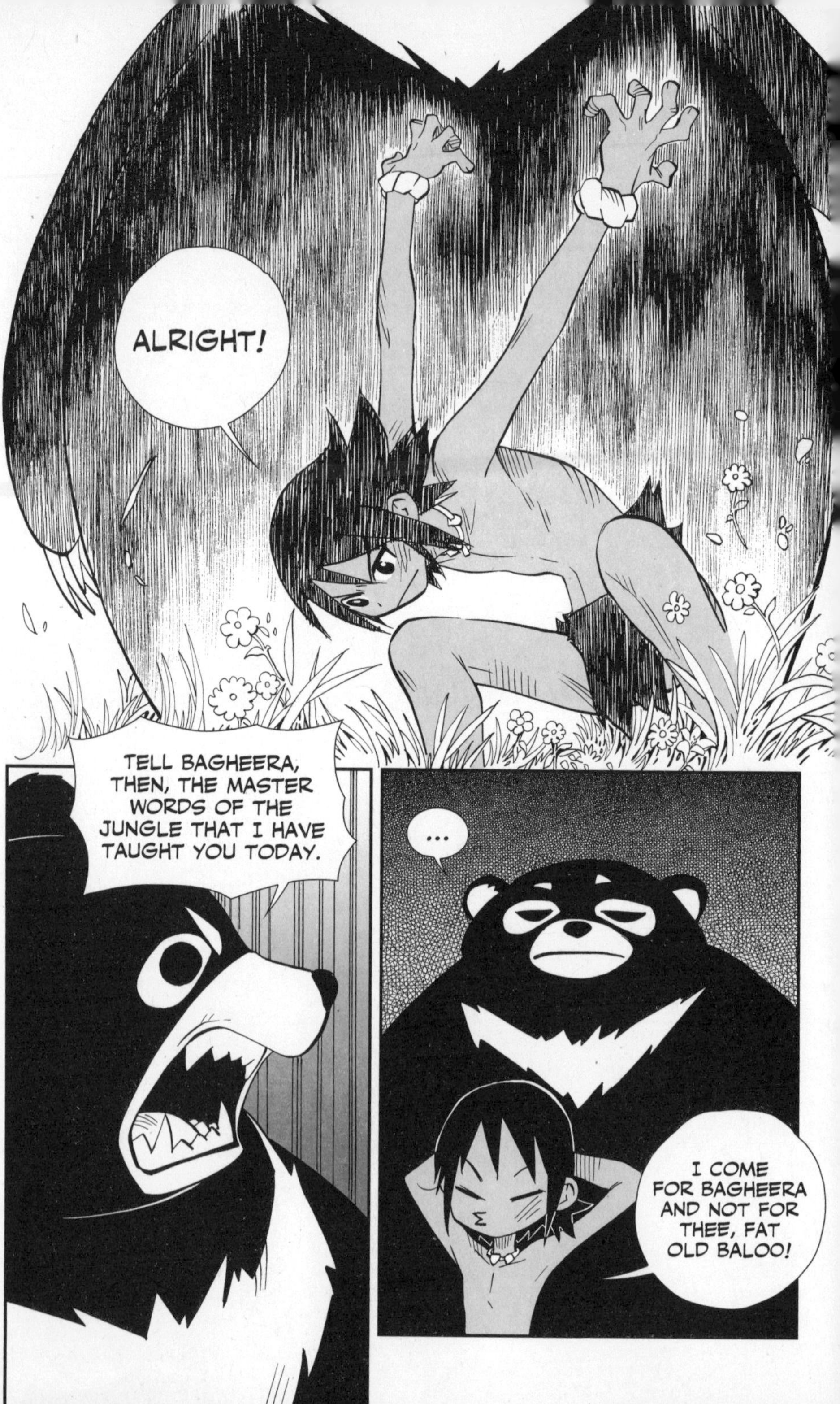
ALRIGHT!
...
I COME FOR BAGHEERA AND NOT FOR THEE, FAT OLD BALOO!
TELL BAGHEERA, THEN, THE MASTER WORDS OF THE JUNGLE THAT I HAVE TAUGHT YOU TODAY.

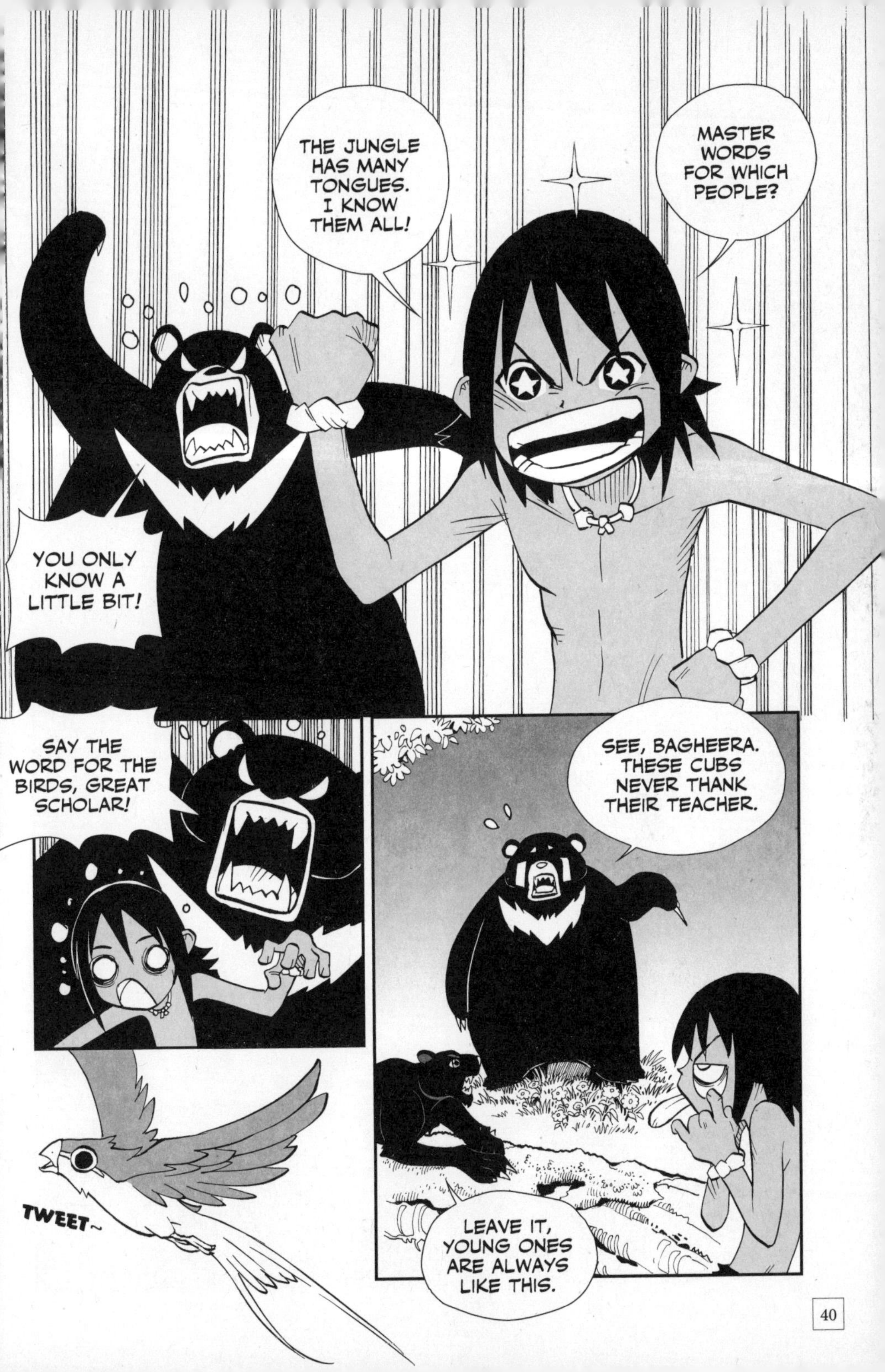
MASTER WORDS FOR WHICH PEOPLE?
THE JUNGLE HAS MANY TONGUES. I KNOW THEM ALL!
YOU ONLY KNOW A LITTLE BIT!
SEE, BAGHEERA. THESE CUBS NEVER THANK THEIR TEACHER.
LEAVE IT, YOUNG ONES ARE ALWAYS LIKE THIS.
SAY THE WORD FOR THE BIRDS, GREAT SCHOLAR!
TWEET~

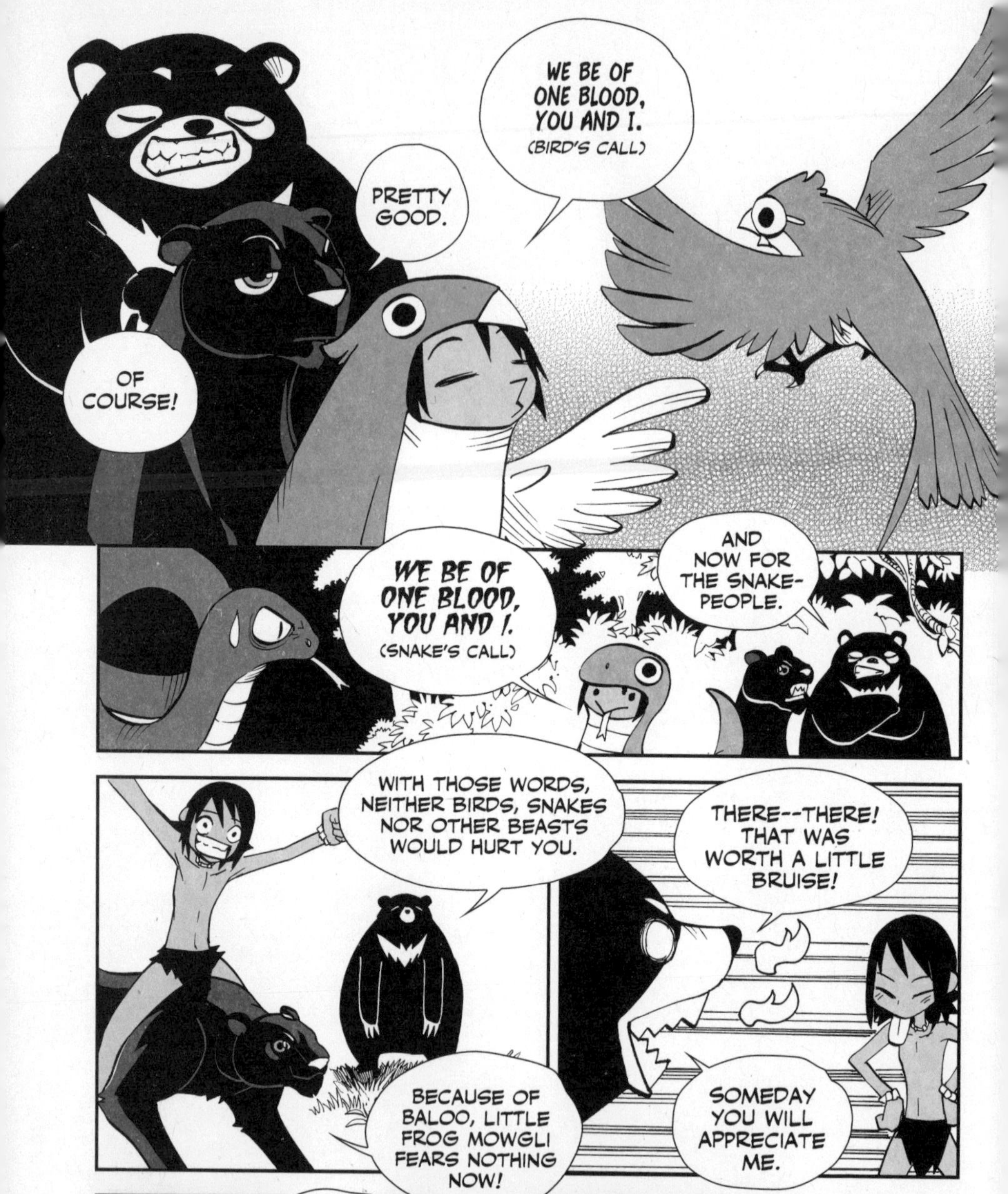
WE BE OF ONE BLOOD, YOU AND I.
(BIRD'S CALL)
PRETTY GOOD.
OF COURSE!
AND NOW FOR THE SNAKE-PEOPLE.
WE BE OF ONE BLOOD, YOU AND I.
(SNAKE'S CALL)
THERE--THERE! THAT WAS WORTH A LITTLE BRUISE!
SOMEDAY YOU WILL APPRECIATE ME.
WITH THOSE WORDS, NEITHER BIRDS, SNAKES NOR OTHER BEASTS WOULD HURT YOU.
BECAUSE OF BALOO, LITTLE FROG MOWGLI FEARS NOTHING NOW!
NOTHING EXCEPT HIS OWN TRIBE
...

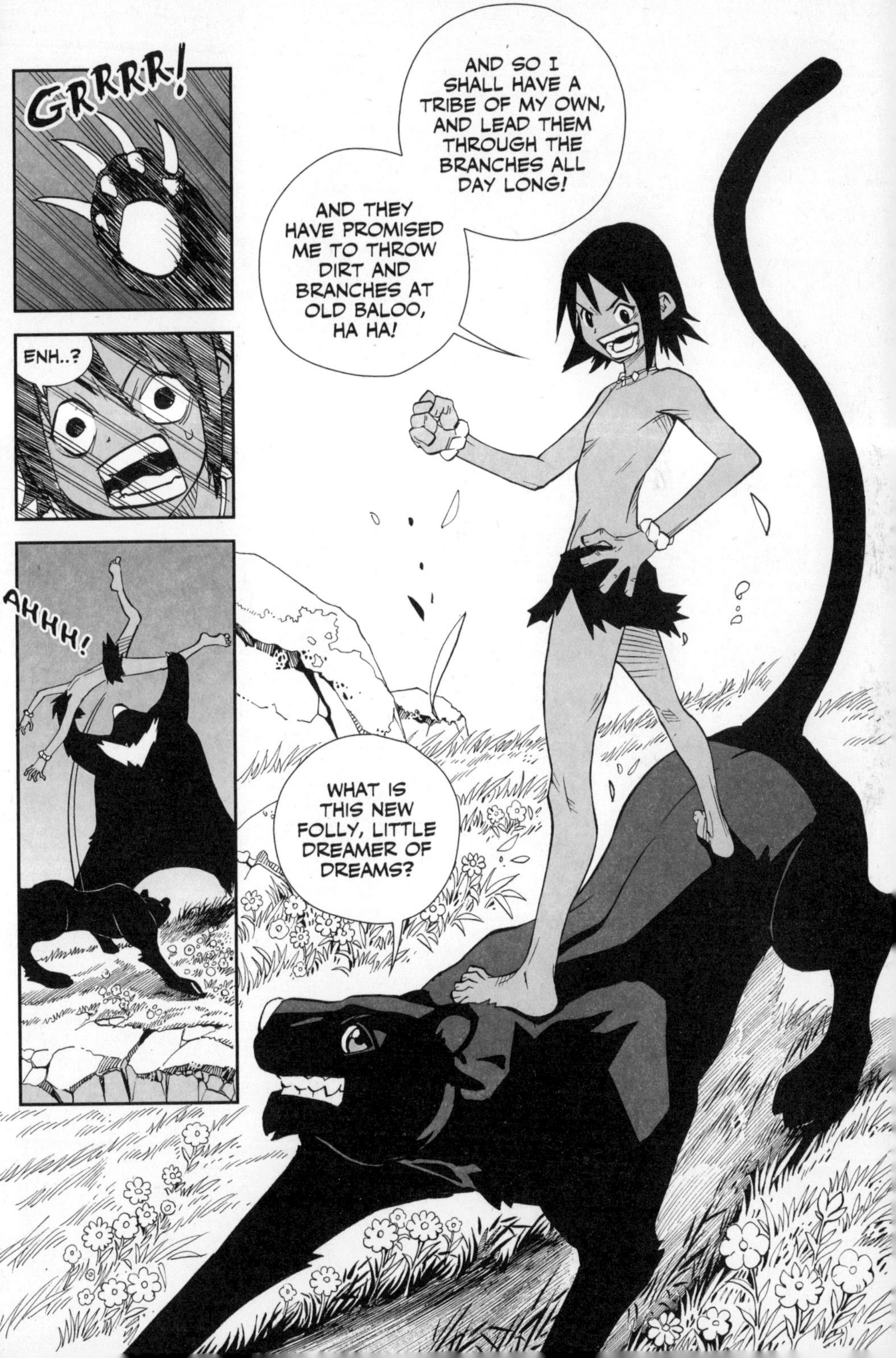
AND SO I SHALL HAVE A TRIBE OF MY OWN, AND LEAD THEM THROUGH THE BRANCHES ALL DAY LONG!
AND THEY HAVE PROMISED ME TO THROW DIRT AND BRANCHES AT OLD BALOO, HA HA!
WHAT IS THIS NEW FOLLY, LITTLE DREAMER OF DREAMS?
GRRRR!
ENH..?
AHHHH!

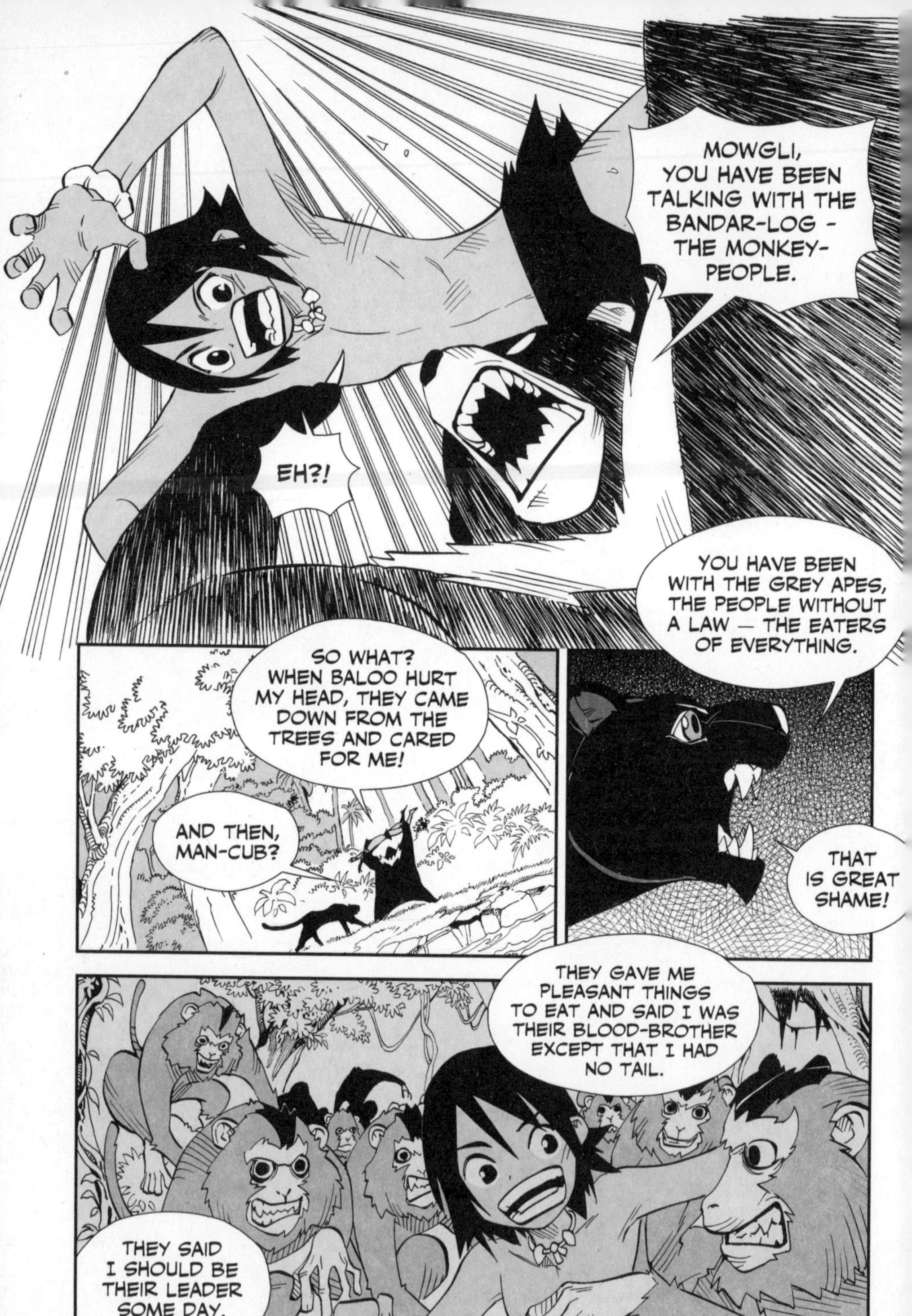
MOWGLI, YOU HAVE BEEN TALKING WITH THE BANDAR-LOG - THE MONKEY-PEOPLE.
EH?!
YOU HAVE BEEN WITH THE GREY APES, THE PEOPLE WITHOUT A LAW — THE EATERS OF EVERYTHING.
THAT IS GREAT SHAME!
SO WHAT? WHEN BALOO HURT MY HEAD, THEY CAME DOWN FROM THE TREES AND CARED FOR ME!
AND THEN, MAN-CUB?
THEY GAVE ME PLEASANT THINGS TO EAT AND SAID I WAS THEIR BLOOD-BROTHER EXCEPT THAT I HAD NO TAIL.
THEY SAID I SHOULD BE THEIR LEADER SOME DAY.

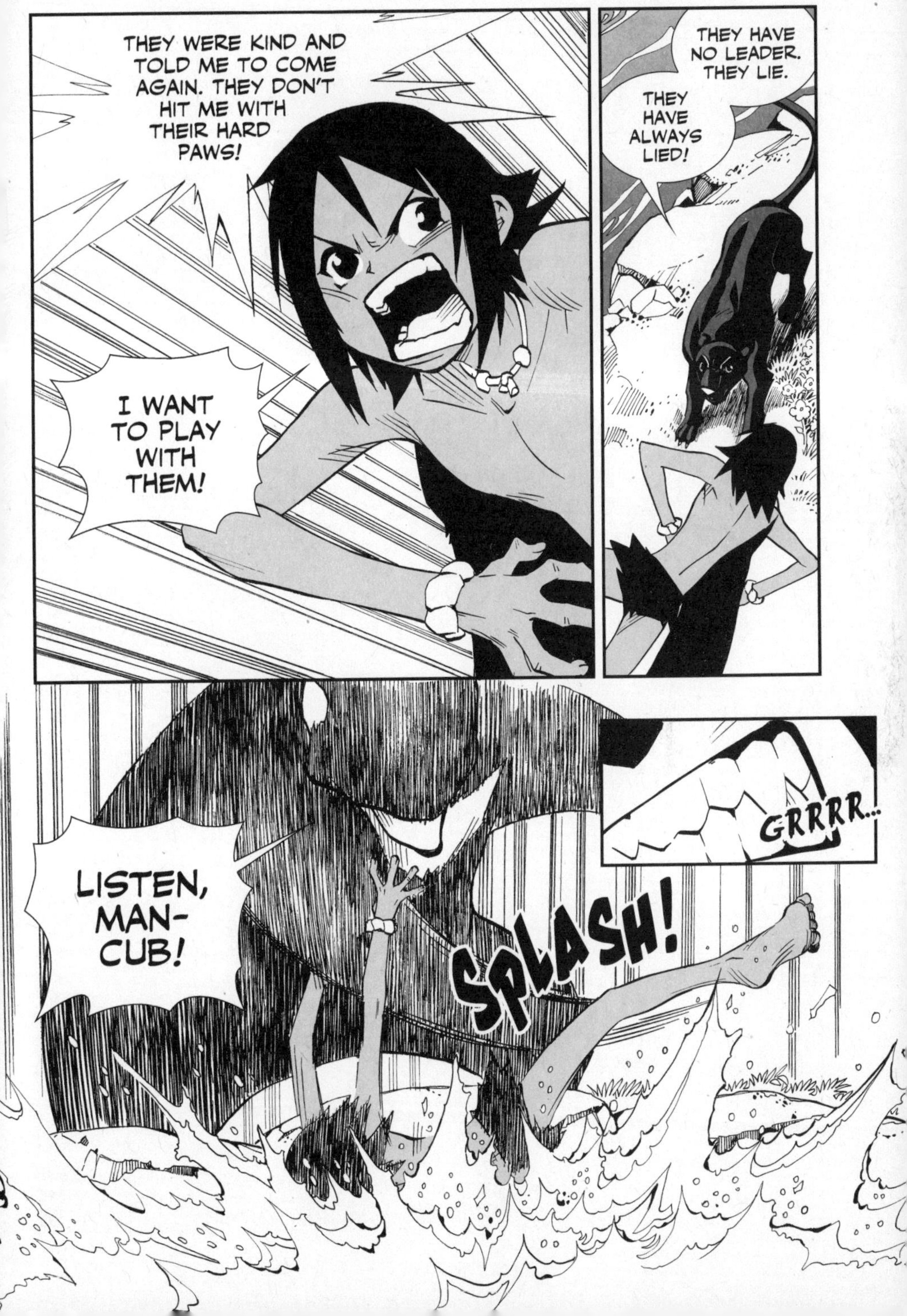
THEY HAVE NO LEADER. THEY LIE.
THEY HAVE ALWAYS LIED!
THEY WERE KIND AND TOLD ME TO COME AGAIN. THEY DON'T HIT ME WITH THEIR HARD PAWS!
I WANT TO PLAY WITH THEM!
GRRRR...
LISTEN, MAN-CUB!
SPLASH!

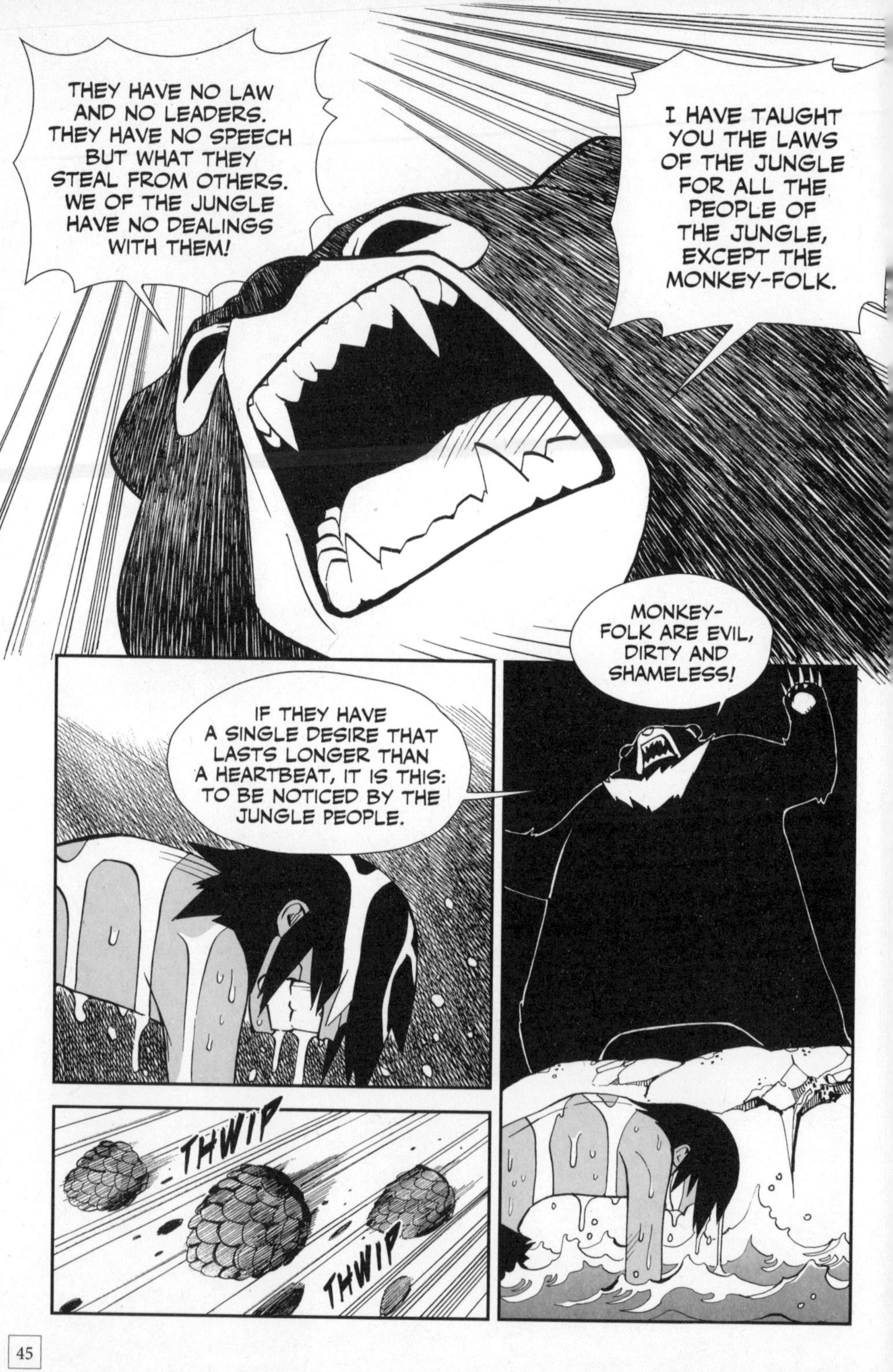
I HAVE TAUGHT YOU THE LAWS OF THE JUNGLE FOR ALL THE PEOPLE OF THE JUNGLE, EXCEPT THE MONKEY-FOLK.
THEY HAVE NO LAW AND NO LEADERS. THEY HAVE NO SPEECH BUT WHAT THEY STEAL FROM OTHERS. WE OF THE JUNGLE HAVE NO DEALINGS WITH THEM!
MONKEY-FOLK ARE EVIL, DIRTY AND SHAMELESS!
IF THEY HAVE A SINGLE DESIRE THAT LASTS LONGER THAN A HEARTBEAT, IT IS THIS: TO BE NOTICED BY THE JUNGLE PEOPLE.
THWIP
THWIP

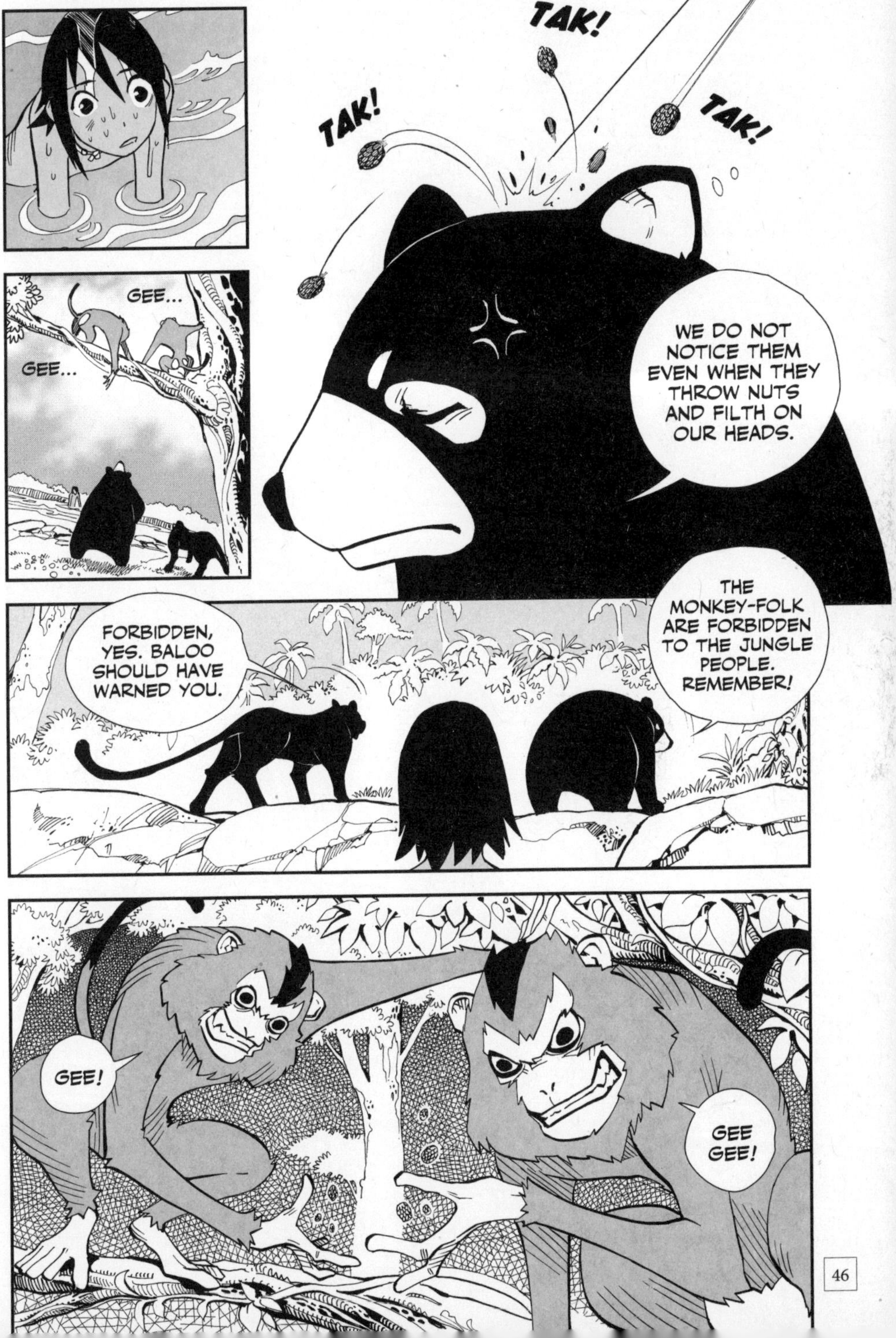
TAK!
TAK!
TAK!
WE DO NOT NOTICE THEM EVEN WHEN THEY THROW NUTS AND FILTH ON OUR HEADS.
GEE...
GEE...
THE MONKEY-FOLK ARE FORBIDDEN TO THE JUNGLE PEOPLE. REMEMBER!
FORBIDDEN, YES. BALOO SHOULD HAVE WARNED YOU.
GEE GEE!
GEE!

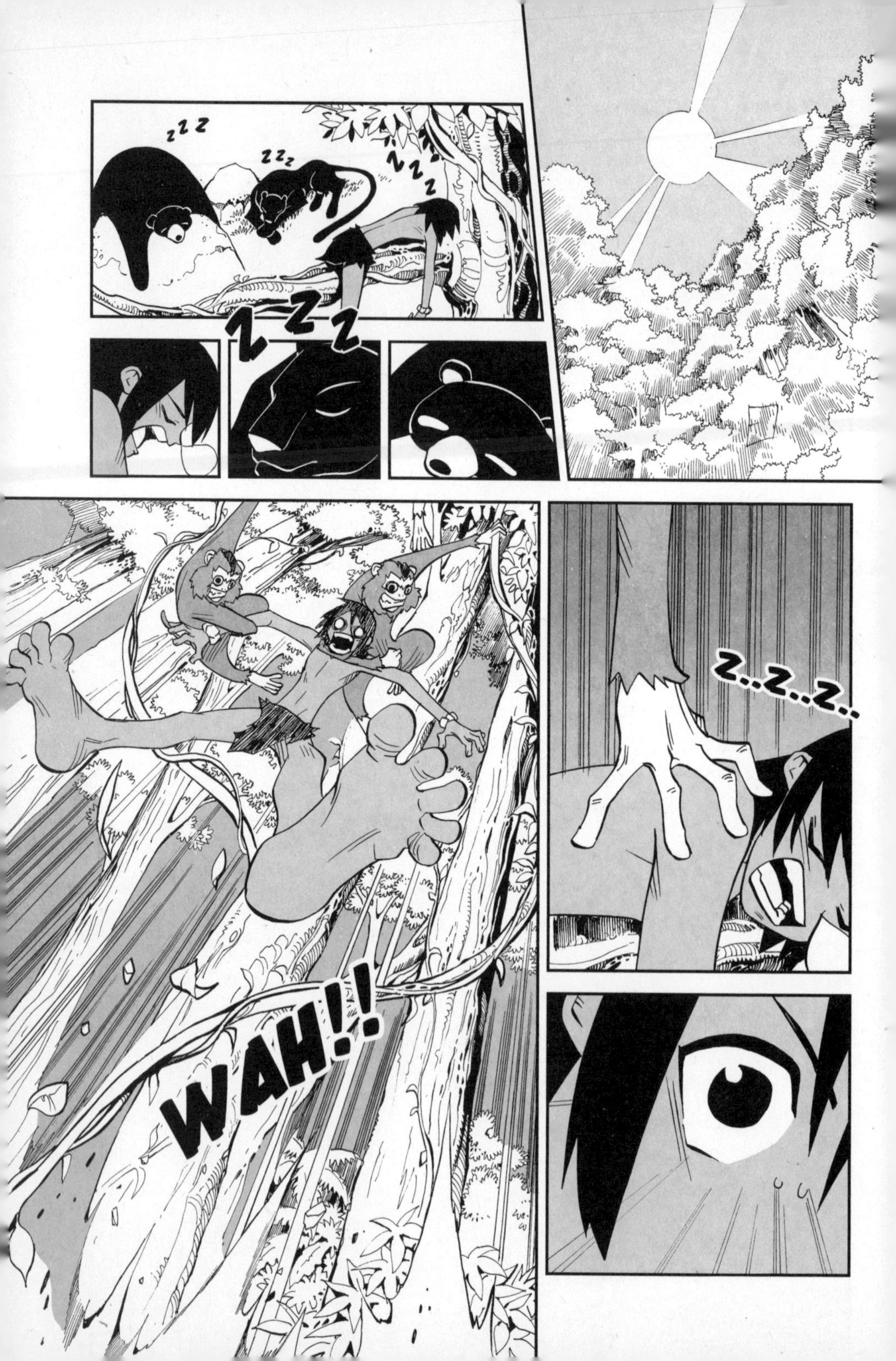
ZZZ
ZZZ
ZZZ
ZZZ
Z..Z..Z..
WAH!!

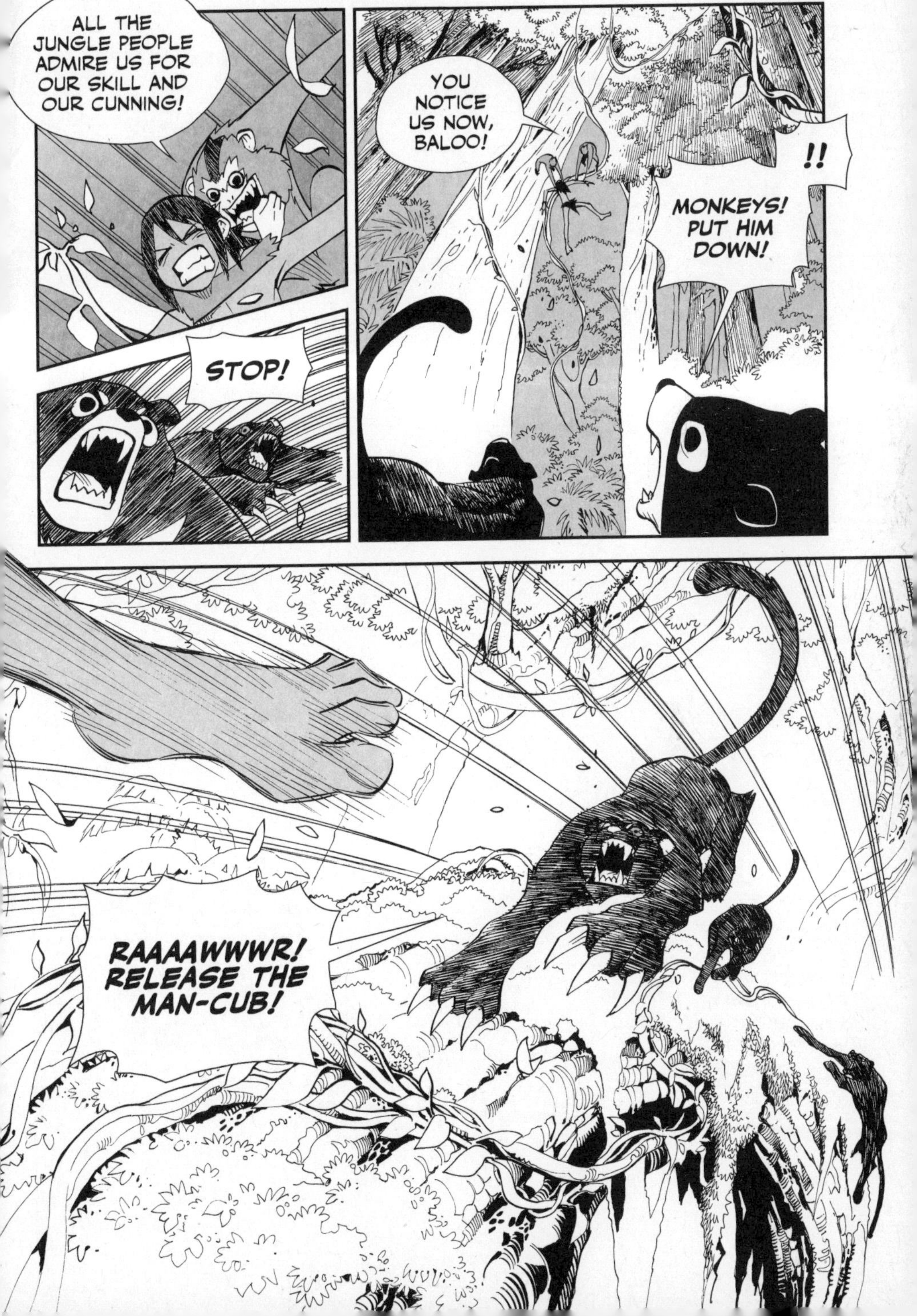
!!
MONKEYS! PUT HIM DOWN!
YOU NOTICE US NOW, BALOO!
ALL THE JUNGLE PEOPLE ADMIRE US FOR OUR SKILL AND OUR CUNNING!
STOP!
RAAAAWWWR! RELEASE THE MAN-CUB!

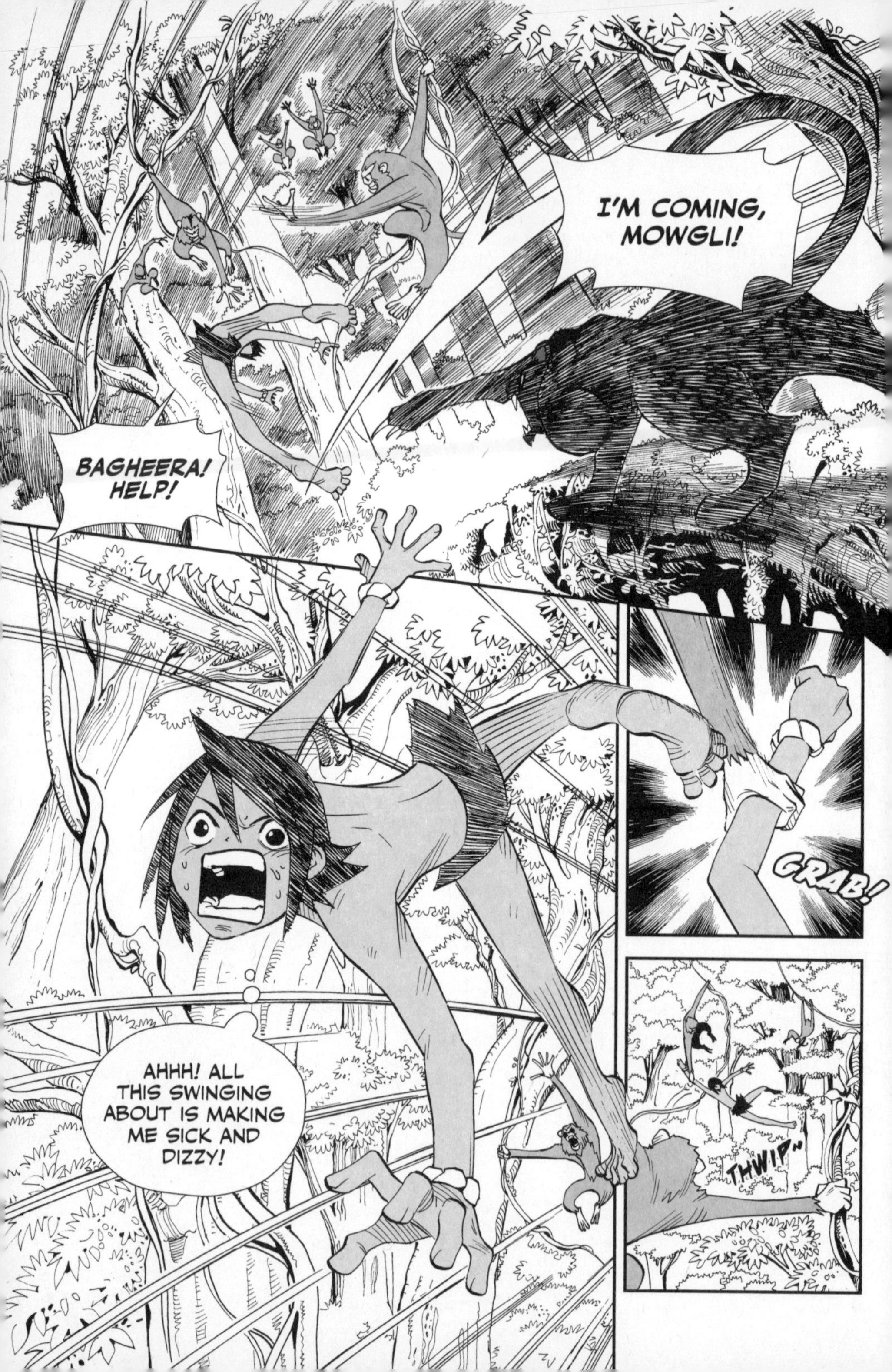
I'M COMING, MOWGLI!
BAGHEERA! HELP!
GRAB!
THWIP
AHHH! ALL THIS SWINGING ABOUT IS MAKING ME SICK AND DIZZY!

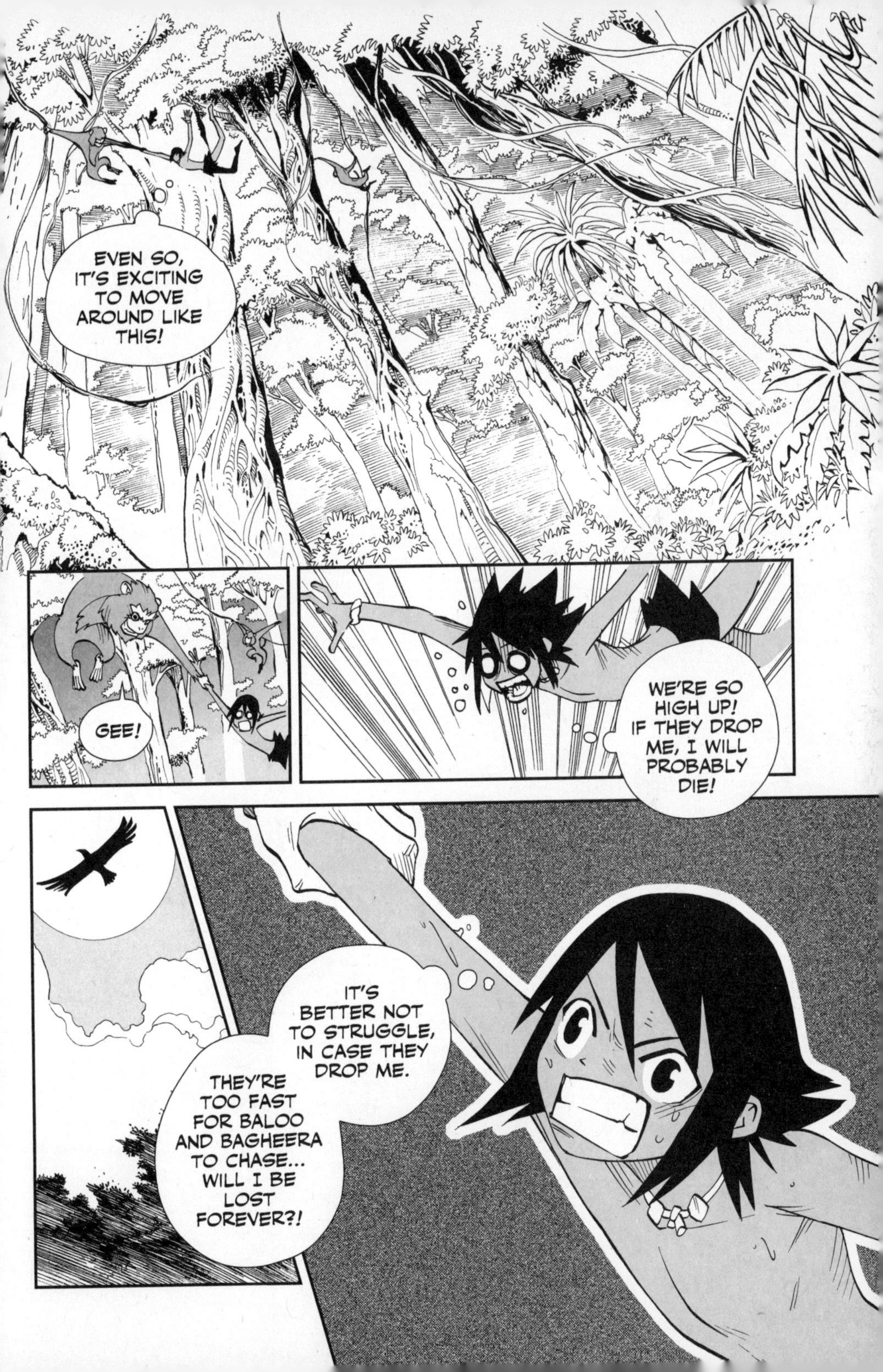
EVEN SO, IT'S EXCITING TO MOVE AROUND LIKE THIS!
WE'RE SO HIGH UP! IF THEY DROP ME, I WILL PROBABLY DIE!
GEE!
IT'S BETTER NOT TO STRUGGLE, IN CASE THEY DROP ME.
THEY'RE TOO FAST FOR BALOO AND BAGHEERA TO CHASE... WILL I BE LOST FOREVER?!

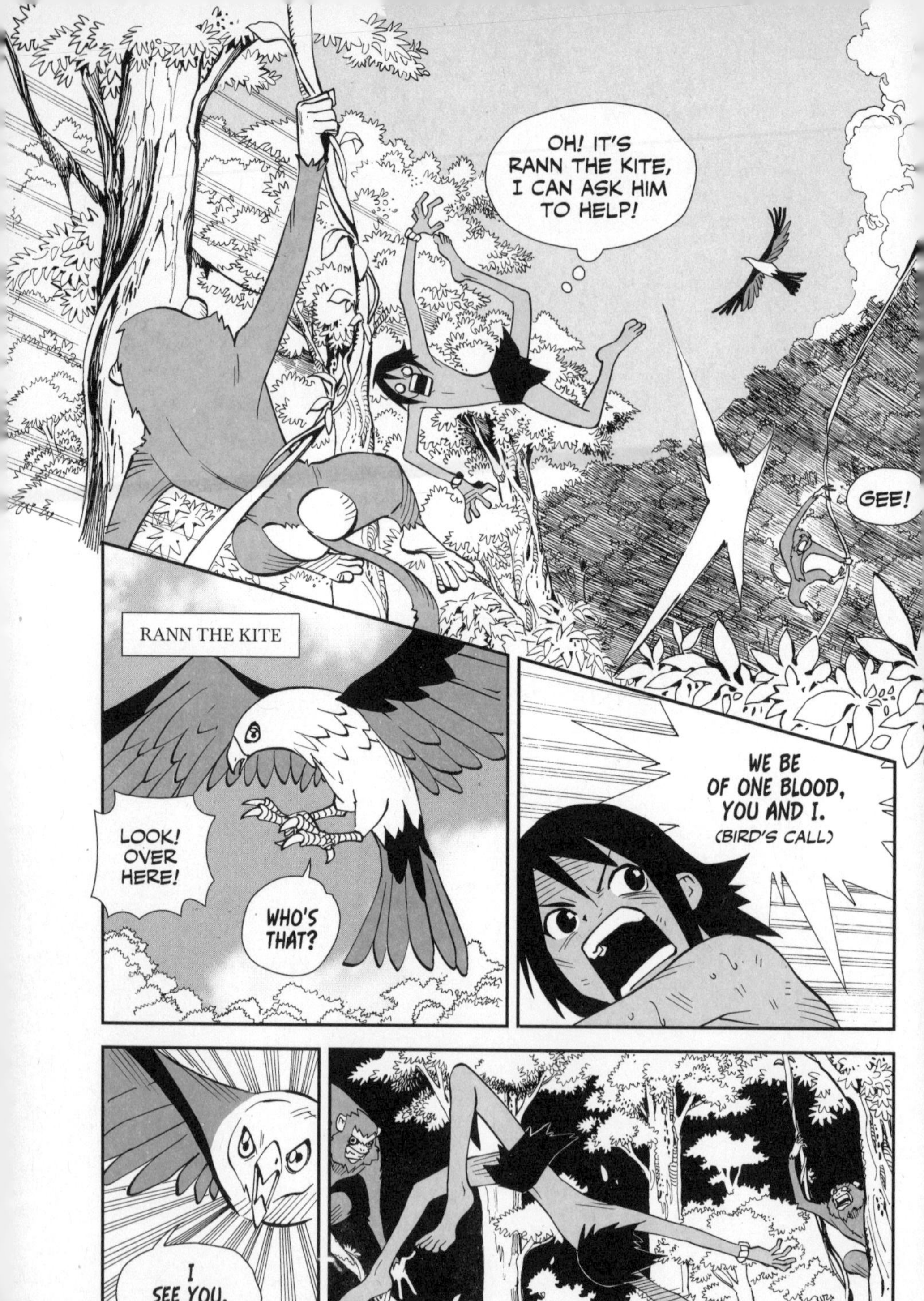

OH! IT'S RANN THE KITE, I CAN ASK HIM TO HELP!
GEE!
WE BE OF ONE BLOOD, YOU AND I.
(BIRD'S CALL)
RANN THE KITE
LOOK! OVER HERE!
WHO'S THAT?
I SEE YOU, BROTHER.

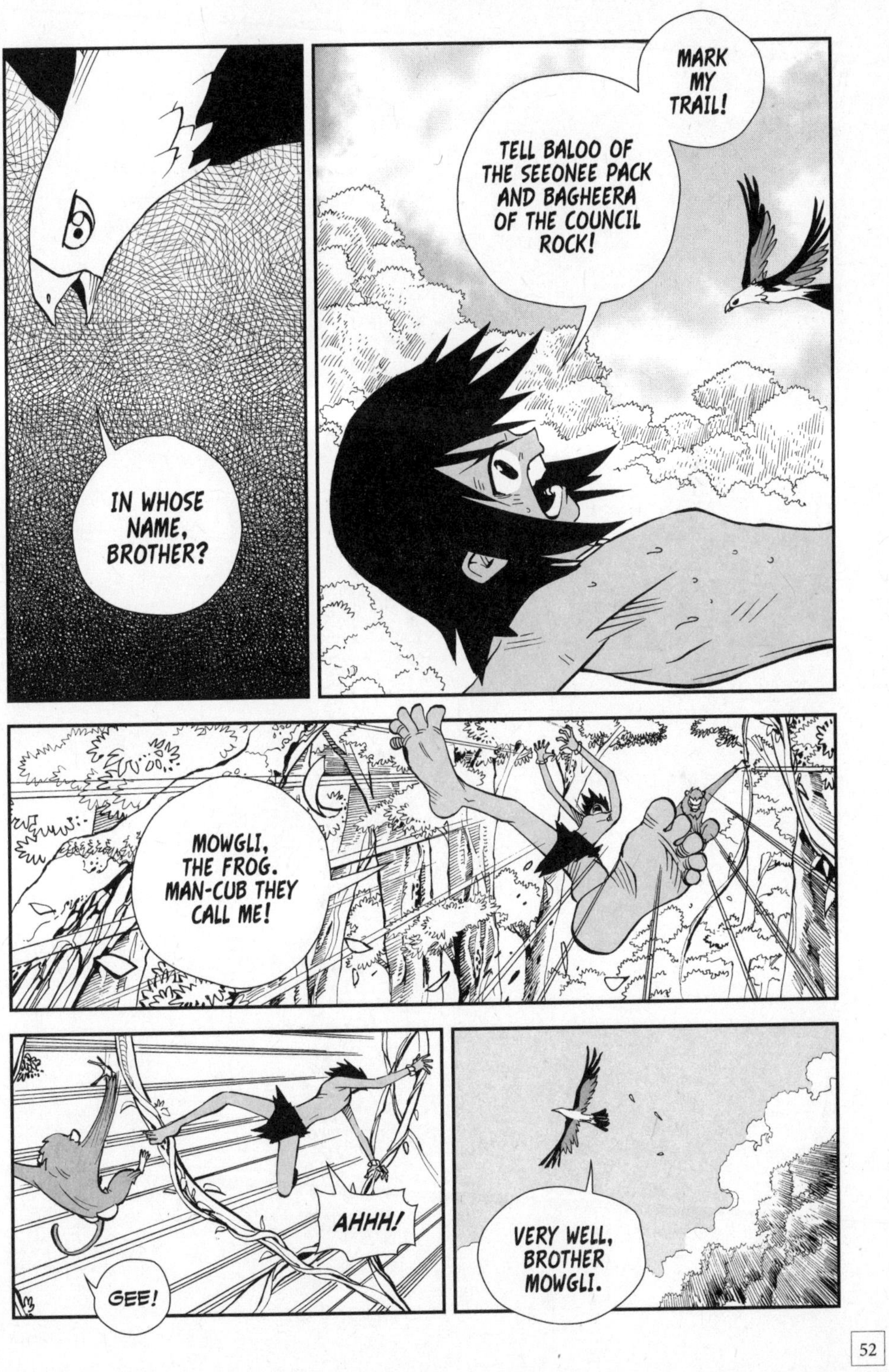
MARK MY TRAIL!
TELL BALOO OF THE SEEONEE PACK AND BAGHEERA OF THE COUNCIL ROCK!
IN WHOSE NAME, BROTHER?
MOWGLI, THE FROG. MAN-CUB THEY CALL ME!
VERY WELL, BROTHER MOWGLI.
AHHH!
GEE!

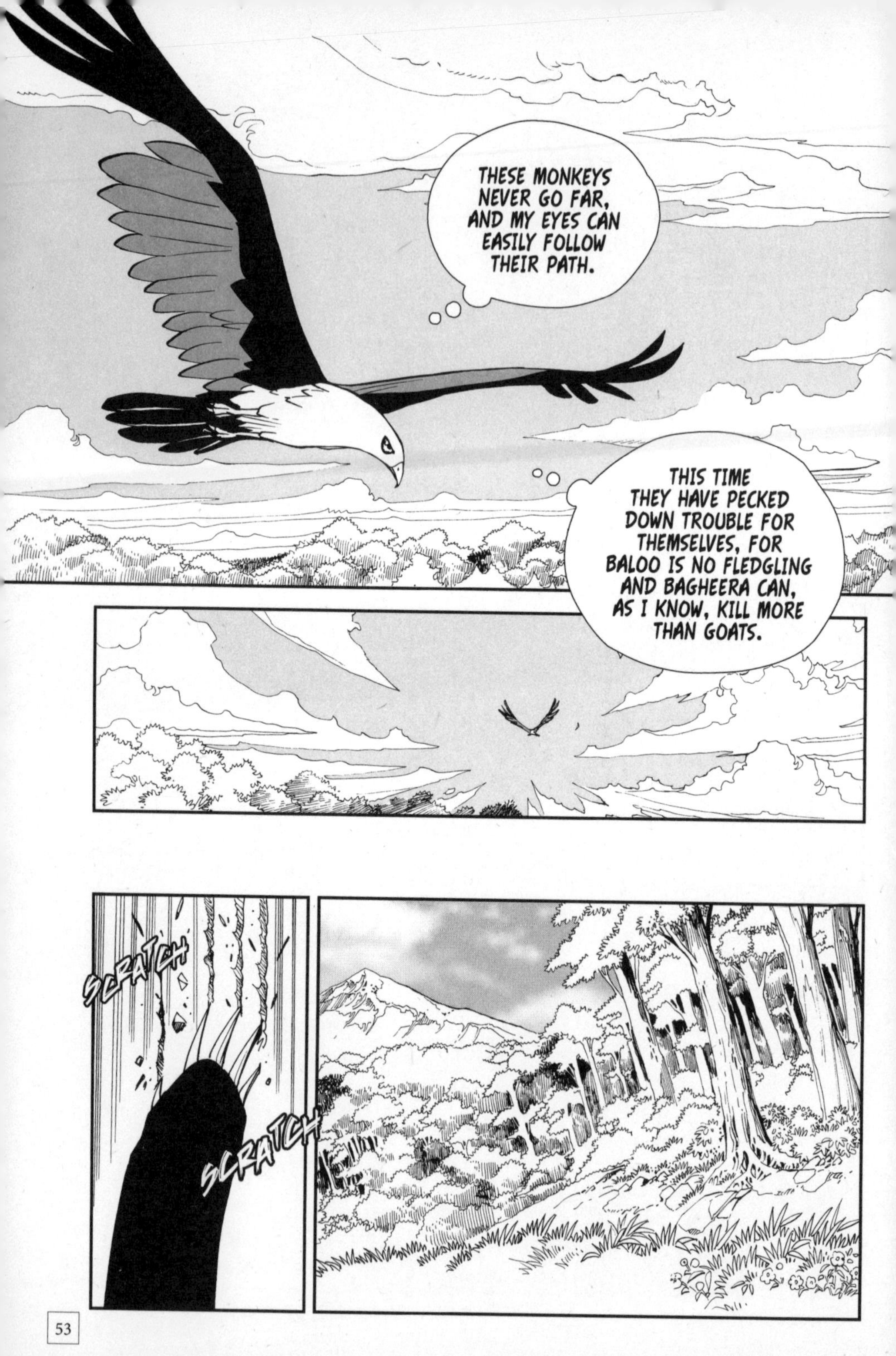
THESE MONKEYS NEVER GO FAR, AND MY EYES CAN EASILY FOLLOW THEIR PATH.
THIS TIME THEY HAVE PECKED DOWN TROUBLE FOR THEMSELVES, FOR BALOO IS NO FLEDGLING AND BAGHEERA CAN, AS I KNOW, KILL MORE THAN GOATS.
SCRATCH
SCRATCH

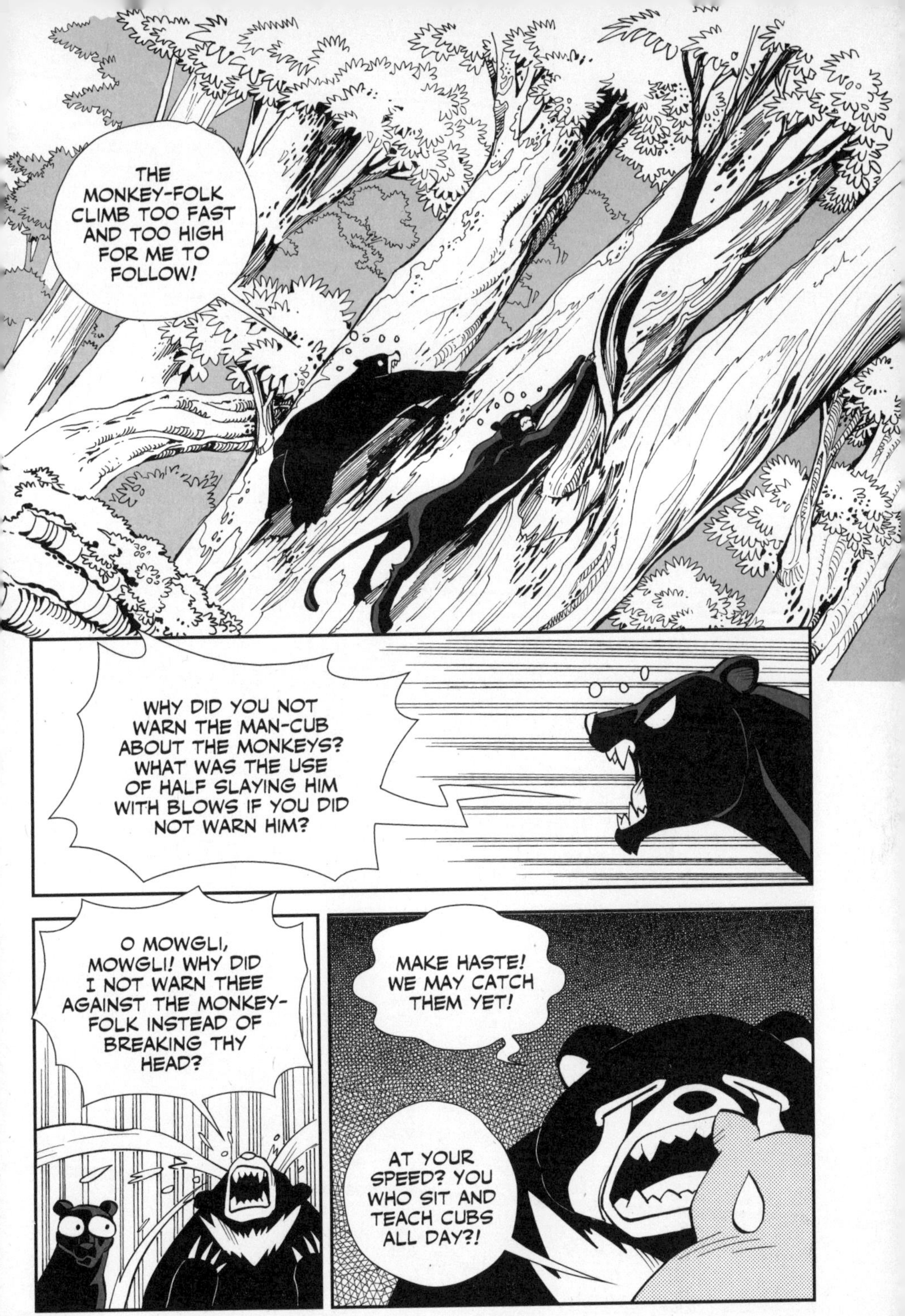
THE MONKEY-FOLK CLIMB TOO FAST AND TOO HIGH FOR ME TO FOLLOW!
WHY DID YOU NOT WARN THE MAN-CUB ABOUT THE MONKEYS? WHAT WAS THE USE OF HALF SLAYING HIM WITH BLOWS IF YOU DID NOT WARN HIM?
MAKE HASTE! WE MAY CATCH THEM YET!
AT YOUR SPEED? YOU WHO SIT AND TEACH CUBS ALL DAY?!
O MOWGLI, MOWGLI! WHY DID I NOT WARN THEE AGAINST THE MONKEY-FOLK INSTEAD OF BREAKING THY HEAD?

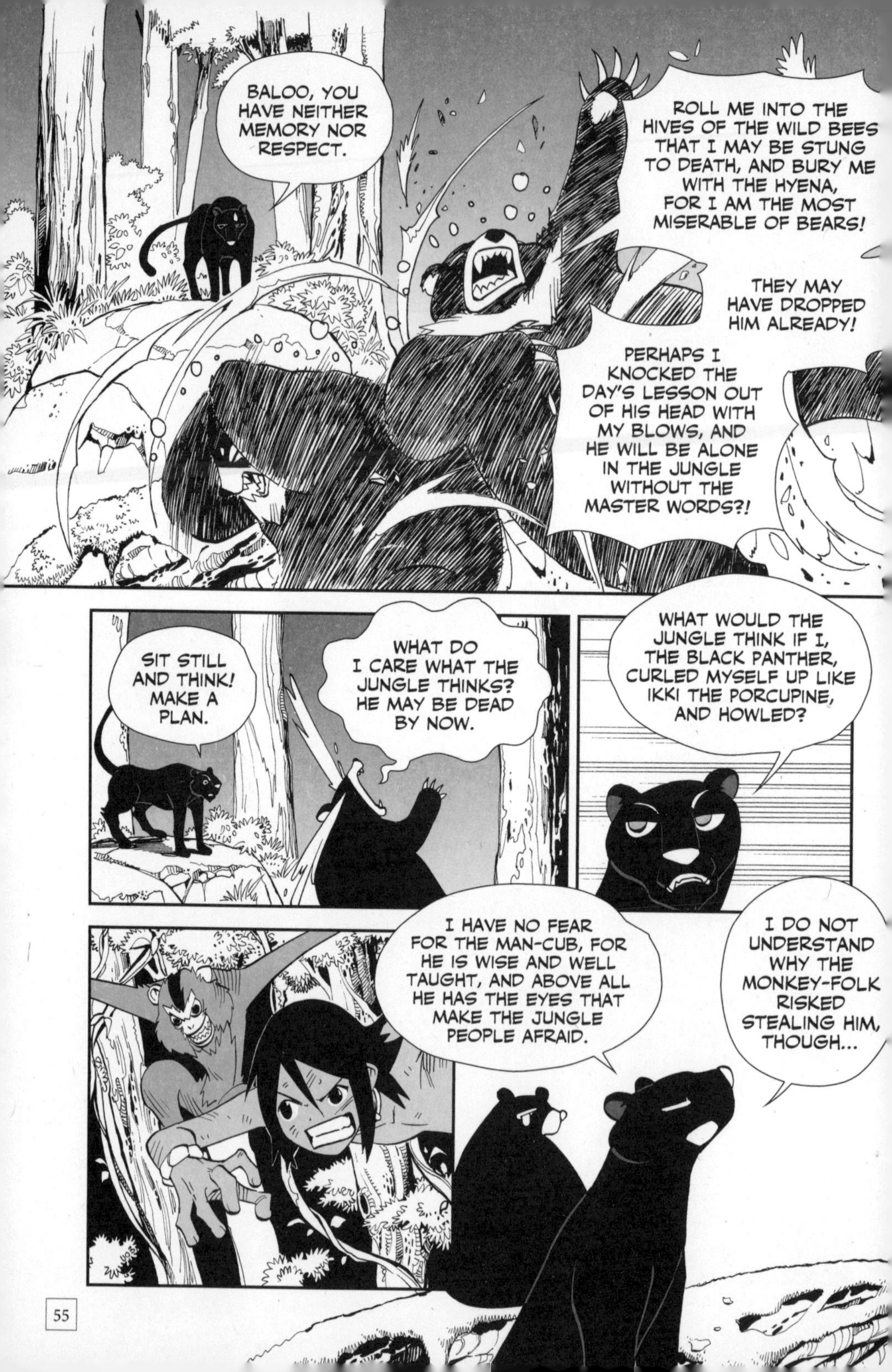
ROLL ME INTO THE HIVES OF THE WILD BEES THAT I MAY BE STUNG TO DEATH, AND BURY ME WITH THE HYENA, FOR I AM THE MOST MISERABLE OF BEARS!
THEY MAY HAVE DROPPED HIM ALREADY!
PERHAPS I KNOCKED THE DAY'S LESSON OUT OF HIS HEAD WITH MY BLOWS, AND HE WILL BE ALONE IN THE JUNGLE WITHOUT THE MASTER WORDS?!
BALOO, YOU HAVE NEITHER MEMORY NOR RESPECT.
WHAT WOULD THE JUNGLE THINK IF I, THE BLACK PANTHER, CURLED MYSELF UP LIKE IKKI THE PORCUPINE, AND HOWLED?
WHAT DO I CARE WHAT THE JUNGLE THINKS? HE MAY BE DEAD BY NOW.
SIT STILL AND THINK! MAKE A PLAN.
I DO NOT UNDERSTAND WHY THE MONKEY-FOLK RISKED STEALING HIM, THOUGH...
I HAVE NO FEAR FOR THE MAN-CUB, FOR HE IS WISE AND WELL TAUGHT, AND ABOVE ALL HE HAS THE EYES THAT MAKE THE JUNGLE PEOPLE AFRAID.

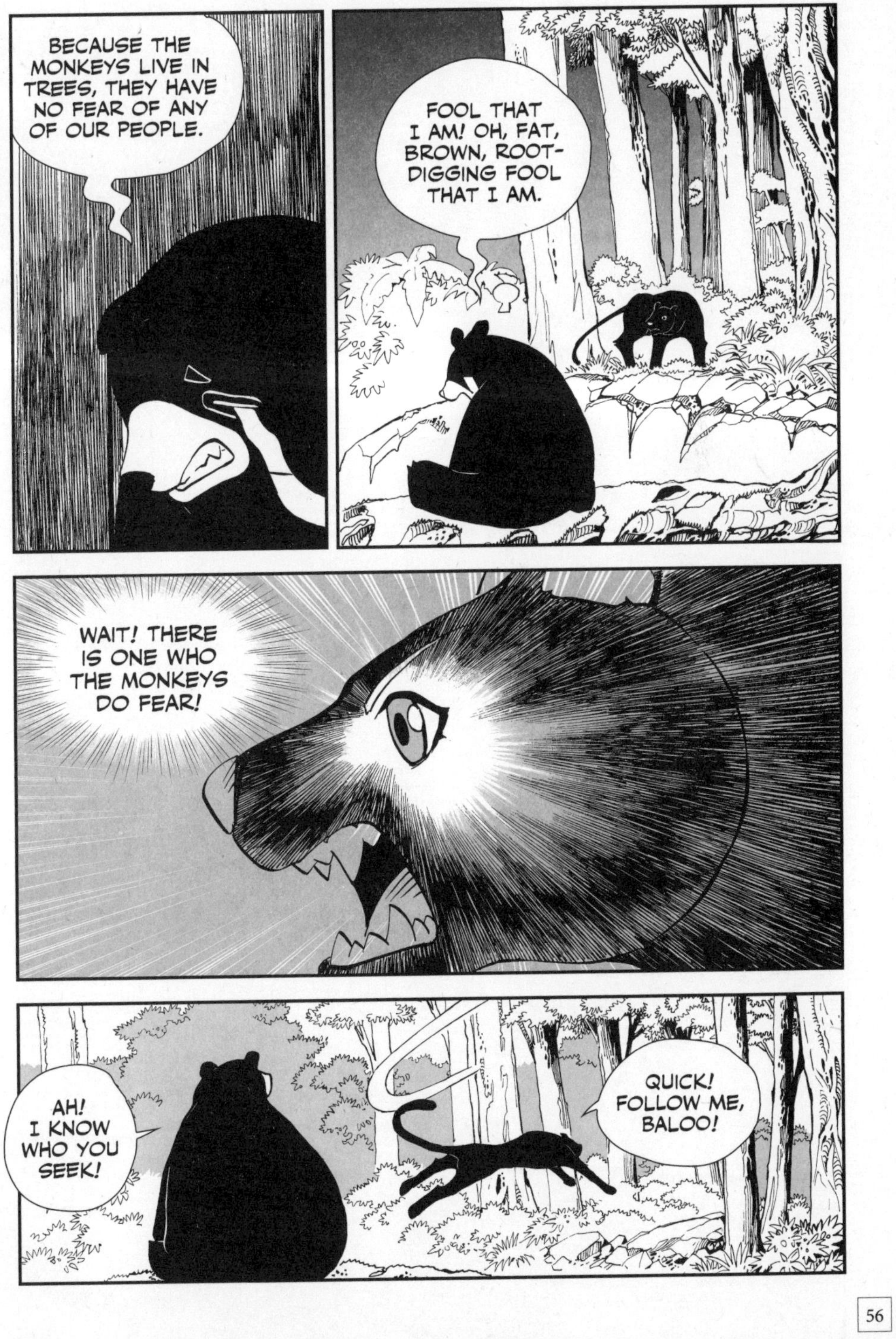
FOOL THAT I AM! OH, FAT, BROWN, ROOT-DIGGING FOOL THAT I AM.
BECAUSE THE MONKEYS LIVE IN TREES, THEY HAVE NO FEAR OF ANY OF OUR PEOPLE.
WAIT! THERE IS ONE WHO THE MONKEYS DO FEAR!
QUICK! FOLLOW ME, BALOO!
AH! I KNOW WHO YOU SEEK!

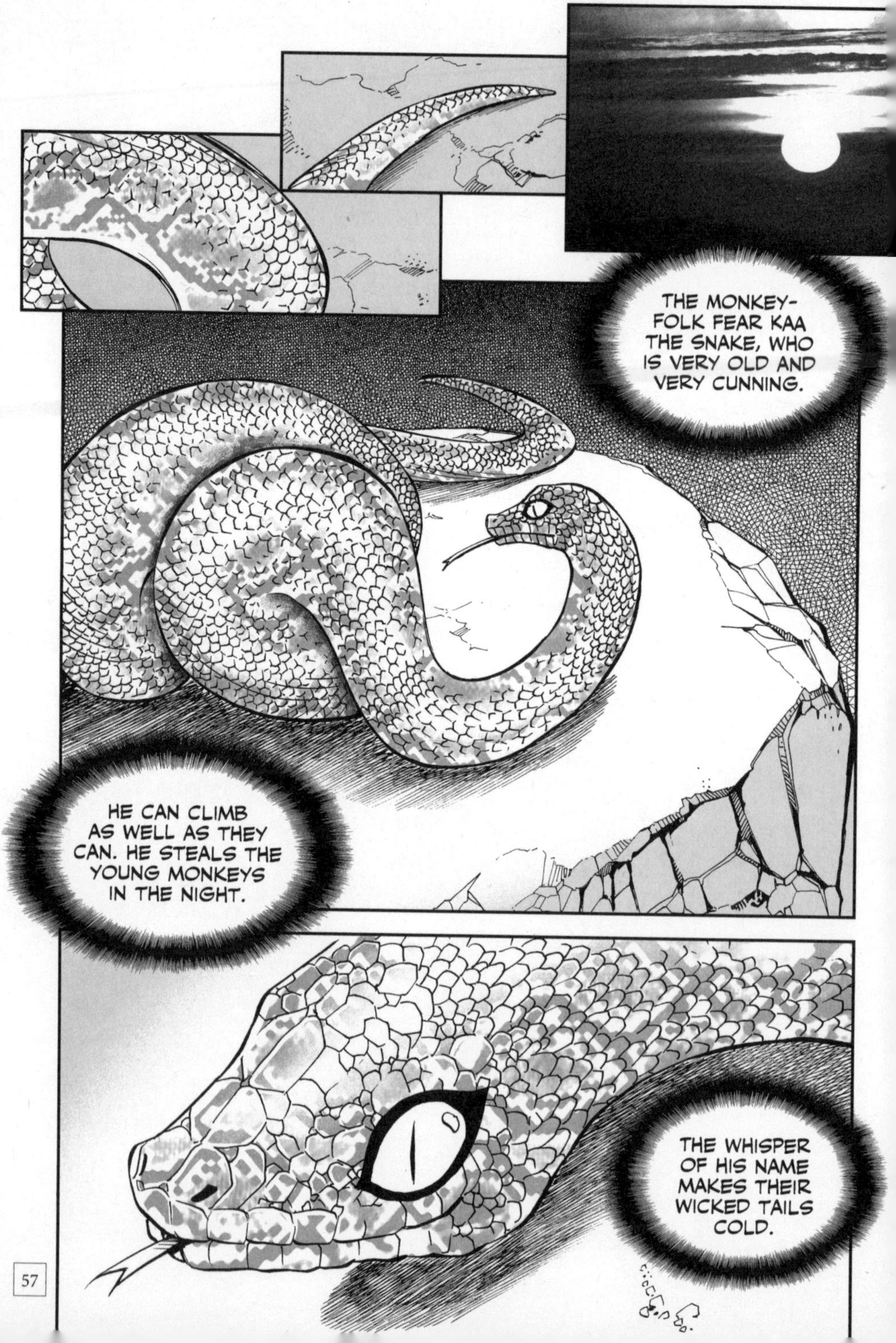
THE MONKEY-FOLK FEAR KAA THE SNAKE, WHO IS VERY OLD AND VERY CUNNING.
HE CAN CLIMB AS WELL AS THEY CAN. HE STEALS THE YOUNG MONKEYS IN THE NIGHT.
THE WHISPER OF HIS NAME MAKES THEIR WICKED TAILS COLD.

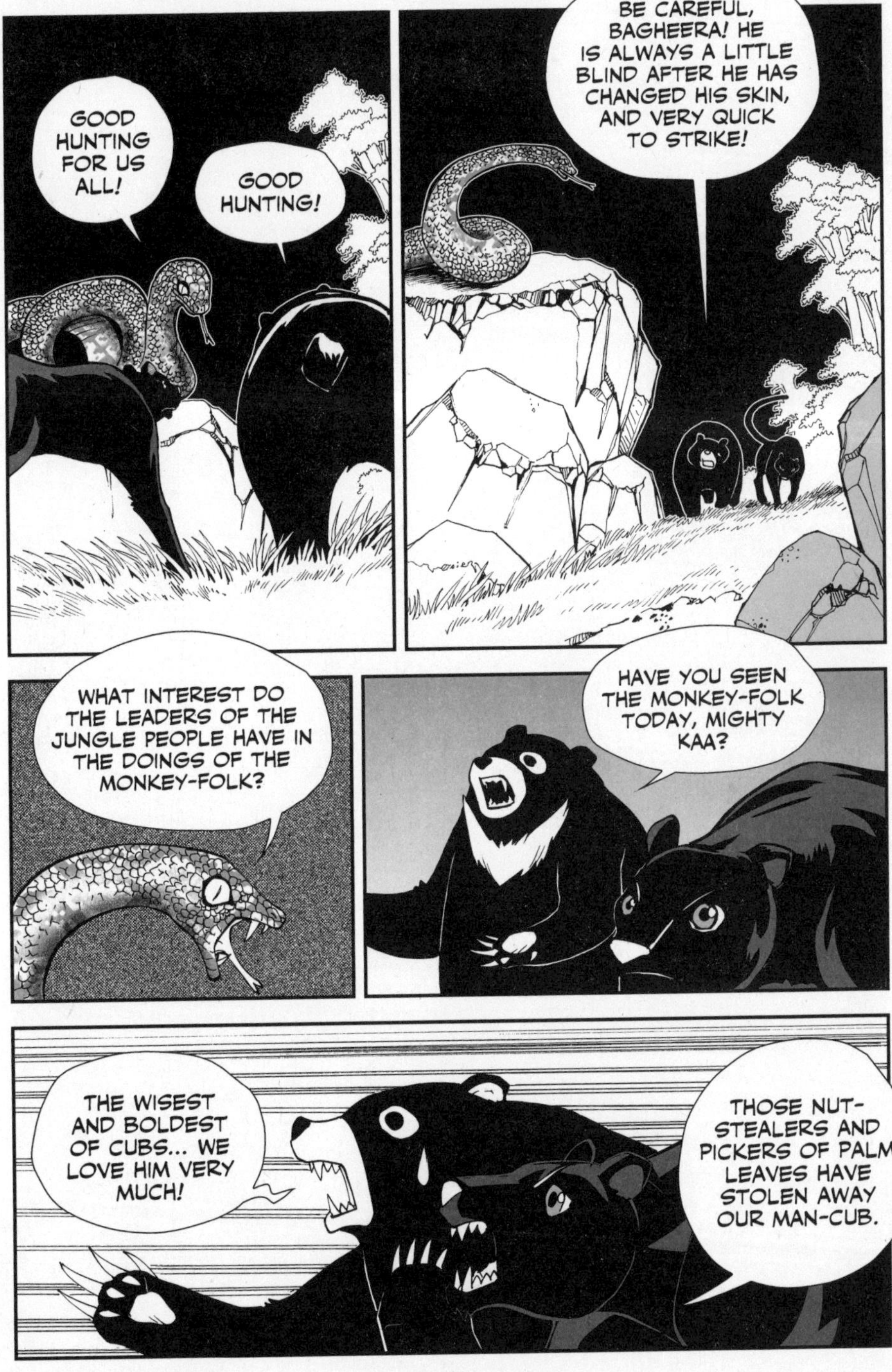
BE CAREFUL, BAGHEERA! HE IS ALWAYS A LITTLE BLIND AFTER HE HAS CHANGED HIS SKIN, AND VERY QUICK TO STRIKE!
GOOD HUNTING!
GOOD HUNTING FOR US ALL!
HAVE YOU SEEN THE MONKEY-FOLK TODAY, MIGHTY KAA?
WHAT INTEREST DO THE LEADERS OF THE JUNGLE PEOPLE HAVE IN THE DOINGS OF THE MONKEY-FOLK?
THOSE NUT-STEALERS AND PICKERS OF PALM LEAVES HAVE STOLEN AWAY OUR MAN-CUB.
THE WISEST AND BOLDEST OF CUBS... WE LOVE HIM VERY MUCH!

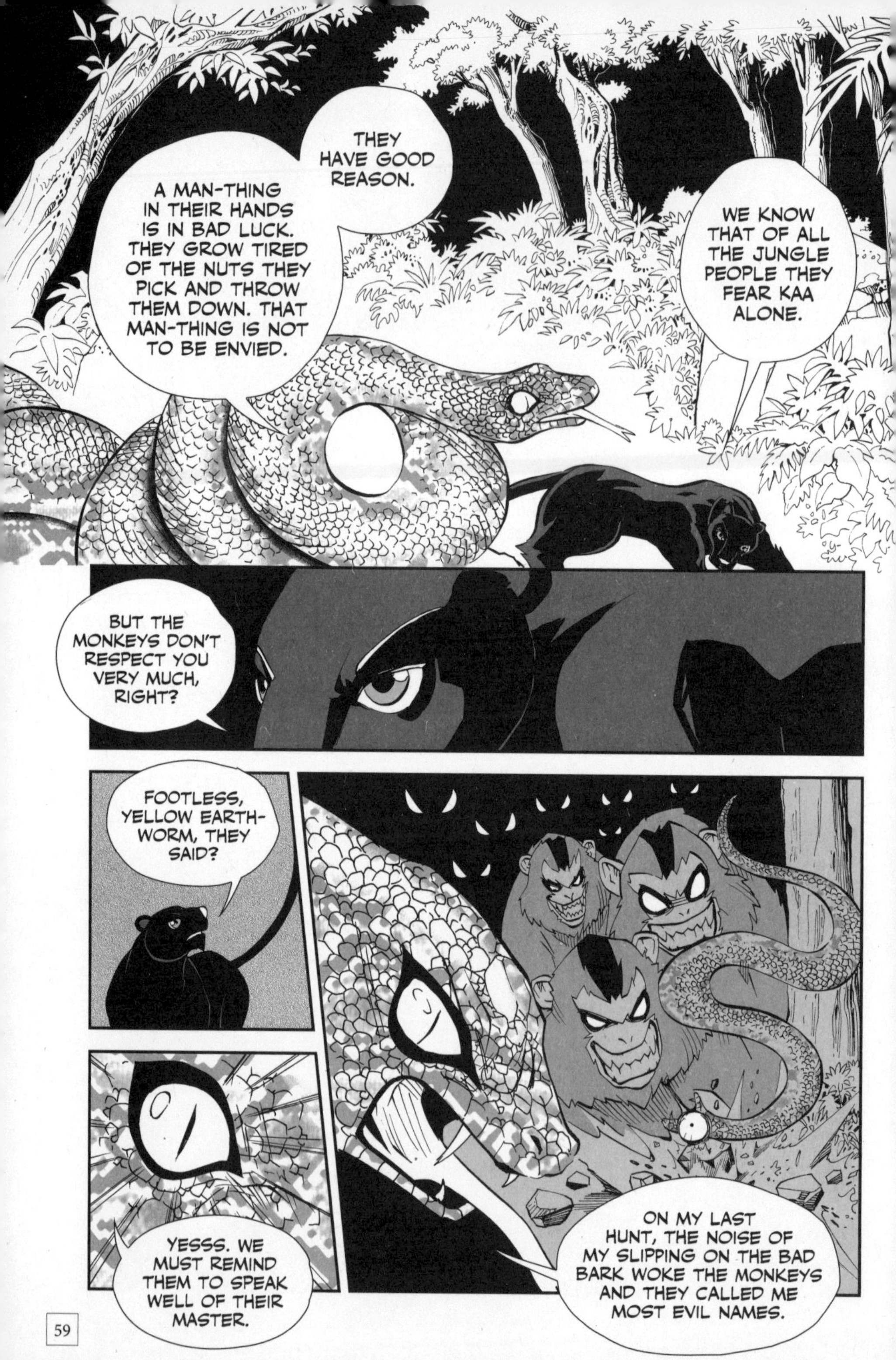
WE KNOW THAT OF ALL THE JUNGLE PEOPLE THEY FEAR KAA ALONE.
THEY HAVE GOOD REASON.
A MAN-THING IN THEIR HANDS IS IN BAD LUCK. THEY GROW TIRED OF THE NUTS THEY PICK AND THROW THEM DOWN. THAT MAN-THING IS NOT TO BE ENVIED.
BUT THE MONKEYS DON'T RESPECT YOU VERY MUCH, RIGHT?
ON MY LAST HUNT, THE NOISE OF MY SLIPPING ON THE BAD BARK WOKE THE MONKEYS AND THEY CALLED ME MOST EVIL NAMES.
FOOTLESS, YELLOW EARTH-WORM, THEY SAID?
YESSS. WE MUST REMIND THEM TO SPEAK WELL OF THEIR MASTER.

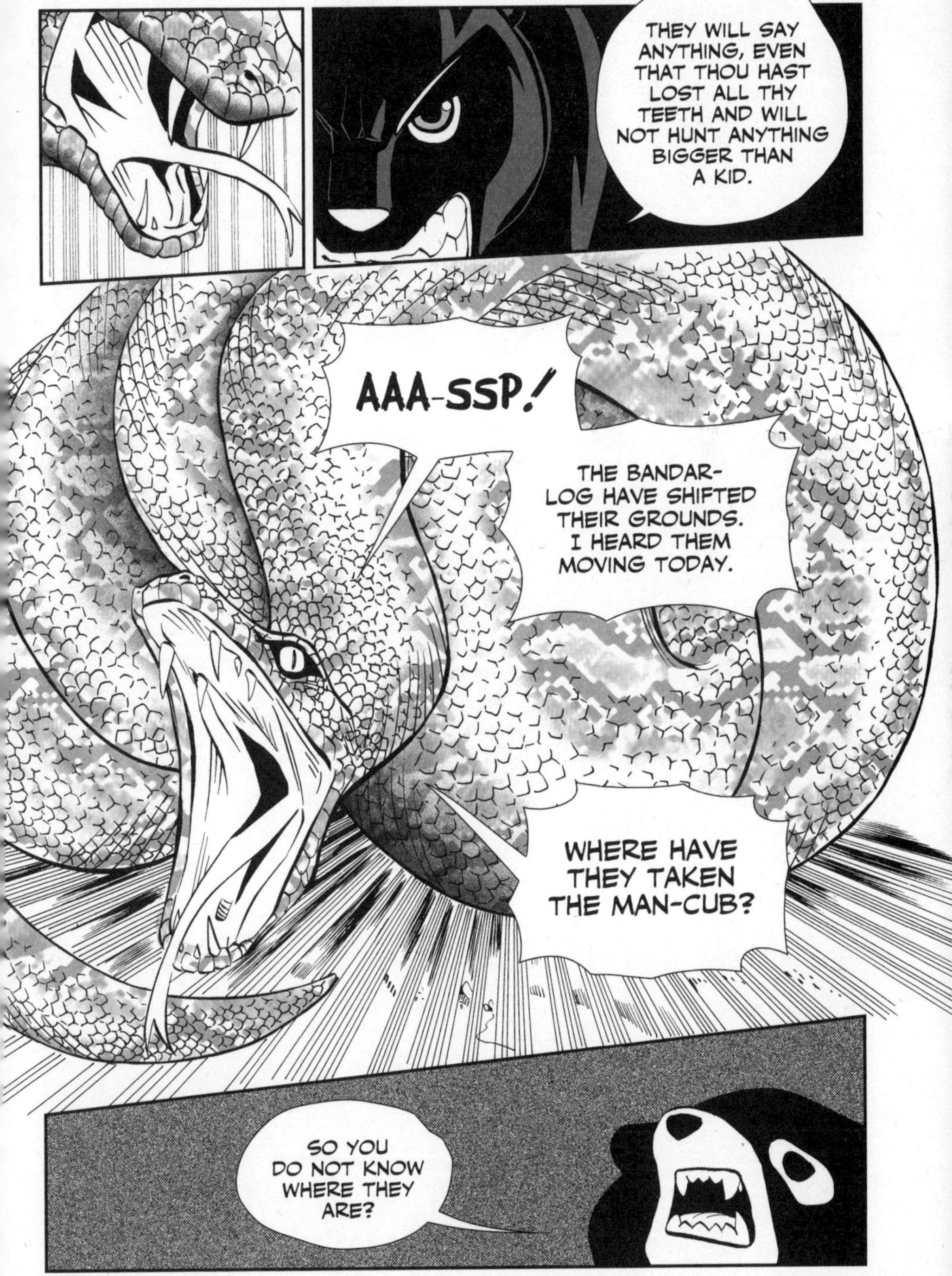
THEY WILL SAY ANYTHING, EVEN THAT THOU HAST LOST ALL THY TEETH AND WILL NOT HUNT ANYTHING BIGGER THAN A KID.
AAA-SSP!
THE BANDAR-LOG HAVE SHIFTED THEIR GROUNDS. I HEARD THEM MOVING TODAY.
WHERE HAVE THEY TAKEN THE MAN-CUB?
SO YOU DO NOT KNOW WHERE THEY ARE?

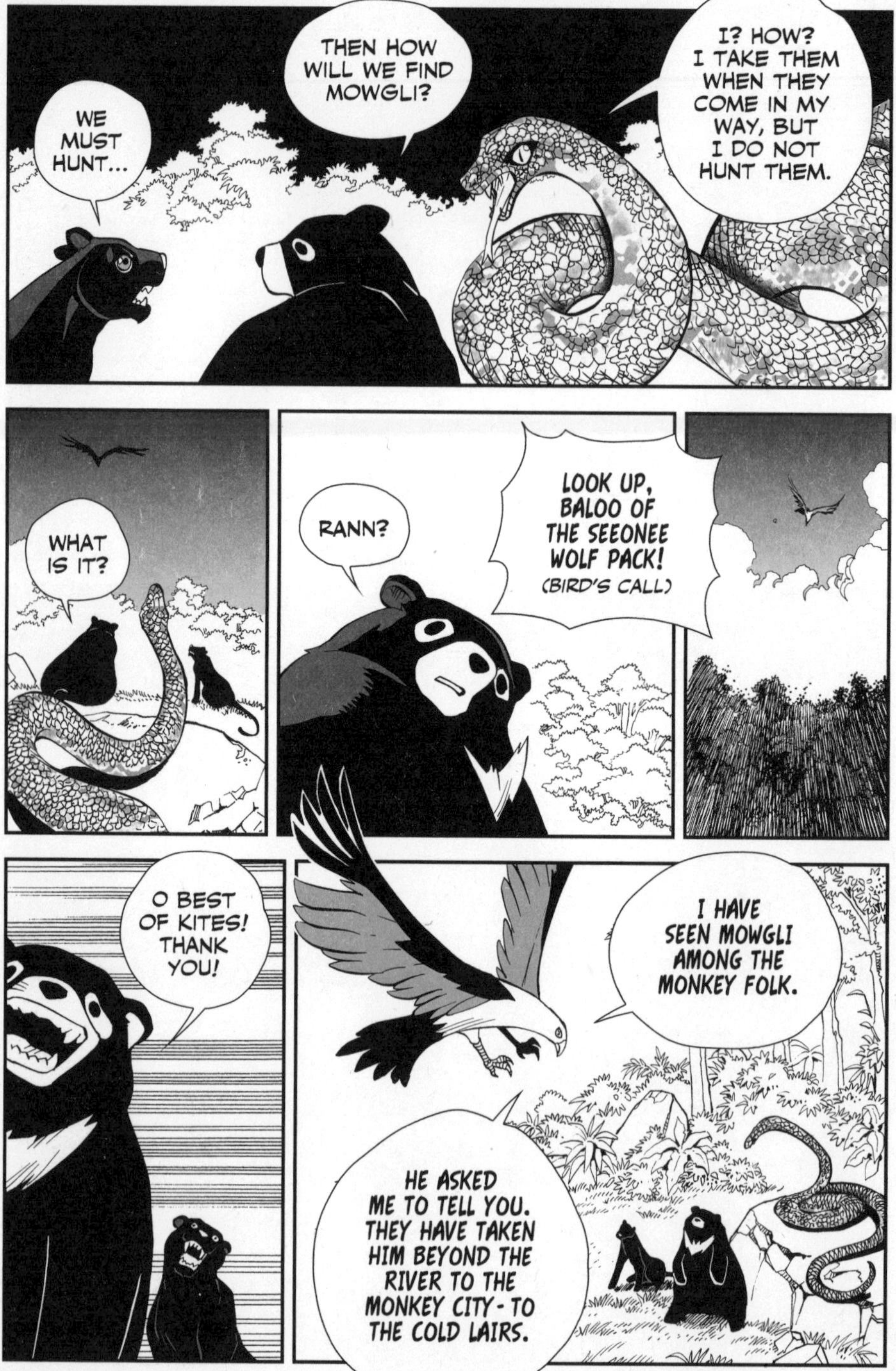
I? HOW? I TAKE THEM WHEN THEY COME IN MY WAY, BUT I DO NOT HUNT THEM.
THEN HOW WILL WE FIND MOWGLI?
WE MUST HUNT...
LOOK UP, BALOO OF THE SEEONEE WOLF PACK! (BIRD'S CALL)
RANN?
WHAT IS IT?
I HAVE SEEN MOWGLI AMONG THE MONKEY FOLK.
HE ASKED ME TO TELL YOU. THEY HAVE TAKEN HIM BEYOND THE RIVER TO THE MONKEY CITY - TO THE COLD LAIRS.
O BEST OF KITES! THANK YOU!

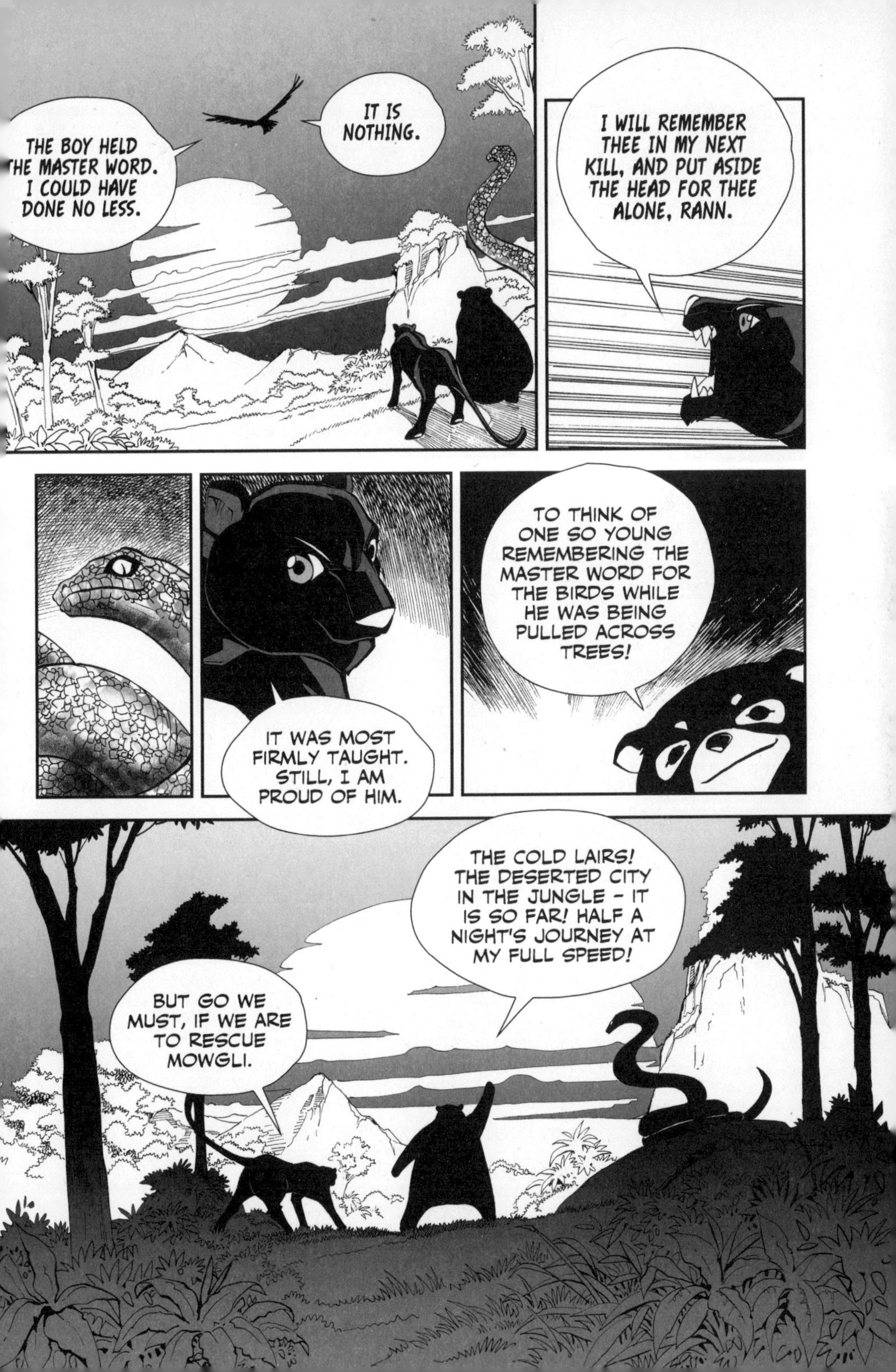
I WILL REMEMBER THEE IN MY NEXT KILL, AND PUT ASIDE THE HEAD FOR THEE ALONE, RANN.
IT IS NOTHING.
THE BOY HELD THE MASTER WORD. I COULD HAVE DONE NO LESS.
TO THINK OF ONE SO YOUNG REMEMBERING THE MASTER WORD FOR THE BIRDS WHILE HE WAS BEING PULLED ACROSS TREES!
IT WAS MOST FIRMLY TAUGHT. STILL, I AM PROUD OF HIM.
THE COLD LAIRS! THE DESERTED CITY IN THE JUNGLE - IT IS SO FAR! HALF A NIGHT'S JOURNEY AT MY FULL SPEED!
BUT GO WE MUST, IF WE ARE TO RESCUE MOWGLI.

ROAD-SONG OF THE BANDAR-LOG

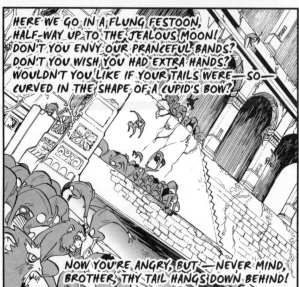

HERE WE GO IN A FLUNG FESTOON,
HALF-WAY UP TO THE JEALOUS MOON!
DON'T YOU ENVY OUR PRANCEFUL BANDS?
DON'T YOU WISH YOU HAD EXTRA HANDS?
WOULDN'T YOU LIKE IF YOUR TAILS WERE —SO—
CURVED IN THE SHAPE OF A CUPID'S BOW?

NOW YOU'RE ANGRY, BUT —NEVER MIND,
BROTHER, THY TAIL HANGS DOWN BEHIND!

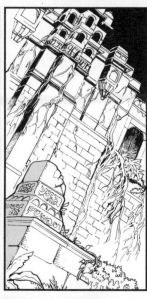

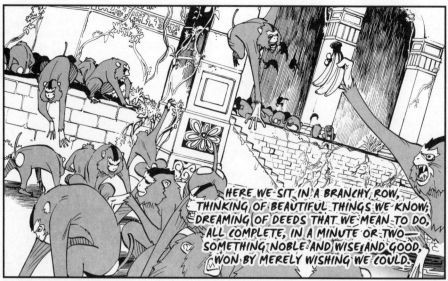

HERE WE SIT IN A BRANCHY ROW,
THINKING OF BEAUTIFUL THINGS WE KNOW;
DREAMING OF DEEDS THAT WE MEAN TO DO,
ALL COMPLETE, IN A MINUTE OR TWO—
SOMETHING NOBLE AND WISE AND GOOD,
WON BY MERELY WISHING WE COULD.

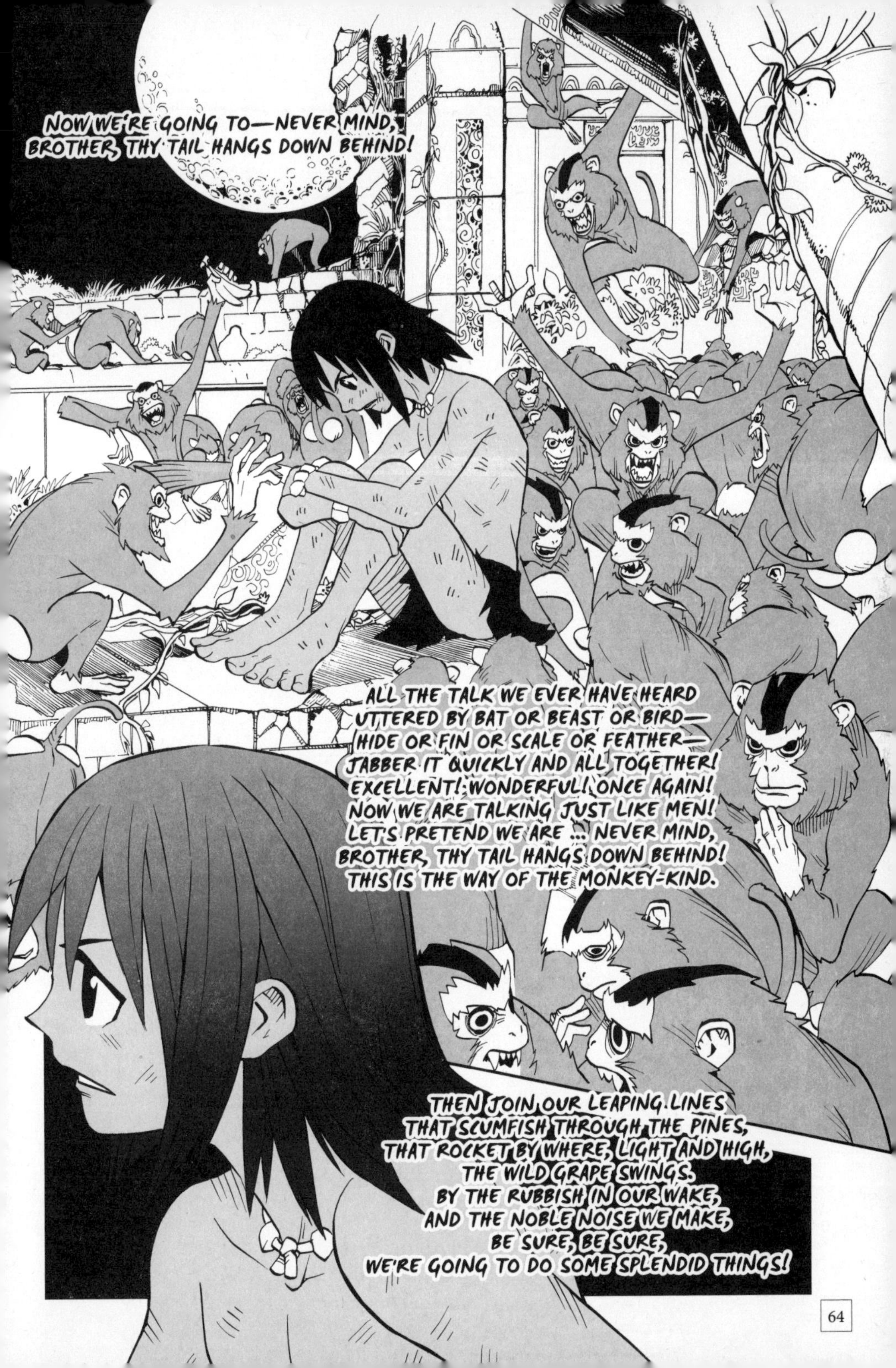
NOW WE'RE GOING TO—NEVER MIND, BROTHER, THY TAIL HANGS DOWN BEHIND!
ALL THE TALK WE EVER HAVE HEARD
UTTERED BY BAT OR BEAST OR BIRD—
HIDE OR FIN OR SCALE OR FEATHER—
JABBER IT QUICKLY AND ALL TOGETHER!
EXCELLENT! WONDERFUL! ONCE AGAIN!
NOW WE ARE TALKING JUST LIKE MEN!
LET'S PRETEND WE ARE ... NEVER MIND,
BROTHER, THY TAIL HANGS DOWN BEHIND!
THIS IS THE WAY OF THE MONKEY-KIND.
THEN JOIN OUR LEAPING LINES
THAT SCUMFISH THROUGH THE PINES,
THAT ROCKET BY WHERE, LIGHT AND HIGH,
THE WILD GRAPE SWINGS.
BY THE RUBBISH IN OUR WAKE,
AND THE NOBLE NOISE WE MAKE,
BE SURE, BE SURE,
WE'RE GOING TO DO SOME SPLENDID THINGS!

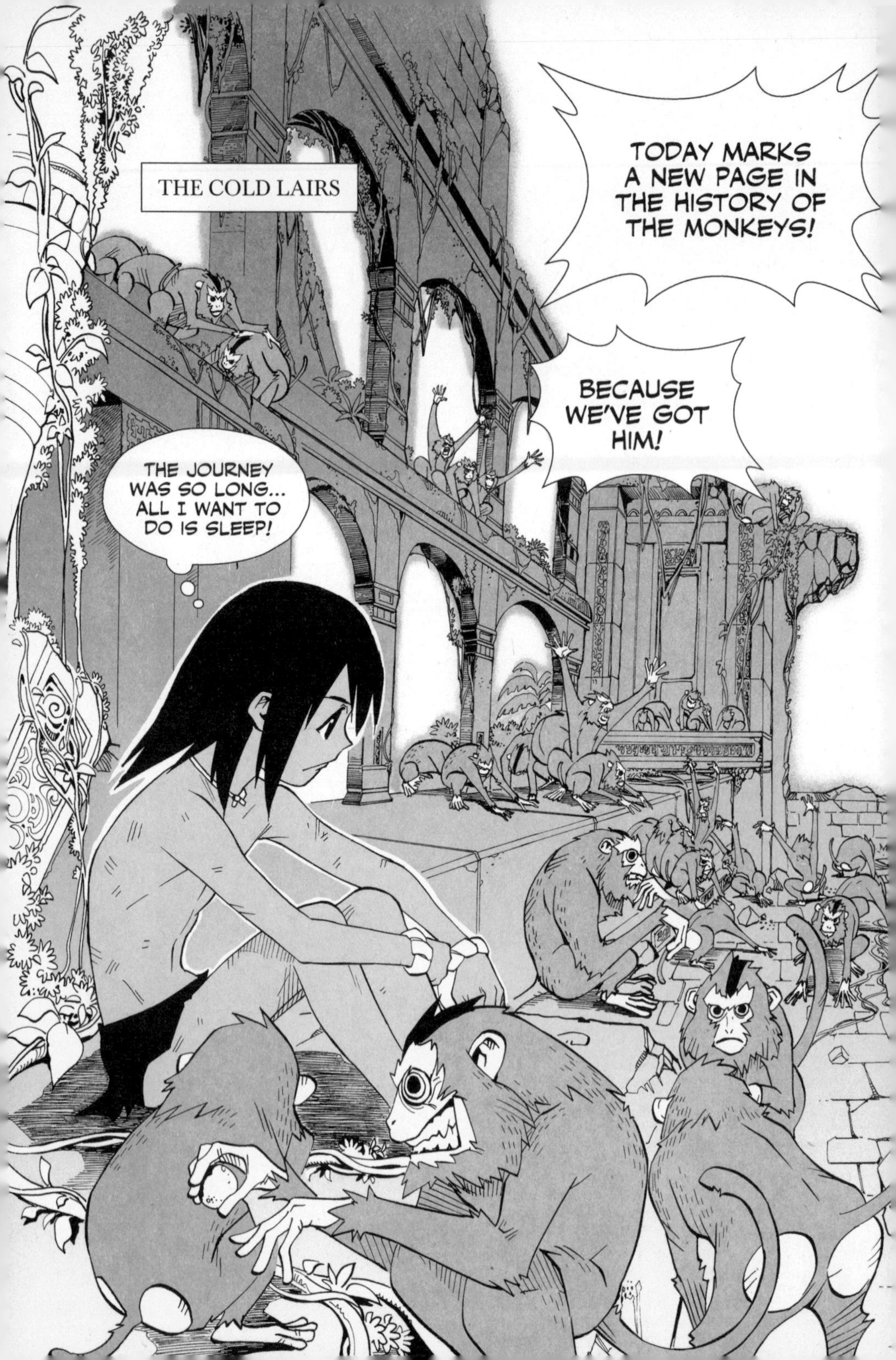
TODAY MARKS A NEW PAGE IN THE HISTORY OF THE MONKEYS!
THE COLD LAIRS
BECAUSE WE'VE GOT HIM!
THE JOURNEY WAS SO LONG... ALL I WANT TO DO IS SLEEP!

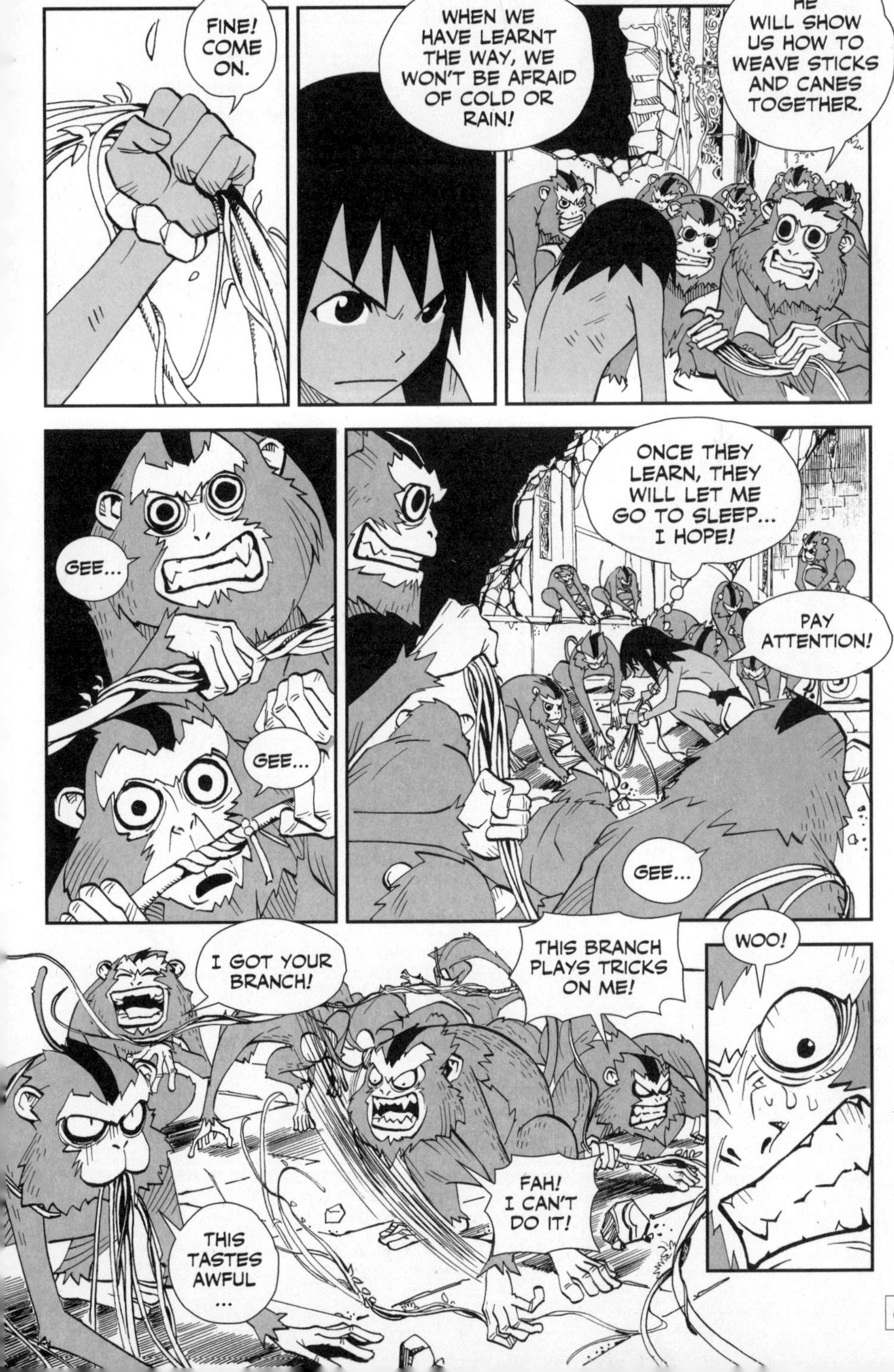
HE WILL SHOW US HOW TO WEAVE STICKS AND CANES TOGETHER.
WHEN WE HAVE LEARNT THE WAY, WE WON'T BE AFRAID OF COLD OR RAIN!
FINE! COME ON.
ONCE THEY LEARN, THEY WILL LET ME GO TO SLEEP... I HOPE!
PAY ATTENTION!
GEE...
GEE...
GEE...
WOO!
THIS BRANCH PLAYS TRICKS ON ME!
I GOT YOUR BRANCH!
FAH! I CAN'T DO IT!
THIS TASTES AWFUL ...

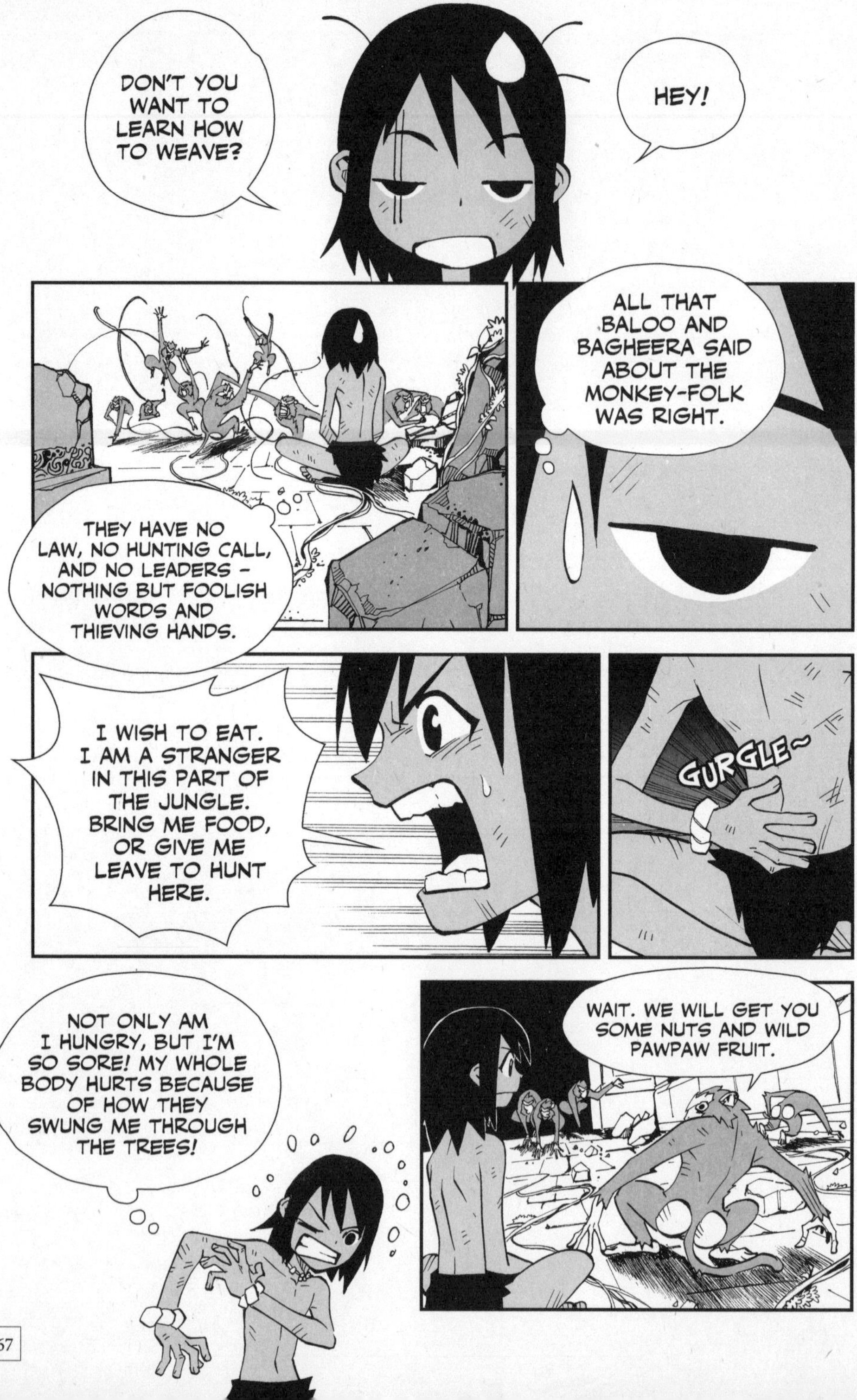
HEY!
DON'T YOU WANT TO LEARN HOW TO WEAVE?
ALL THAT BALOO AND BAGHEERA SAID ABOUT THE MONKEY-FOLK WAS RIGHT.
THEY HAVE NO LAW, NO HUNTING CALL, AND NO LEADERS – NOTHING BUT FOOLISH WORDS AND THIEVING HANDS.
GURGLE~
I WISH TO EAT. I AM A STRANGER IN THIS PART OF THE JUNGLE. BRING ME FOOD, OR GIVE ME LEAVE TO HUNT HERE.
WAIT. WE WILL GET YOU SOME NUTS AND WILD PAWPAW FRUIT.
NOT ONLY AM I HUNGRY, BUT I'M SO SORE! MY WHOLE BODY HURTS BECAUSE OF HOW THEY SWUNG ME THROUGH THE TREES!

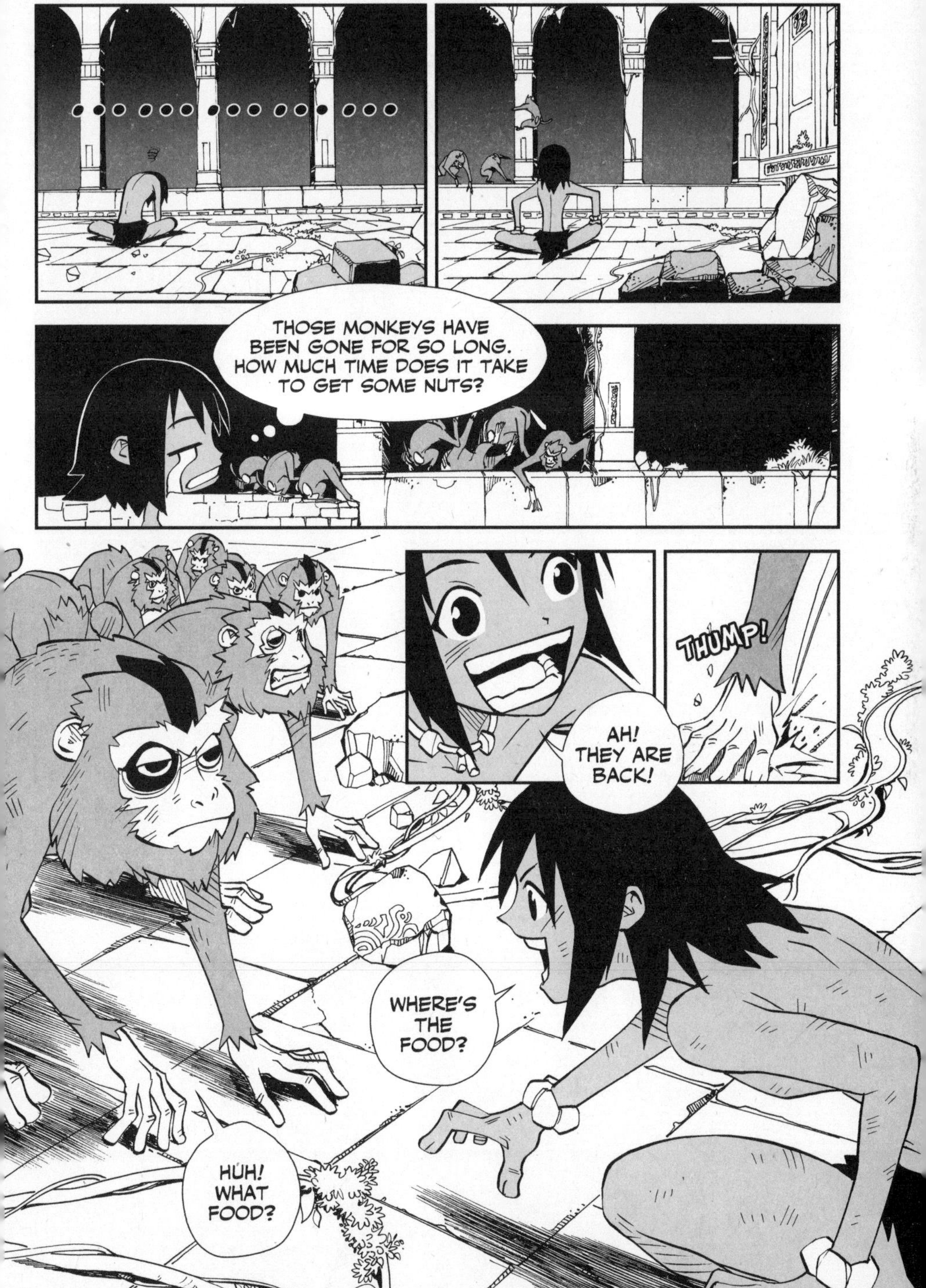
THOSE MONKEYS HAVE BEEN GONE FOR SO LONG. HOW MUCH TIME DOES IT TAKE TO GET SOME NUTS?
THUMP!
AH! THEY ARE BACK!
WHERE'S THE FOOD?
HUH! WHAT FOOD?

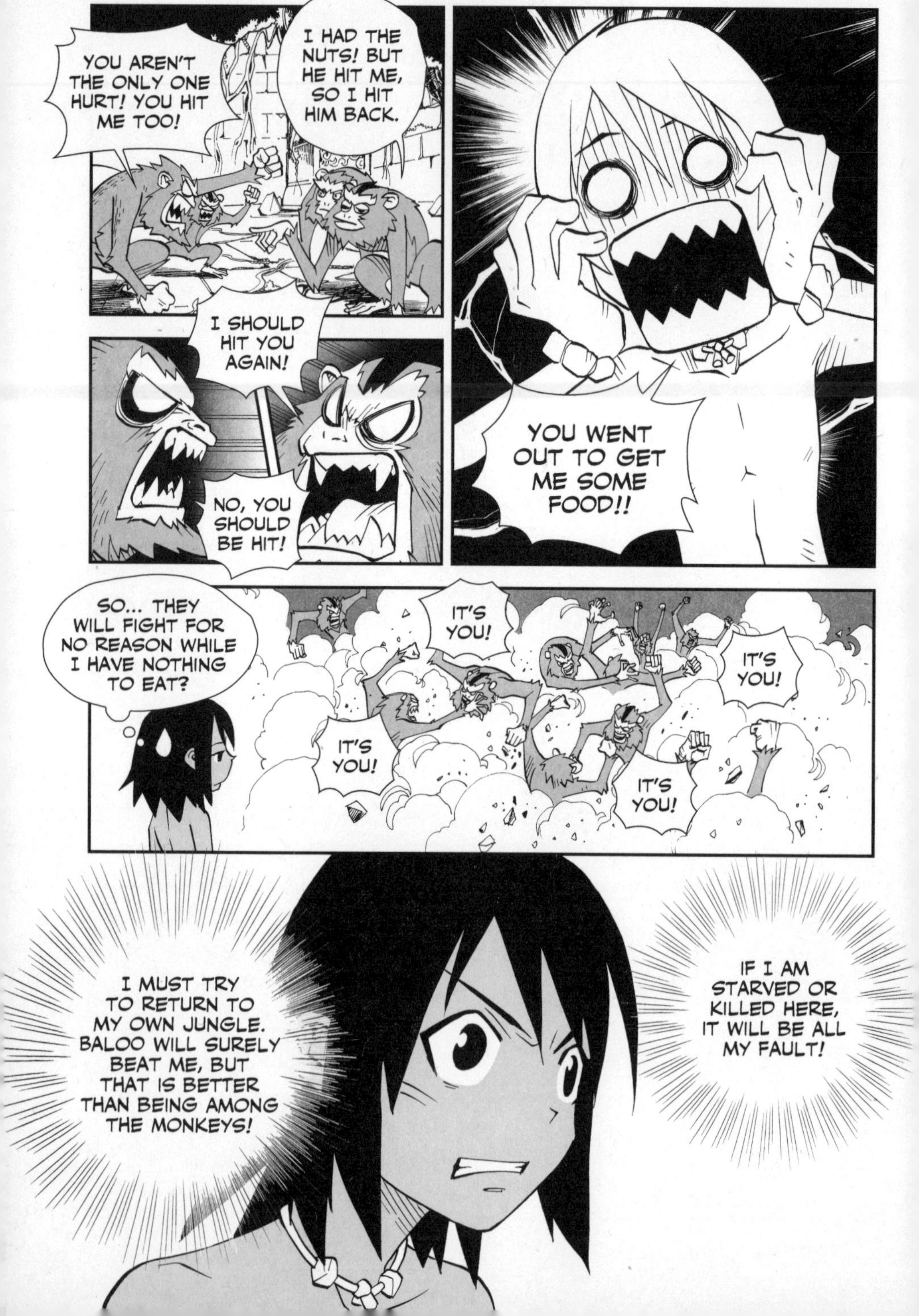

YOU WENT OUT TO GET ME SOME FOOD!!
I HAD THE NUTS! BUT HE HIT ME, SO I HIT HIM BACK.
YOU AREN'T THE ONLY ONE HURT! YOU HIT ME TOO!
I SHOULD HIT YOU AGAIN!
NO, YOU SHOULD BE HIT!
IT'S YOU!
IT'S YOU!
IT'S YOU!
IT'S YOU!
SO... THEY WILL FIGHT FOR NO REASON WHILE I HAVE NOTHING TO EAT?
IF I AM STARVED OR KILLED HERE, IT WILL BE ALL MY FAULT!
I MUST TRY TO RETURN TO MY OWN JUNGLE. BALOO WILL SURELY BEAT ME, BUT THAT IS BETTER THAN BEING AMONG THE MONKEYS!

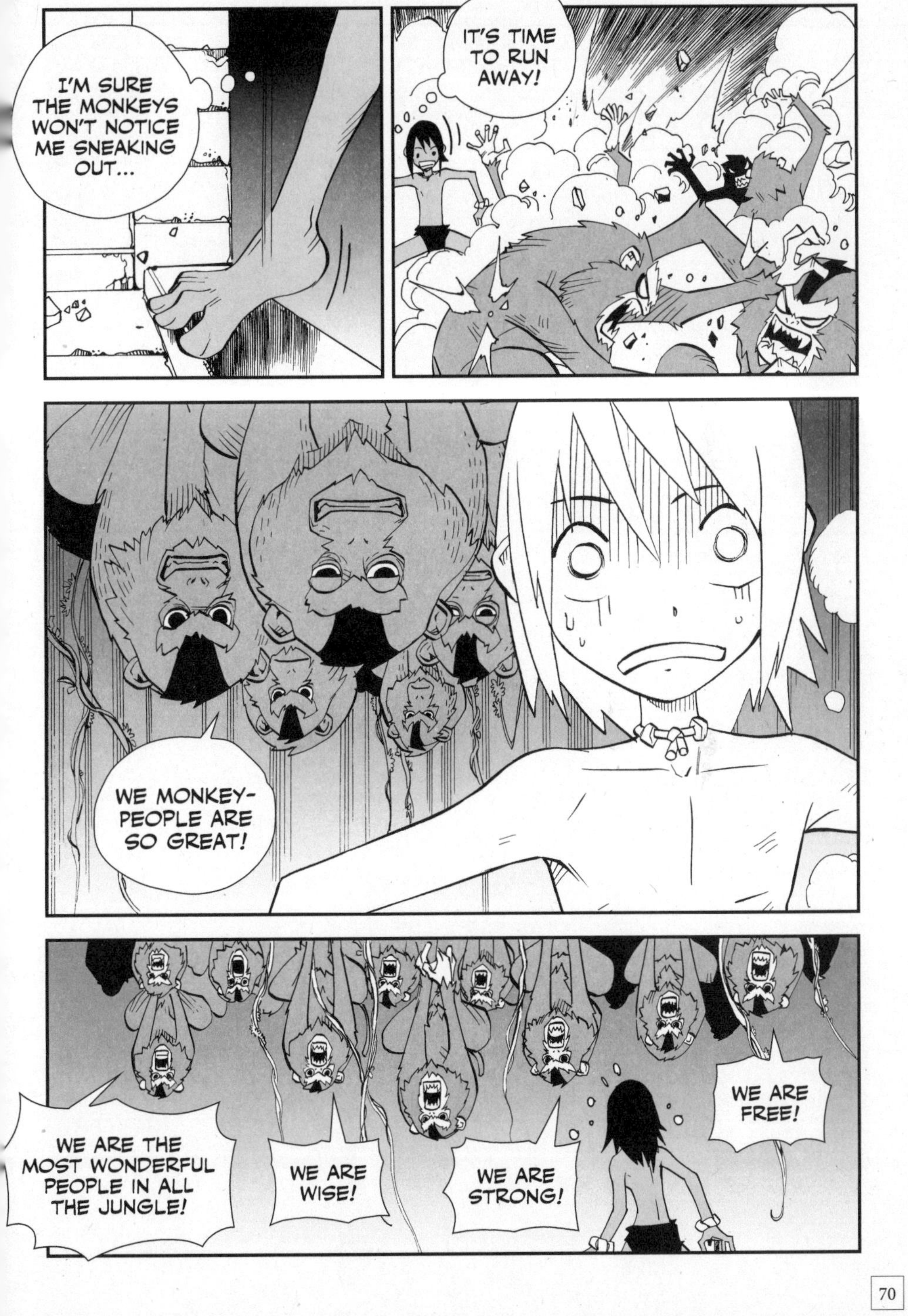
IT'S TIME TO RUN AWAY!
I'M SURE THE MONKEYS WON'T NOTICE ME SNEAKING OUT...
WE MONKEY-PEOPLE ARE SO GREAT!
WE ARE FREE!
WE ARE STRONG!
WE ARE WISE!
WE ARE THE MOST WONDERFUL PEOPLE IN ALL THE JUNGLE!

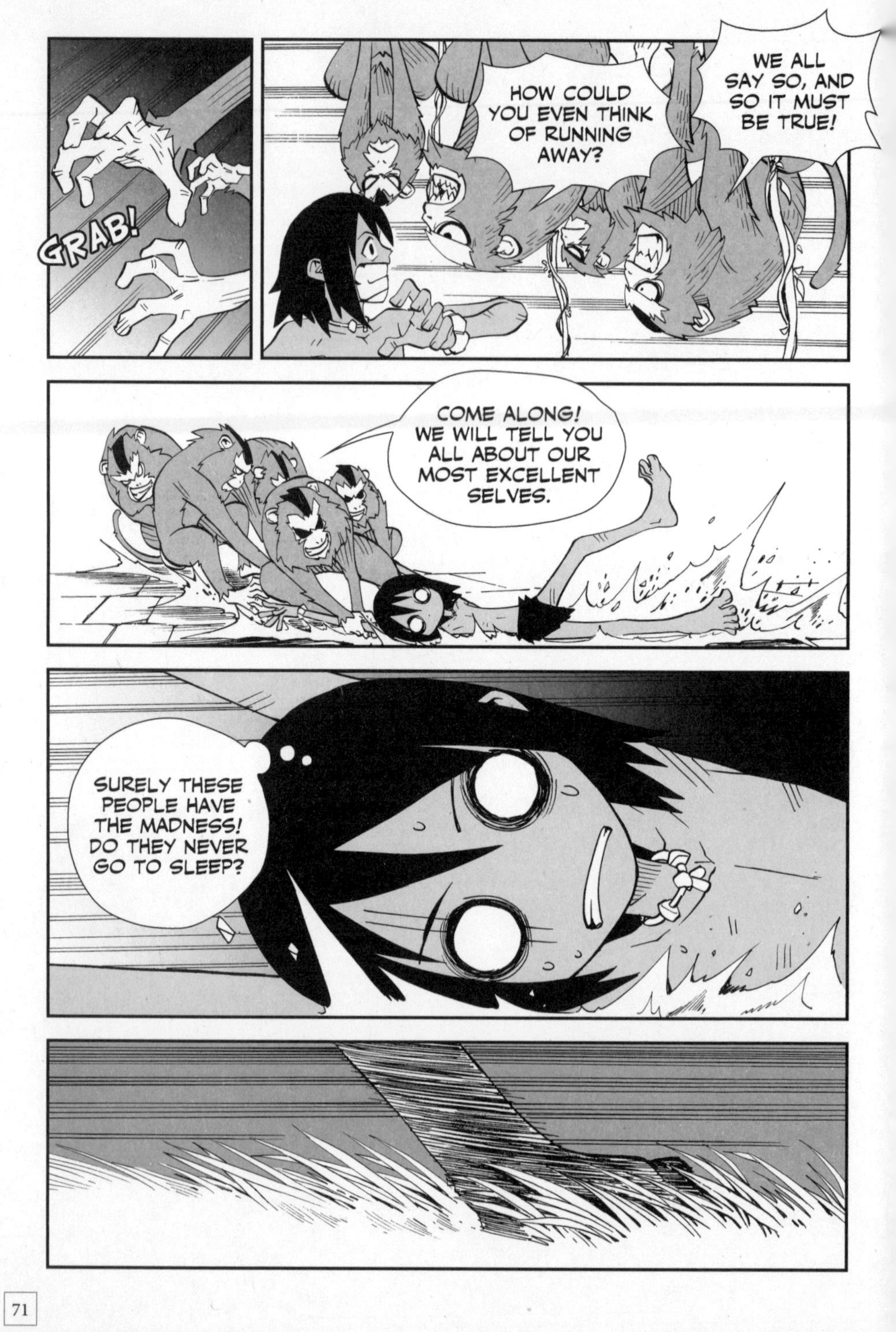
WE ALL SAY SO, AND SO IT MUST BE TRUE!
HOW COULD YOU EVEN THINK OF RUNNING AWAY?
GRAB!
COME ALONG! WE WILL TELL YOU ALL ABOUT OUR MOST EXCELLENT SELVES.
SURELY THESE PEOPLE HAVE THE MADNESS! DO THEY NEVER GO TO SLEEP?

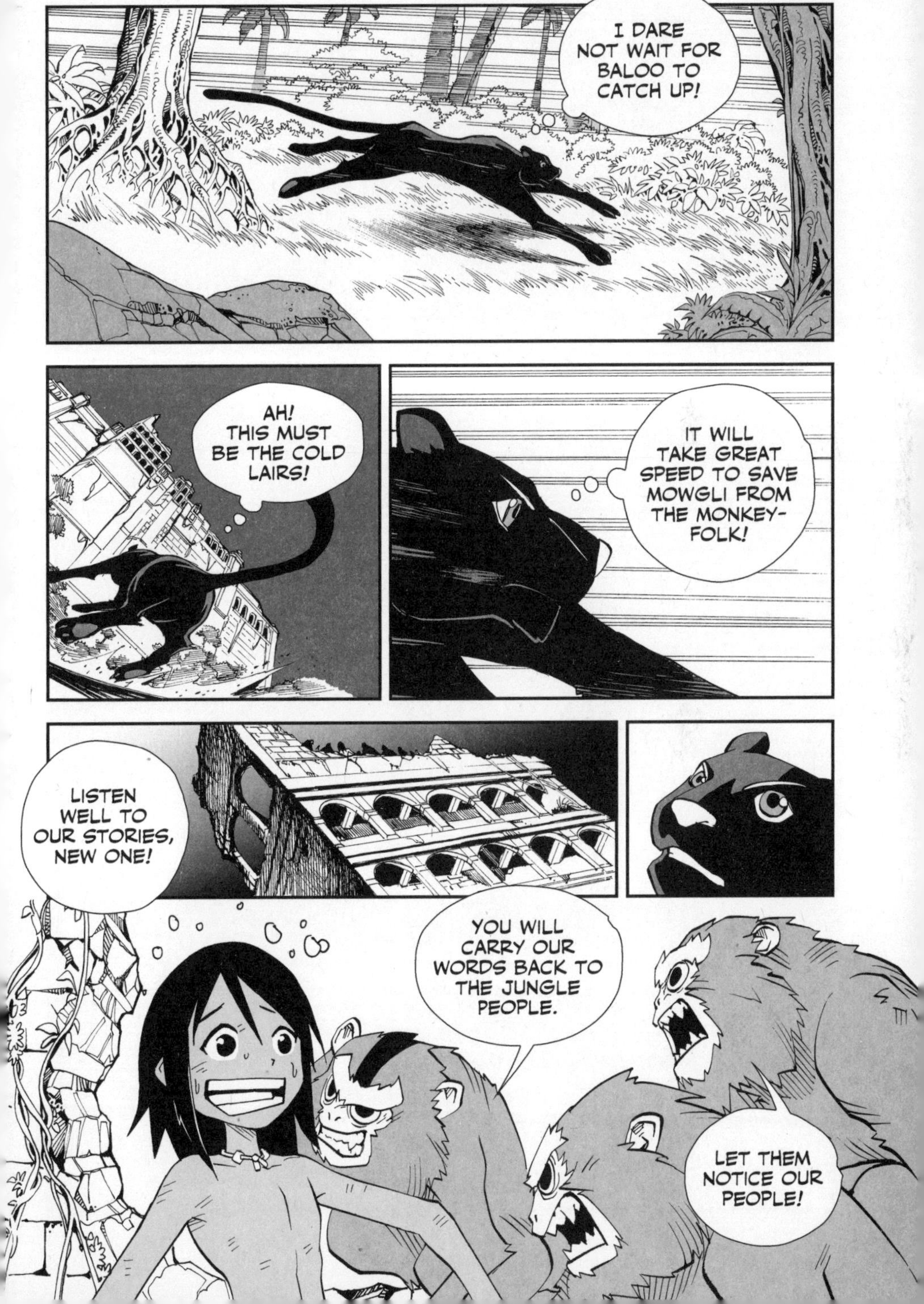
I DARE NOT WAIT FOR BALOO TO CATCH UP!
IT WILL TAKE GREAT SPEED TO SAVE MOWGLI FROM THE MONKEY-FOLK!
AH! THIS MUST BE THE COLD LAIRS!
LISTEN WELL TO OUR STORIES, NEW ONE!
YOU WILL CARRY OUR WORDS BACK TO THE JUNGLE PEOPLE.
LET THEM NOTICE OUR PEOPLE!

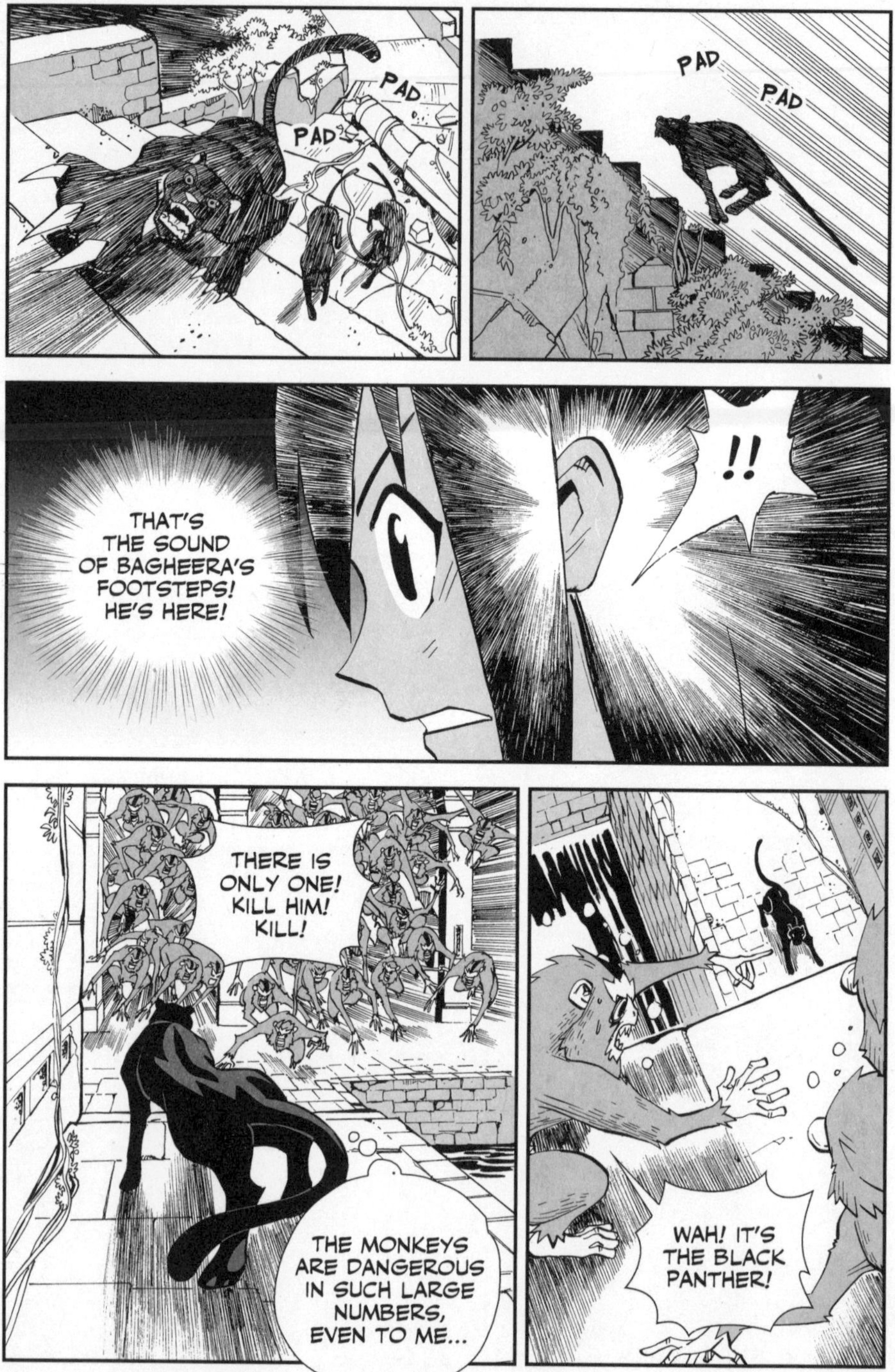
PAD
PAD
PAD
PAD
!!
THAT'S THE SOUND OF BAGHEERA'S FOOTSTEPS! HE'S HERE!
WAH! IT'S THE BLACK PANTHER!
THERE IS ONLY ONE! KILL HIM! KILL!
THE MONKEYS ARE DANGEROUS IN SUCH LARGE NUMBERS, EVEN TO ME...

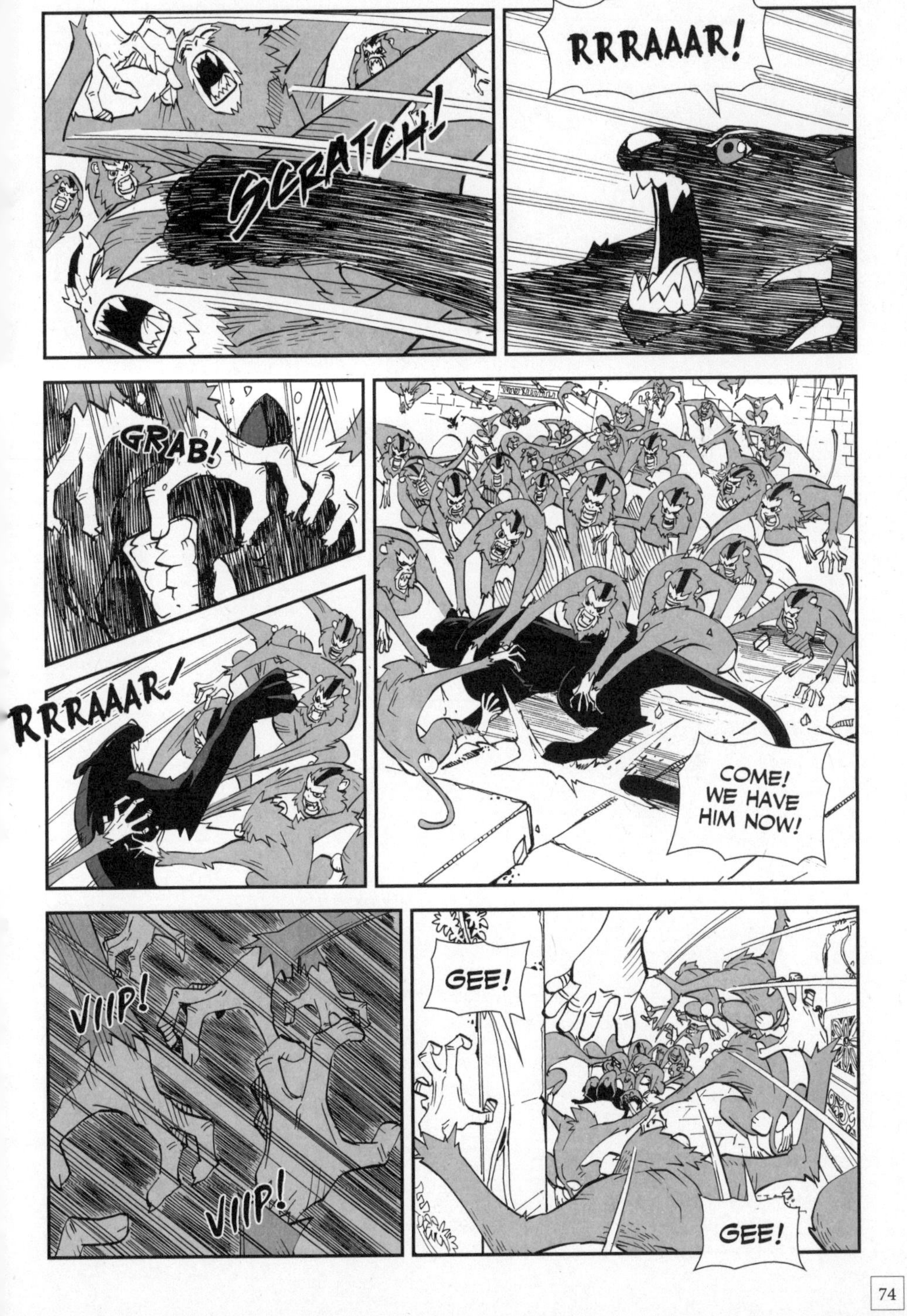
RRRAAAR!
SCRATCH!
COME! WE HAVE HIM NOW!
GRAB!
RRRAAAR!
GEE!
GEE!
VIIP!
VIIP!

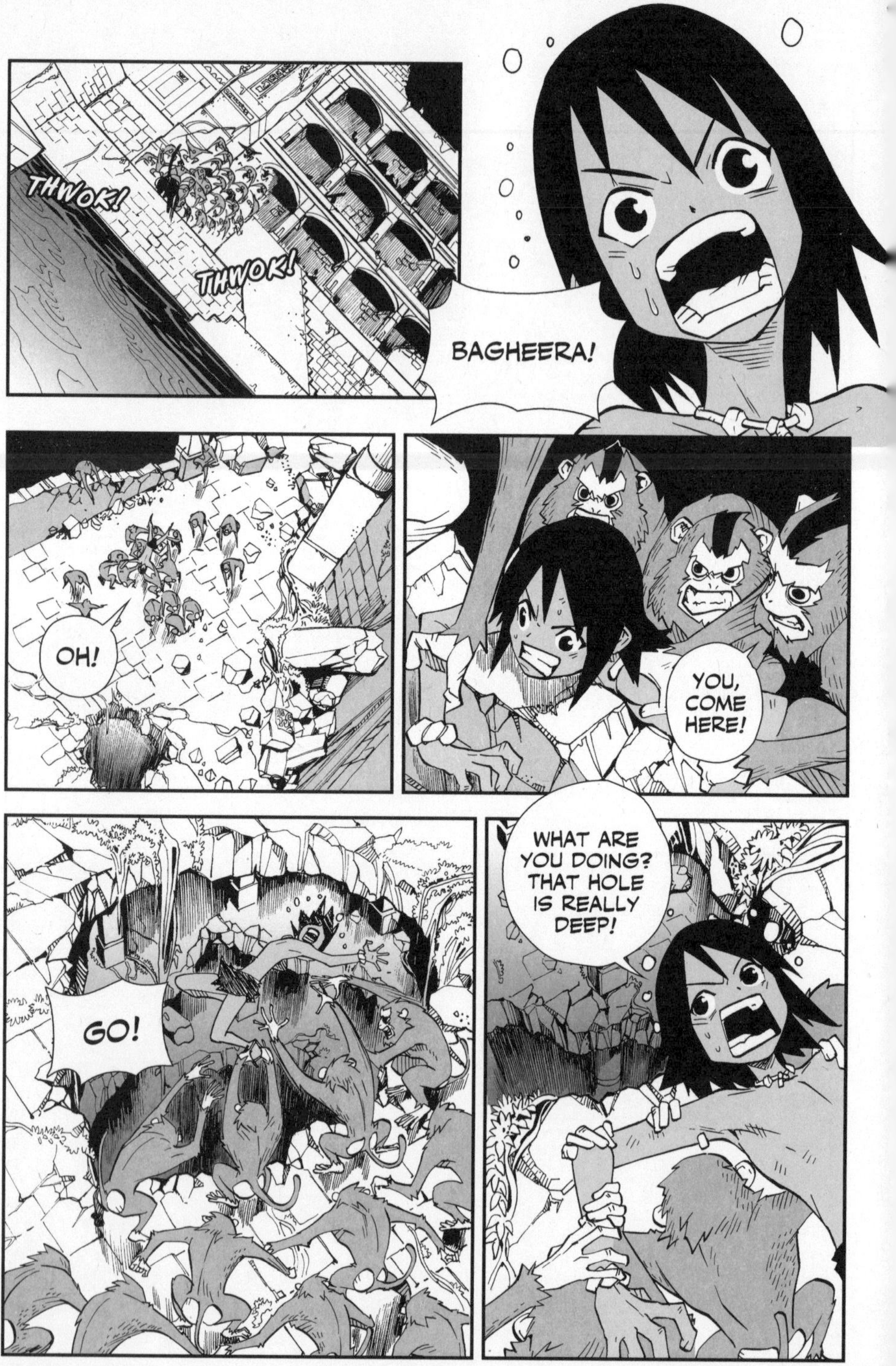
BAGHEERA!
THWOK!
THWOK!
YOU, COME HERE!
OH!
WHAT ARE YOU DOING? THAT HOLE IS REALLY DEEP!
GO!

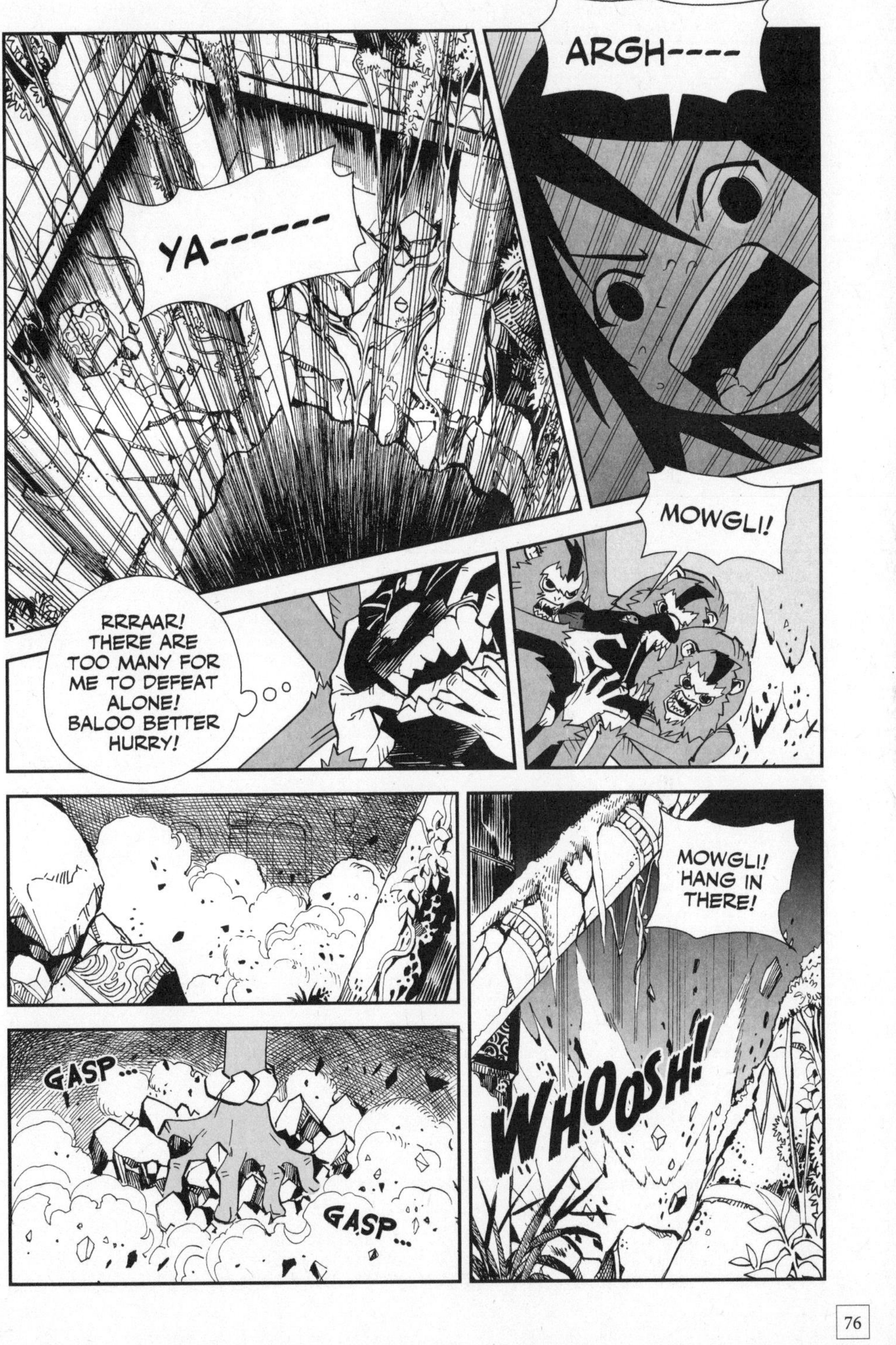

ARGH----
YA-------
MOWGLI!
RRRAAR! THERE ARE TOO MANY FOR ME TO DEFEAT ALONE! BALOO BETTER HURRY!
MOWGLI! HANG IN THERE!
WHOOSH!
GASP...
GASP...

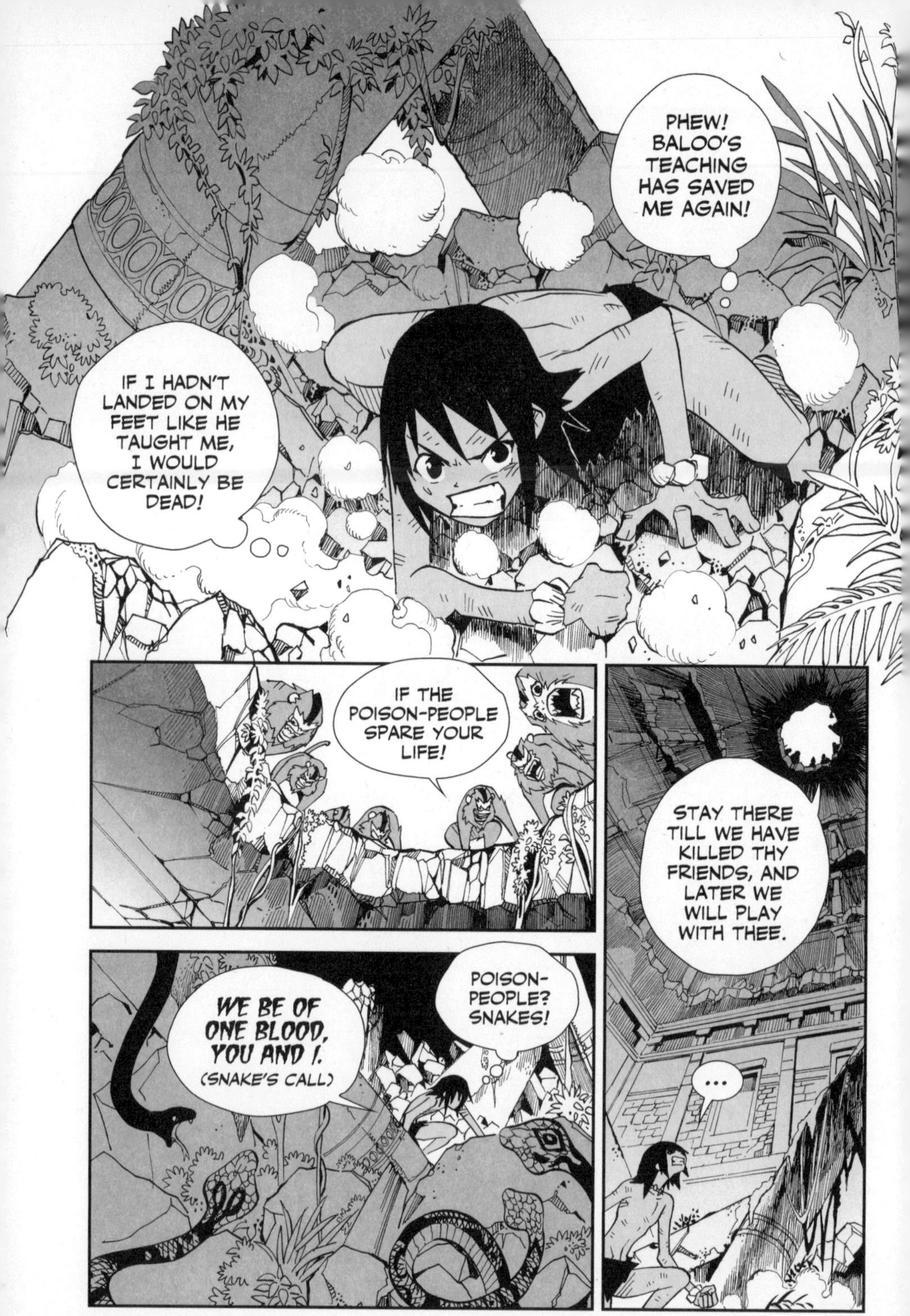
PHEW! BALOO'S TEACHING HAS SAVED ME AGAIN!
IF I HADN'T LANDED ON MY FEET LIKE HE TAUGHT ME, I WOULD CERTAINLY BE DEAD!
STAY THERE TILL WE HAVE KILLED THY FRIENDS, AND LATER WE WILL PLAY WITH THEE.
...
IF THE POISON-PEOPLE SPARE YOUR LIFE!
POISON-PEOPLE? SNAKES!
WE BE OF ONE BLOOD, YOU AND I.
(SNAKE'S CALL)

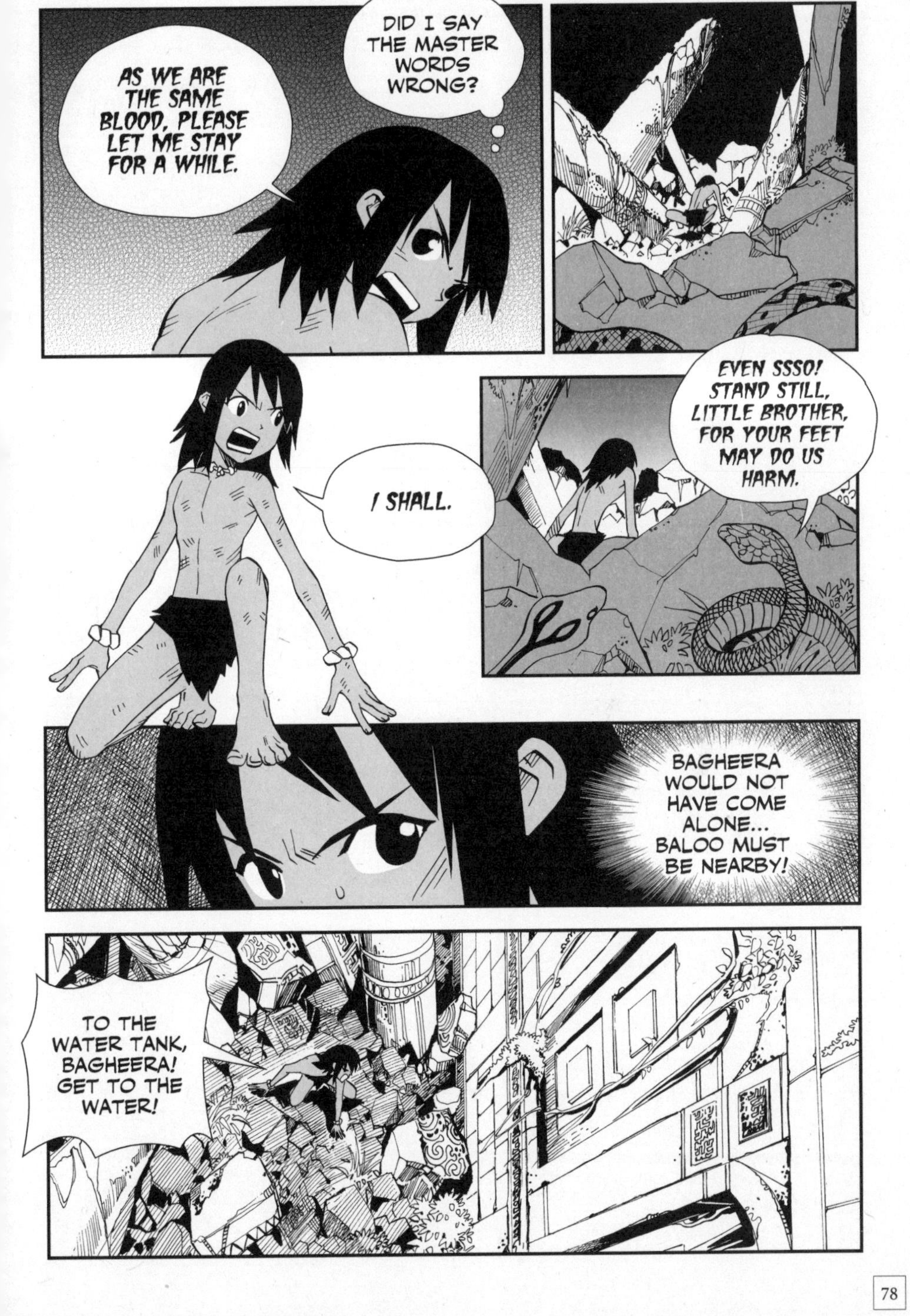
DID I SAY THE MASTER WORDS WRONG?
AS WE ARE THE SAME BLOOD, PLEASE LET ME STAY FOR A WHILE.
EVEN SSSO! STAND STILL, LITTLE BROTHER, FOR YOUR FEET MAY DO US HARM.
I SHALL.
BAGHEERA WOULD NOT HAVE COME ALONE... BALOO MUST BE NEARBY!
TO THE WATER TANK, BAGHEERA! GET TO THE WATER!

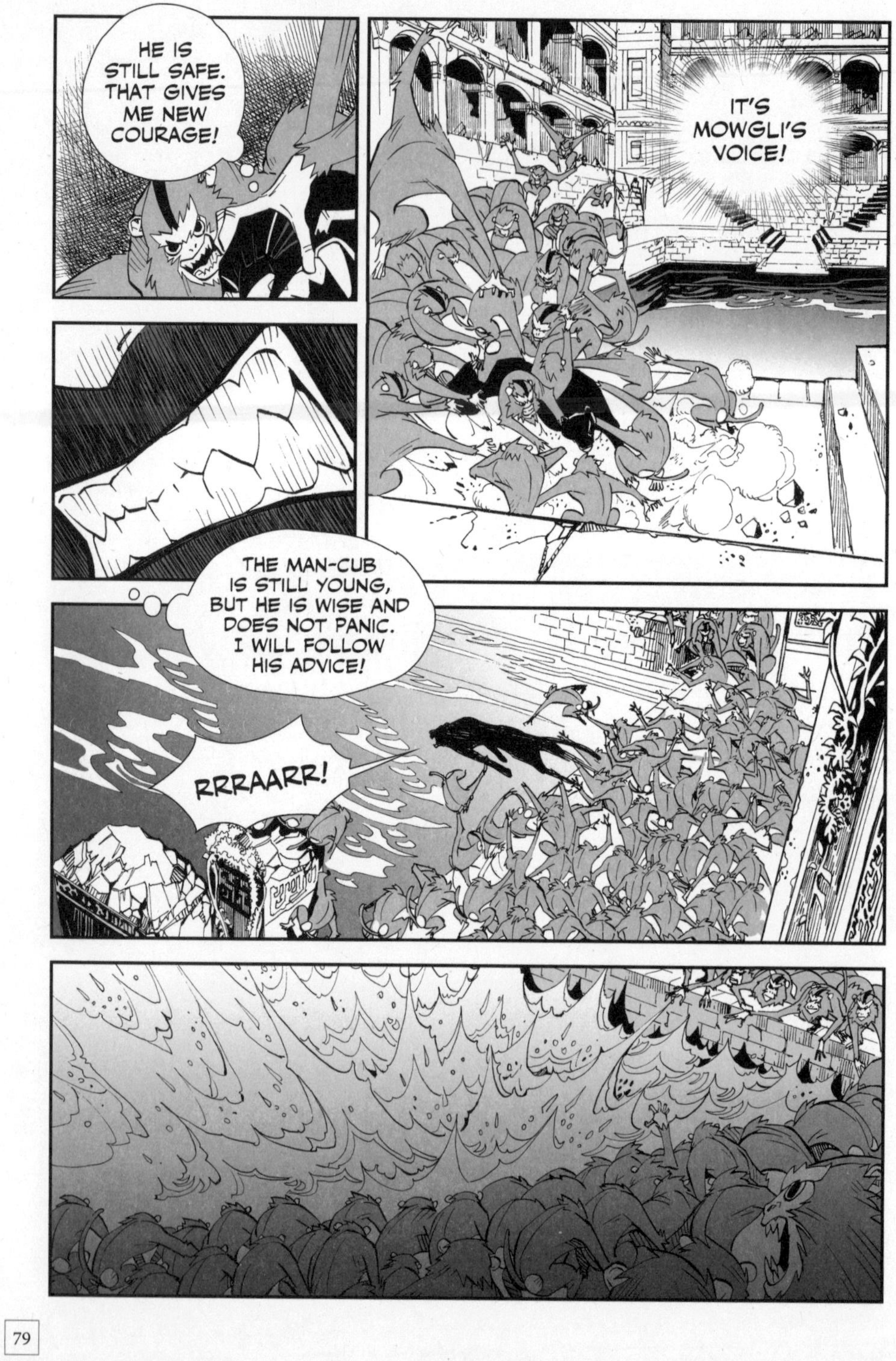
IT'S MOWGLI'S VOICE!
HE IS STILL SAFE. THAT GIVES ME NEW COURAGE!
THE MAN-CUB IS STILL YOUNG, BUT HE IS WISE AND DOES NOT PANIC. I WILL FOLLOW HIS ADVICE!
RRRAARR!

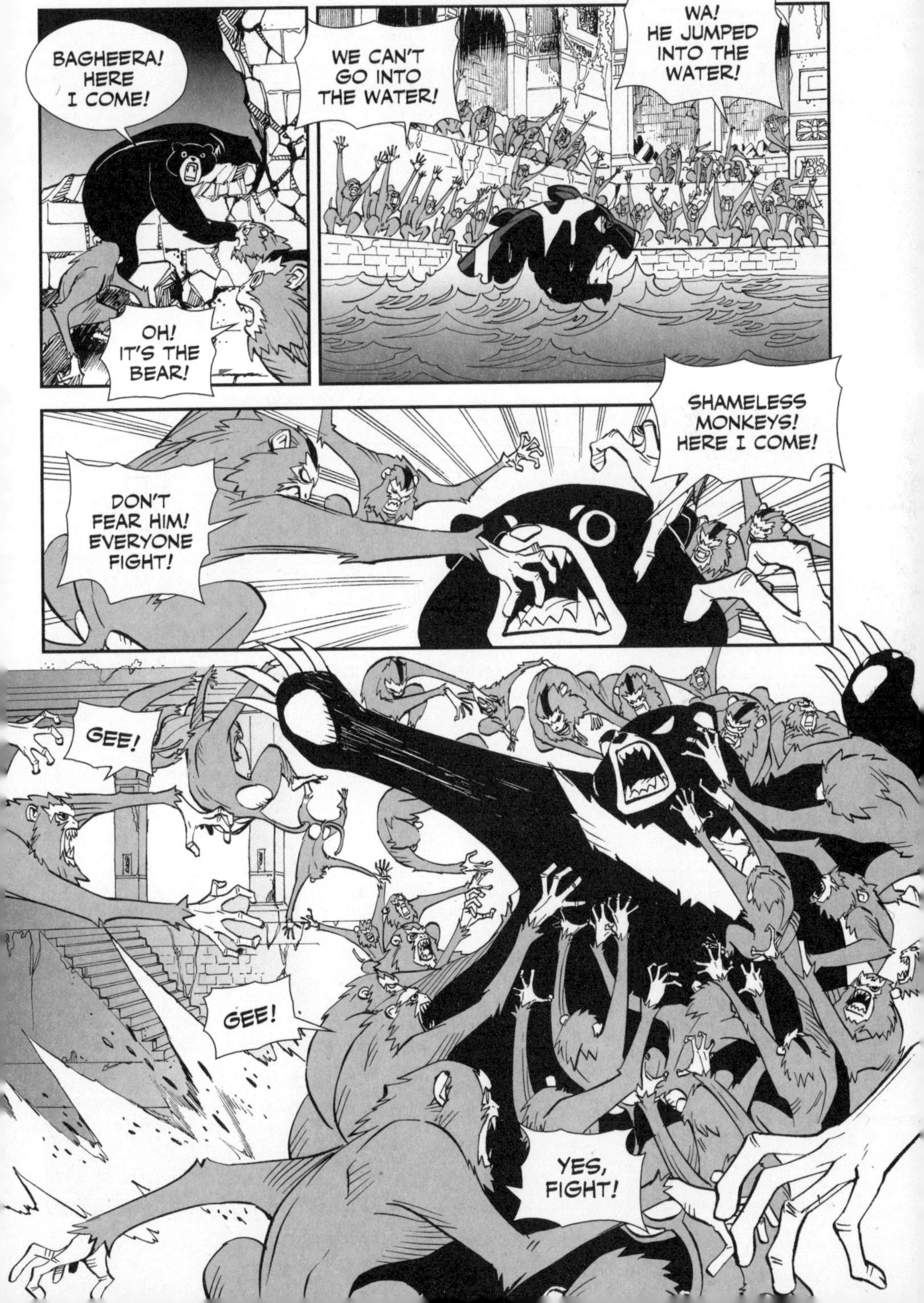
WA! HE JUMPED INTO THE WATER!
WE CAN'T GO INTO THE WATER!
BAGHEERA! HERE I COME!
OH! IT'S THE BEAR!
SHAMELESS MONKEYS! HERE I COME!
DON'T FEAR HIM! EVERYONE FIGHT!
GEE!
GEE!
YES, FIGHT!

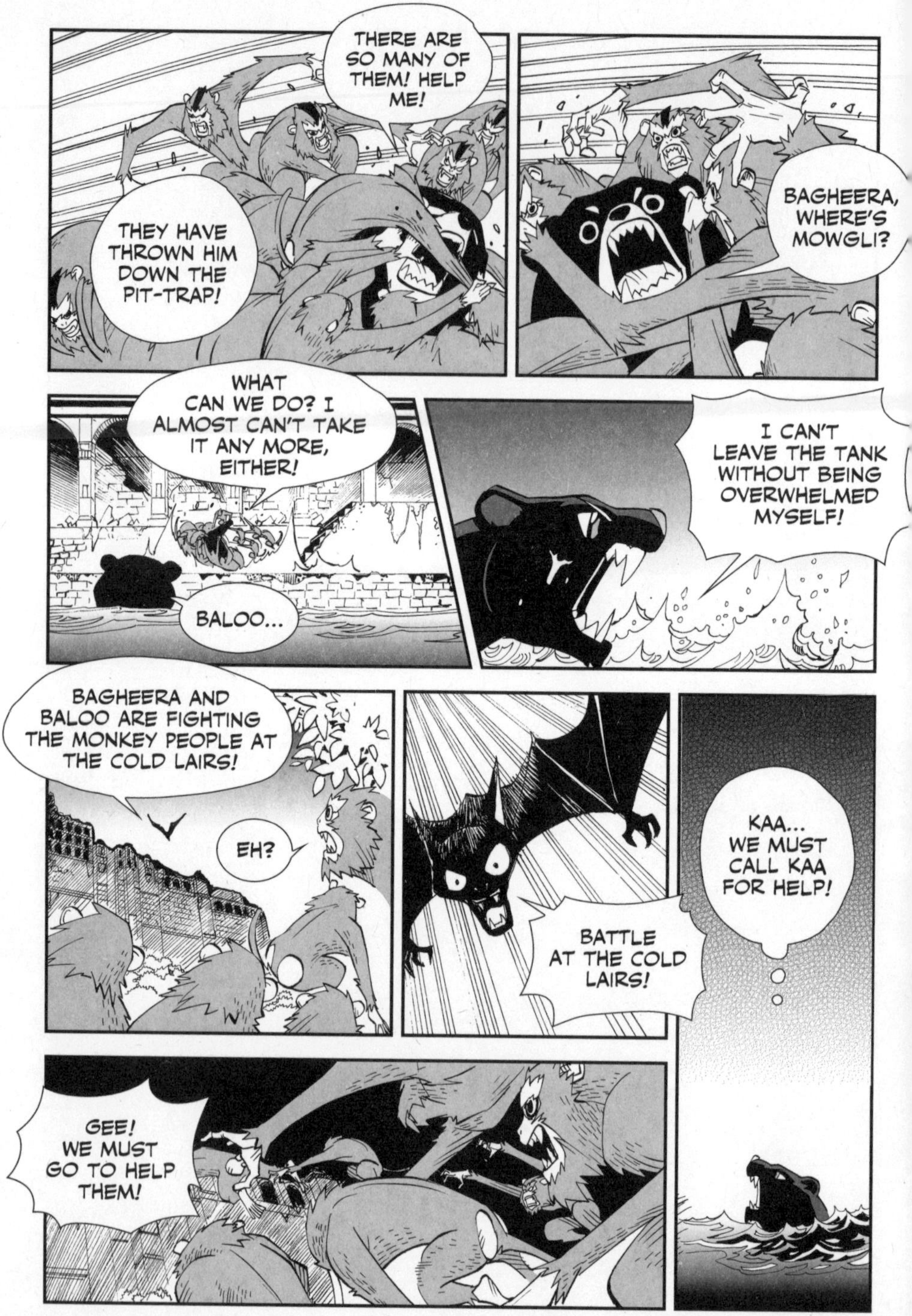

BAGHEERA, WHERE'S MOWGLI?
THERE ARE SO MANY OF THEM! HELP ME!
THEY HAVE THROWN HIM DOWN THE PIT-TRAP!
I CAN'T LEAVE THE TANK WITHOUT BEING OVERWHELMED MYSELF!
WHAT CAN WE DO? I ALMOST CAN'T TAKE IT ANY MORE, EITHER!
BALOO...
KAA... WE MUST CALL KAA FOR HELP!
BATTLE AT THE COLD LAIRS!
BAGHEERA AND BALOO ARE FIGHTING THE MONKEY PEOPLE AT THE COLD LAIRS!
EH?
GEE! WE MUST GO TO HELP THEM!

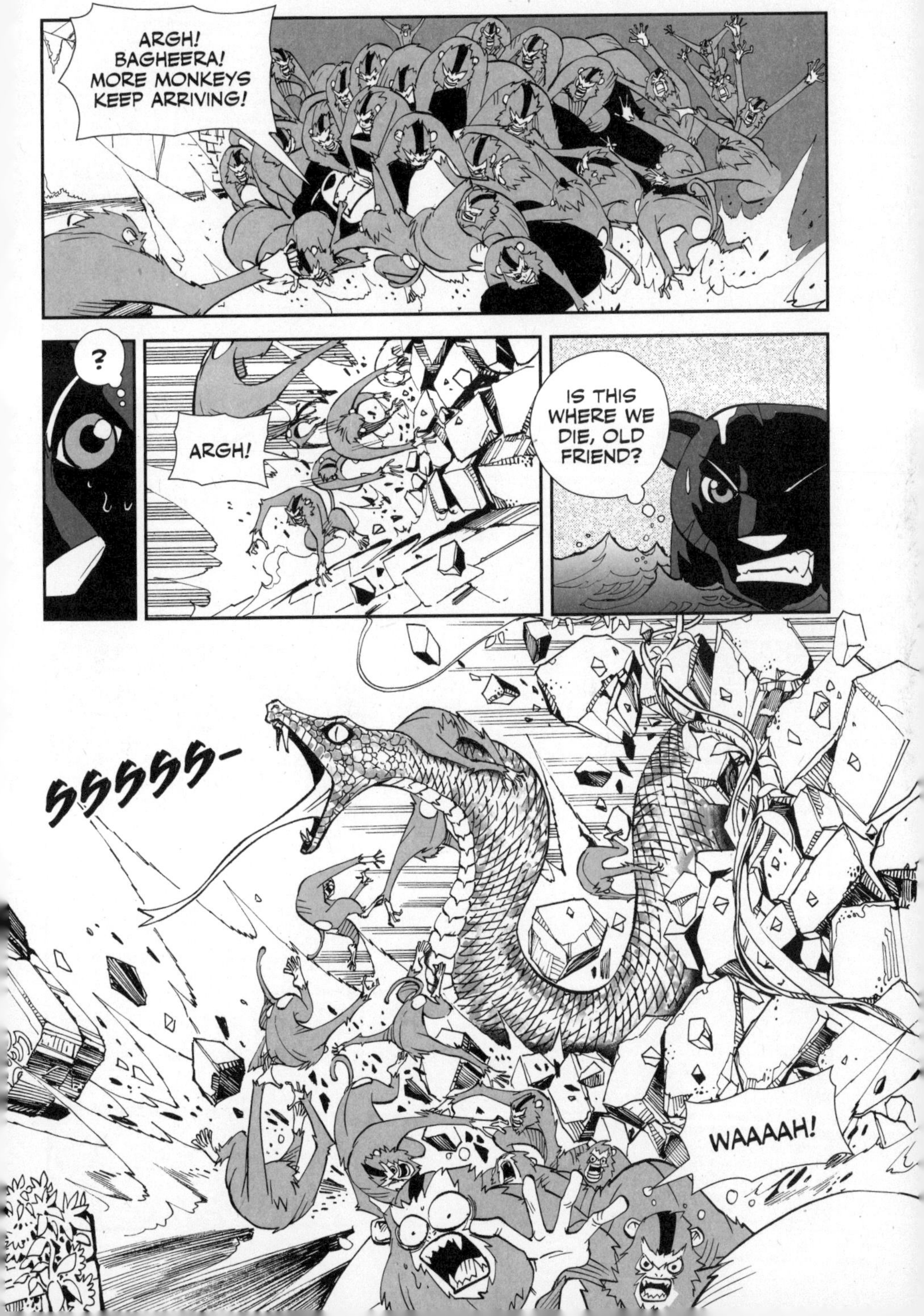
ARGH! BAGHEERA! MORE MONKEYS KEEP ARRIVING!
IS THIS WHERE WE DIE, OLD FRIEND?
ARGH!
?
SSSSS-
WAAAAH!

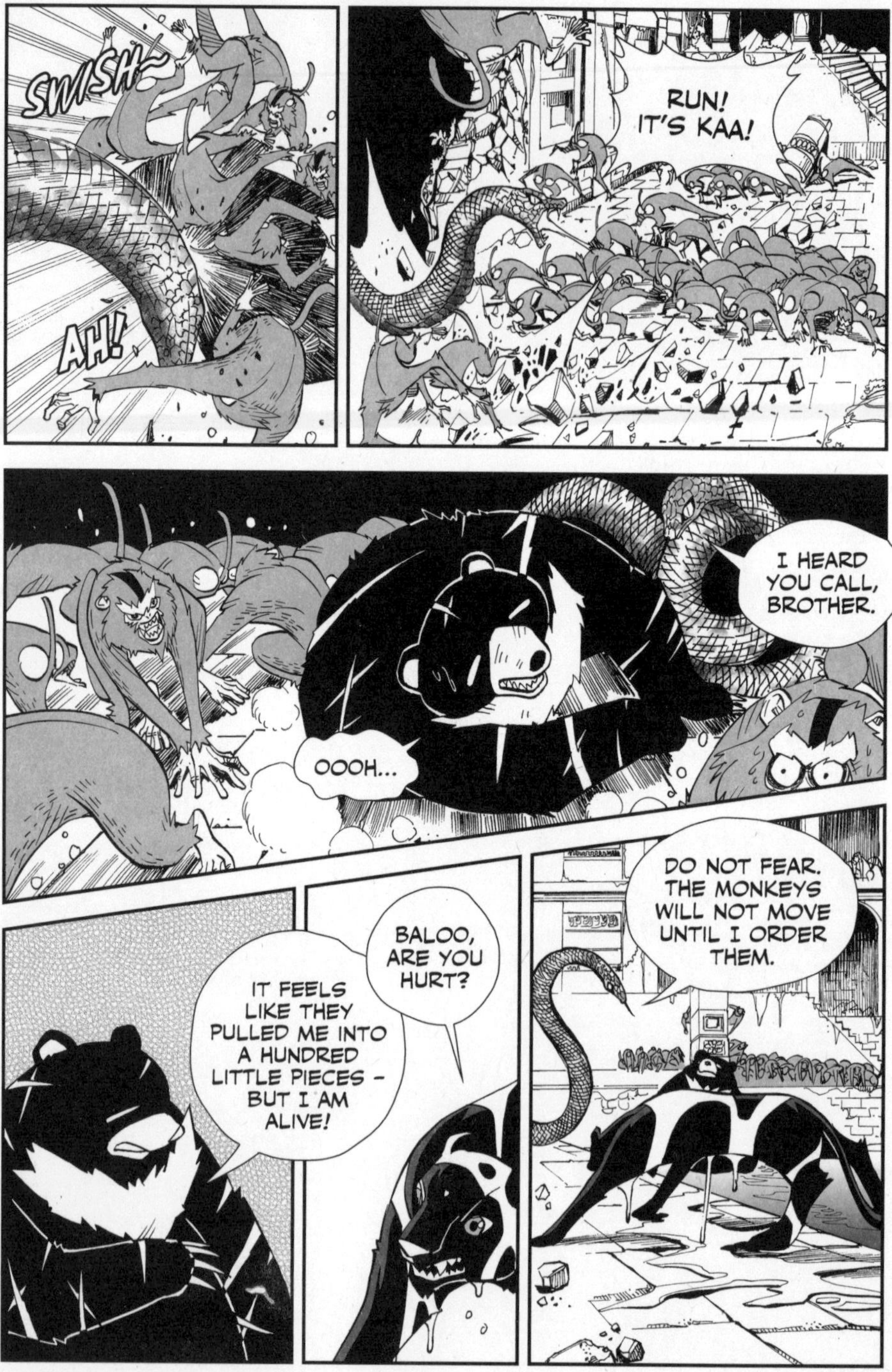
RUN! IT'S KAA!
SWISH
AH!
I HEARD YOU CALL, BROTHER.
OOOH...
DO NOT FEAR. THE MONKEYS WILL NOT MOVE UNTIL I ORDER THEM.
BALOO, ARE YOU HURT?
IT FEELS LIKE THEY PULLED ME INTO A HUNDRED LITTLE PIECES - BUT I AM ALIVE!

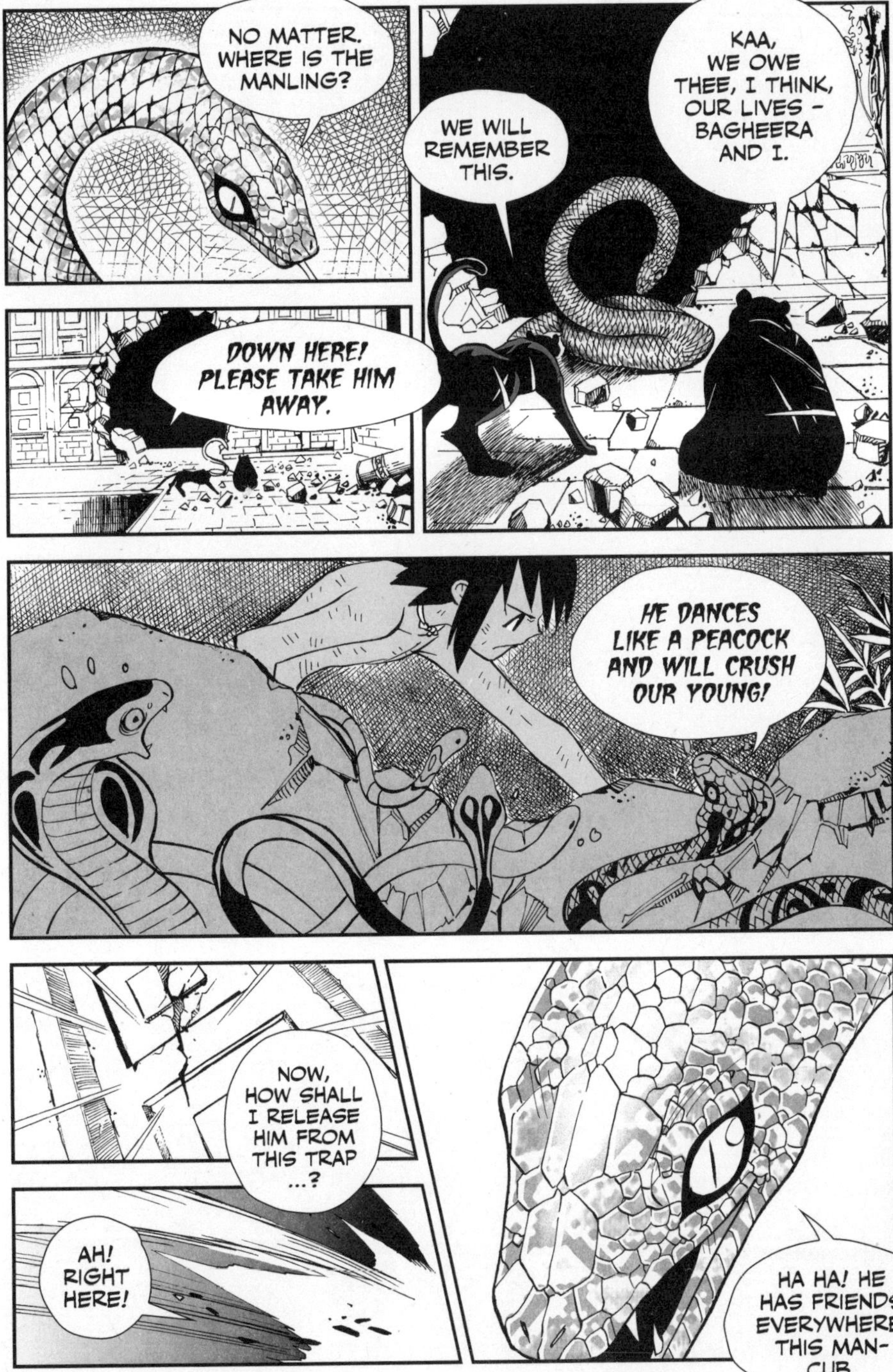
KAA, WE OWE THEE, I THINK, OUR LIVES - BAGHEERA AND I.
WE WILL REMEMBER THIS.
NO MATTER. WHERE IS THE MANLING?
DOWN HERE! PLEASE TAKE HIM AWAY.
HE DANCES LIKE A PEACOCK AND WILL CRUSH OUR YOUNG!
HA HA! HE HAS FRIENDS EVERYWHERE, THIS MAN-CUB.
NOW, HOW SHALL I RELEASE HIM FROM THIS TRAP ...?
AH! RIGHT HERE!

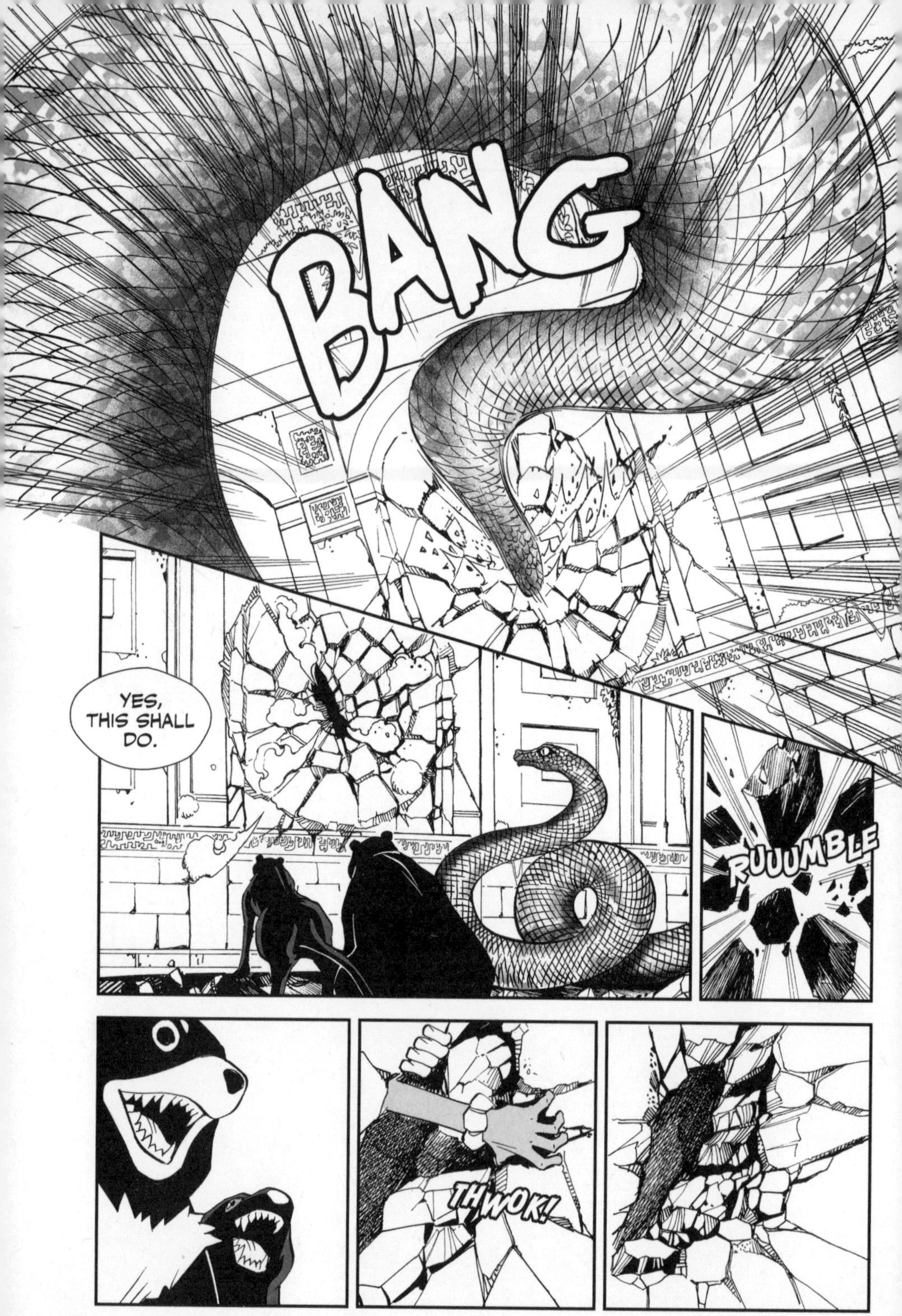
BANG
RUUUMBLE
YES, THIS SHALL DO.
THWOK!

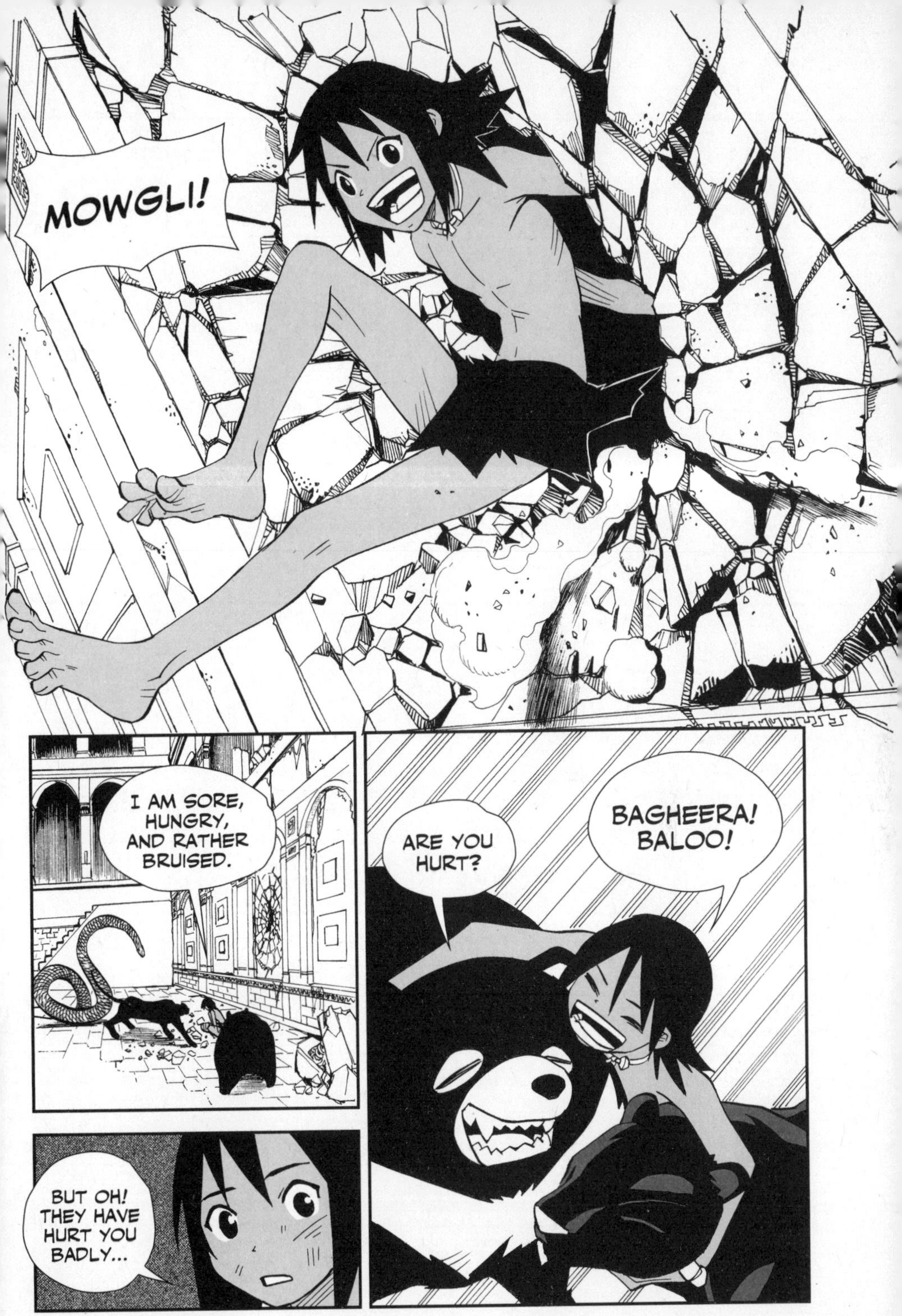
MOWGLI!
BAGHEERA! BALOO!
ARE YOU HURT?
I AM SORE, HUNGRY, AND RATHER BRUISED.
BUT OH! THEY HAVE HURT YOU BADLY...

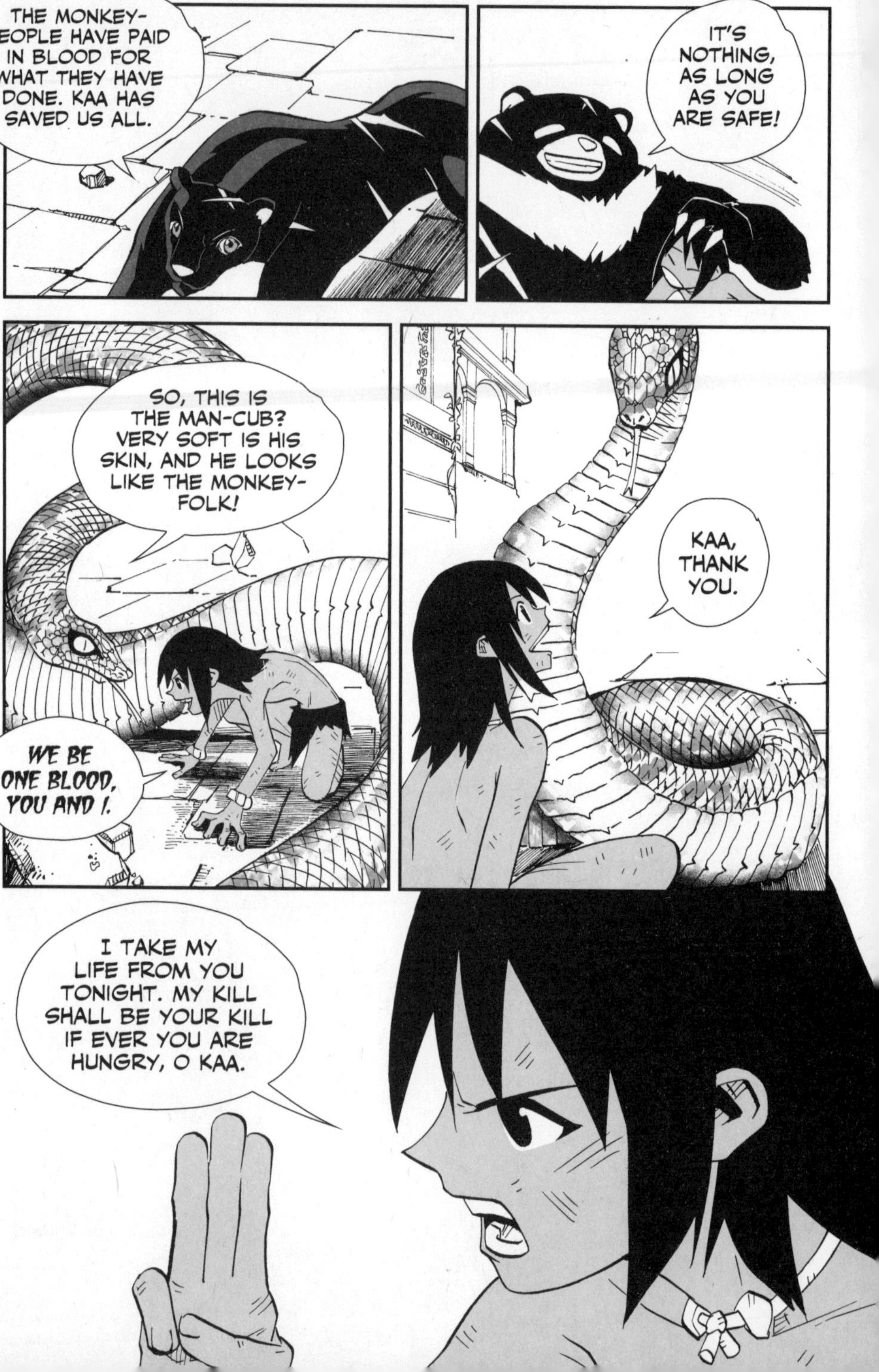
IT'S NOTHING, AS LONG AS YOU ARE SAFE!
THE MONKEY-PEOPLE HAVE PAID IN BLOOD FOR WHAT THEY HAVE DONE. KAA HAS SAVED US ALL.
KAA, THANK YOU.
SO, THIS IS THE MAN-CUB? VERY SOFT IS HIS SKIN, AND HE LOOKS LIKE THE MONKEY-FOLK!
WE BE ONE BLOOD, YOU AND I.
I TAKE MY LIFE FROM YOU TONIGHT. MY KILL SHALL BE YOUR KILL IF EVER YOU ARE HUNGRY, O KAA.

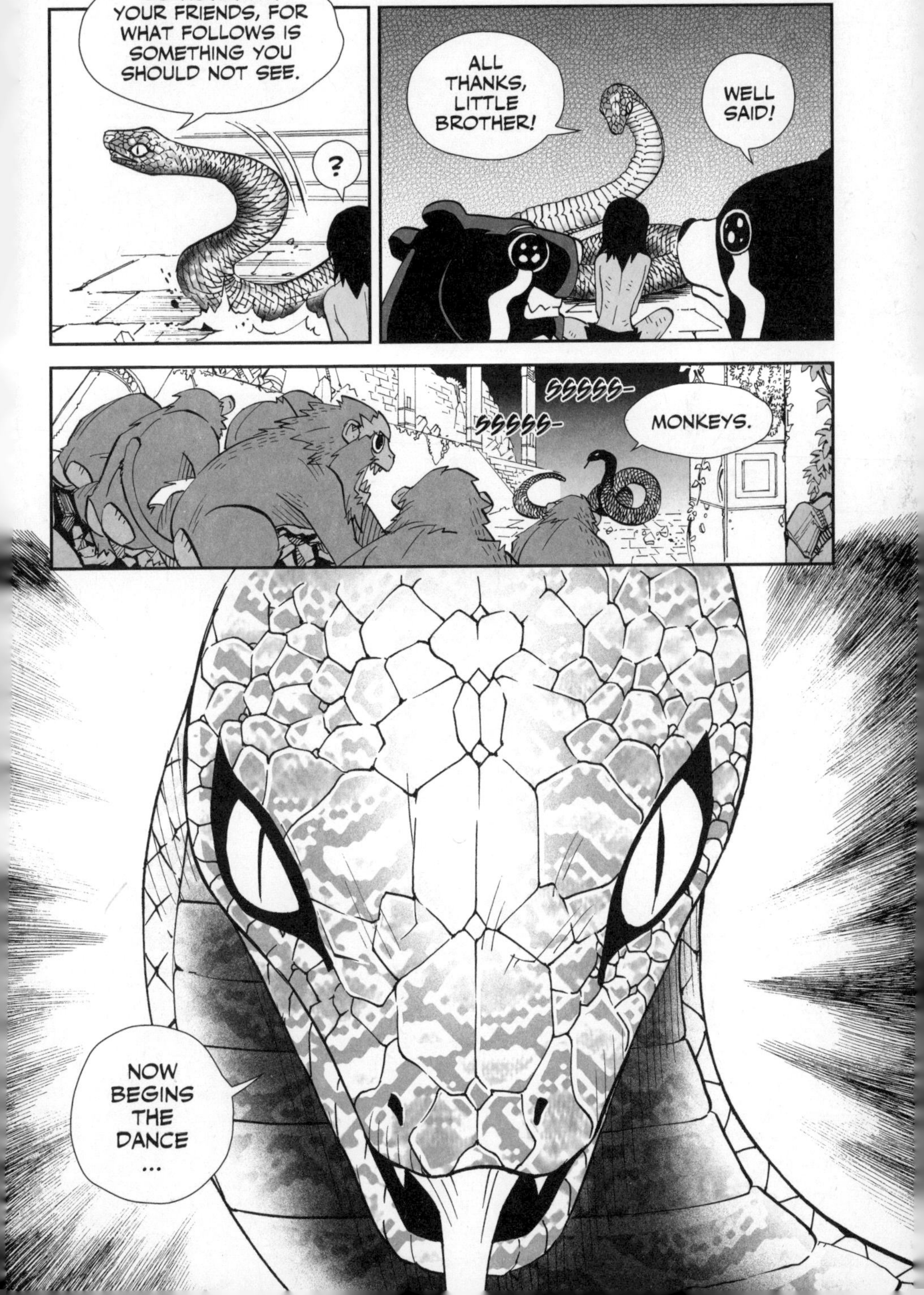
WELL SAID!
ALL THANKS, LITTLE BROTHER!
GO NOW WITH YOUR FRIENDS, FOR WHAT FOLLOWS IS SOMETHING YOU SHOULD NOT SEE.
?
SSSSS-
SSSSS-
MONKEYS.
NOW BEGINS THE DANCE ...

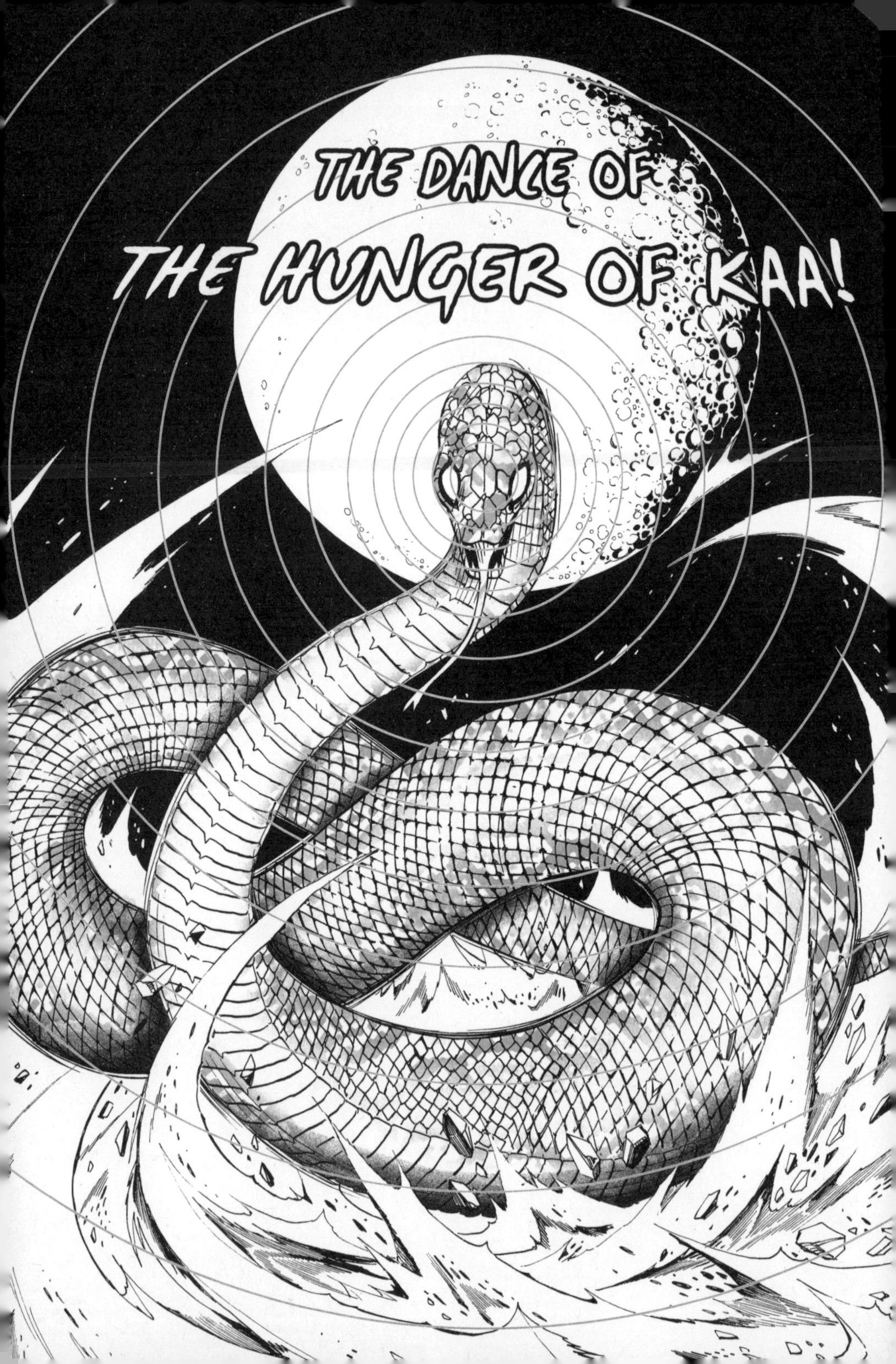
THE DANCE OF
THE HUNGER OF KAA!

AH
MONKEY-FOLK!
CAN YOU STIR YOUR FOOT OR HAND WITHOUT MY ORDER? SPEAK!
WE CANNOT.
GOOD!
COME ALL ONE STEP CLOSER TOWARDS ME.
UNDER-STOOD.
ONE STEP CLOSER.

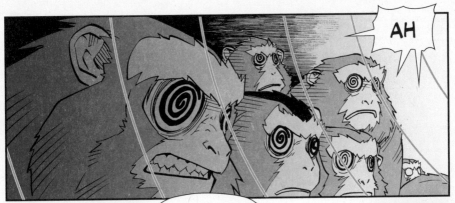

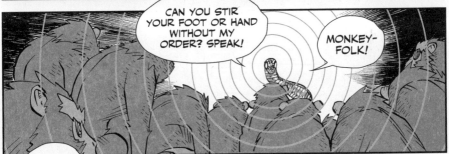

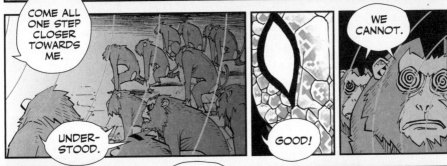

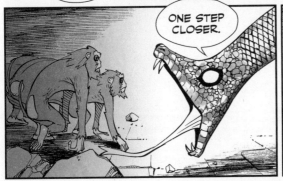

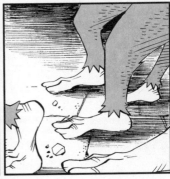

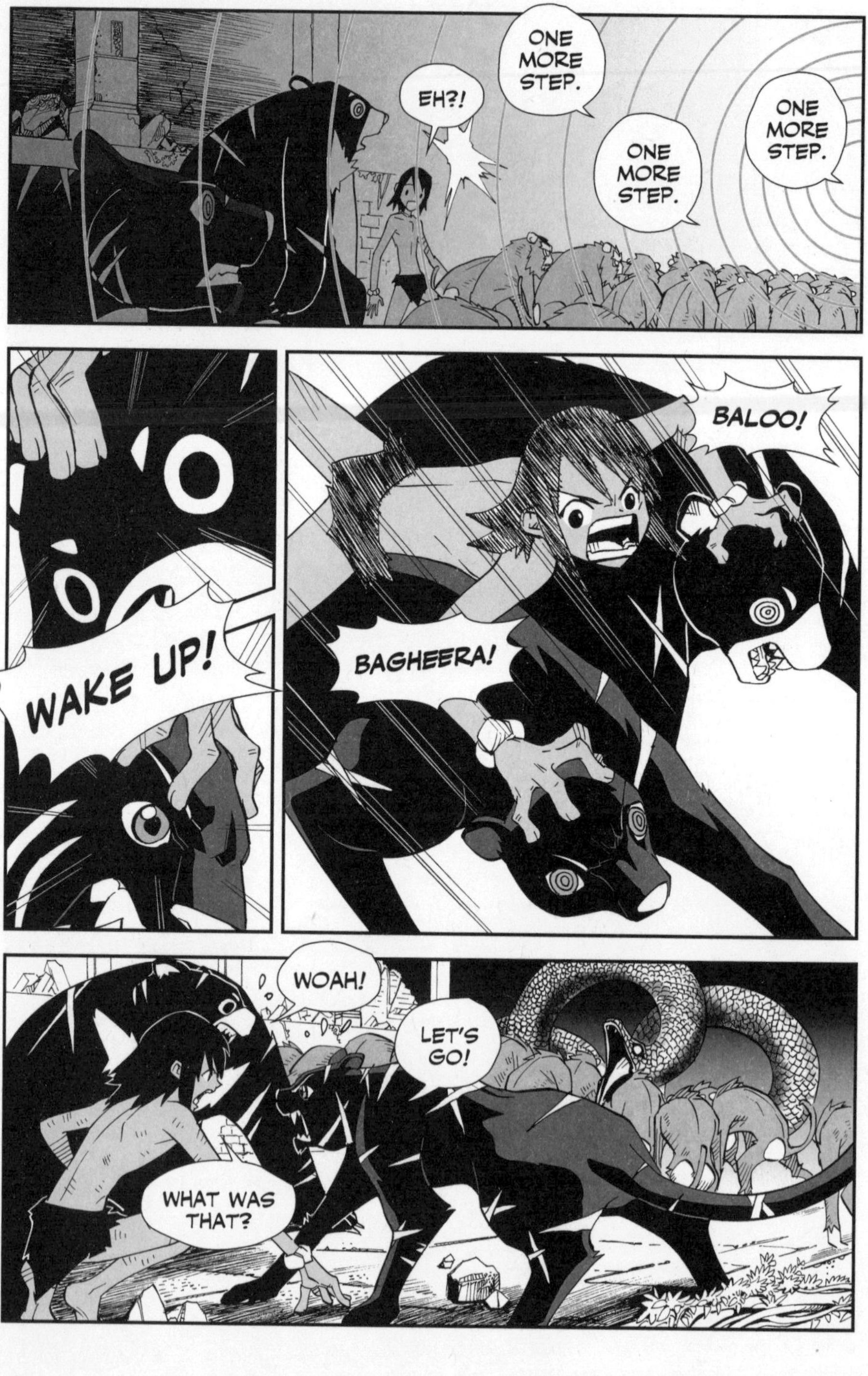
ONE MORE STEP.
ONE MORE STEP.
ONE MORE STEP.
EH?!
BALOO!
BAGHEERA!
WAKE UP!
WOAH!
LET'S GO!
WHAT WAS THAT?

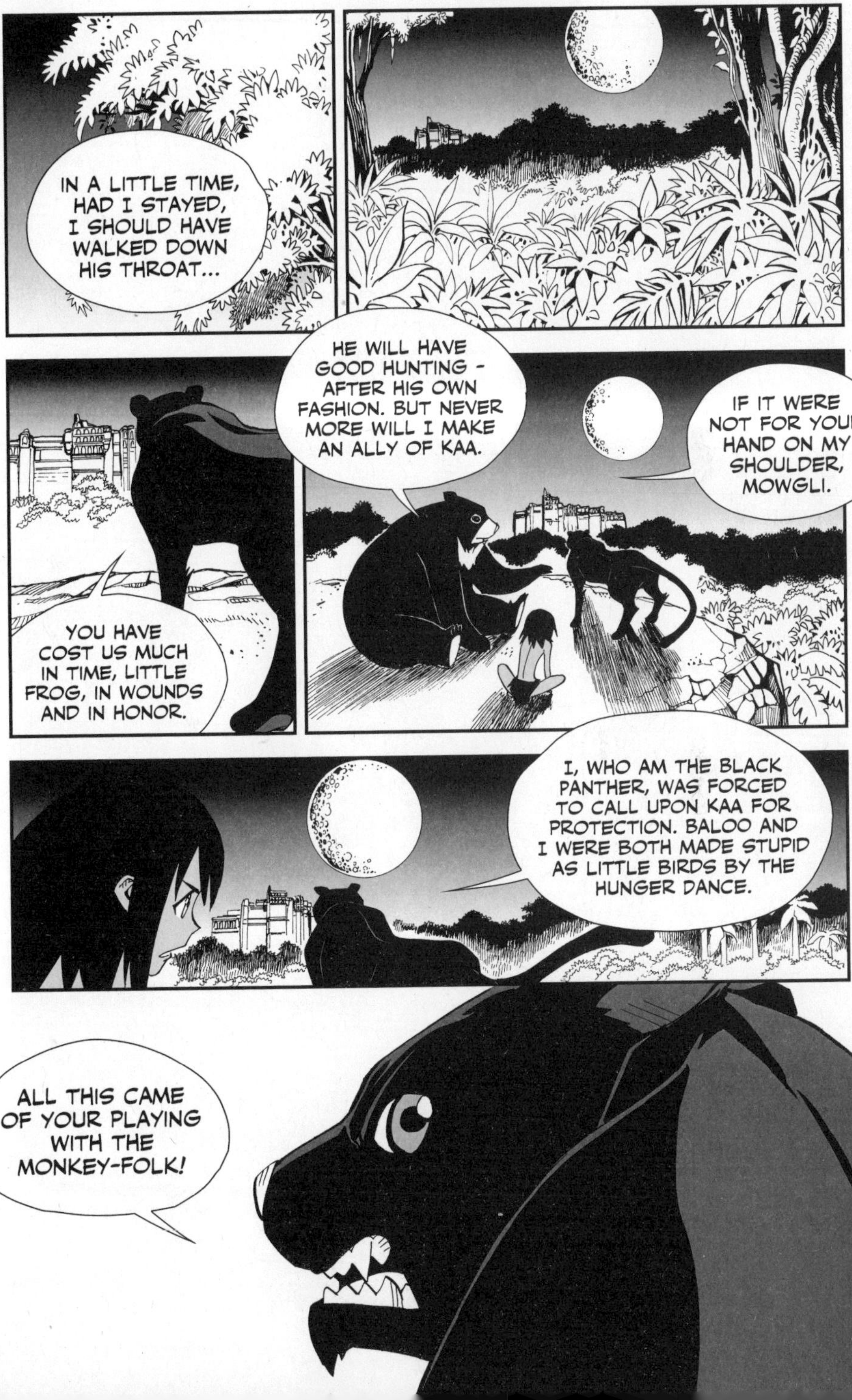
IN A LITTLE TIME, HAD I STAYED, I SHOULD HAVE WALKED DOWN HIS THROAT...
HE WILL HAVE GOOD HUNTING - AFTER HIS OWN FASHION. BUT NEVER MORE WILL I MAKE AN ALLY OF KAA.
IF IT WERE NOT FOR YOUR HAND ON MY SHOULDER, MOWGLI.
YOU HAVE COST US MUCH IN TIME, LITTLE FROG, IN WOUNDS AND IN HONOR.
I, WHO AM THE BLACK PANTHER, WAS FORCED TO CALL UPON KAA FOR PROTECTION. BALOO AND I WERE BOTH MADE STUPID AS LITTLE BIRDS BY THE HUNGER DANCE.
ALL THIS CAME OF YOUR PLAYING WITH THE MONKEY-FOLK!

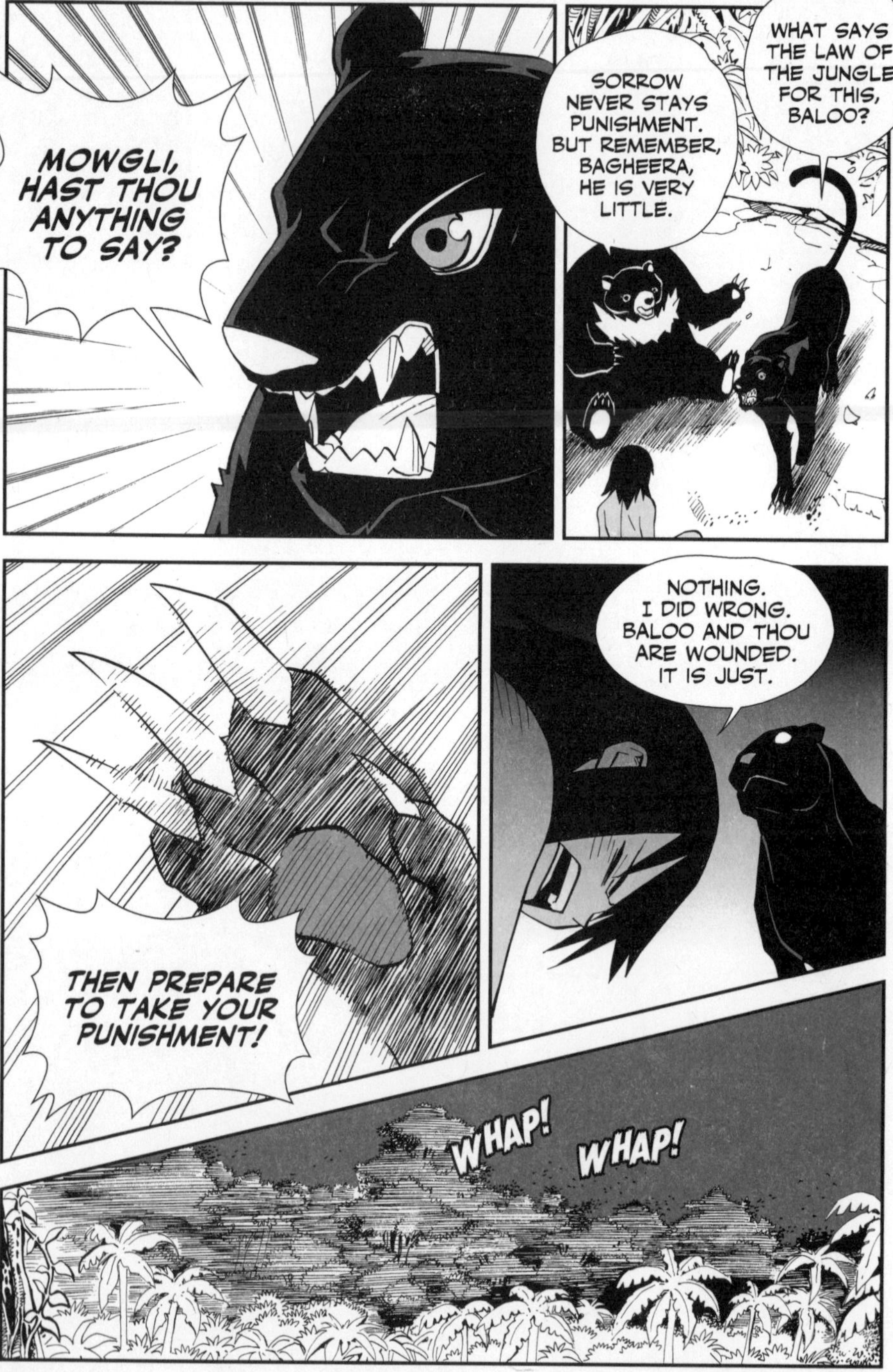
WHAT SAYS THE LAW OF THE JUNGLE FOR THIS, BALOO?
SORROW NEVER STAYS PUNISHMENT. BUT REMEMBER, BAGHEERA, HE IS VERY LITTLE.
MOWGLI, HAST THOU ANYTHING TO SAY?
NOTHING. I DID WRONG. BALOO AND THOU ARE WOUNDED. IT IS JUST.
THEN PREPARE TO TAKE YOUR PUNISHMENT!
WHAP!
WHAP!

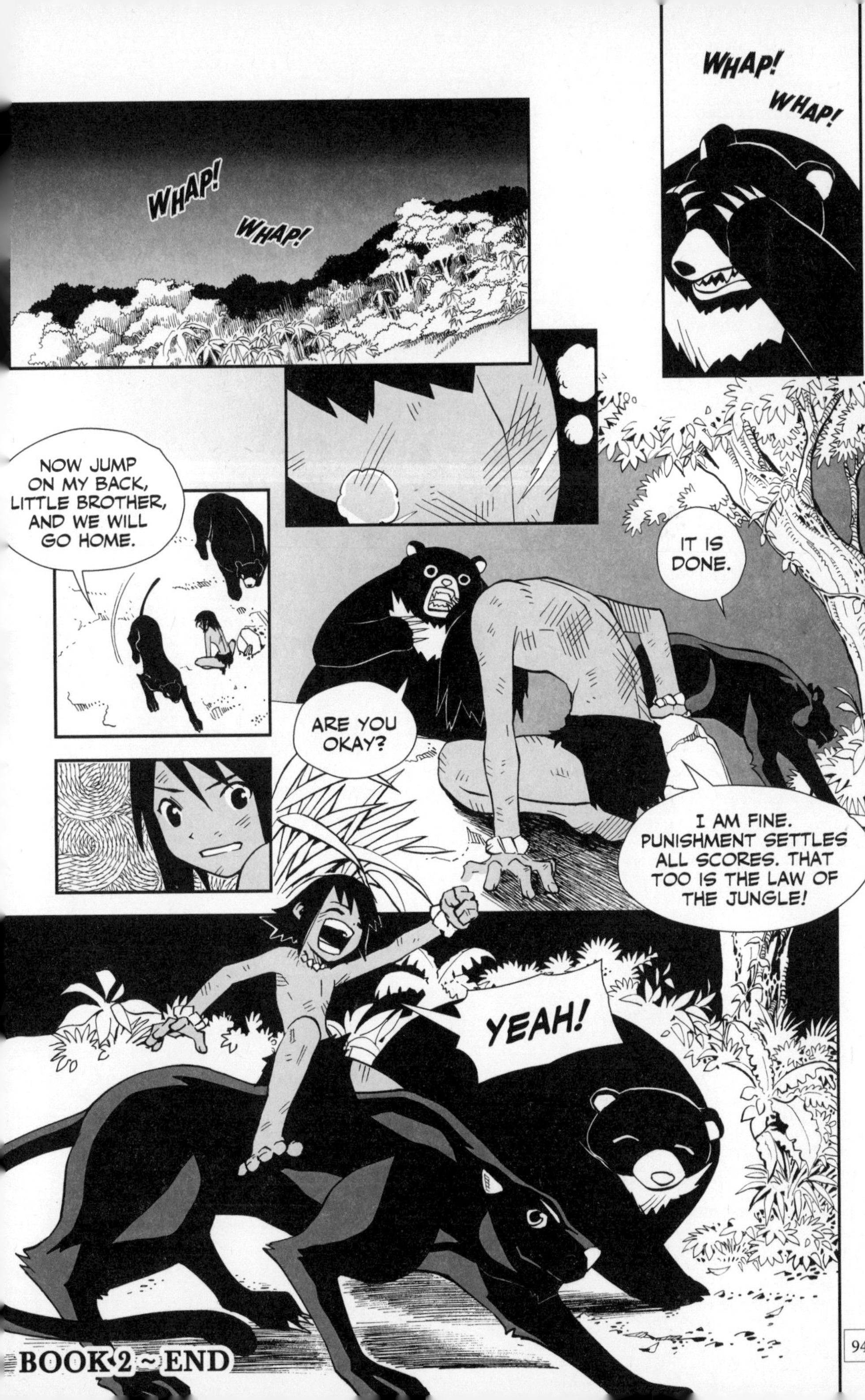
WHAP!
WHAP!
WHAP!
WHAP!
IT IS DONE.
ARE YOU OKAY?
I AM FINE. PUNISHMENT SETTLES ALL SCORES. THAT TOO IS THE LAW OF THE JUNGLE!
NOW JUMP ON MY BACK, LITTLE BROTHER, AND WE WILL GO HOME.
YEAH!
BOOK 2 ~ END

BOOK 3: TIGER! TIGER!

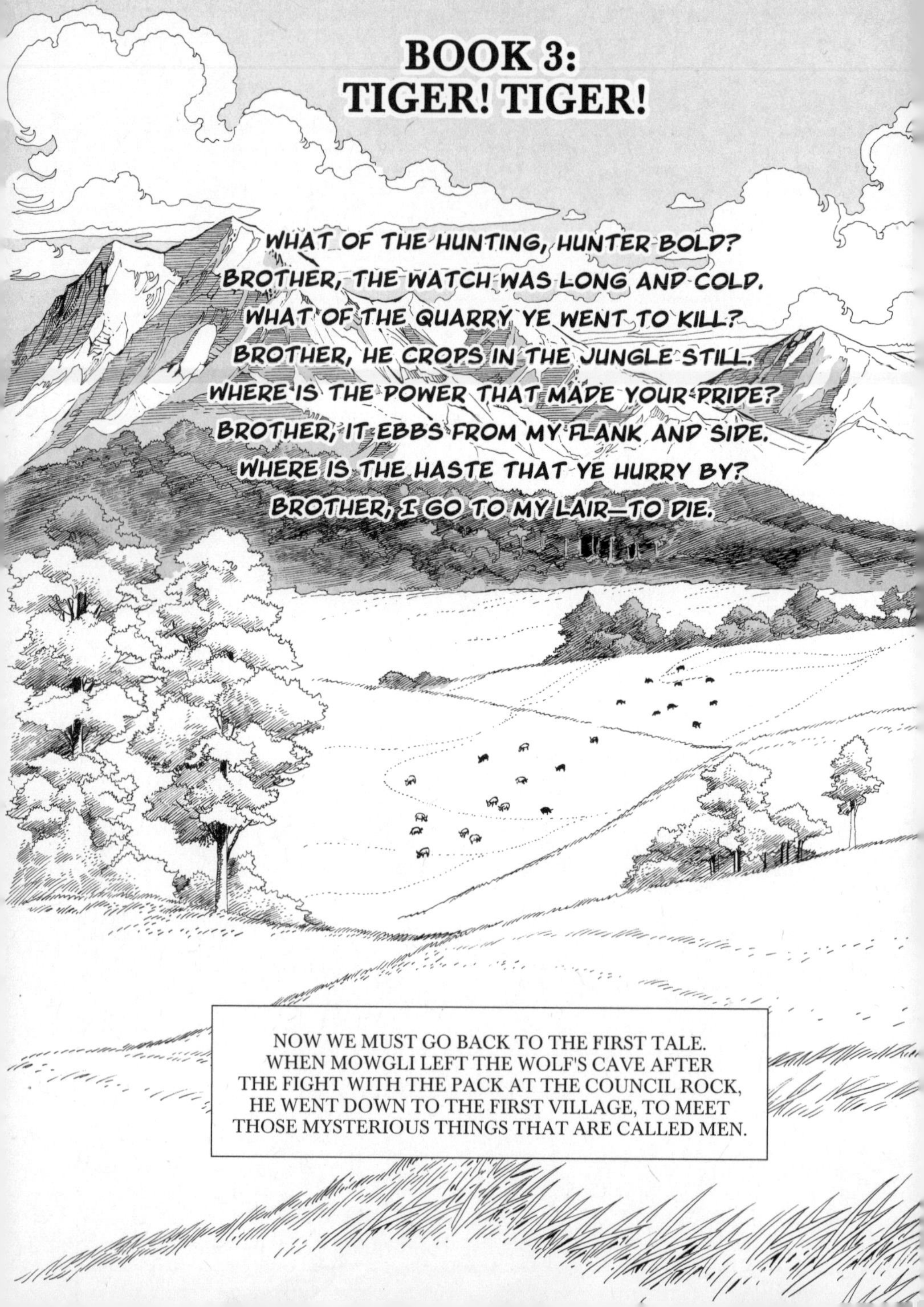
WHAT OF THE HUNTING, HUNTER BOLD?
BROTHER, THE WATCH WAS LONG AND COLD.
WHAT OF THE QUARRY YE WENT TO KILL?
BROTHER, HE CROPS IN THE JUNGLE STILL.
WHERE IS THE POWER THAT MADE YOUR PRIDE?
BROTHER, IT EBBS FROM MY FLANK AND SIDE.
WHERE IS THE HASTE THAT YE HURRY BY?
BROTHER, I GO TO MY LAIR—TO DIE.
NOW WE MUST GO BACK TO THE FIRST TALE. WHEN MOWGLI LEFT THE WOLF'S CAVE AFTER THE FIGHT WITH THE PACK AT THE COUNCIL ROCK, HE WENT DOWN TO THE FIRST VILLAGE, TO MEET THOSE MYSTERIOUS THINGS THAT ARE CALLED MEN.

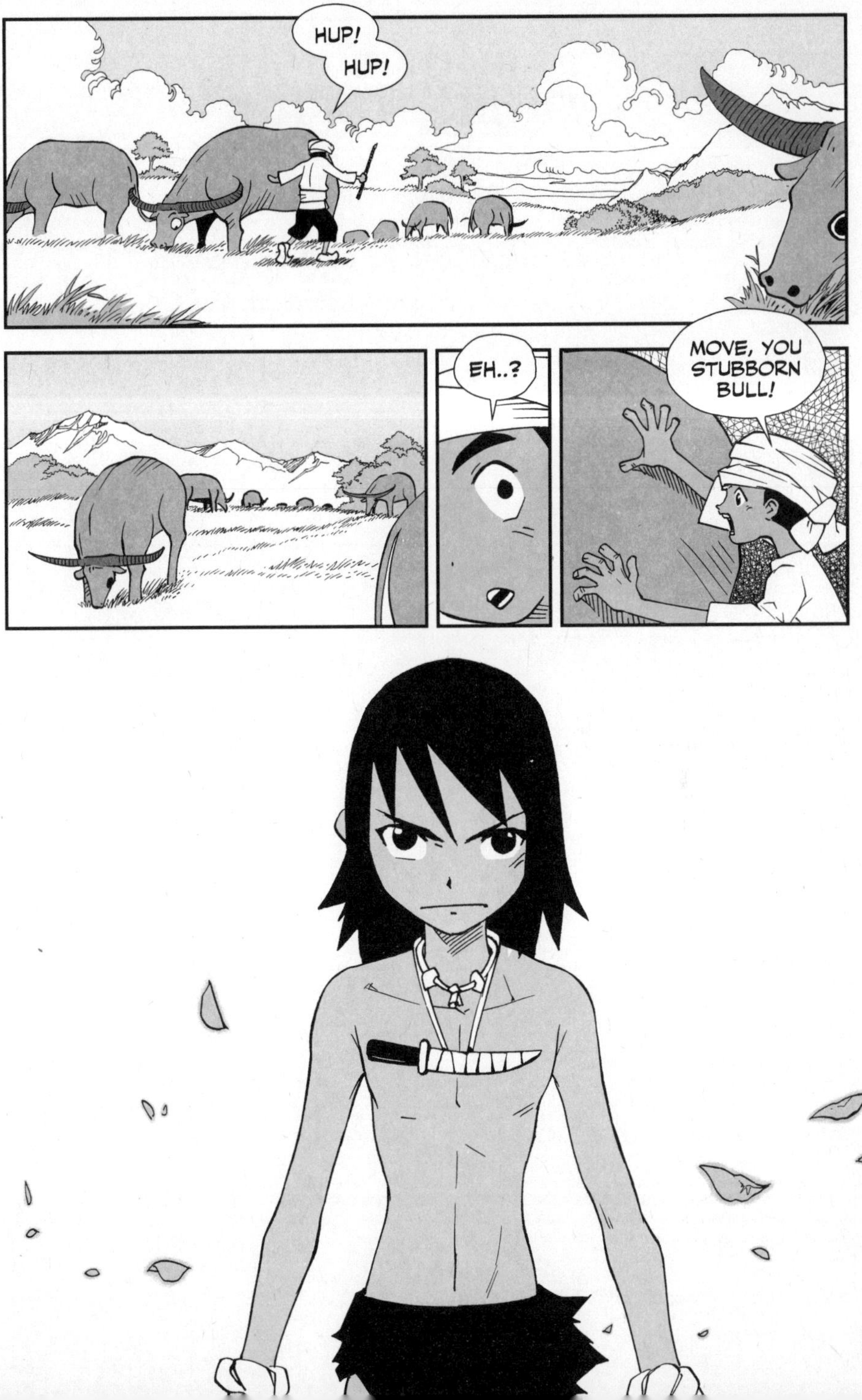
HUP!
HUP!
MOVE, YOU STUBBORN BULL!
EH..?

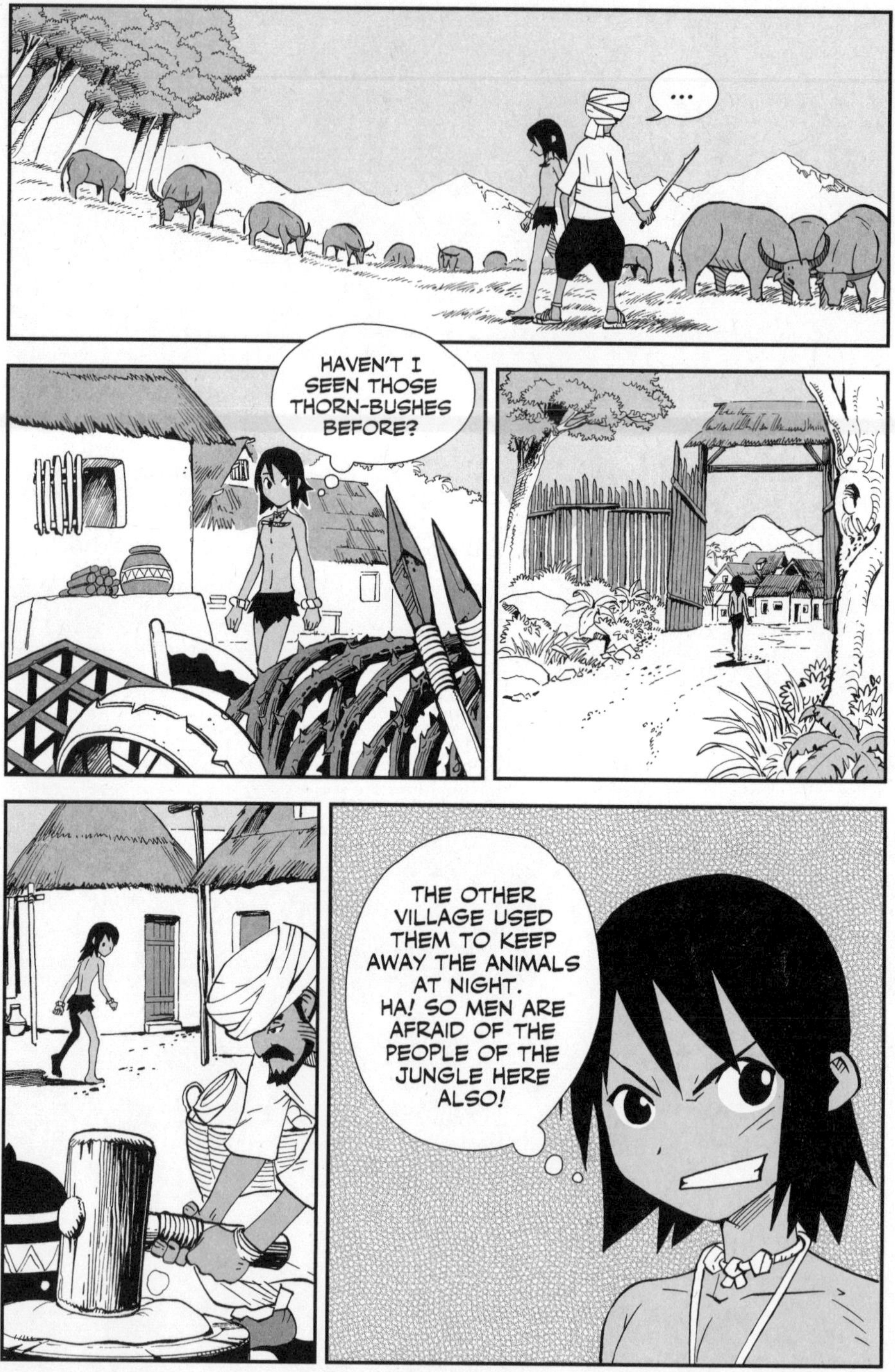
...
HAVEN'T I SEEN THOSE THORN-BUSHES BEFORE?
THE OTHER VILLAGE USED THEM TO KEEP AWAY THE ANIMALS AT NIGHT. HA! SO MEN ARE AFRAID OF THE PEOPLE OF THE JUNGLE HERE ALSO!

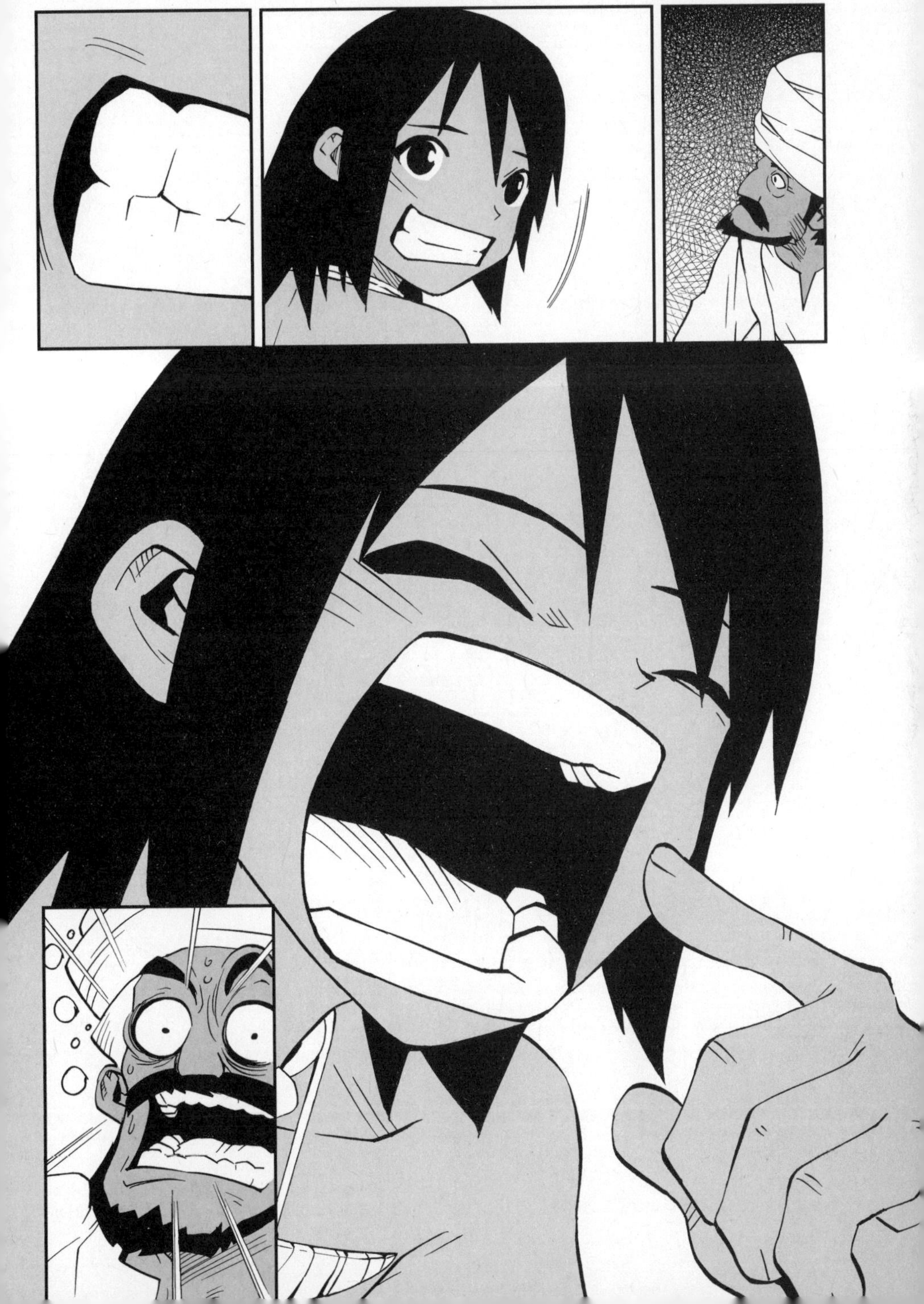

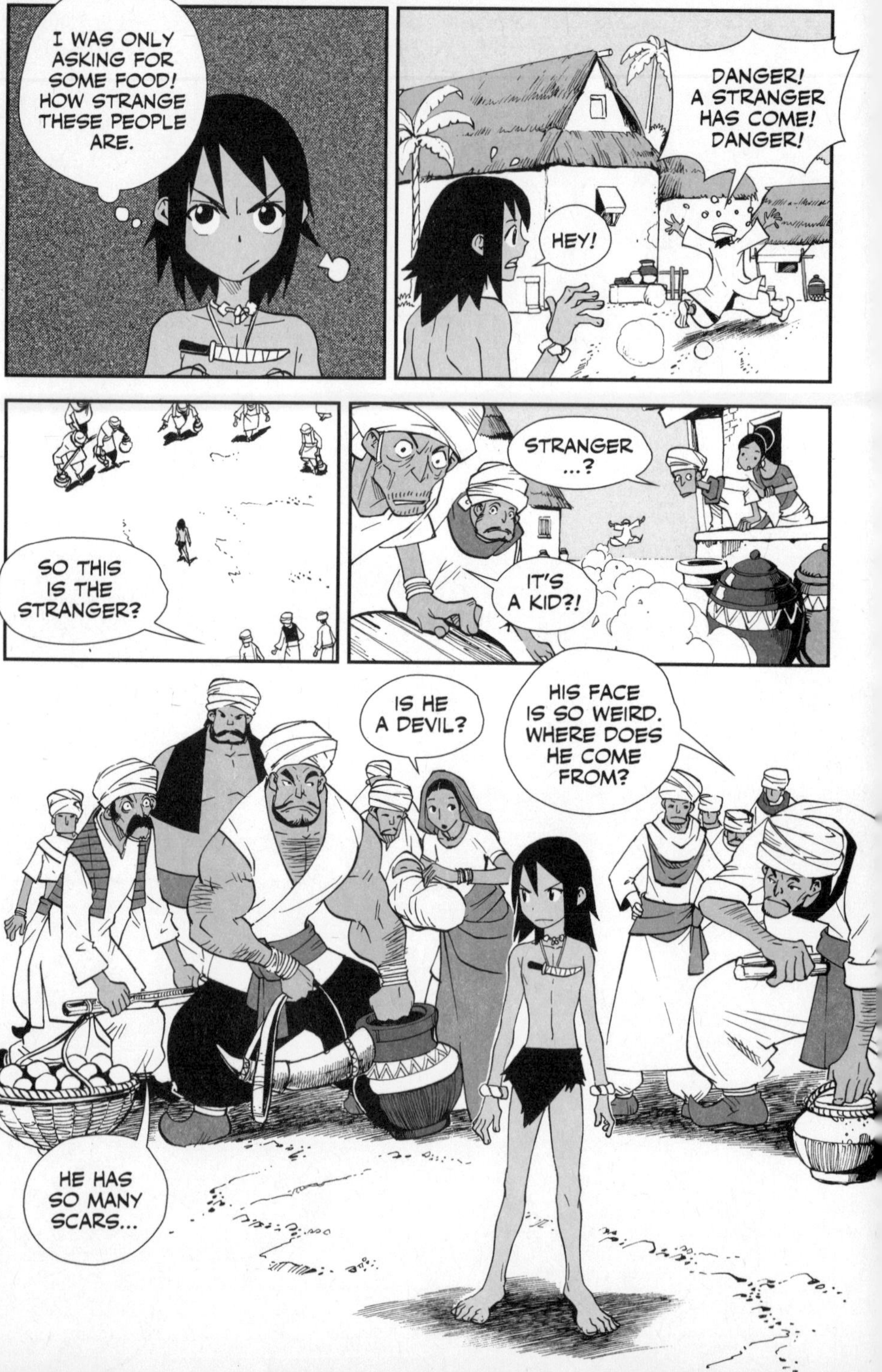
DANGER! A STRANGER HAS COME! DANGER!
HEY!
I WAS ONLY ASKING FOR SOME FOOD! HOW STRANGE THESE PEOPLE ARE.
STRANGER ...?
IT'S A KID?!
SO THIS IS THE STRANGER?
HIS FACE IS SO WEIRD. WHERE DOES HE COME FROM?
IS HE A DEVIL?
HE HAS SO MANY SCARS...

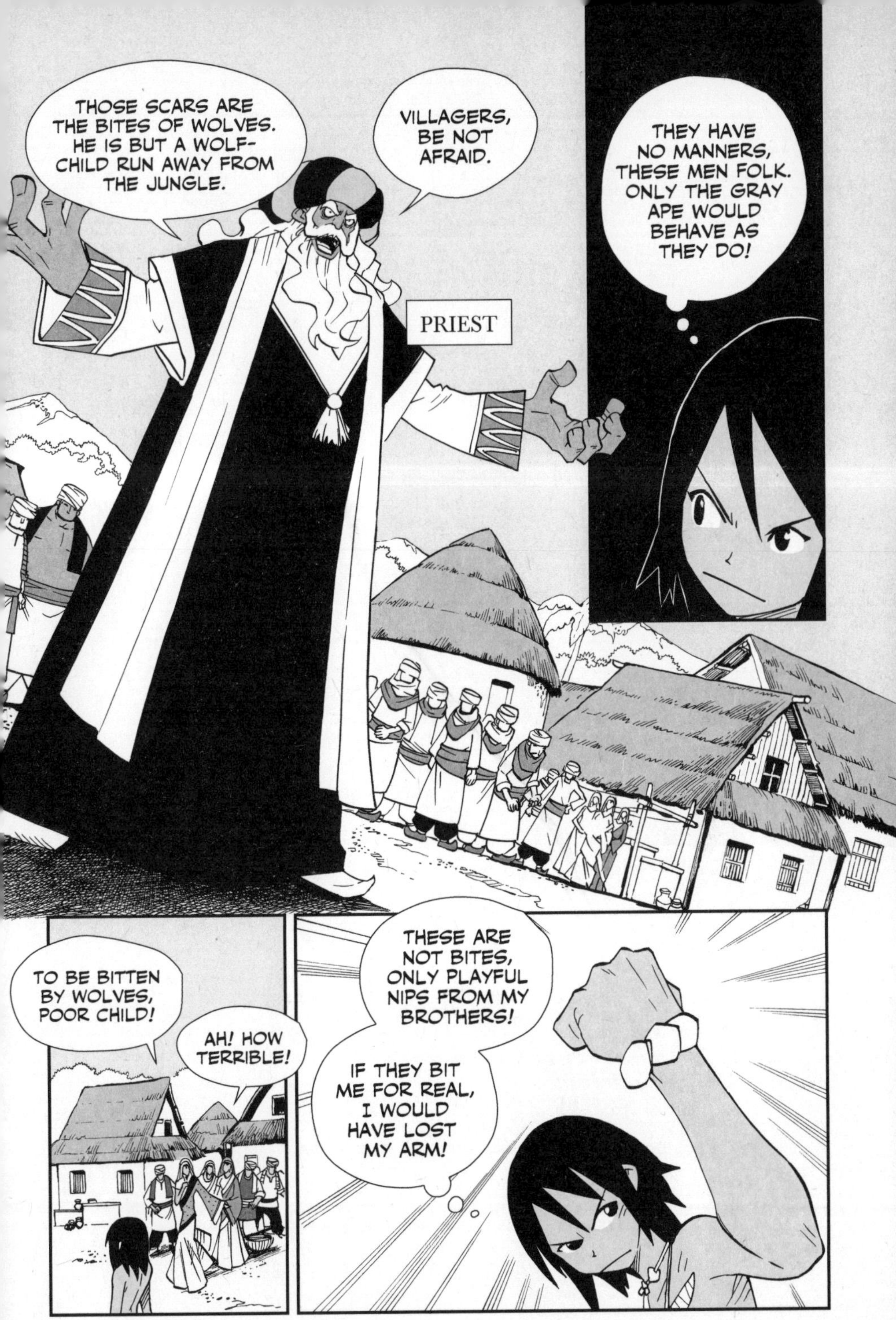
THEY HAVE NO MANNERS, THESE MEN FOLK. ONLY THE GRAY APE WOULD BEHAVE AS THEY DO!
VILLAGERS, BE NOT AFRAID.
THOSE SCARS ARE THE BITES OF WOLVES. HE IS BUT A WOLF-CHILD RUN AWAY FROM THE JUNGLE.
PRIEST
THESE ARE NOT BITES, ONLY PLAYFUL NIPS FROM MY BROTHERS!
IF THEY BIT ME FOR REAL, I WOULD HAVE LOST MY ARM!
TO BE BITTEN BY WOLVES, POOR CHILD!
AH! HOW TERRIBLE!

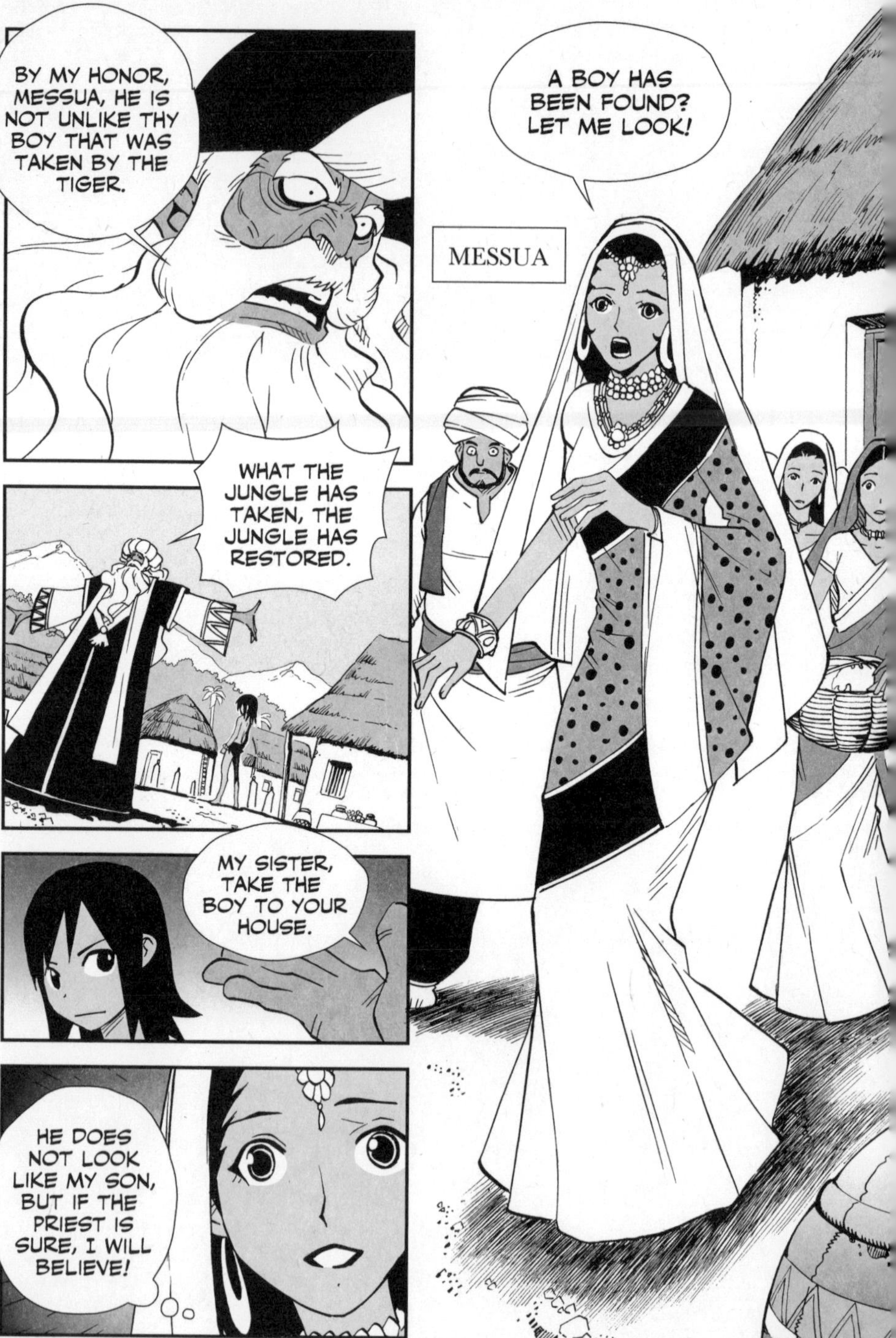
A BOY HAS BEEN FOUND? LET ME LOOK!
MESSUA
BY MY HONOR, MESSUA, HE IS NOT UNLIKE THY BOY THAT WAS TAKEN BY THE TIGER.
WHAT THE JUNGLE HAS TAKEN, THE JUNGLE HAS RESTORED.
MY SISTER, TAKE THE BOY TO YOUR HOUSE.
HE DOES NOT LOOK LIKE MY SON, BUT IF THE PRIEST IS SURE, I WILL BELIEVE!

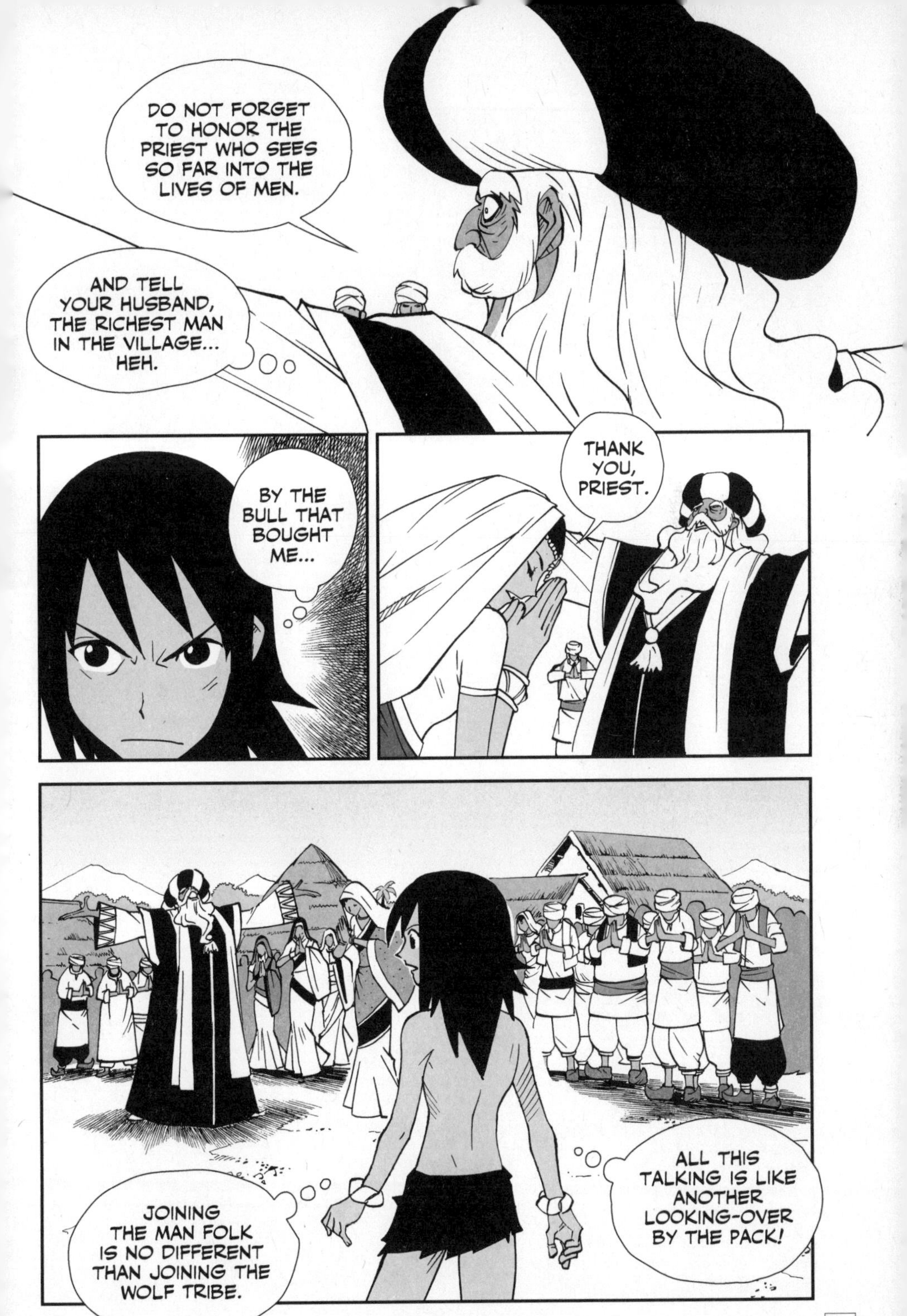
DO NOT FORGET TO HONOR THE PRIEST WHO SEES SO FAR INTO THE LIVES OF MEN.
AND TELL YOUR HUSBAND, THE RICHEST MAN IN THE VILLAGE... HEH.
THANK YOU, PRIEST.
BY THE BULL THAT BOUGHT ME...
ALL THIS TALKING IS LIKE ANOTHER LOOKING-OVER BY THE PACK!
JOINING THE MAN FOLK IS NO DIFFERENT THAN JOINING THE WOLF TRIBE.

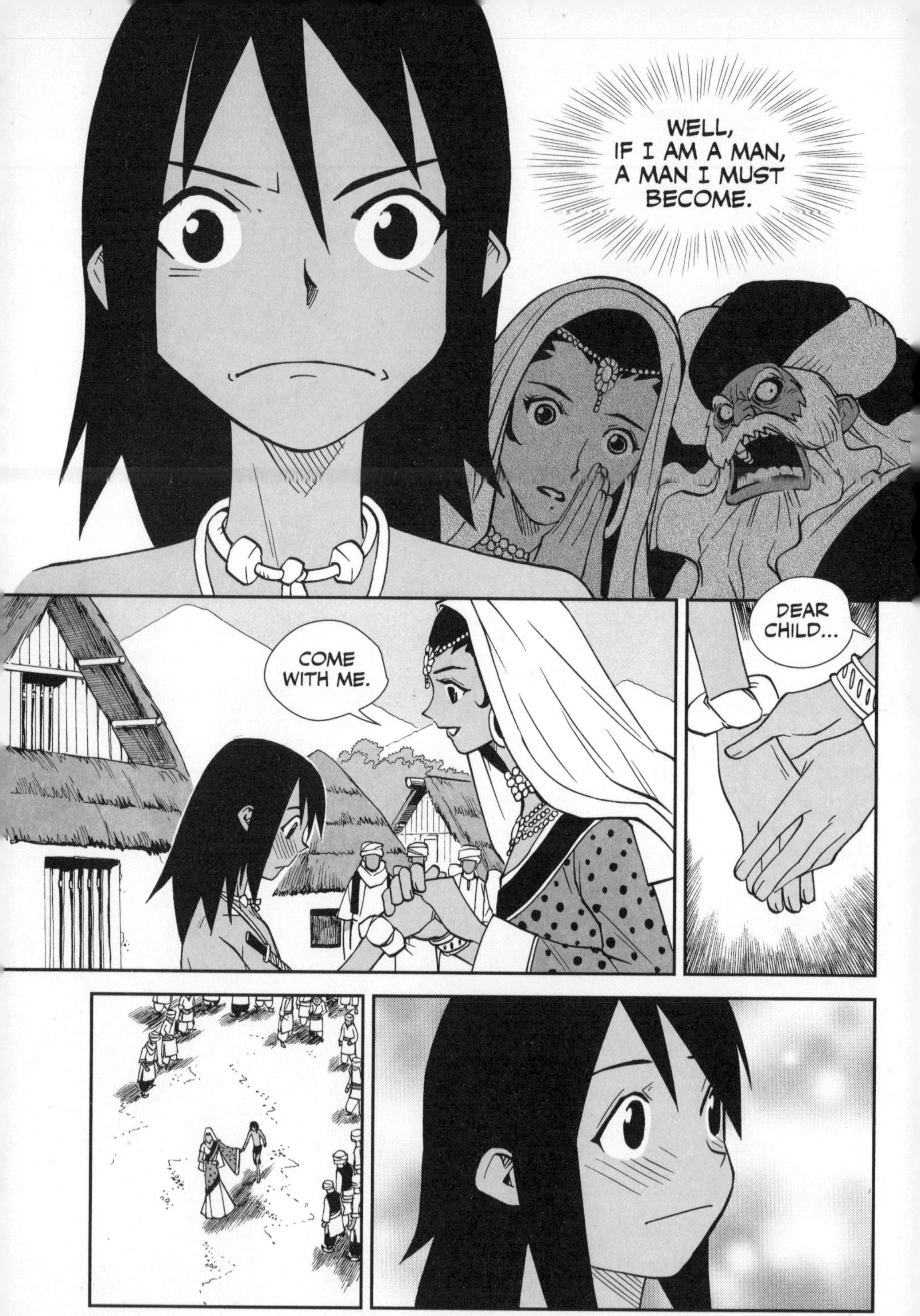
WELL, IF I AM A MAN, A MAN I MUST BECOME.
DEAR CHILD...
COME WITH ME.

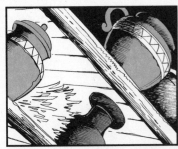

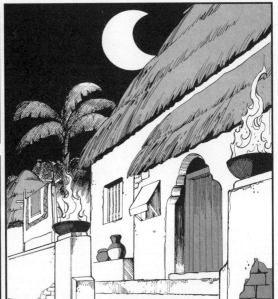

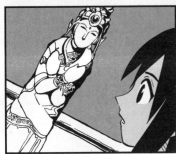

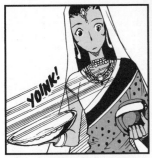

YOINK!

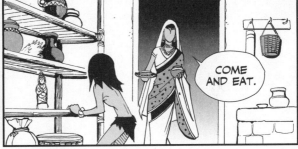

COME AND EAT.

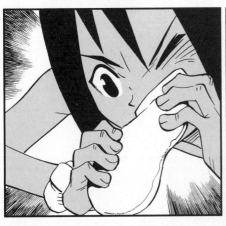

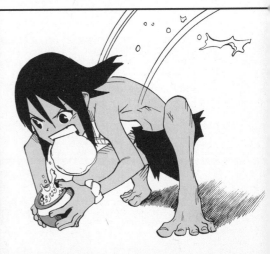

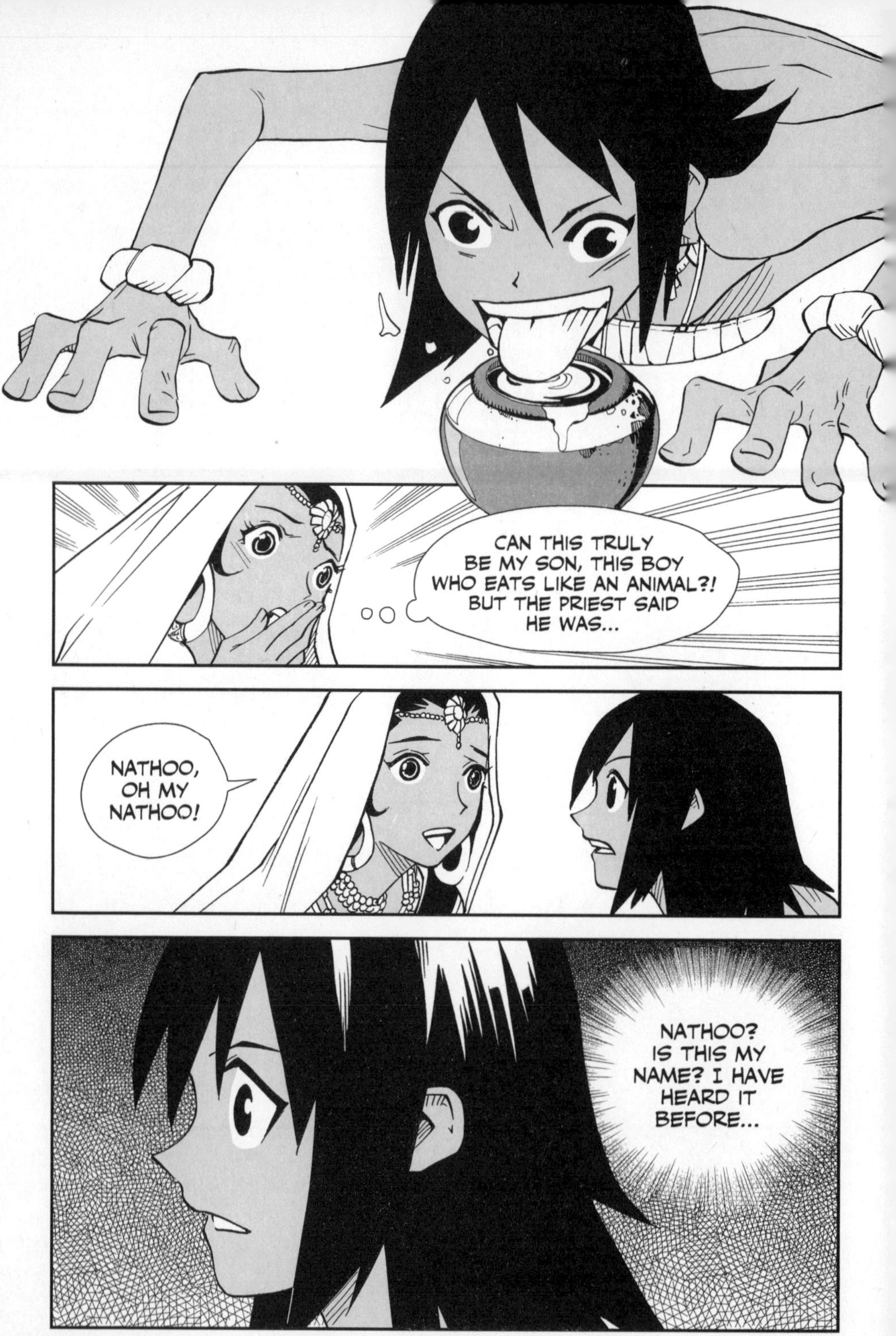
CAN THIS TRULY BE MY SON, THIS BOY WHO EATS LIKE AN ANIMAL?! BUT THE PRIEST SAID HE WAS...
NATHOO, OH MY NATHOO!
NATHOO? IS THIS MY NAME? I HAVE HEARD IT BEFORE...

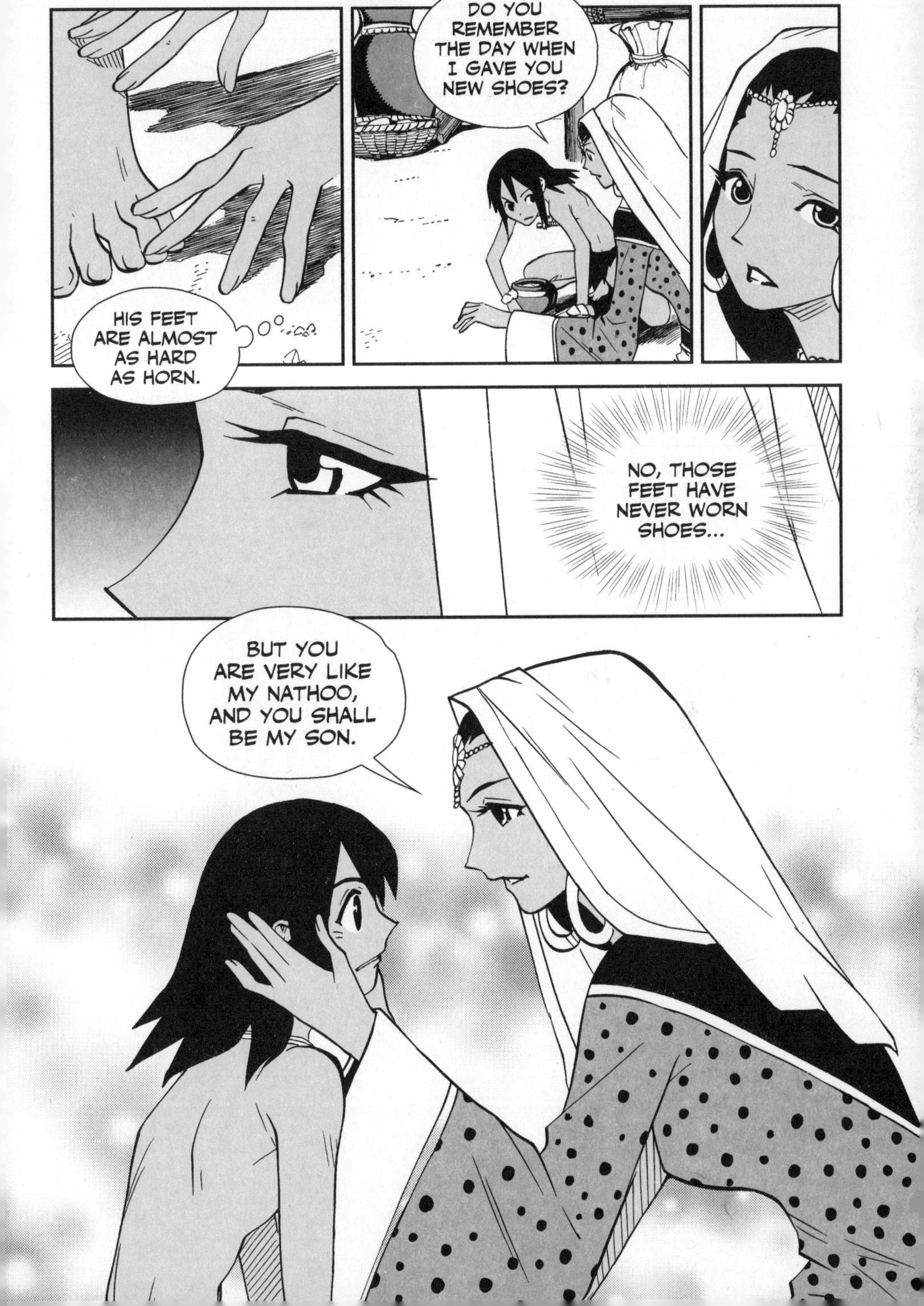
DO YOU REMEMBER THE DAY WHEN I GAVE YOU NEW SHOES?
HIS FEET ARE ALMOST AS HARD AS HORN.
NO, THOSE FEET HAVE NEVER WORN SHOES...
BUT YOU ARE VERY LIKE MY NATHOO, AND YOU SHALL BE MY SON.

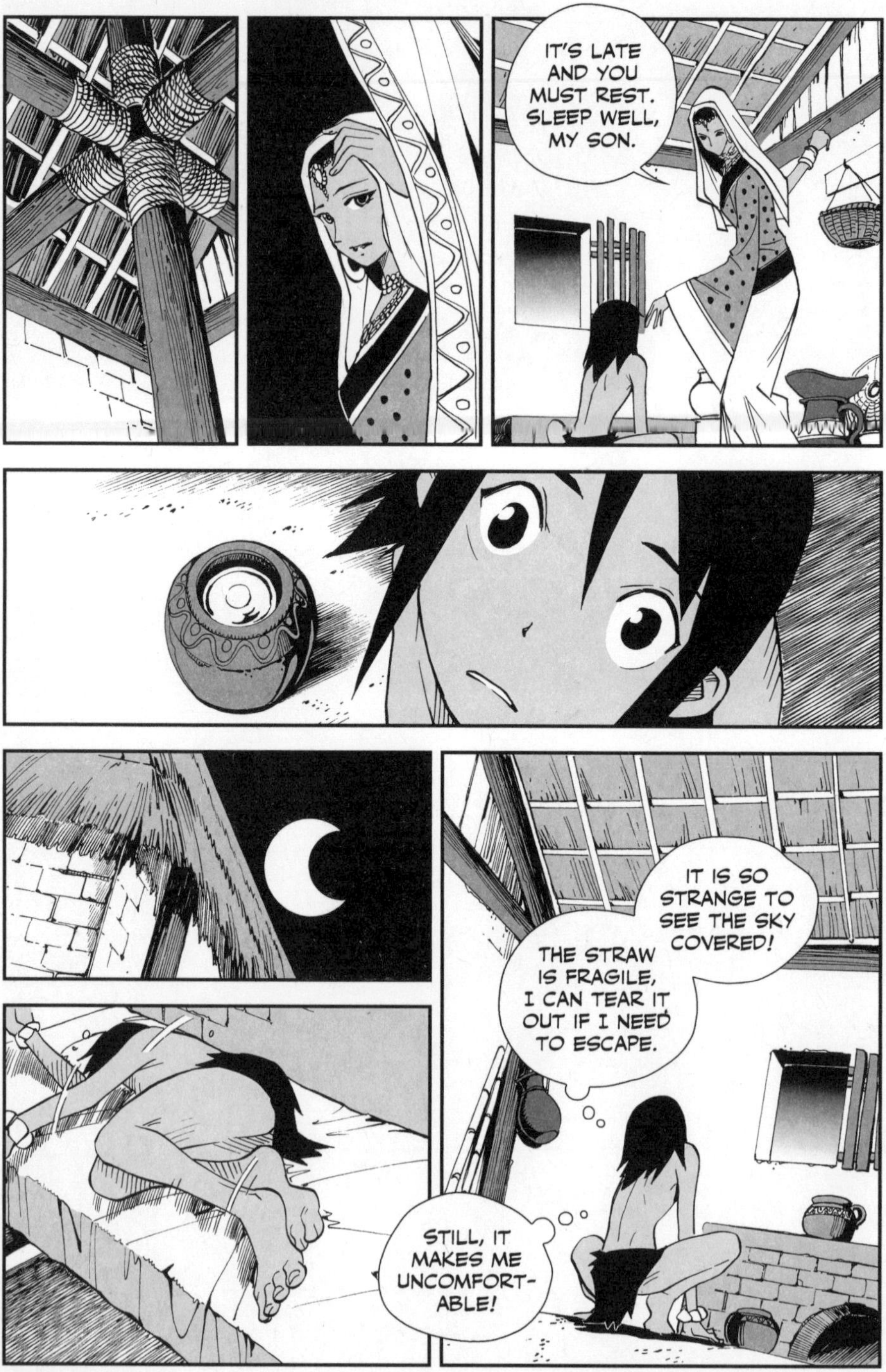
IT'S LATE AND YOU MUST REST. SLEEP WELL, MY SON.
IT IS SO STRANGE TO SEE THE SKY COVERED!
THE STRAW IS FRAGILE, I CAN TEAR IT OUT IF I NEED TO ESCAPE.
STILL, IT MAKES ME UNCOMFORT-ABLE!

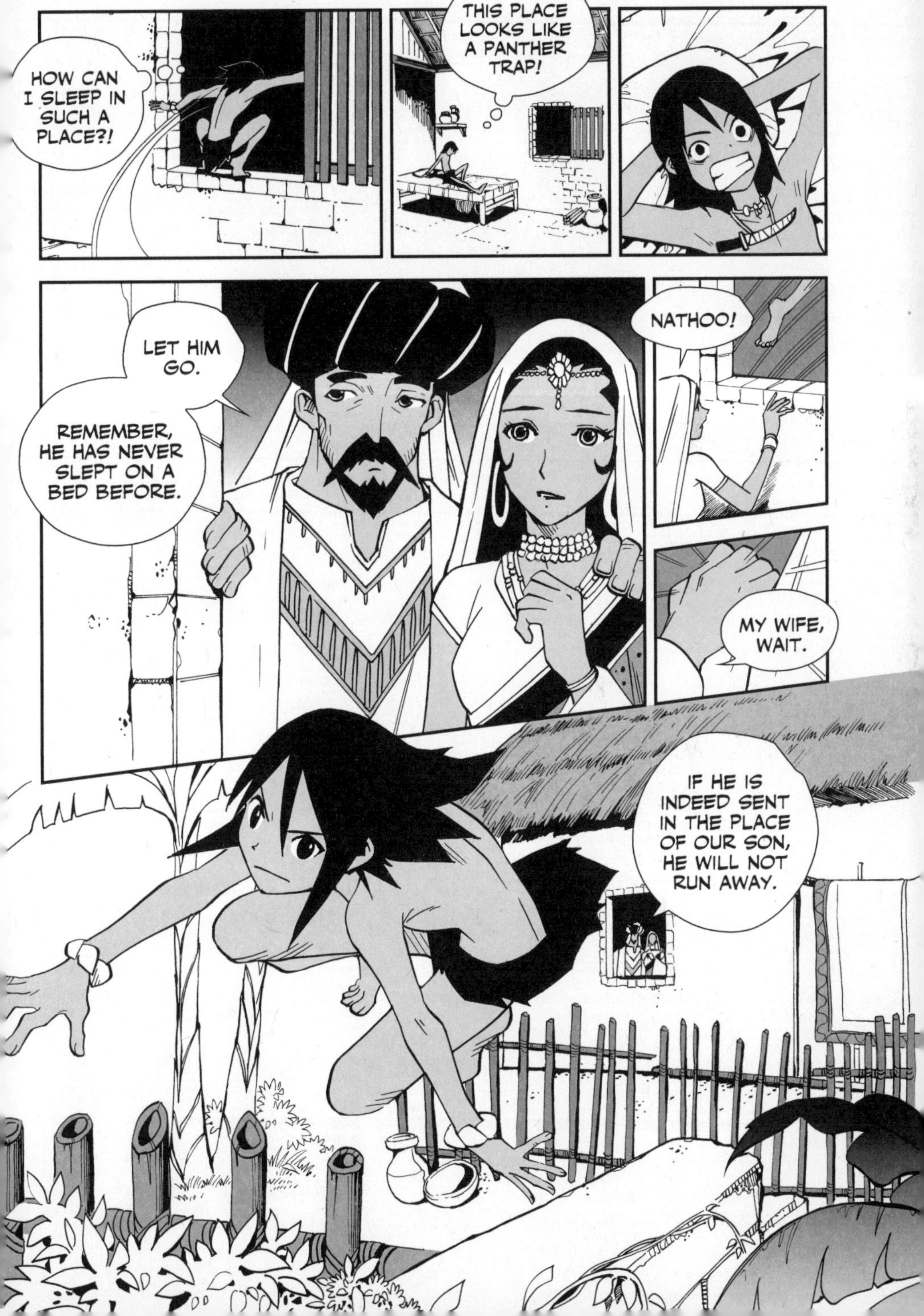
THIS PLACE LOOKS LIKE A PANTHER TRAP!
HOW CAN I SLEEP IN SUCH A PLACE?!
NATHOO!
MY WIFE, WAIT.
LET HIM GO.
REMEMBER, HE HAS NEVER SLEPT ON A BED BEFORE.
IF HE IS INDEED SENT IN THE PLACE OF OUR SON, HE WILL NOT RUN AWAY.

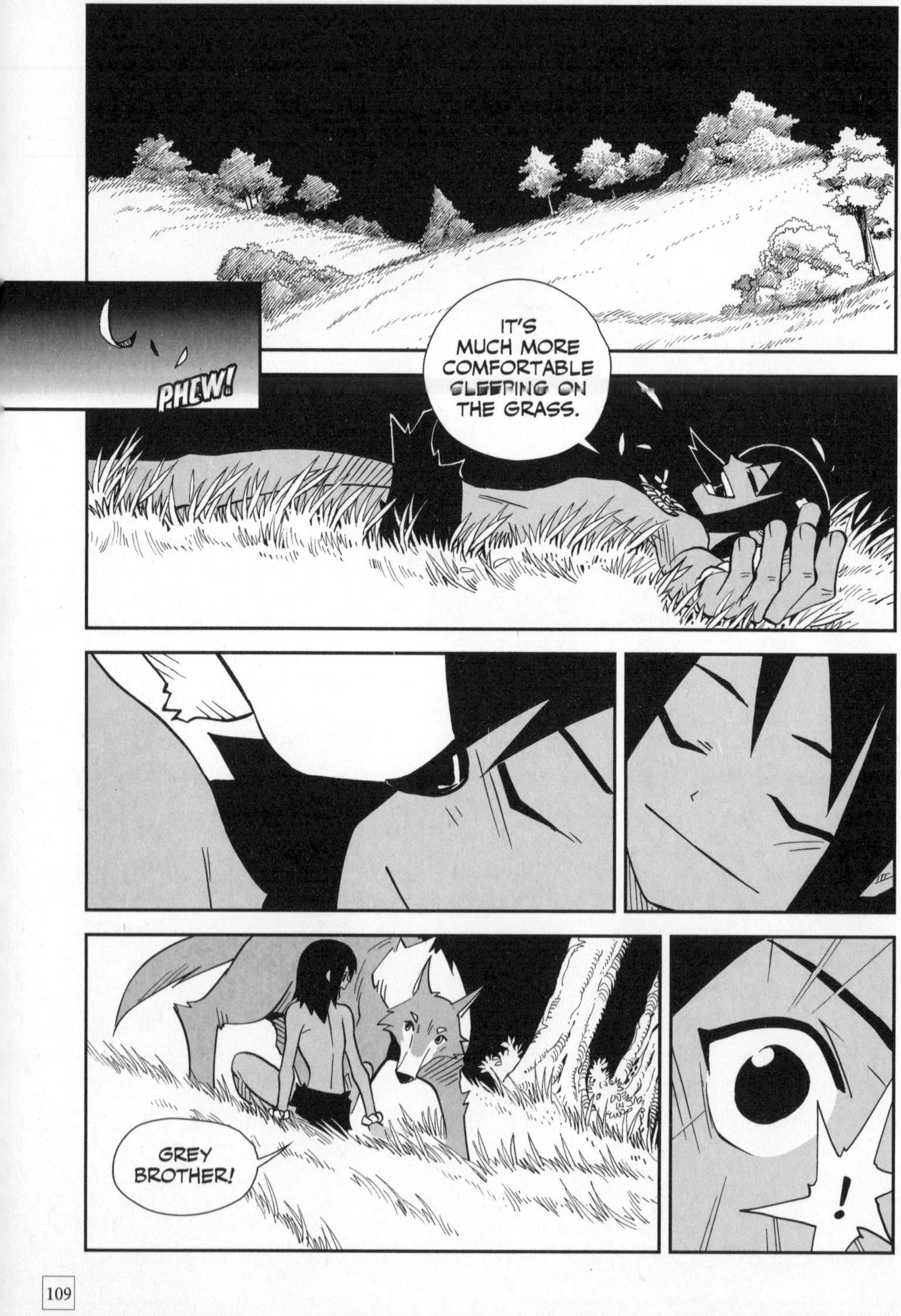
IT'S MUCH MORE COMFORTABLE SLEEPING ON THE GRASS.
PHEW!
!
GREY BROTHER!

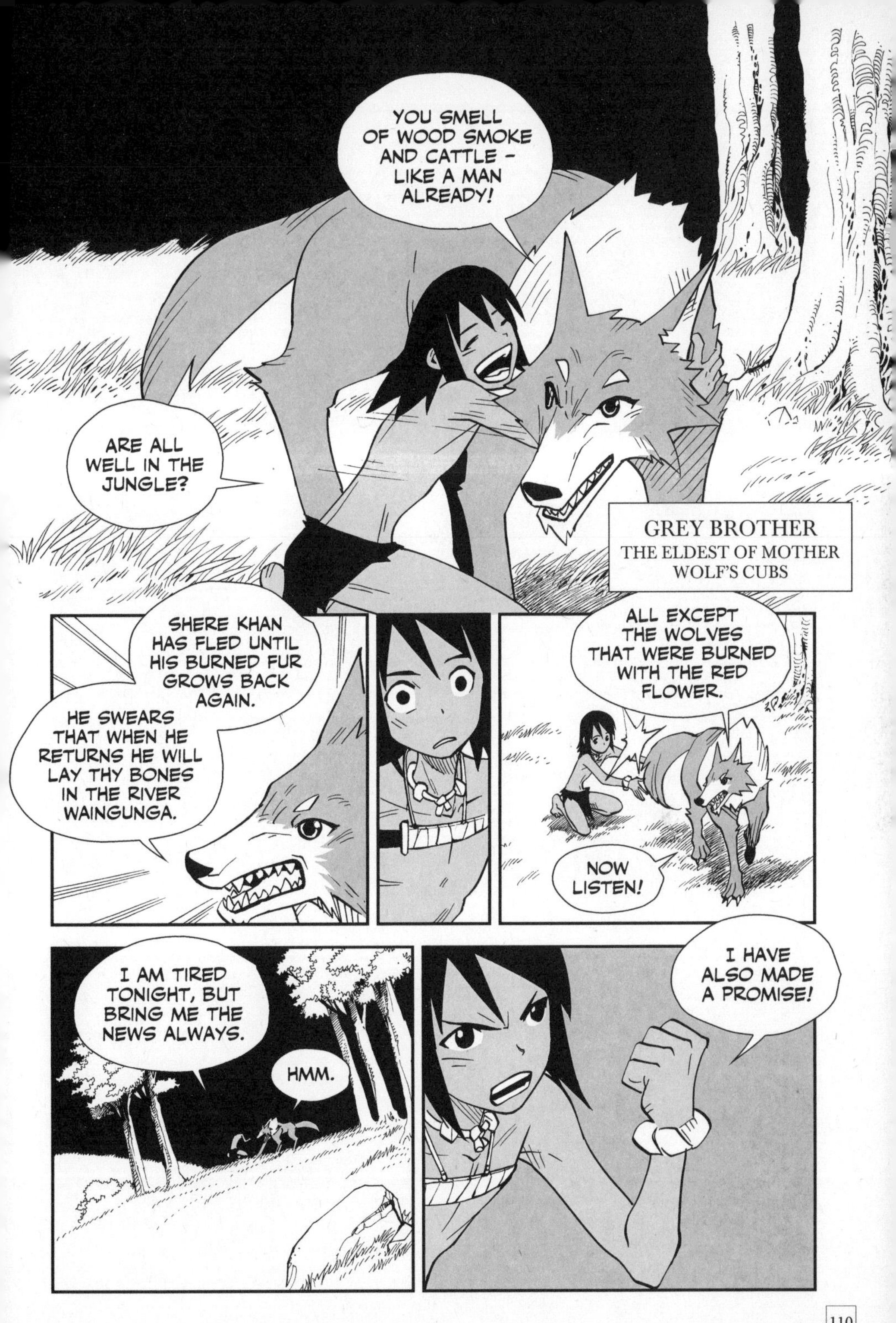
YOU SMELL OF WOOD SMOKE AND CATTLE – LIKE A MAN ALREADY!
ARE ALL WELL IN THE JUNGLE?
GREY BROTHER
THE ELDEST OF MOTHER WOLF'S CUBS
ALL EXCEPT THE WOLVES THAT WERE BURNED WITH THE RED FLOWER.
NOW LISTEN!
SHERE KHAN HAS FLED UNTIL HIS BURNED FUR GROWS BACK AGAIN.
HE SWEARS THAT WHEN HE RETURNS HE WILL LAY THY BONES IN THE RIVER WAINGUNGA.
I HAVE ALSO MADE A PROMISE!
I AM TIRED TONIGHT, BUT BRING ME THE NEWS ALWAYS.
HMM.

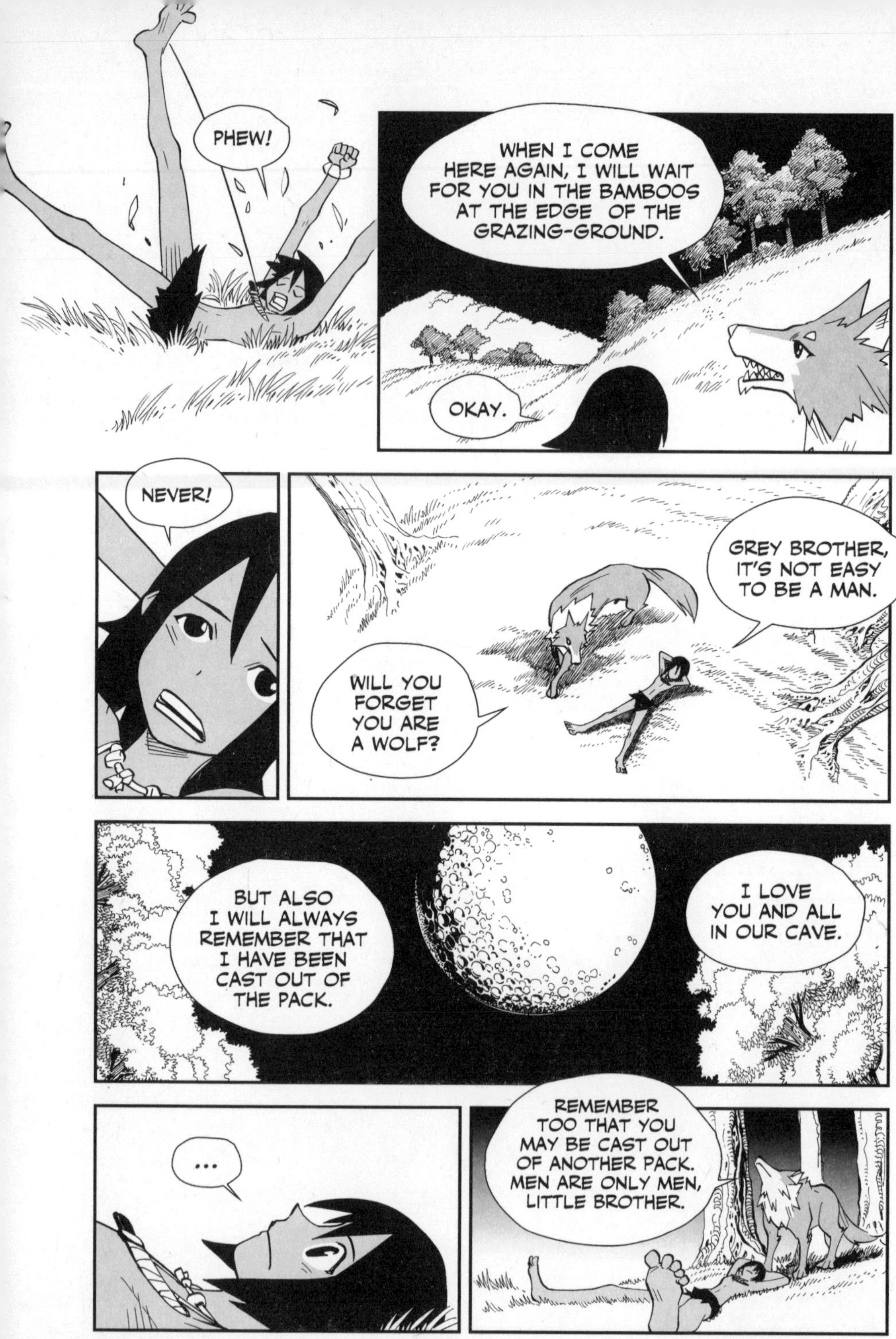

WHEN I COME HERE AGAIN, I WILL WAIT FOR YOU IN THE BAMBOOS AT THE EDGE OF THE GRAZING-GROUND.
OKAY.
PHEW!
GREY BROTHER, IT'S NOT EASY TO BE A MAN.
WILL YOU FORGET YOU ARE A WOLF?
NEVER!
I LOVE YOU AND ALL IN OUR CAVE.
BUT ALSO I WILL ALWAYS REMEMBER THAT I HAVE BEEN CAST OUT OF THE PACK.
REMEMBER TOO THAT YOU MAY BE CAST OUT OF ANOTHER PACK. MEN ARE ONLY MEN, LITTLE BROTHER.
...

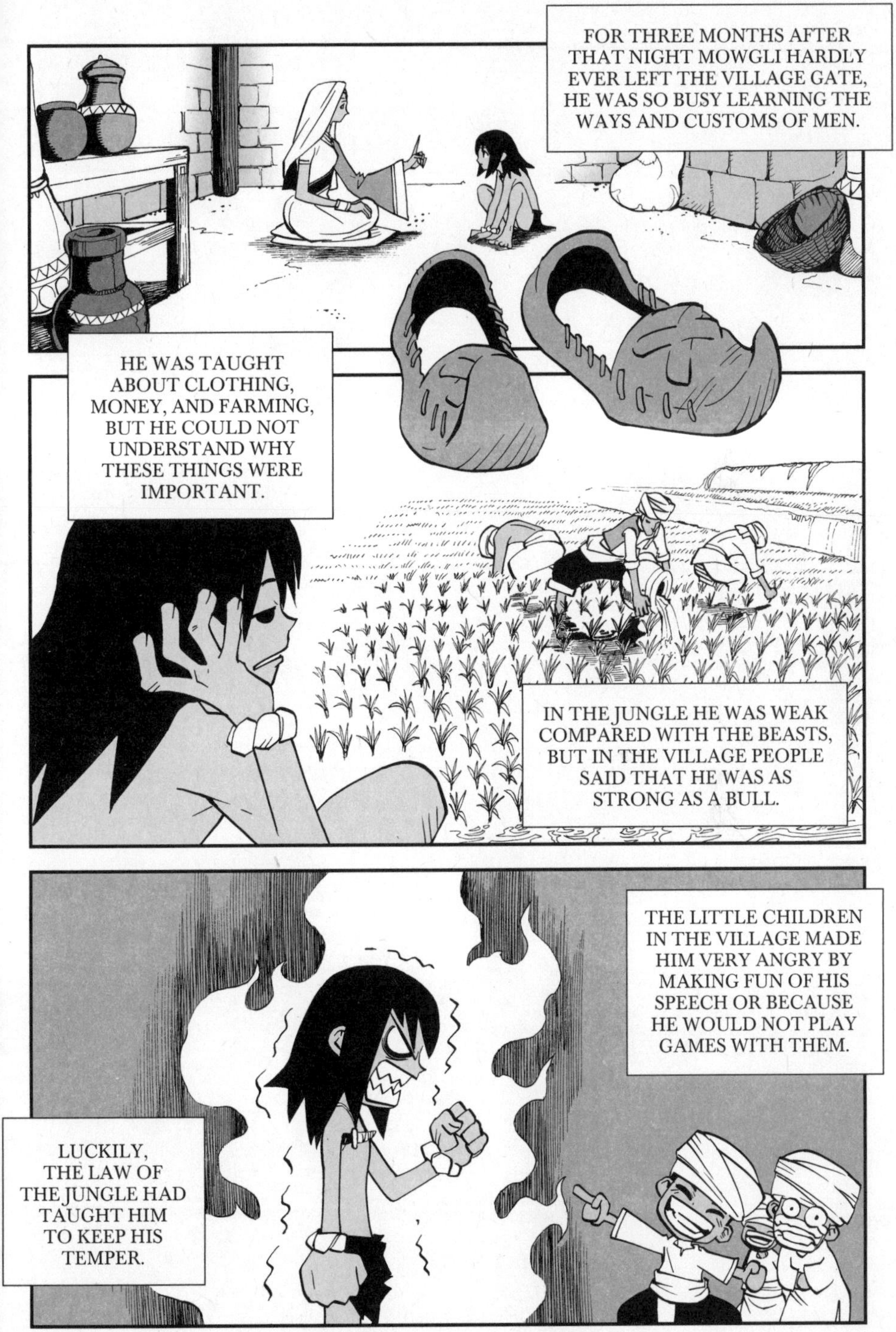
FOR THREE MONTHS AFTER THAT NIGHT MOWGLI HARDLY EVER LEFT THE VILLAGE GATE, HE WAS SO BUSY LEARNING THE WAYS AND CUSTOMS OF MEN.
HE WAS TAUGHT ABOUT CLOTHING, MONEY, AND FARMING, BUT HE COULD NOT UNDERSTAND WHY THESE THINGS WERE IMPORTANT.
IN THE JUNGLE HE WAS WEAK COMPARED WITH THE BEASTS, BUT IN THE VILLAGE PEOPLE SAID THAT HE WAS AS STRONG AS A BULL.
THE LITTLE CHILDREN IN THE VILLAGE MADE HIM VERY ANGRY BY MAKING FUN OF HIS SPEECH OR BECAUSE HE WOULD NOT PLAY GAMES WITH THEM.
LUCKILY, THE LAW OF THE JUNGLE HAD TAUGHT HIM TO KEEP HIS TEMPER.

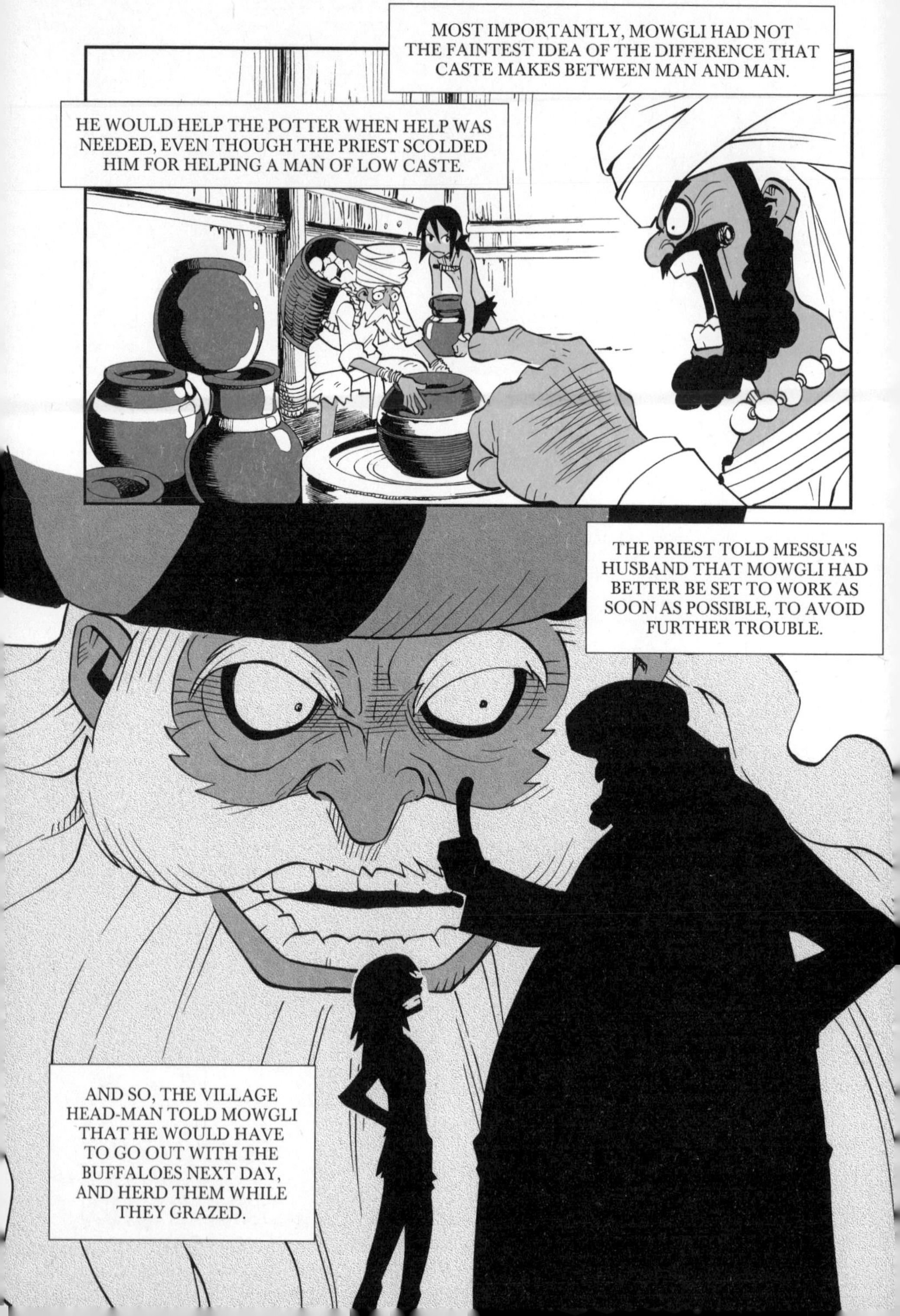
MOST IMPORTANTLY, MOWGLI HAD NOT THE FAINTEST IDEA OF THE DIFFERENCE THAT CASTE MAKES BETWEEN MAN AND MAN.
HE WOULD HELP THE POTTER WHEN HELP WAS NEEDED, EVEN THOUGH THE PRIEST SCOLDED HIM FOR HELPING A MAN OF LOW CASTE.
THE PRIEST TOLD MESSUA'S HUSBAND THAT MOWGLI HAD BETTER BE SET TO WORK AS SOON AS POSSIBLE, TO AVOID FURTHER TROUBLE.
AND SO, THE VILLAGE HEAD-MAN TOLD MOWGLI THAT HE WOULD HAVE TO GO OUT WITH THE BUFFALOES NEXT DAY, AND HERD THEM WHILE THEY GRAZED.

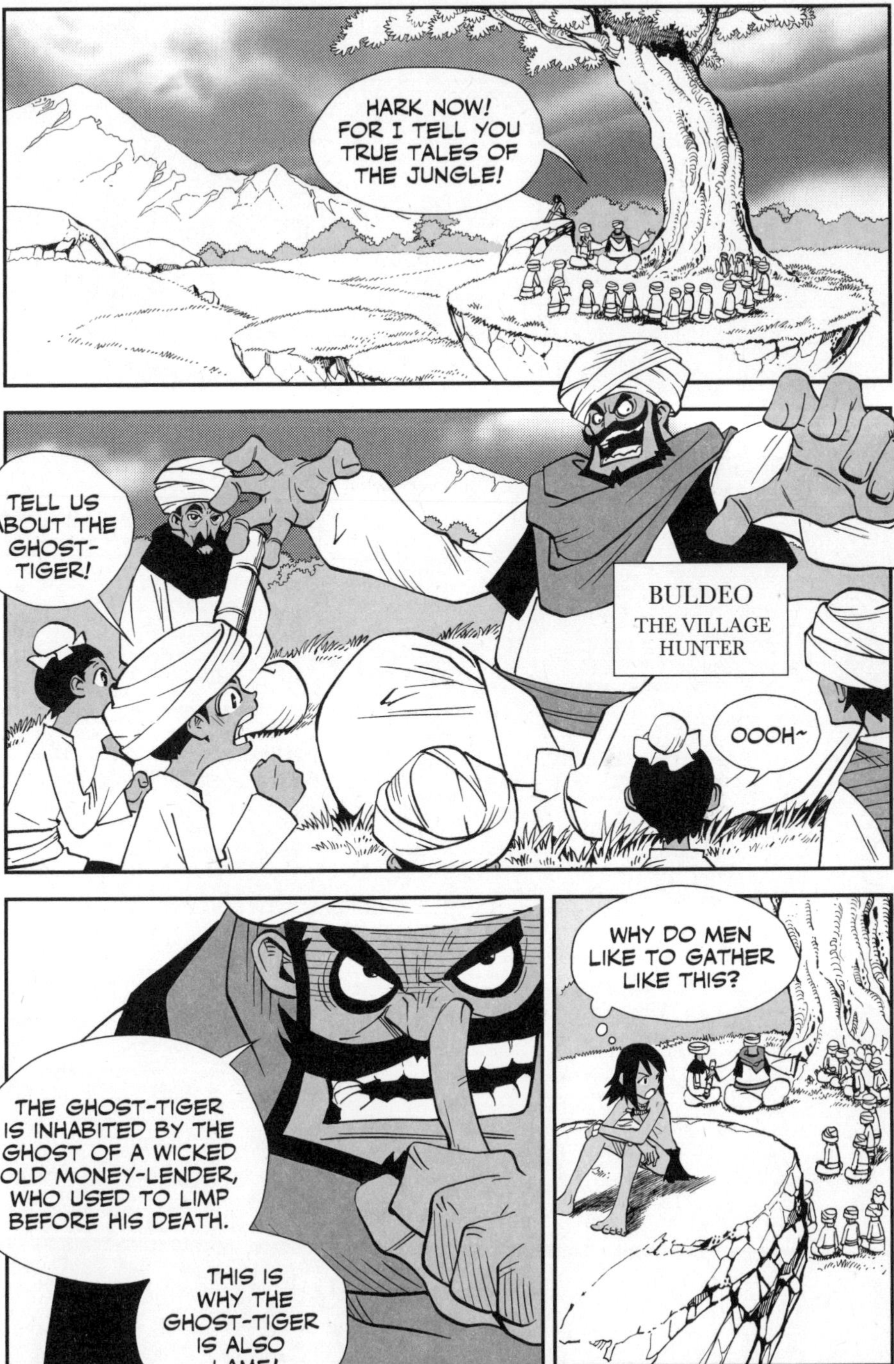
HARK NOW! FOR I TELL YOU TRUE TALES OF THE JUNGLE!
BULDEO THE VILLAGE HUNTER
TELL US ABOUT THE GHOST-TIGER!
OOOH~
WHY DO MEN LIKE TO GATHER LIKE THIS?
THE GHOST-TIGER IS INHABITED BY THE GHOST OF A WICKED OLD MONEY-LENDER, WHO USED TO LIMP BEFORE HIS DEATH.
THIS IS WHY THE GHOST-TIGER IS ALSO LAME!

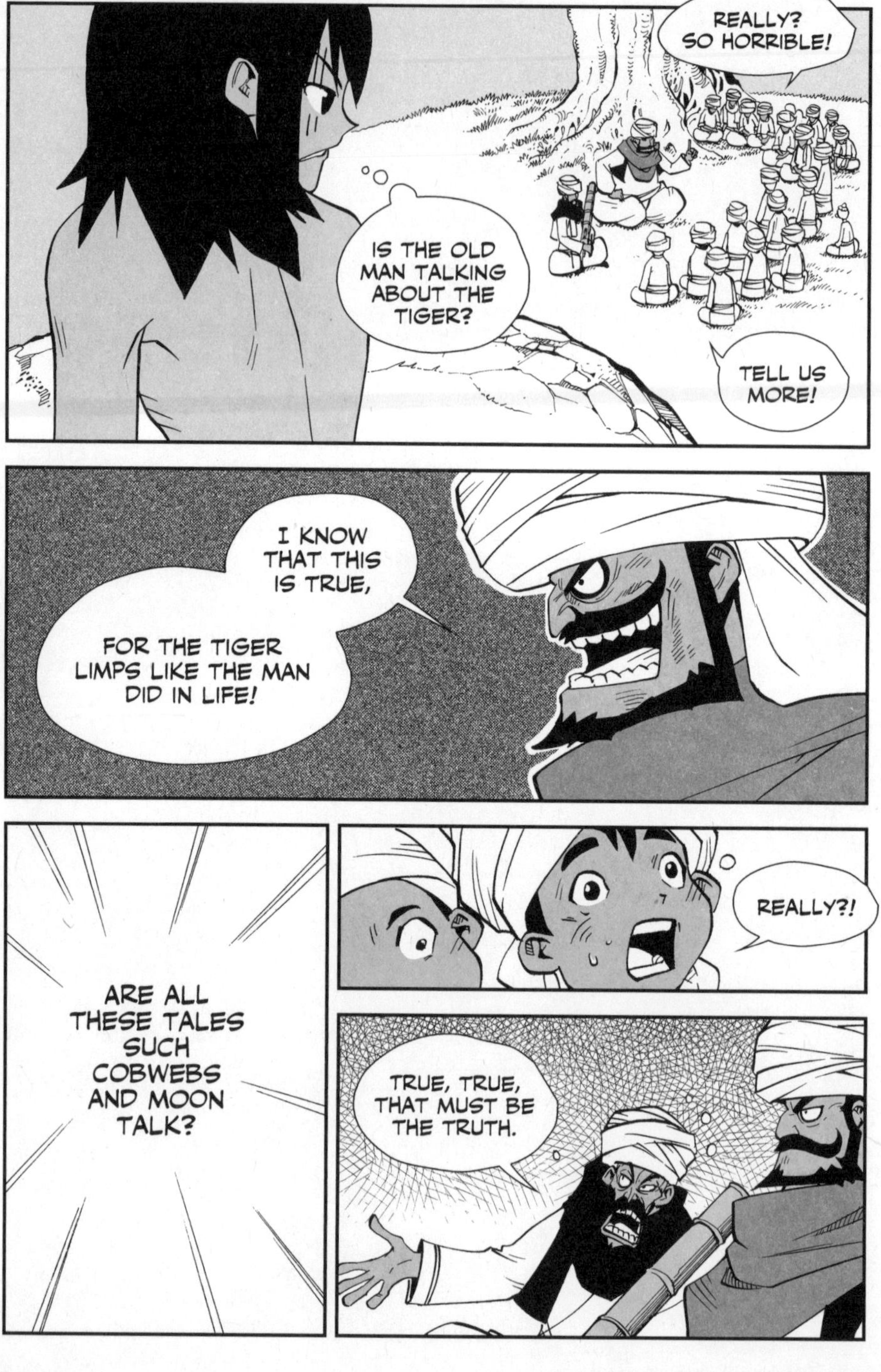
REALLY? SO HORRIBLE!
IS THE OLD MAN TALKING ABOUT THE TIGER?
TELL US MORE!
I KNOW THAT THIS IS TRUE,
FOR THE TIGER LIMPS LIKE THE MAN DID IN LIFE!
REALLY?!
TRUE, TRUE, THAT MUST BE THE TRUTH.
ARE ALL THESE TALES SUCH COBWEBS AND MOON TALK?

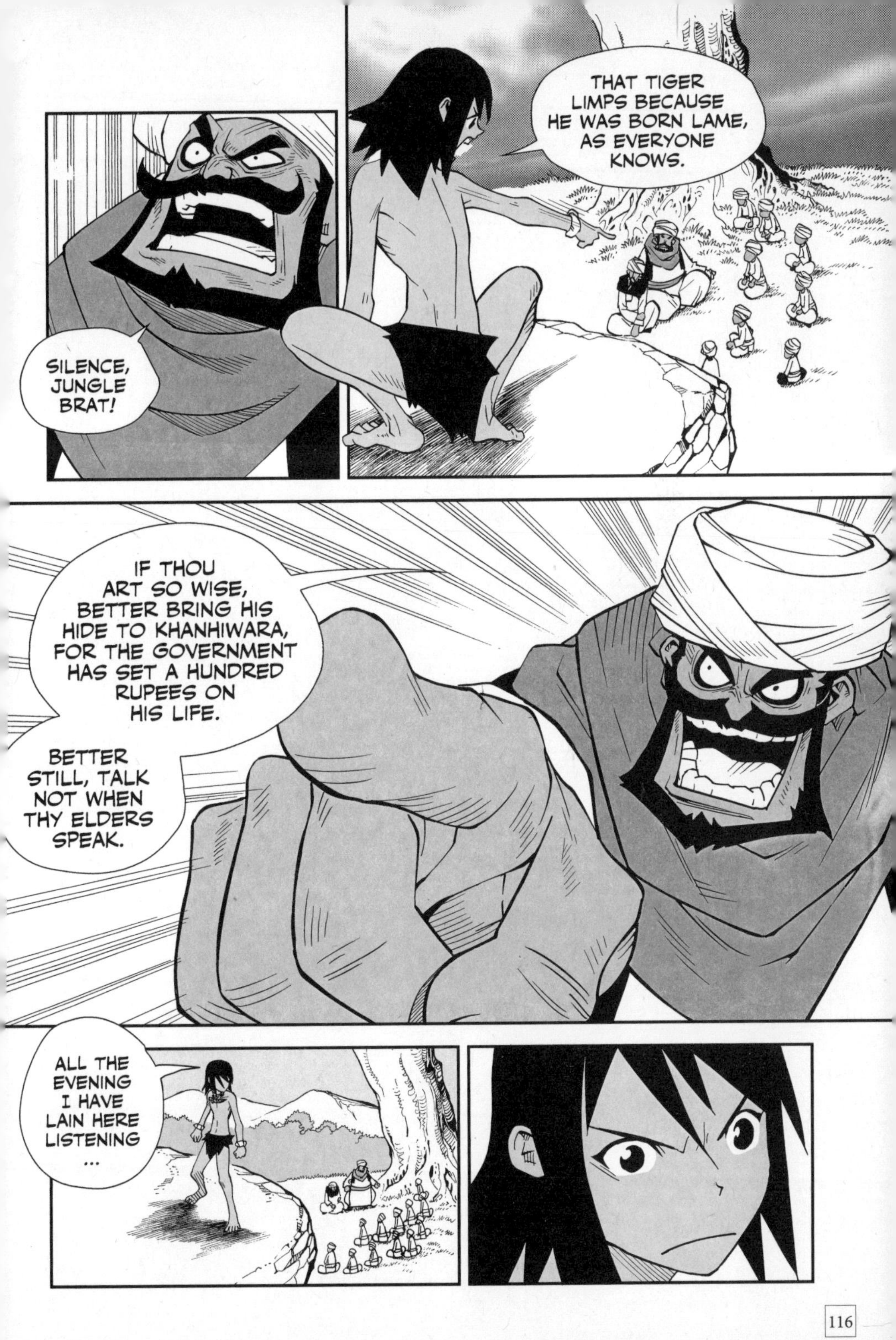
THAT TIGER LIMPS BECAUSE HE WAS BORN LAME, AS EVERYONE KNOWS.
SILENCE, JUNGLE BRAT!
IF THOU ART SO WISE, BETTER BRING HIS HIDE TO KHANHIWARA, FOR THE GOVERNMENT HAS SET A HUNDRED RUPEES ON HIS LIFE.
BETTER STILL, TALK NOT WHEN THY ELDERS SPEAK.
ALL THE EVENING I HAVE LAIN HERE LISTENING ...

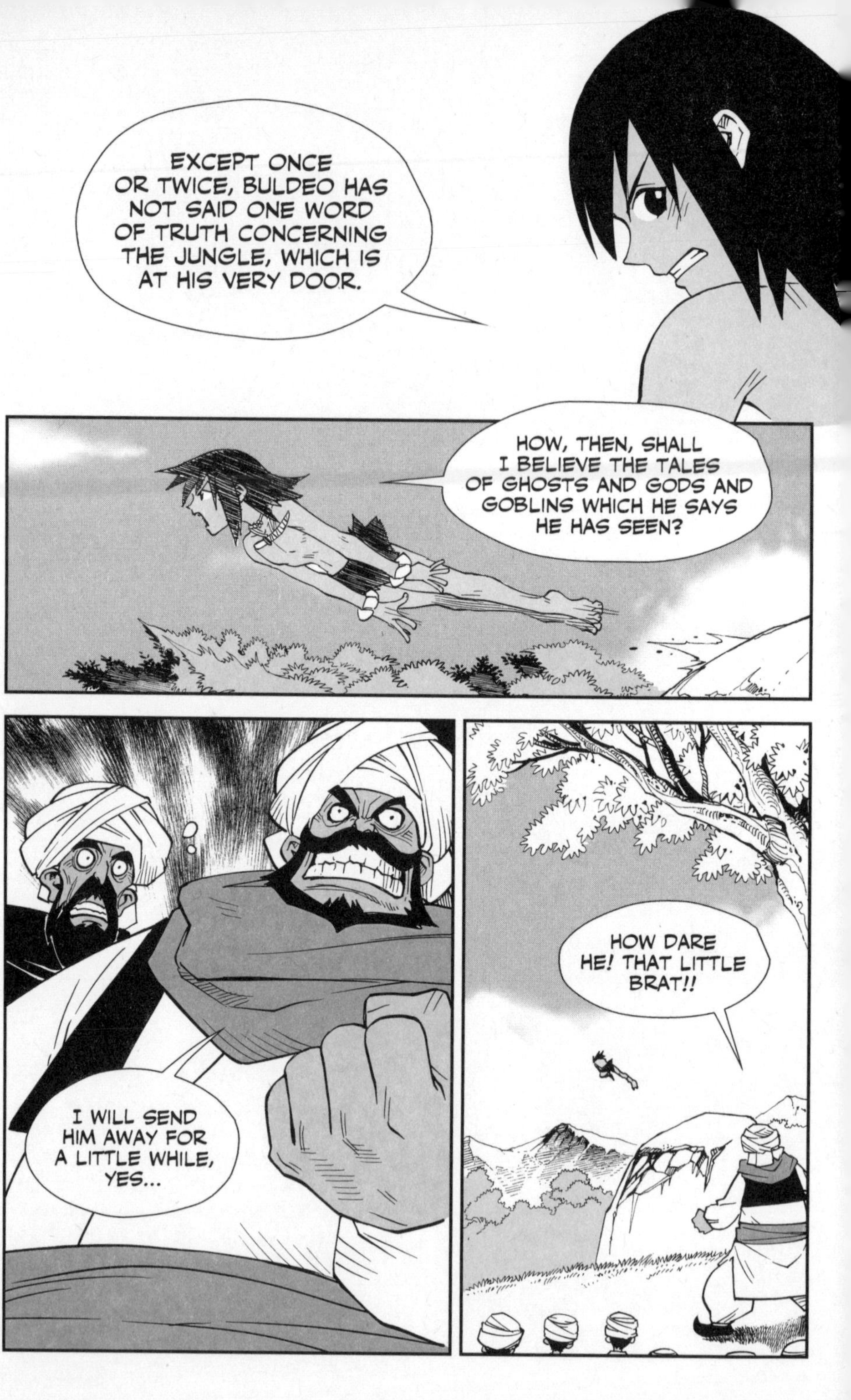
EXCEPT ONCE OR TWICE, BULDEO HAS NOT SAID ONE WORD OF TRUTH CONCERNING THE JUNGLE, WHICH IS AT HIS VERY DOOR.
HOW, THEN, SHALL I BELIEVE THE TALES OF GHOSTS AND GODS AND GOBLINS WHICH HE SAYS HE HAS SEEN?
HOW DARE HE! THAT LITTLE BRAT!!
I WILL SEND HIM AWAY FOR A LITTLE WHILE, YES...

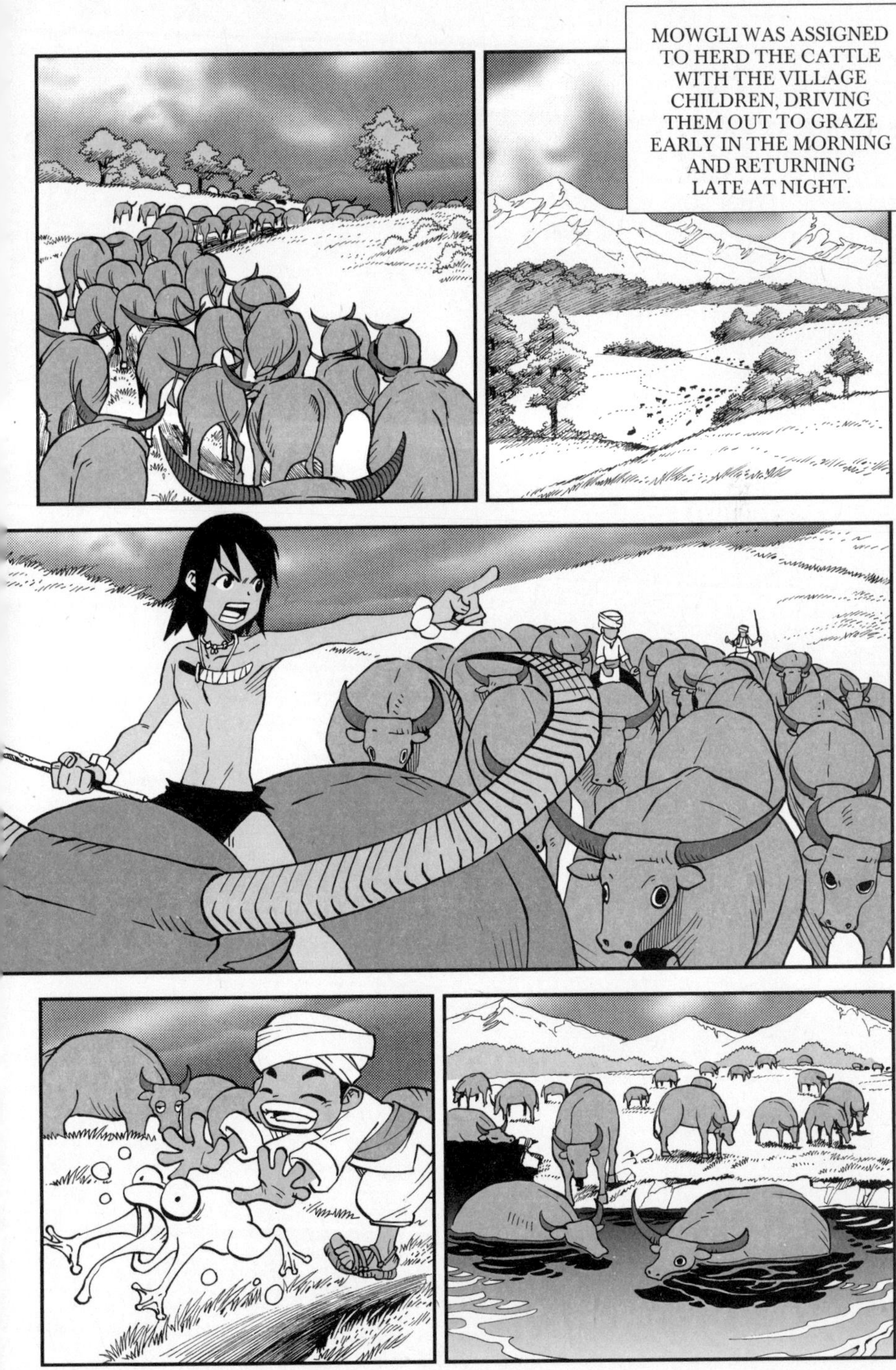
MOWGLI WAS ASSIGNED TO HERD THE CATTLE WITH THE VILLAGE CHILDREN, DRIVING THEM OUT TO GRAZE EARLY IN THE MORNING AND RETURNING LATE AT NIGHT.

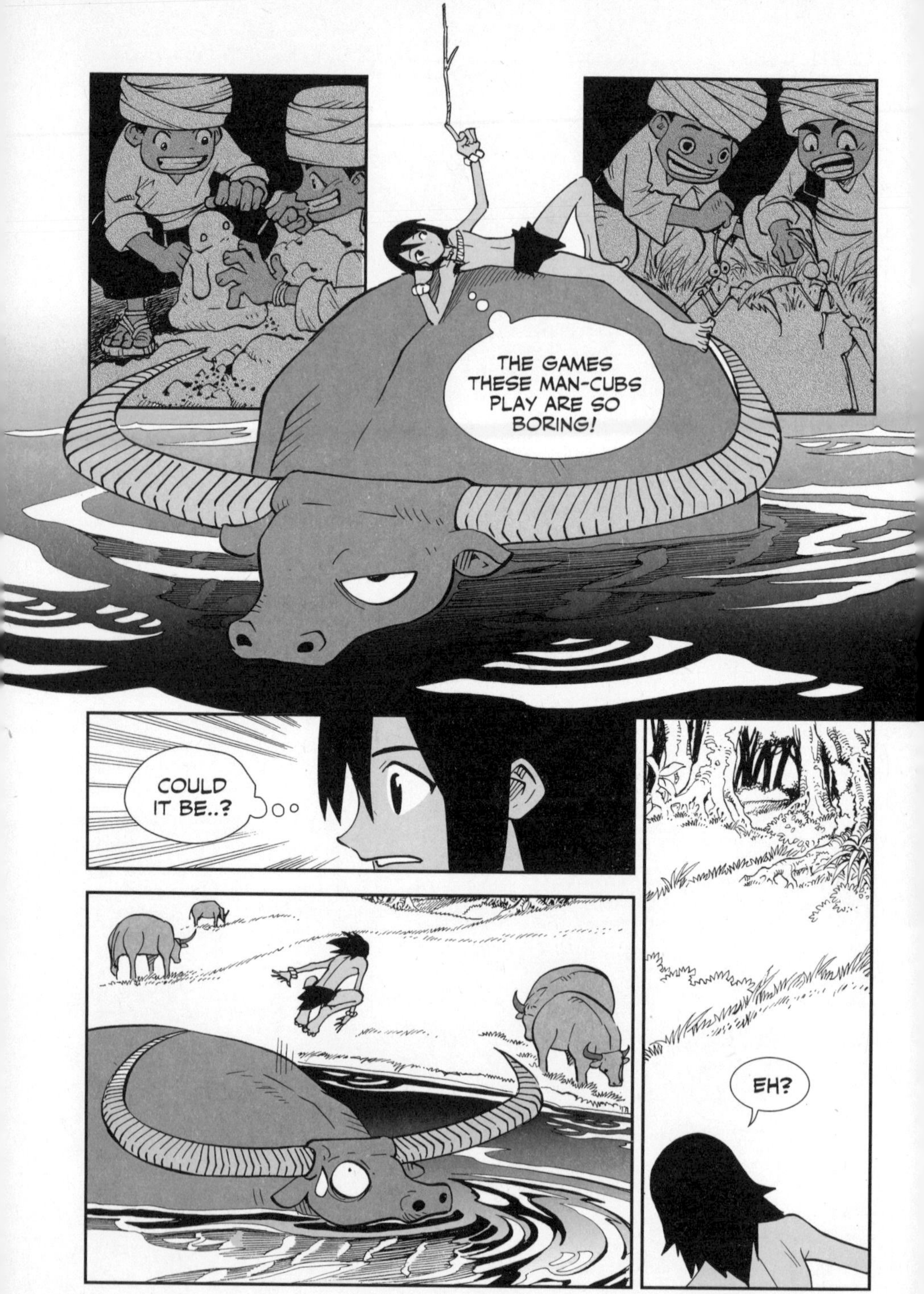
THE GAMES THESE MAN-CUBS PLAY ARE SO BORING!
EH?
COULD IT BE..?

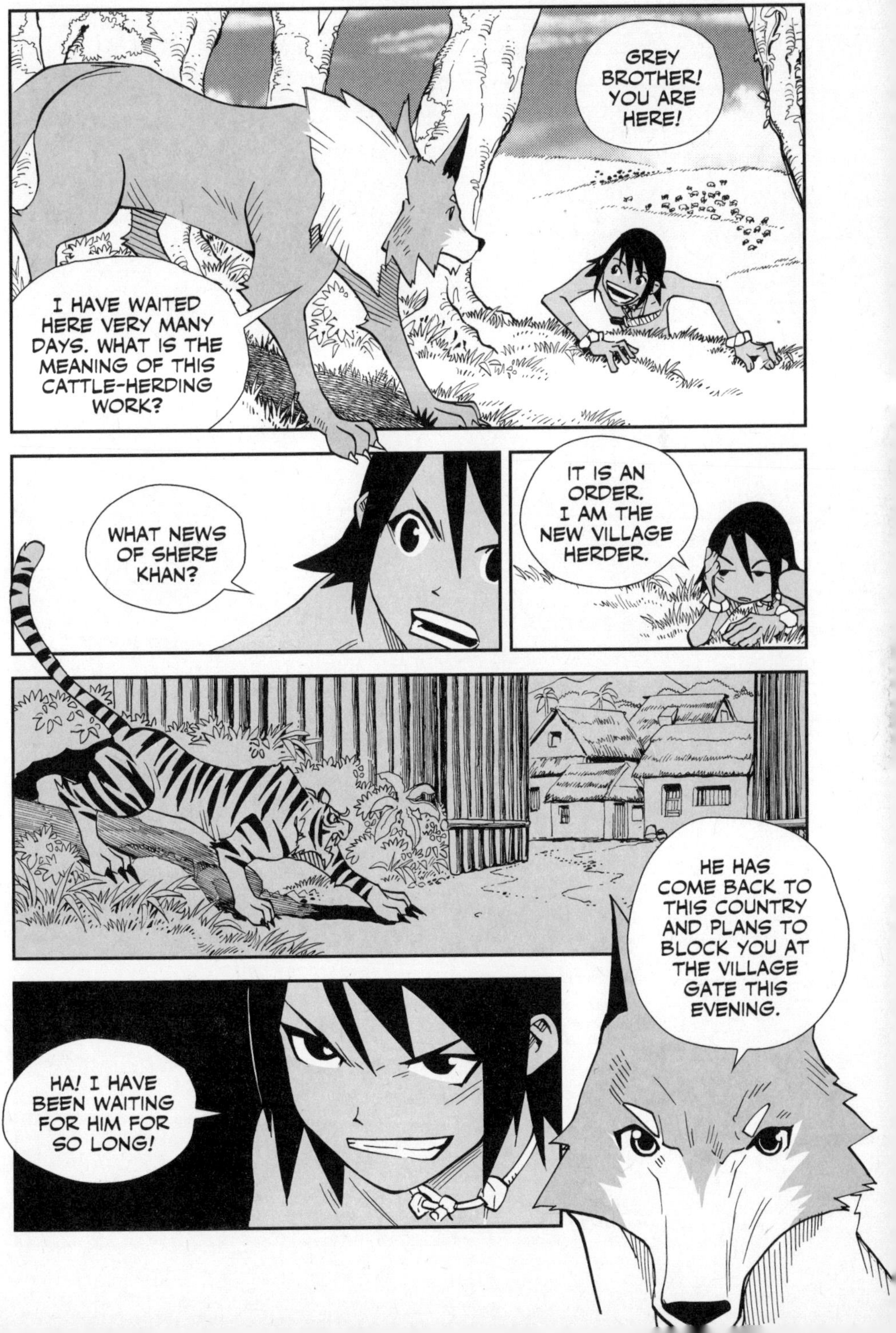
GREY BROTHER! YOU ARE HERE!
I HAVE WAITED HERE VERY MANY DAYS. WHAT IS THE MEANING OF THIS CATTLE-HERDING WORK?
IT IS AN ORDER. I AM THE NEW VILLAGE HERDER.
WHAT NEWS OF SHERE KHAN?
HE HAS COME BACK TO THIS COUNTRY AND PLANS TO BLOCK YOU AT THE VILLAGE GATE THIS EVENING.
HA! I HAVE BEEN WAITING FOR HIM FOR SO LONG!

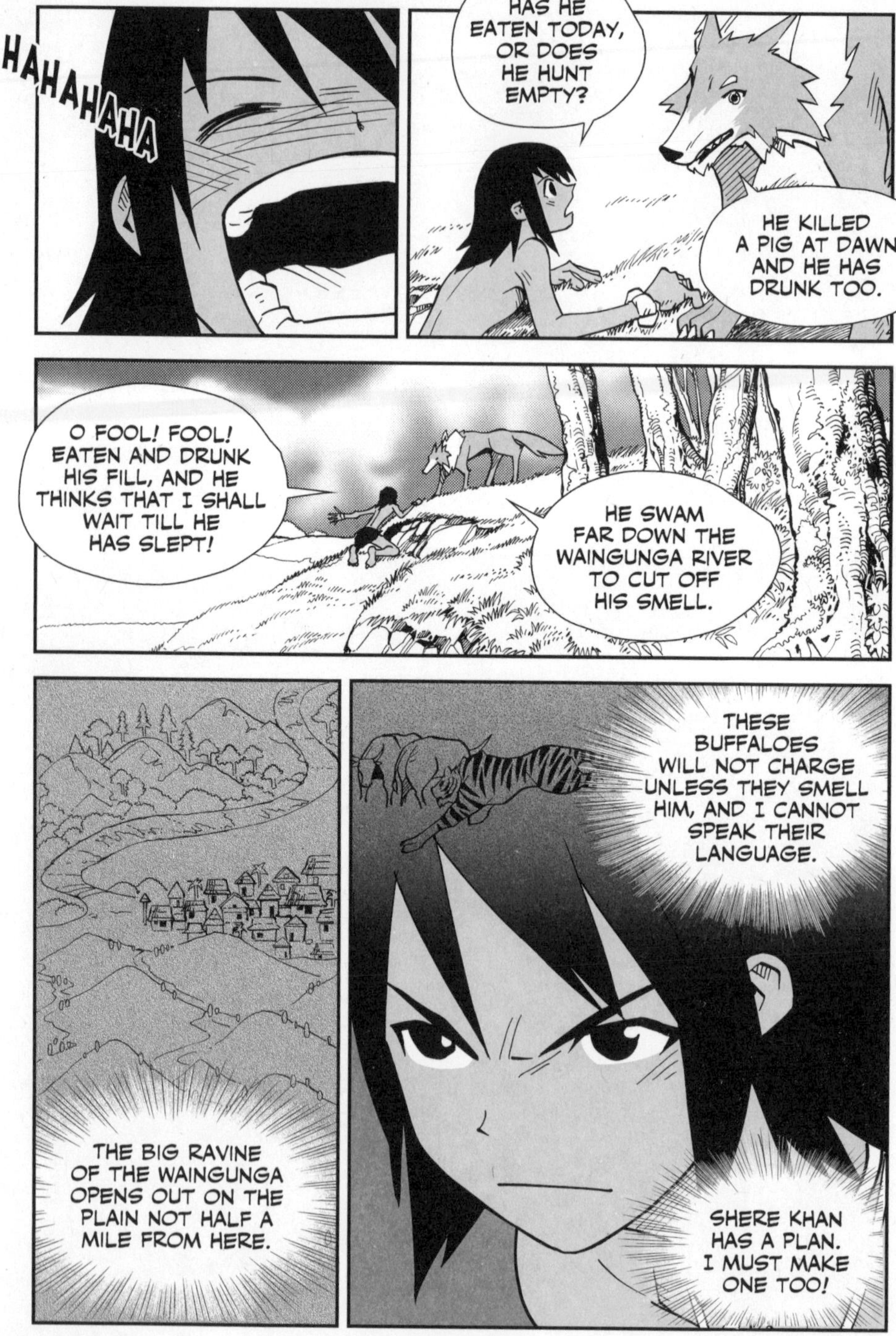
HAHAHAHAHA
HAS HE EATEN TODAY, OR DOES HE HUNT EMPTY?
HE KILLED A PIG AT DAWN AND HE HAS DRUNK TOO.
O FOOL! FOOL! EATEN AND DRUNK HIS FILL, AND HE THINKS THAT I SHALL WAIT TILL HE HAS SLEPT!
HE SWAM FAR DOWN THE WAINGUNGA RIVER TO CUT OFF HIS SMELL.
THE BIG RAVINE OF THE WAINGUNGA OPENS OUT ON THE PLAIN NOT HALF A MILE FROM HERE.
THESE BUFFALOES WILL NOT CHARGE UNLESS THEY SMELL HIM, AND I CANNOT SPEAK THEIR LANGUAGE.
SHERE KHAN HAS A PLAN. I MUST MAKE ONE TOO!

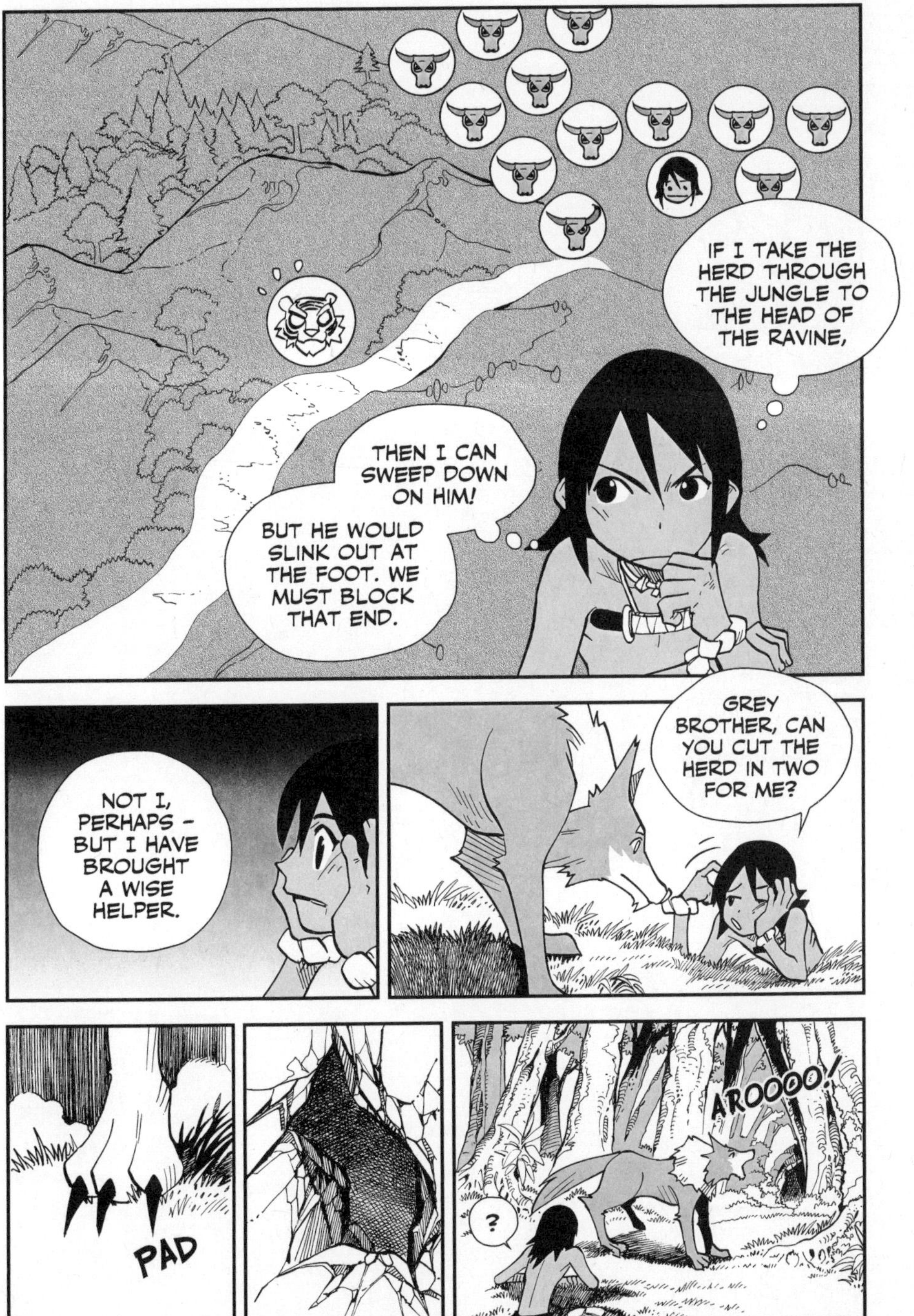
IF I TAKE THE HERD THROUGH THE JUNGLE TO THE HEAD OF THE RAVINE,
THEN I CAN SWEEP DOWN ON HIM!
BUT HE WOULD SLINK OUT AT THE FOOT. WE MUST BLOCK THAT END.
GREY BROTHER, CAN YOU CUT THE HERD IN TWO FOR ME?
NOT I, PERHAPS - BUT I HAVE BROUGHT A WISE HELPER.
AROOOO!
?
PAD

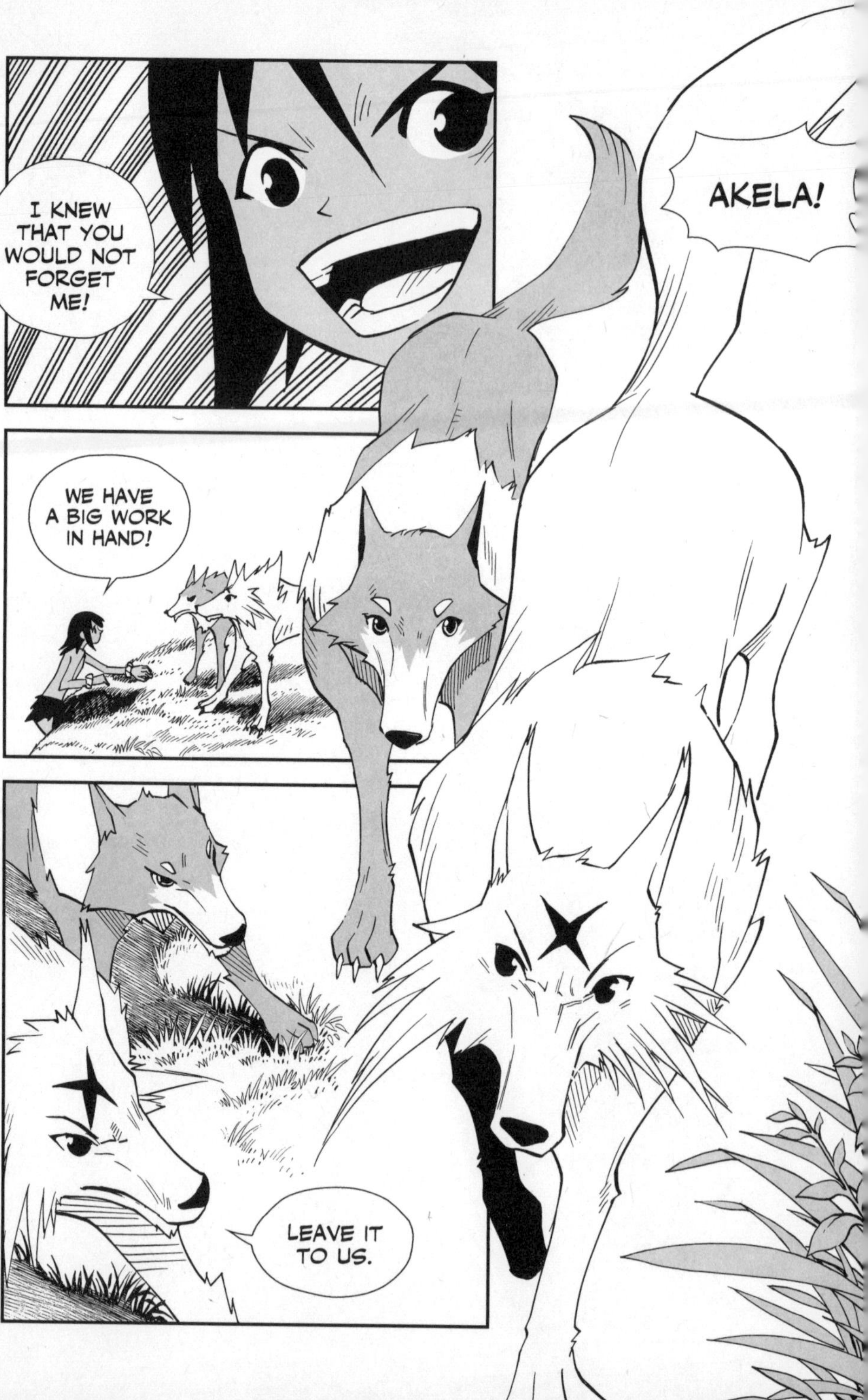
AKELA!
I KNEW THAT YOU WOULD NOT FORGET ME!
WE HAVE A BIG WORK IN HAND!
LEAVE IT TO US.

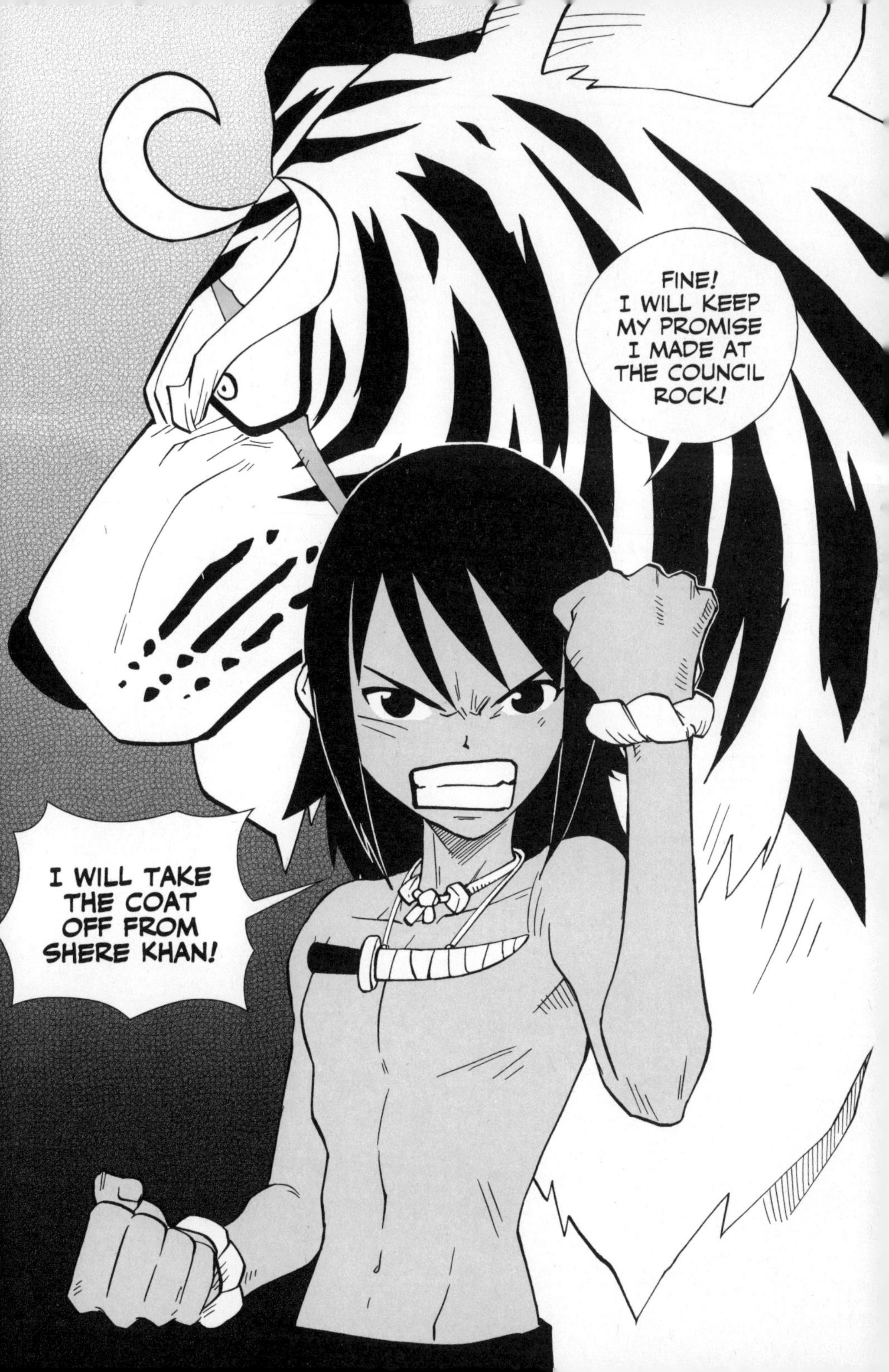
FINE! I WILL KEEP MY PROMISE I MADE AT THE COUNCIL ROCK!
I WILL TAKE THE COAT OFF FROM SHERE KHAN!

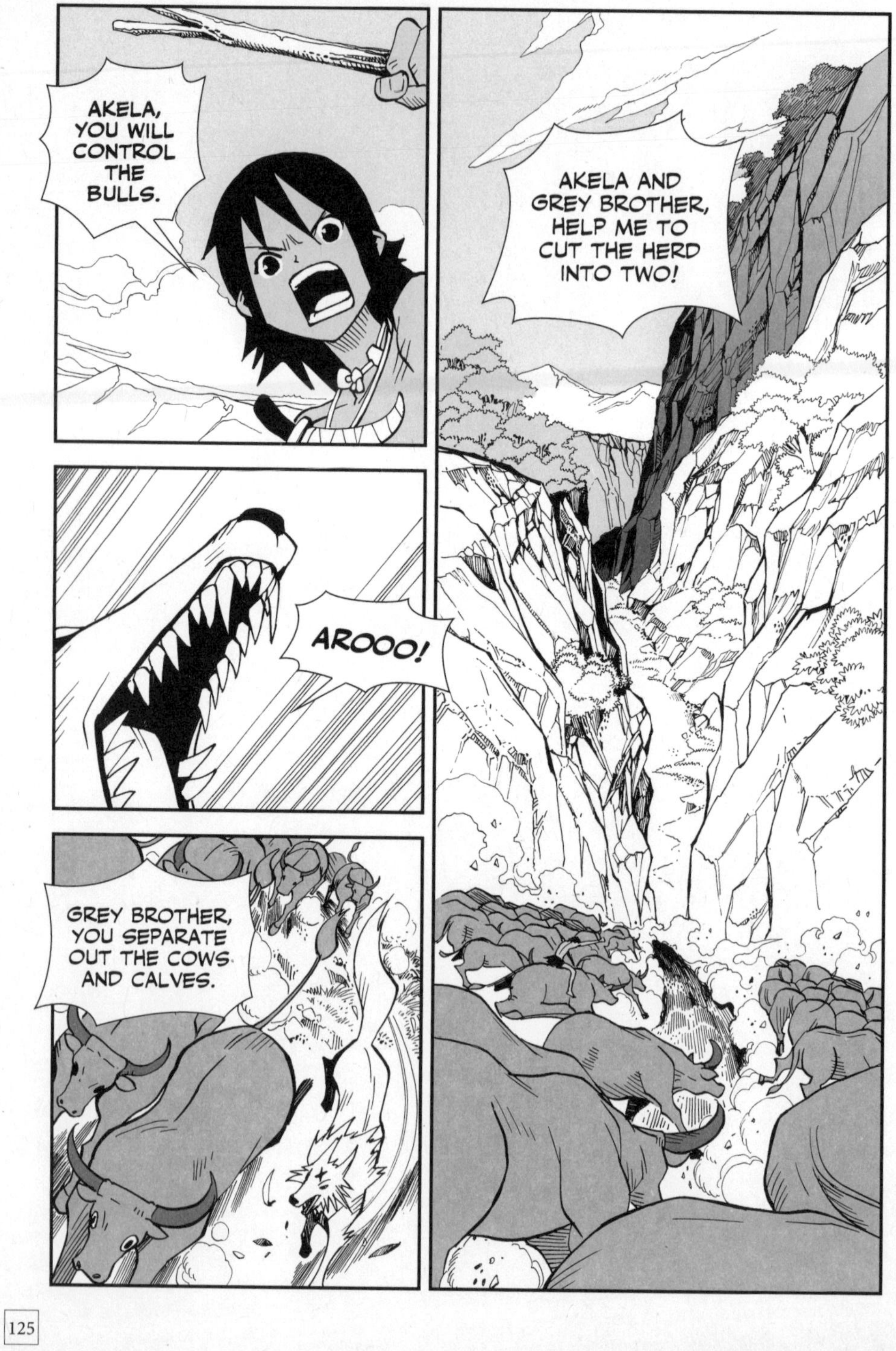
AKELA AND GREY BROTHER, HELP ME TO CUT THE HERD INTO TWO!
AKELA, YOU WILL CONTROL THE BULLS.
AROOO!
GREY BROTHER, YOU SEPARATE OUT THE COWS AND CALVES.

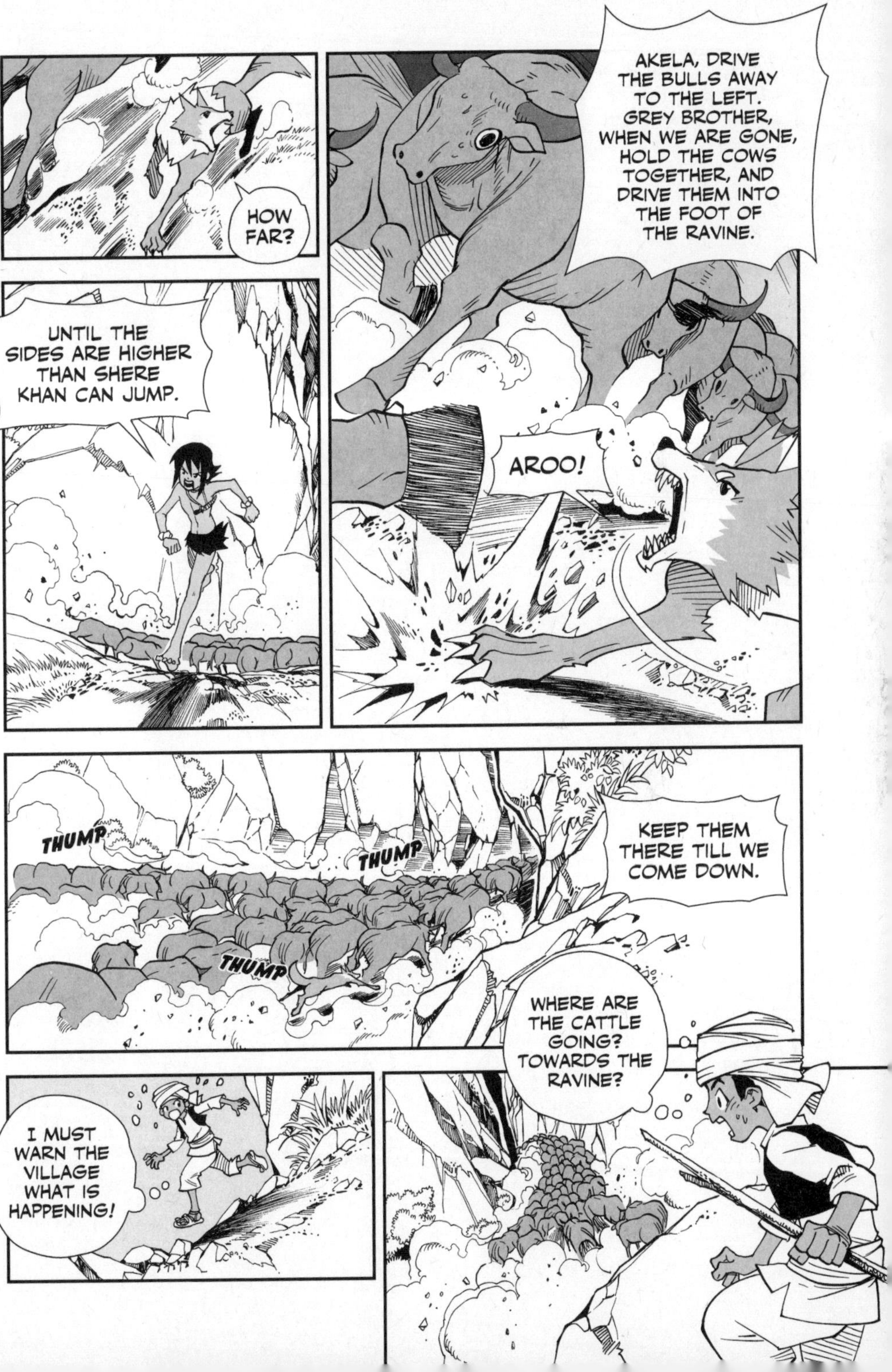
AKELA, DRIVE THE BULLS AWAY TO THE LEFT. GREY BROTHER, WHEN WE ARE GONE, HOLD THE COWS TOGETHER, AND DRIVE THEM INTO THE FOOT OF THE RAVINE.
AROO!
HOW FAR?
UNTIL THE SIDES ARE HIGHER THAN SHERE KHAN CAN JUMP.
KEEP THEM THERE TILL WE COME DOWN.
THUMP
THUMP
THUMP
WHERE ARE THE CATTLE GOING? TOWARDS THE RAVINE?
I MUST WARN THE VILLAGE WHAT IS HAPPENING!

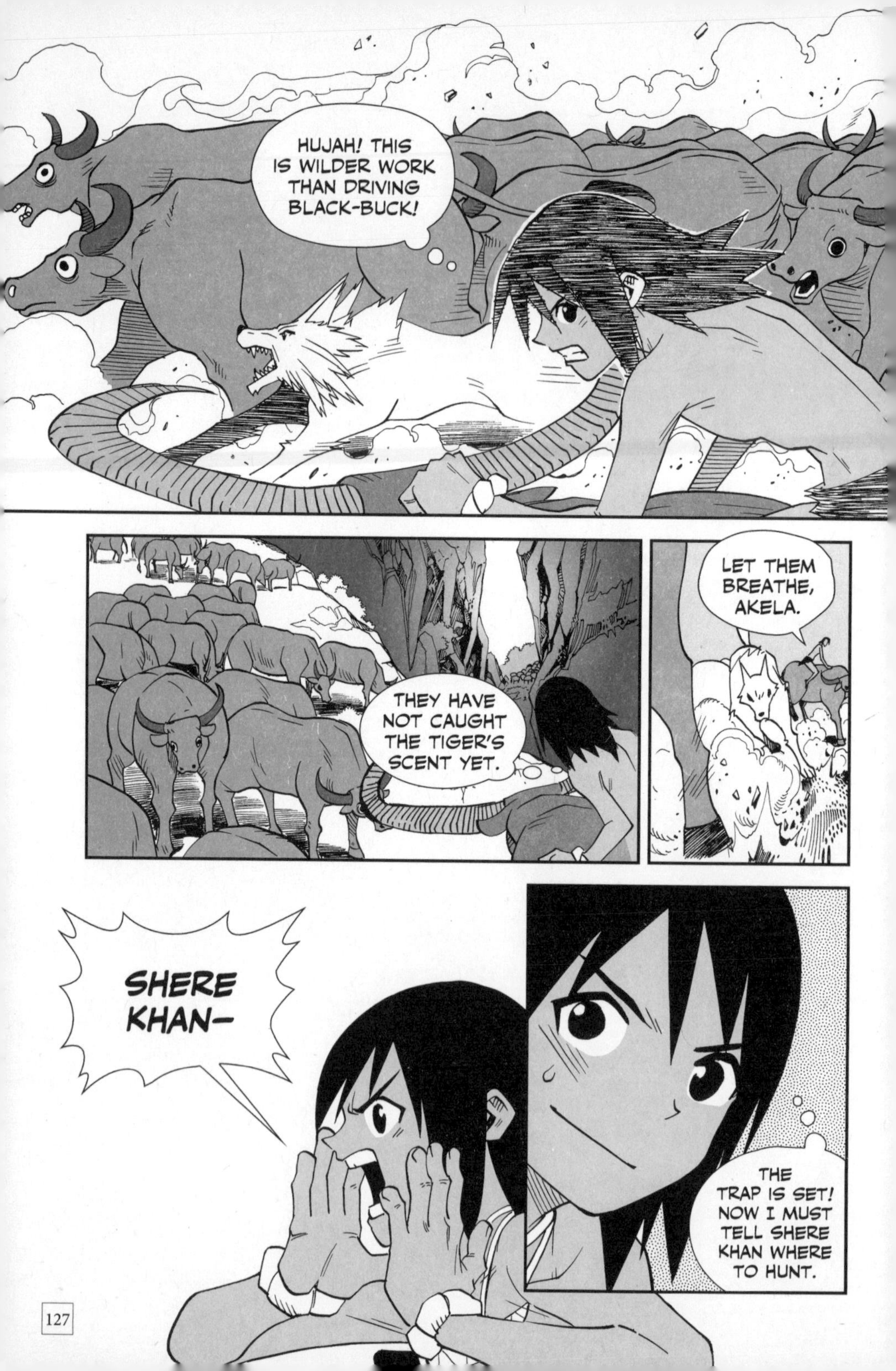
HUJAH! THIS IS WILDER WORK THAN DRIVING BLACK-BUCK!
LET THEM BREATHE, AKELA.
THEY HAVE NOT CAUGHT THE TIGER'S SCENT YET.
THE TRAP IS SET! NOW I MUST TELL SHERE KHAN WHERE TO HUNT.
SHERE KHAN-

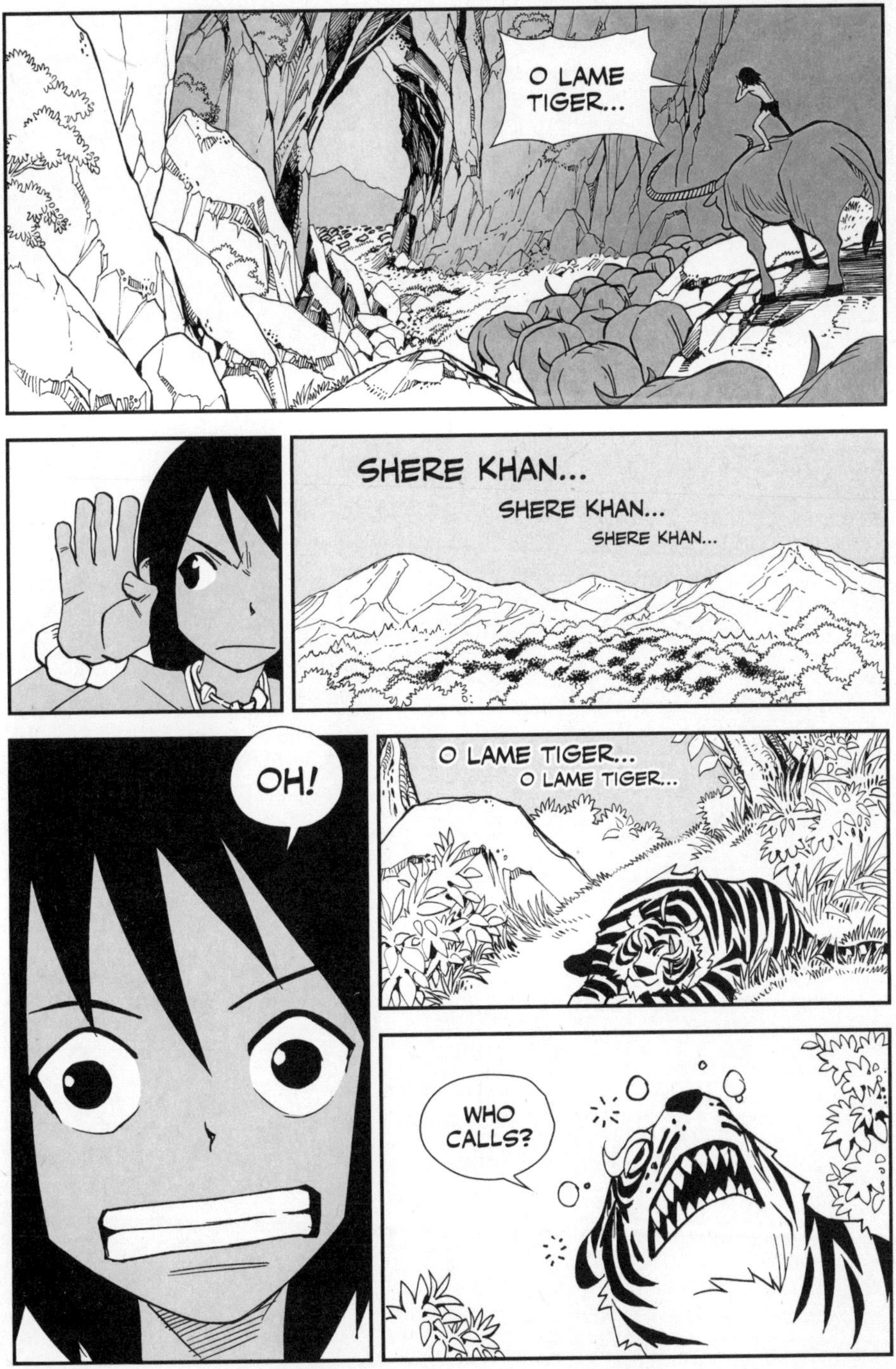
O LAME TIGER...
SHERE KHAN...
SHERE KHAN...
SHERE KHAN...
O LAME TIGER...
O LAME TIGER...
WHO CALLS?
OH!

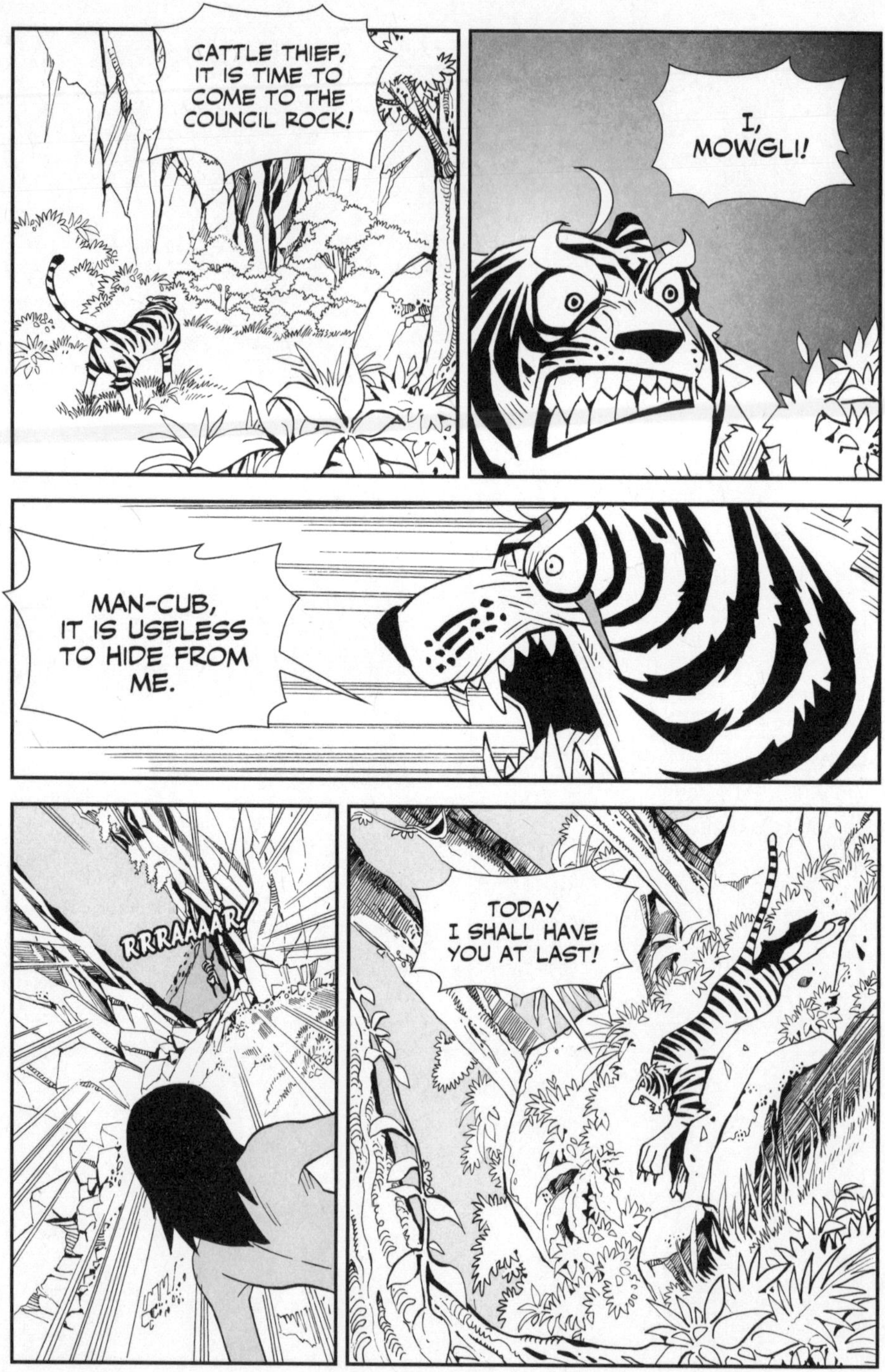
I, MOWGLI!
CATTLE THIEF, IT IS TIME TO COME TO THE COUNCIL ROCK!
MAN-CUB, IT IS USELESS TO HIDE FROM ME.
TODAY I SHALL HAVE YOU AT LAST!
RRRAAAAR!

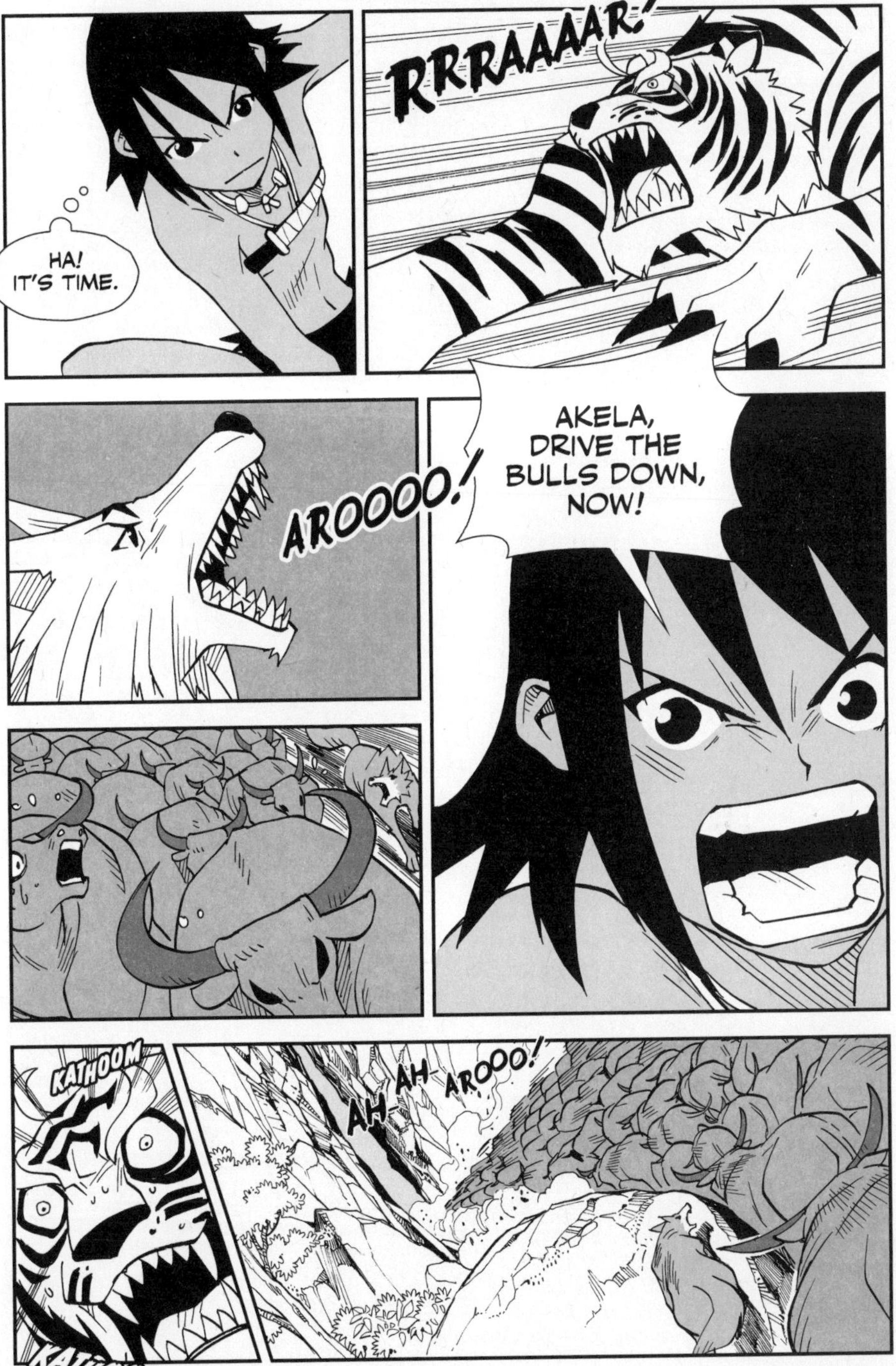
RRRAAAAR!
HA! IT'S TIME.
AKELA, DRIVE THE BULLS DOWN, NOW!
AROOOO!
AH-AH-AROOO!
KATHOOM
KATHOOM

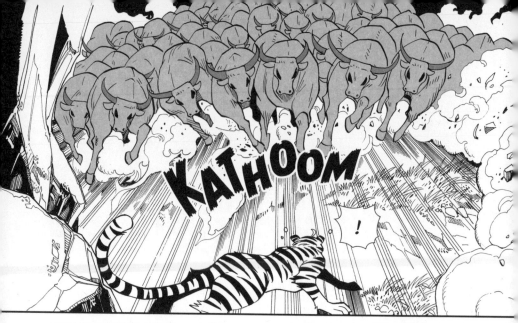

KATHOOM

!

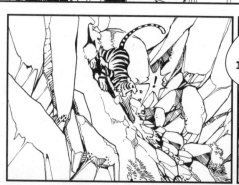

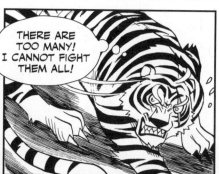

THERE ARE TOO MANY! I CANNOT FIGHT THEM ALL!

AAAH!

AROO! AROO!

I SHALL ESCAPE... NO! COWS ARE STAMPEDING FROM THE OTHER DIRECTION!

KATHOOM

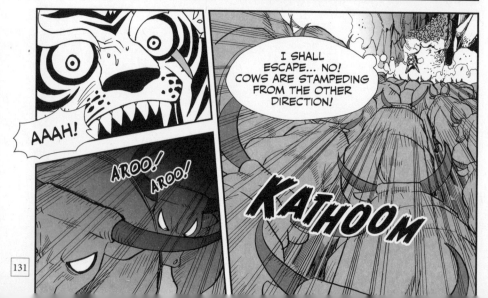

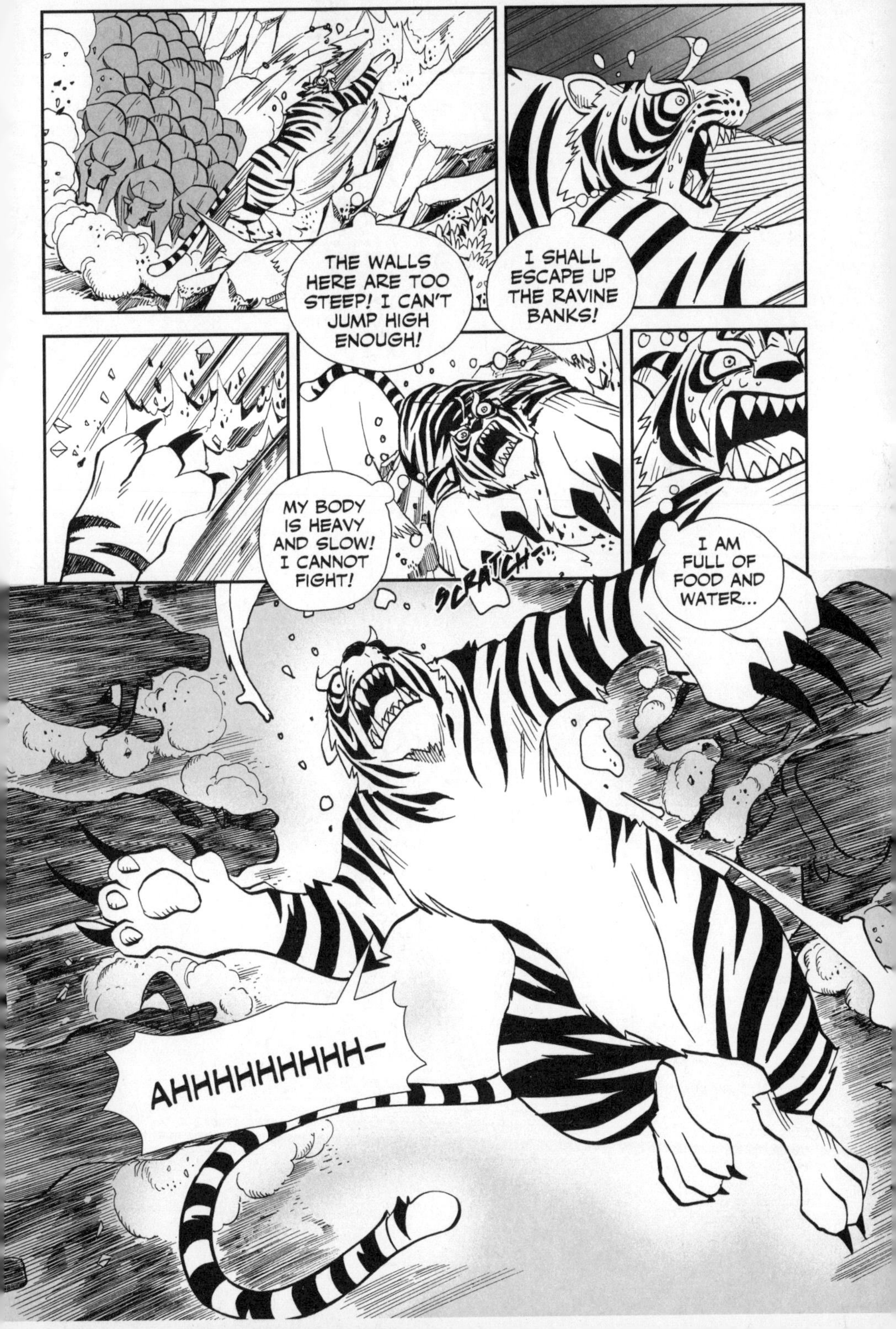
I SHALL ESCAPE UP THE RAVINE BANKS!
THE WALLS HERE ARE TOO STEEP! I CAN'T JUMP HIGH ENOUGH!
I AM FULL OF FOOD AND WATER...
MY BODY IS HEAVY AND SLOW! I CANNOT FIGHT!
SCRATCH
AHHHHHHHHH-

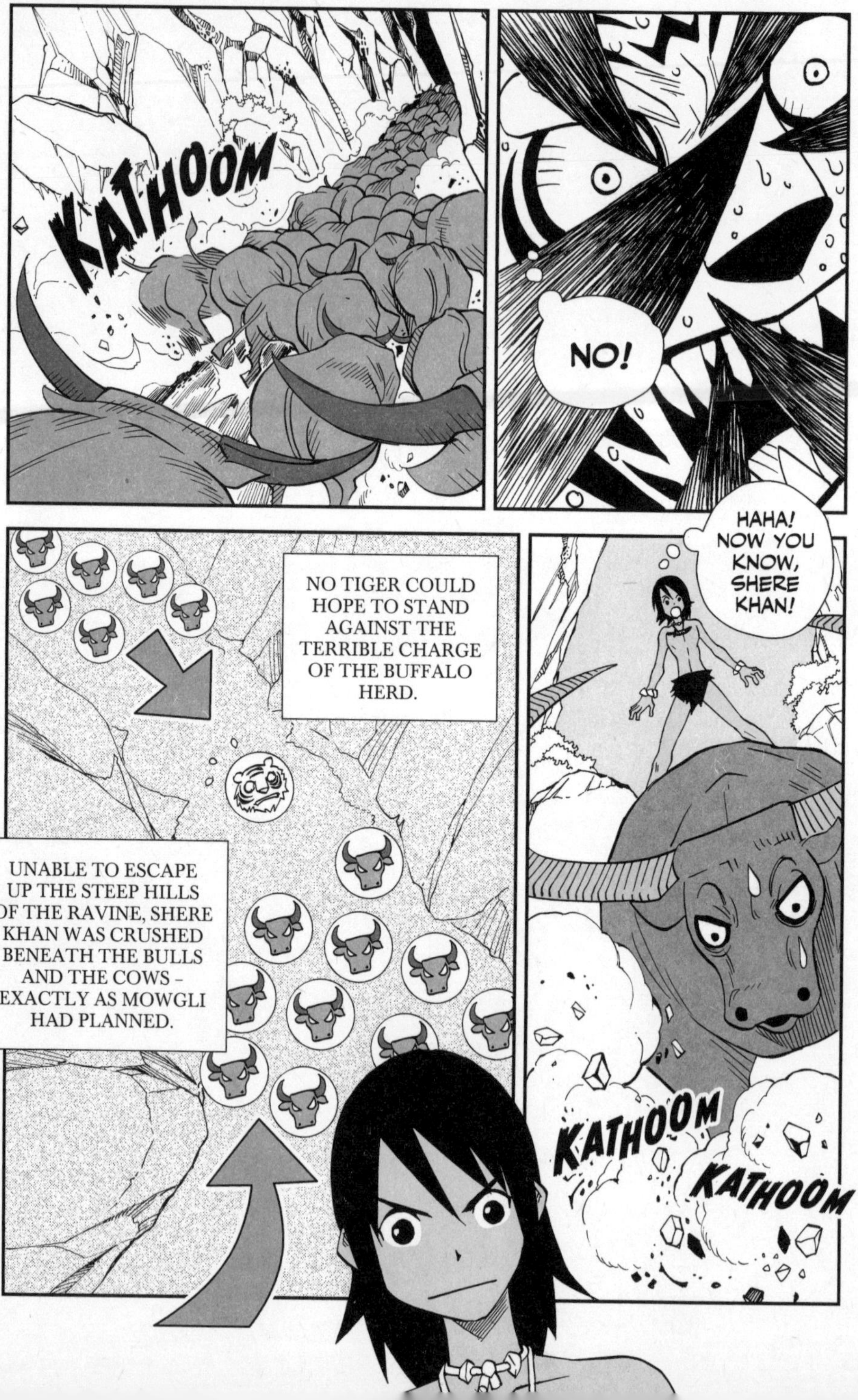
NO!
KATHOOM
HAHA! NOW YOU KNOW, SHERE KHAN!
KATHOOM
KATHOOM
NO TIGER COULD HOPE TO STAND AGAINST THE TERRIBLE CHARGE OF THE BUFFALO HERD.
UNABLE TO ESCAPE UP THE STEEP HILLS OF THE RAVINE, SHERE KHAN WAS CRUSHED BENEATH THE BULLS AND THE COWS – EXACTLY AS MOWGLI HAD PLANNED.

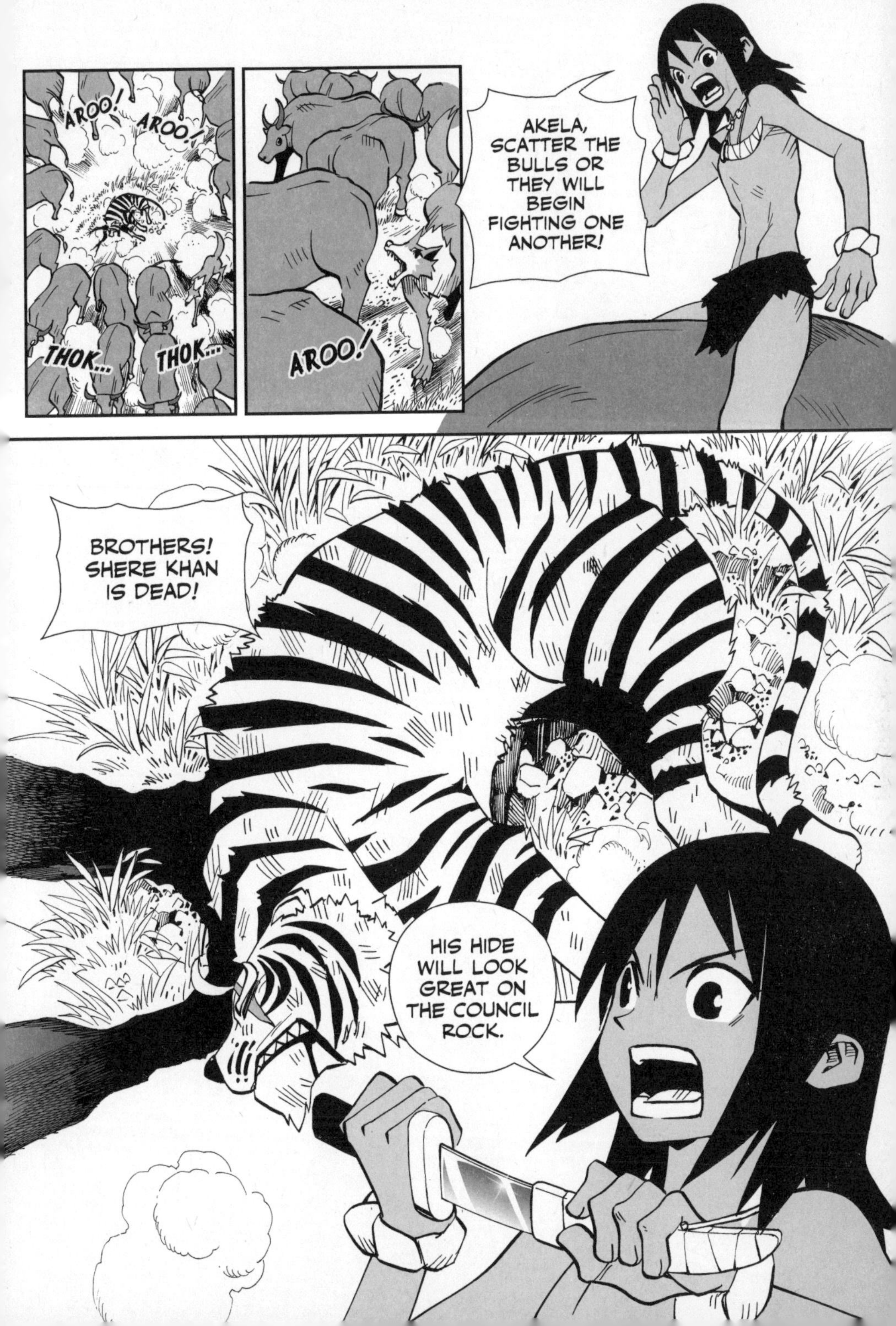

AKELA, SCATTER THE BULLS OR THEY WILL BEGIN FIGHTING ONE ANOTHER!
AROO!
AROO!
AROO!
THOK...
THOK...
BROTHERS! SHERE KHAN IS DEAD!
HIS HIDE WILL LOOK GREAT ON THE COUNCIL ROCK.

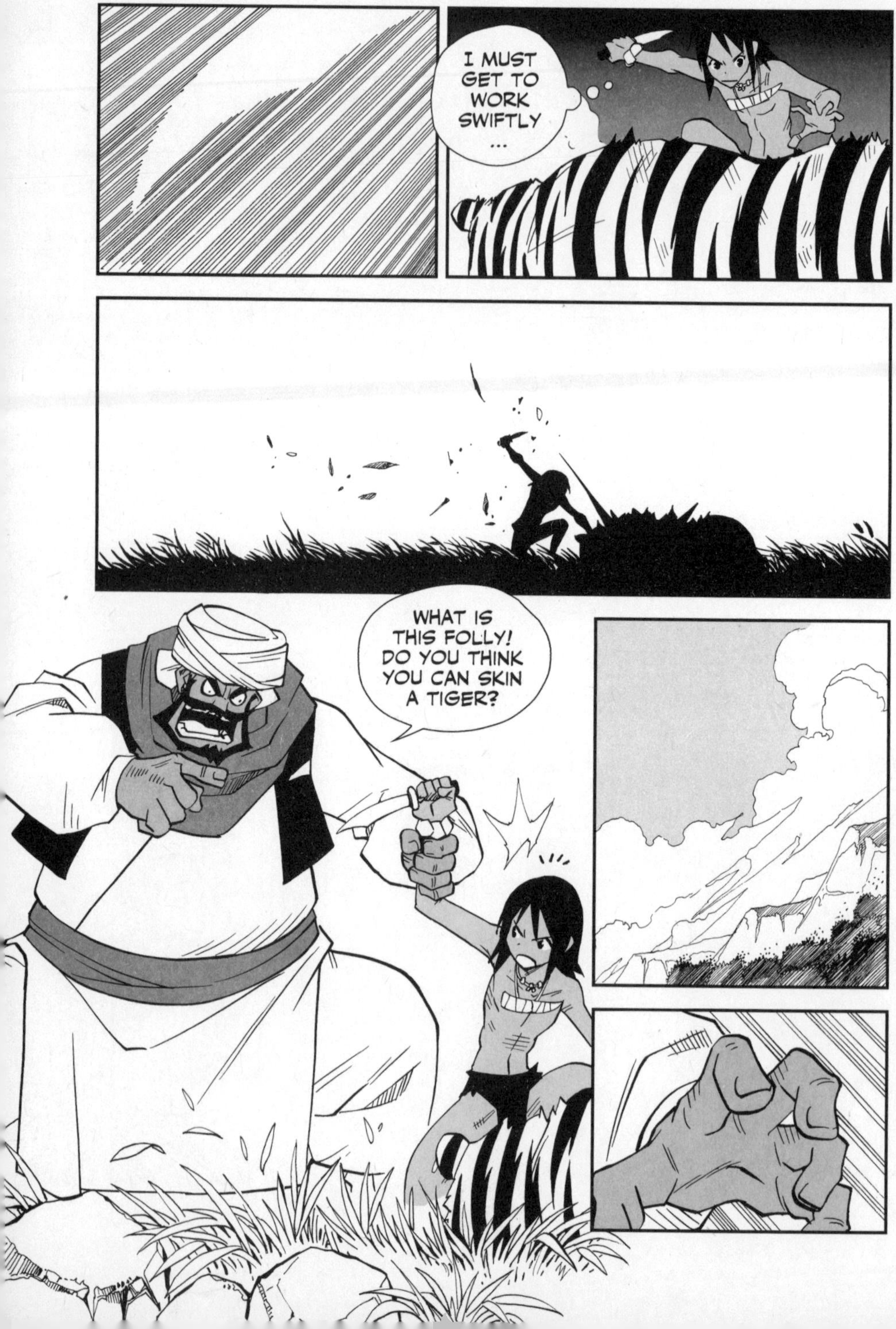
I MUST GET TO WORK SWIFTLY ...
WHAT IS THIS FOLLY! DO YOU THINK YOU CAN SKIN A TIGER?

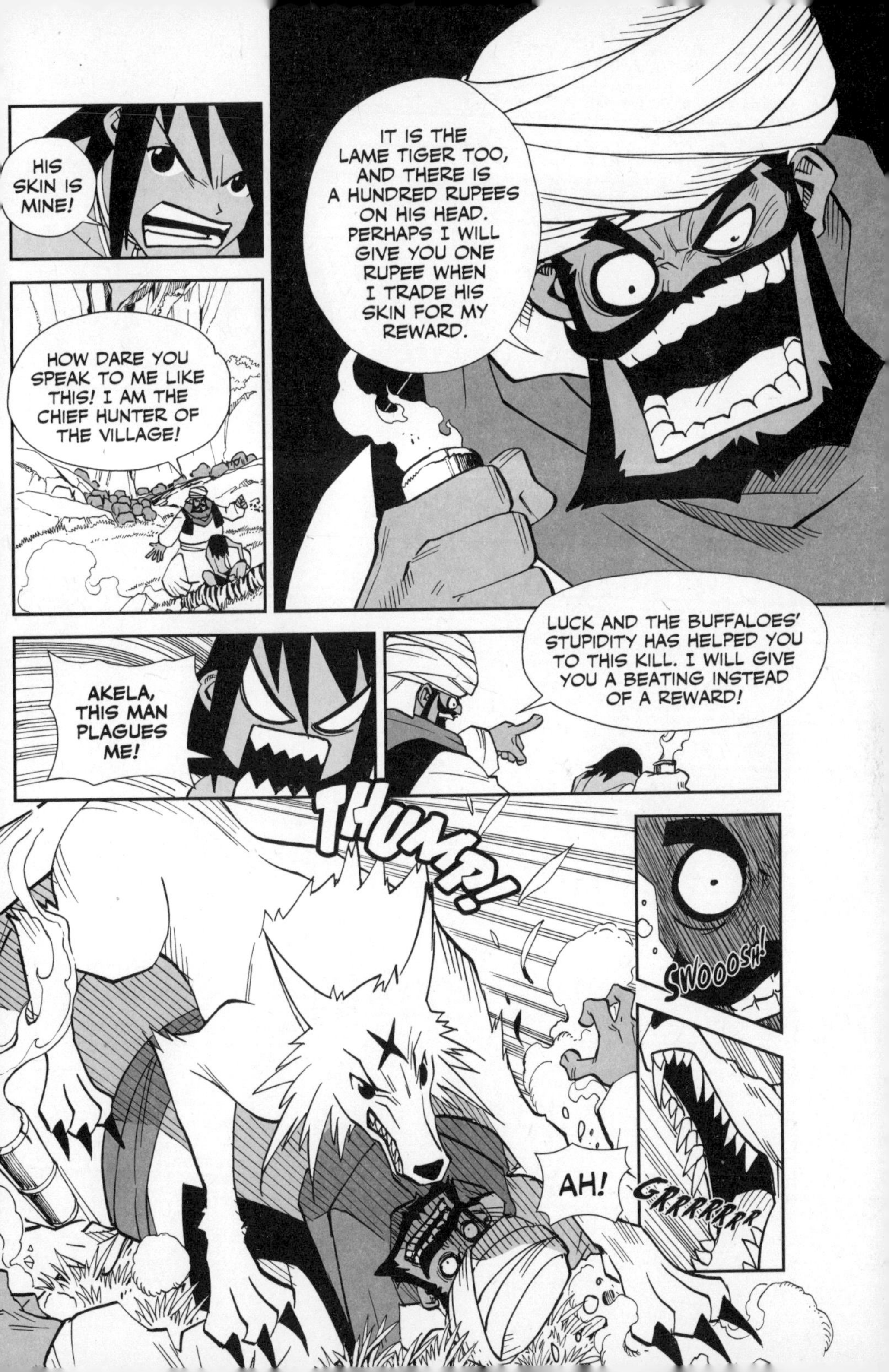
IT IS THE LAME TIGER TOO, AND THERE IS A HUNDRED RUPEES ON HIS HEAD. PERHAPS I WILL GIVE YOU ONE RUPEE WHEN I TRADE HIS SKIN FOR MY REWARD.
HIS SKIN IS MINE!
HOW DARE YOU SPEAK TO ME LIKE THIS! I AM THE CHIEF HUNTER OF THE VILLAGE!
LUCK AND THE BUFFALOES' STUPIDITY HAS HELPED YOU TO THIS KILL. I WILL GIVE YOU A BEATING INSTEAD OF A REWARD!
AKELA, THIS MAN PLAGUES ME!
SWOOOSH!
GRRRRRRR
THUMP!
AH!

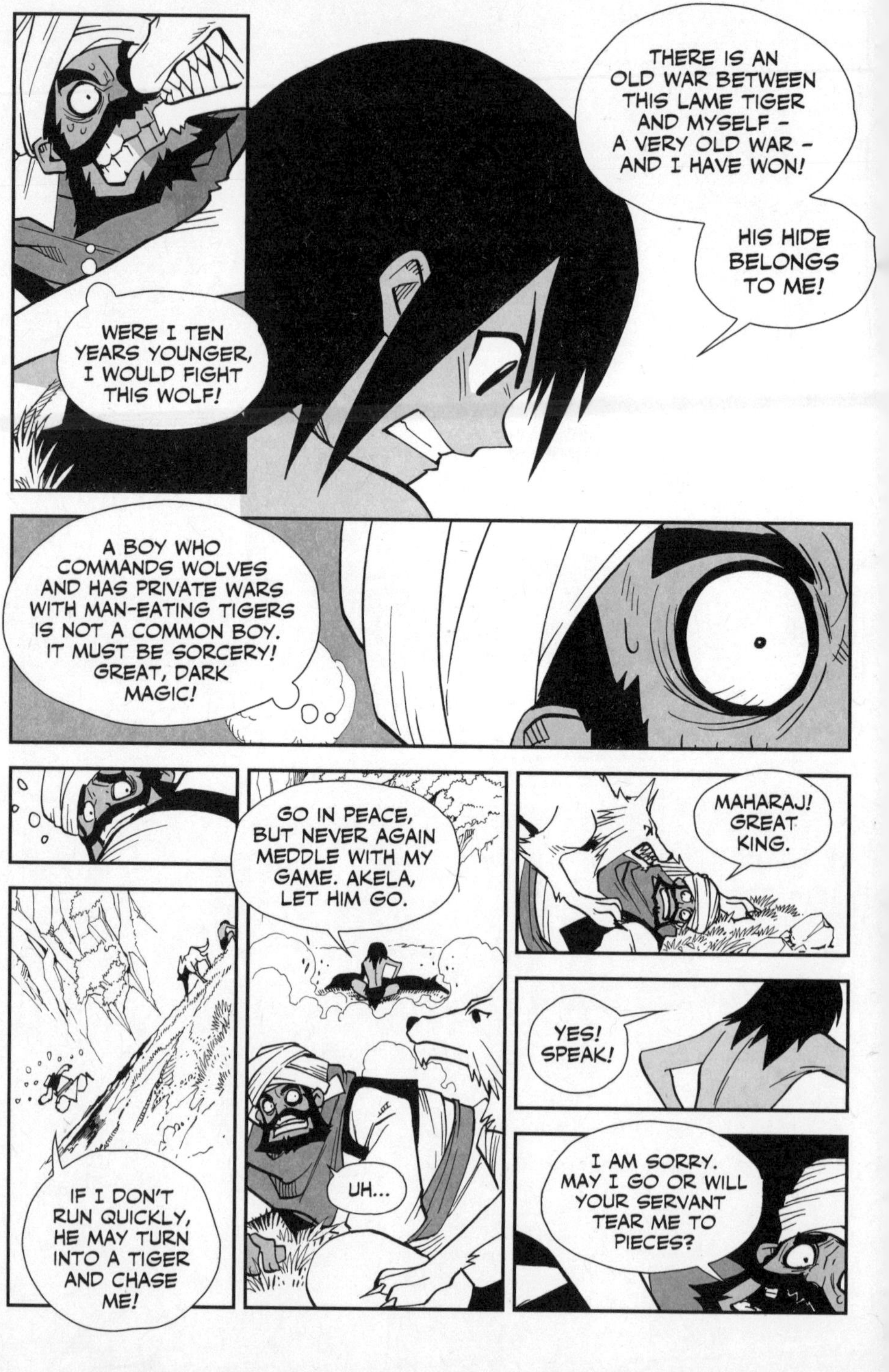
THERE IS AN OLD WAR BETWEEN THIS LAME TIGER AND MYSELF - A VERY OLD WAR - AND I HAVE WON!
HIS HIDE BELONGS TO ME!
WERE I TEN YEARS YOUNGER, I WOULD FIGHT THIS WOLF!
A BOY WHO COMMANDS WOLVES AND HAS PRIVATE WARS WITH MAN-EATING TIGERS IS NOT A COMMON BOY. IT MUST BE SORCERY! GREAT, DARK MAGIC!
MAHARAJ! GREAT KING.
YES! SPEAK!
I AM SORRY. MAY I GO OR WILL YOUR SERVANT TEAR ME TO PIECES?
GO IN PEACE, BUT NEVER AGAIN MEDDLE WITH MY GAME. AKELA, LET HIM GO.
UH...
IF I DON'T RUN QUICKLY, HE MAY TURN INTO A TIGER AND CHASE ME!

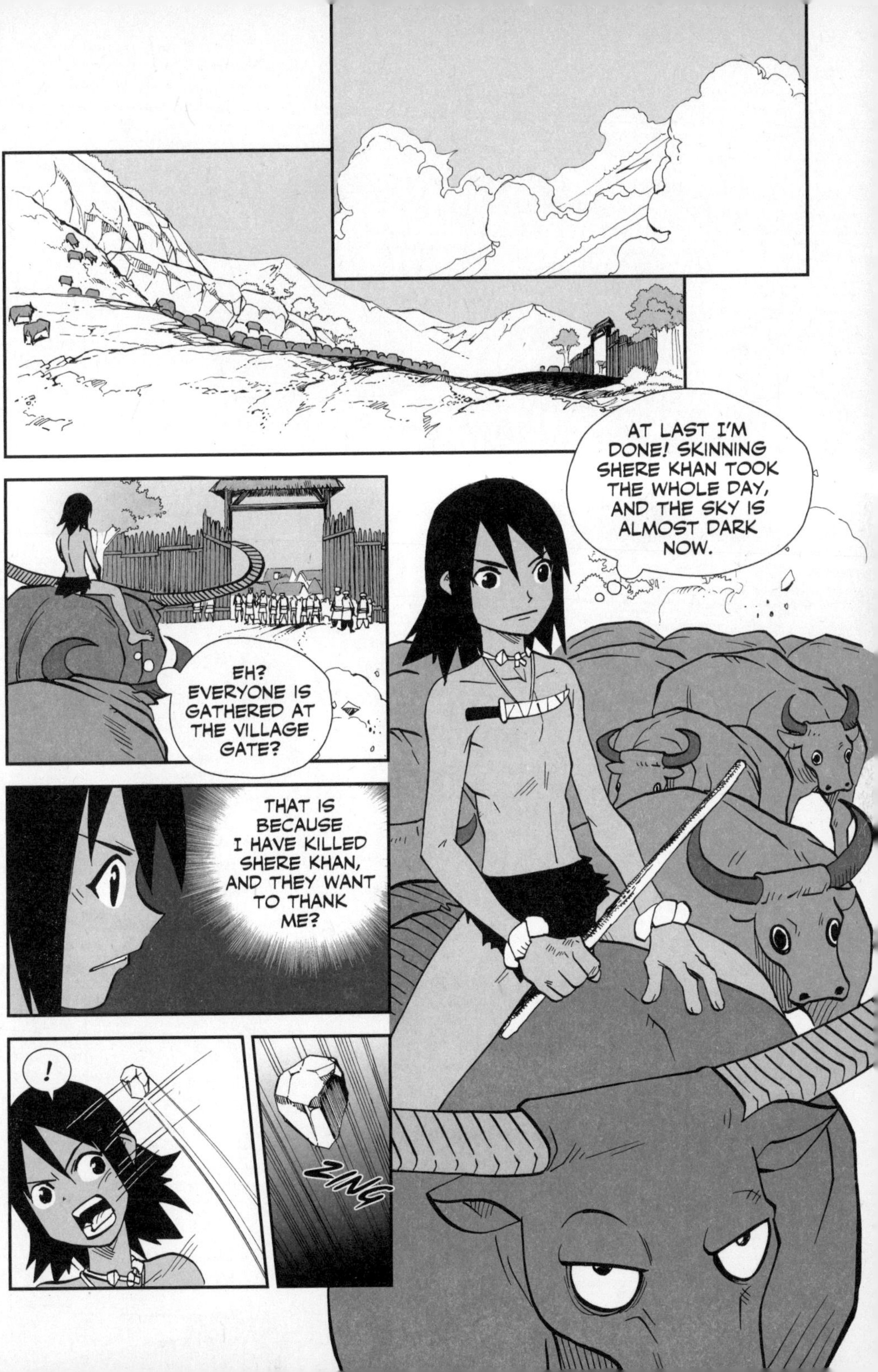
AT LAST I'M DONE! SKINNING SHERE KHAN TOOK THE WHOLE DAY, AND THE SKY IS ALMOST DARK NOW.
EH? EVERYONE IS GATHERED AT THE VILLAGE GATE?
THAT IS BECAUSE I HAVE KILLED SHERE KHAN, AND THEY WANT TO THANK ME?
ZING
!

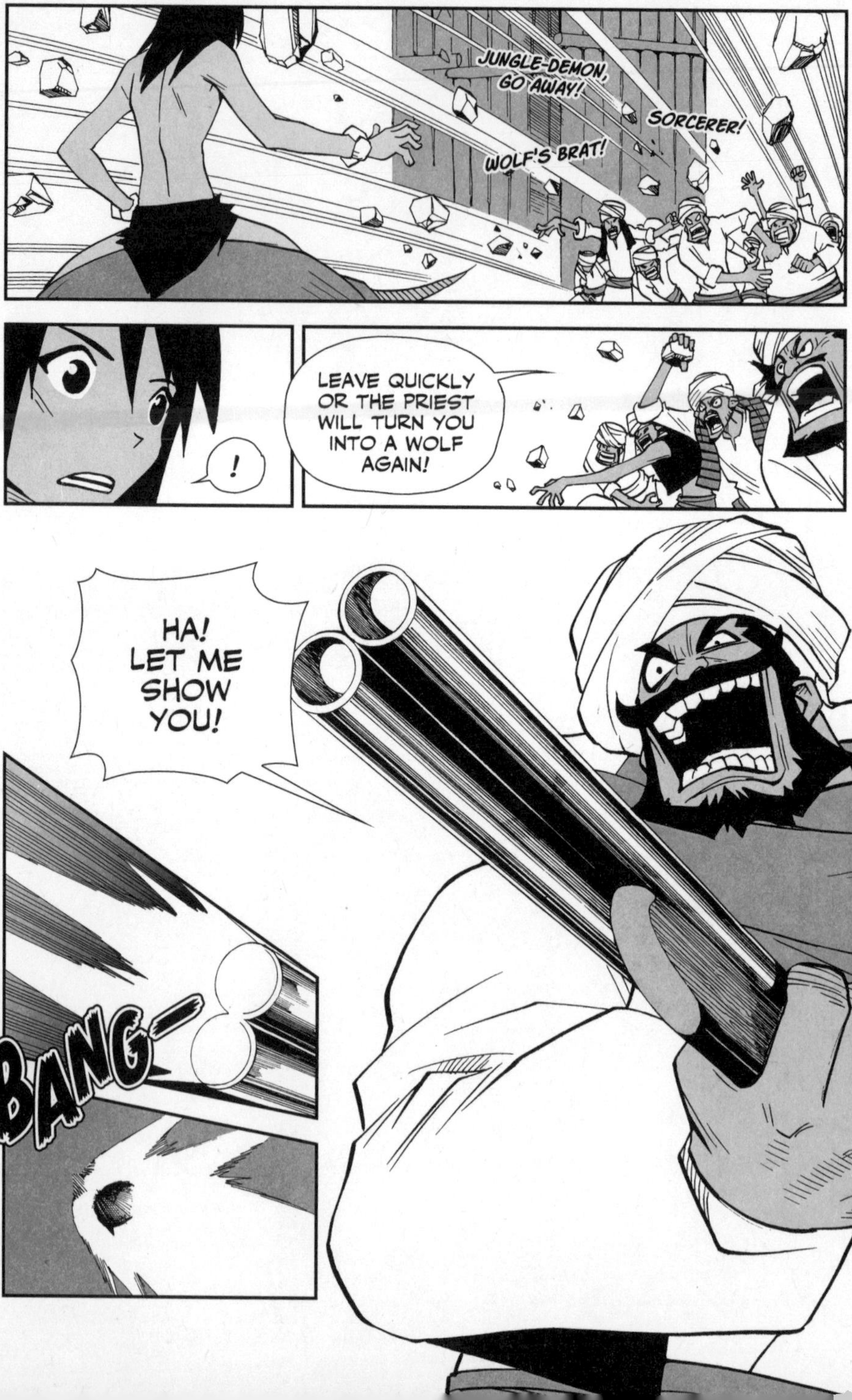

JUNGLE-DEMON, GO AWAY!
SORCERER!
WOLF'S BRAT!
LEAVE QUICKLY OR THE PRIEST WILL TURN YOU INTO A WOLF AGAIN!
!
HA! LET ME SHOW YOU!
BANG-

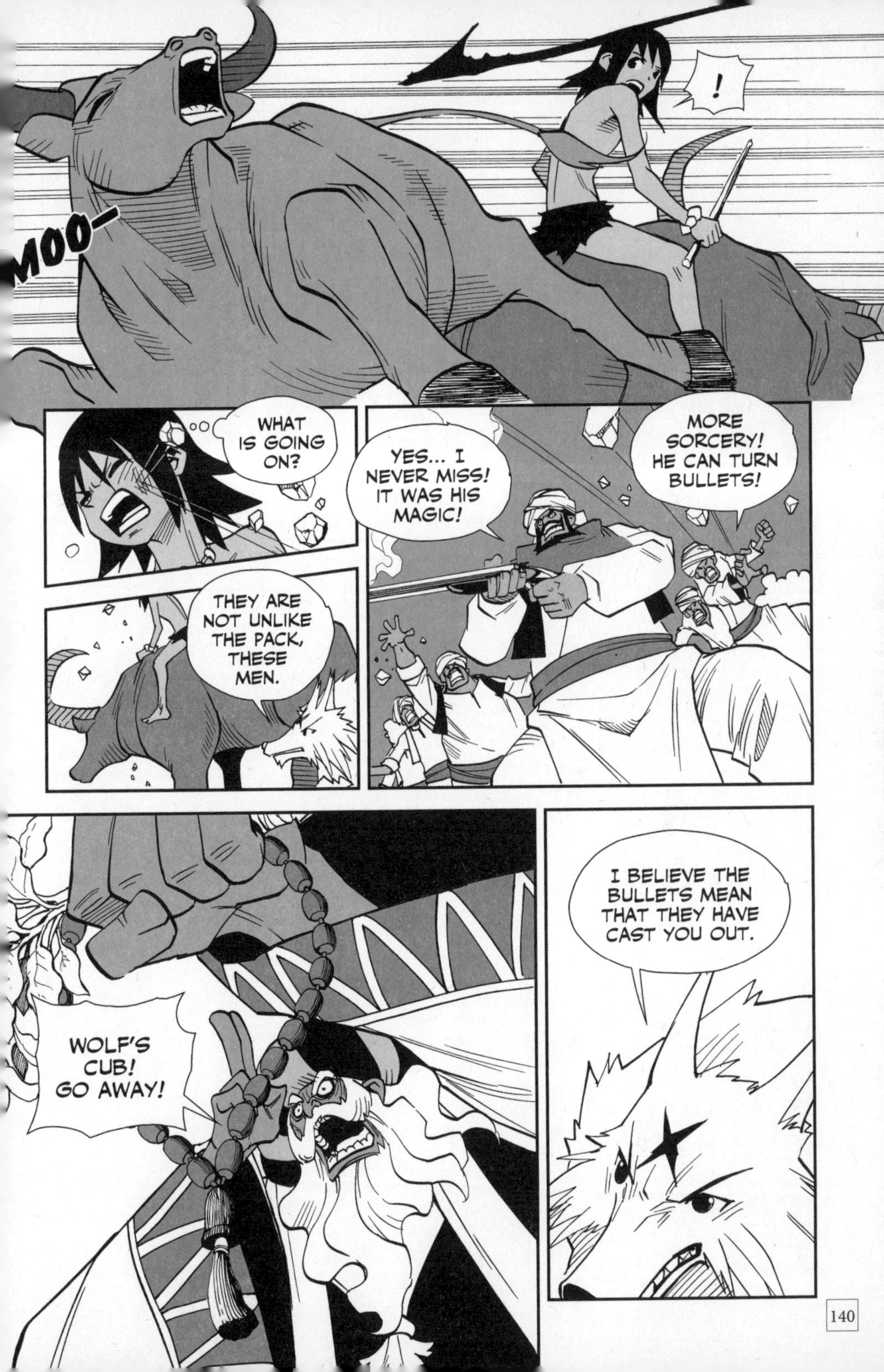
!
MOO—
MORE SORCERY! HE CAN TURN BULLETS!
YES... I NEVER MISS! IT WAS HIS MAGIC!
WHAT IS GOING ON?
THEY ARE NOT UNLIKE THE PACK, THESE MEN.
I BELIEVE THE BULLETS MEAN THAT THEY HAVE CAST YOU OUT.
WOLF'S CUB! GO AWAY!

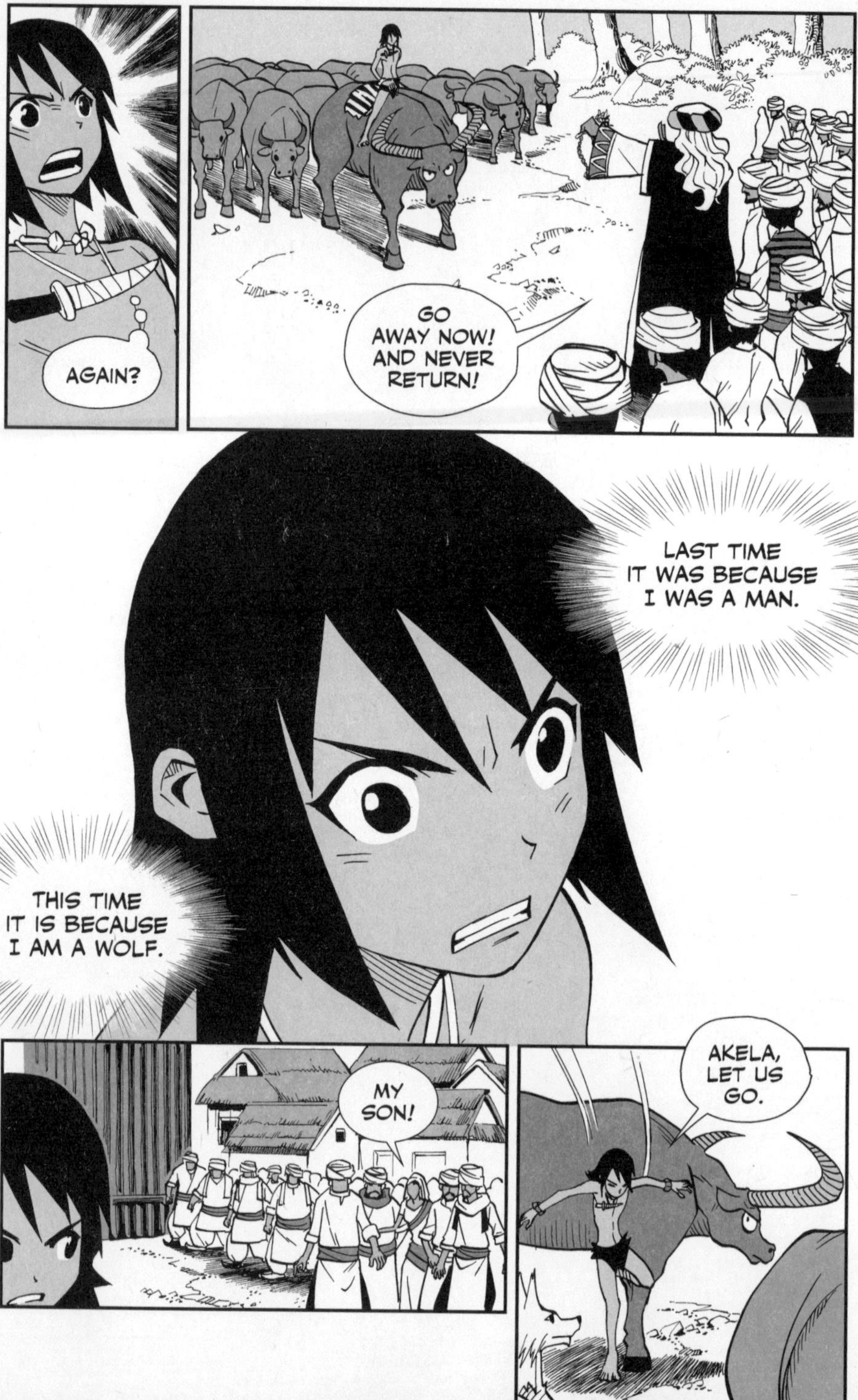
GO AWAY NOW! AND NEVER RETURN!
AGAIN?
LAST TIME IT WAS BECAUSE I WAS A MAN.
THIS TIME IT IS BECAUSE I AM A WOLF.
AKELA, LET US GO.
MY SON!

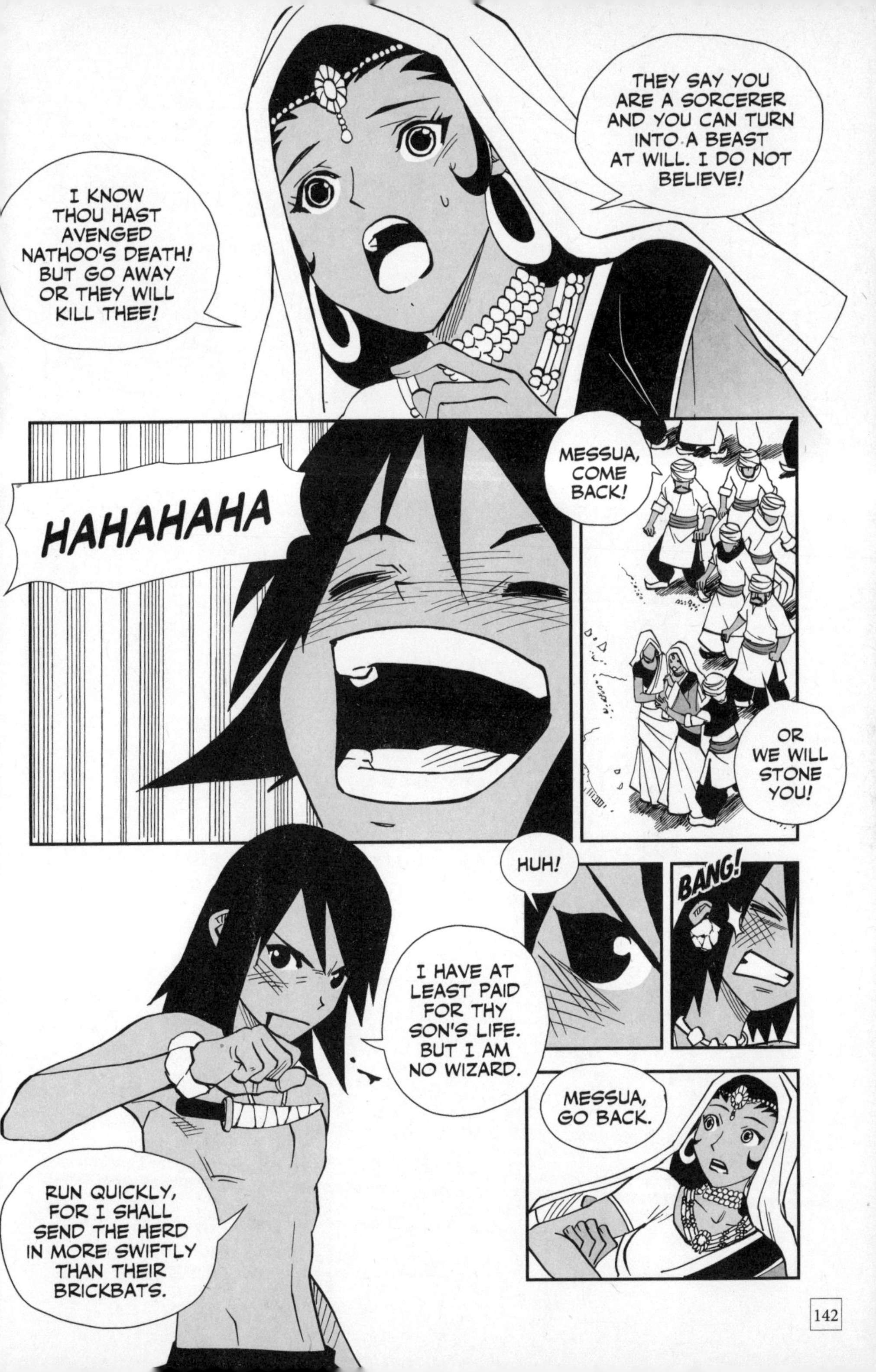
THEY SAY YOU ARE A SORCERER AND YOU CAN TURN INTO A BEAST AT WILL. I DO NOT BELIEVE!
I KNOW THOU HAST AVENGED NATHOO'S DEATH! BUT GO AWAY OR THEY WILL KILL THEE!
MESSUA, COME BACK!
OR WE WILL STONE YOU!
HAHAHAHA
BANG!
HUH!
MESSUA, GO BACK.
I HAVE AT LEAST PAID FOR THY SON'S LIFE. BUT I AM NO WIZARD.
RUN QUICKLY, FOR I SHALL SEND THE HERD IN MORE SWIFTLY THAN THEIR BRICKBATS.

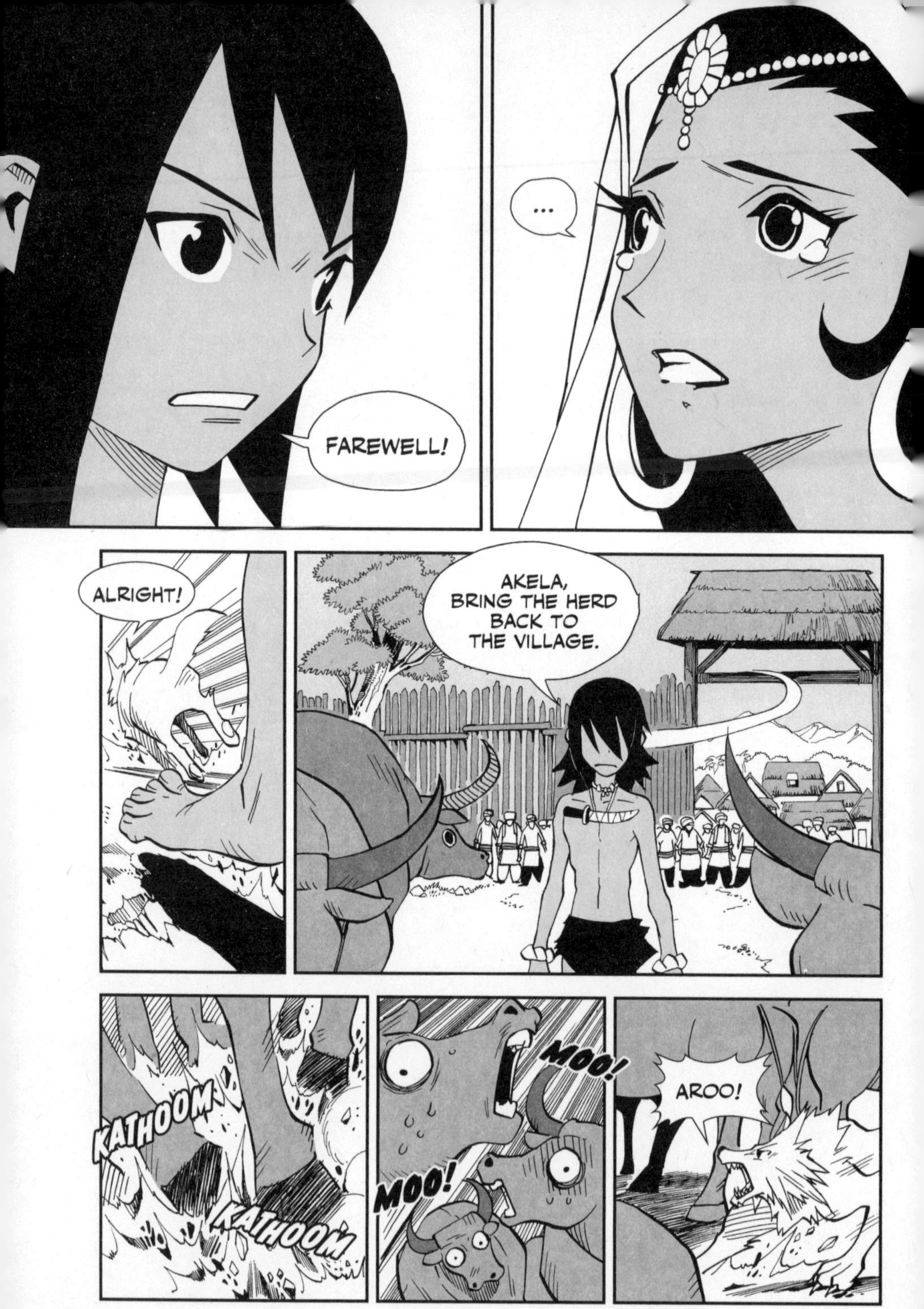
...
FAREWELL!
AKELA, BRING THE HERD BACK TO THE VILLAGE.
ALRIGHT!
AROO!
MOO!
MOO!
KATHOOM
KATHOOM

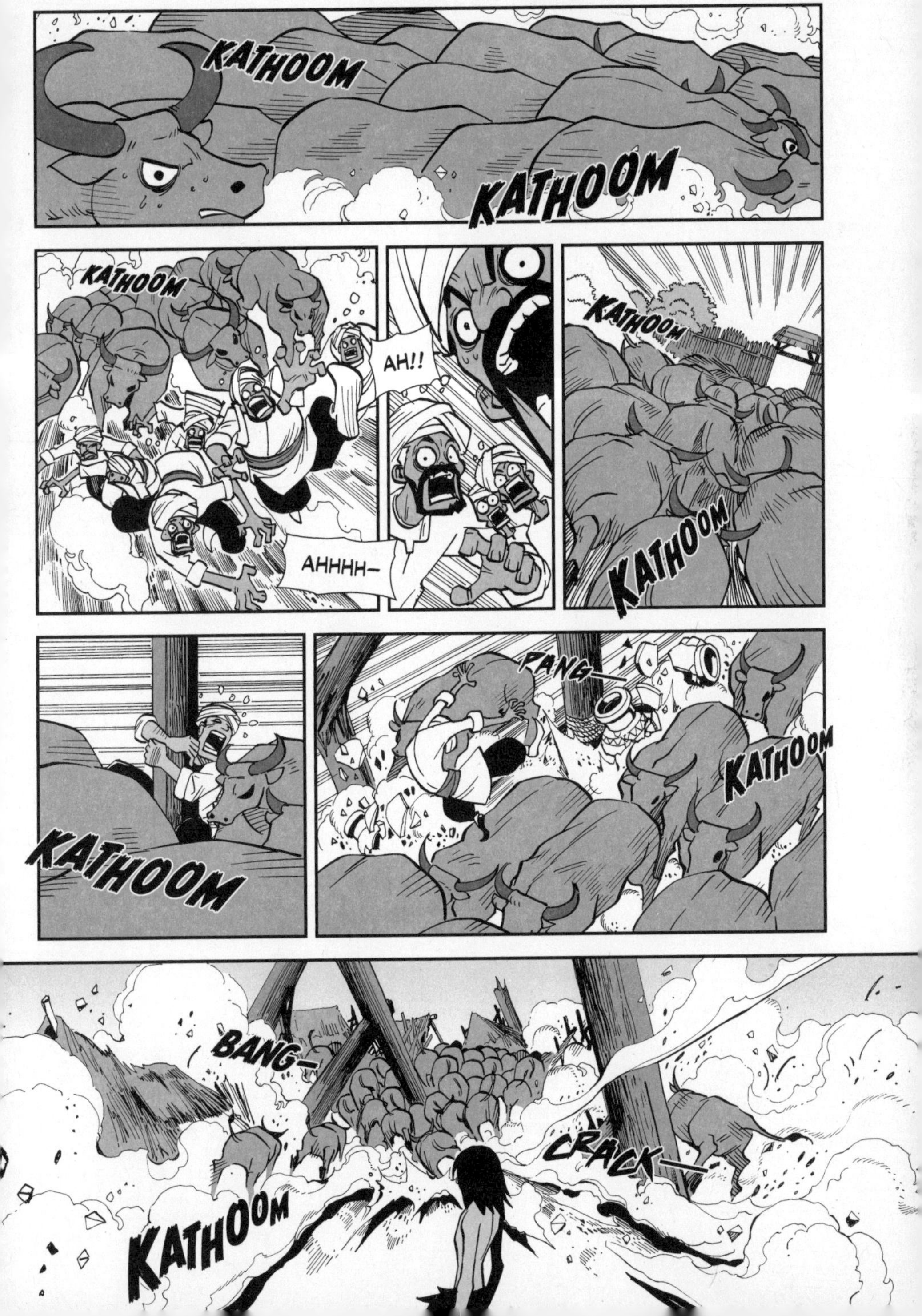
KATHOOM
KATHOOM
KATHOOM
KATHOOM
AH!!
KATHOOM
AHHHH-
PANG—
KATHOOM
KATHOOM
BANG-
CRACK—
KATHOOM

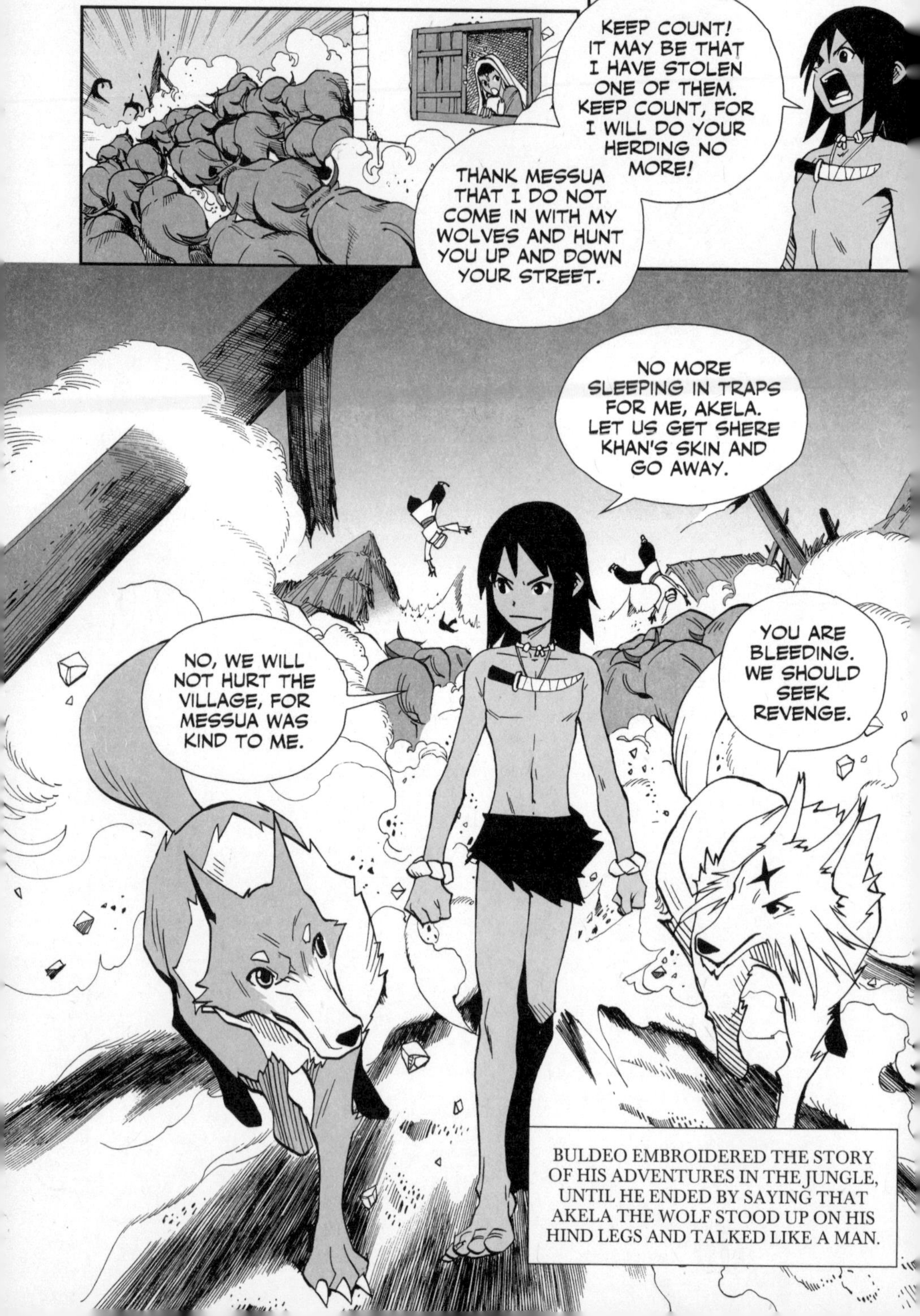
KEEP COUNT! IT MAY BE THAT I HAVE STOLEN ONE OF THEM. KEEP COUNT, FOR I WILL DO YOUR HERDING NO MORE!
THANK MESSUA THAT I DO NOT COME IN WITH MY WOLVES AND HUNT YOU UP AND DOWN YOUR STREET.
NO MORE SLEEPING IN TRAPS FOR ME, AKELA. LET US GET SHERE KHAN'S SKIN AND GO AWAY.
YOU ARE BLEEDING. WE SHOULD SEEK REVENGE.
NO, WE WILL NOT HURT THE VILLAGE, FOR MESSUA WAS KIND TO ME.
BULDEO EMBROIDERED THE STORY OF HIS ADVENTURES IN THE JUNGLE, UNTIL HE ENDED BY SAYING THAT AKELA THE WOLF STOOD UP ON HIS HIND LEGS AND TALKED LIKE A MAN.

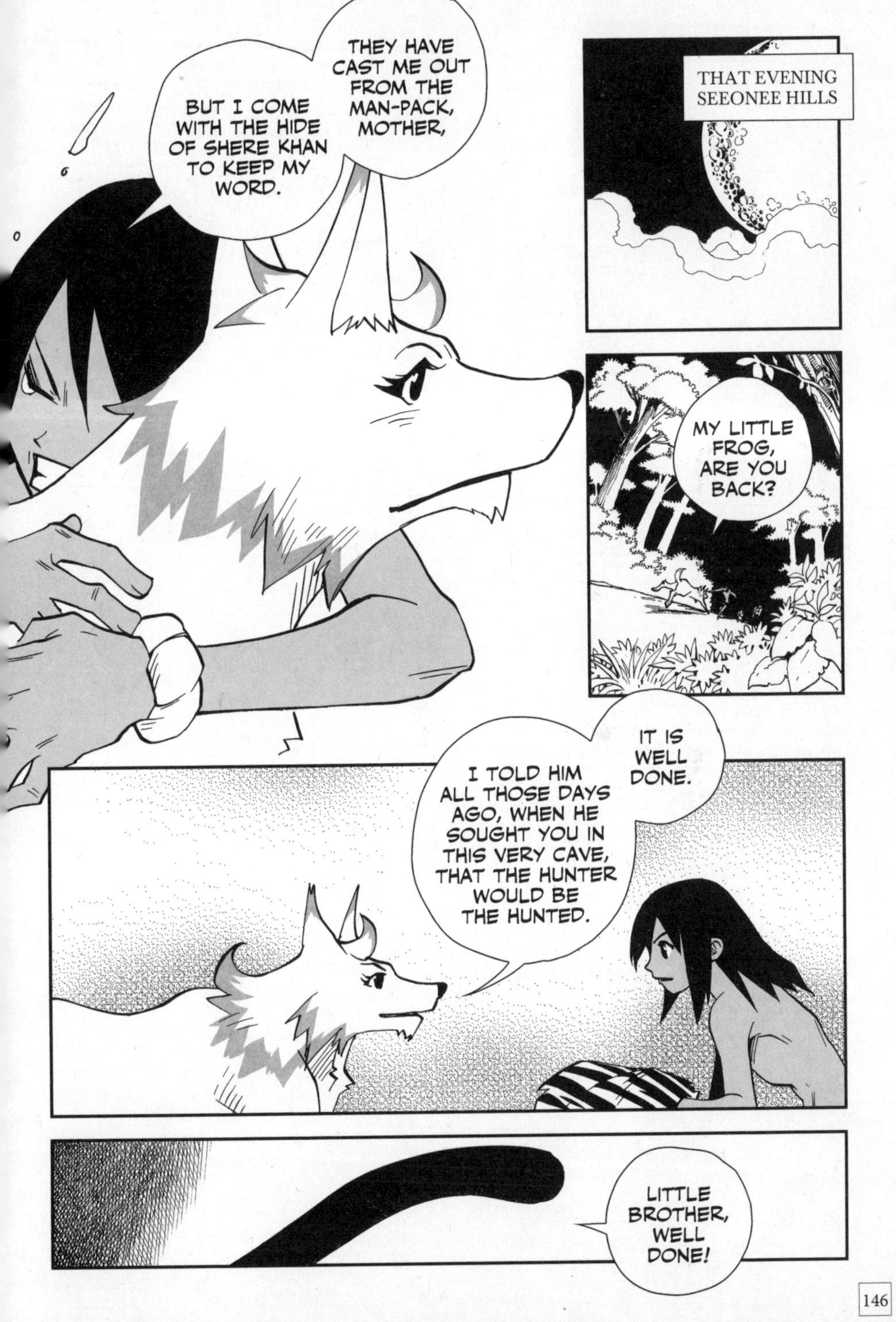
THAT EVENING
SEEONEE HILLS
MY LITTLE FROG, ARE YOU BACK?
THEY HAVE CAST ME OUT FROM THE MAN-PACK, MOTHER,
BUT I COME WITH THE HIDE OF SHERE KHAN TO KEEP MY WORD.
IT IS WELL DONE.
I TOLD HIM ALL THOSE DAYS AGO, WHEN HE SOUGHT YOU IN THIS VERY CAVE, THAT THE HUNTER WOULD BE THE HUNTED.
LITTLE BROTHER, WELL DONE!

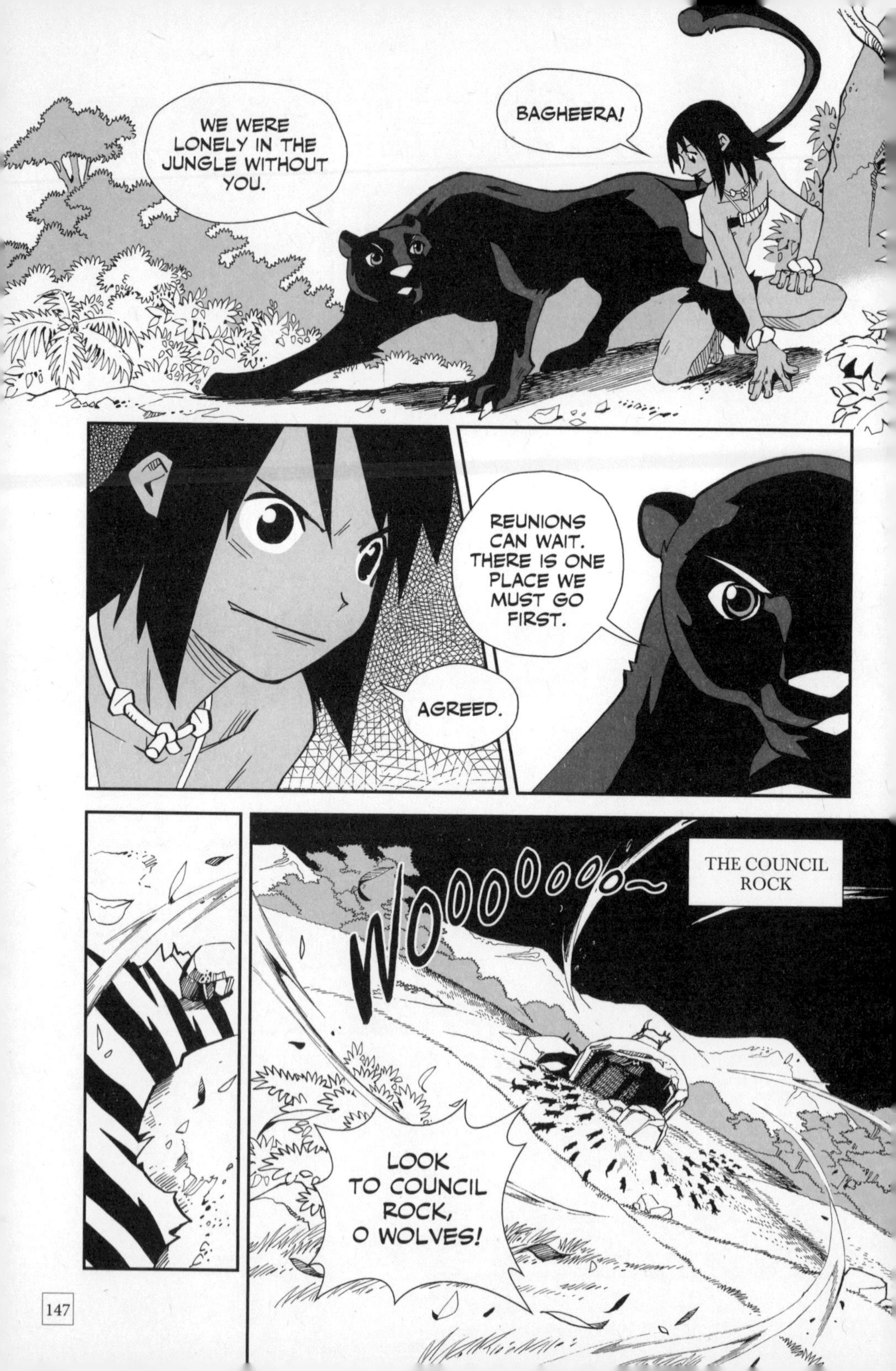
BAGHEERA!
WE WERE LONELY IN THE JUNGLE WITHOUT YOU.
REUNIONS CAN WAIT. THERE IS ONE PLACE WE MUST GO FIRST.
AGREED.
THE COUNCIL ROCK
WOOOOOOO~
LOOK TO COUNCIL ROCK, O WOLVES!

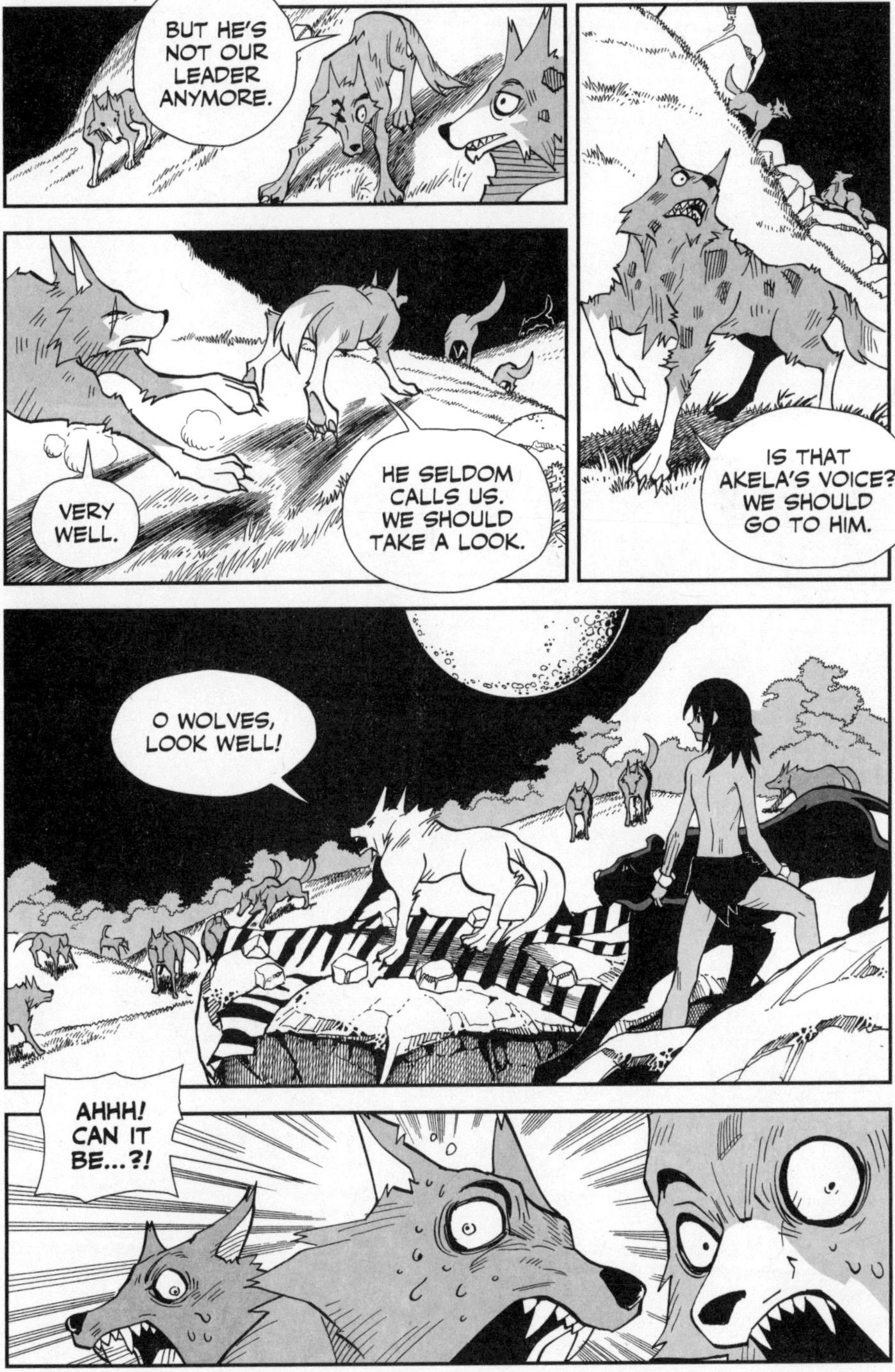
IS THAT AKELA'S VOICE? WE SHOULD GO TO HIM.
BUT HE'S NOT OUR LEADER ANYMORE.
HE SELDOM CALLS US. WE SHOULD TAKE A LOOK.
VERY WELL.
O WOLVES, LOOK WELL!
AHHH! CAN IT BE...?!

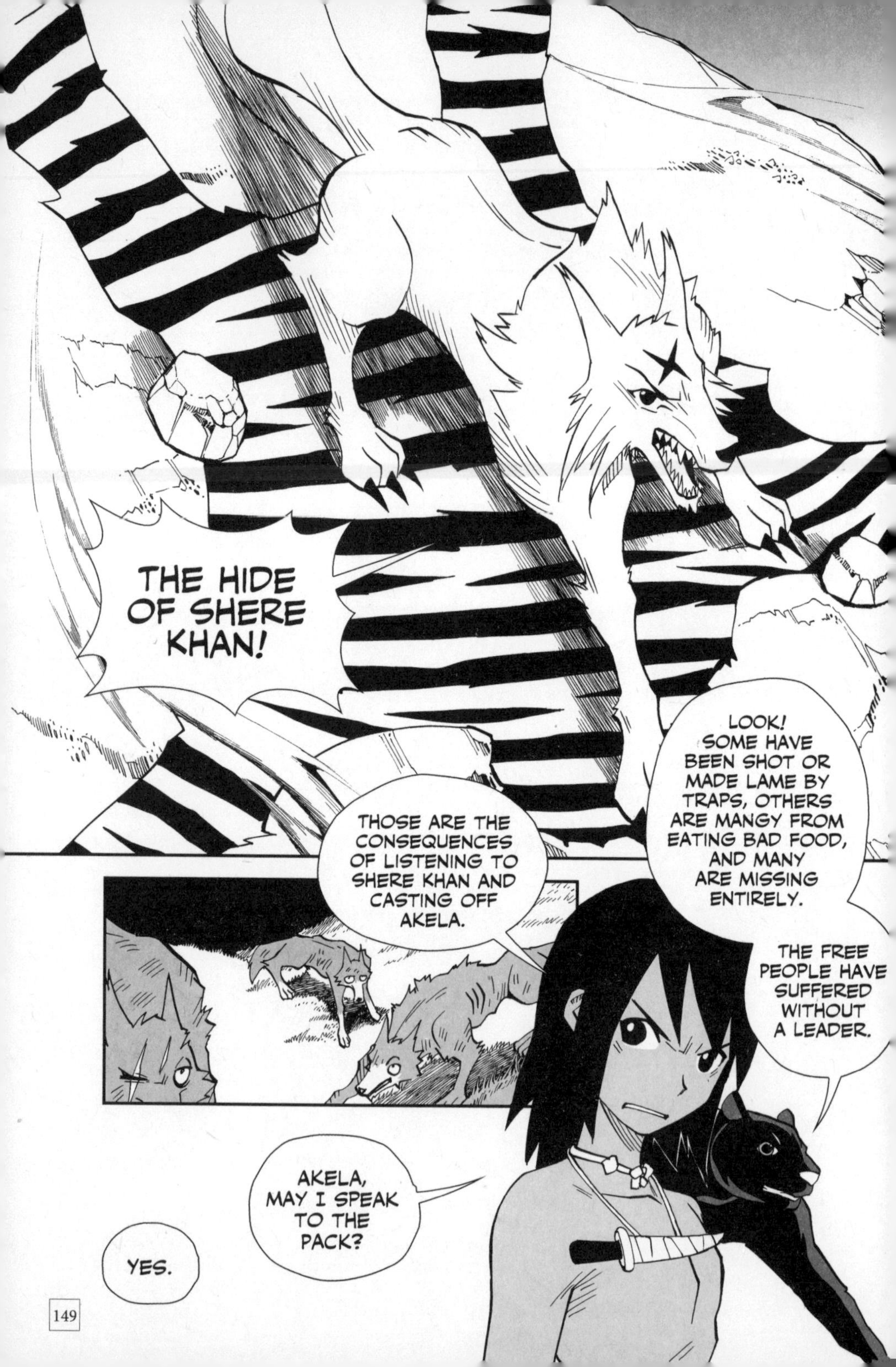
THE HIDE OF SHERE KHAN!
LOOK! SOME HAVE BEEN SHOT OR MADE LAME BY TRAPS, OTHERS ARE MANGY FROM EATING BAD FOOD, AND MANY ARE MISSING ENTIRELY.
THOSE ARE THE CONSEQUENCES OF LISTENING TO SHERE KHAN AND CASTING OFF AKELA.
THE FREE PEOPLE HAVE SUFFERED WITHOUT A LEADER.
AKELA, MAY I SPEAK TO THE PACK?
YES.

MOWGLI'S SONG

THAT HE SANG AT THE COUNCIL ROCK
WHEN HE DANCED ON SHERE KHAN'S HIDE

THE SONG OF MOWGLI — I, MOWGLI, AM SINGING.
LET THE JUNGLE LISTEN TO THE THINGS I HAVE DONE.

SHERE KHAN SAID HE WOULD KILL — WOULD KILL!
AT THE GATES IN THE TWILIGHT HE WOULD KILL MOWGLI, THE FROG!

HE ATE AND HE DRANK. DRINK DEEP, SHERE KHAN,
FOR WHEN WILT THOU DRINK AGAIN? SLEEP AND DREAM OF THE KILL.

I AM ALONE ON THE GRAZING-GROUNDS. GRAY BROTHER, COME TO ME!
COME TO ME, LONE WOLF, FOR THERE IS BIG GAME AFOOT!

BRING UP THE GREAT BULL BUFFALOES, THE BLUE-SKINNED
HERD BULLS WITH THE ANGRY EYES.
DRIVE THEM TO AND FRO AS I ORDER.

SLEEPEST THOU STILL, SHERE KHAN? WAKE, OH, WAKE!
HERE COME I, AND THE BULLS ARE BEHIND.

RAMA, THE KING OF THE BUFFALOES, STAMPED WITH HIS FOOT.
WATERS OF THE WAINGUNGA, WHITHER WENT SHERE KHAN?

HE IS NOT IKKI TO DIG HOLES, NOR MAO, THE PEACOCK,
THAT HE SHOULD FLY. HE IS NOT MANG THE BAT,
TO HANG IN THE BRANCHES. LITTLE BAMBOOS THAT CREAK TOGETHER,
TELL ME WHERE HE RAN?

OW! HE IS THERE. AHOO! HE IS THERE.
UNDER THE FEET OF RAMA LIES THE LAME ONE! UP, SHERE KHAN!

UP AND KILL! HERE IS MEAT; BREAK THE NECKS OF THE BULLS!

HSH! HE IS ASLEEP. WE WILL NOT WAKE HIM,
FOR HIS STRENGTH IS VERY GREAT.
THE KITES HAVE COME DOWN TO SEE IT.
THE BLACK ANTS HAVE COME UP TO KNOW IT.
THERE IS A GREAT ASSEMBLY IN HIS HONOR.

ALALA! I HAVE NO CLOTH TO WRAP ME.
THE KITES WILL SEE THAT I AM NAKED.
I AM ASHAMED TO MEET ALL THESE PEOPLE.

LEND ME THY COAT, SHERE KHAN.
LEND ME THY GAY STRIPED COAT THAT I MAY GO TO THE COUNCIL ROCK.

BY THE BULL THAT BOUGHT ME I MADE A PROMISE — A LITTLE PROMISE.
ONLY THY COAT IS LACKING BEFORE I KEEP MY WORD.

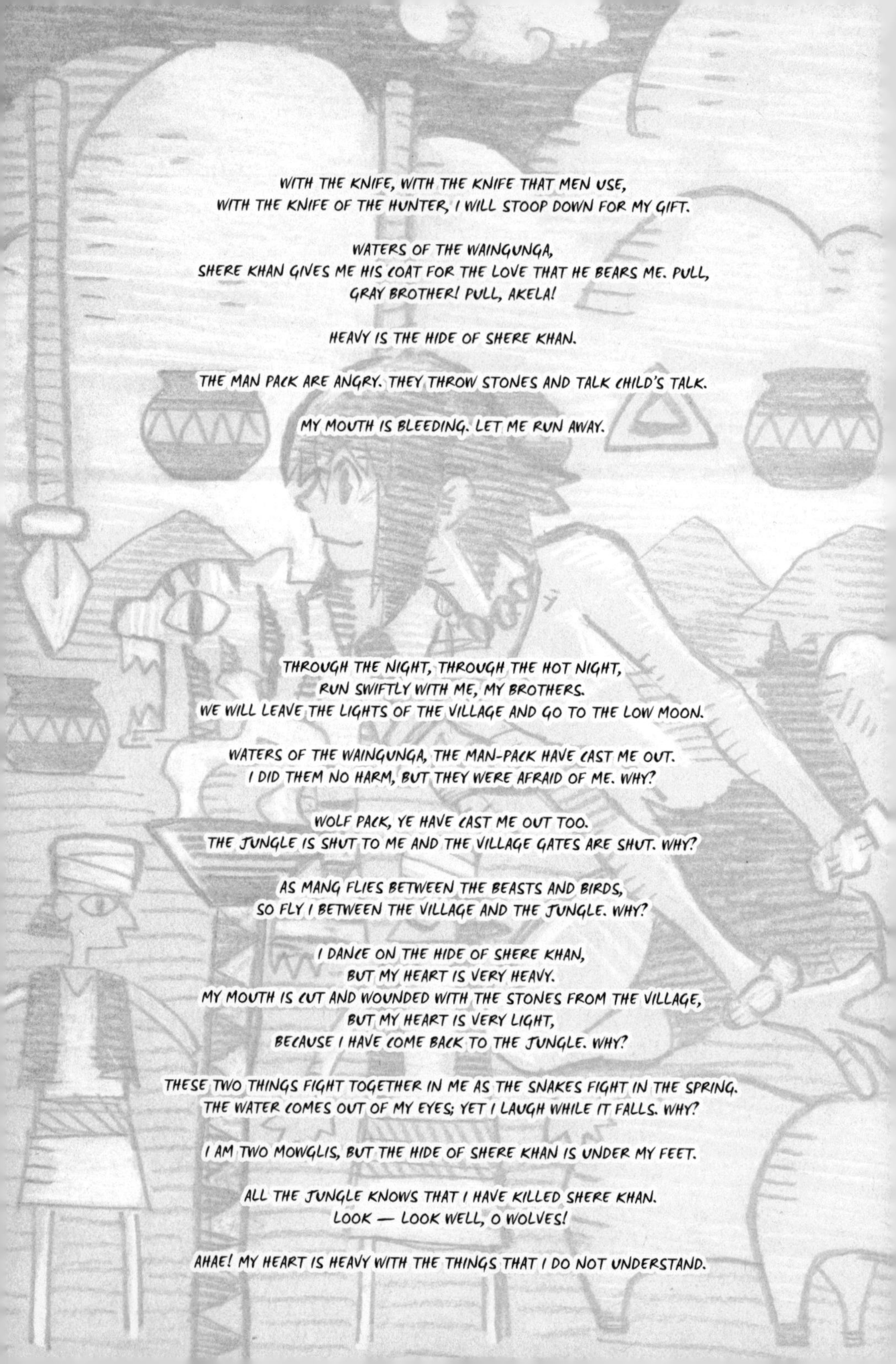

WITH THE KNIFE, WITH THE KNIFE THAT MEN USE,
WITH THE KNIFE OF THE HUNTER, I WILL STOOP DOWN FOR MY GIFT.

WATERS OF THE WAINGUNGA,
SHERE KHAN GIVES ME HIS COAT FOR THE LOVE THAT HE BEARS ME. PULL,
GRAY BROTHER! PULL, AKELA!

HEAVY IS THE HIDE OF SHERE KHAN.

THE MAN PACK ARE ANGRY. THEY THROW STONES AND TALK CHILD'S TALK.

MY MOUTH IS BLEEDING. LET ME RUN AWAY.

THROUGH THE NIGHT, THROUGH THE HOT NIGHT,
RUN SWIFTLY WITH ME, MY BROTHERS.
WE WILL LEAVE THE LIGHTS OF THE VILLAGE AND GO TO THE LOW MOON.

WATERS OF THE WAINGUNGA, THE MAN-PACK HAVE CAST ME OUT.
I DID THEM NO HARM, BUT THEY WERE AFRAID OF ME. WHY?

WOLF PACK, YE HAVE CAST ME OUT TOO.
THE JUNGLE IS SHUT TO ME AND THE VILLAGE GATES ARE SHUT. WHY?

AS MANG FLIES BETWEEN THE BEASTS AND BIRDS,
SO FLY I BETWEEN THE VILLAGE AND THE JUNGLE. WHY?

I DANCE ON THE HIDE OF SHERE KHAN,
BUT MY HEART IS VERY HEAVY.
MY MOUTH IS CUT AND WOUNDED WITH THE STONES FROM THE VILLAGE,
BUT MY HEART IS VERY LIGHT,
BECAUSE I HAVE COME BACK TO THE JUNGLE. WHY?

THESE TWO THINGS FIGHT TOGETHER IN ME AS THE SNAKES FIGHT IN THE SPRING.
THE WATER COMES OUT OF MY EYES; YET I LAUGH WHILE IT FALLS. WHY?

I AM TWO MOWGLIS, BUT THE HIDE OF SHERE KHAN IS UNDER MY FEET.

ALL THE JUNGLE KNOWS THAT I HAVE KILLED SHERE KHAN.
LOOK — LOOK WELL, O WOLVES!

AHAE! MY HEART IS HEAVY WITH THE THINGS THAT I DO NOT UNDERSTAND.

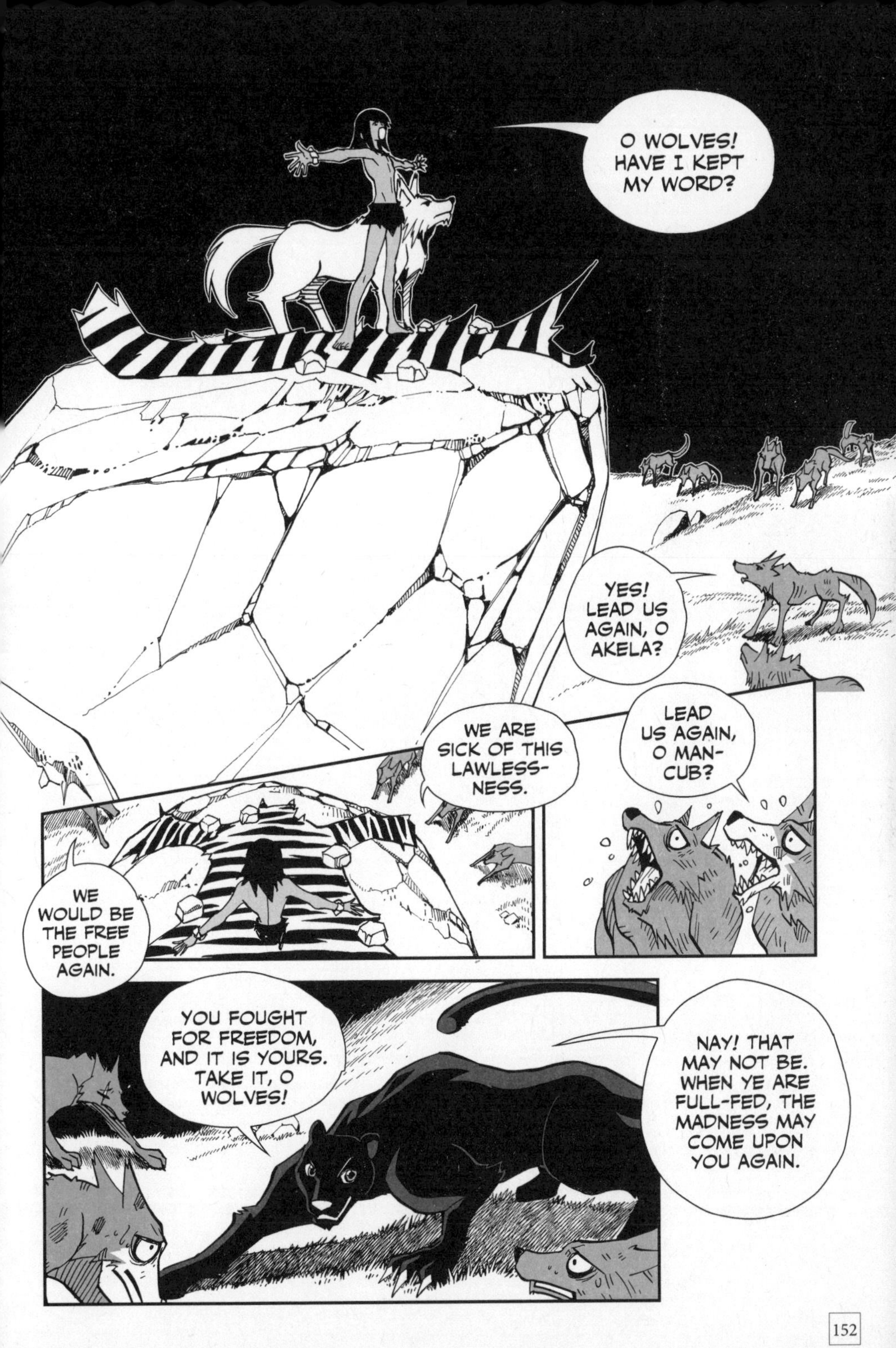
O WOLVES! HAVE I KEPT MY WORD?
YES! LEAD US AGAIN, O AKELA?
LEAD US AGAIN, O MAN-CUB?
WE ARE SICK OF THIS LAWLESS-NESS.
WE WOULD BE THE FREE PEOPLE AGAIN.
YOU FOUGHT FOR FREEDOM, AND IT IS YOURS. TAKE IT, O WOLVES!
NAY! THAT MAY NOT BE. WHEN YE ARE FULL-FED, THE MADNESS MAY COME UPON YOU AGAIN.

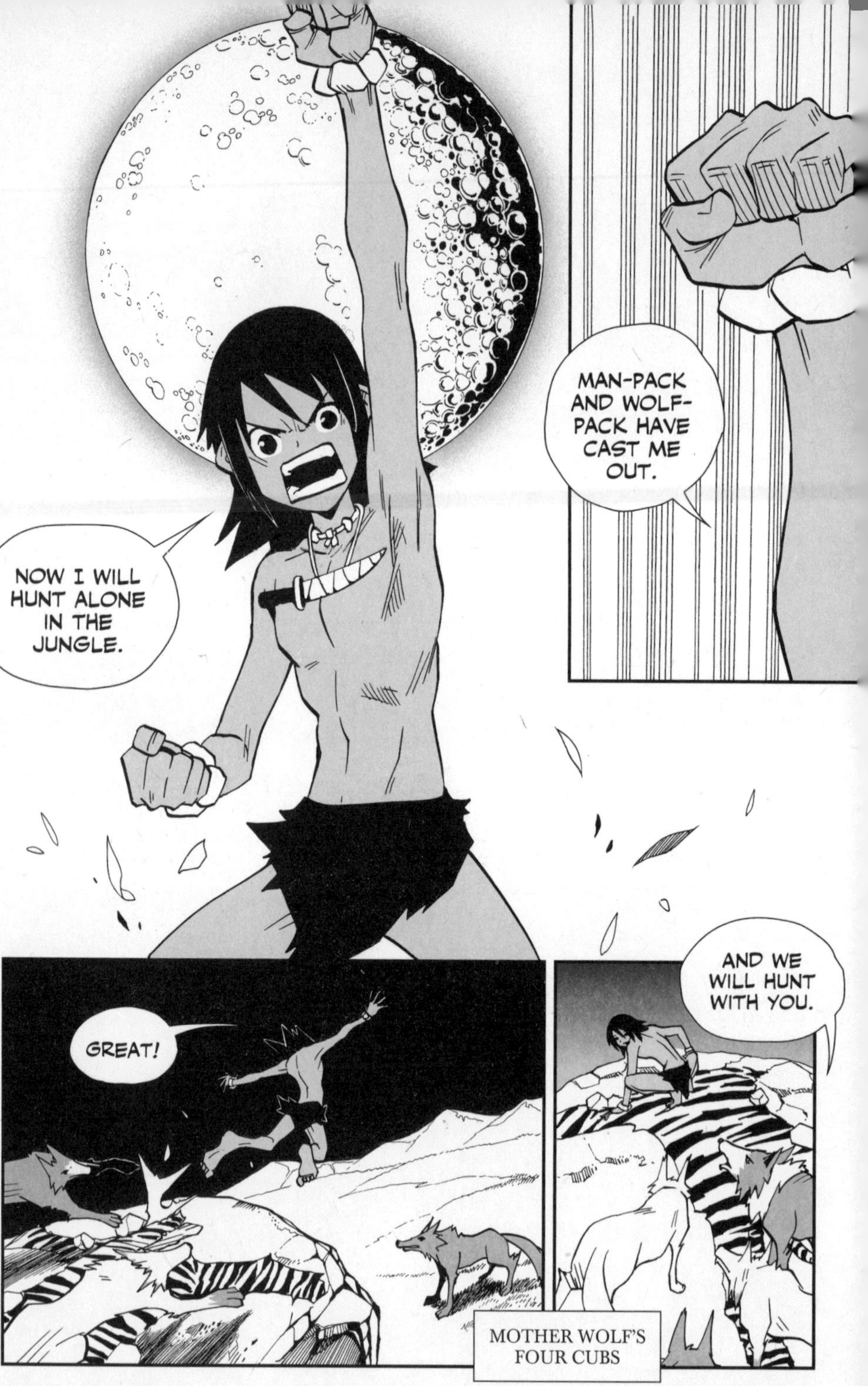
MAN-PACK AND WOLF-PACK HAVE CAST ME OUT.
NOW I WILL HUNT ALONE IN THE JUNGLE.
AND WE WILL HUNT WITH YOU.
MOTHER WOLF'S FOUR CUBS
GREAT!

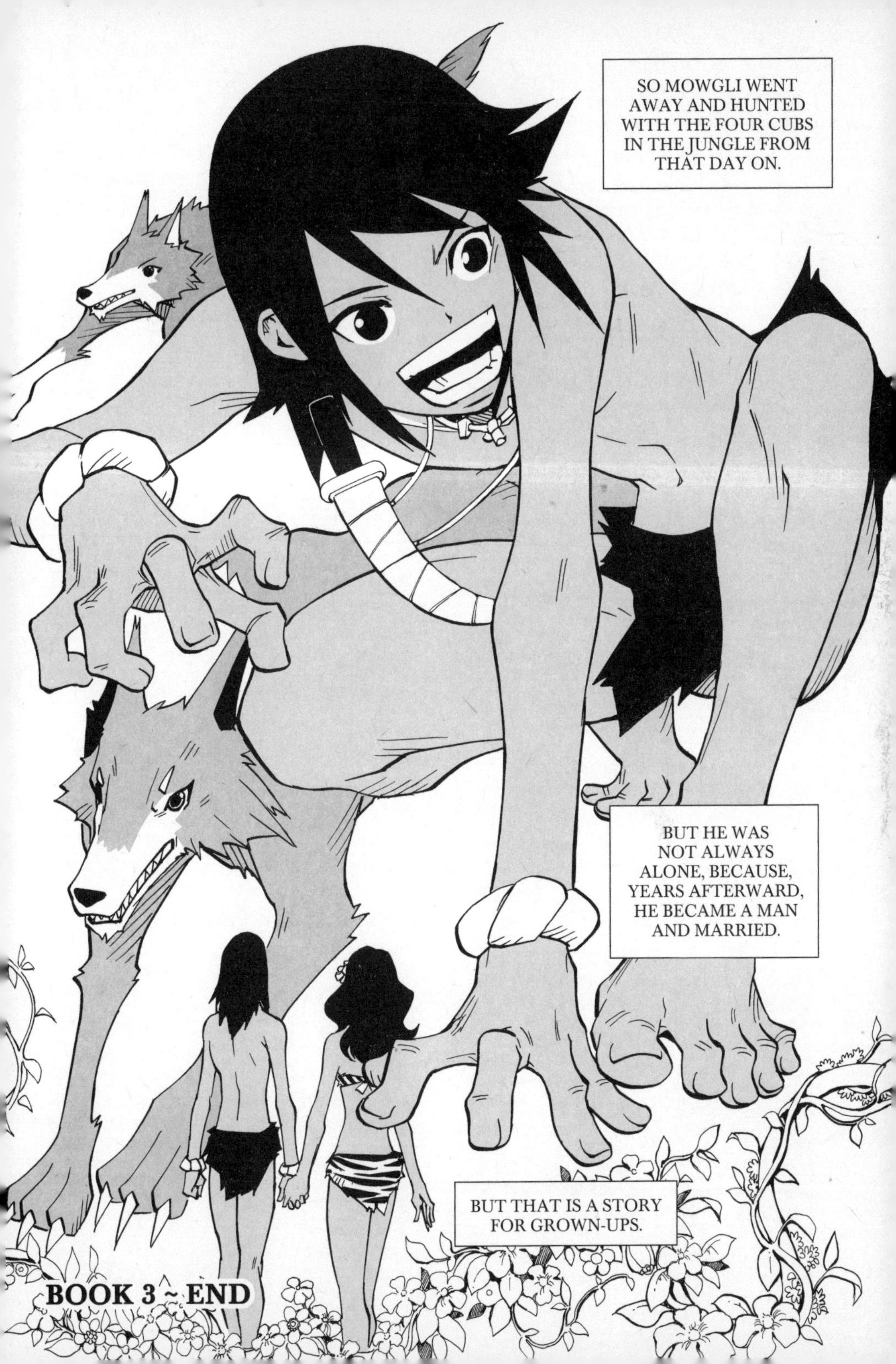
SO MOWGLI WENT AWAY AND HUNTED WITH THE FOUR CUBS IN THE JUNGLE FROM THAT DAY ON.
BUT HE WAS NOT ALWAYS ALONE, BECAUSE, YEARS AFTERWARD, HE BECAME A MAN AND MARRIED.
BUT THAT IS A STORY FOR GROWN-UPS.
BOOK 3 ~ END

BOOK 4: THE WHITE SEAL

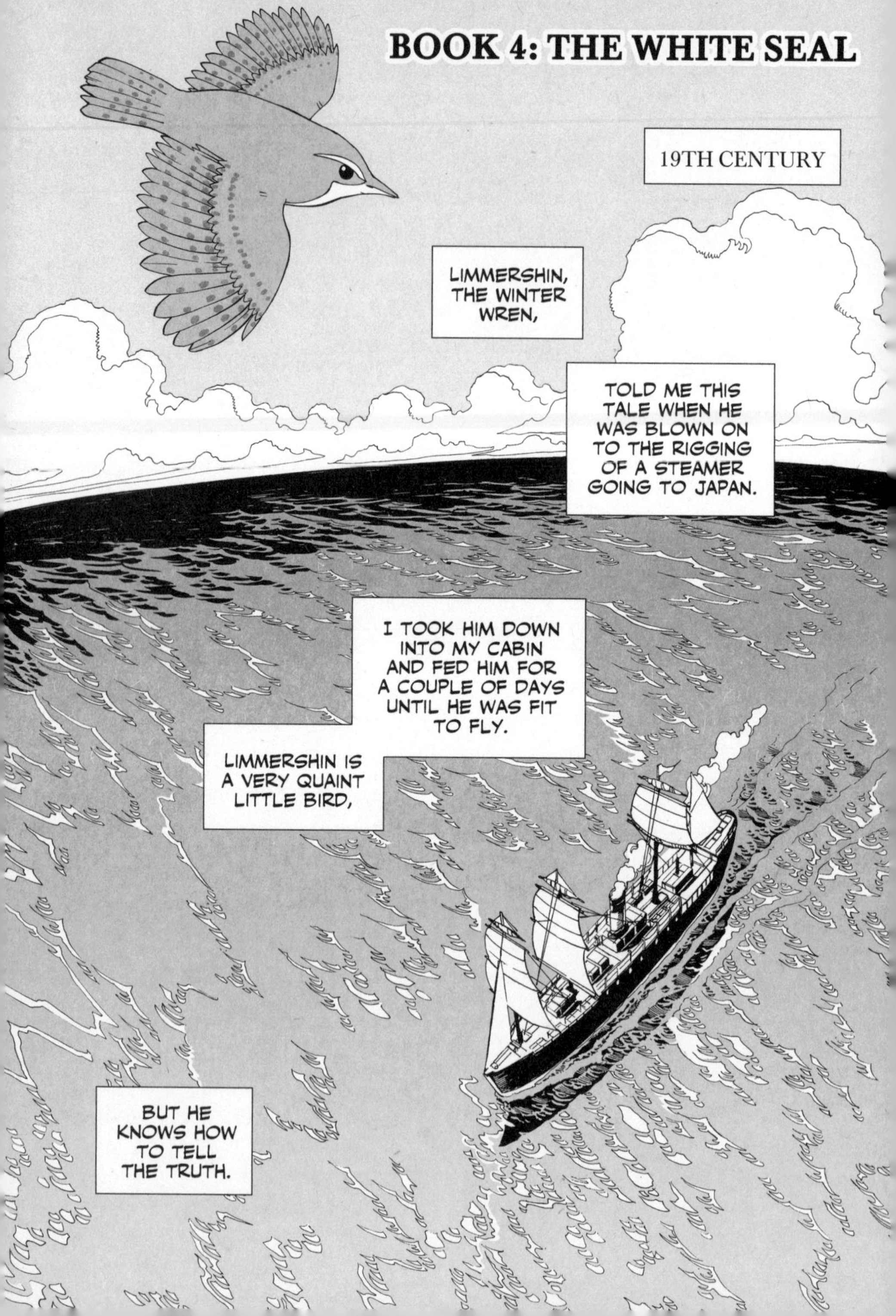
19TH CENTURY
LIMMERSHIN, THE WINTER WREN,
TOLD ME THIS TALE WHEN HE WAS BLOWN ON TO THE RIGGING OF A STEAMER GOING TO JAPAN.
I TOOK HIM DOWN INTO MY CABIN AND FED HIM FOR A COUPLE OF DAYS UNTIL HE WAS FIT TO FLY.
LIMMERSHIN IS A VERY QUAINT LITTLE BIRD,
BUT HE KNOWS HOW TO TELL THE TRUTH.

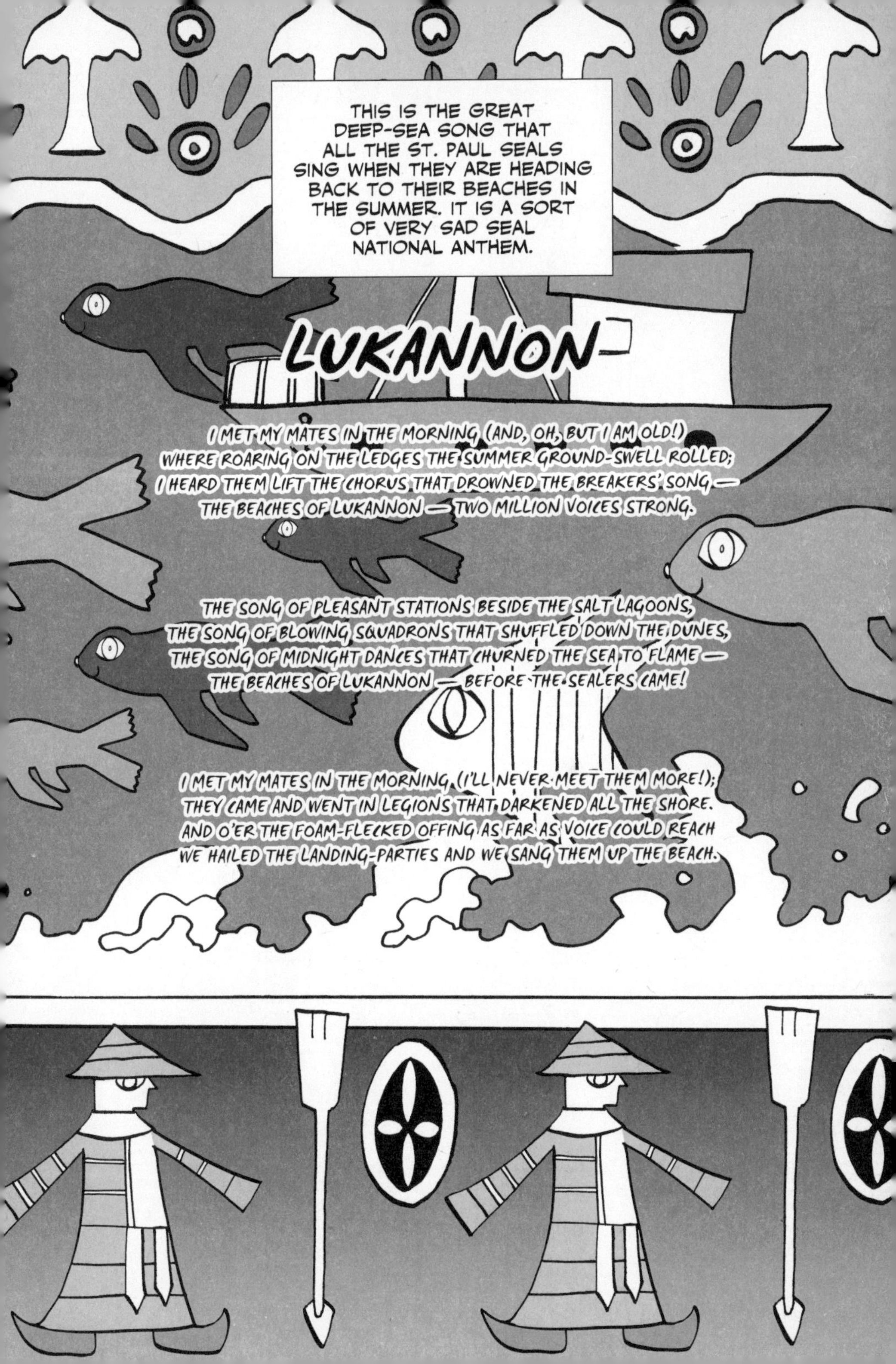
THIS IS THE GREAT DEEP-SEA SONG THAT ALL THE ST. PAUL SEALS SING WHEN THEY ARE HEADING BACK TO THEIR BEACHES IN THE SUMMER. IT IS A SORT OF VERY SAD SEAL NATIONAL ANTHEM.
LUKANNON
I MET MY MATES IN THE MORNING (AND, OH, BUT I AM OLD!)
WHERE ROARING ON THE LEDGES THE SUMMER GROUND-SWELL ROLLED;
I HEARD THEM LIFT THE CHORUS THAT DROWNED THE BREAKERS' SONG —
THE BEACHES OF LUKANNON — TWO MILLION VOICES STRONG.
THE SONG OF PLEASANT STATIONS BESIDE THE SALT LAGOONS,
THE SONG OF BLOWING SQUADRONS THAT SHUFFLED DOWN THE DUNES,
THE SONG OF MIDNIGHT DANCES THAT CHURNED THE SEA TO FLAME —
THE BEACHES OF LUKANNON — BEFORE THE SEALERS CAME!
I MET MY MATES IN THE MORNING (I'LL NEVER MEET THEM MORE!);
THEY CAME AND WENT IN LEGIONS THAT DARKENED ALL THE SHORE.
AND O'ER THE FOAM-FLECKED OFFING AS FAR AS VOICE COULD REACH
WE HAILED THE LANDING-PARTIES AND WE SANG THEM UP THE BEACH.

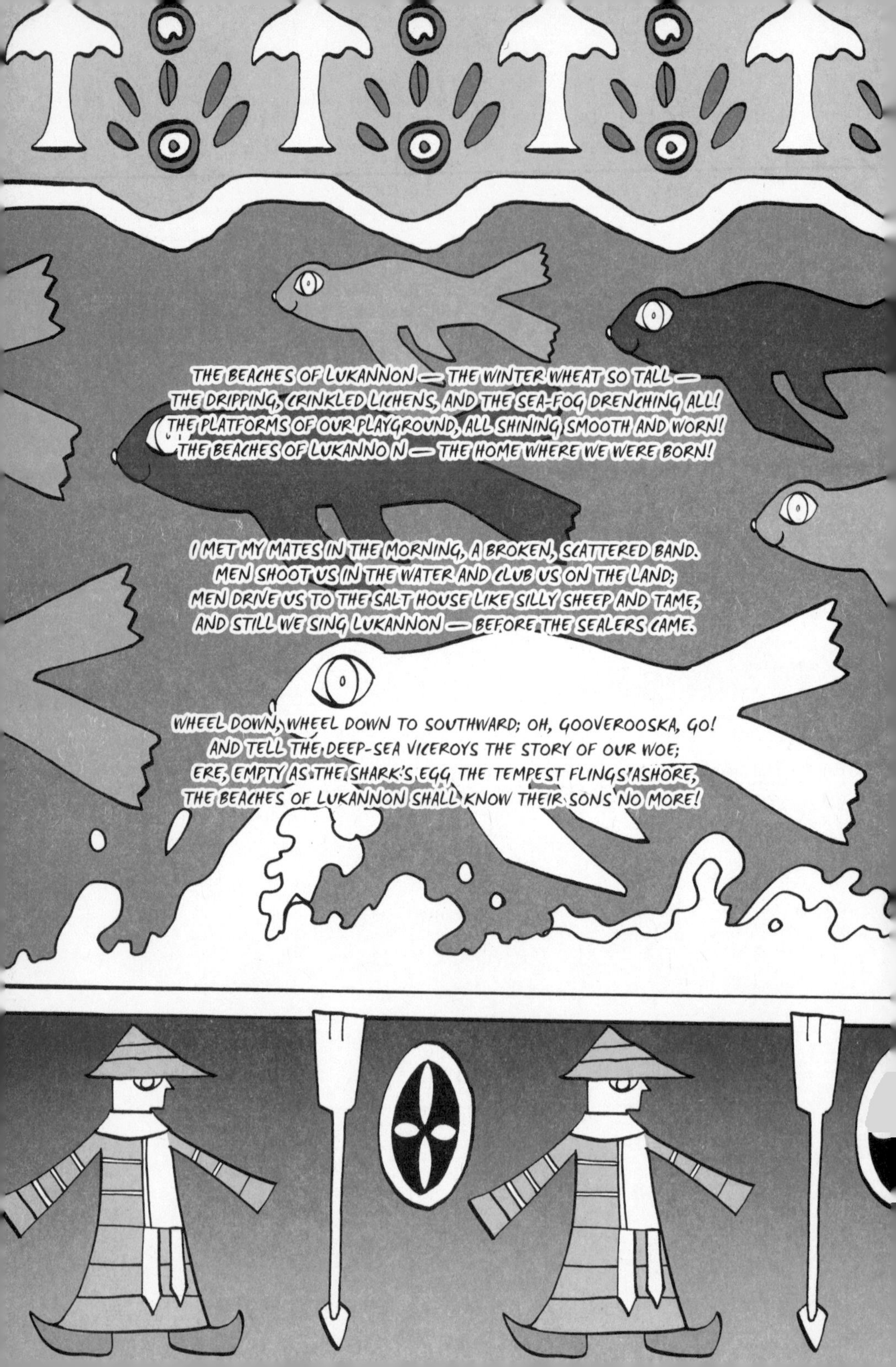
THE BEACHES OF LUKANNON — THE WINTER WHEAT SO TALL —
THE DRIPPING, CRINKLED LICHENS, AND THE SEA-FOG DRENCHING ALL!
THE PLATFORMS OF OUR PLAYGROUND, ALL SHINING SMOOTH AND WORN!
THE BEACHES OF LUKANNON — THE HOME WHERE WE WERE BORN!
I MET MY MATES IN THE MORNING, A BROKEN, SCATTERED BAND.
MEN SHOOT US IN THE WATER AND CLUB US ON THE LAND;
MEN DRIVE US TO THE SALT HOUSE LIKE SILLY SHEEP AND TAME,
AND STILL WE SING LUKANNON — BEFORE THE SEALERS CAME.
WHEEL DOWN, WHEEL DOWN TO SOUTHWARD; OH, GOOVEROOSKA, GO!
AND TELL THE DEEP-SEA VICEROYS THE STORY OF OUR WOE;
ERE, EMPTY AS THE SHARK'S EGG THE TEMPEST FLINGS ASHORE,
THE BEACHES OF LUKANNON SHALL KNOW THEIR SONS NO MORE!

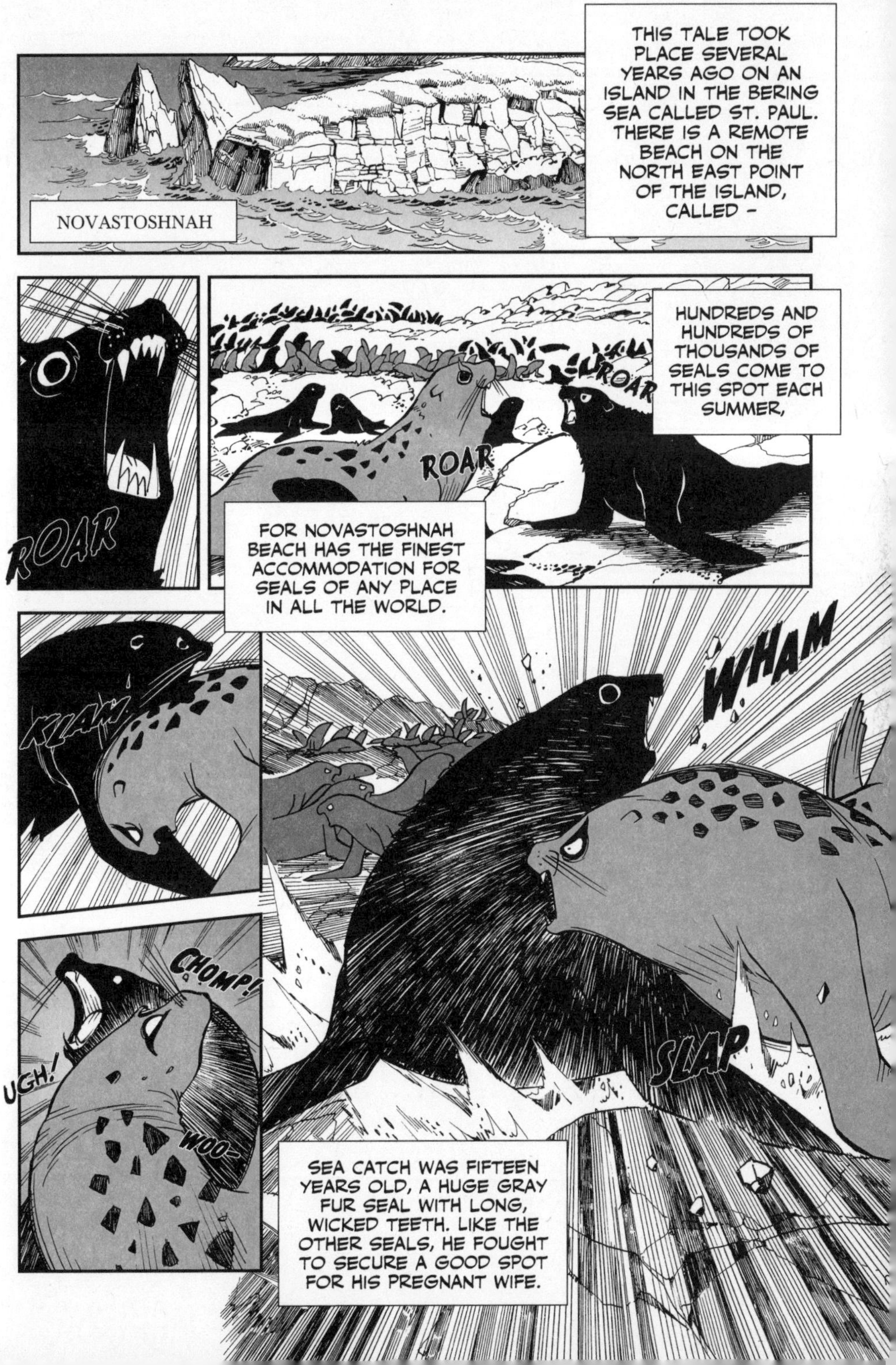
THIS TALE TOOK PLACE SEVERAL YEARS AGO ON AN ISLAND IN THE BERING SEA CALLED ST. PAUL. THERE IS A REMOTE BEACH ON THE NORTH EAST POINT OF THE ISLAND, CALLED –
NOVASTOSHNAH
HUNDREDS AND HUNDREDS OF THOUSANDS OF SEALS COME TO THIS SPOT EACH SUMMER,
UROAR
ROAR
FOR NOVASTOSHNAH BEACH HAS THE FINEST ACCOMMODATION FOR SEALS OF ANY PLACE IN ALL THE WORLD.
ROAR
WHAM
SLAP
SEA CATCH WAS FIFTEEN YEARS OLD, A HUGE GRAY FUR SEAL WITH LONG, WICKED TEETH. LIKE THE OTHER SEALS, HE FOUGHT TO SECURE A GOOD SPOT FOR HIS PREGNANT WIFE.
KLAM
CHOMP!
UGH!
WOO-

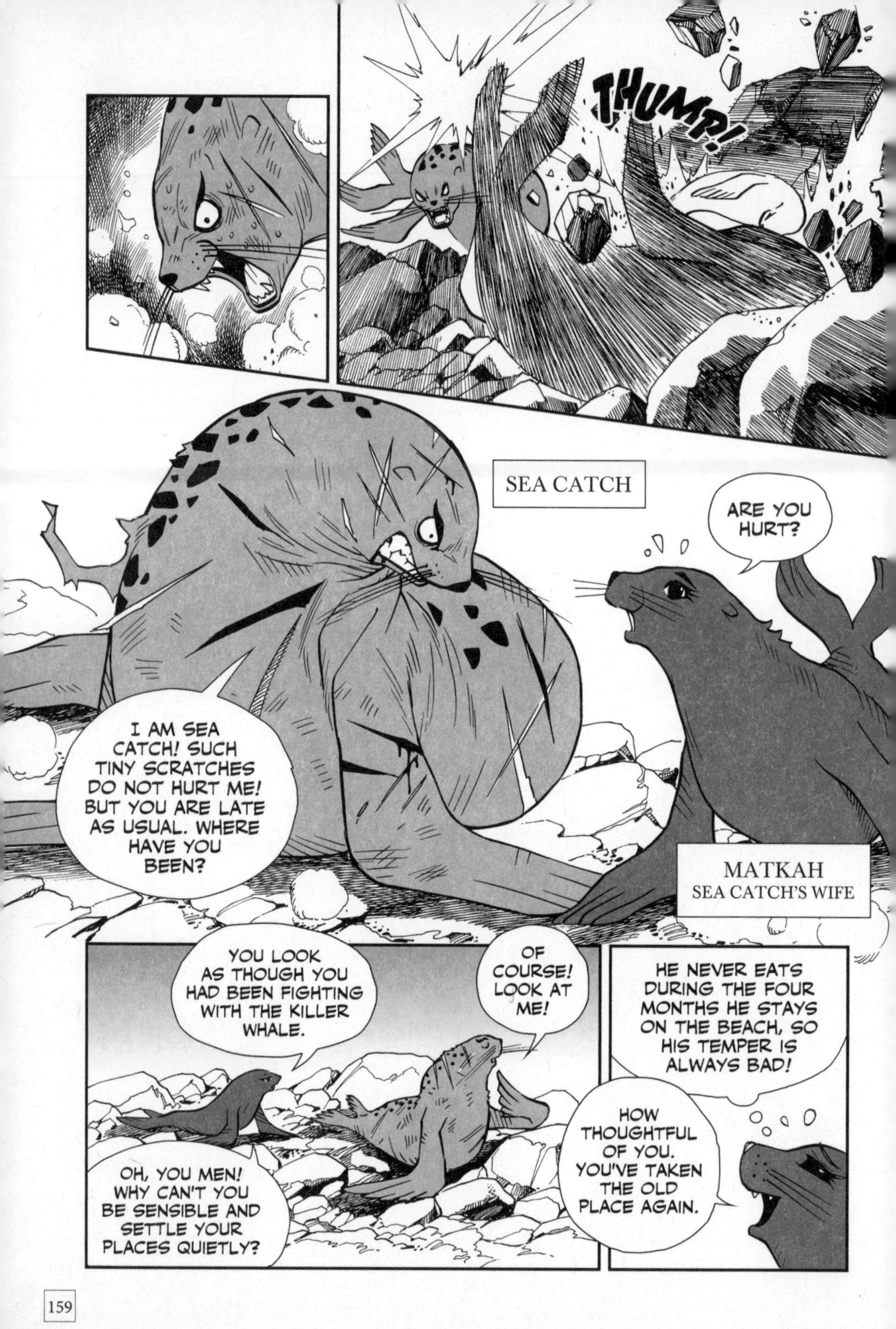
THUMP!
SEA CATCH
ARE YOU HURT?
MATKAH SEA CATCH'S WIFE
I AM SEA CATCH! SUCH TINY SCRATCHES DO NOT HURT ME! BUT YOU ARE LATE AS USUAL. WHERE HAVE YOU BEEN?
HE NEVER EATS DURING THE FOUR MONTHS HE STAYS ON THE BEACH, SO HIS TEMPER IS ALWAYS BAD!
HOW THOUGHTFUL OF YOU. YOU'VE TAKEN THE OLD PLACE AGAIN.
YOU LOOK AS THOUGH YOU HAD BEEN FIGHTING WITH THE KILLER WHALE.
OF COURSE! LOOK AT ME!
OH, YOU MEN! WHY CAN'T YOU BE SENSIBLE AND SETTLE YOUR PLACES QUIETLY?

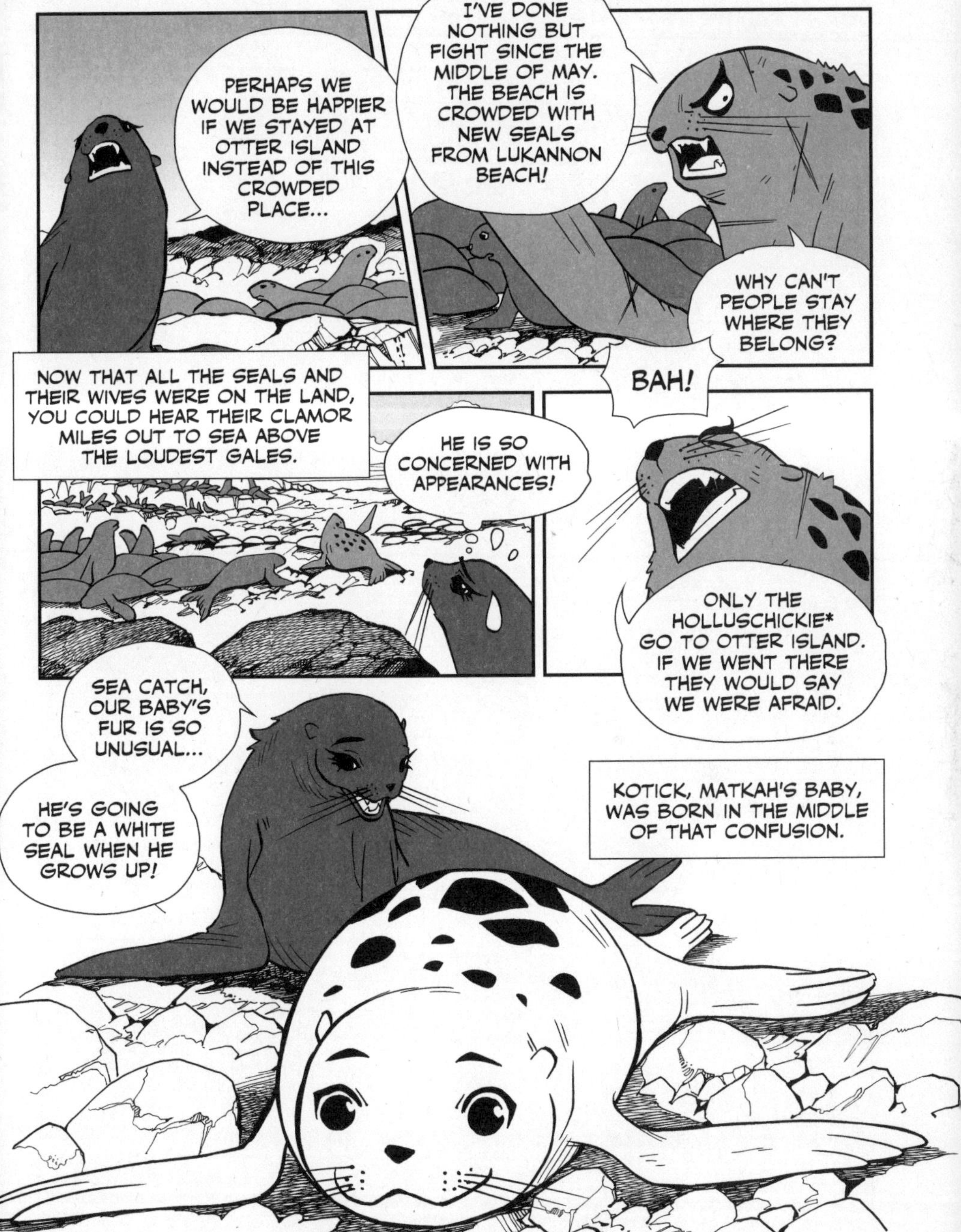
I'VE DONE NOTHING BUT FIGHT SINCE THE MIDDLE OF MAY. THE BEACH IS CROWDED WITH NEW SEALS FROM LUKANNON BEACH!
WHY CAN'T PEOPLE STAY WHERE THEY BELONG?
BAH!
PERHAPS WE WOULD BE HAPPIER IF WE STAYED AT OTTER ISLAND INSTEAD OF THIS CROWDED PLACE...
ONLY THE HOLLUSCHICKIE* GO TO OTTER ISLAND. IF WE WENT THERE THEY WOULD SAY WE WERE AFRAID.
NOW THAT ALL THE SEALS AND THEIR WIVES WERE ON THE LAND, YOU COULD HEAR THEIR CLAMOR MILES OUT TO SEA ABOVE THE LOUDEST GALES.
HE IS SO CONCERNED WITH APPEARANCES!
KOTICK, MATKAH'S BABY, WAS BORN IN THE MIDDLE OF THAT CONFUSION.
SEA CATCH, OUR BABY'S FUR IS SO UNUSUAL...
HE'S GOING TO BE A WHITE SEAL WHEN HE GROWS UP!

***NOTE:** HOLLUSCHICKIE – A YOUNG MALE SEAL

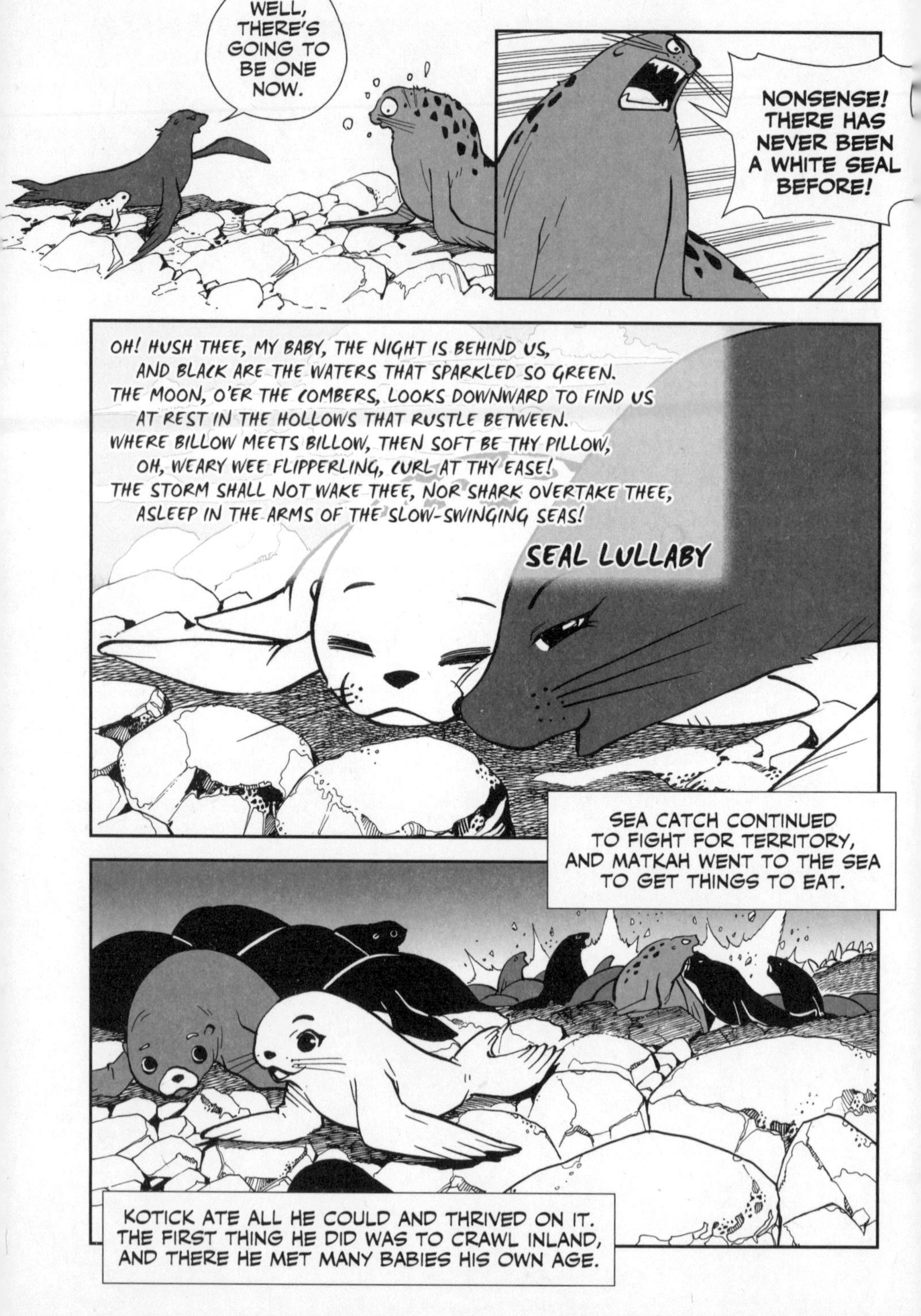
NONSENSE! THERE HAS NEVER BEEN A WHITE SEAL BEFORE!
WELL, THERE'S GOING TO BE ONE NOW.
OH! HUSH THEE, MY BABY, THE NIGHT IS BEHIND US,
AND BLACK ARE THE WATERS THAT SPARKLED SO GREEN.
THE MOON, O'ER THE COMBERS, LOOKS DOWNWARD TO FIND US
AT REST IN THE HOLLOWS THAT RUSTLE BETWEEN.
WHERE BILLOW MEETS BILLOW, THEN SOFT BE THY PILLOW,
OH, WEARY WEE FLIPPERLING, CURL AT THY EASE!
THE STORM SHALL NOT WAKE THEE, NOR SHARK OVERTAKE THEE,
ASLEEP IN THE ARMS OF THE SLOW-SWINGING SEAS!
SEAL LULLABY
SEA CATCH CONTINUED TO FIGHT FOR TERRITORY, AND MATKAH WENT TO THE SEA TO GET THINGS TO EAT.
KOTICK ATE ALL HE COULD AND THRIVED ON IT. THE FIRST THING HE DID WAS TO CRAWL INLAND, AND THERE HE MET MANY BABIES HIS OWN AGE.

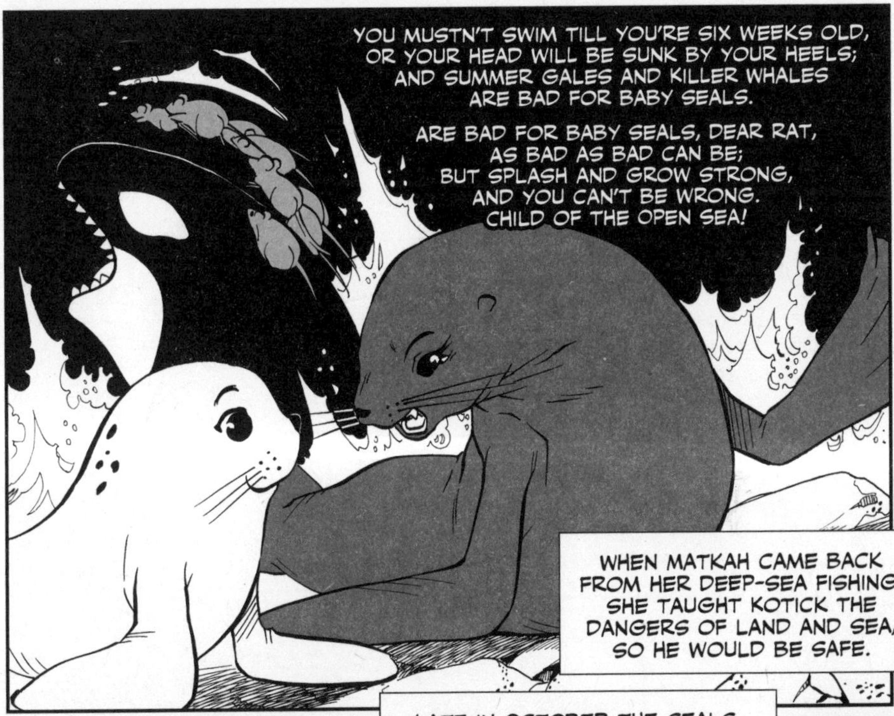
YOU MUSTN'T SWIM TILL YOU'RE SIX WEEKS OLD, OR YOUR HEAD WILL BE SUNK BY YOUR HEELS; AND SUMMER GALES AND KILLER WHALES ARE BAD FOR BABY SEALS.
ARE BAD FOR BABY SEALS, DEAR RAT, AS BAD AS BAD CAN BE; BUT SPLASH AND GROW STRONG, AND YOU CAN'T BE WRONG. CHILD OF THE OPEN SEA!
WHEN MATKAH CAME BACK FROM HER DEEP-SEA FISHING, SHE TAUGHT KOTICK THE DANGERS OF LAND AND SEA, SO HE WOULD BE SAFE.

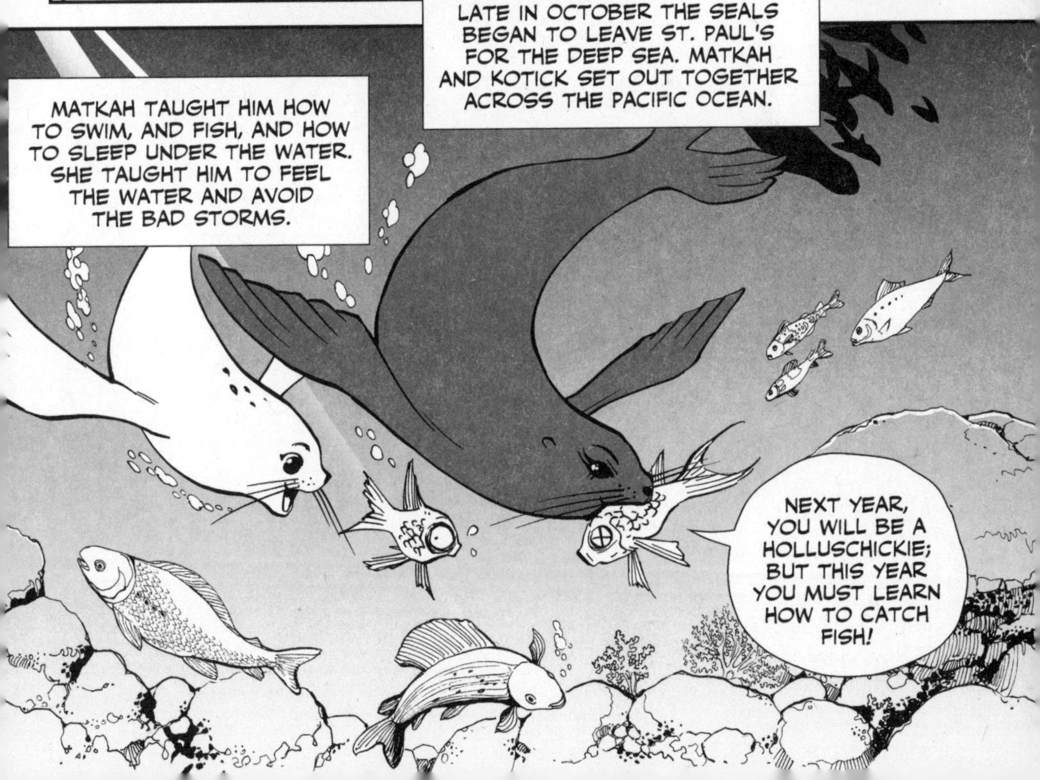
LATE IN OCTOBER THE SEALS BEGAN TO LEAVE ST. PAUL'S FOR THE DEEP SEA. MATKAH AND KOTICK SET OUT TOGETHER ACROSS THE PACIFIC OCEAN.
MATKAH TAUGHT HIM HOW TO SWIM, AND FISH, AND HOW TO SLEEP UNDER THE WATER. SHE TAUGHT HIM TO FEEL THE WATER AND AVOID THE BAD STORMS.
NEXT YEAR, YOU WILL BE A HOLLUSCHICKIE; BUT THIS YEAR YOU MUST LEARN HOW TO CATCH FISH!

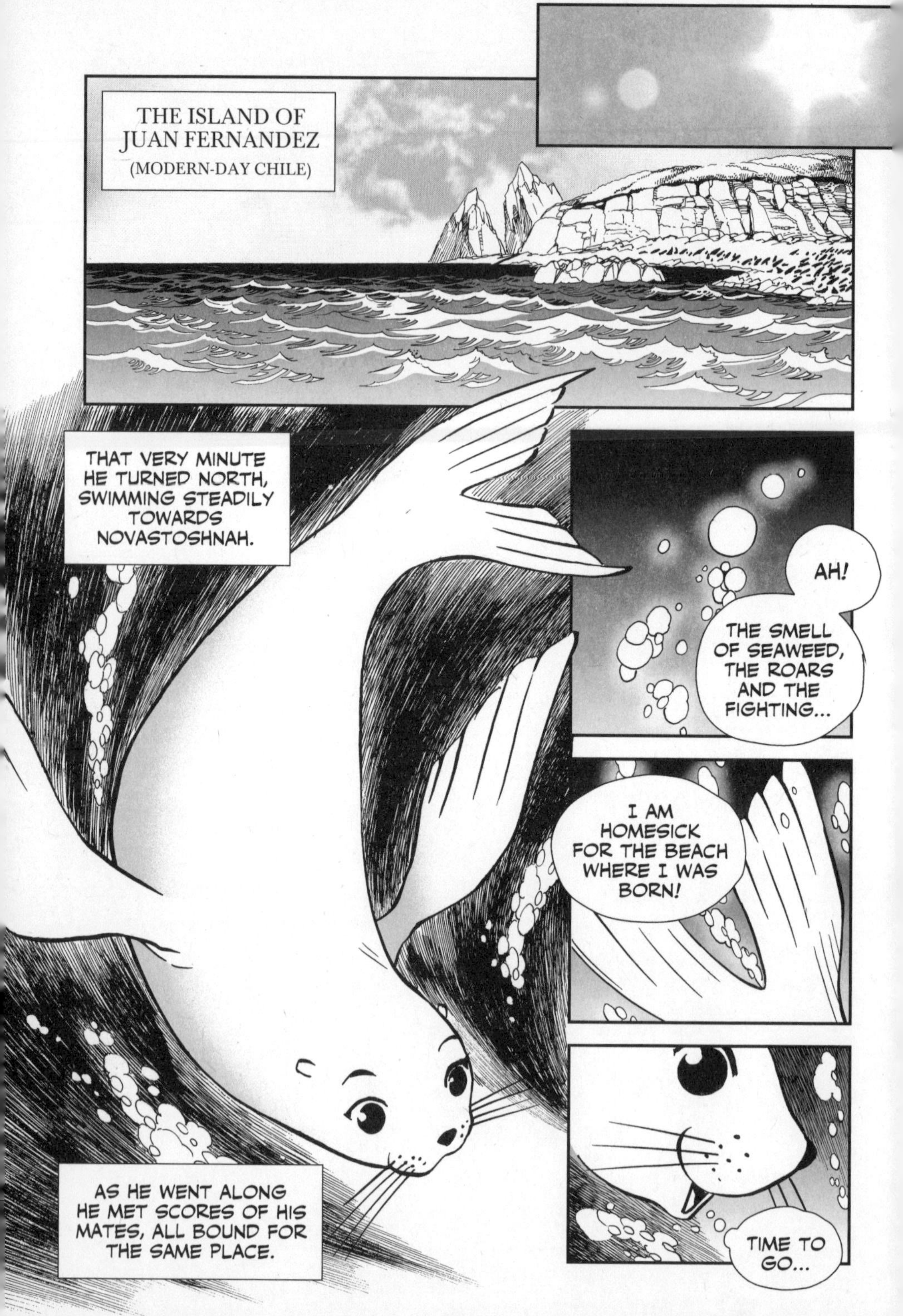
THE ISLAND OF JUAN FERNANDEZ (MODERN-DAY CHILE)
AH!
THE SMELL OF SEAWEED, THE ROARS AND THE FIGHTING...
I AM HOMESICK FOR THE BEACH WHERE I WAS BORN!
TIME TO GO...
THAT VERY MINUTE HE TURNED NORTH, SWIMMING STEADILY TOWARDS NOVASTOSHNAH.
AS HE WENT ALONG HE MET SCORES OF HIS MATES, ALL BOUND FOR THE SAME PLACE.

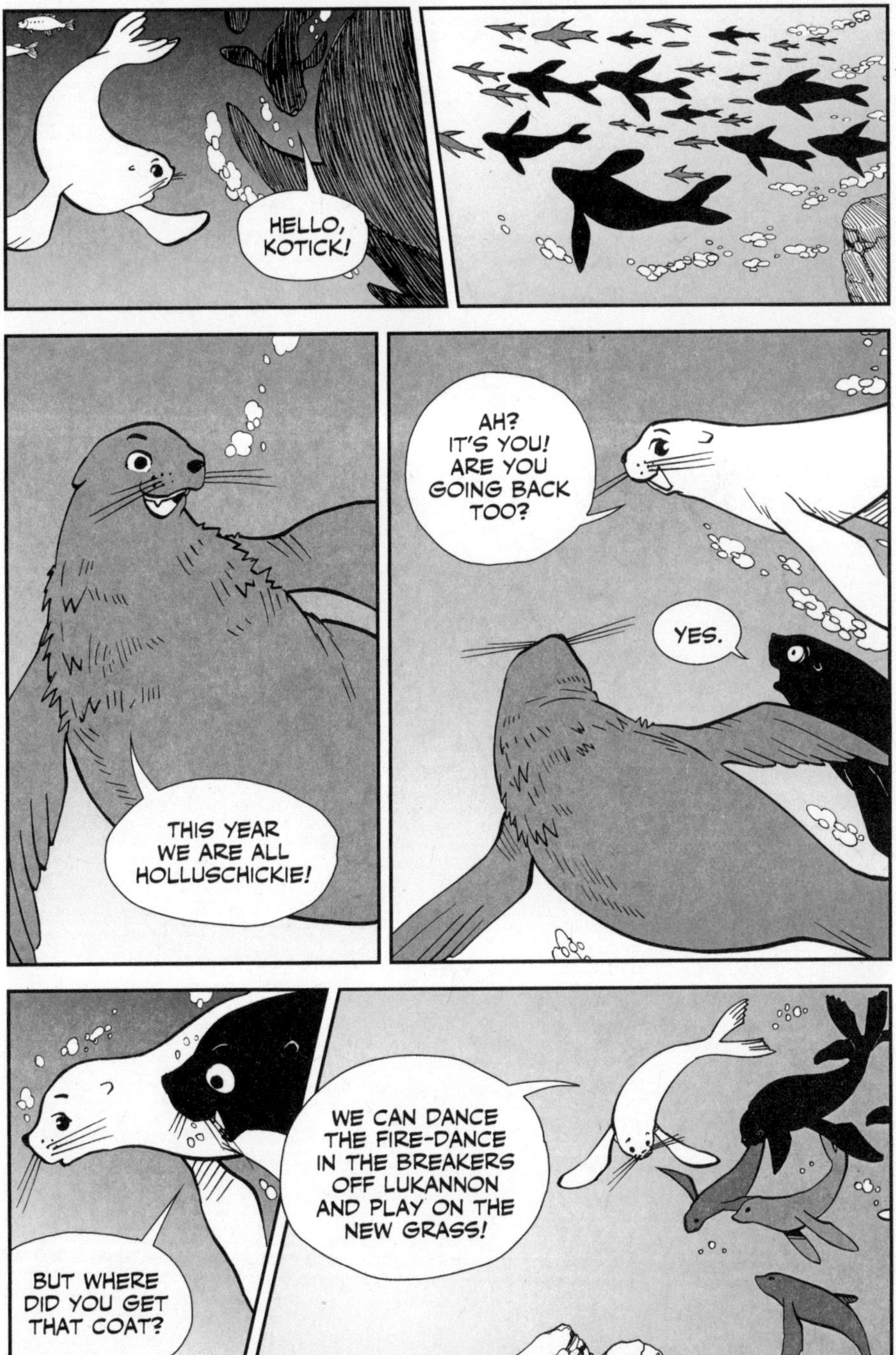
HELLO, KOTICK!
AH? IT'S YOU! ARE YOU GOING BACK TOO?
YES.
THIS YEAR WE ARE ALL HOLLUSCHICKIE!
WE CAN DANCE THE FIRE-DANCE IN THE BREAKERS OFF LUKANNON AND PLAY ON THE NEW GRASS!
BUT WHERE DID YOU GET THAT COAT?

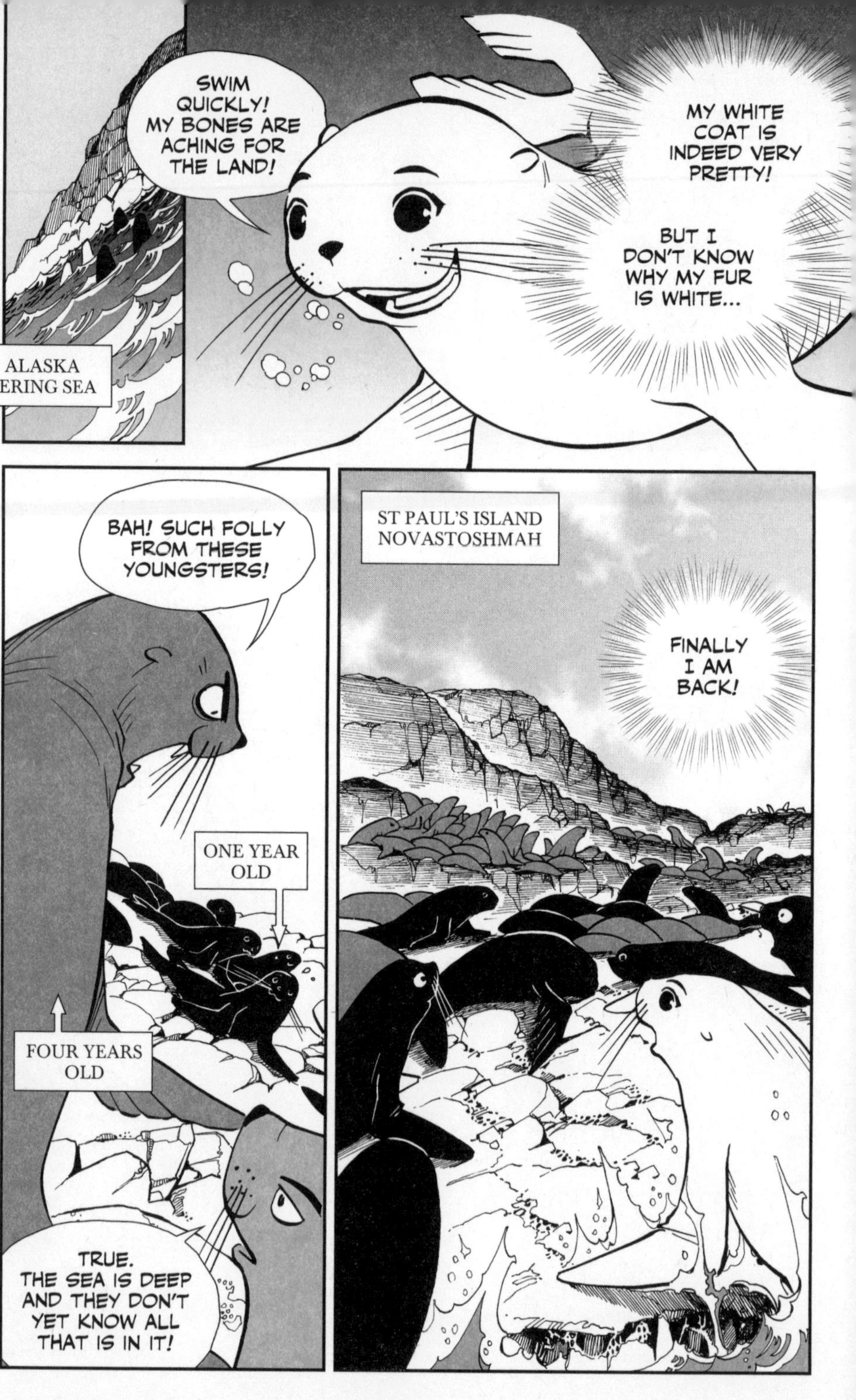

MY WHITE COAT IS INDEED VERY PRETTY!
BUT I DON'T KNOW WHY MY FUR IS WHITE...
SWIM QUICKLY! MY BONES ARE ACHING FOR THE LAND!
ALASKA BERING SEA
ST PAUL'S ISLAND NOVASTOSHMAH
FINALLY I AM BACK!
BAH! SUCH FOLLY FROM THESE YOUNGSTERS!
ONE YEAR OLD
FOUR YEARS OLD
TRUE. THE SEA IS DEEP AND THEY DON'T YET KNOW ALL THAT IS IN IT!

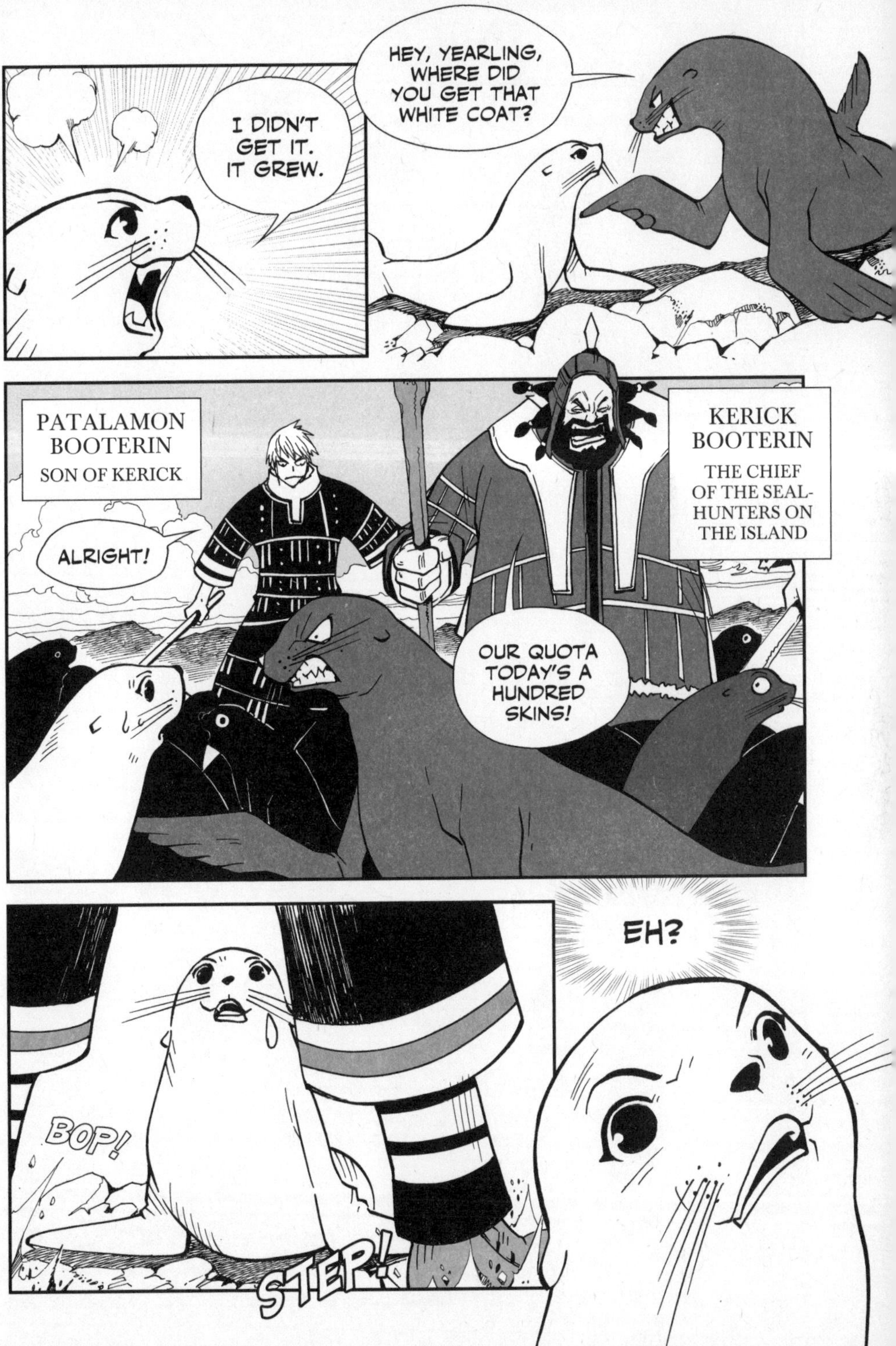

HEY, YEARLING, WHERE DID YOU GET THAT WHITE COAT?
I DIDN'T GET IT. IT GREW.
KERICK BOOTERIN
THE CHIEF OF THE SEAL-HUNTERS ON THE ISLAND
PATALAMON BOOTERIN
SON OF KERICK
OUR QUOTA TODAY'S A HUNDRED SKINS!
ALRIGHT!
EH?
BOP!
STEP!

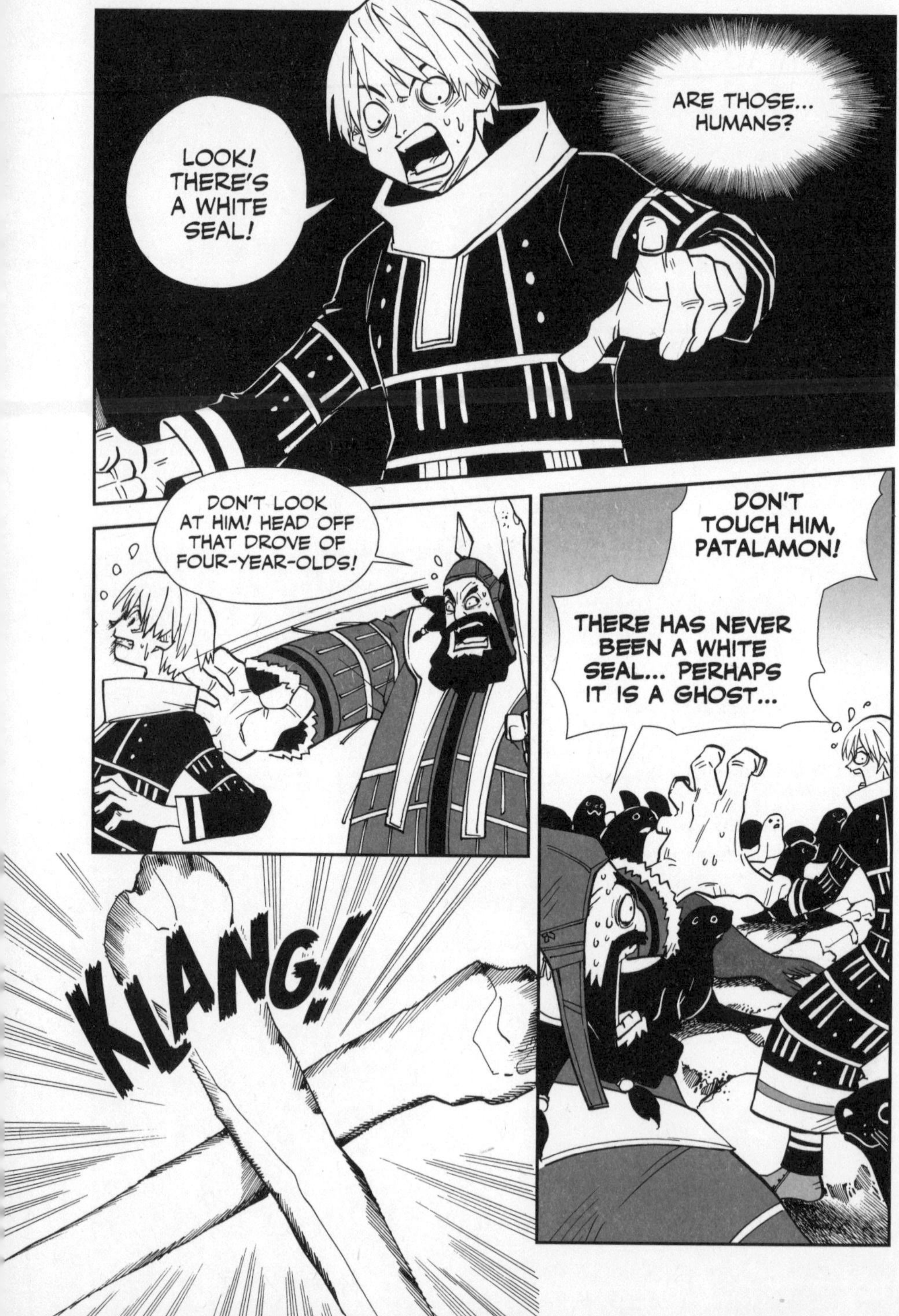
ARE THOSE... HUMANS?
LOOK! THERE'S A WHITE SEAL!
DON'T TOUCH HIM, PATALAMON!
THERE HAS NEVER BEEN A WHITE SEAL... PERHAPS IT IS A GHOST...
DON'T LOOK AT HIM! HEAD OFF THAT DROVE OF FOUR-YEAR-OLDS!
KLANG!

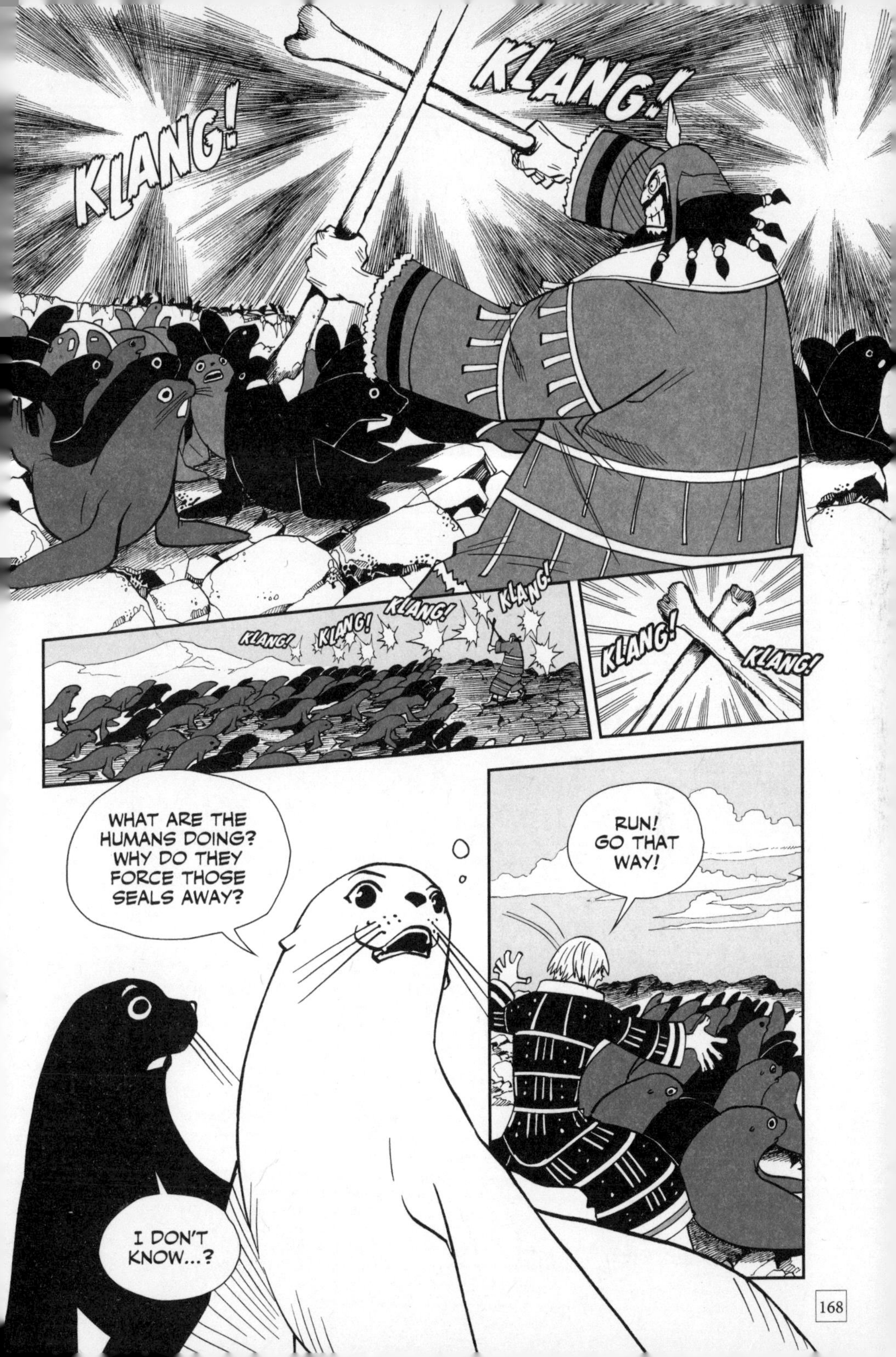
KLANG!
KLANG!
KLANG!
KLANG!
KLANG!
KLANG!
KLANG!
KLANG!
RUN! GO THAT WAY!
WHAT ARE THE HUMANS DOING? WHY DO THEY FORCE THOSE SEALS AWAY?
I DON'T KNOW...?

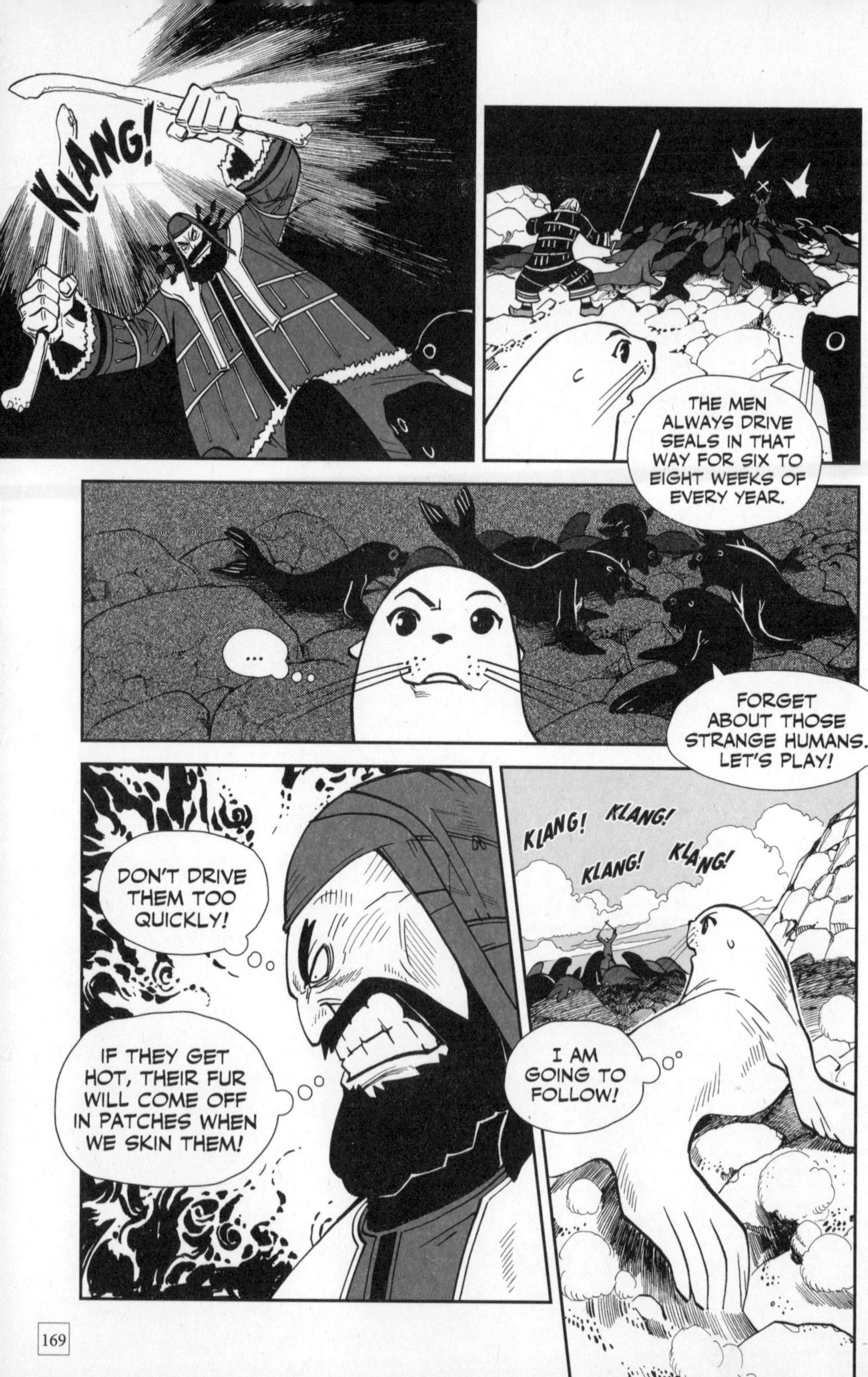
THE MEN ALWAYS DRIVE SEALS IN THAT WAY FOR SIX TO EIGHT WEEKS OF EVERY YEAR.
KLANG!
...
FORGET ABOUT THOSE STRANGE HUMANS. LET'S PLAY!
KLANG! KLANG!
KLANG! KLANG!
I AM GOING TO FOLLOW!
DON'T DRIVE THEM TOO QUICKLY!
IF THEY GET HOT, THEIR FUR WILL COME OFF IN PATCHES WHEN WE SKIN THEM!

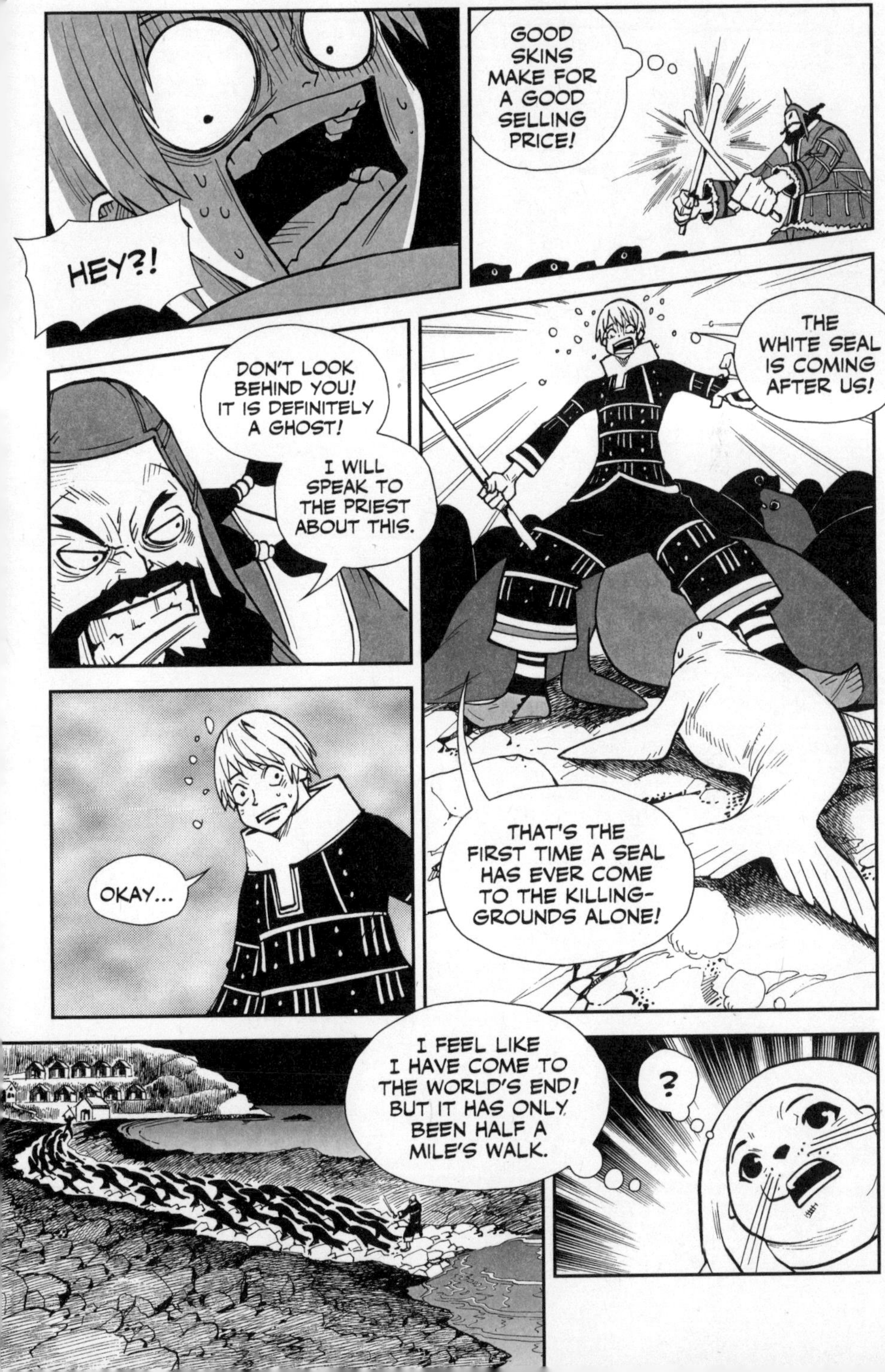
GOOD SKINS MAKE FOR A GOOD SELLING PRICE!
HEY?!
THE WHITE SEAL IS COMING AFTER US!
THAT'S THE FIRST TIME A SEAL HAS EVER COME TO THE KILLING-GROUNDS ALONE!
DON'T LOOK BEHIND YOU! IT IS DEFINITELY A GHOST!
I WILL SPEAK TO THE PRIEST ABOUT THIS.
OKAY...
?
I FEEL LIKE I HAVE COME TO THE WORLD'S END! BUT IT HAS ONLY BEEN HALF A MILE'S WALK.

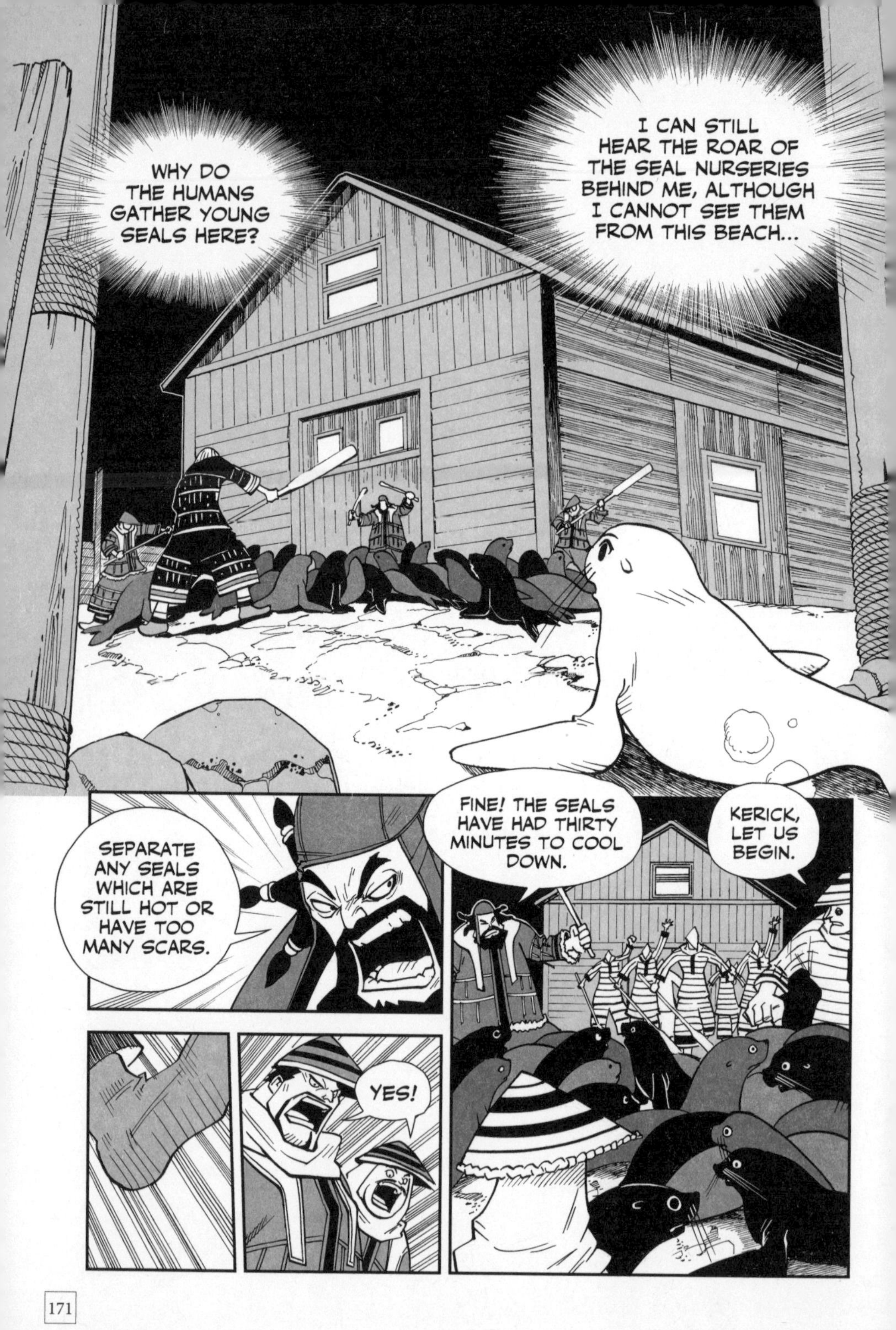
I CAN STILL HEAR THE ROAR OF THE SEAL NURSERIES BEHIND ME, ALTHOUGH I CANNOT SEE THEM FROM THIS BEACH...
WHY DO THE HUMANS GATHER YOUNG SEALS HERE?
KERICK, LET US BEGIN.
FINE! THE SEALS HAVE HAD THIRTY MINUTES TO COOL DOWN.
SEPARATE ANY SEALS WHICH ARE STILL HOT OR HAVE TOO MANY SCARS.
YES!

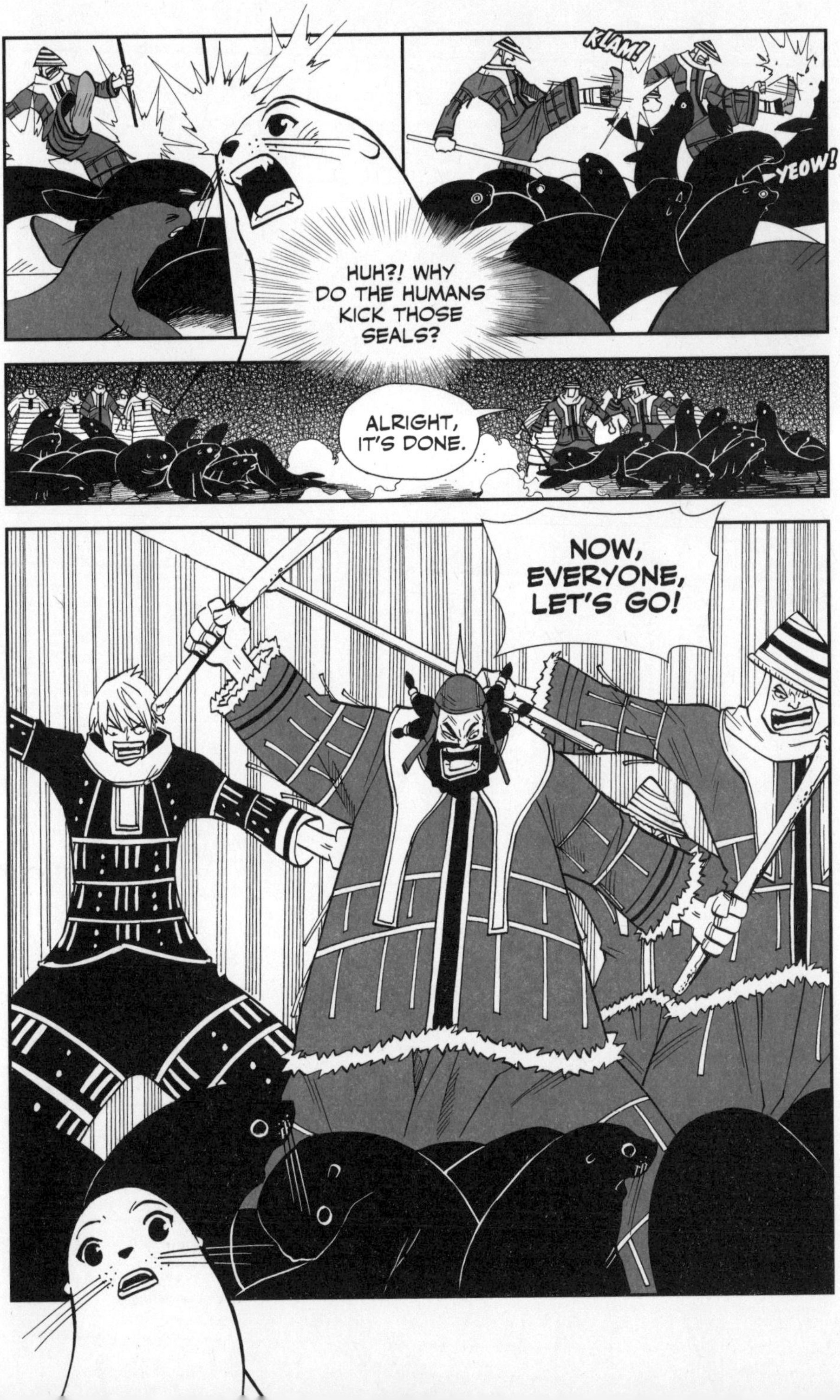
KLAM!
YEOW!
HUH?! WHY DO THE HUMANS KICK THOSE SEALS?
ALRIGHT, IT'S DONE.
NOW, EVERYONE, LET'S GO!

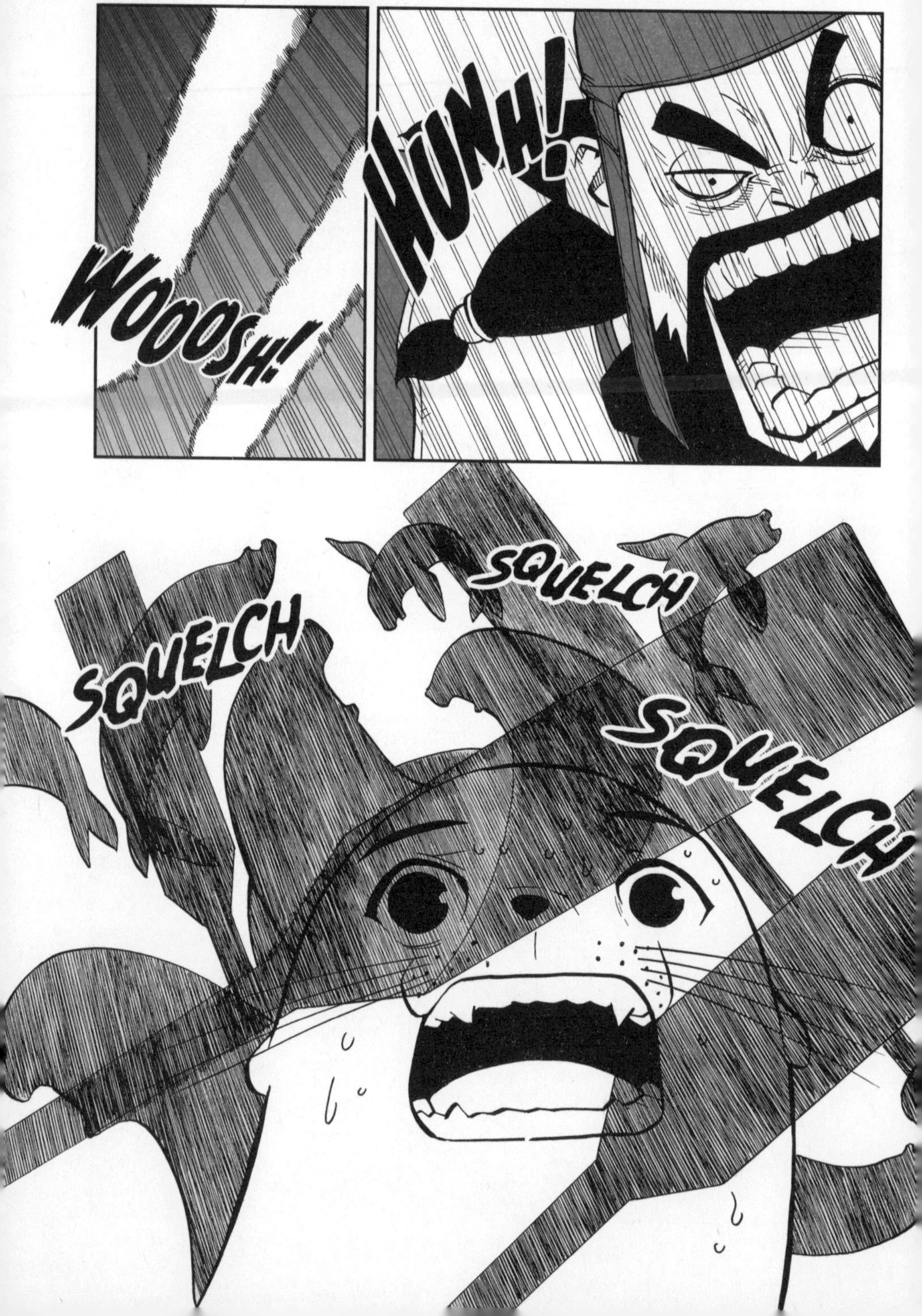
HUNH!
WOOOSH!
SQUELCH
SQUELCH
SQUELCH

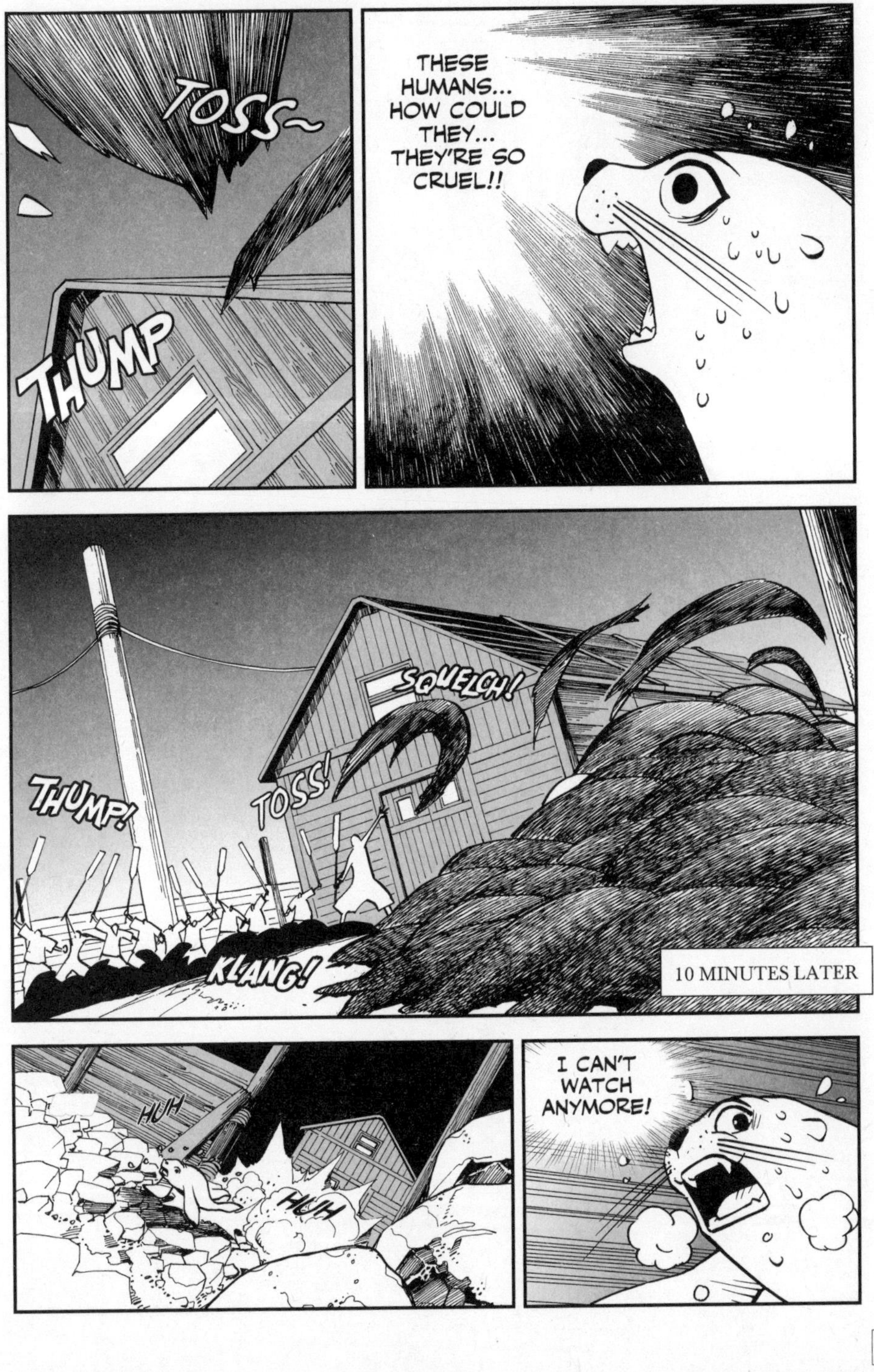
THESE HUMANS... HOW COULD THEY... THEY'RE SO CRUEL!!
TOSS~
THUMP
SQUELCH!
TOSS!
THUMP!
10 MINUTES LATER
KLANG!
I CAN'T WATCH ANYMORE!
HUH
HUH

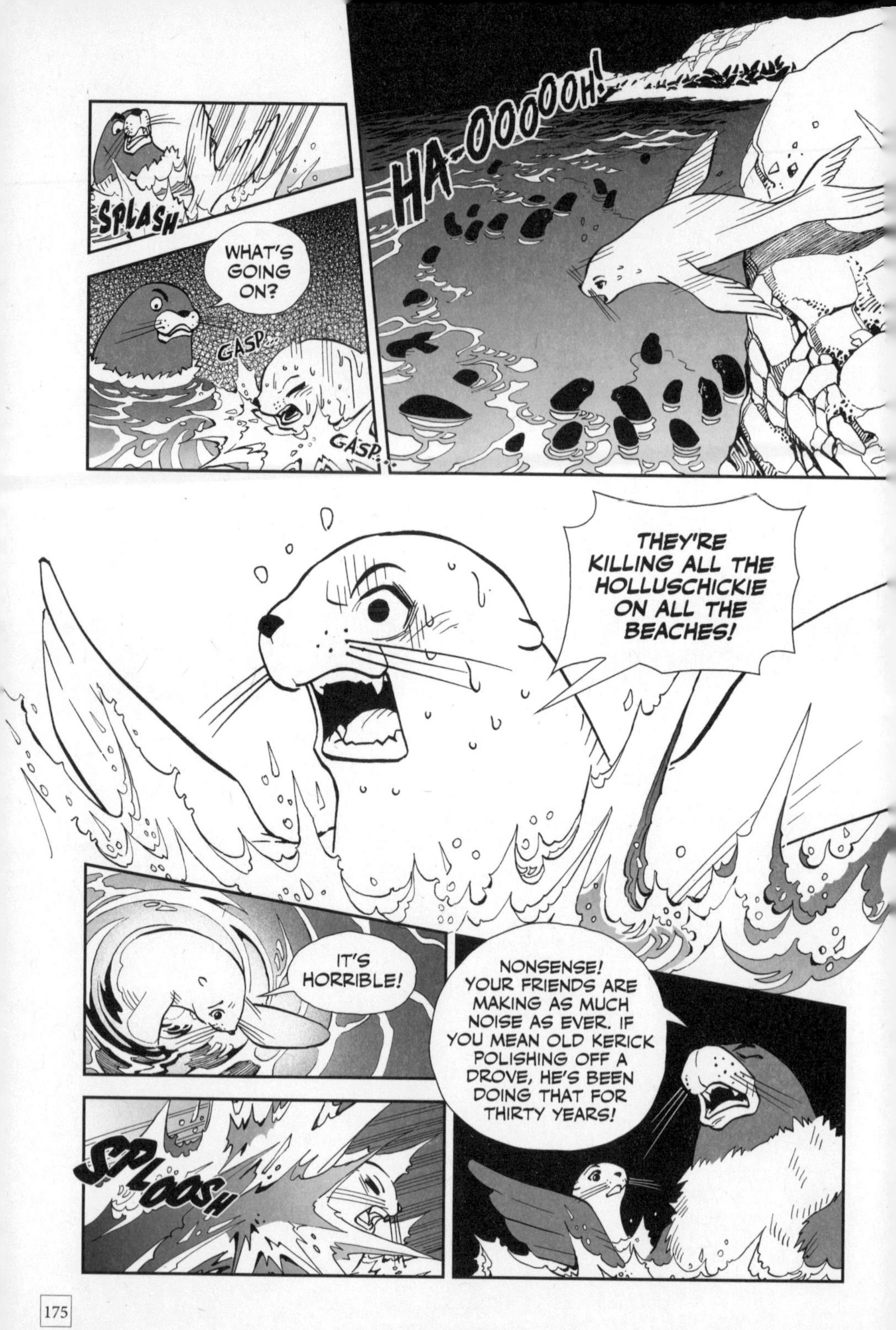
HA-OOOOOH!
SPLASH
WHAT'S GOING ON?
GASP...
GASP...
THEY'RE KILLING ALL THE HOLLUSCHICKIE ON ALL THE BEACHES!
NONSENSE! YOUR FRIENDS ARE MAKING AS MUCH NOISE AS EVER. IF YOU MEAN OLD KERICK POLISHING OFF A DROVE, HE'S BEEN DOING THAT FOR THIRTY YEARS!
IT'S HORRIBLE!
SPLOOSH

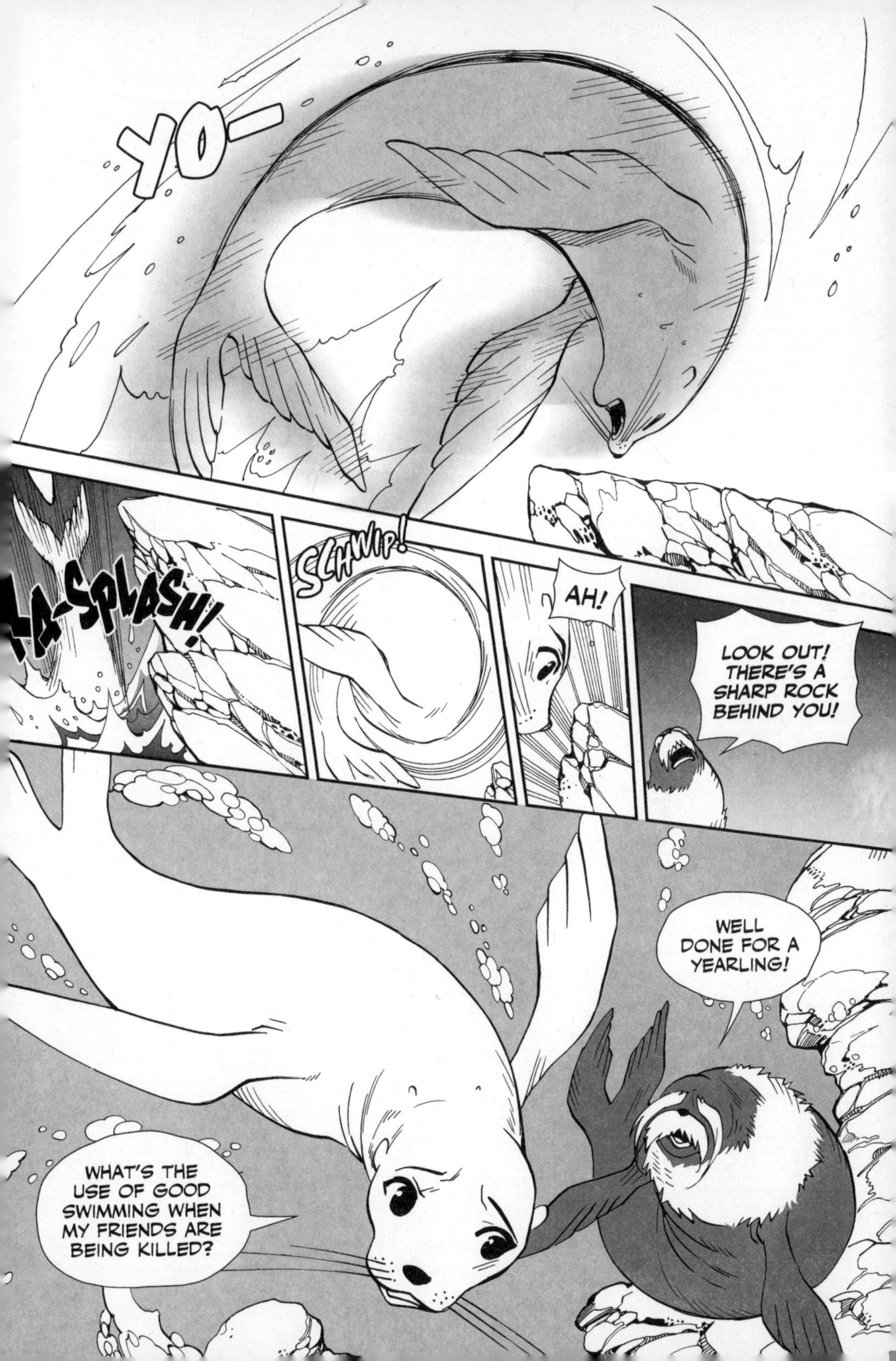
YO-
LOOK OUT! THERE'S A SHARP ROCK BEHIND YOU!
AH!
SCHWIP!
SPLASH!
WELL DONE FOR A YEARLING!
WHAT'S THE USE OF GOOD SWIMMING WHEN MY FRIENDS ARE BEING KILLED?

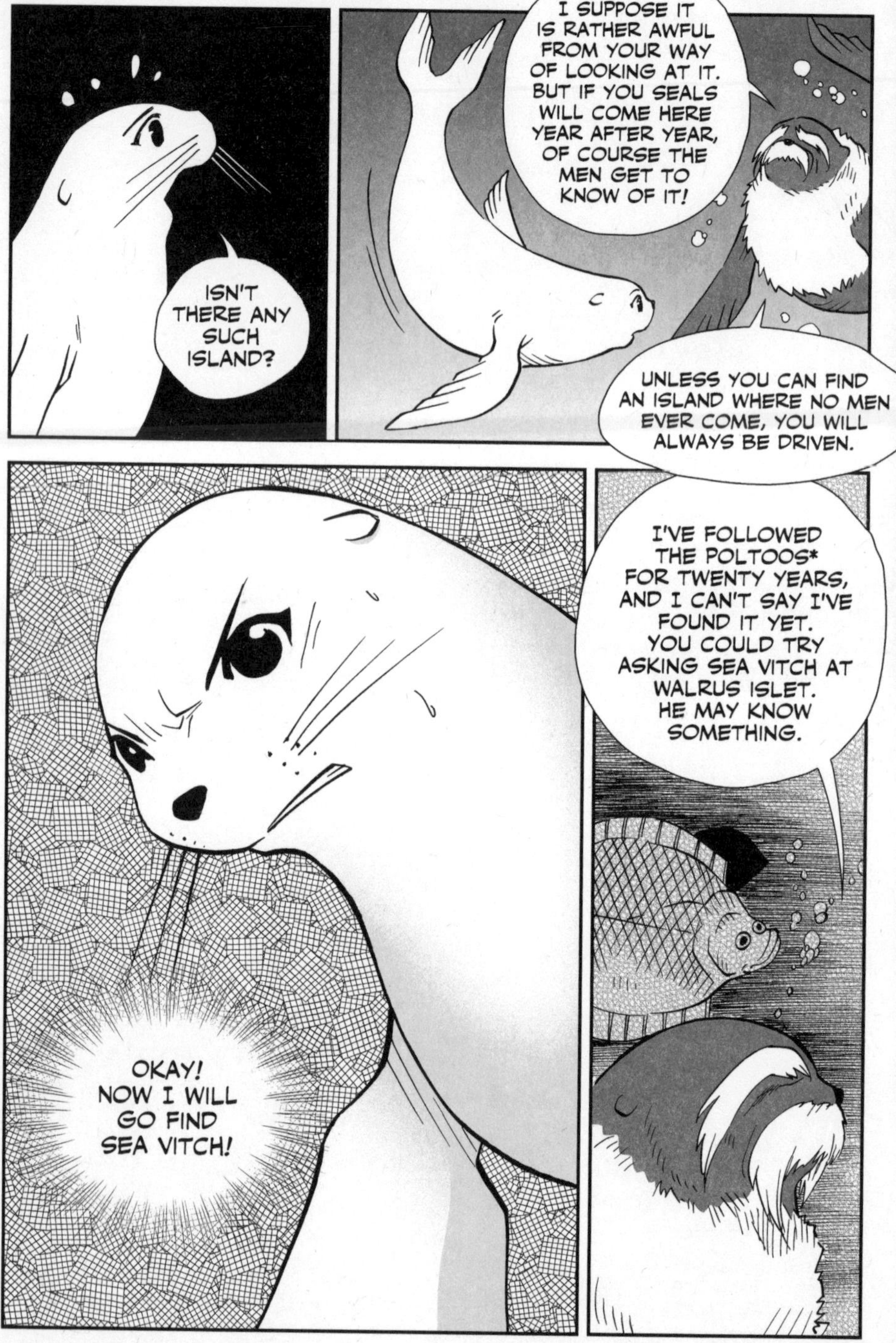
I SUPPOSE IT IS RATHER AWFUL FROM YOUR WAY OF LOOKING AT IT. BUT IF YOU SEALS WILL COME HERE YEAR AFTER YEAR, OF COURSE THE MEN GET TO KNOW OF IT!
UNLESS YOU CAN FIND AN ISLAND WHERE NO MEN EVER COME, YOU WILL ALWAYS BE DRIVEN.
ISN'T THERE ANY SUCH ISLAND?
I'VE FOLLOWED THE POLTOOS* FOR TWENTY YEARS, AND I CAN'T SAY I'VE FOUND IT YET. YOU COULD TRY ASKING SEA VITCH AT WALRUS ISLET. HE MAY KNOW SOMETHING.
OKAY! NOW I WILL GO FIND SEA VITCH!

*NOTE: POLTOOS - HALIBUT

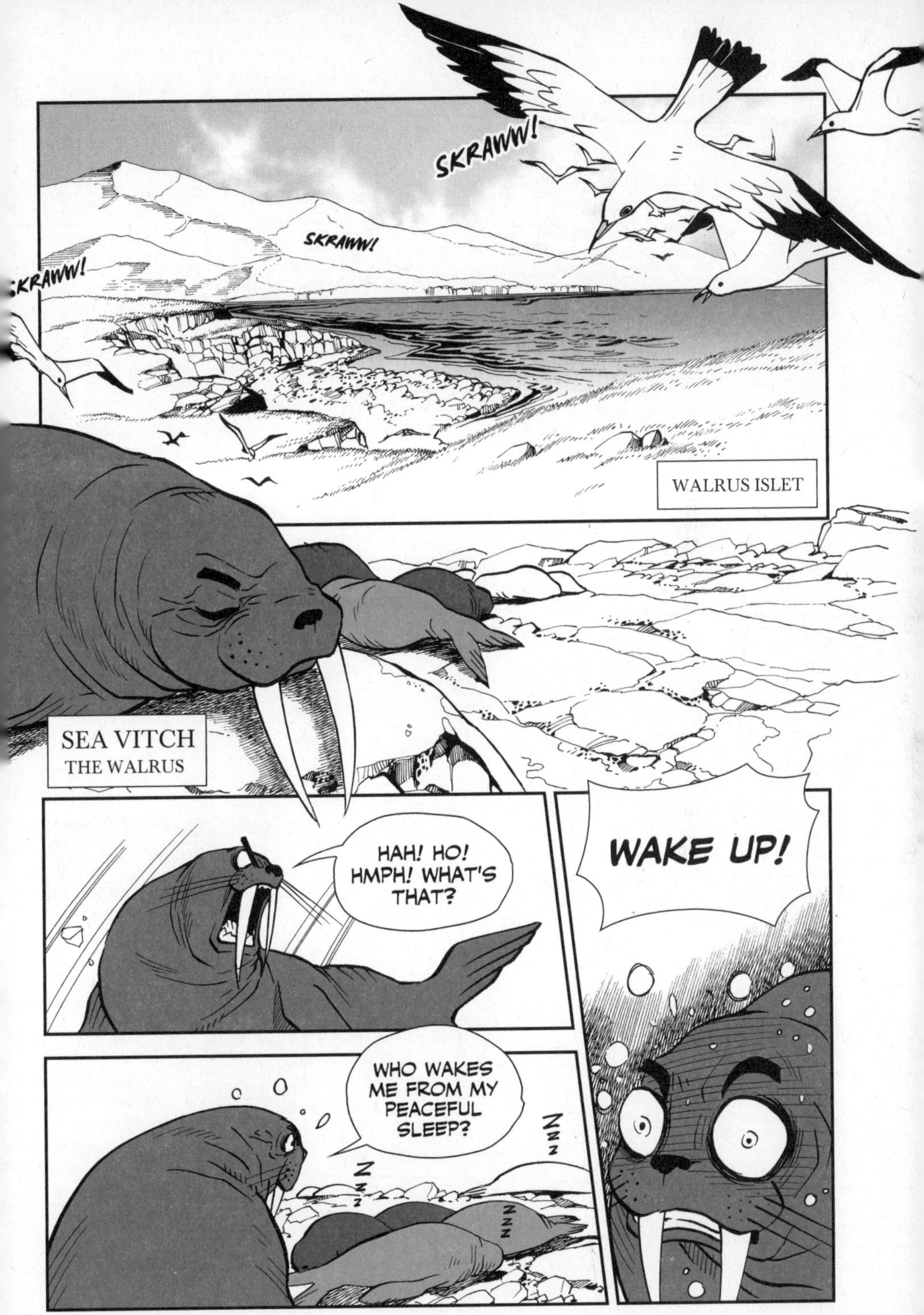

SKRAWW!
SKRAWW!
SKRAWW!
WALRUS ISLET
SEA VITCH THE WALRUS
WAKE UP!
HAH! HO! HMPH! WHAT'S THAT?
WHO WAKES ME FROM MY PEACEFUL SLEEP?
ZZZ
ZZZ
ZZZ

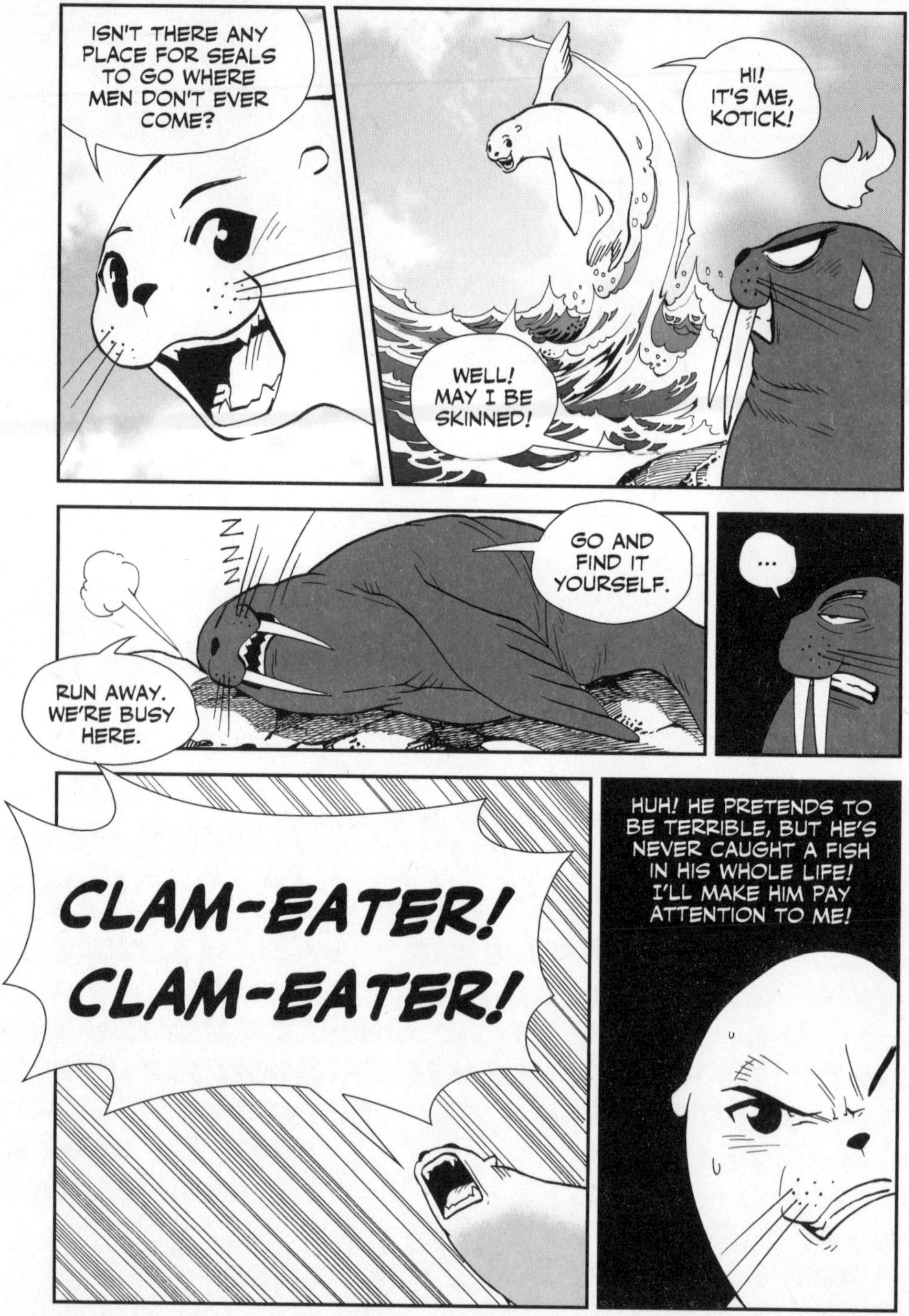
HI! IT'S ME, KOTICK!
WELL! MAY I BE SKINNED!
ISN'T THERE ANY PLACE FOR SEALS TO GO WHERE MEN DON'T EVER COME?
...
GO AND FIND IT YOURSELF.
RUN AWAY. WE'RE BUSY HERE.
ZZZ
HUH! HE PRETENDS TO BE TERRIBLE, BUT HE'S NEVER CAUGHT A FISH IN HIS WHOLE LIFE! I'LL MAKE HIM PAY ATTENTION TO ME!
CLAM-EATER! CLAM-EATER!

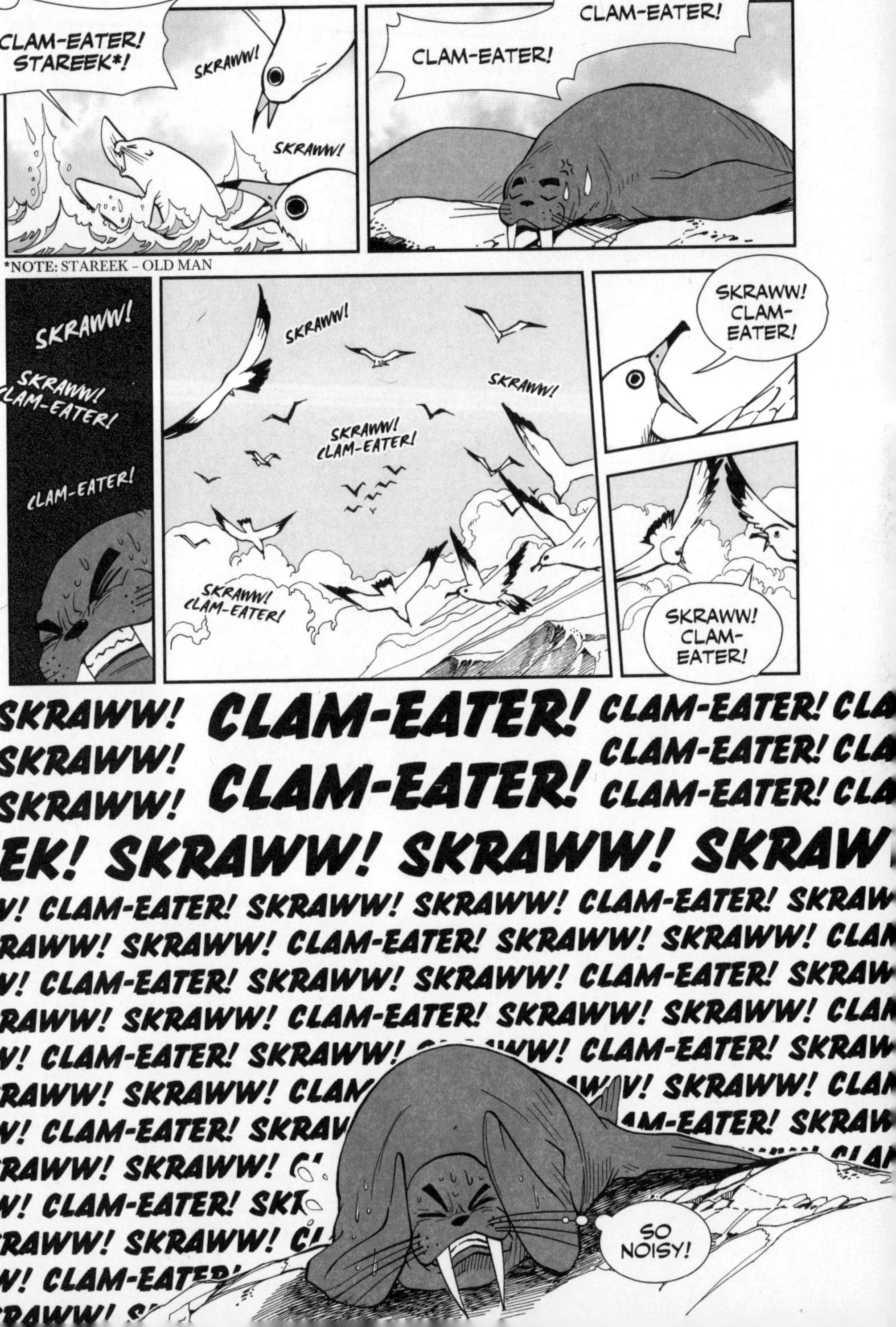
CLAM-EATER!
CLAM-EATER!
CLAM-EATER! STAREEK*!
SKRAWW!
SKRAWW!
SKRAWW! CLAM-EATER!
SKRAWW! CLAM-EATER!
SKRAWW!
SKRAWW!
SKRAWW! CLAM-EATER!
SKRAWW! CLAM-EATER!
SKRAWW!
SKRAWW! CLAM-EATER!
CLAM-EATER!
SKRAWW! CLAM-EATER! CLAM-EATER!
SKRAWW! CLAM-EATER!
SKRAWW! CLAM-EATER! CLAM-EATER!
SKRAWW! SKRAWW!
CLAM-EATER! SKRAWW! SKRAWW! CLAM-EATER!
SKRAWW! CLAM-EATER! SKRAWW! SKRAWW!
CLAM-EATER! SKRAWW! SKRAWW! CLAM-EATER!
SKRAWW! SKRAWW! CLAM-EATER! SKRAWW! SKRAWW!
CLAM-EATER! SKRAWW! CLAM-EATER!
SKRAWW! SKRAWW!
CLAM-EATER!
SKRAWW! SKRAWW!
CLAM-EATER!
SKRAWW! SKRAWW!
SO NOISY!
*NOTE: STAREEK – OLD MAN

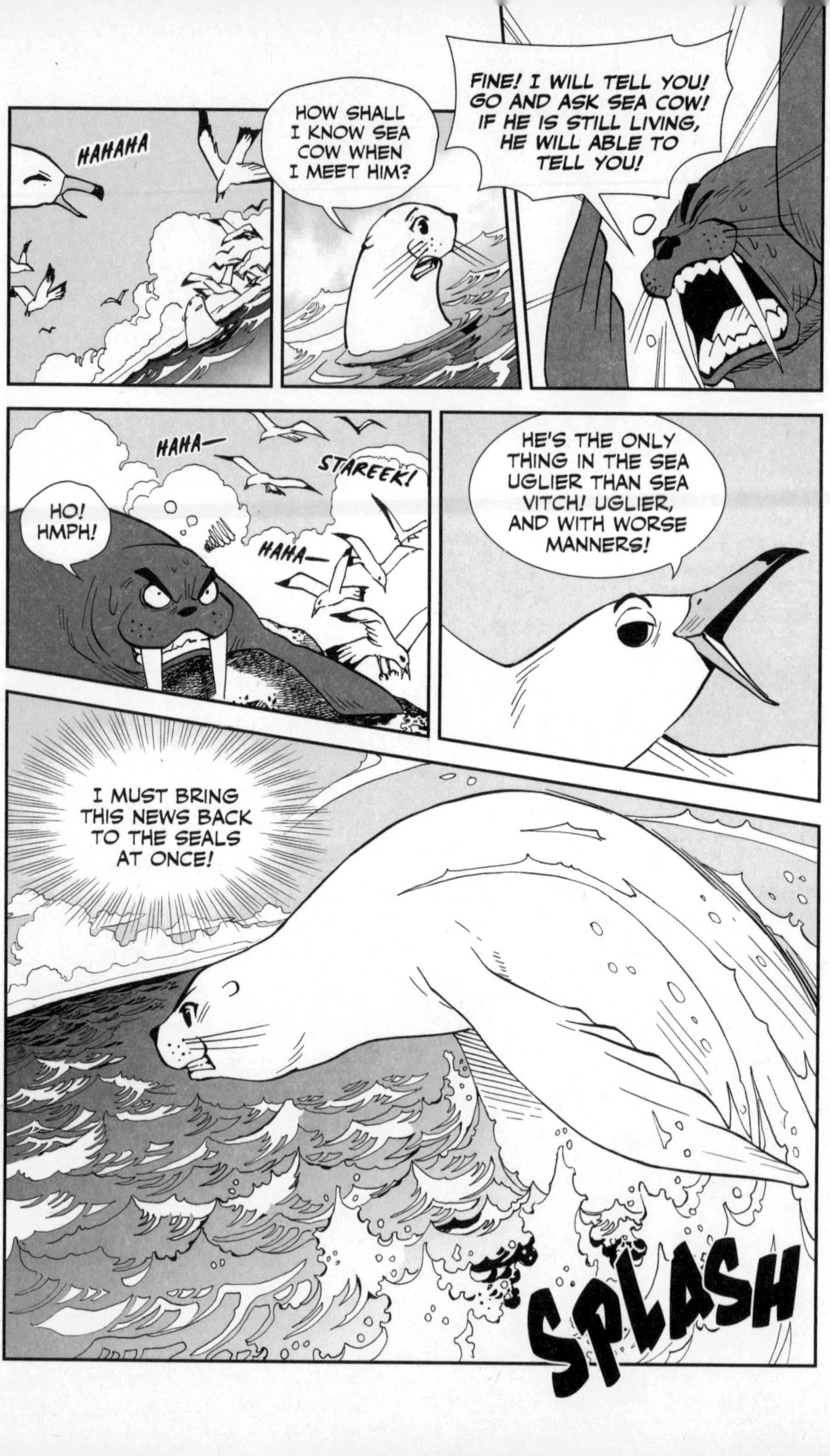
FINE! I WILL TELL YOU! GO AND ASK SEA COW! IF HE IS STILL LIVING, HE WILL ABLE TO TELL YOU!
HOW SHALL I KNOW SEA COW WHEN I MEET HIM?
HAHAHA
HE'S THE ONLY THING IN THE SEA UGLIER THAN SEA VITCH! UGLIER, AND WITH WORSE MANNERS!
STAREEK!
HAHA—
HAHA—
HO! HMPH!
I MUST BRING THIS NEWS BACK TO THE SEALS AT ONCE!
SPLASH

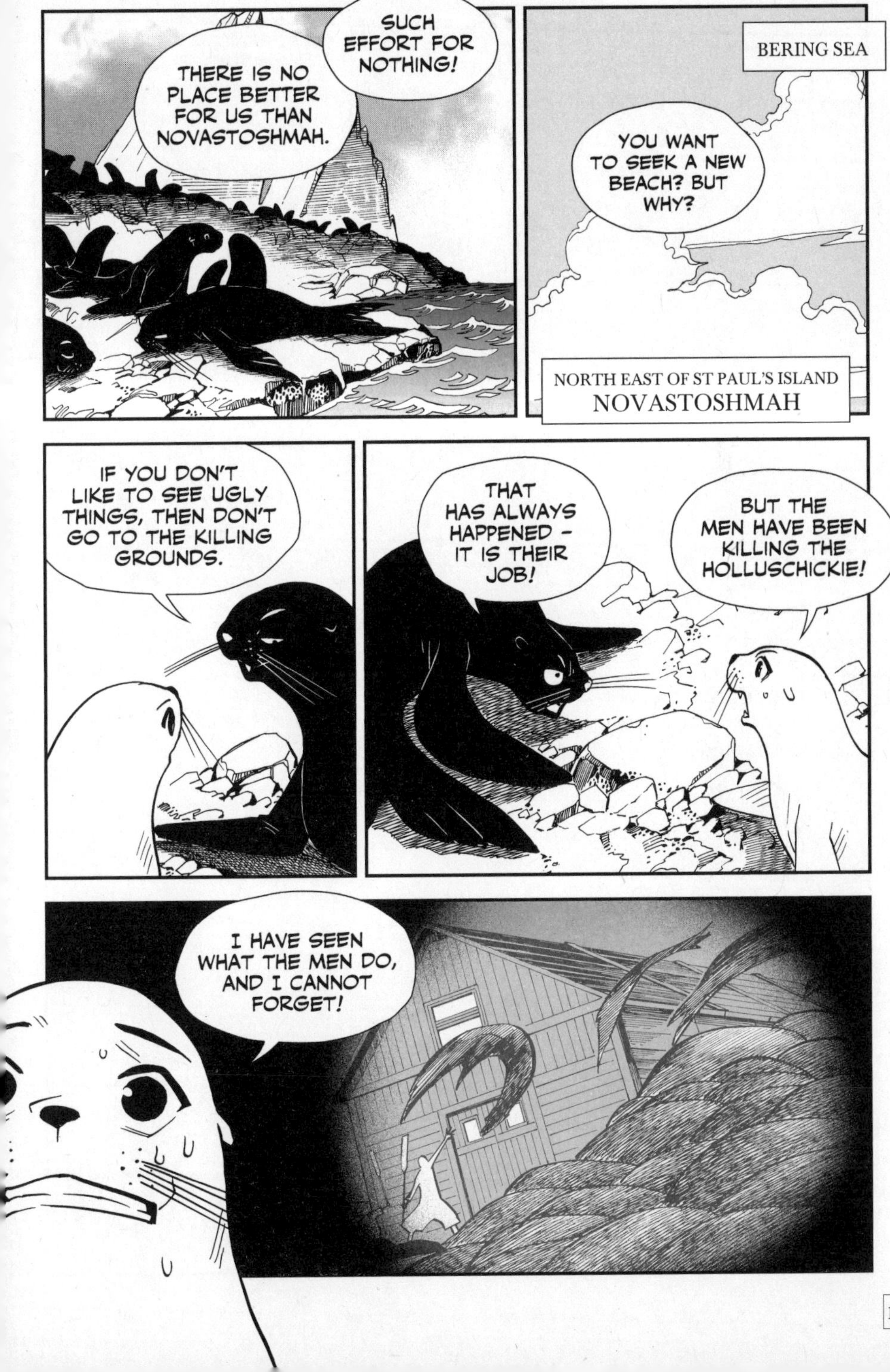
BERING SEA
YOU WANT TO SEEK A NEW BEACH? BUT WHY?
NORTH EAST OF ST PAUL'S ISLAND
NOVASTOSHMAH
SUCH EFFORT FOR NOTHING!
THERE IS NO PLACE BETTER FOR US THAN NOVASTOSHMAH.
BUT THE MEN HAVE BEEN KILLING THE HOLLUSCHICKIE!
THAT HAS ALWAYS HAPPENED - IT IS THEIR JOB!
IF YOU DON'T LIKE TO SEE UGLY THINGS, THEN DON'T GO TO THE KILLING GROUNDS.
I HAVE SEEN WHAT THE MEN DO, AND I CANNOT FORGET!

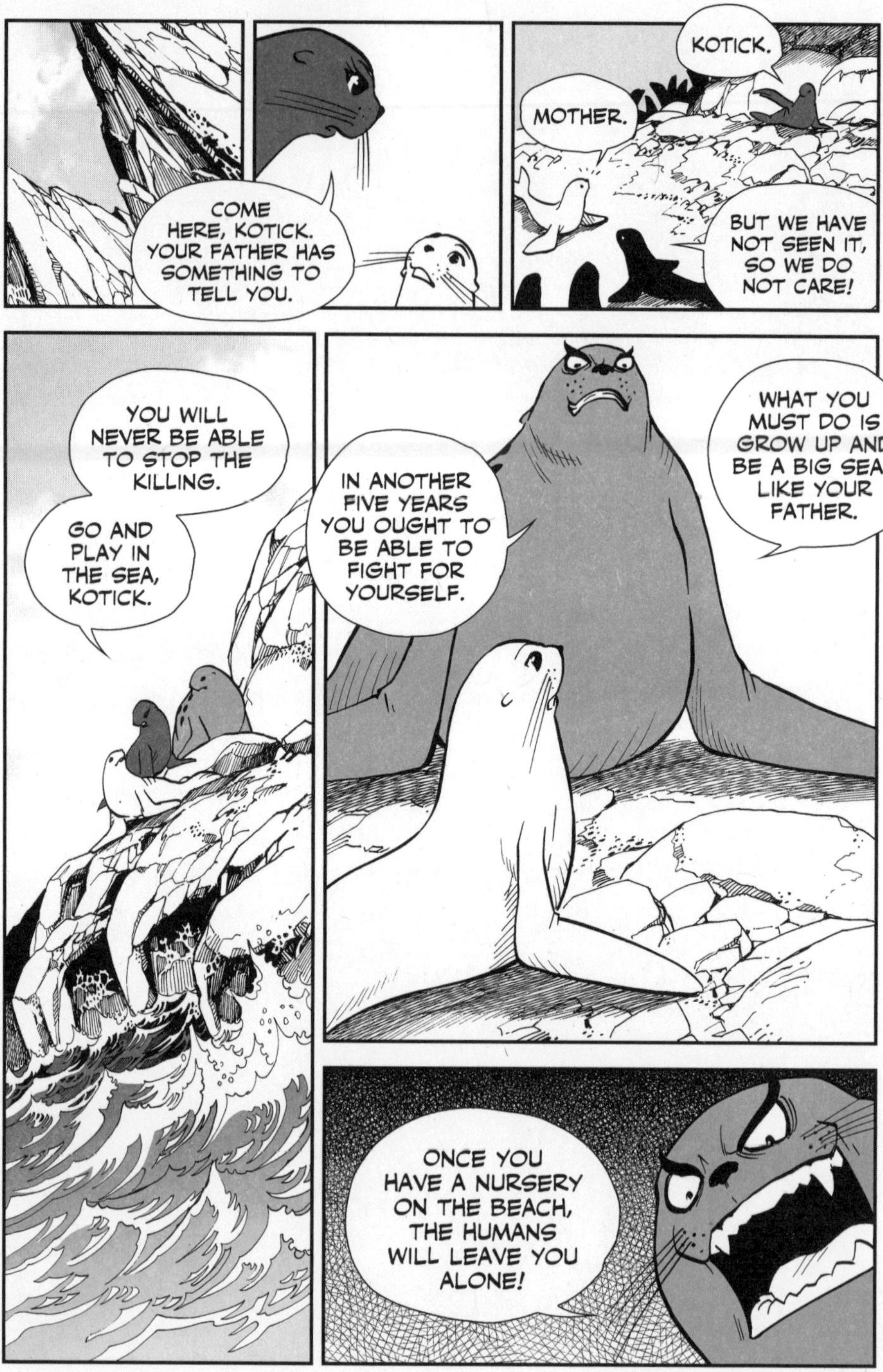

KOTICK.
MOTHER.
BUT WE HAVE NOT SEEN IT, SO WE DO NOT CARE!
COME HERE, KOTICK. YOUR FATHER HAS SOMETHING TO TELL YOU.
WHAT YOU MUST DO IS GROW UP AND BE A BIG SEAL LIKE YOUR FATHER.
IN ANOTHER FIVE YEARS YOU OUGHT TO BE ABLE TO FIGHT FOR YOURSELF.
ONCE YOU HAVE A NURSERY ON THE BEACH, THE HUMANS WILL LEAVE YOU ALONE!
YOU WILL NEVER BE ABLE TO STOP THE KILLING.
GO AND PLAY IN THE SEA, KOTICK.

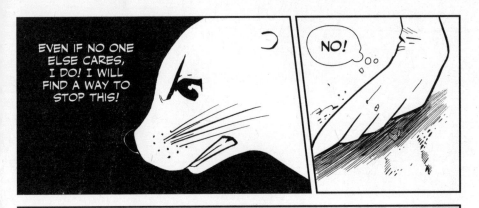

EVEN IF NO ONE ELSE CARES, I DO! I WILL FIND A WAY TO STOP THIS!

NO!

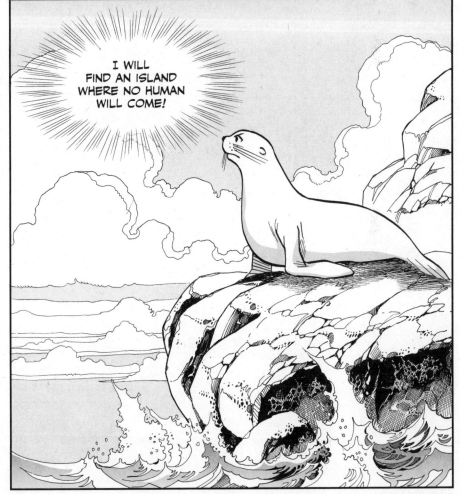

I WILL FIND AN ISLAND WHERE NO HUMAN WILL COME!

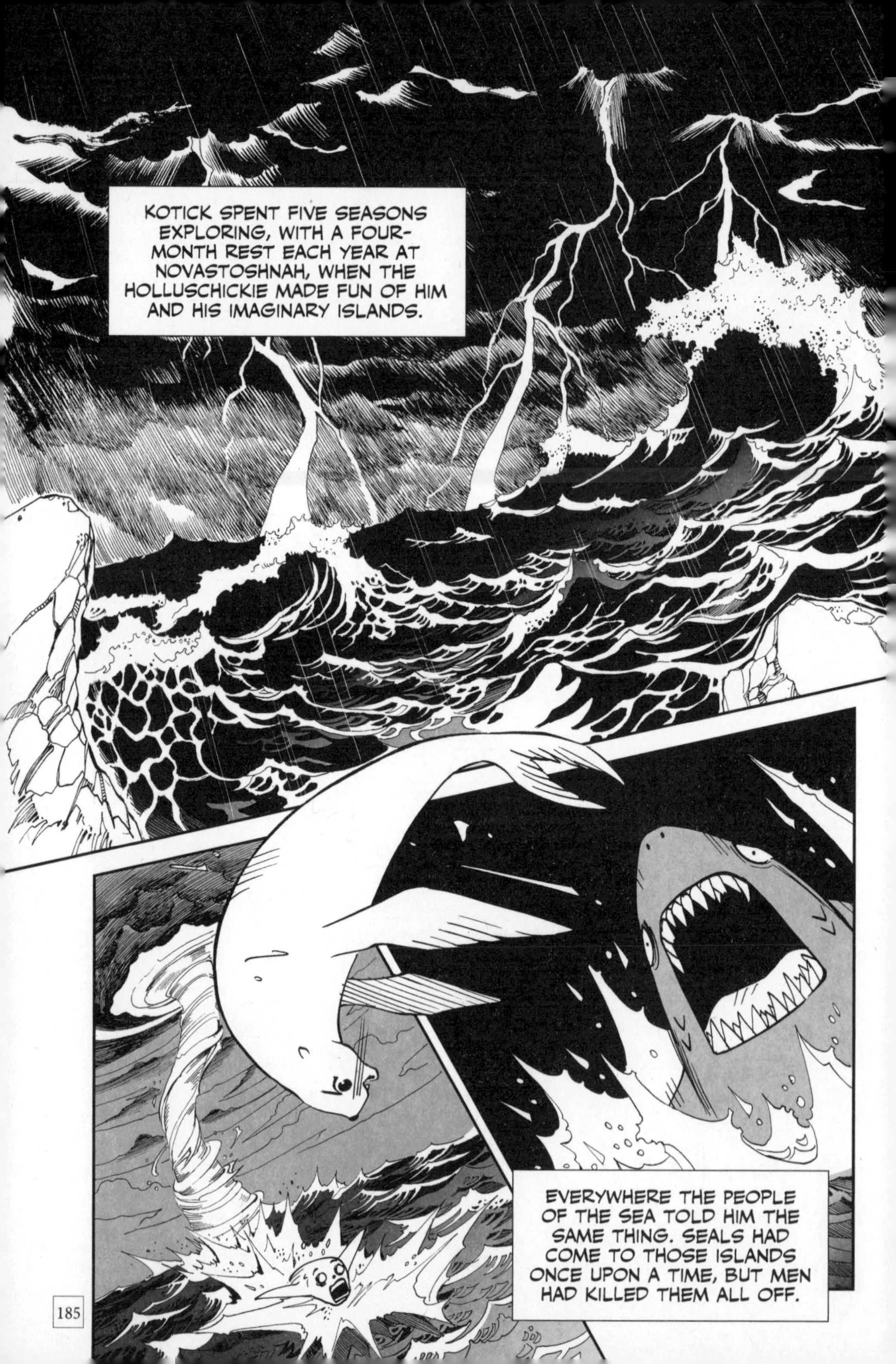
KOTICK SPENT FIVE SEASONS EXPLORING, WITH A FOUR-MONTH REST EACH YEAR AT NOVASTOSHNAH, WHEN THE HOLLUSCHICKIE MADE FUN OF HIM AND HIS IMAGINARY ISLANDS.
EVERYWHERE THE PEOPLE OF THE SEA TOLD HIM THE SAME THING. SEALS HAD COME TO THOSE ISLANDS ONCE UPON A TIME, BUT MEN HAD KILLED THEM ALL OFF.

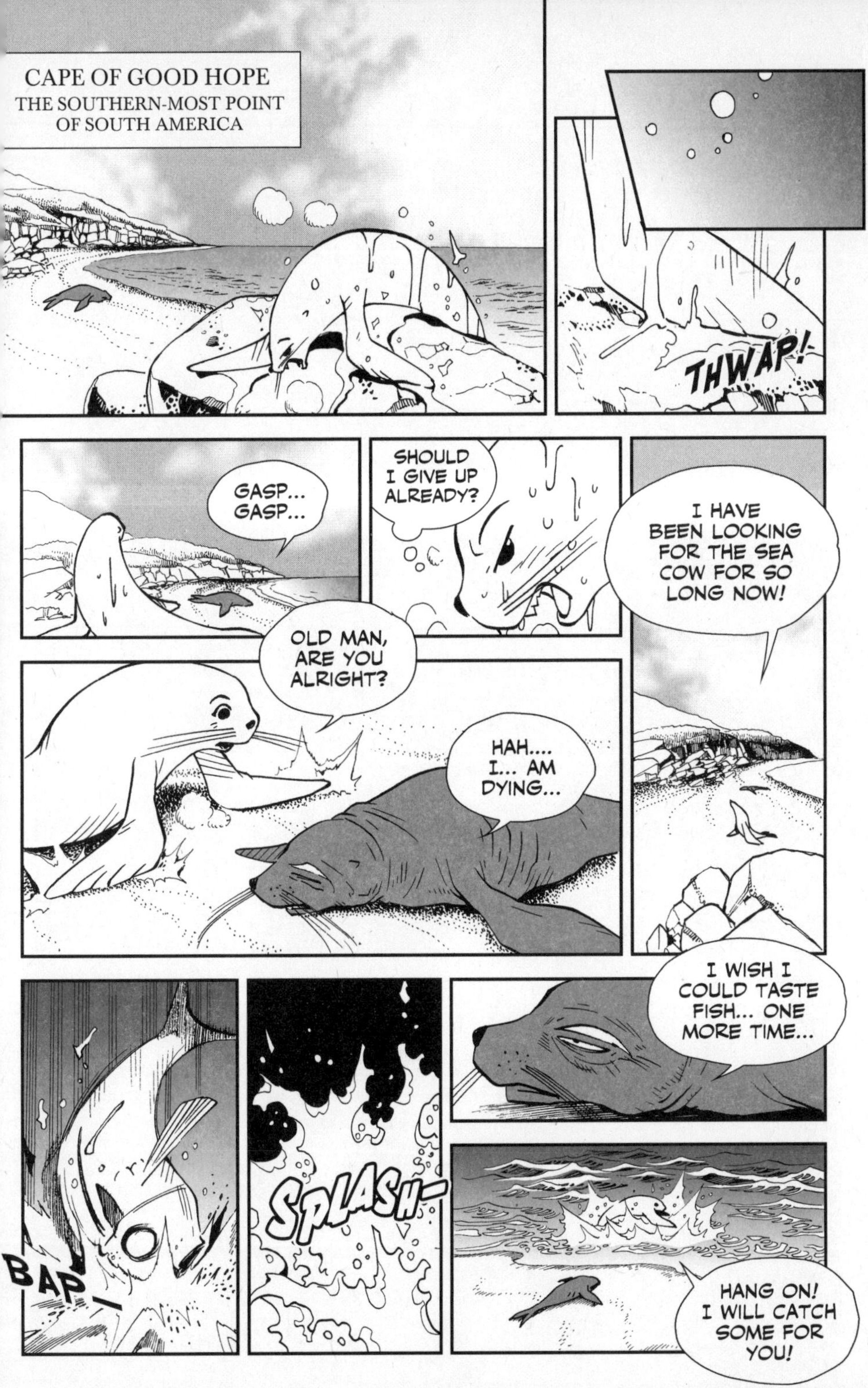
THWAP!
CAPE OF GOOD HOPE
THE SOUTHERN-MOST POINT
OF SOUTH AMERICA
I HAVE BEEN LOOKING FOR THE SEA COW FOR SO LONG NOW!
SHOULD I GIVE UP ALREADY?
GASP... GASP...
OLD MAN, ARE YOU ALRIGHT?
HAH.... I... AM DYING...
I WISH I COULD TASTE FISH... ONE MORE TIME...
HANG ON! I WILL CATCH SOME FOR YOU!
SPLASH-
BAP-

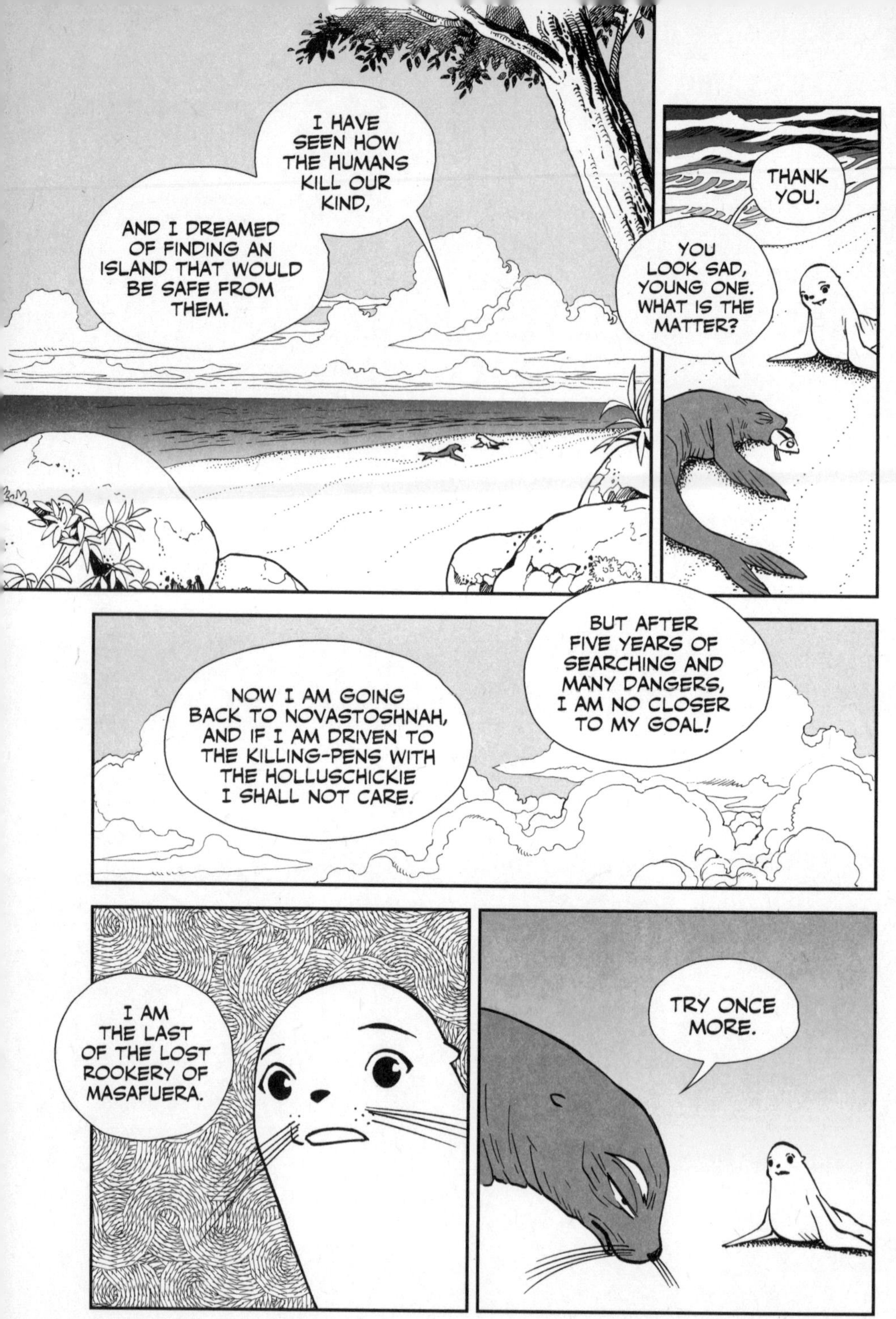
THANK YOU.
YOU LOOK SAD, YOUNG ONE. WHAT IS THE MATTER?
I HAVE SEEN HOW THE HUMANS KILL OUR KIND,
AND I DREAMED OF FINDING AN ISLAND THAT WOULD BE SAFE FROM THEM.
BUT AFTER FIVE YEARS OF SEARCHING AND MANY DANGERS, I AM NO CLOSER TO MY GOAL!
NOW I AM GOING BACK TO NOVASTOSHNAH, AND IF I AM DRIVEN TO THE KILLING-PENS WITH THE HOLLUSCHICKIE I SHALL NOT CARE.
TRY ONCE MORE.
I AM THE LAST OF THE LOST ROOKERY OF MASAFUERA.

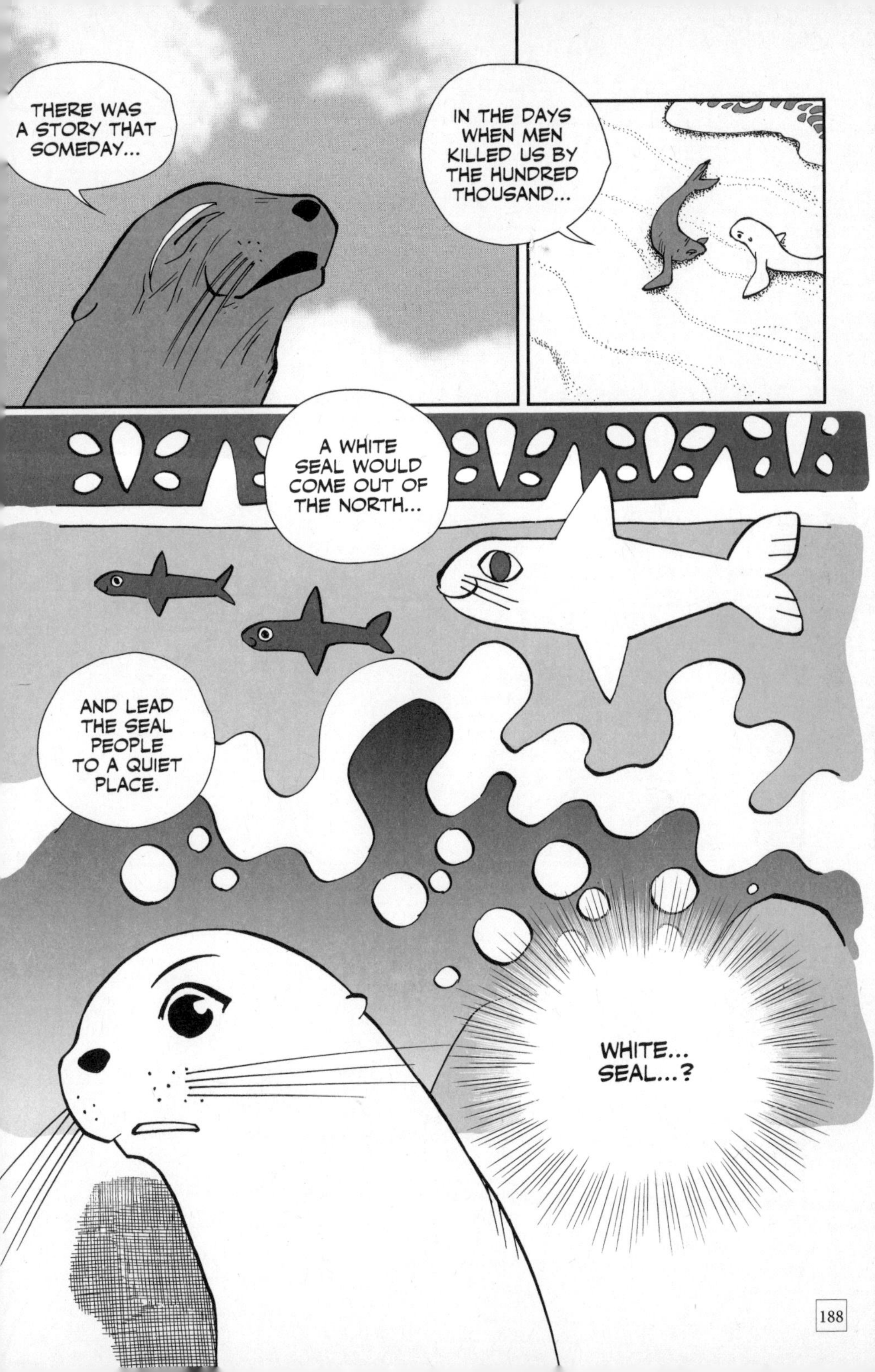

IN THE DAYS WHEN MEN KILLED US BY THE HUNDRED THOUSAND...
THERE WAS A STORY THAT SOMEDAY...
A WHITE SEAL WOULD COME OUT OF THE NORTH...
AND LEAD THE SEAL PEOPLE TO A QUIET PLACE.
WHITE... SEAL...?

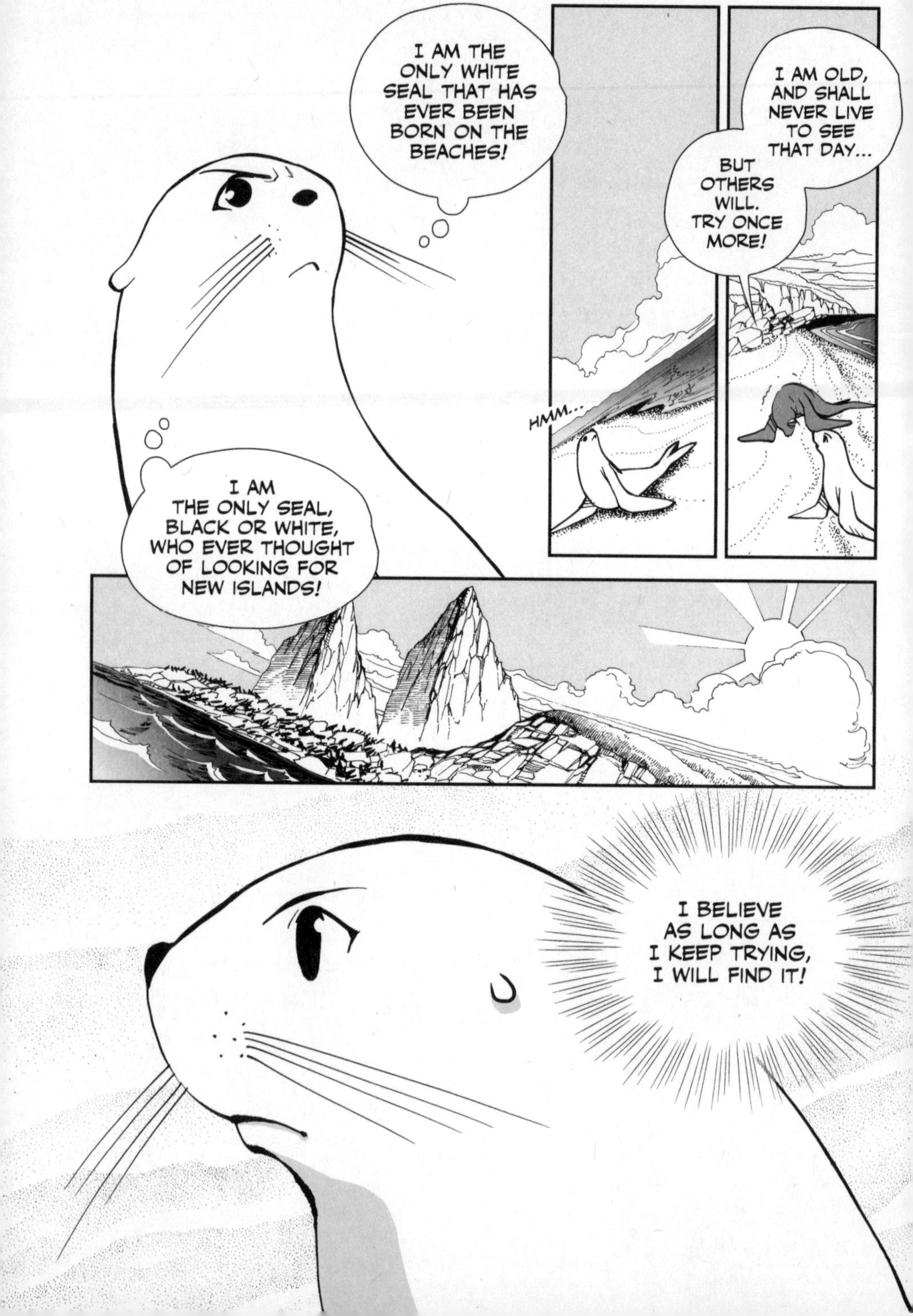
I AM OLD, AND SHALL NEVER LIVE TO SEE THAT DAY...
BUT OTHERS WILL. TRY ONCE MORE!
HMM...
I AM THE ONLY WHITE SEAL THAT HAS EVER BEEN BORN ON THE BEACHES!
I AM THE ONLY SEAL, BLACK OR WHITE, WHO EVER THOUGHT OF LOOKING FOR NEW ISLANDS!
I BELIEVE AS LONG AS I KEEP TRYING, I WILL FIND IT!

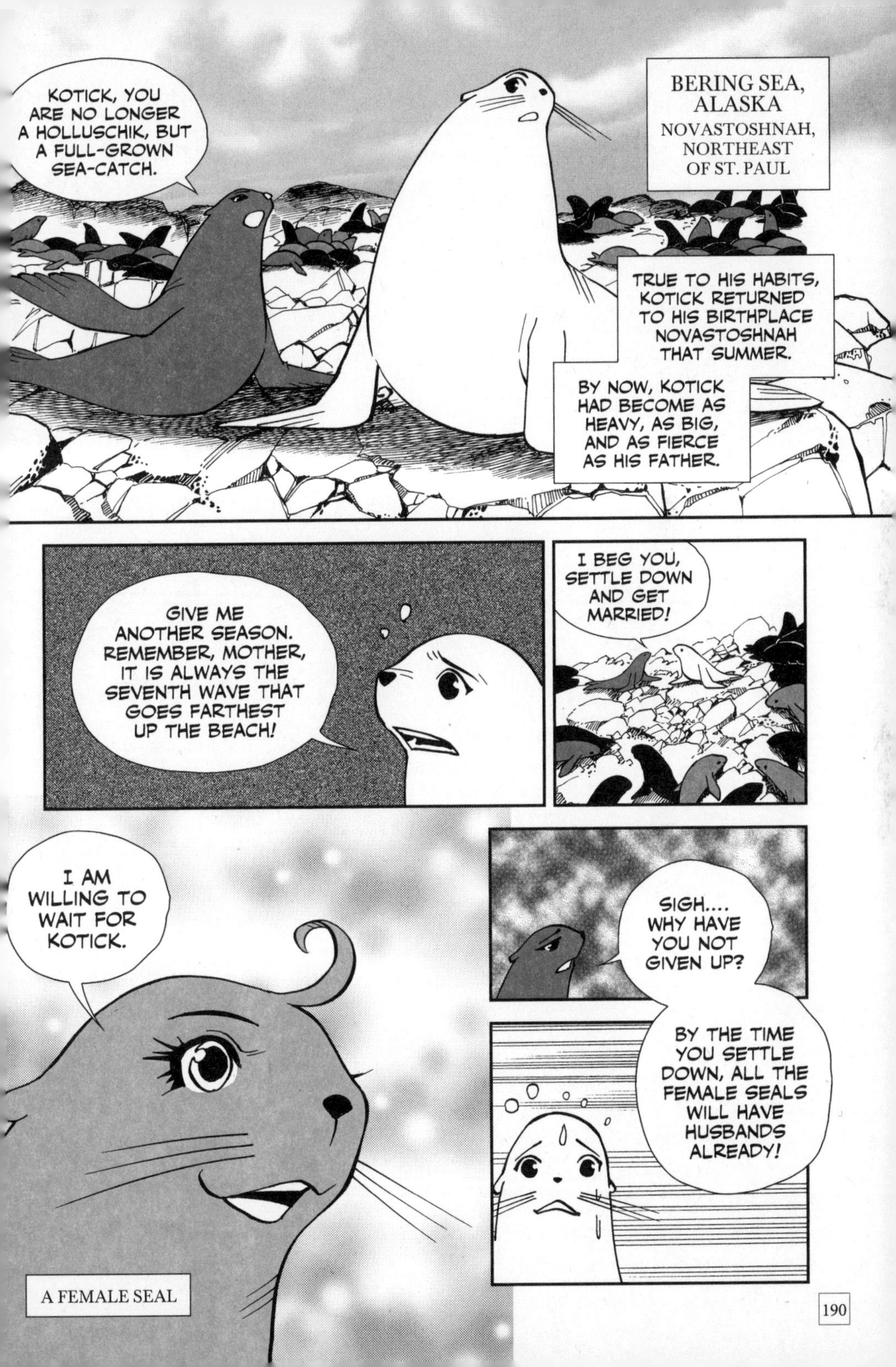

BERING SEA, ALASKA
NOVASTOSHNAH, NORTHEAST OF ST. PAUL
KOTICK, YOU ARE NO LONGER A HOLLUSCHIK, BUT A FULL-GROWN SEA-CATCH.
TRUE TO HIS HABITS, KOTICK RETURNED TO HIS BIRTHPLACE NOVASTOSHNAH THAT SUMMER.
BY NOW, KOTICK HAD BECOME AS HEAVY, AS BIG, AND AS FIERCE AS HIS FATHER.
I BEG YOU, SETTLE DOWN AND GET MARRIED!
GIVE ME ANOTHER SEASON. REMEMBER, MOTHER, IT IS ALWAYS THE SEVENTH WAVE THAT GOES FARTHEST UP THE BEACH!
SIGH.... WHY HAVE YOU NOT GIVEN UP?
BY THE TIME YOU SETTLE DOWN, ALL THE FEMALE SEALS WILL HAVE HUSBANDS ALREADY!
I AM WILLING TO WAIT FOR KOTICK.
A FEMALE SEAL

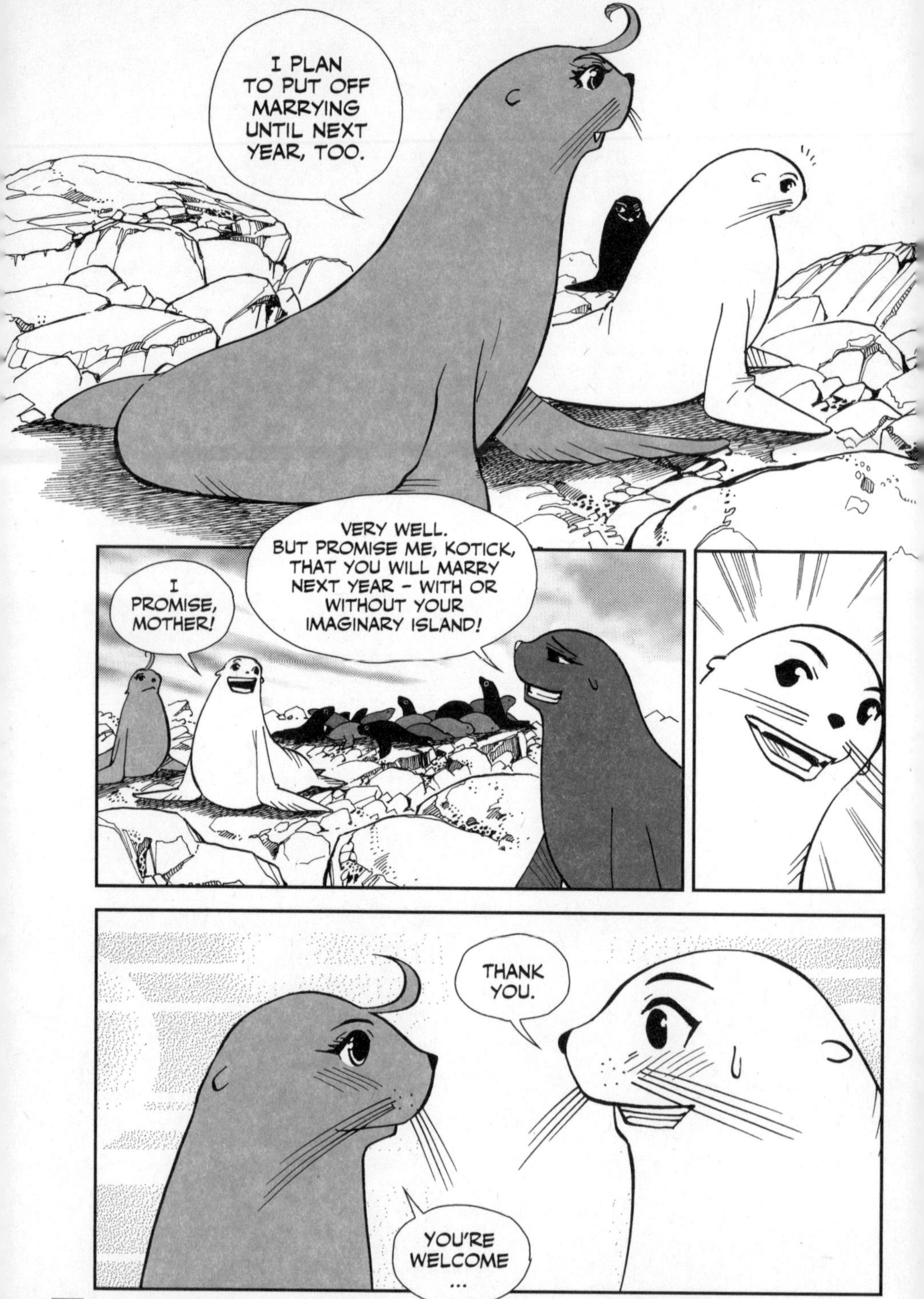
I PLAN TO PUT OFF MARRYING UNTIL NEXT YEAR, TOO.
VERY WELL. BUT PROMISE ME, KOTICK, THAT YOU WILL MARRY NEXT YEAR - WITH OR WITHOUT YOUR IMAGINARY ISLAND!
I PROMISE, MOTHER!
THANK YOU.
YOU'RE WELCOME ...

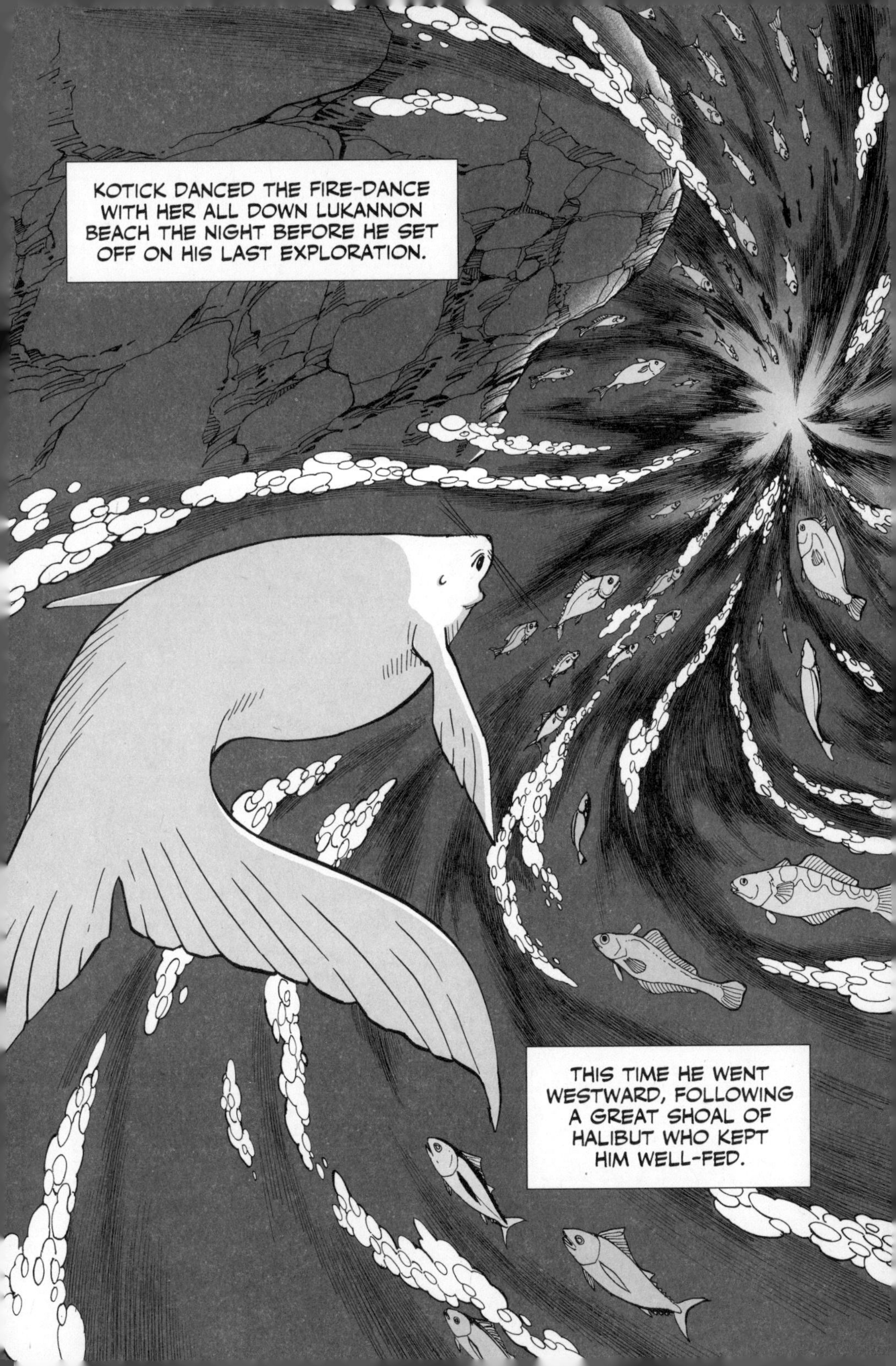
KOTICK DANCED THE FIRE-DANCE WITH HER ALL DOWN LUKANNON BEACH THE NIGHT BEFORE HE SET OFF ON HIS LAST EXPLORATION.
THIS TIME HE WENT WESTWARD, FOLLOWING A GREAT SHOAL OF HALIBUT WHO KEPT HIM WELL-FED.

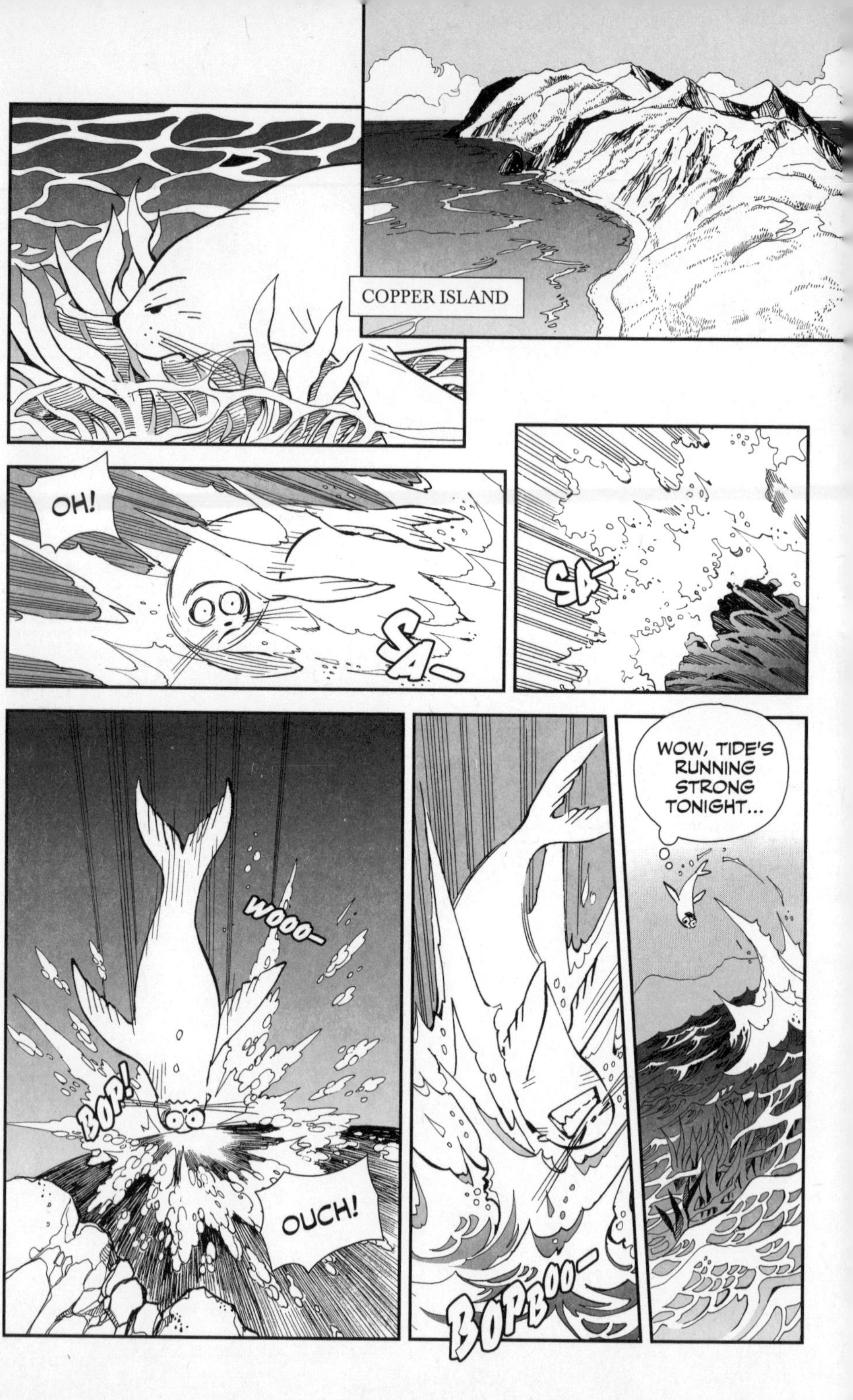
COPPER ISLAND
SA-
OH!
SA-
WOW, TIDE'S RUNNING STRONG TONIGHT...
BOPBOO-
WOOO-
BOP!
OUCH!

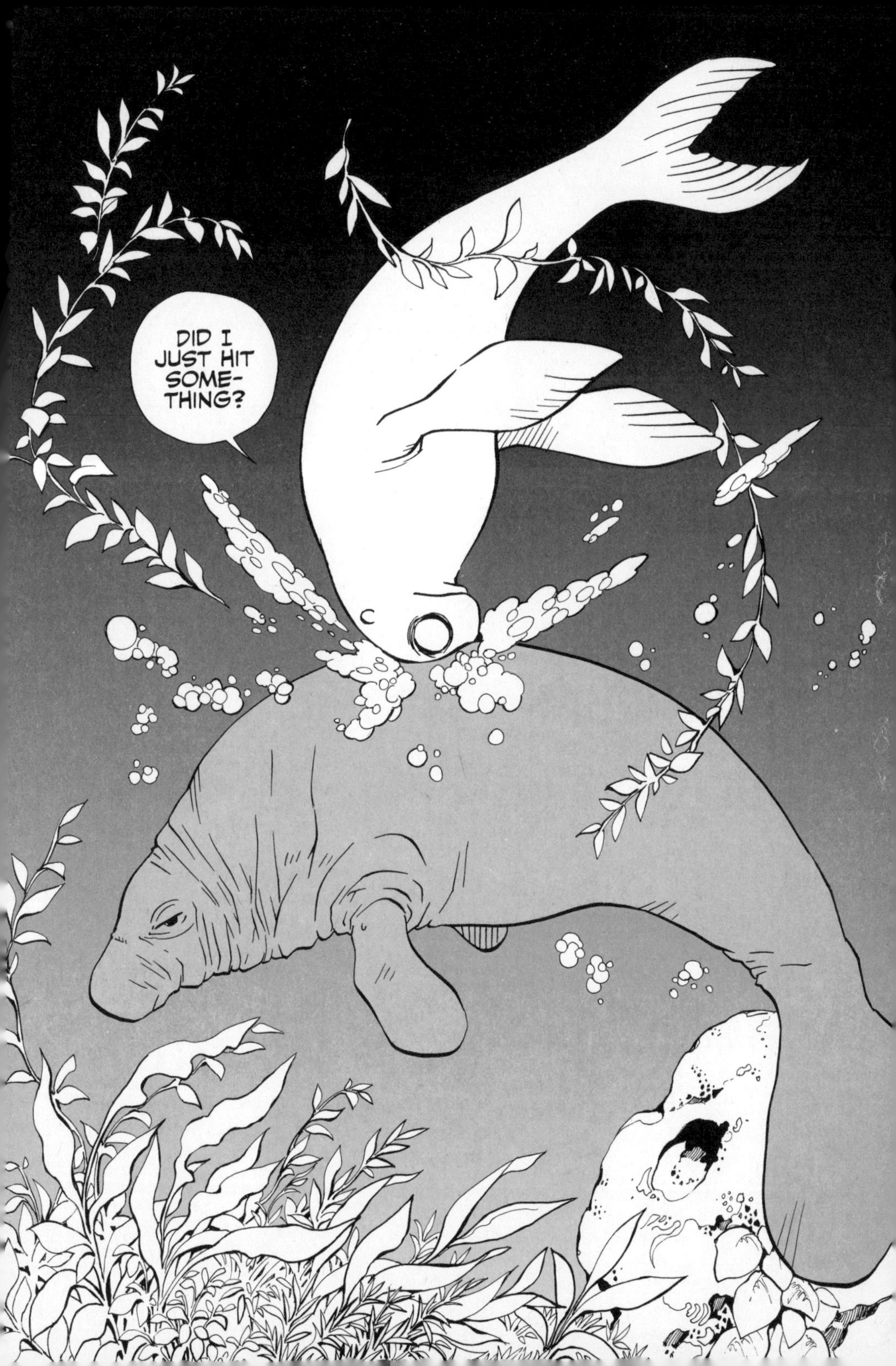
DID I JUST HIT SOME-THING?

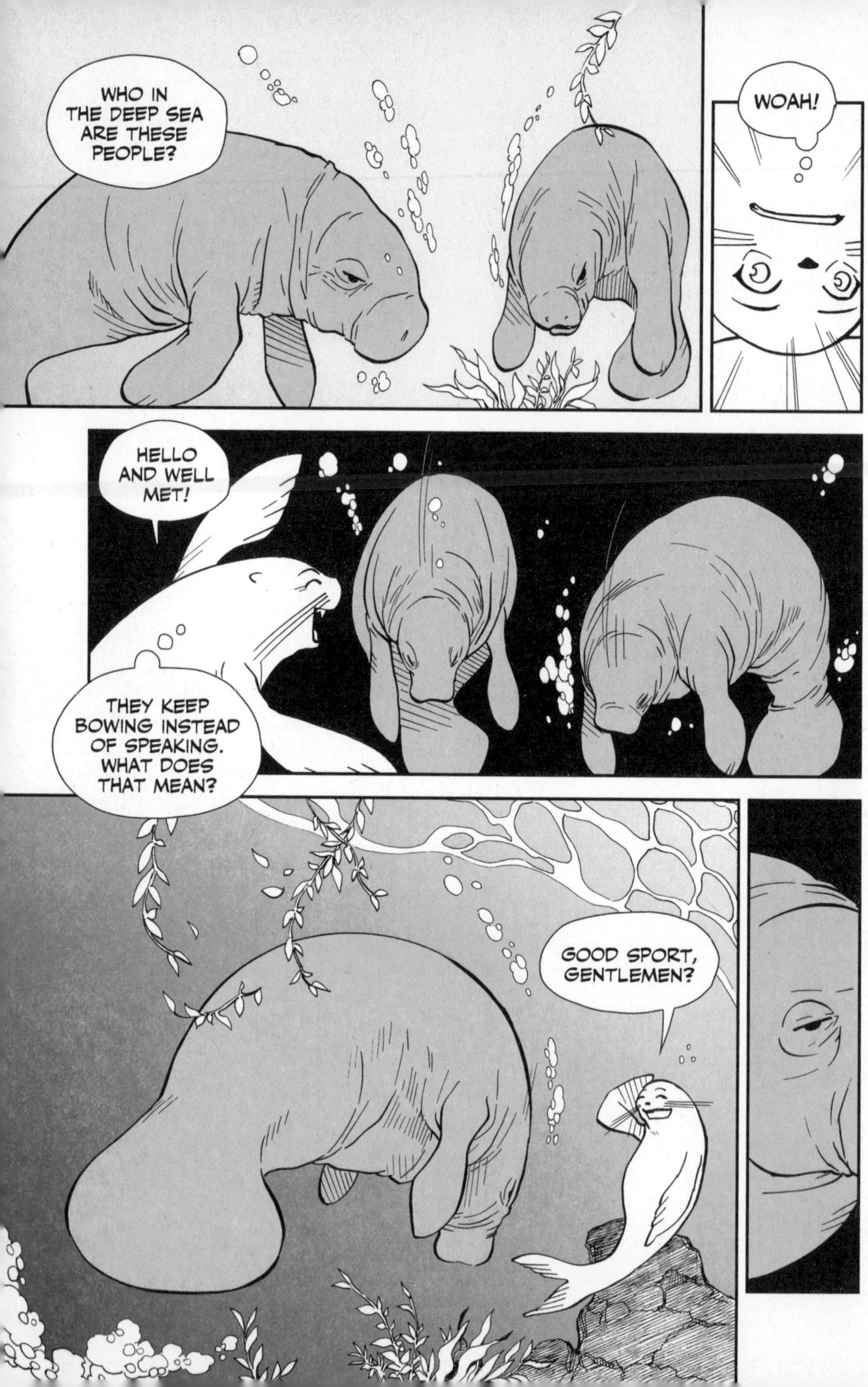
WOAH!
WHO IN THE DEEP SEA ARE THESE PEOPLE?
HELLO AND WELL MET!
THEY KEEP BOWING INSTEAD OF SPEAKING. WHAT DOES THAT MEAN?
GOOD SPORT, GENTLEMEN?

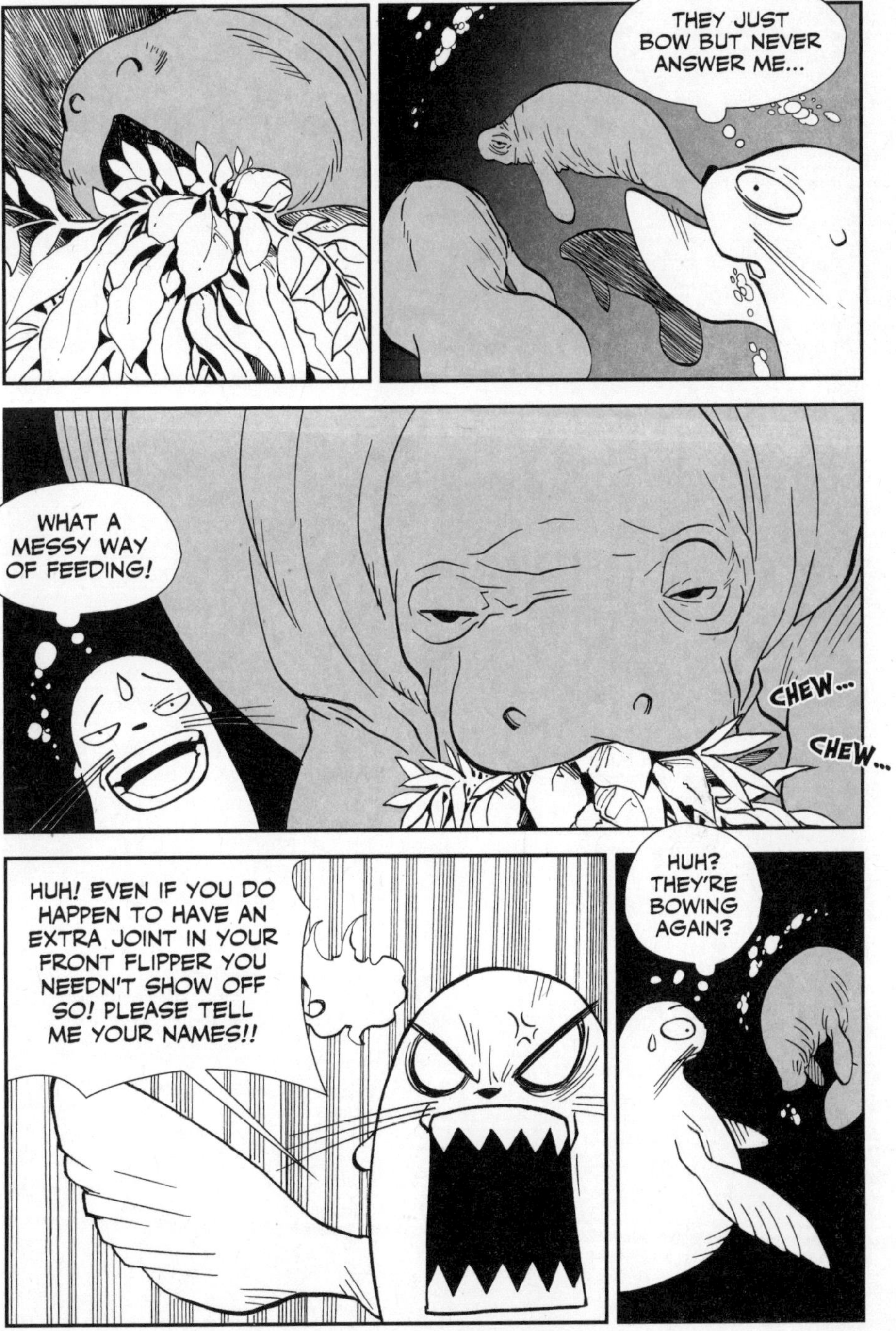
THEY JUST BOW BUT NEVER ANSWER ME...
WHAT A MESSY WAY OF FEEDING!
CHEW...
CHEW...
HUH? THEY'RE BOWING AGAIN?
HUH! EVEN IF YOU DO HAPPEN TO HAVE AN EXTRA JOINT IN YOUR FRONT FLIPPER YOU NEEDN'T SHOW OFF SO! PLEASE TELL ME YOUR NAMES!!

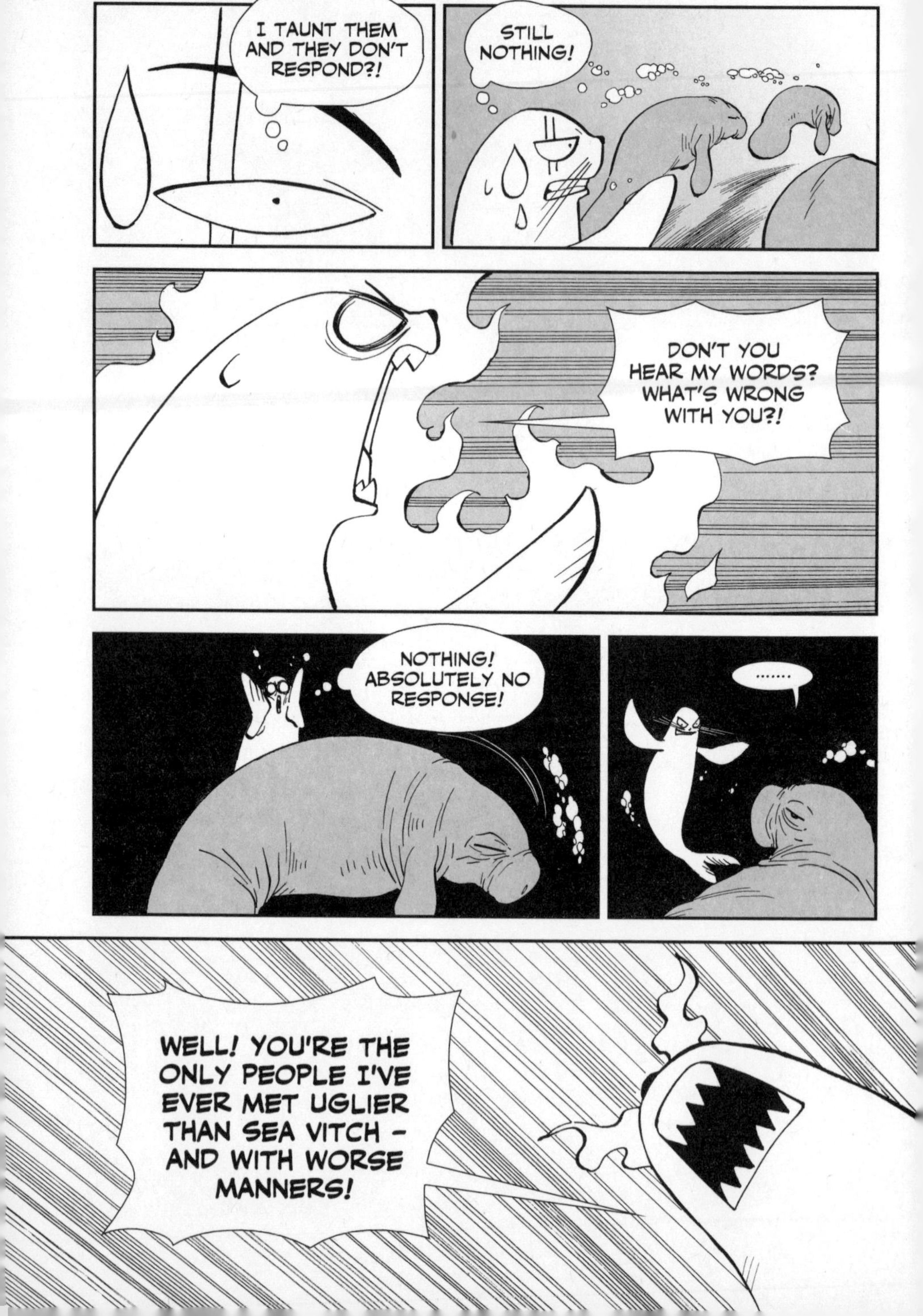
STILL NOTHING!
I TAUNT THEM AND THEY DON'T RESPOND?!
DON'T YOU HEAR MY WORDS? WHAT'S WRONG WITH YOU?!
....
NOTHING! ABSOLUTELY NO RESPONSE!
WELL! YOU'RE THE ONLY PEOPLE I'VE EVER MET UGLIER THAN SEA VITCH - AND WITH WORSE MANNERS!

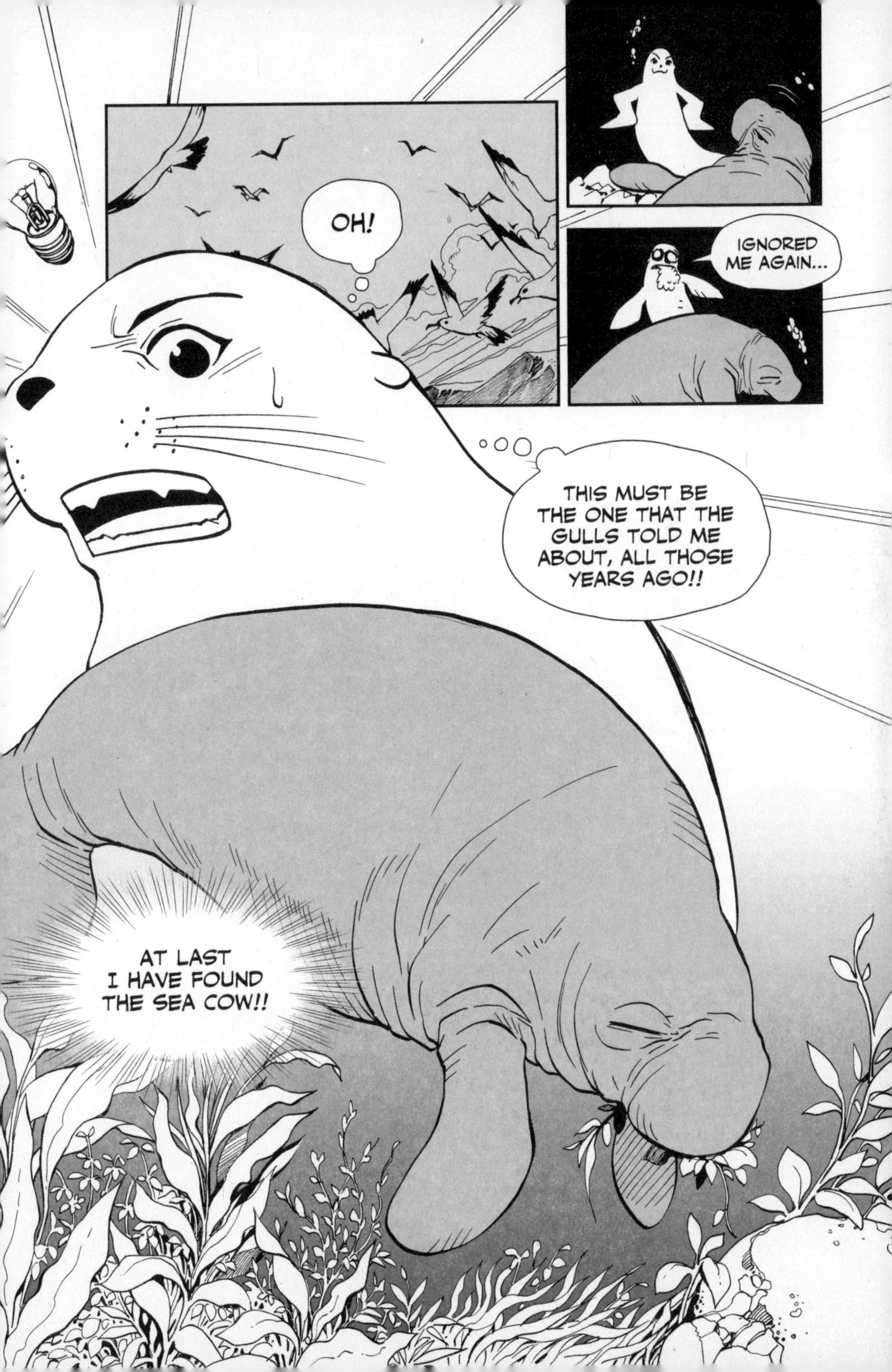

IGNORED ME AGAIN...
OH!
THIS MUST BE THE ONE THAT THE GULLS TOLD ME ABOUT, ALL THOSE YEARS AGO!!
AT LAST I HAVE FOUND THE SEA COW!!

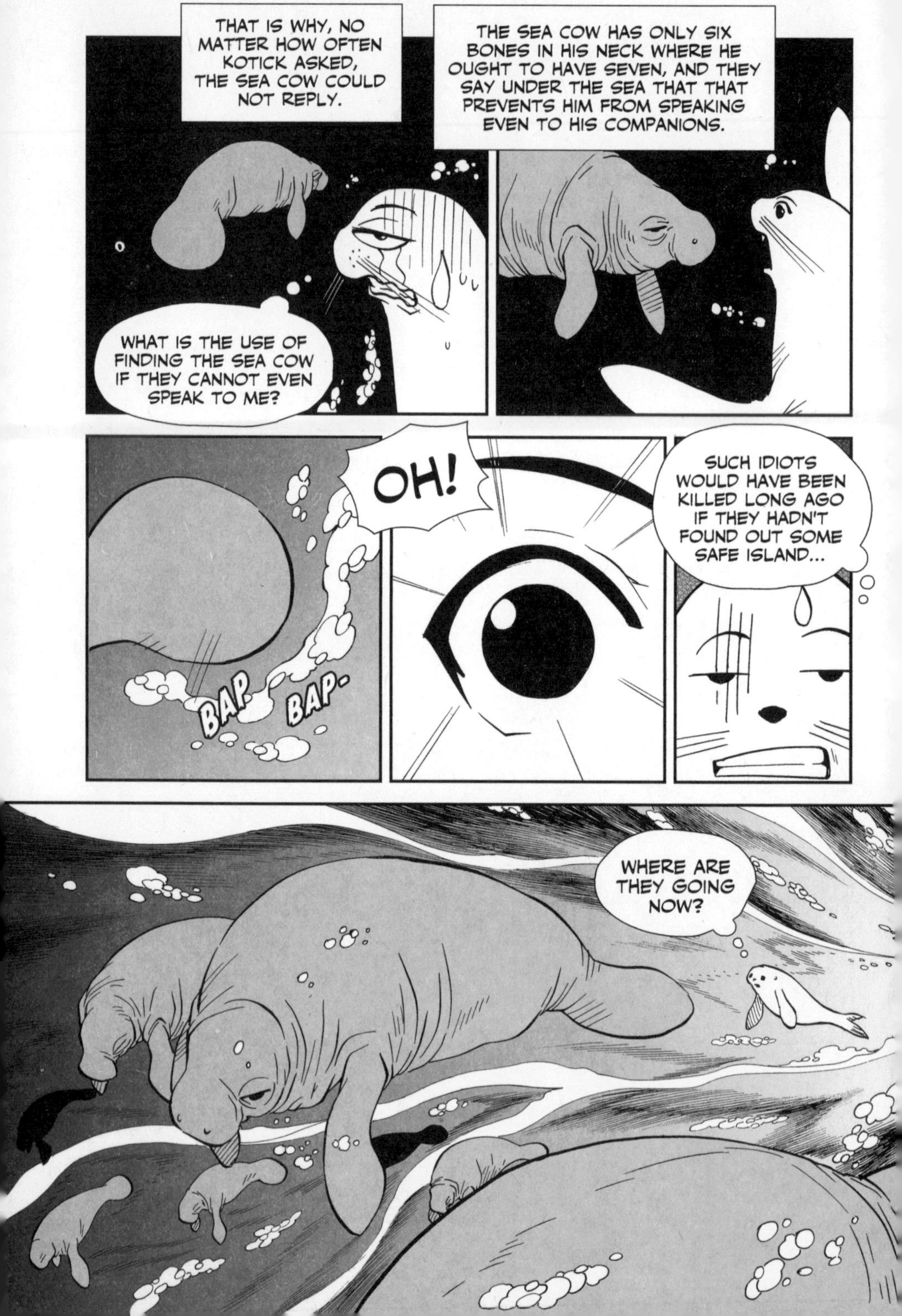
THE SEA COW HAS ONLY SIX BONES IN HIS NECK WHERE HE OUGHT TO HAVE SEVEN, AND THEY SAY UNDER THE SEA THAT THAT PREVENTS HIM FROM SPEAKING EVEN TO HIS COMPANIONS.
THAT IS WHY, NO MATTER HOW OFTEN KOTICK ASKED, THE SEA COW COULD NOT REPLY.
WHAT IS THE USE OF FINDING THE SEA COW IF THEY CANNOT EVEN SPEAK TO ME?
SUCH IDIOTS WOULD HAVE BEEN KILLED LONG AGO IF THEY HADN'T FOUND OUT SOME SAFE ISLAND...
OH!
BAP
BAP-
WHERE ARE THEY GOING NOW?

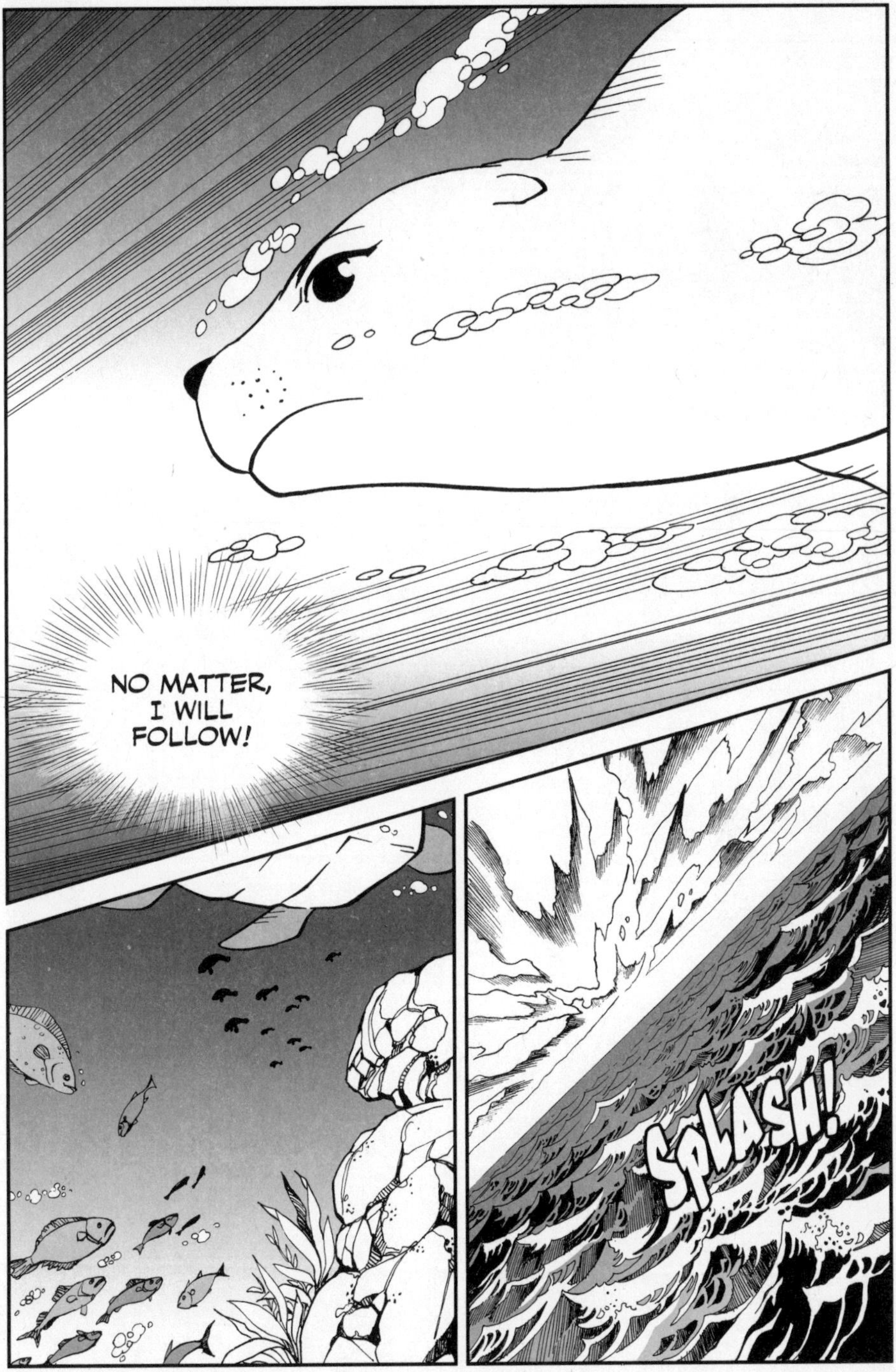
NO MATTER,
I WILL
FOLLOW!
SPLASH!

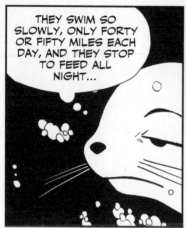

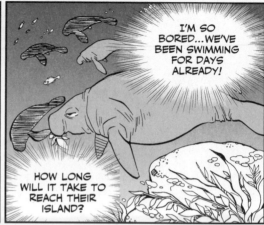

I'M SO BORED...WE'VE BEEN SWIMMING FOR DAYS ALREADY!
HOW LONG WILL IT TAKE TO REACH THEIR ISLAND?
THEY SWIM SO SLOWLY, ONLY FORTY OR FIFTY MILES EACH DAY, AND THEY STOP TO FEED ALL NIGHT...
ARGH! CAN'T YOU SWIM FASTER!?
EH?!
IS THIS A WARM CURRENT?!

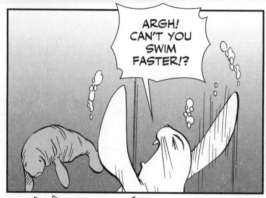

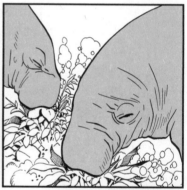

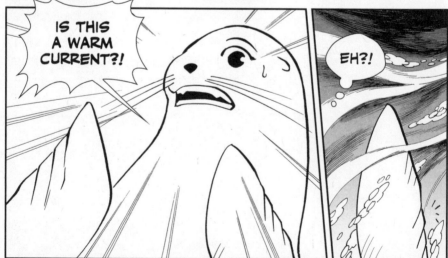

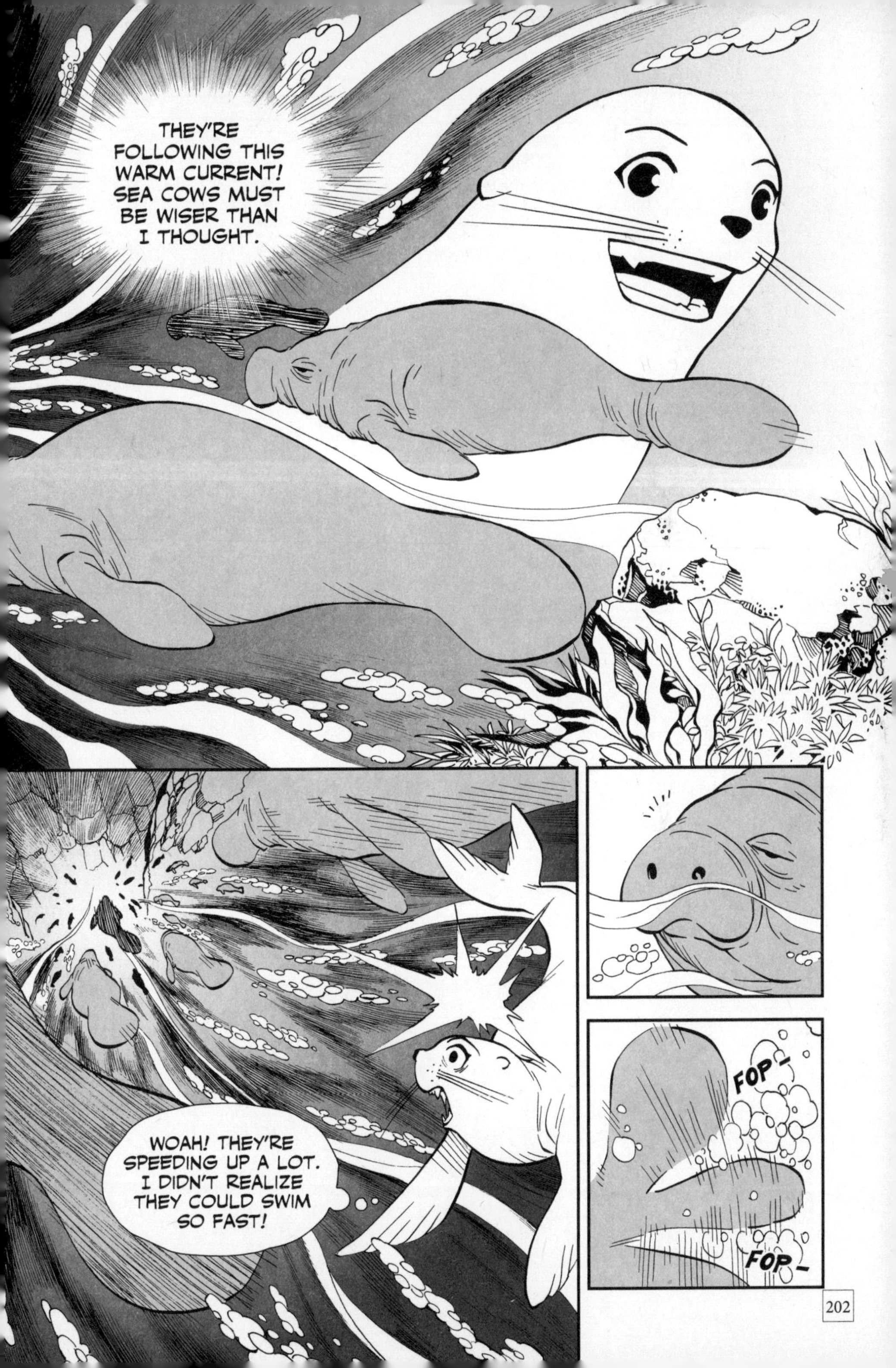
THEY'RE FOLLOWING THIS WARM CURRENT! SEA COWS MUST BE WISER THAN I THOUGHT.
FOP-
FOP-
WOAH! THEY'RE SPEEDING UP A LOT. I DIDN'T REALIZE THEY COULD SWIM SO FAST!

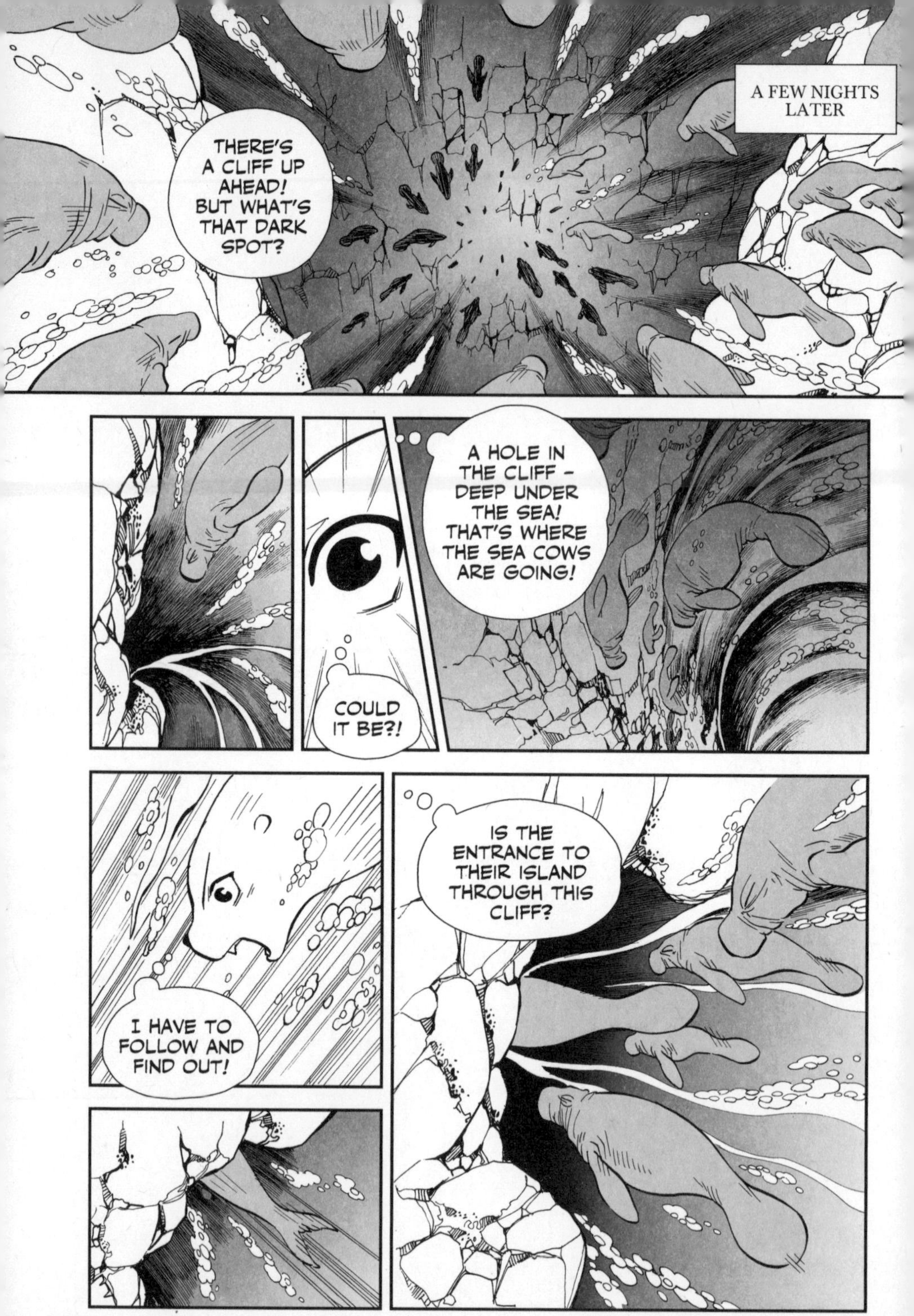
A FEW NIGHTS LATER
THERE'S A CLIFF UP AHEAD! BUT WHAT'S THAT DARK SPOT?
A HOLE IN THE CLIFF - DEEP UNDER THE SEA! THAT'S WHERE THE SEA COWS ARE GOING!
COULD IT BE?!
IS THE ENTRANCE TO THEIR ISLAND THROUGH THIS CLIFF?
I HAVE TO FOLLOW AND FIND OUT!

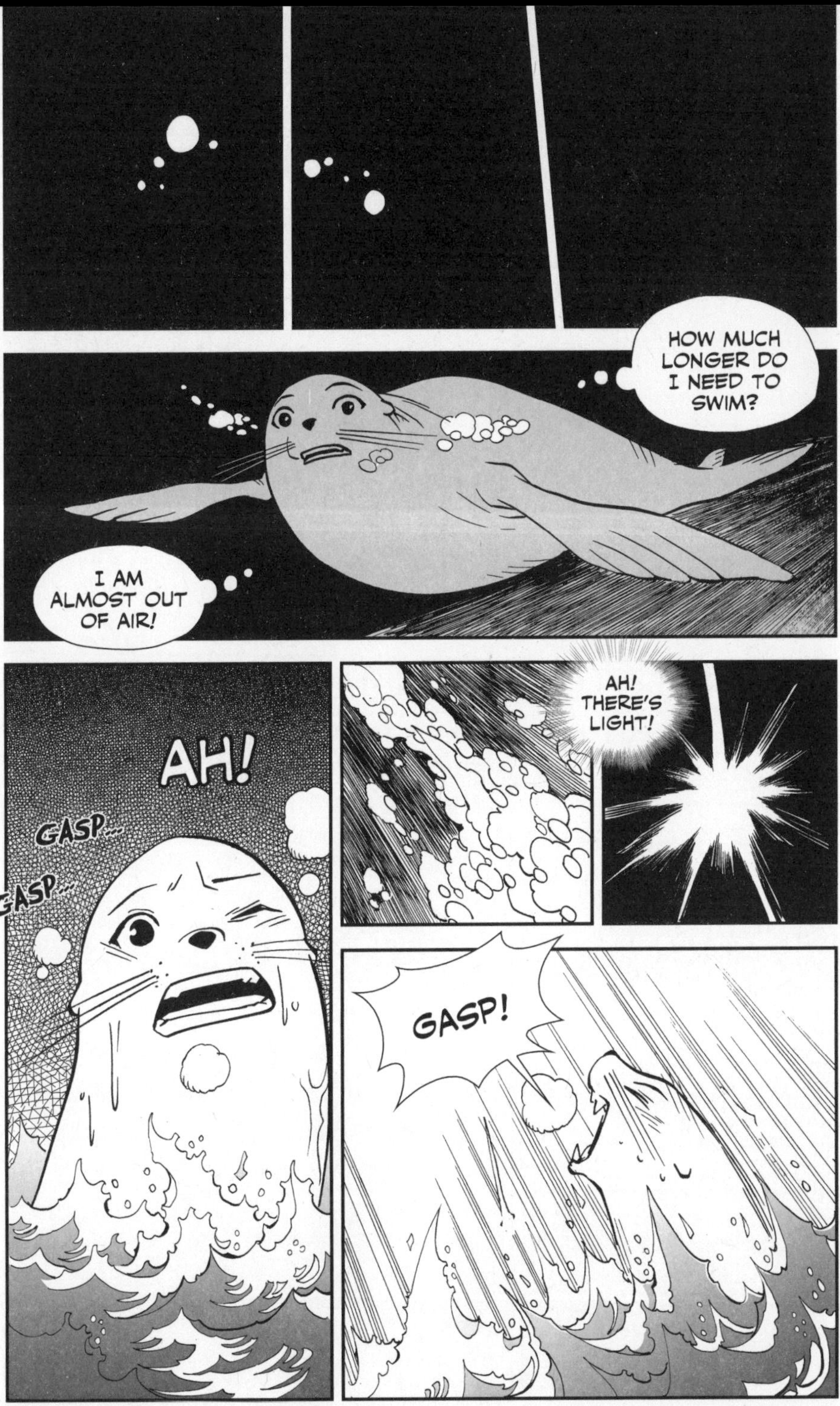
HOW MUCH LONGER DO I NEED TO SWIM?
I AM ALMOST OUT OF AIR!
AH! THERE'S LIGHT!
GASP!
AH!
GASP...
GASP...

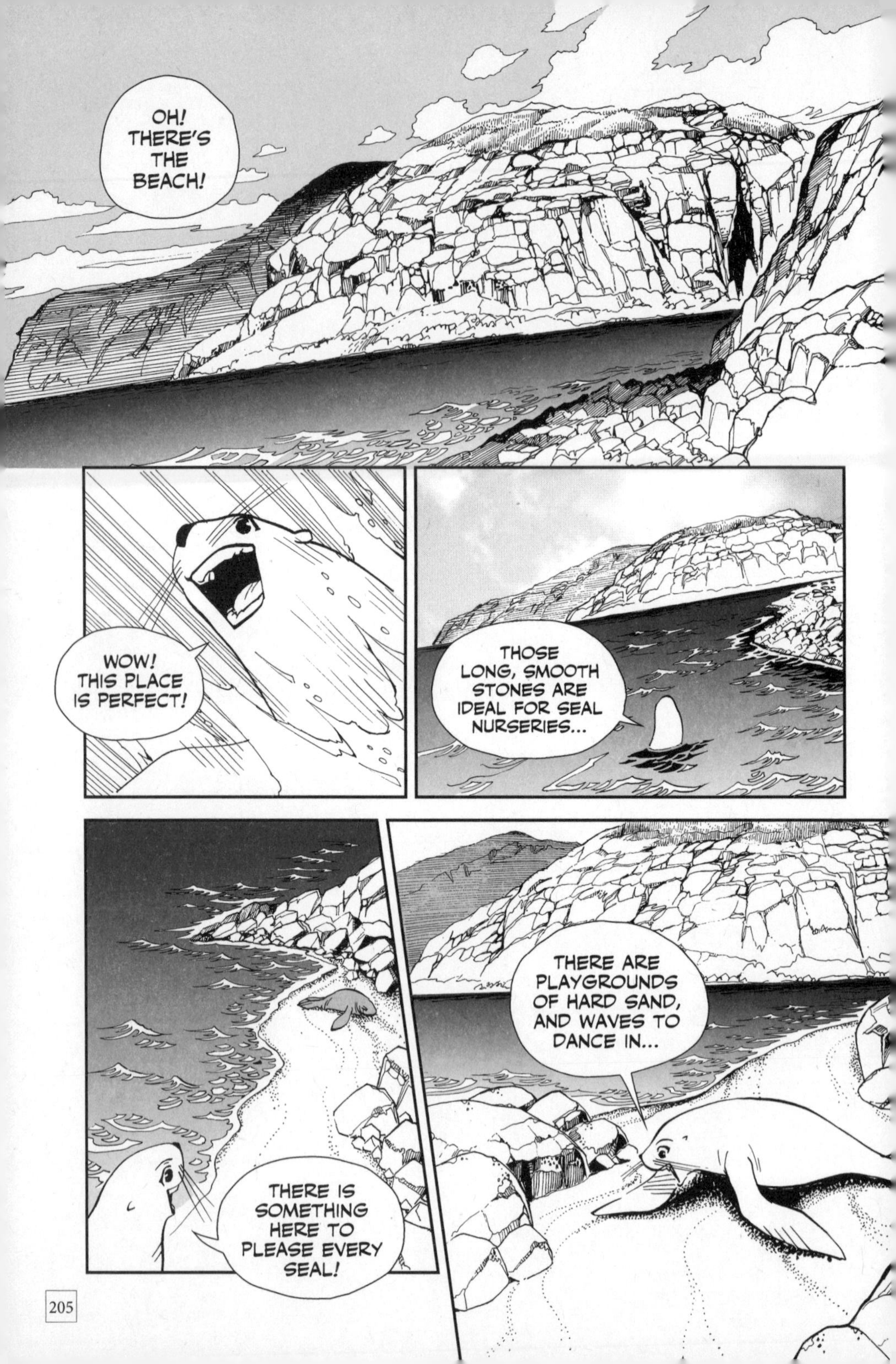
OH! THERE'S THE BEACH!
THOSE LONG, SMOOTH STONES ARE IDEAL FOR SEAL NURSERIES...
WOW! THIS PLACE IS PERFECT!
THERE ARE PLAYGROUNDS OF HARD SAND, AND WAVES TO DANCE IN...
THERE IS SOMETHING HERE TO PLEASE EVERY SEAL!

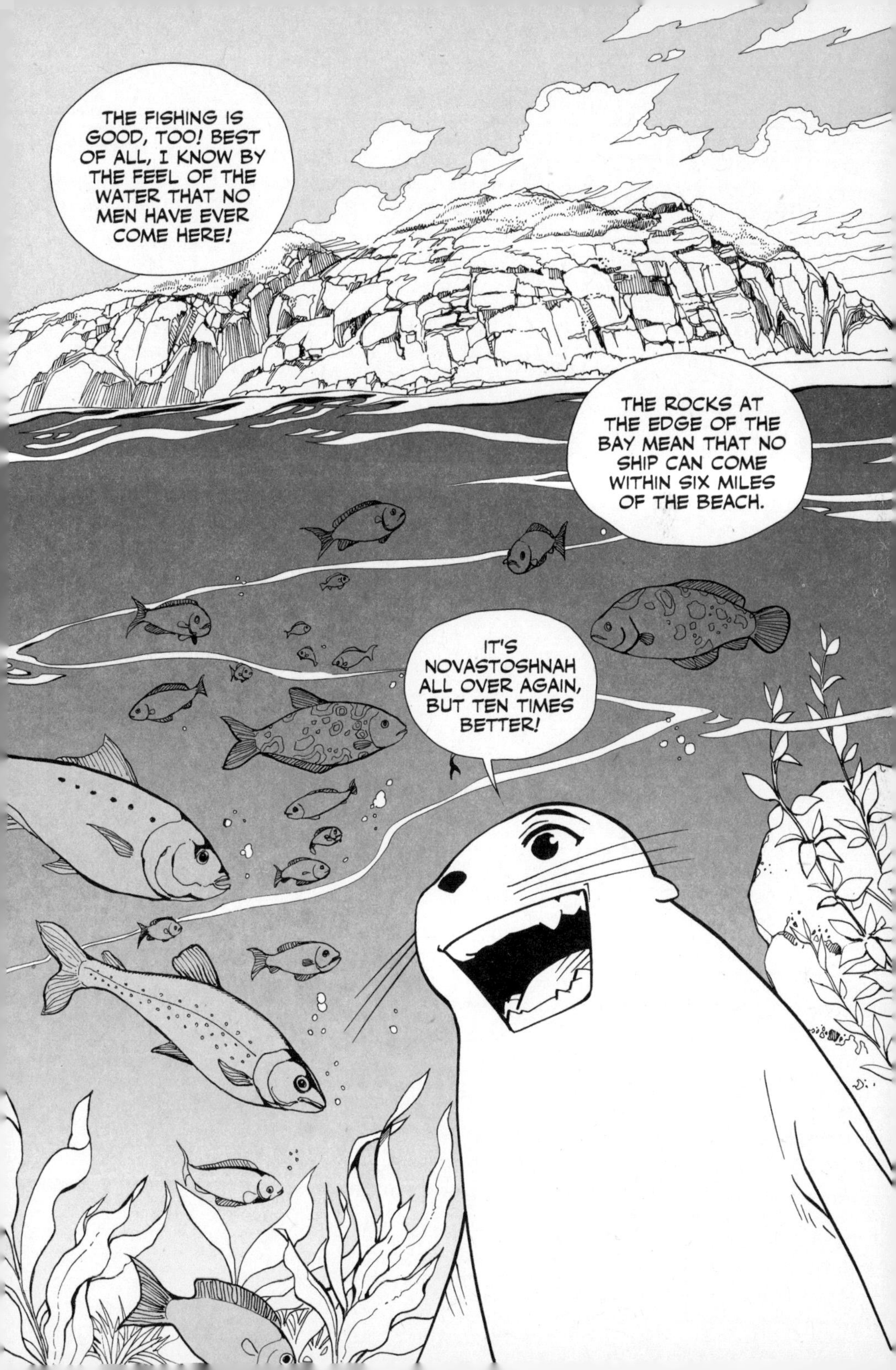
THE FISHING IS GOOD, TOO! BEST OF ALL, I KNOW BY THE FEEL OF THE WATER THAT NO MEN HAVE EVER COME HERE!
THE ROCKS AT THE EDGE OF THE BAY MEAN THAT NO SHIP CAN COME WITHIN SIX MILES OF THE BEACH.
IT'S NOVASTOSHNAH ALL OVER AGAIN, BUT TEN TIMES BETTER!

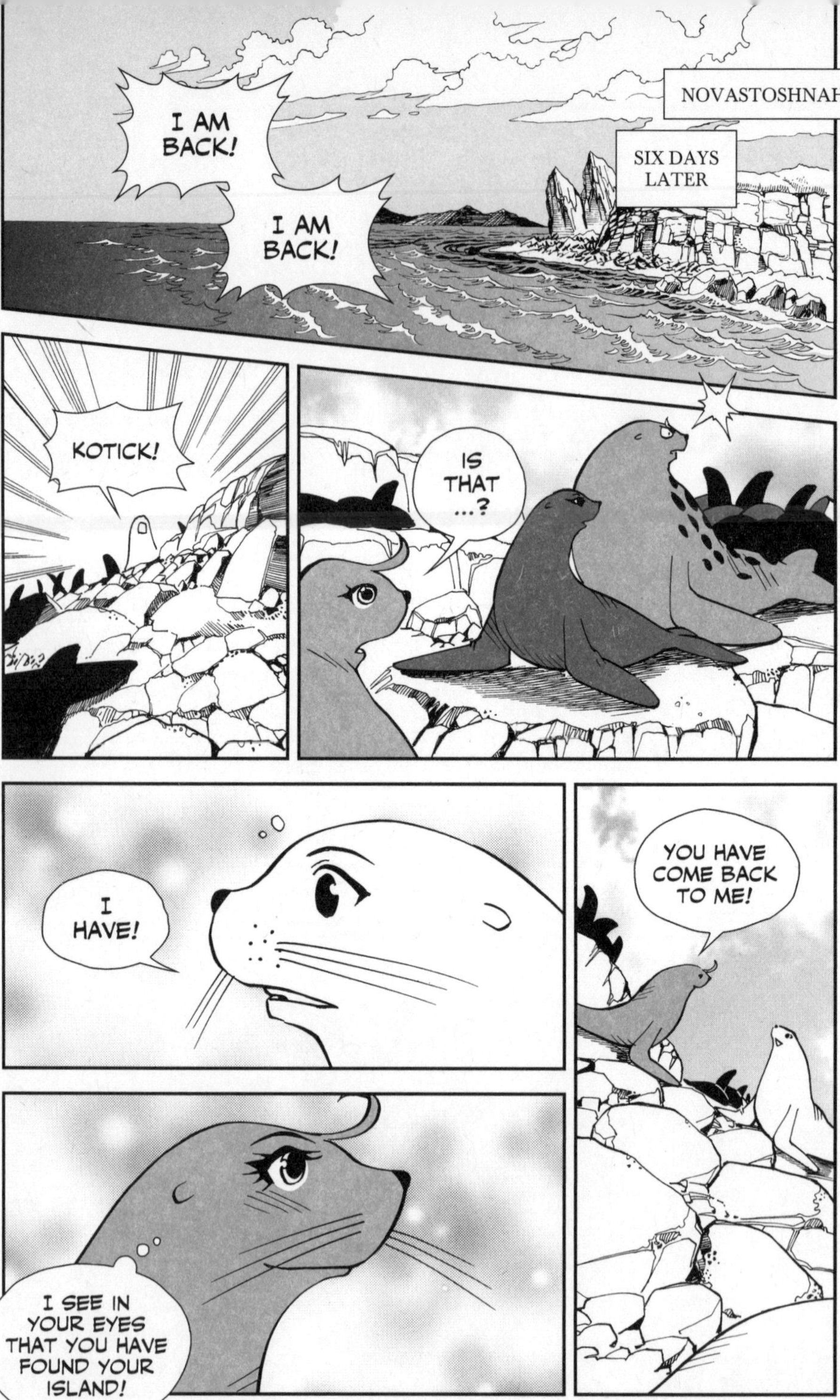
NOVASTOSHNAH
SIX DAYS LATER
I AM BACK!
I AM BACK!
IS THAT ...?
KOTICK!
YOU HAVE COME BACK TO ME!
I HAVE!
I SEE IN YOUR EYES THAT YOU HAVE FOUND YOUR ISLAND!

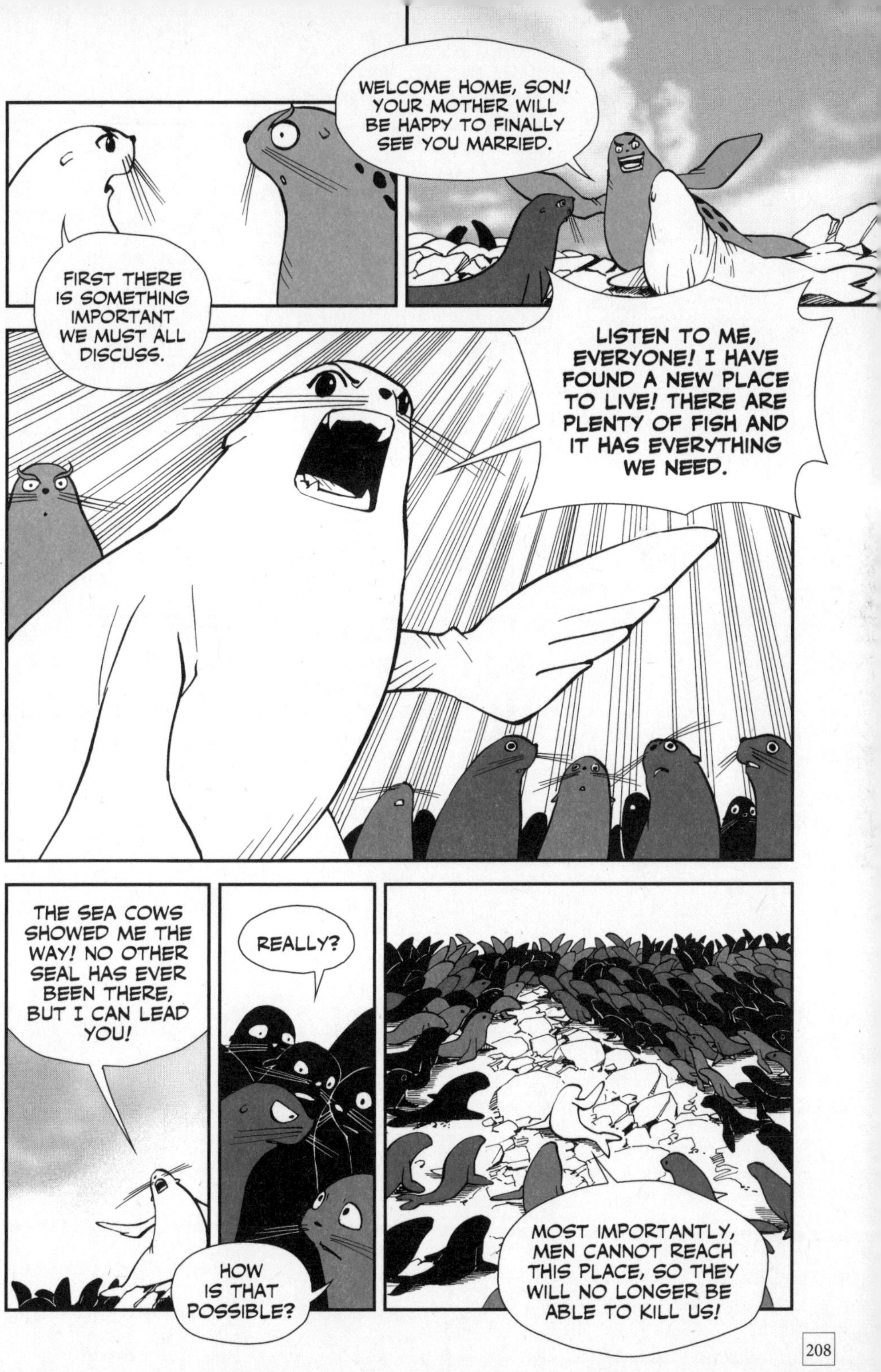
WELCOME HOME, SON! YOUR MOTHER WILL BE HAPPY TO FINALLY SEE YOU MARRIED.
FIRST THERE IS SOMETHING IMPORTANT WE MUST ALL DISCUSS.
LISTEN TO ME, EVERYONE! I HAVE FOUND A NEW PLACE TO LIVE! THERE ARE PLENTY OF FISH AND IT HAS EVERYTHING WE NEED.
MOST IMPORTANTLY, MEN CANNOT REACH THIS PLACE, SO THEY WILL NO LONGER BE ABLE TO KILL US!
REALLY?
HOW IS THAT POSSIBLE?
THE SEA COWS SHOWED ME THE WAY! NO OTHER SEAL HAS EVER BEEN THERE, BUT I CAN LEAD YOU!

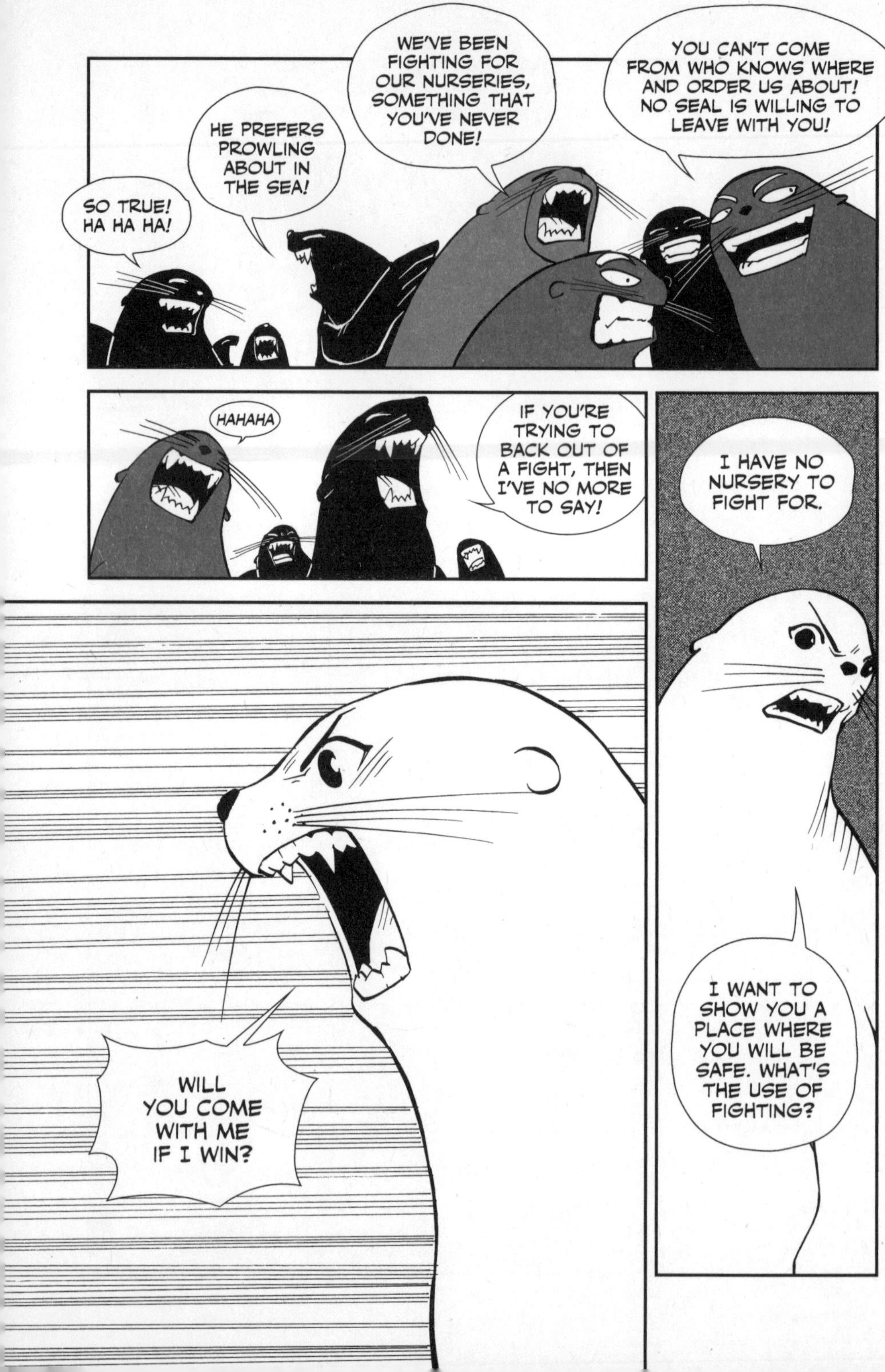
YOU CAN'T COME FROM WHO KNOWS WHERE AND ORDER US ABOUT! NO SEAL IS WILLING TO LEAVE WITH YOU!
WE'VE BEEN FIGHTING FOR OUR NURSERIES, SOMETHING THAT YOU'VE NEVER DONE!
HE PREFERS PROWLING ABOUT IN THE SEA!
SO TRUE! HA HA HA!
I HAVE NO NURSERY TO FIGHT FOR.
I WANT TO SHOW YOU A PLACE WHERE YOU WILL BE SAFE. WHAT'S THE USE OF FIGHTING?
IF YOU'RE TRYING TO BACK OUT OF A FIGHT, THEN I'VE NO MORE TO SAY!
HAHAHA
WILL YOU COME WITH ME IF I WIN?

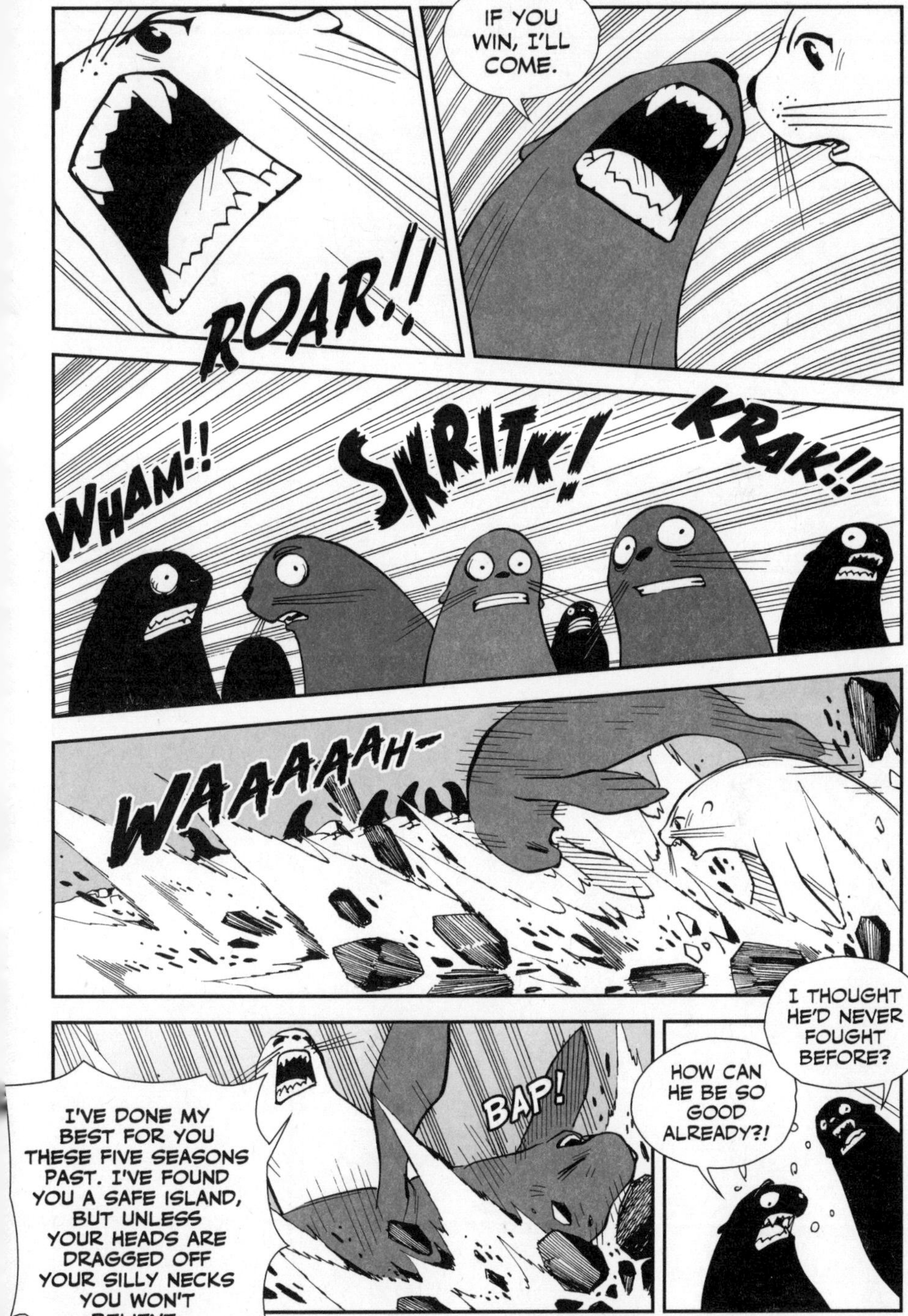
IF YOU WIN, I'LL COME.
ROAR!!
KRAK!!
SKRITK!
WHAM!!
WAAAAAH-
I THOUGHT HE'D NEVER FOUGHT BEFORE?
HOW CAN HE BE SO GOOD ALREADY?!
BAP!
I'VE DONE MY BEST FOR YOU THESE FIVE SEASONS PAST. I'VE FOUND YOU A SAFE ISLAND, BUT UNLESS YOUR HEADS ARE DRAGGED OFF YOUR SILLY NECKS YOU WON'T BELIEVE.

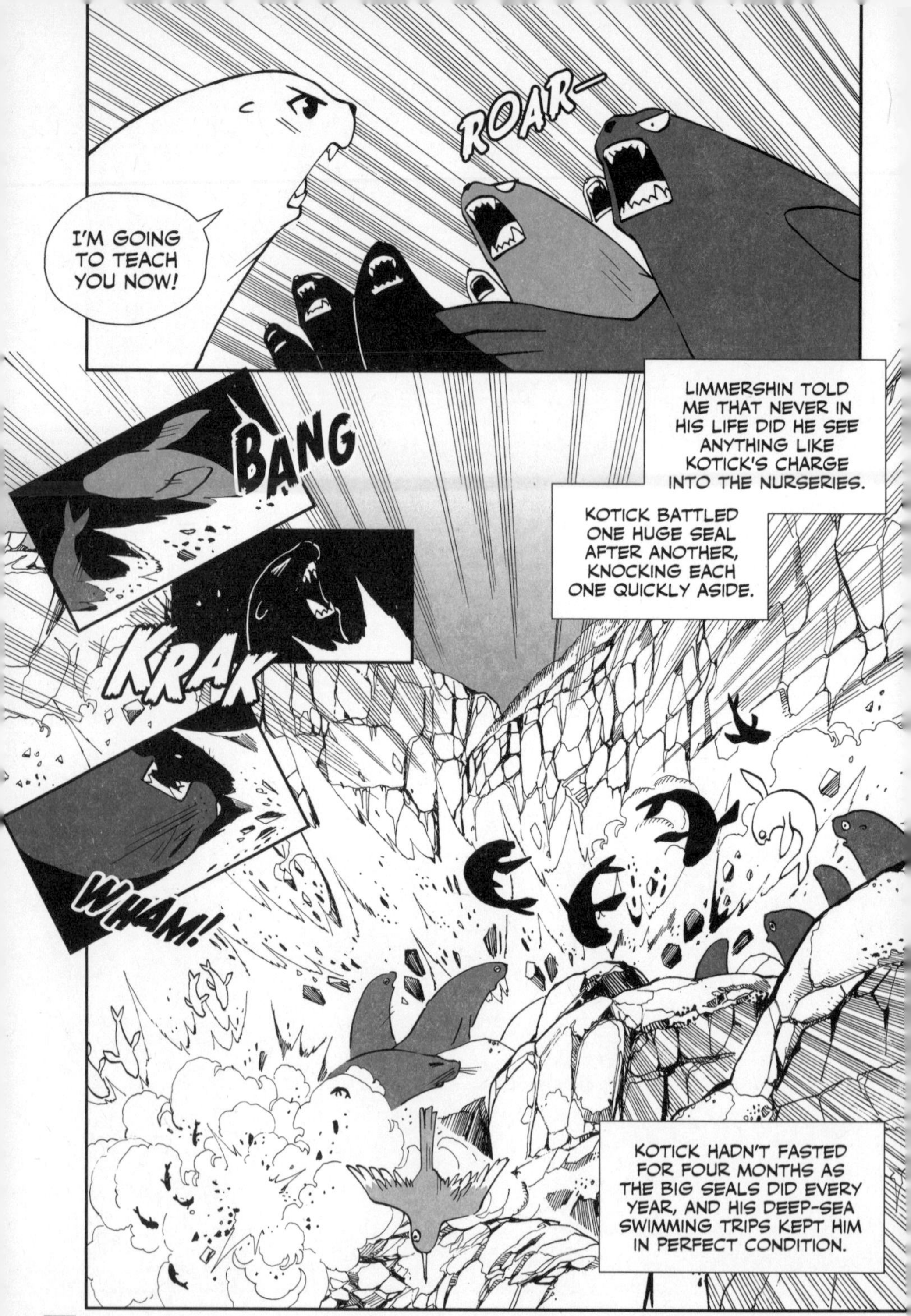
ROAR—
I'M GOING TO TEACH YOU NOW!
LIMMERSHIN TOLD ME THAT NEVER IN HIS LIFE DID HE SEE ANYTHING LIKE KOTICK'S CHARGE INTO THE NURSERIES.
KOTICK BATTLED ONE HUGE SEAL AFTER ANOTHER, KNOCKING EACH ONE QUICKLY ASIDE.
BANG
KRAK
WHAM!
KOTICK HADN'T FASTED FOR FOUR MONTHS AS THE BIG SEALS DID EVERY YEAR, AND HIS DEEP-SEA SWIMMING TRIPS KEPT HIM IN PERFECT CONDITION.

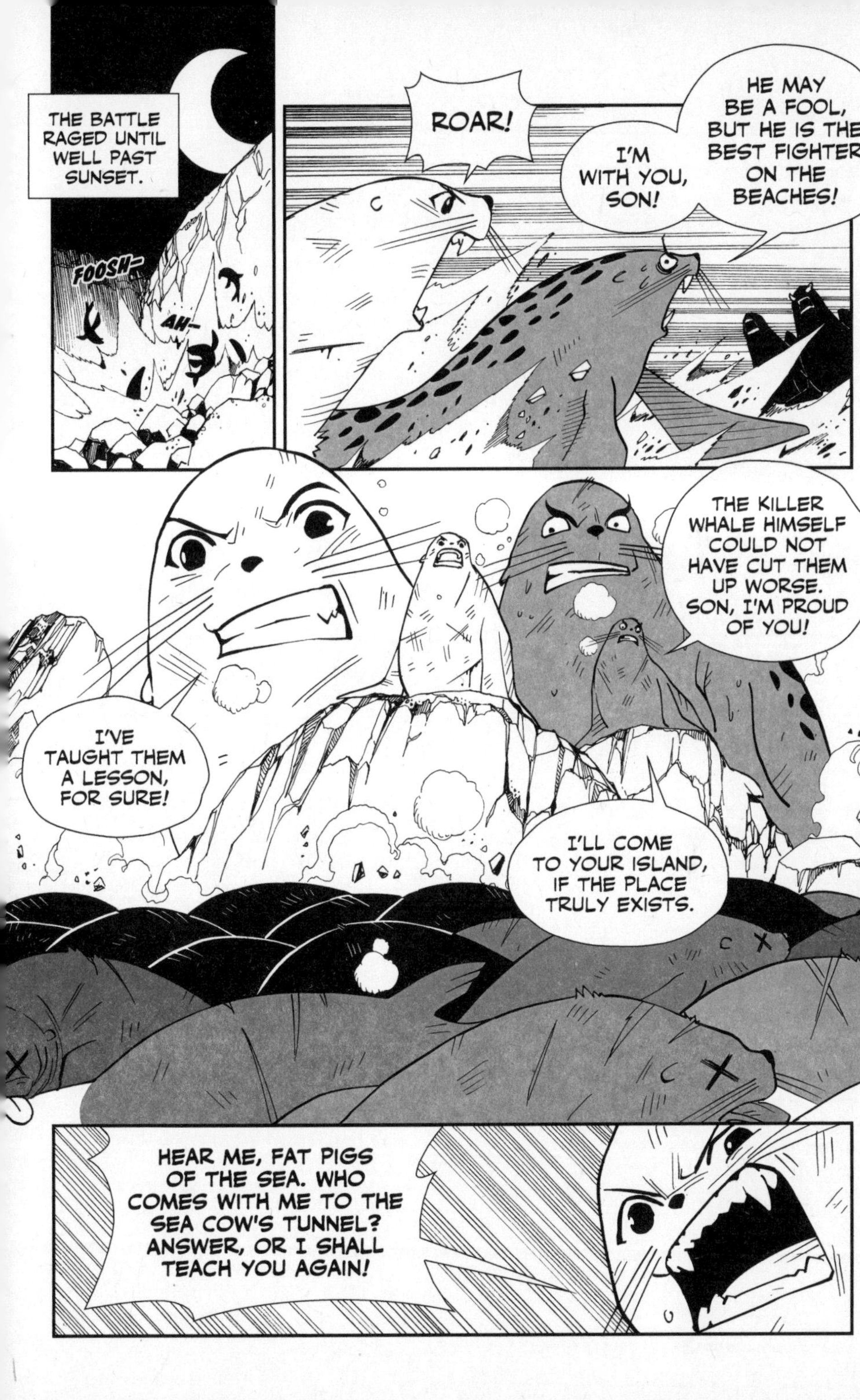
HE MAY BE A FOOL, BUT HE IS THE BEST FIGHTER ON THE BEACHES!
ROAR!
I'M WITH YOU, SON!
THE BATTLE RAGED UNTIL WELL PAST SUNSET.
FOOSH-
AH-
THE KILLER WHALE HIMSELF COULD NOT HAVE CUT THEM UP WORSE. SON, I'M PROUD OF YOU!
I'VE TAUGHT THEM A LESSON, FOR SURE!
I'LL COME TO YOUR ISLAND, IF THE PLACE TRULY EXISTS.
HEAR ME, FAT PIGS OF THE SEA. WHO COMES WITH ME TO THE SEA COW'S TUNNEL? ANSWER, OR I SHALL TEACH YOU AGAIN!

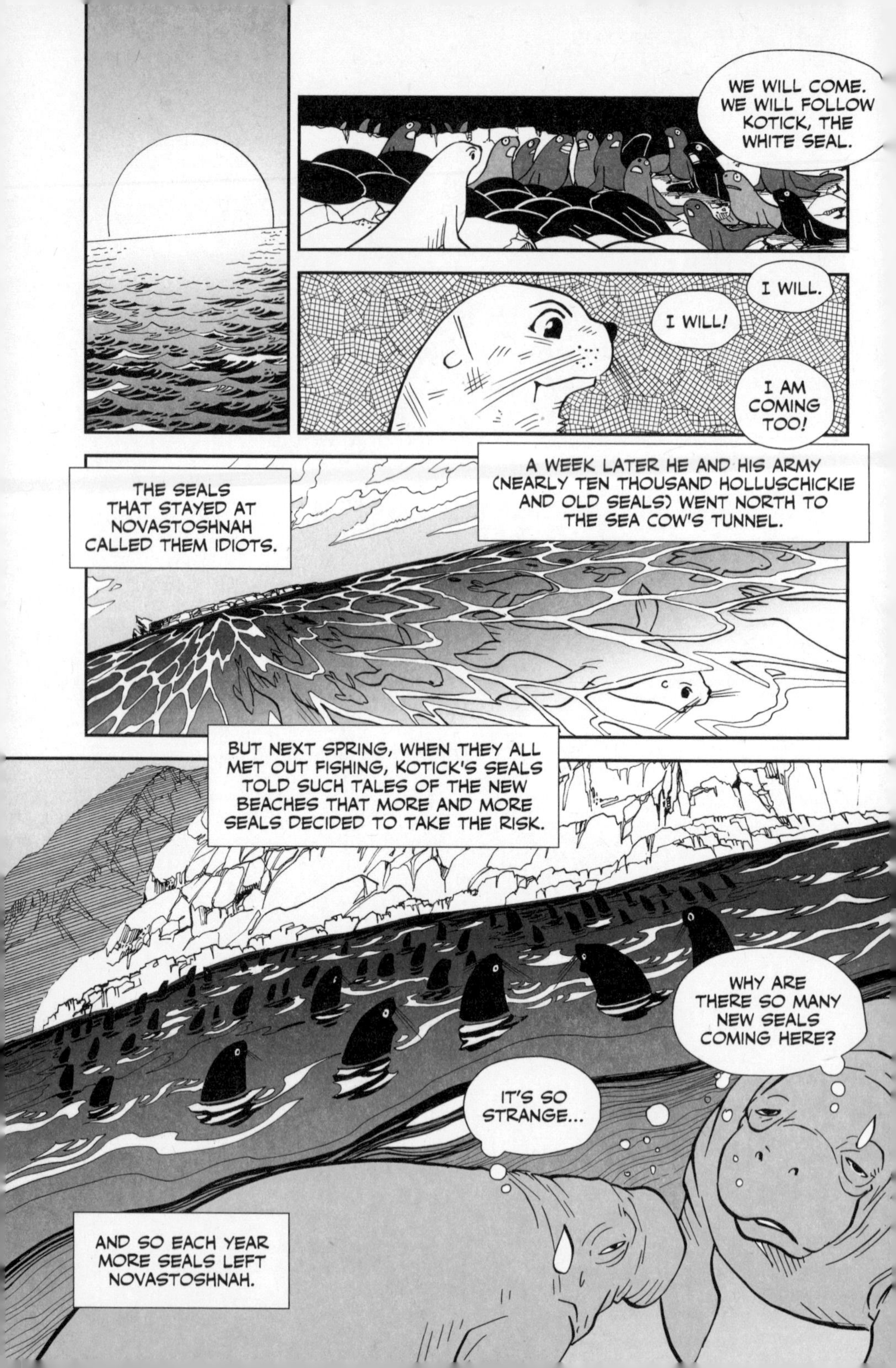
WE WILL COME. WE WILL FOLLOW KOTICK, THE WHITE SEAL.
I WILL.
I WILL!
I AM COMING TOO!
A WEEK LATER HE AND HIS ARMY (NEARLY TEN THOUSAND HOLLUSCHICKIE AND OLD SEALS) WENT NORTH TO THE SEA COW'S TUNNEL.
THE SEALS THAT STAYED AT NOVASTOSHNAH CALLED THEM IDIOTS.
BUT NEXT SPRING, WHEN THEY ALL MET OUT FISHING, KOTICK'S SEALS TOLD SUCH TALES OF THE NEW BEACHES THAT MORE AND MORE SEALS DECIDED TO TAKE THE RISK.
WHY ARE THERE SO MANY NEW SEALS COMING HERE?
IT'S SO STRANGE...
AND SO EACH YEAR MORE SEALS LEFT NOVASTOSHNAH.

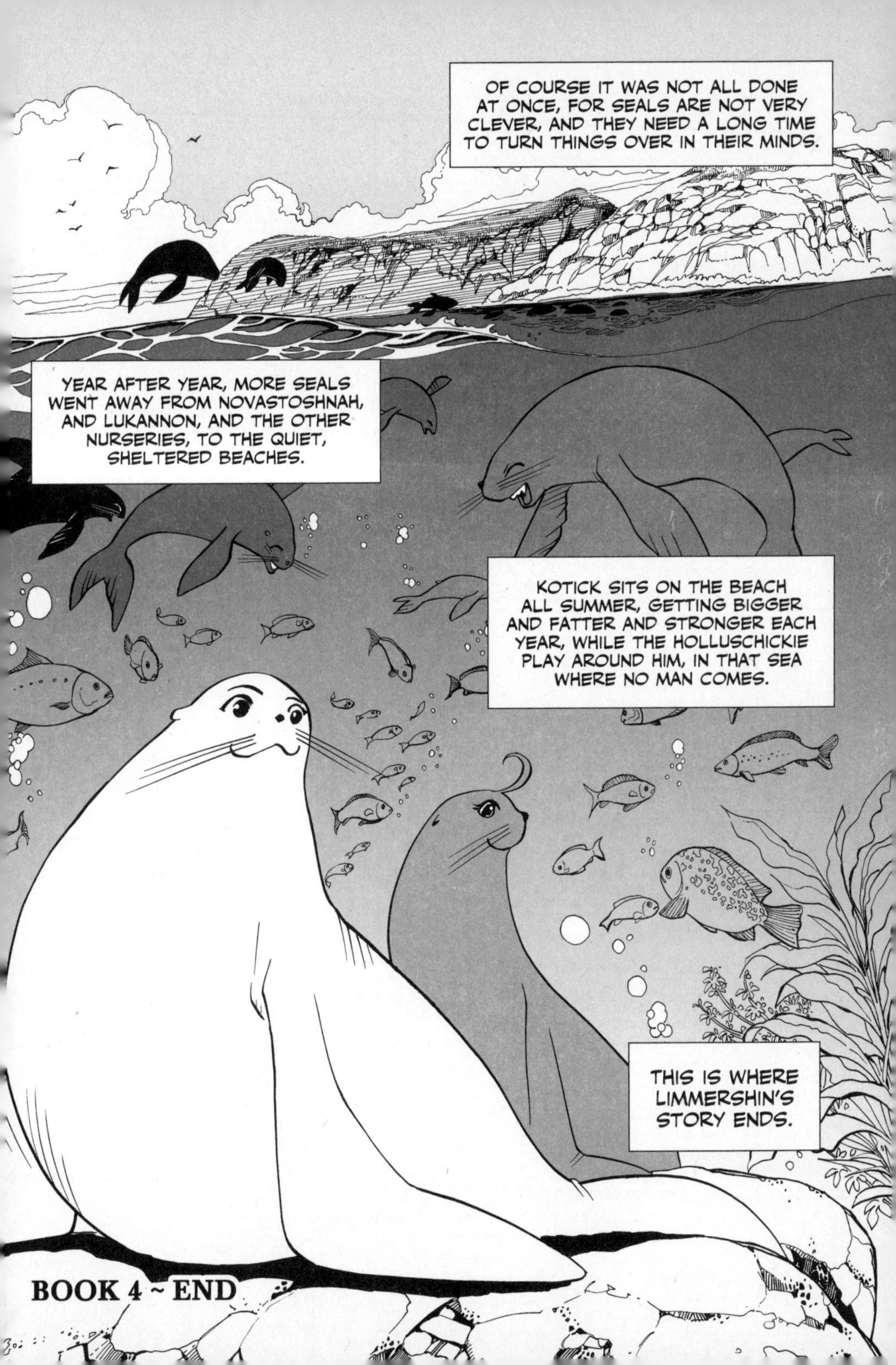
OF COURSE IT WAS NOT ALL DONE AT ONCE, FOR SEALS ARE NOT VERY CLEVER, AND THEY NEED A LONG TIME TO TURN THINGS OVER IN THEIR MINDS.
YEAR AFTER YEAR, MORE SEALS WENT AWAY FROM NOVASTOSHNAH, AND LUKANNON, AND THE OTHER NURSERIES, TO THE QUIET, SHELTERED BEACHES.
KOTICK SITS ON THE BEACH ALL SUMMER, GETTING BIGGER AND FATTER AND STRONGER EACH YEAR, WHILE THE HOLLUSCHICKIE PLAY AROUND HIM, IN THAT SEA WHERE NO MAN COMES.
THIS IS WHERE LIMMERSHIN'S STORY ENDS.
BOOK 4 ~ END

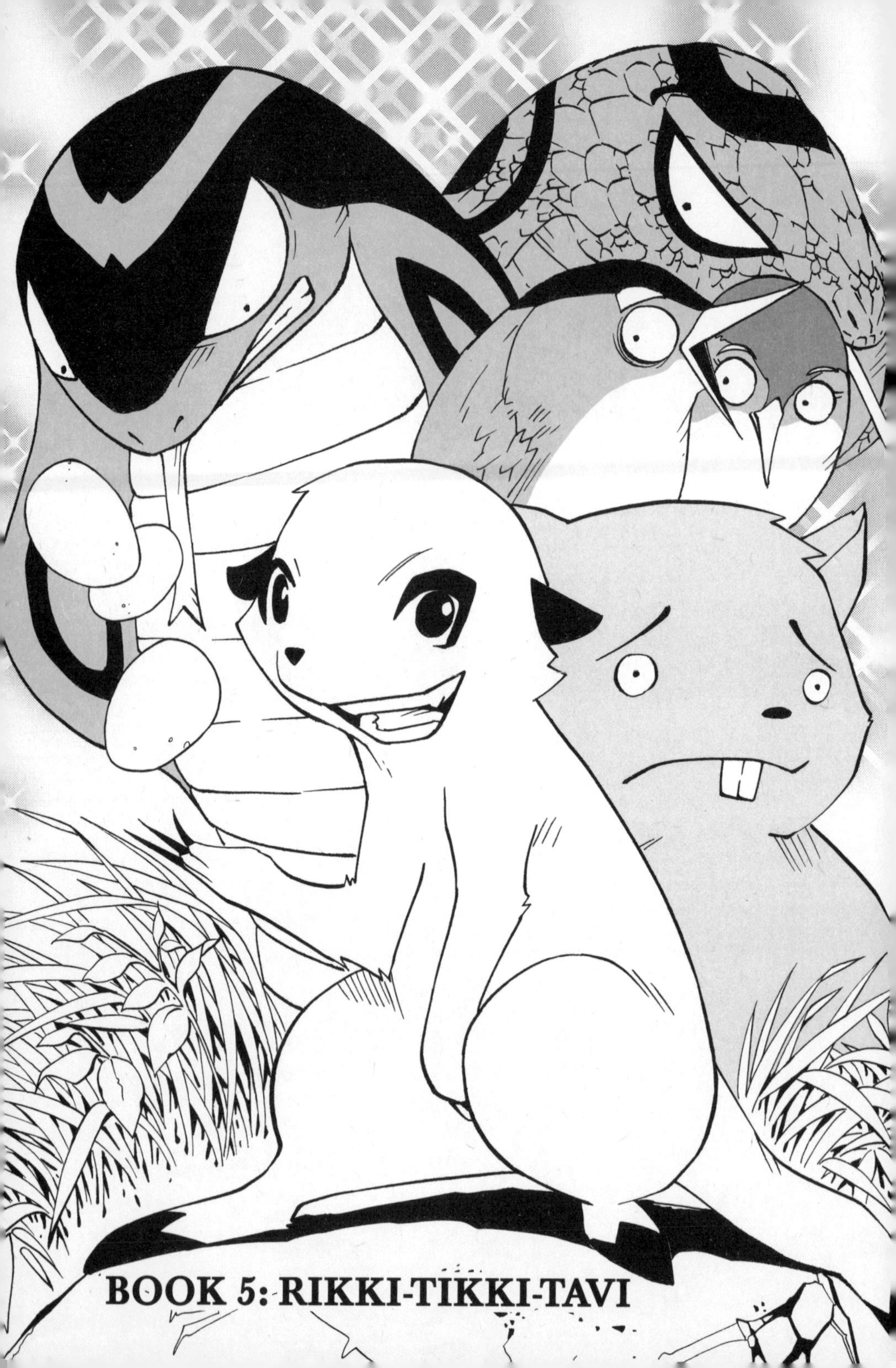

BOOK 5: RIKKI-TIKKI-TAVI

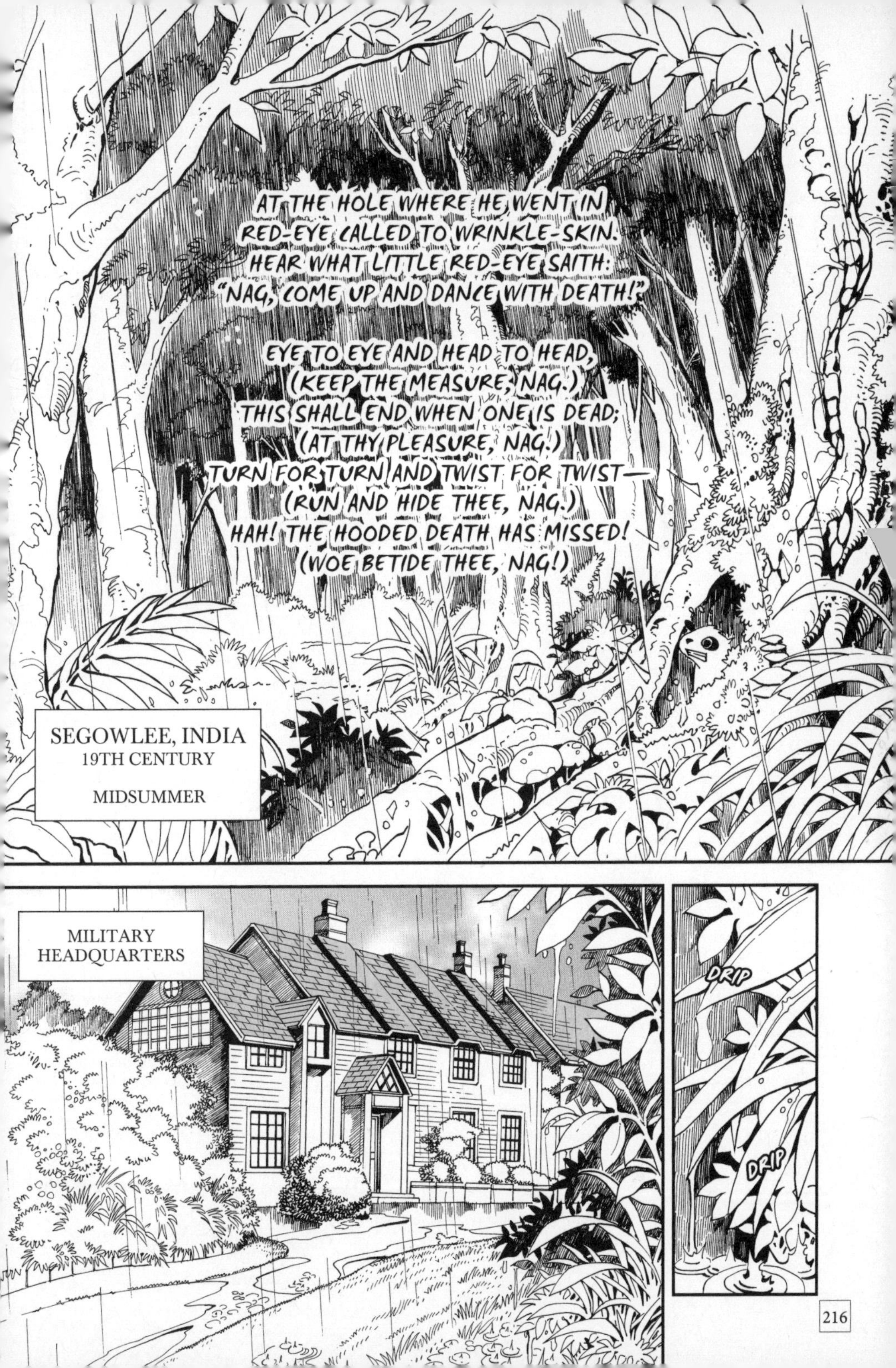
AT THE HOLE WHERE HE WENT IN
RED-EYE CALLED TO WRINKLE-SKIN.
HEAR WHAT LITTLE RED-EYE SAITH:
"NAG, COME UP AND DANCE WITH DEATH!"

EYE TO EYE AND HEAD TO HEAD,
(KEEP THE MEASURE, NAG.)
THIS SHALL END WHEN ONE IS DEAD;
(AT THY PLEASURE, NAG.)
TURN FOR TURN AND TWIST FOR TWIST—
(RUN AND HIDE THEE, NAG.)
HAH! THE HOODED DEATH HAS MISSED!
(WOE BETIDE THEE, NAG!)
SEGOWLEE, INDIA
19TH CENTURY
MIDSUMMER
DRIP
DRIP
MILITARY
HEADQUARTERS

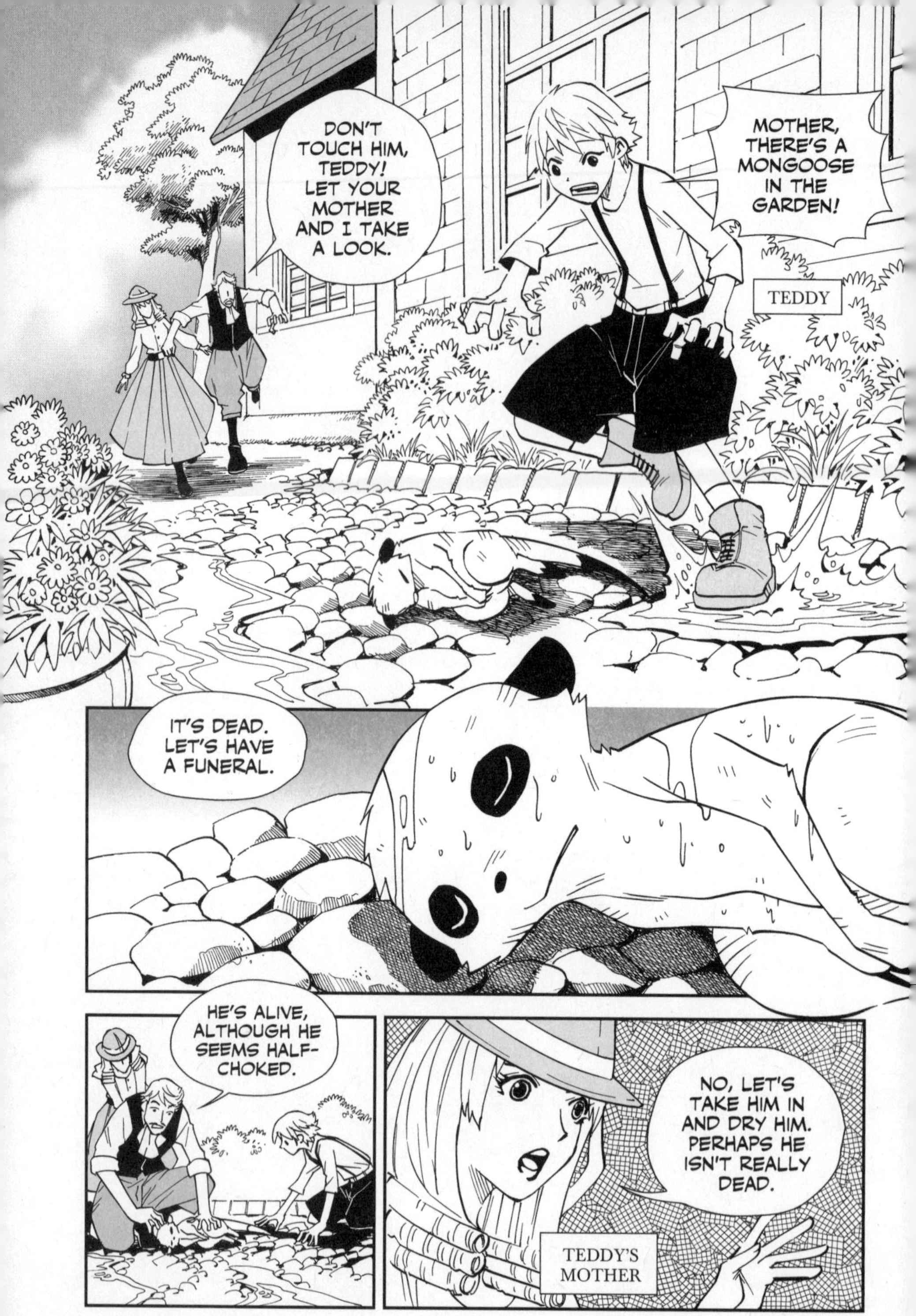
MOTHER, THERE'S A MONGOOSE IN THE GARDEN!
TEDDY
DON'T TOUCH HIM, TEDDY! LET YOUR MOTHER AND I TAKE A LOOK.
IT'S DEAD. LET'S HAVE A FUNERAL.
NO, LET'S TAKE HIM IN AND DRY HIM. PERHAPS HE ISN'T REALLY DEAD.
TEDDY'S MOTHER
HE'S ALIVE, ALTHOUGH HE SEEMS HALF-CHOKED.

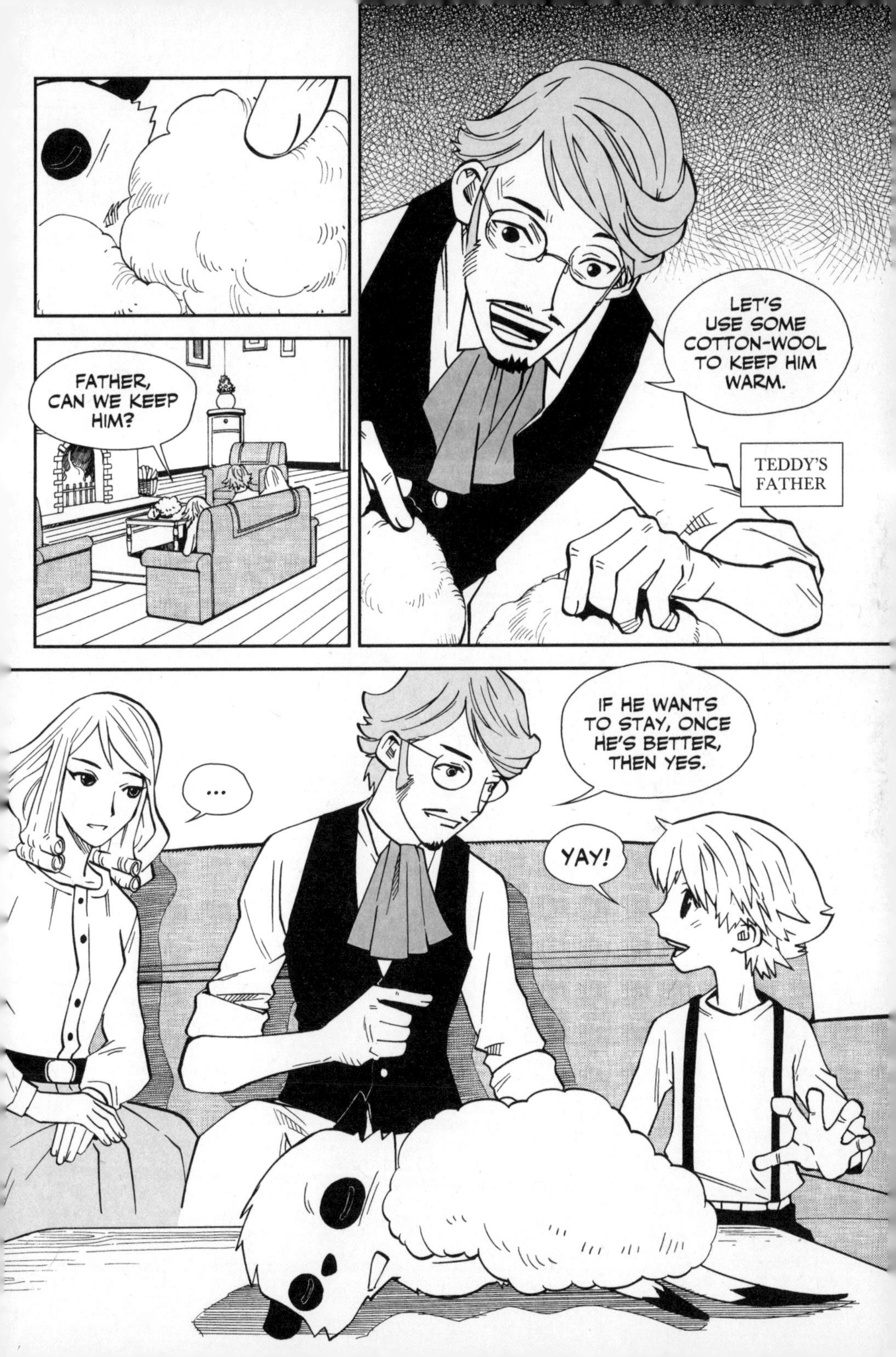
LET'S USE SOME COTTON-WOOL TO KEEP HIM WARM.
TEDDY'S FATHER
FATHER, CAN WE KEEP HIM?
IF HE WANTS TO STAY, ONCE HE'S BETTER, THEN YES.
YAY!
...

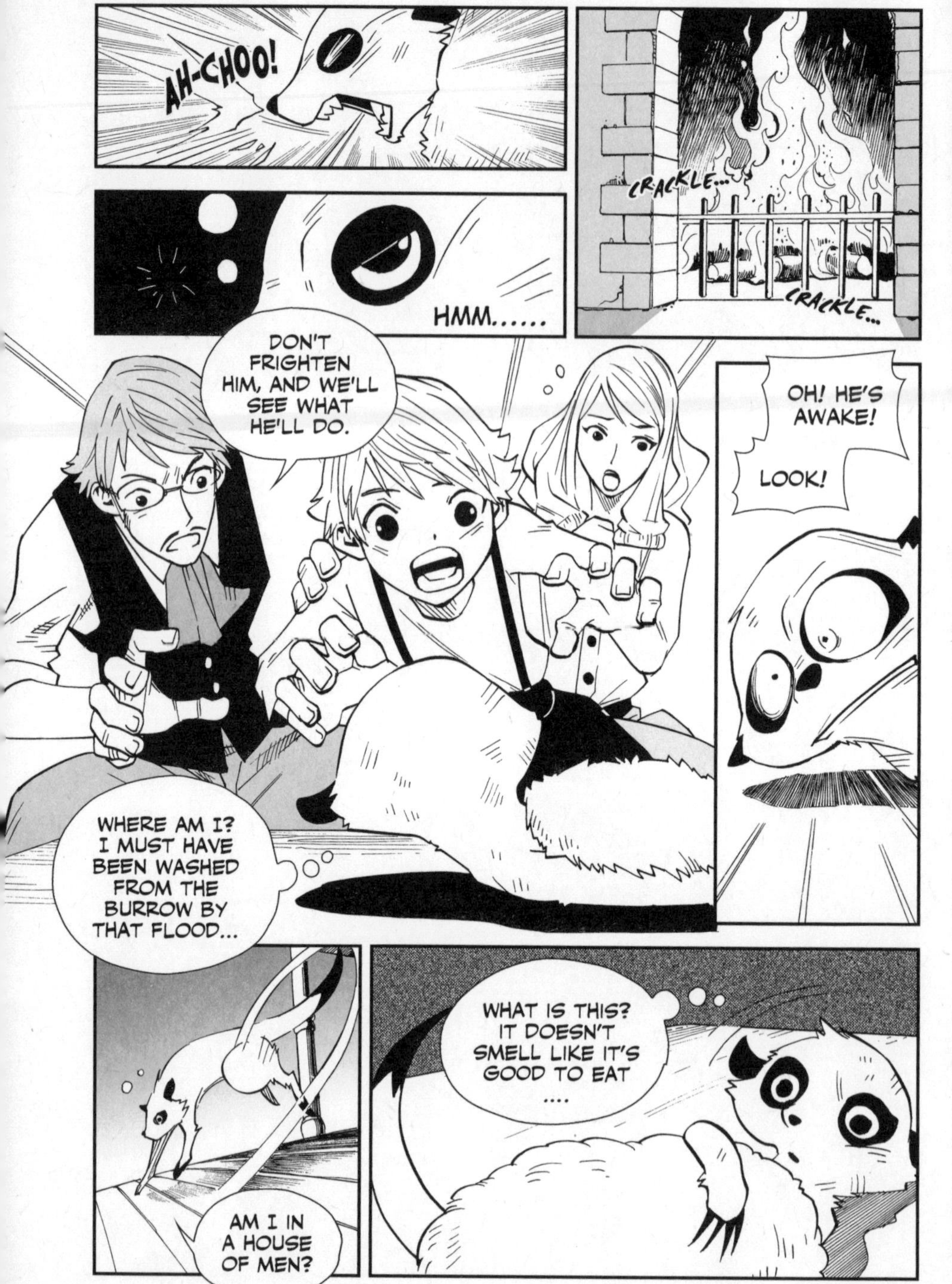
CRACKLE...
CRACKLE...
AH-CHOO!
HMM......
OH! HE'S AWAKE!
LOOK!
DON'T FRIGHTEN HIM, AND WE'LL SEE WHAT HE'LL DO.
WHERE AM I? I MUST HAVE BEEN WASHED FROM THE BURROW BY THAT FLOOD...
WHAT IS THIS? IT DOESN'T SMELL LIKE IT'S GOOD TO EAT ....
AM I IN A HOUSE OF MEN?

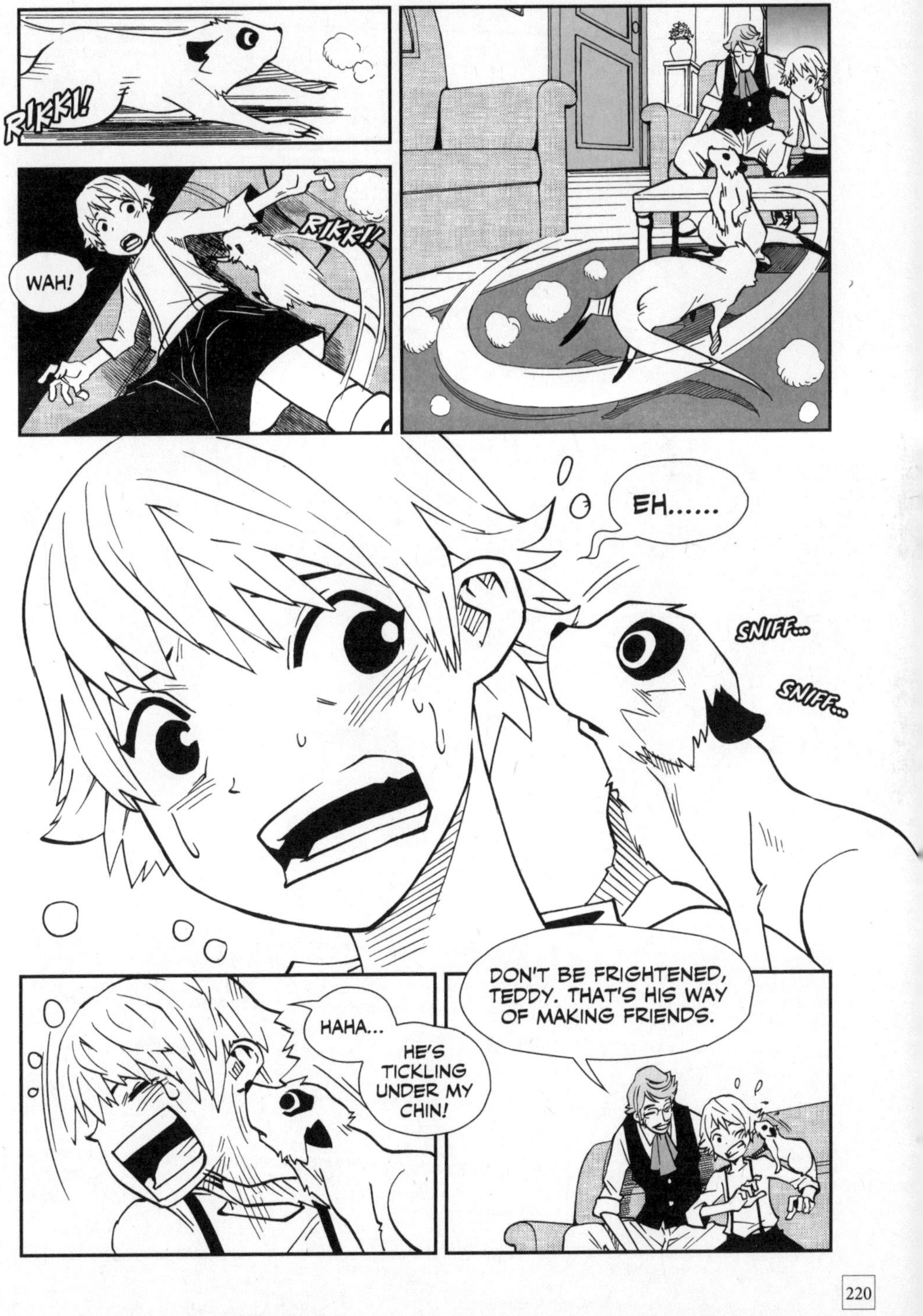
RIKKI!
RIKKI!
WAH!
EH......
SNIFF...
SNIFF...
DON'T BE FRIGHTENED, TEDDY. THAT'S HIS WAY OF MAKING FRIENDS.
HAHA...
HE'S TICKLING UNDER MY CHIN!

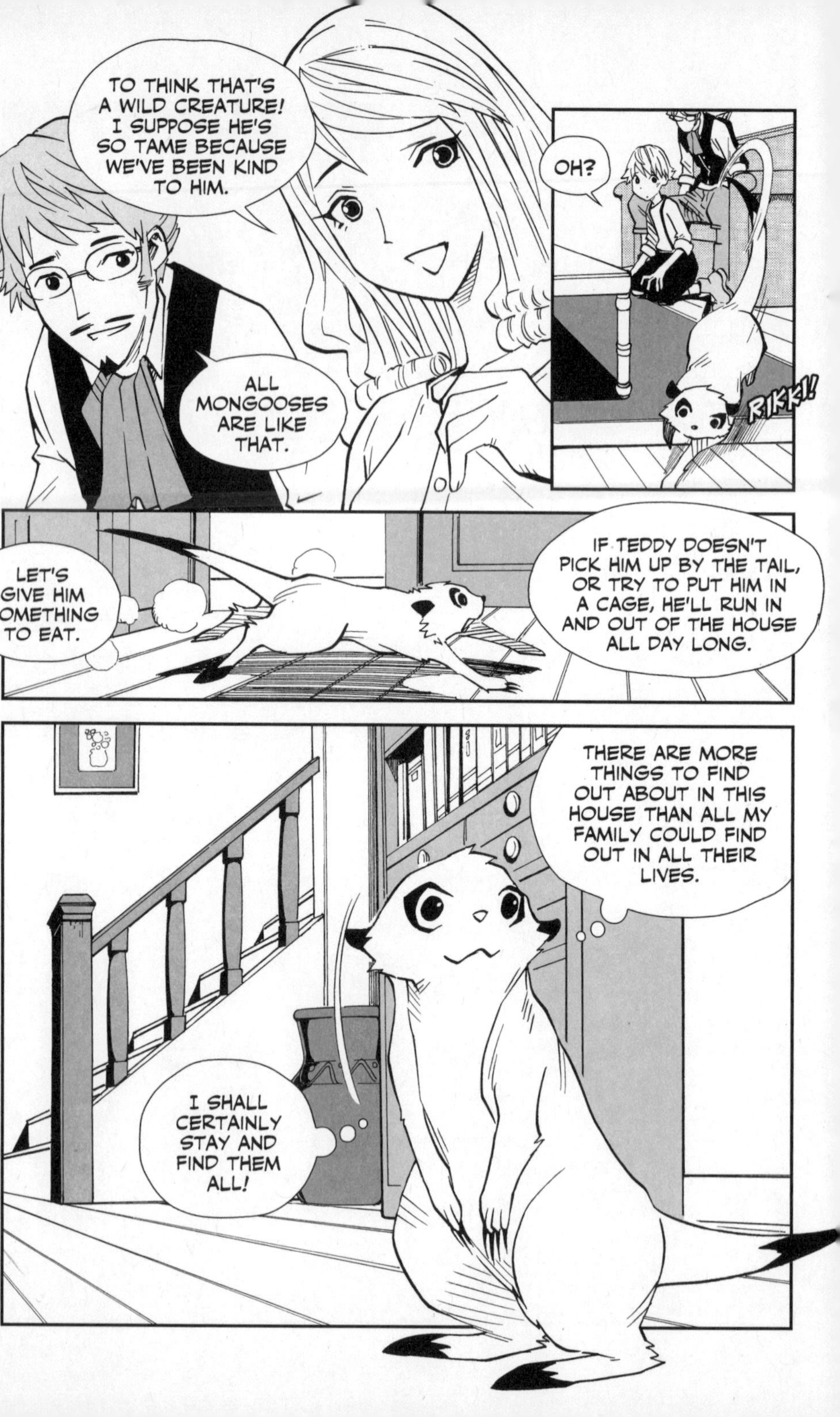
OH?
RIKKI!
TO THINK THAT'S A WILD CREATURE! I SUPPOSE HE'S SO TAME BECAUSE WE'VE BEEN KIND TO HIM.
ALL MONGOOSES ARE LIKE THAT.
IF TEDDY DOESN'T PICK HIM UP BY THE TAIL, OR TRY TO PUT HIM IN A CAGE, HE'LL RUN IN AND OUT OF THE HOUSE ALL DAY LONG.
LET'S GIVE HIM SOMETHING TO EAT.
THERE ARE MORE THINGS TO FIND OUT ABOUT IN THIS HOUSE THAN ALL MY FAMILY COULD FIND OUT IN ALL THEIR LIVES.
I SHALL CERTAINLY STAY AND FIND THEM ALL!

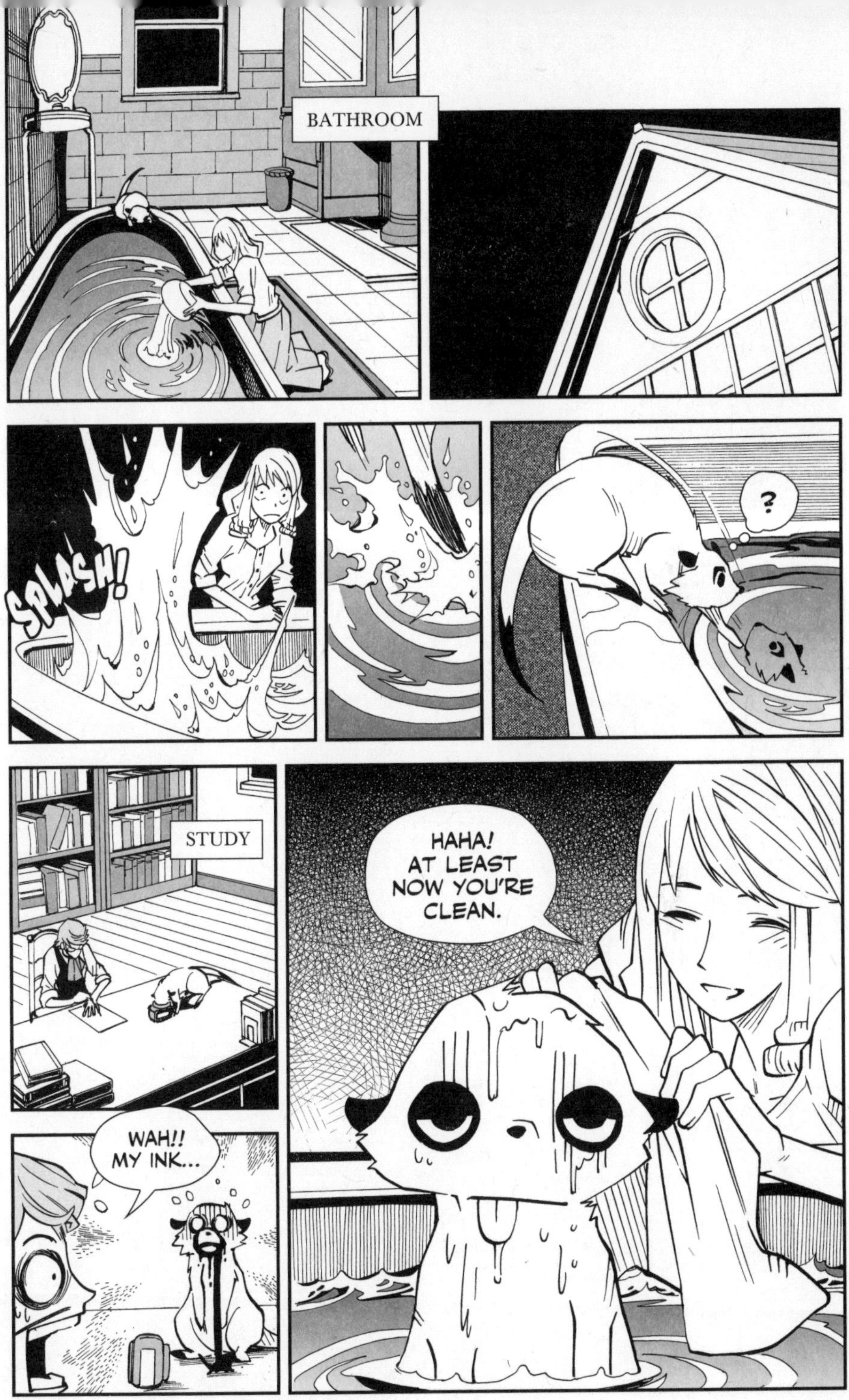
BATHROOM
?
SPLASH!
HAHA! AT LEAST NOW YOU'RE CLEAN.
STUDY
WAH!! MY INK...

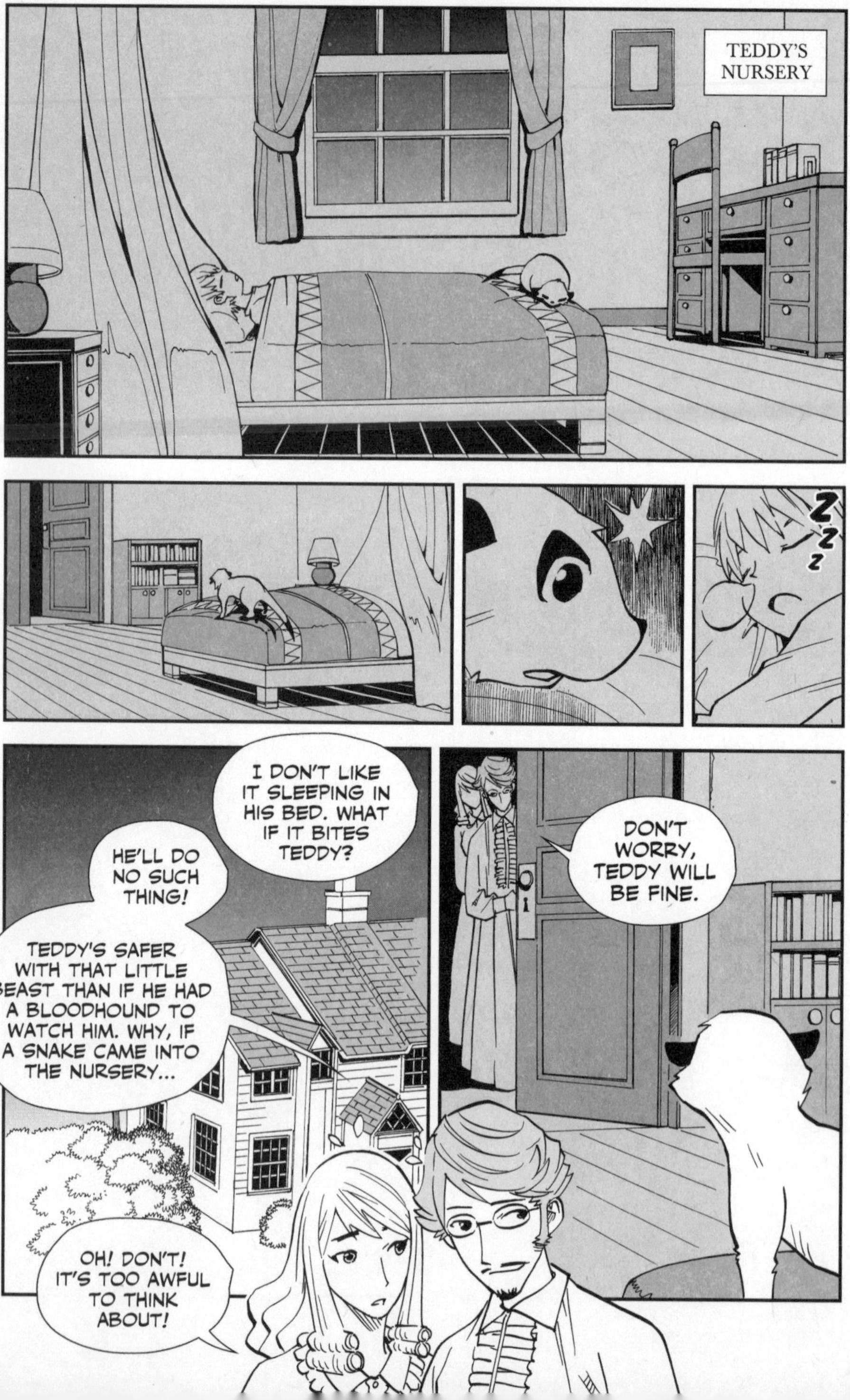
TEDDY'S NURSERY
Z Z Z
DON'T WORRY, TEDDY WILL BE FINE.
I DON'T LIKE IT SLEEPING IN HIS BED. WHAT IF IT BITES TEDDY?
HE'LL DO NO SUCH THING!
TEDDY'S SAFER WITH THAT LITTLE BEAST THAN IF HE HAD A BLOODHOUND TO WATCH HIM. WHY, IF A SNAKE CAME INTO THE NURSERY...
OH! DON'T! IT'S TOO AWFUL TO THINK ABOUT!

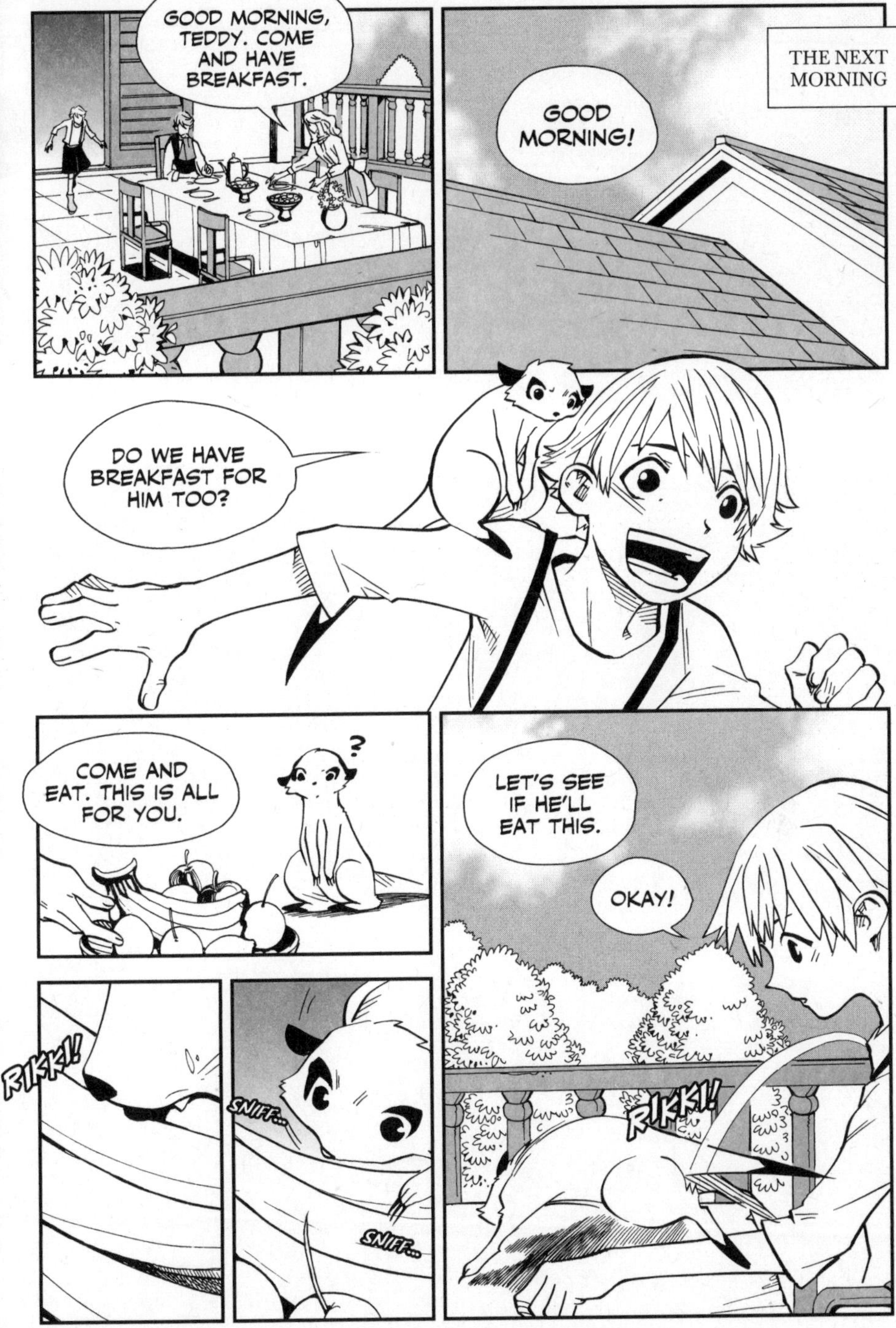
THE NEXT MORNING
GOOD MORNING!
GOOD MORNING, TEDDY. COME AND HAVE BREAKFAST.
DO WE HAVE BREAKFAST FOR HIM TOO?
LET'S SEE IF HE'LL EAT THIS.
OKAY!
RIKKI!
COME AND EAT. THIS IS ALL FOR YOU.
SNIFF...
SNIFF...
RIKKI!

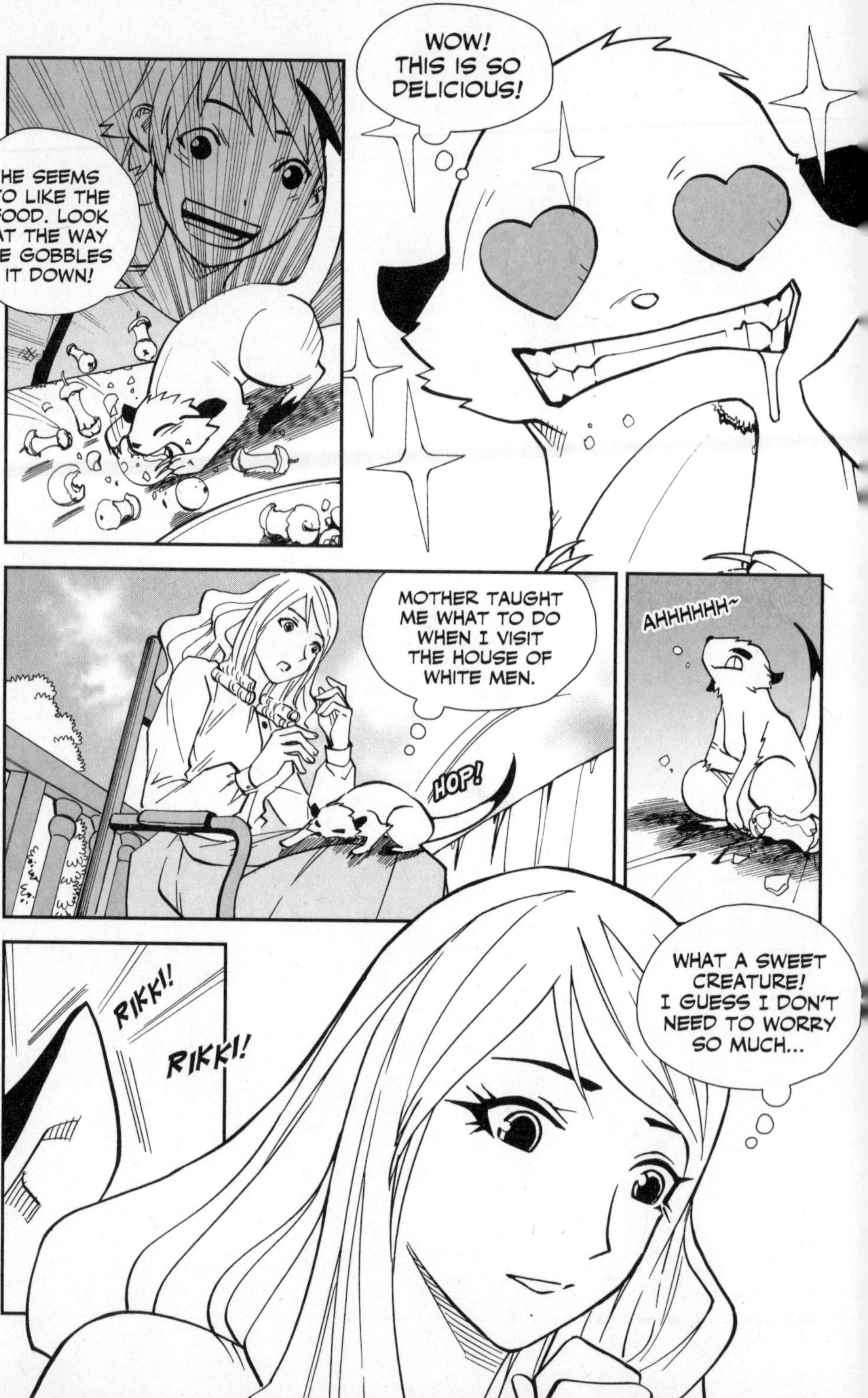
WOW! THIS IS SO DELICIOUS!
HE SEEMS TO LIKE THE FOOD. LOOK AT THE WAY HE GOBBLES IT DOWN!
AHHHHHH~
MOTHER TAUGHT ME WHAT TO DO WHEN I VISIT THE HOUSE OF WHITE MEN.
HOP!
WHAT A SWEET CREATURE! I GUESS I DON'T NEED TO WORRY SO MUCH...
RIKKI!
RIKKI!

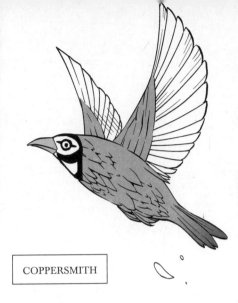

COPPERSMITH

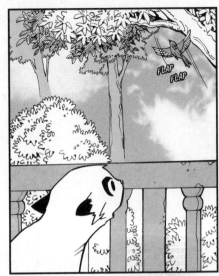

FLAP FLAP

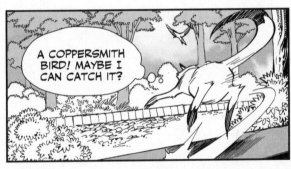

A COPPERSMITH BIRD! MAYBE I CAN CATCH IT?

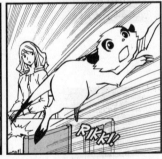

RIKK!

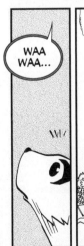

WAA WAA...

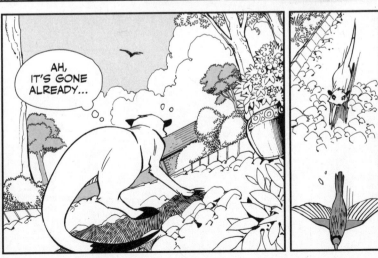

AH, IT'S GONE ALREADY...

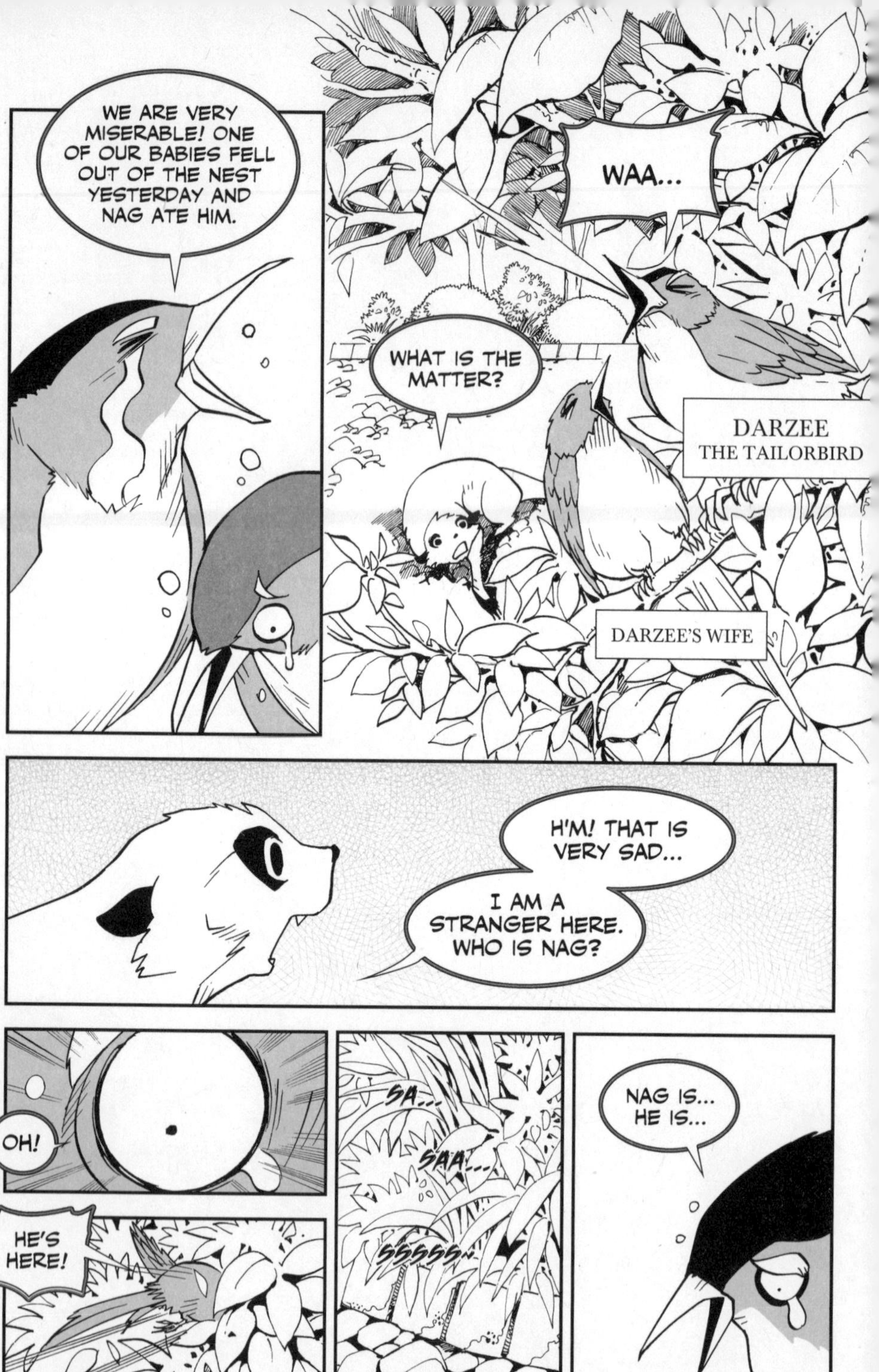
WAA...
WHAT IS THE MATTER?
DARZEE THE TAILORBIRD
DARZEE'S WIFE
WE ARE VERY MISERABLE! ONE OF OUR BABIES FELL OUT OF THE NEST YESTERDAY AND NAG ATE HIM.
H'M! THAT IS VERY SAD...
I AM A STRANGER HERE. WHO IS NAG?
NAG IS... HE IS...
SA...
SAA...
SSSSS...
OH!
HE'S HERE!

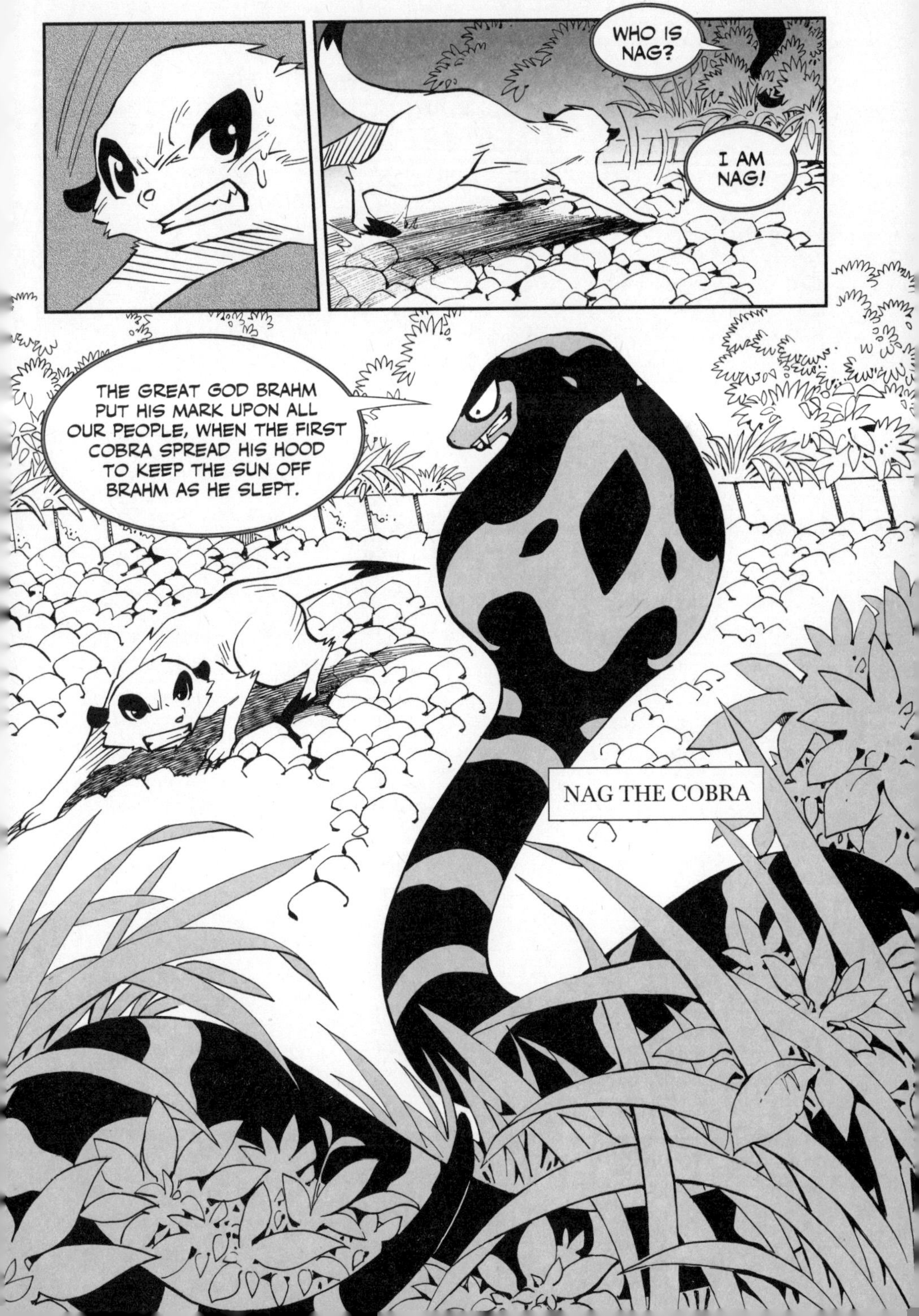
WHO IS NAG?
I AM NAG!
THE GREAT GOD BRAHM PUT HIS MARK UPON ALL OUR PEOPLE, WHEN THE FIRST COBRA SPREAD HIS HOOD TO KEEP THE SUN OFF BRAHM AS HE SLEPT.
NAG THE COBRA

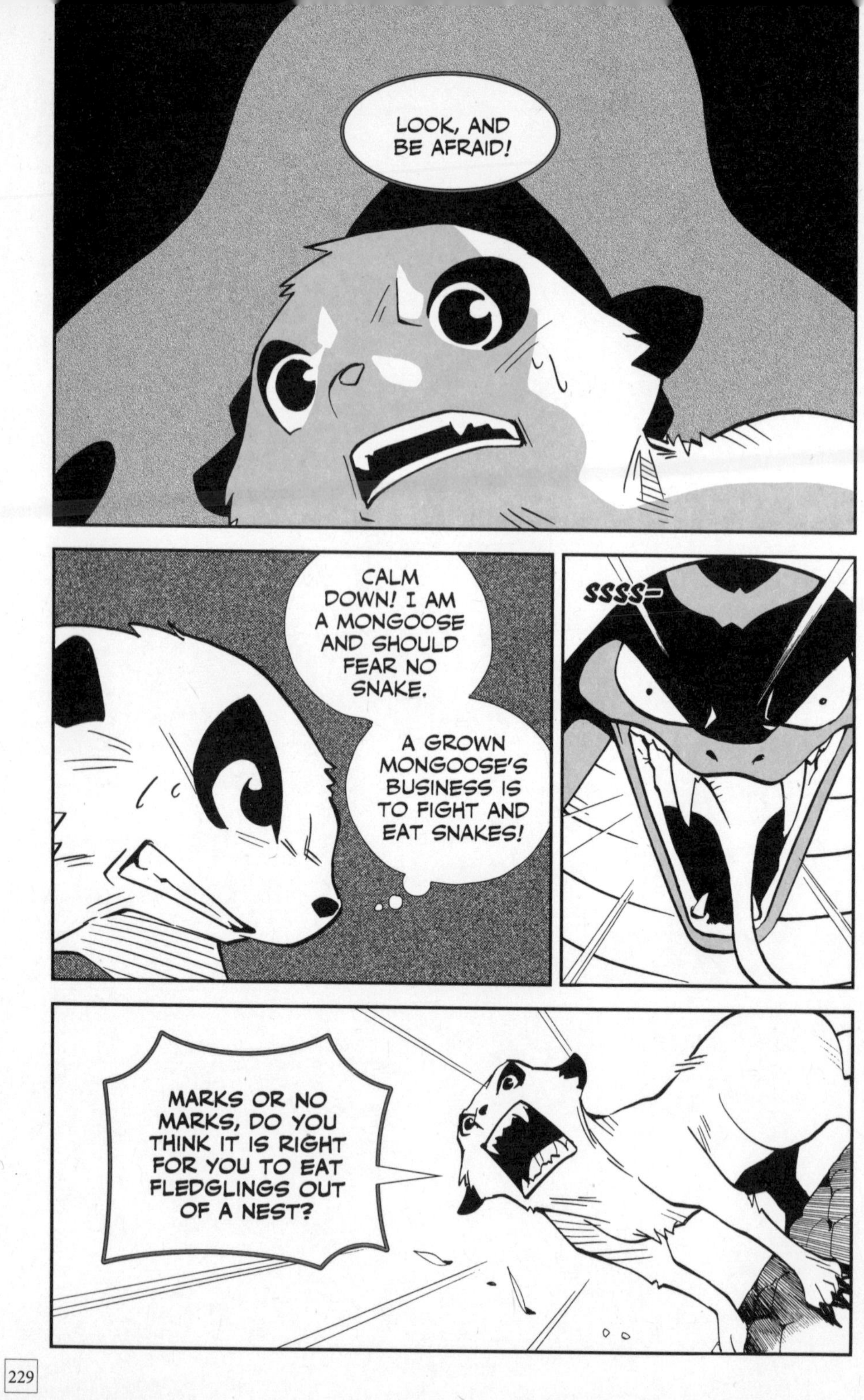
LOOK, AND BE AFRAID!
SSSS-
CALM DOWN! I AM A MONGOOSE AND SHOULD FEAR NO SNAKE.
A GROWN MONGOOSE'S BUSINESS IS TO FIGHT AND EAT SNAKES!
MARKS OR NO MARKS, DO YOU THINK IT IS RIGHT FOR YOU TO EAT FLEDGLINGS OUT OF A NEST?

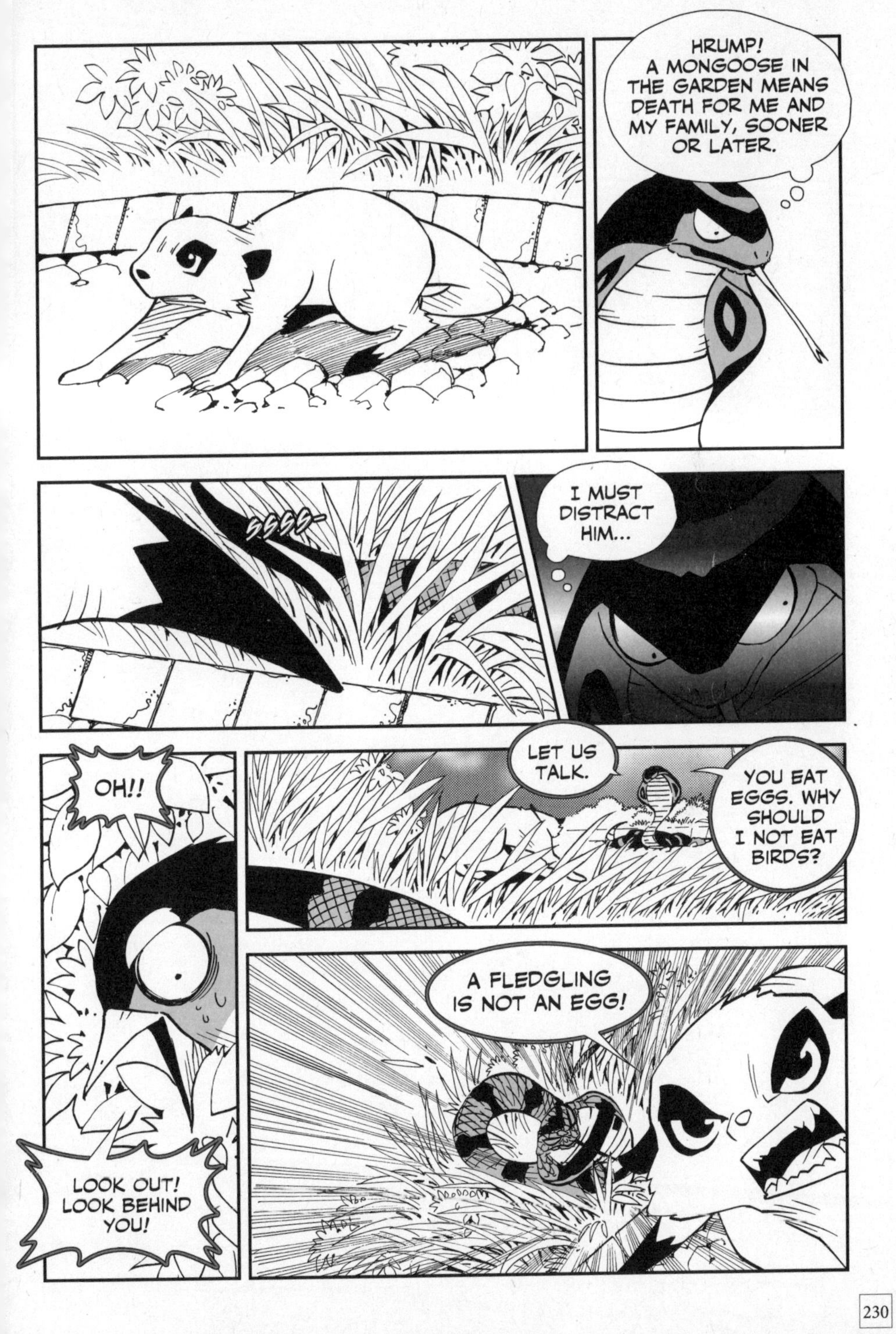
HRUMP! A MONGOOSE IN THE GARDEN MEANS DEATH FOR ME AND MY FAMILY, SOONER OR LATER.
I MUST DISTRACT HIM...
SSSS-
LET US TALK.
YOU EAT EGGS. WHY SHOULD I NOT EAT BIRDS?
A FLEDGLING IS NOT AN EGG!
OH!!
LOOK OUT! LOOK BEHIND YOU!

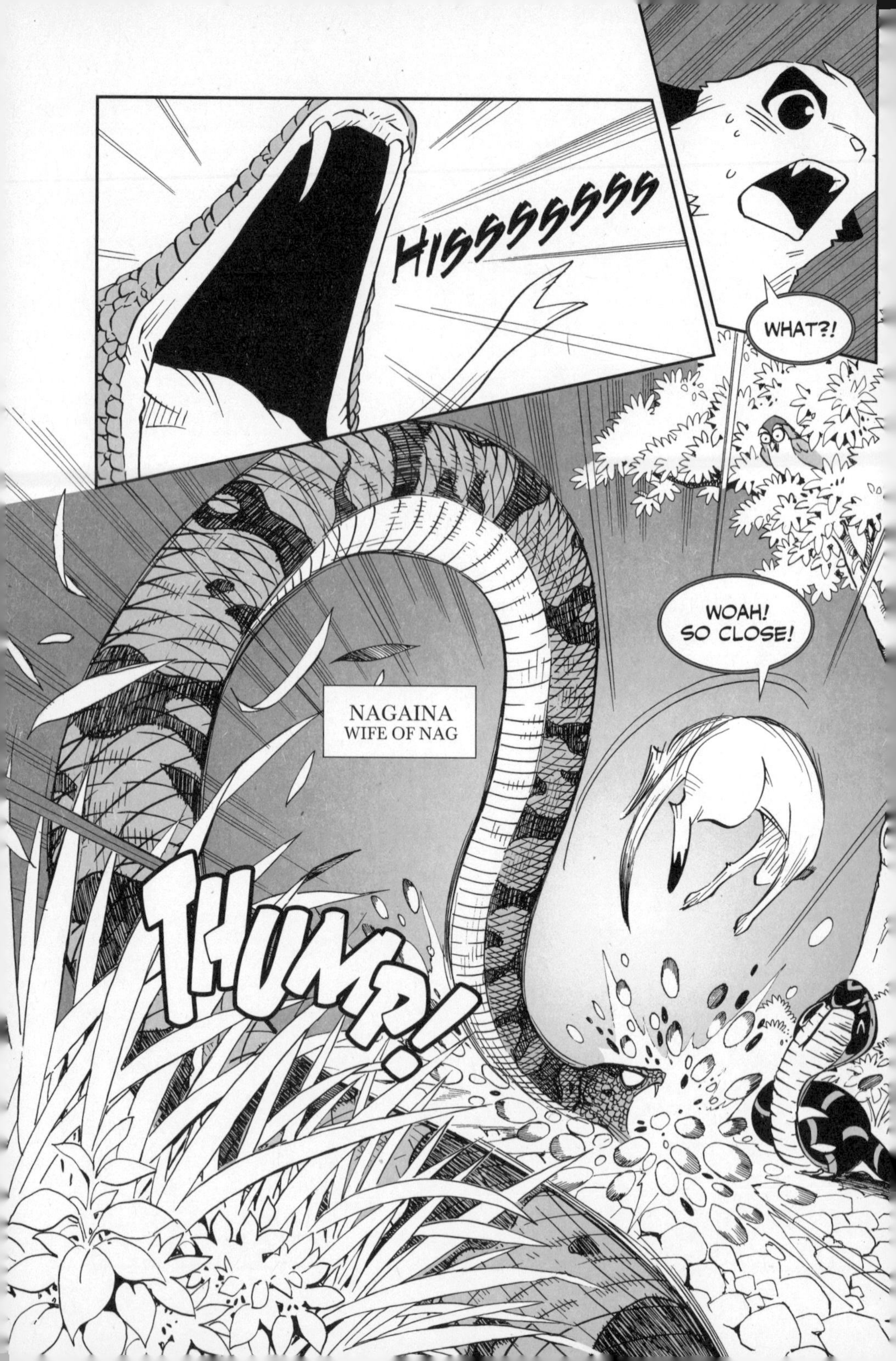
WHAT?!
HISSSSSSSS
WOAH! SO CLOSE!
NAGAINA
WIFE OF NAG
THUMP!

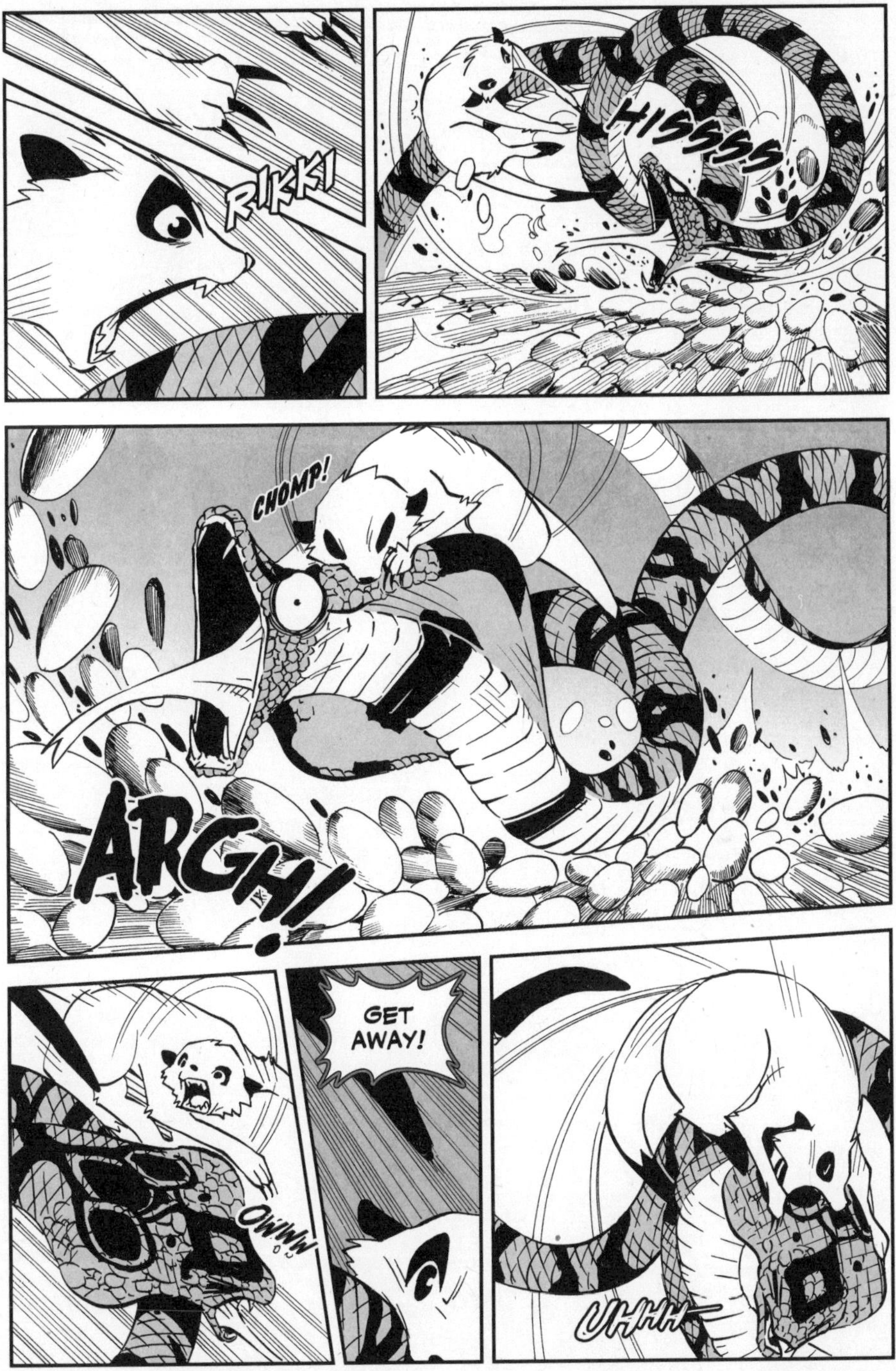
HISSSSS
RIKKI
CHOMP!
ARGH!!
UHHH
GET AWAY!
OWWWW

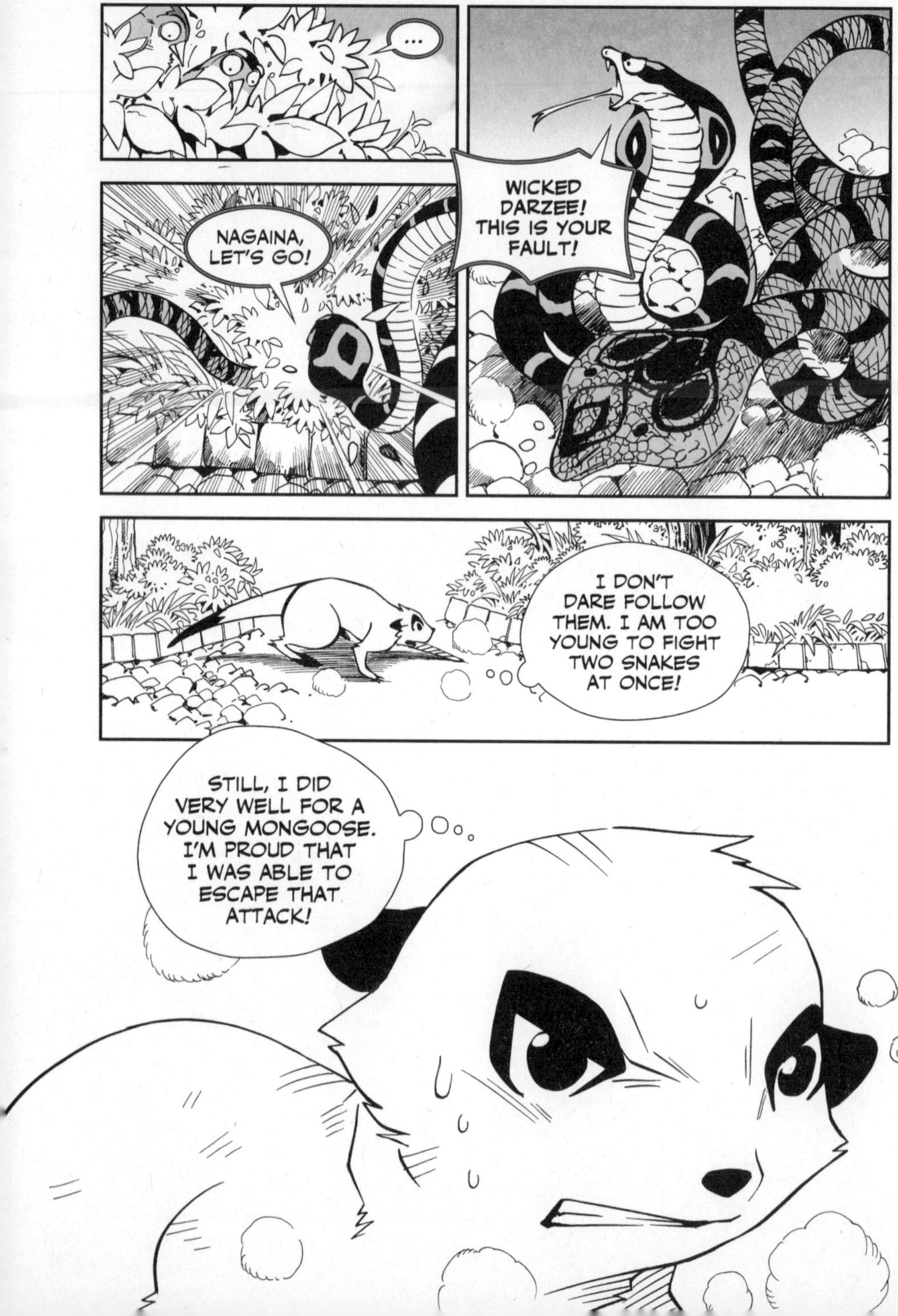
WICKED DARZEE! THIS IS YOUR FAULT!
...
NAGAINA, LET'S GO!
I DON'T DARE FOLLOW THEM. I AM TOO YOUNG TO FIGHT TWO SNAKES AT ONCE!
STILL, I DID VERY WELL FOR A YOUNG MONGOOSE. I'M PROUD THAT I WAS ABLE TO ESCAPE THAT ATTACK!

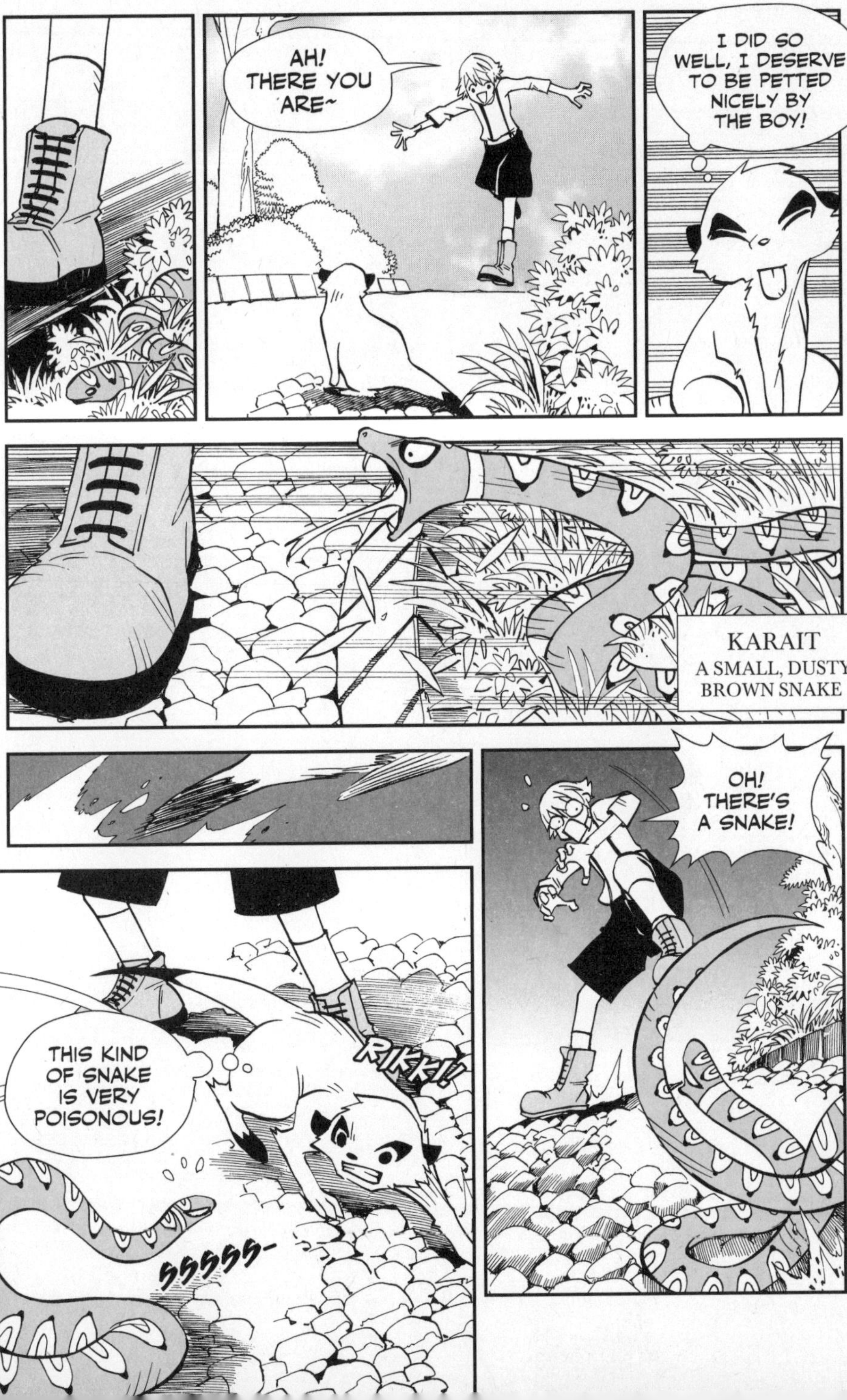
I DID SO WELL, I DESERVE TO BE PETTED NICELY BY THE BOY!
AH! THERE YOU ARE~
KARAIT
A SMALL, DUSTY BROWN SNAKE
OH! THERE'S A SNAKE!
RIKKI!
THIS KIND OF SNAKE IS VERY POISONOUS!
SSSSS-

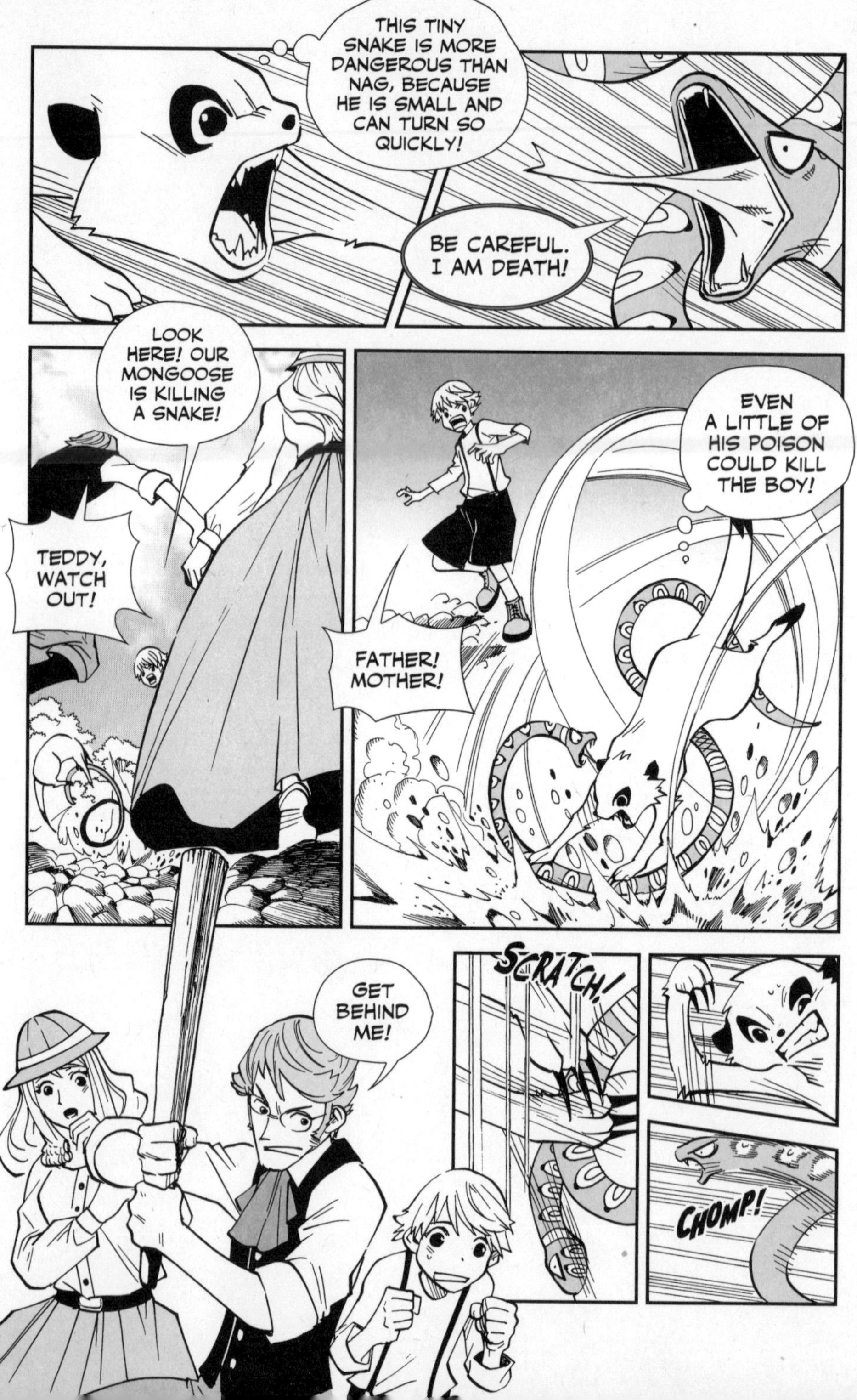
THIS TINY SNAKE IS MORE DANGEROUS THAN NAG, BECAUSE HE IS SMALL AND CAN TURN SO QUICKLY!
BE CAREFUL. I AM DEATH!
EVEN A LITTLE OF HIS POISON COULD KILL THE BOY!
FATHER! MOTHER!
LOOK HERE! OUR MONGOOSE IS KILLING A SNAKE!
TEDDY, WATCH OUT!
CHOMP!
SCRATCH!
GET BEHIND ME!

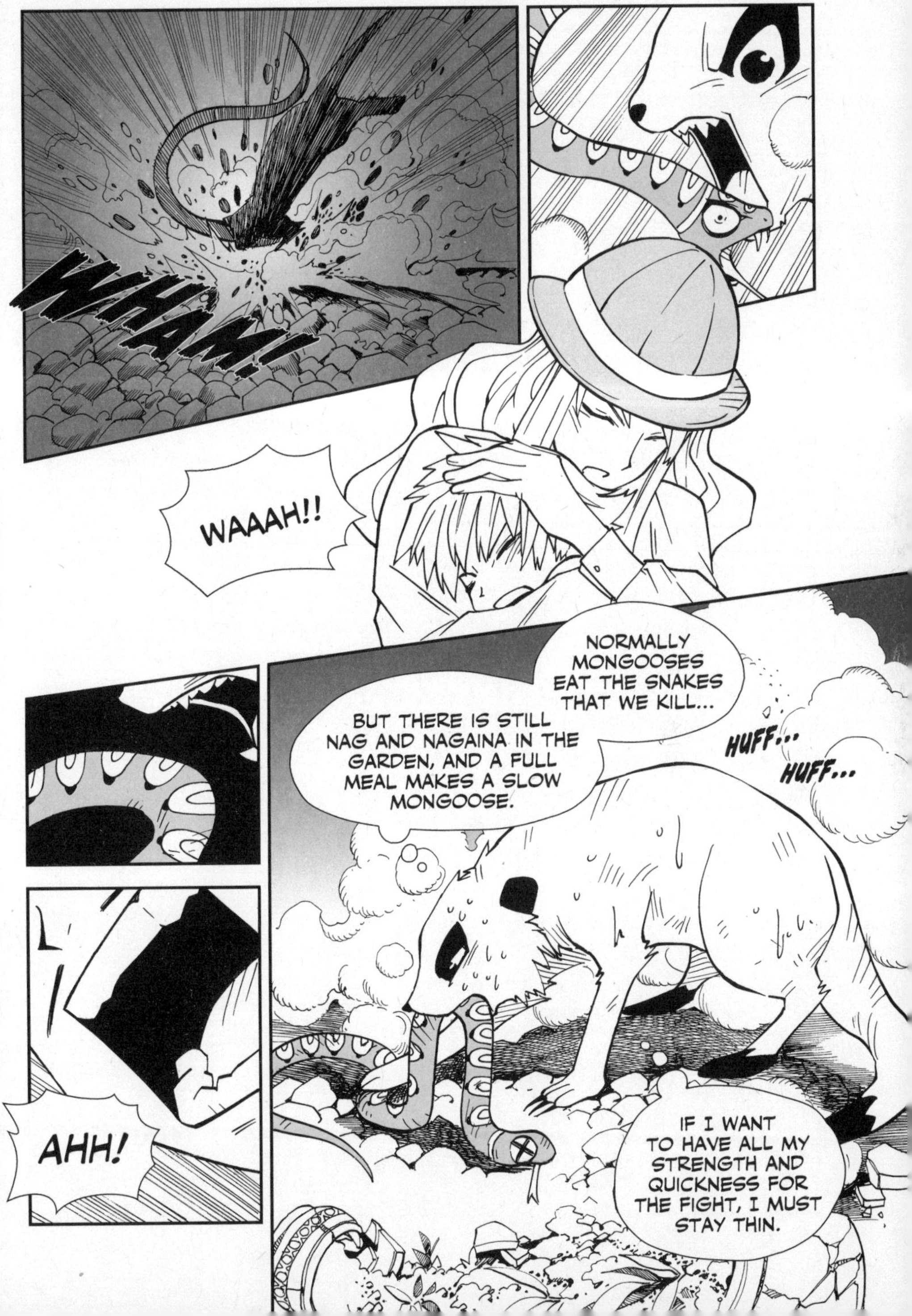
WHAM!
WAAAH!!
NORMALLY MONGOOSES EAT THE SNAKES THAT WE KILL...
BUT THERE IS STILL NAG AND NAGAINA IN THE GARDEN, AND A FULL MEAL MAKES A SLOW MONGOOSE.
HUFF...
HUFF...
IF I WANT TO HAVE ALL MY STRENGTH AND QUICKNESS FOR THE FIGHT, I MUST STAY THIN.
AHH!

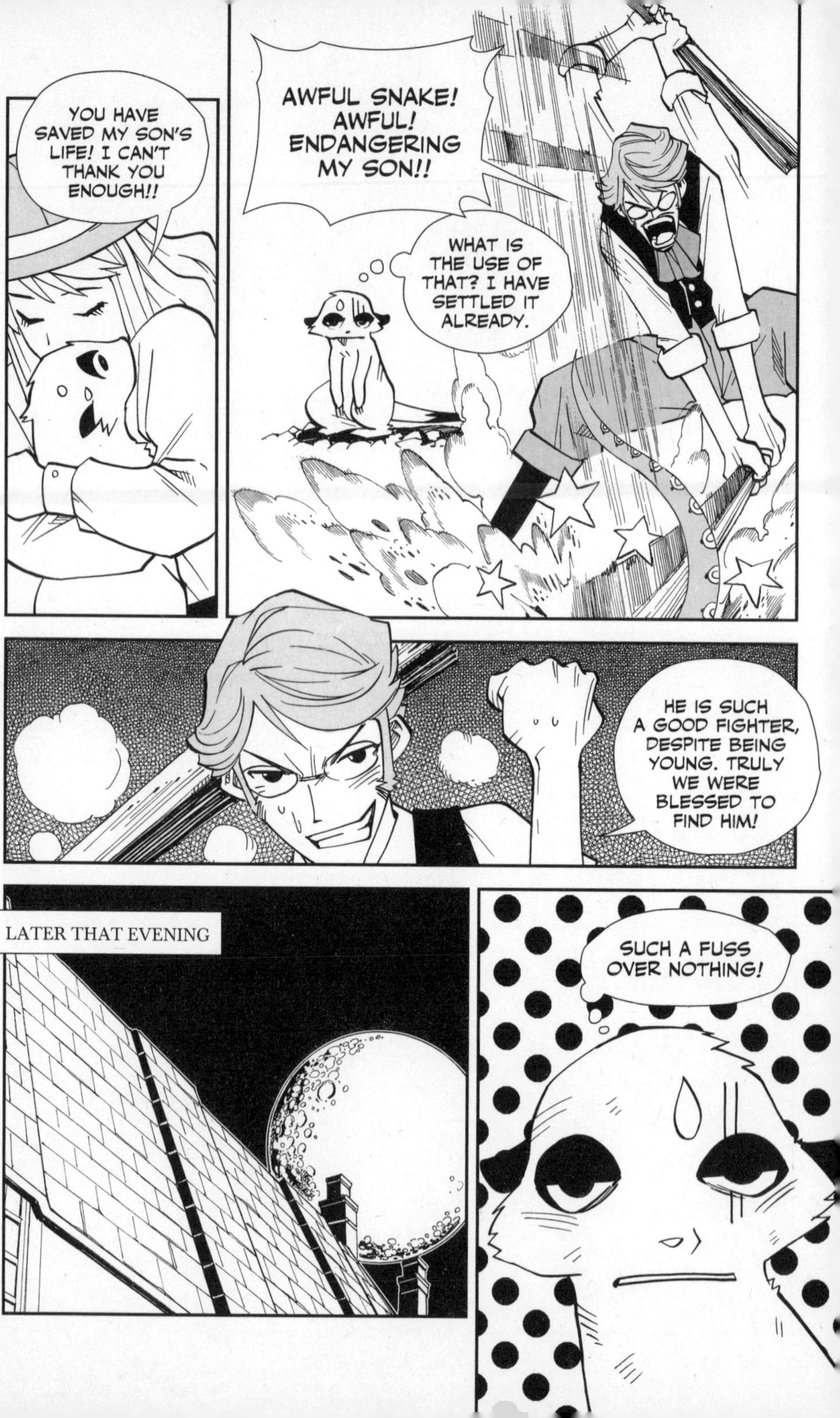
AWFUL SNAKE! AWFUL! ENDANGERING MY SON!!
WHAT IS THE USE OF THAT? I HAVE SETTLED IT ALREADY.
YOU HAVE SAVED MY SON'S LIFE! I CAN'T THANK YOU ENOUGH!!
HE IS SUCH A GOOD FIGHTER, DESPITE BEING YOUNG. TRULY WE WERE BLESSED TO FIND HIM!
SUCH A FUSS OVER NOTHING!
LATER THAT EVENING

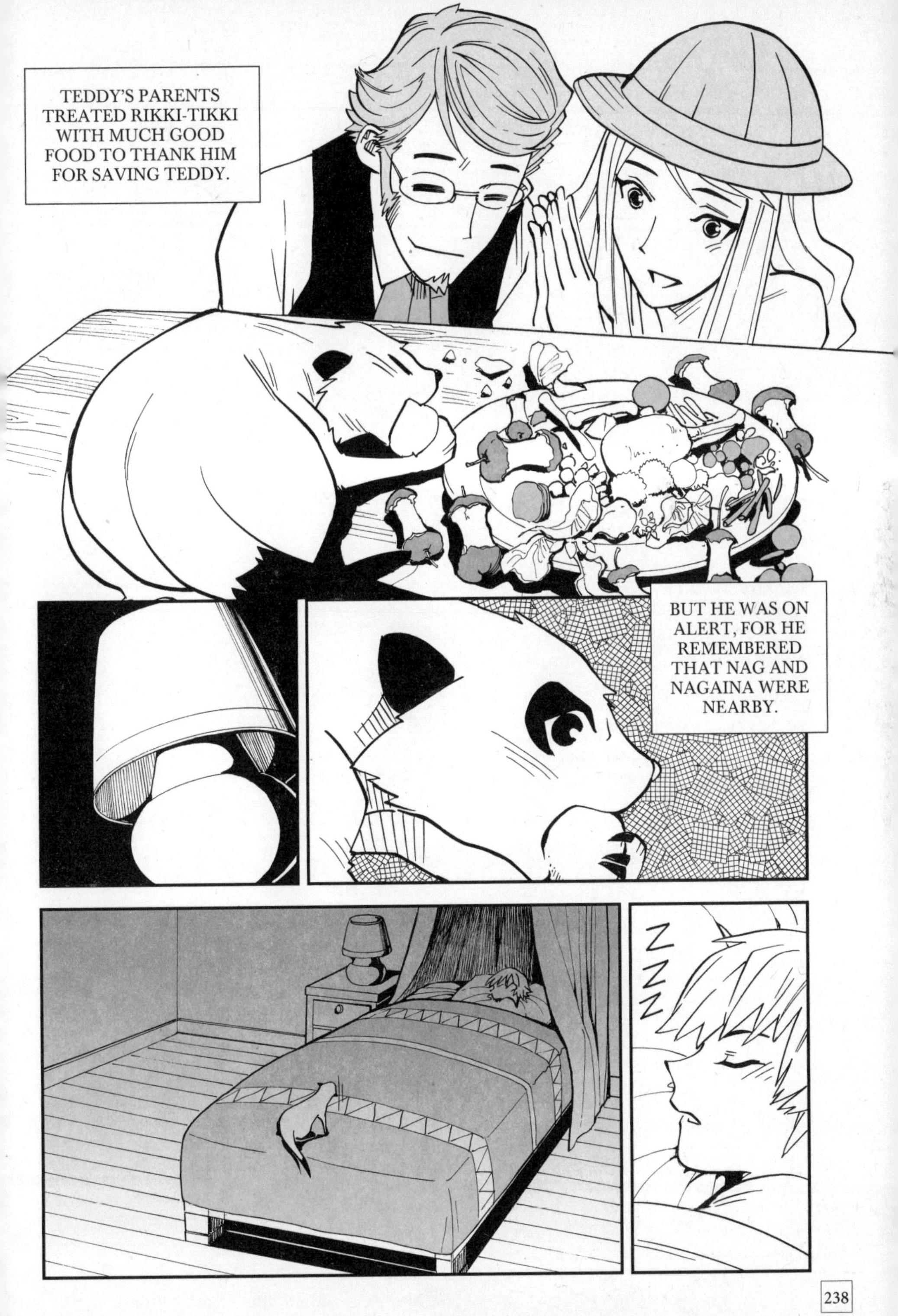
TEDDY'S PARENTS TREATED RIKKI-TIKKI WITH MUCH GOOD FOOD TO THANK HIM FOR SAVING TEDDY.
BUT HE WAS ON ALERT, FOR HE REMEMBERED THAT NAG AND NAGAINA WERE NEARBY.
ZZZ

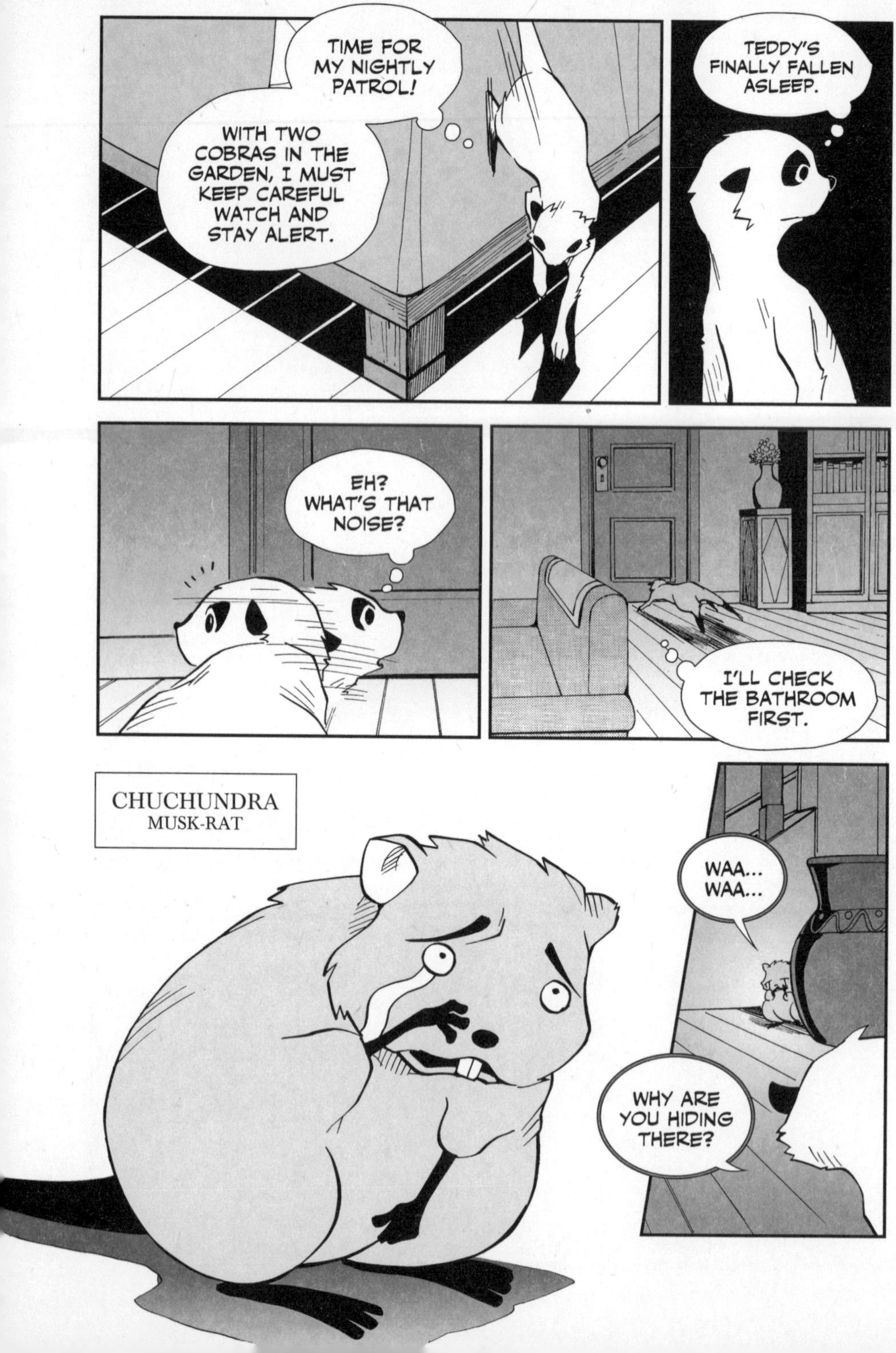
TEDDY'S FINALLY FALLEN ASLEEP.
TIME FOR MY NIGHTLY PATROL!
WITH TWO COBRAS IN THE GARDEN, I MUST KEEP CAREFUL WATCH AND STAY ALERT.
I'LL CHECK THE BATHROOM FIRST.
EH? WHAT'S THAT NOISE?
WAA... WAA...
WHY ARE YOU HIDING THERE?
CHUCHUNDRA
MUSK-RAT

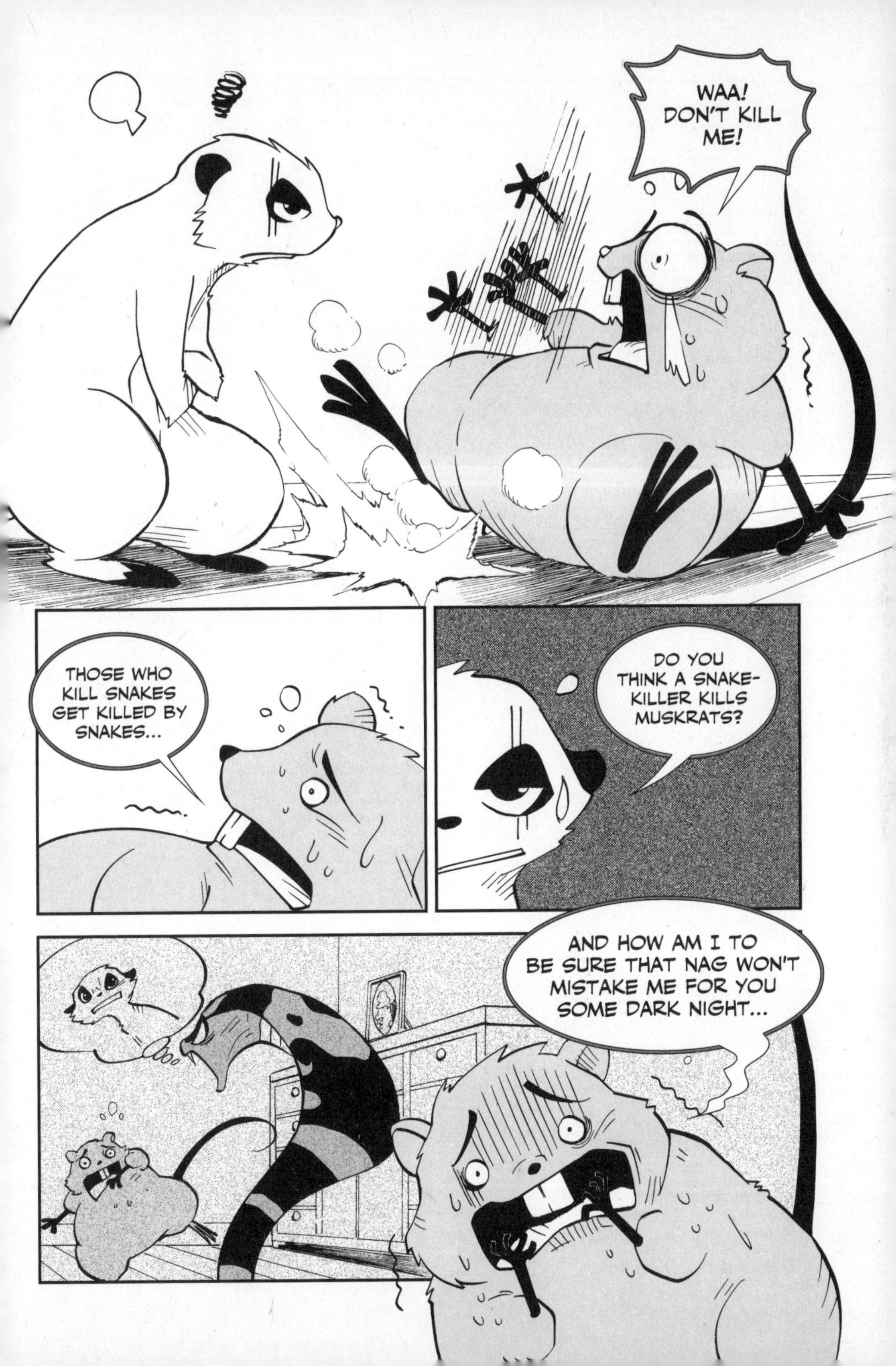
WAA! DON'T KILL ME!
THOSE WHO KILL SNAKES GET KILLED BY SNAKES...
DO YOU THINK A SNAKE-KILLER KILLS MUSKRATS?
AND HOW AM I TO BE SURE THAT NAG WON'T MISTAKE ME FOR YOU SOME DARK NIGHT...

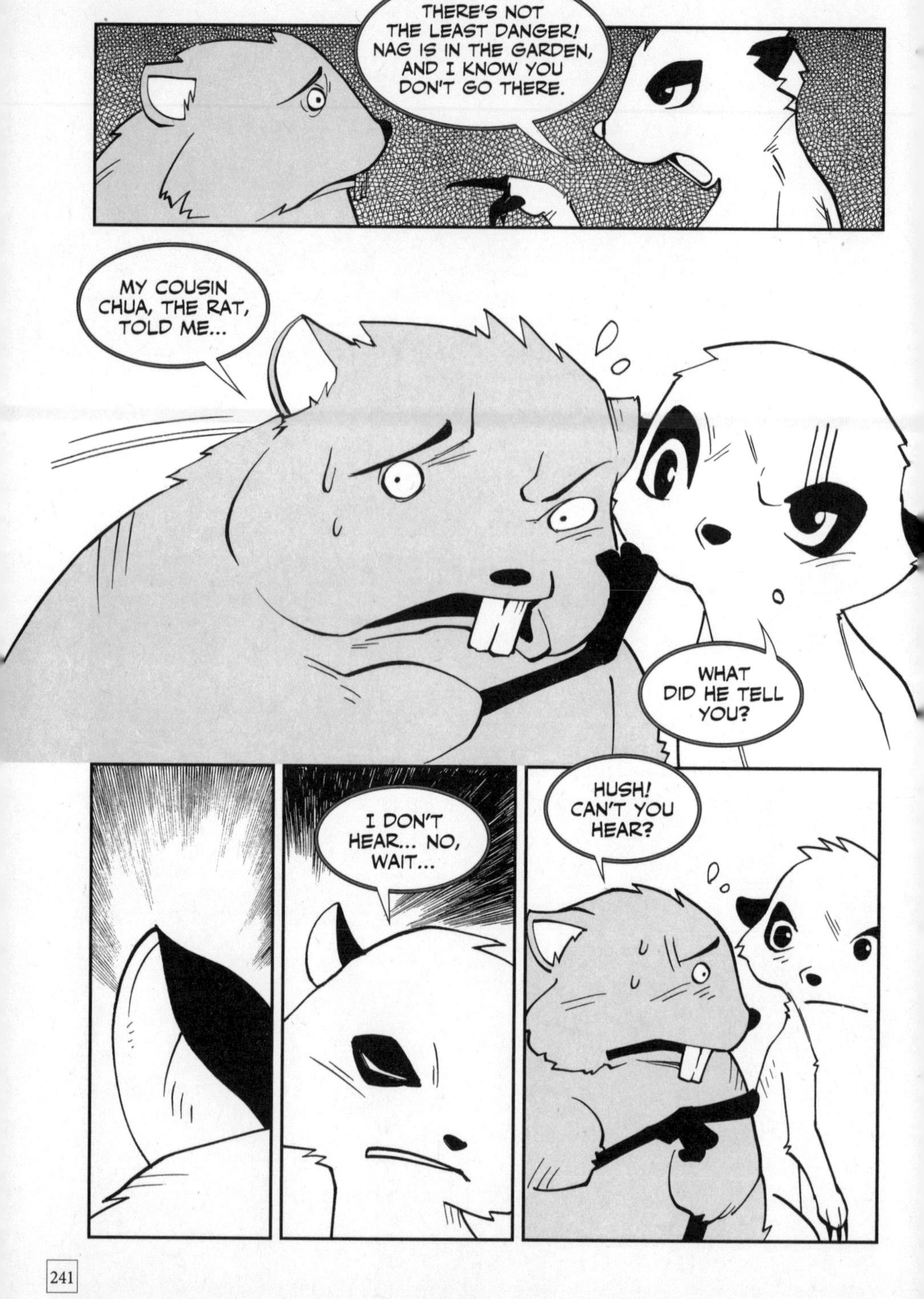
THERE'S NOT THE LEAST DANGER! NAG IS IN THE GARDEN, AND I KNOW YOU DON'T GO THERE.
MY COUSIN CHUA, THE RAT, TOLD ME...
WHAT DID HE TELL YOU?
HUSH! CAN'T YOU HEAR?
I DON'T HEAR... NO, WAIT...

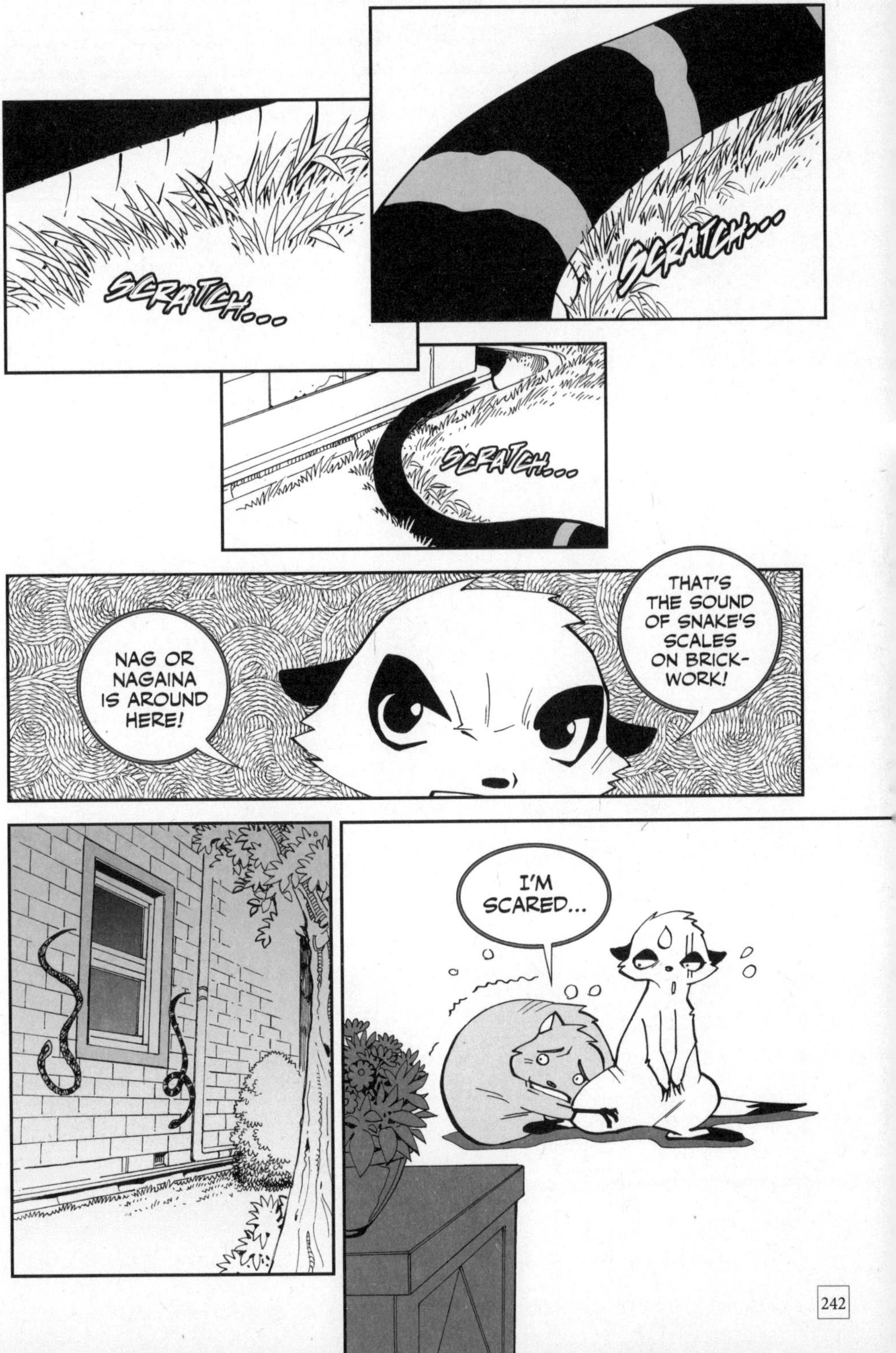
SCRATCH...
SCRATCH...
SCRATCH...
THAT'S THE SOUND OF SNAKE'S SCALES ON BRICK-WORK!
NAG OR NAGAINA IS AROUND HERE!
I'M SCARED...

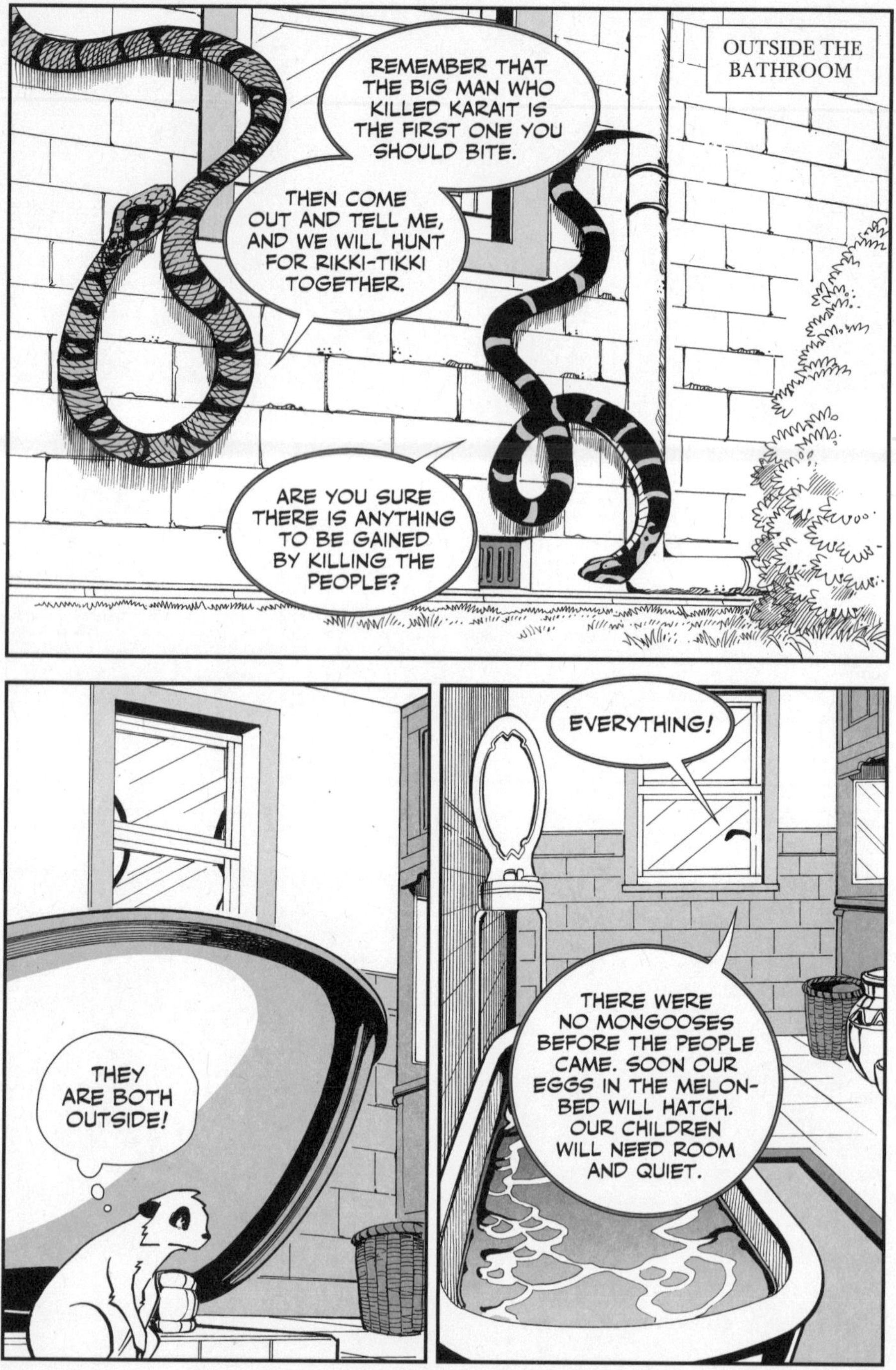
OUTSIDE THE BATHROOM
REMEMBER THAT THE BIG MAN WHO KILLED KARAIT IS THE FIRST ONE YOU SHOULD BITE.
THEN COME OUT AND TELL ME, AND WE WILL HUNT FOR RIKKI-TIKKI TOGETHER.
ARE YOU SURE THERE IS ANYTHING TO BE GAINED BY KILLING THE PEOPLE?
EVERYTHING!
THERE WERE NO MONGOOSES BEFORE THE PEOPLE CAME. SOON OUR EGGS IN THE MELON-BED WILL HATCH. OUR CHILDREN WILL NEED ROOM AND QUIET.
THEY ARE BOTH OUTSIDE!

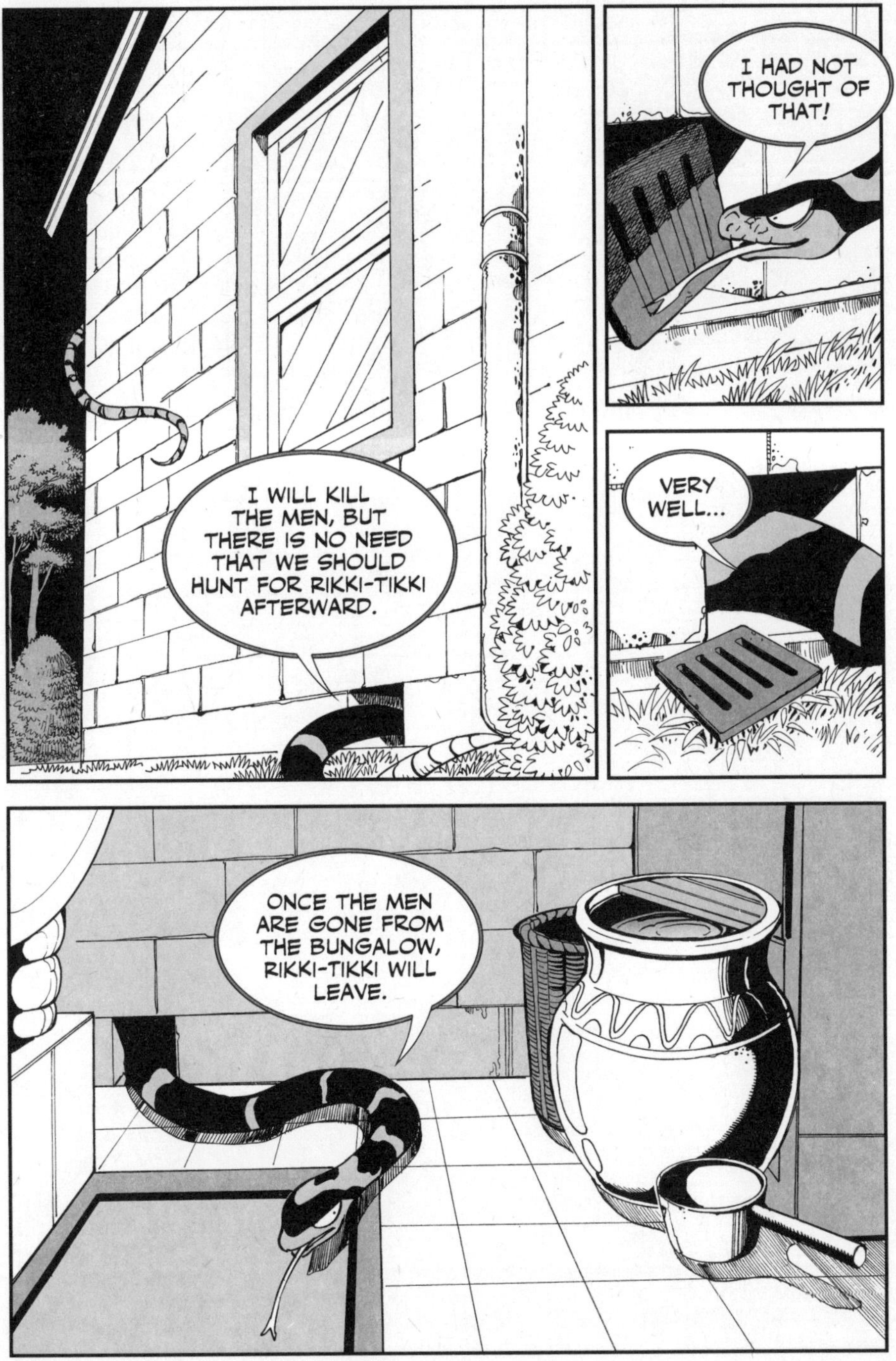
I WILL KILL THE MEN, BUT THERE IS NO NEED THAT WE SHOULD HUNT FOR RIKKI-TIKKI AFTERWARD.
I HAD NOT THOUGHT OF THAT!
VERY WELL...
ONCE THE MEN ARE GONE FROM THE BUNGALOW, RIKKI-TIKKI WILL LEAVE.

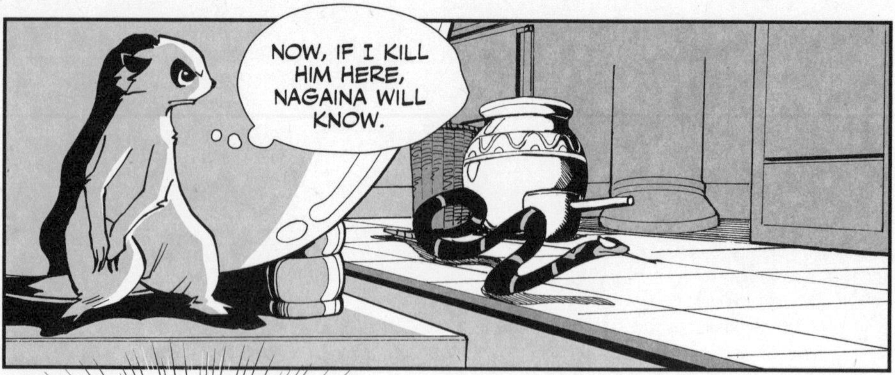
NOW, IF I KILL HIM HERE, NAGAINA WILL KNOW.

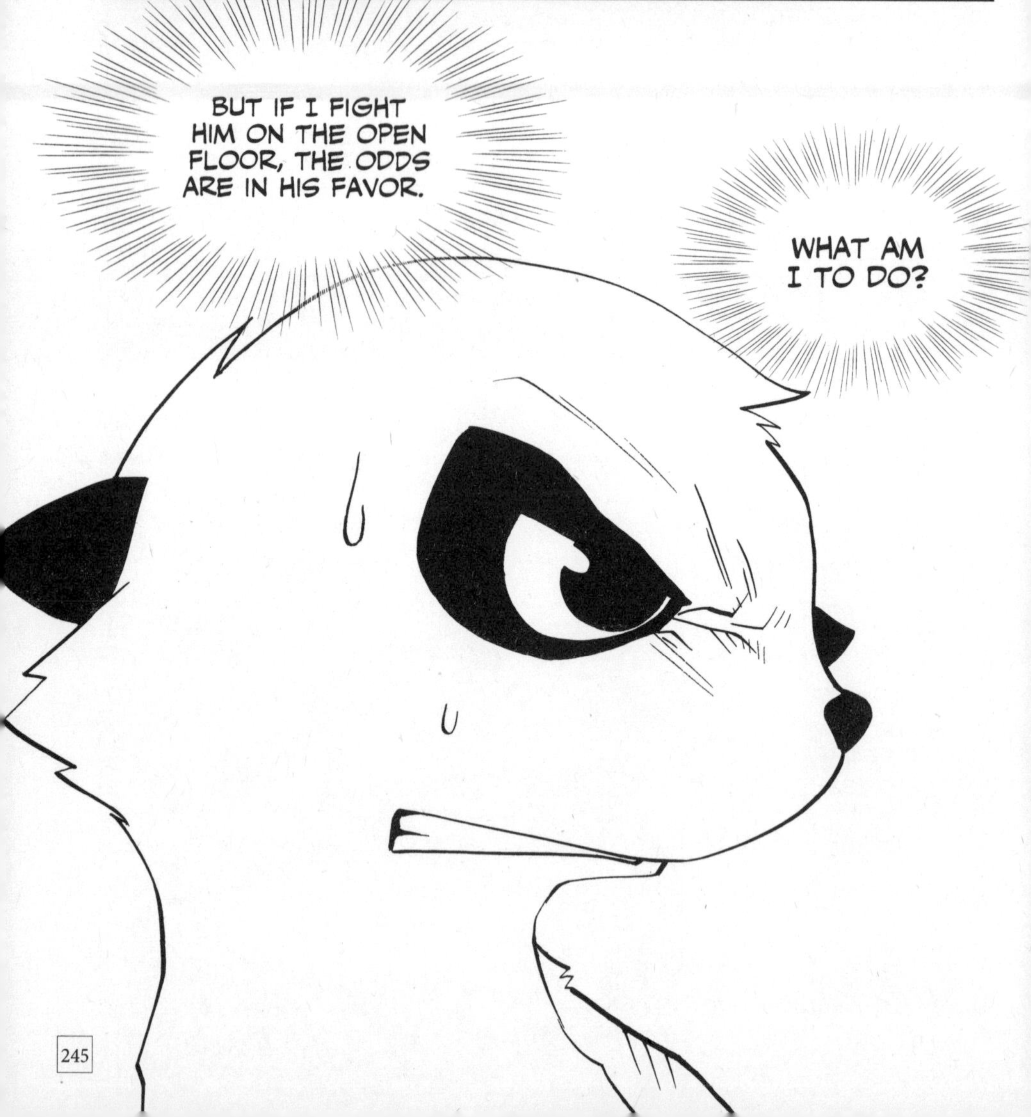
BUT IF I FIGHT HIM ON THE OPEN FLOOR, THE ODDS ARE IN HIS FAVOR.
WHAT AM I TO DO?

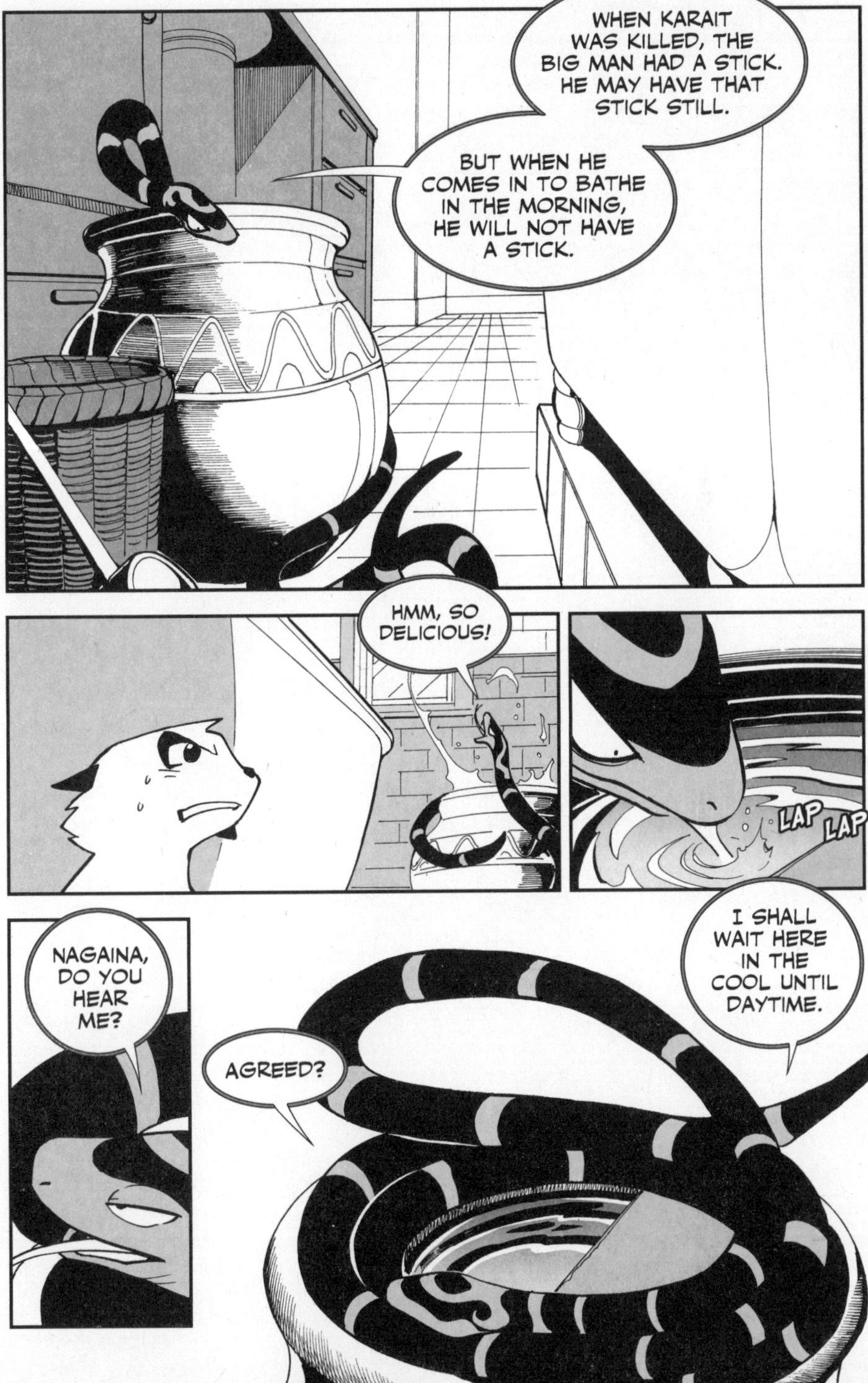
WHEN KARAIT WAS KILLED, THE BIG MAN HAD A STICK. HE MAY HAVE THAT STICK STILL.
BUT WHEN HE COMES IN TO BATHE IN THE MORNING, HE WILL NOT HAVE A STICK.
LAP LAP
HMM, SO DELICIOUS!
I SHALL WAIT HERE IN THE COOL UNTIL DAYTIME.
AGREED?
NAGAINA, DO YOU HEAR ME?

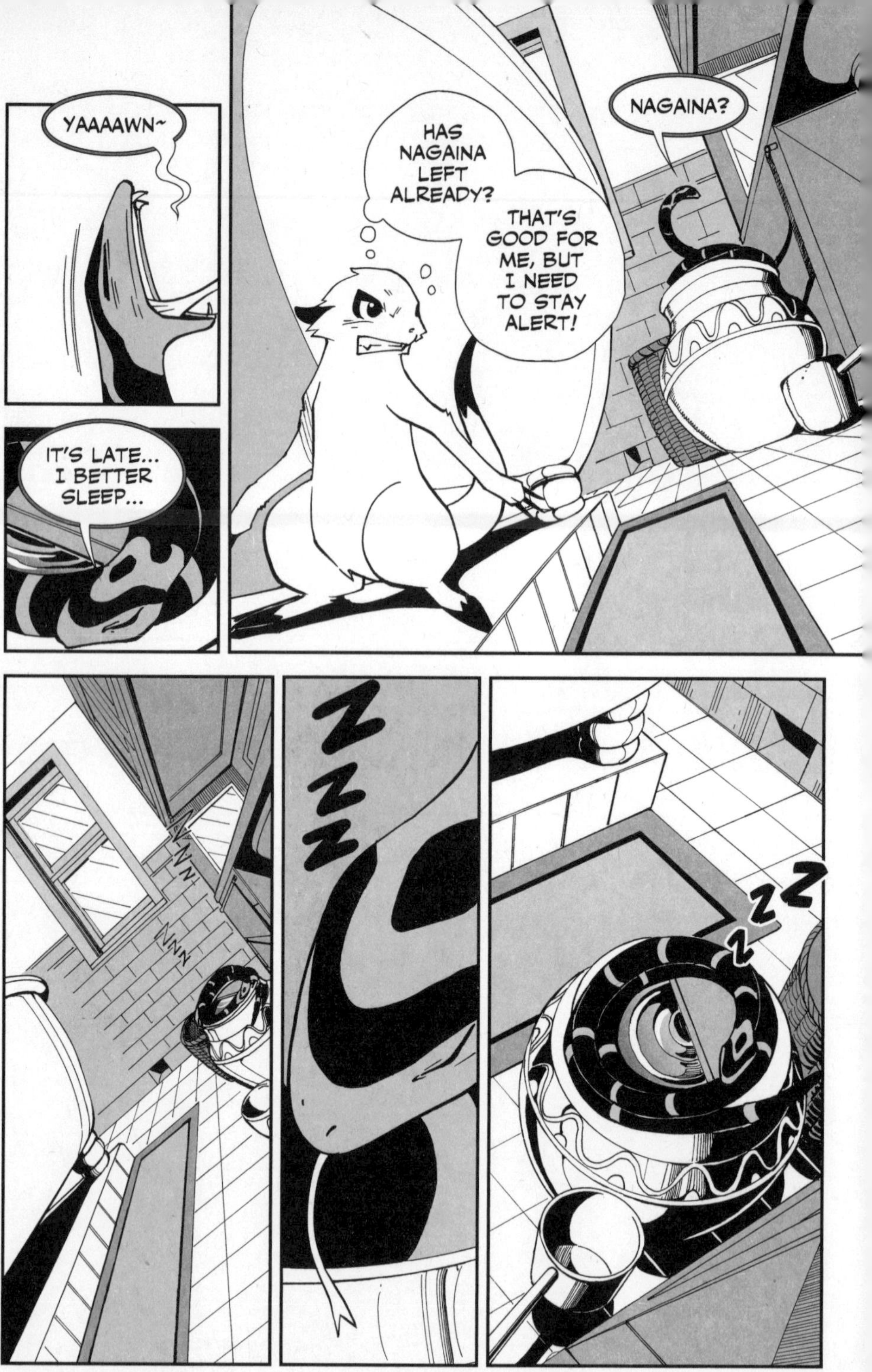
NAGAINA?
HAS NAGAINA LEFT ALREADY?
THAT'S GOOD FOR ME, BUT I NEED TO STAY ALERT!
YAAAAWN~
IT'S LATE... I BETTER SLEEP...
ZZZ
ZZZ
Nnn
Nnn

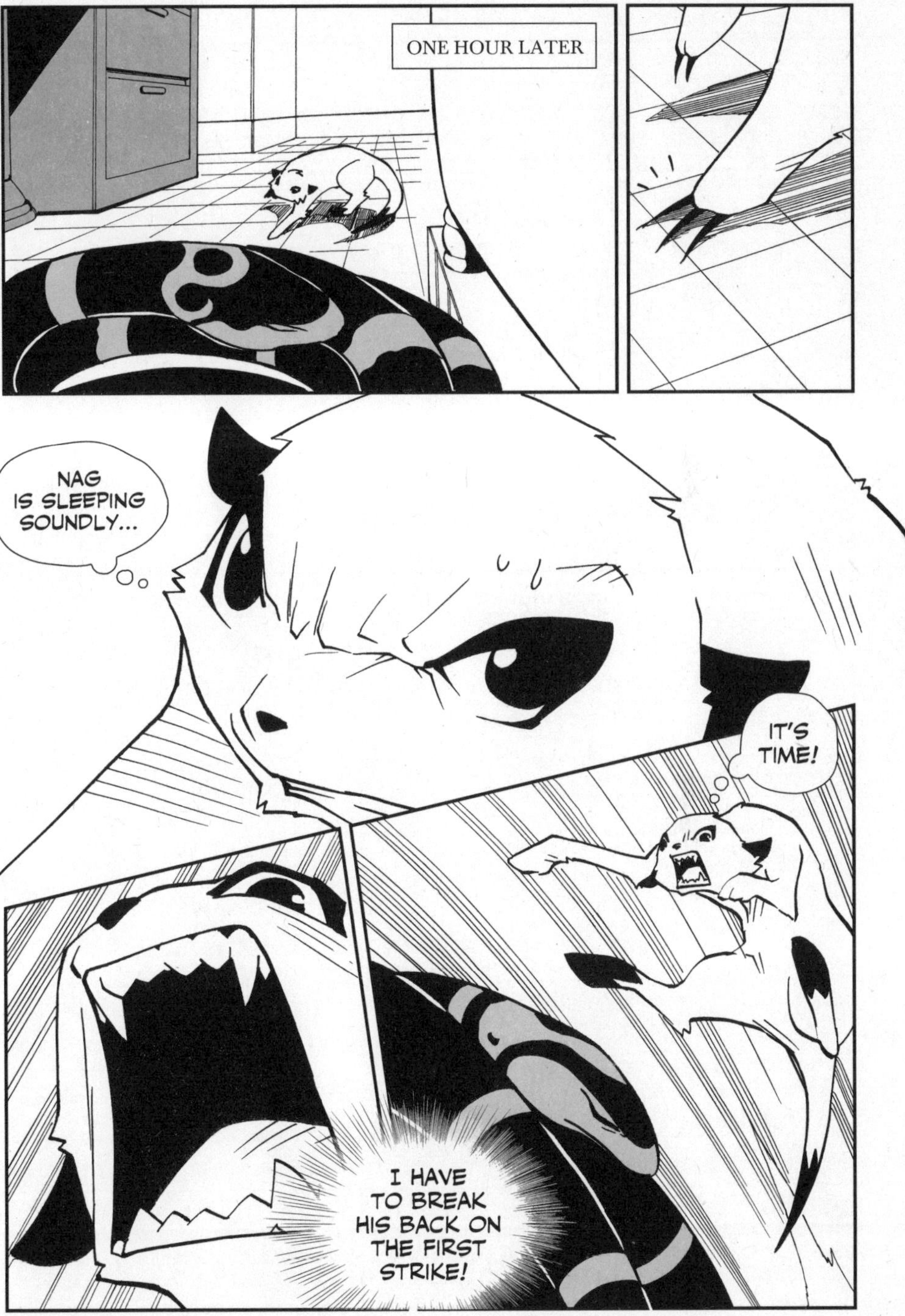
ONE HOUR LATER
NAG IS SLEEPING SOUNDLY...
IT'S TIME!
I HAVE TO BREAK HIS BACK ON THE FIRST STRIKE!

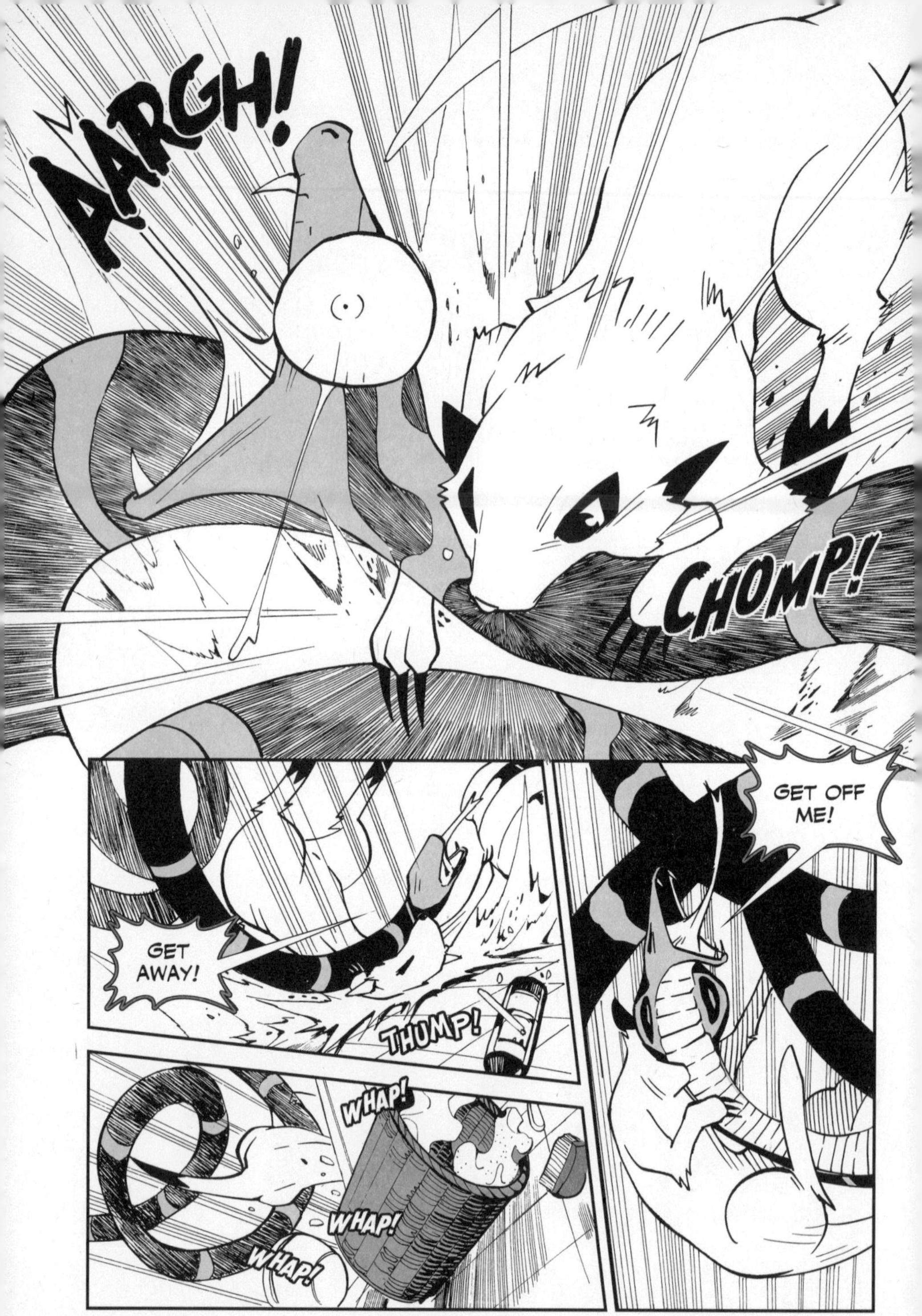
CHOMP!
AARGH!
GET OFF ME!
GET AWAY!
THUMP!
WHAP!
WHAP!
WHAP!

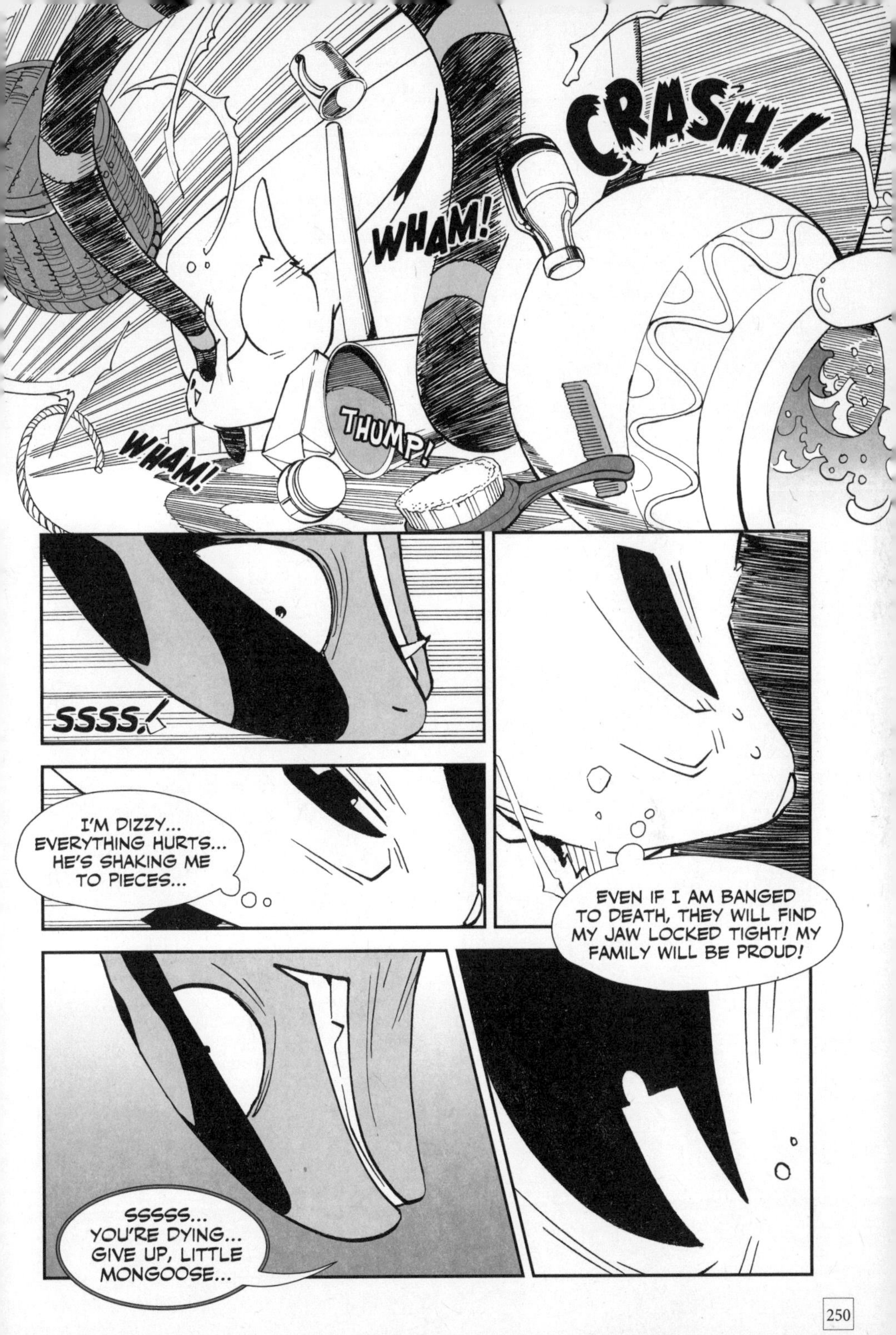
CRASH!
WHAM!
THUMP!
WHAM!
EVEN IF I AM BANGED TO DEATH, THEY WILL FIND MY JAW LOCKED TIGHT! MY FAMILY WILL BE PROUD!
SSSS!
I'M DIZZY... EVERYTHING HURTS... HE'S SHAKING ME TO PIECES...
SSSSS... YOU'RE DYING... GIVE UP, LITTLE MONGOOSE...

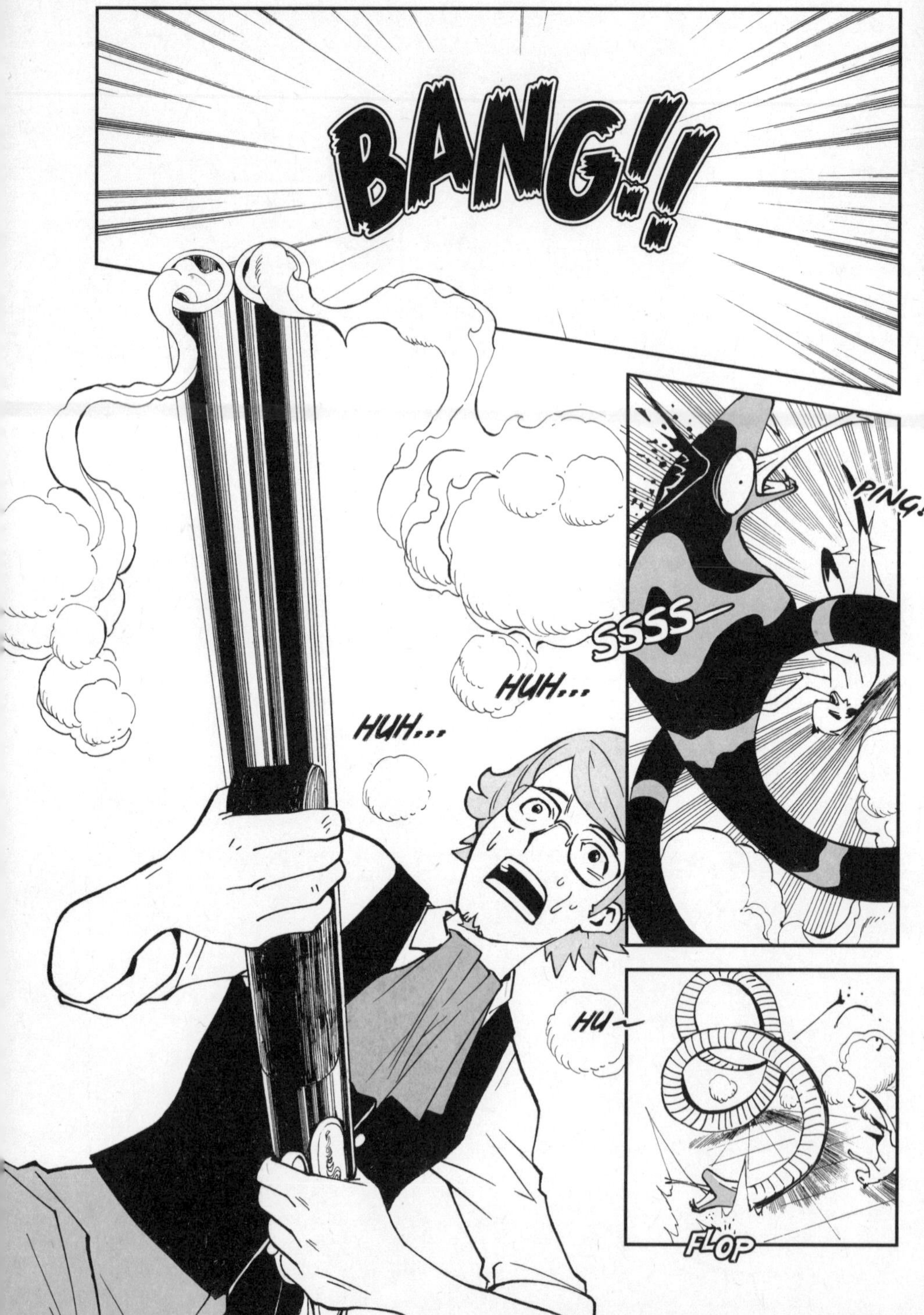
BANG!!
PING!
SSSS
FLOP
HUH...
HUH...
HU~

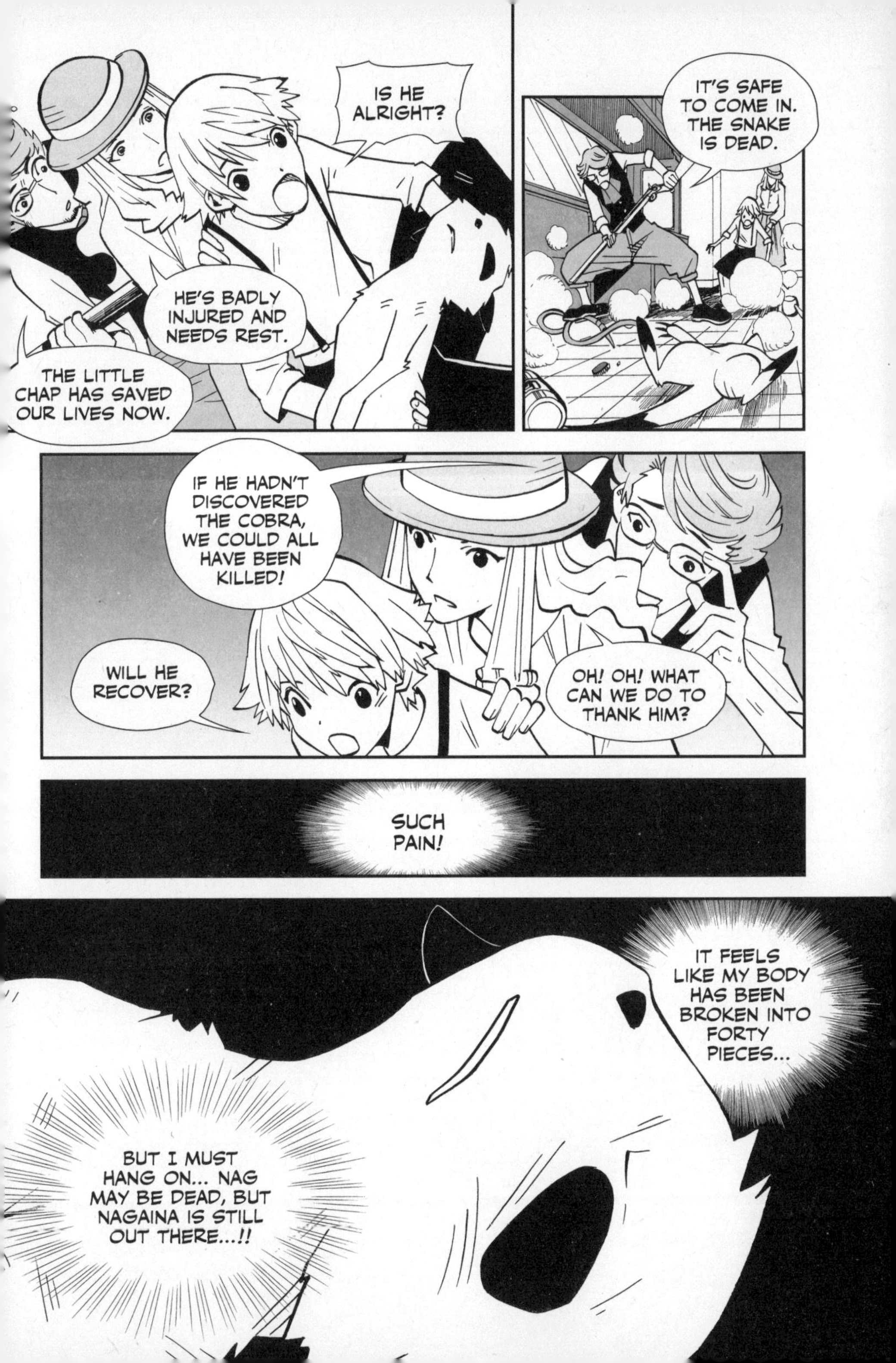
IT'S SAFE TO COME IN. THE SNAKE IS DEAD.
IS HE ALRIGHT?
HE'S BADLY INJURED AND NEEDS REST.
THE LITTLE CHAP HAS SAVED OUR LIVES NOW.
IF HE HADN'T DISCOVERED THE COBRA, WE COULD ALL HAVE BEEN KILLED!
OH! OH! WHAT CAN WE DO TO THANK HIM?
WILL HE RECOVER?
SUCH PAIN!
IT FEELS LIKE MY BODY HAS BEEN BROKEN INTO FORTY PIECES...
BUT I MUST HANG ON... NAG MAY BE DEAD, BUT NAGAINA IS STILL OUT THERE...!!

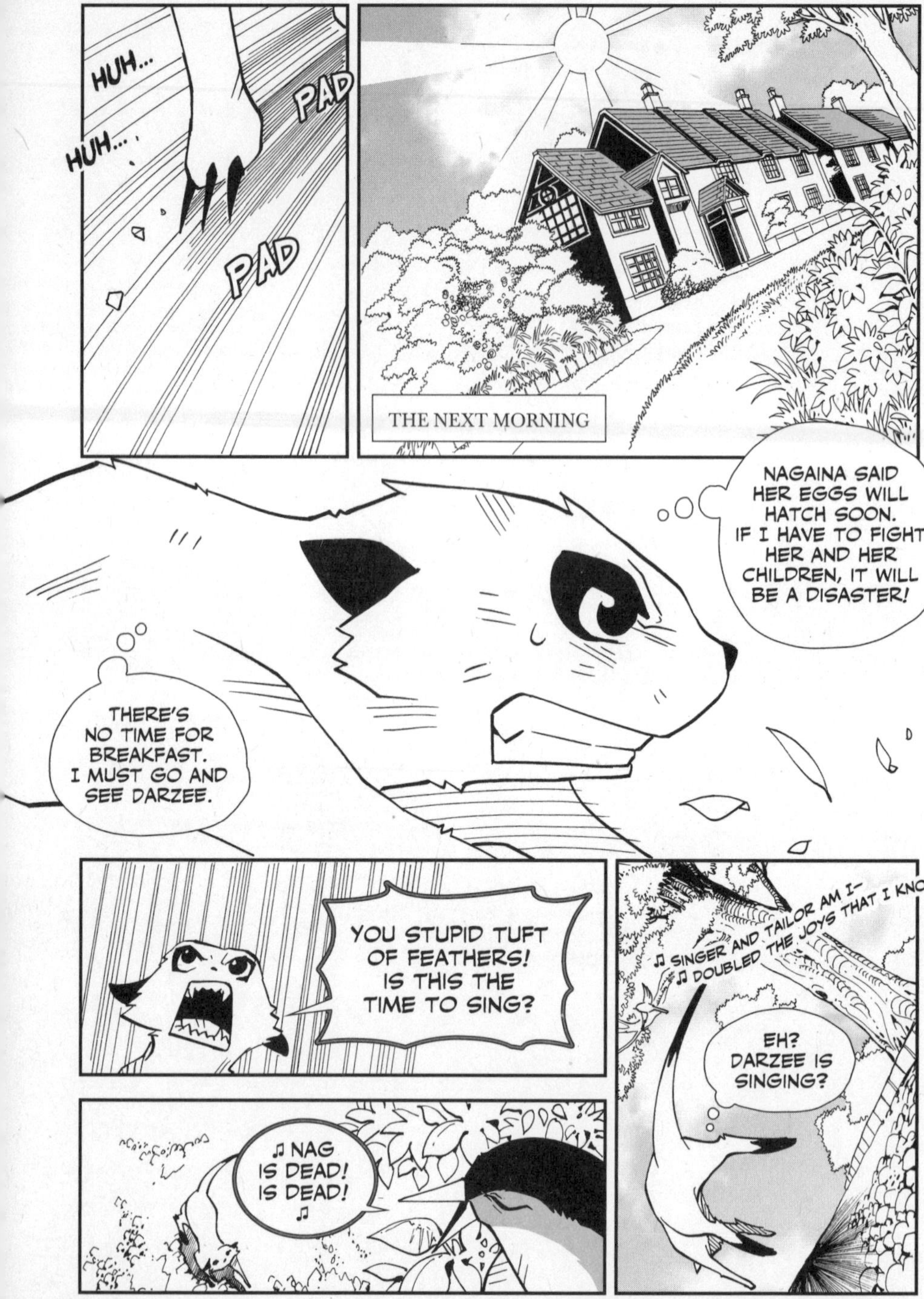
THE NEXT MORNING
HUH...
HUH...
PAD
PAD
NAGAINA SAID HER EGGS WILL HATCH SOON. IF I HAVE TO FIGHT HER AND HER CHILDREN, IT WILL BE A DISASTER!
THERE'S NO TIME FOR BREAKFAST. I MUST GO AND SEE DARZEE.
♫ SINGER AND TAILOR AM I-
♫ DOUBLED THE JOYS THAT I KNOW -
EH? DARZEE IS SINGING?
YOU STUPID TUFT OF FEATHERS! IS THIS THE TIME TO SING?
♫ NAG IS DEAD! IS DEAD! ♫

DARZEE'S CHANT
(SUNG IN HONOR OF RIKKI-TIKKI-TAVI)

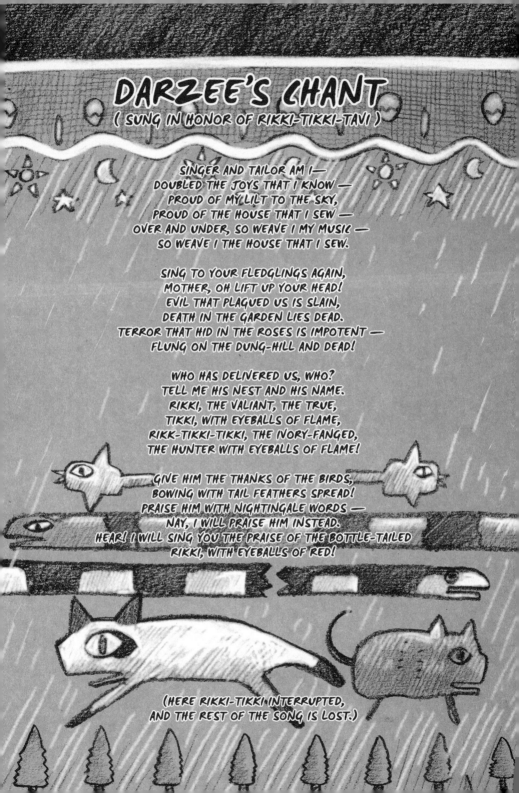

SINGER AND TAILOR AM I—
DOUBLED THE JOYS THAT I KNOW —
PROUD OF MY LILT TO THE SKY,
PROUD OF THE HOUSE THAT I SEW —
OVER AND UNDER, SO WEAVE I MY MUSIC —
SO WEAVE I THE HOUSE THAT I SEW.

SING TO YOUR FLEDGLINGS AGAIN,
MOTHER, OH LIFT UP YOUR HEAD!
EVIL THAT PLAGUED US IS SLAIN,
DEATH IN THE GARDEN LIES DEAD.
TERROR THAT HID IN THE ROSES IS IMPOTENT —
FLUNG ON THE DUNG-HILL AND DEAD!

WHO HAS DELIVERED US, WHO?
TELL ME HIS NEST AND HIS NAME.
RIKKI, THE VALIANT, THE TRUE,
TIKKI, WITH EYEBALLS OF FLAME,
RIKK-TIKKI-TIKKI, THE IVORY-FANGED,
THE HUNTER WITH EYEBALLS OF FLAME!

GIVE HIM THE THANKS OF THE BIRDS,
BOWING WITH TAIL FEATHERS SPREAD!
PRAISE HIM WITH NIGHTINGALE WORDS —
NAY, I WILL PRAISE HIM INSTEAD.
HEAR! I WILL SING YOU THE PRAISE OF THE BOTTLE-TAILED
RIKKI, WITH EYEBALLS OF RED!

(HERE RIKKI-TIKKI INTERRUPTED,
AND THE REST OF THE SONG IS LOST.)

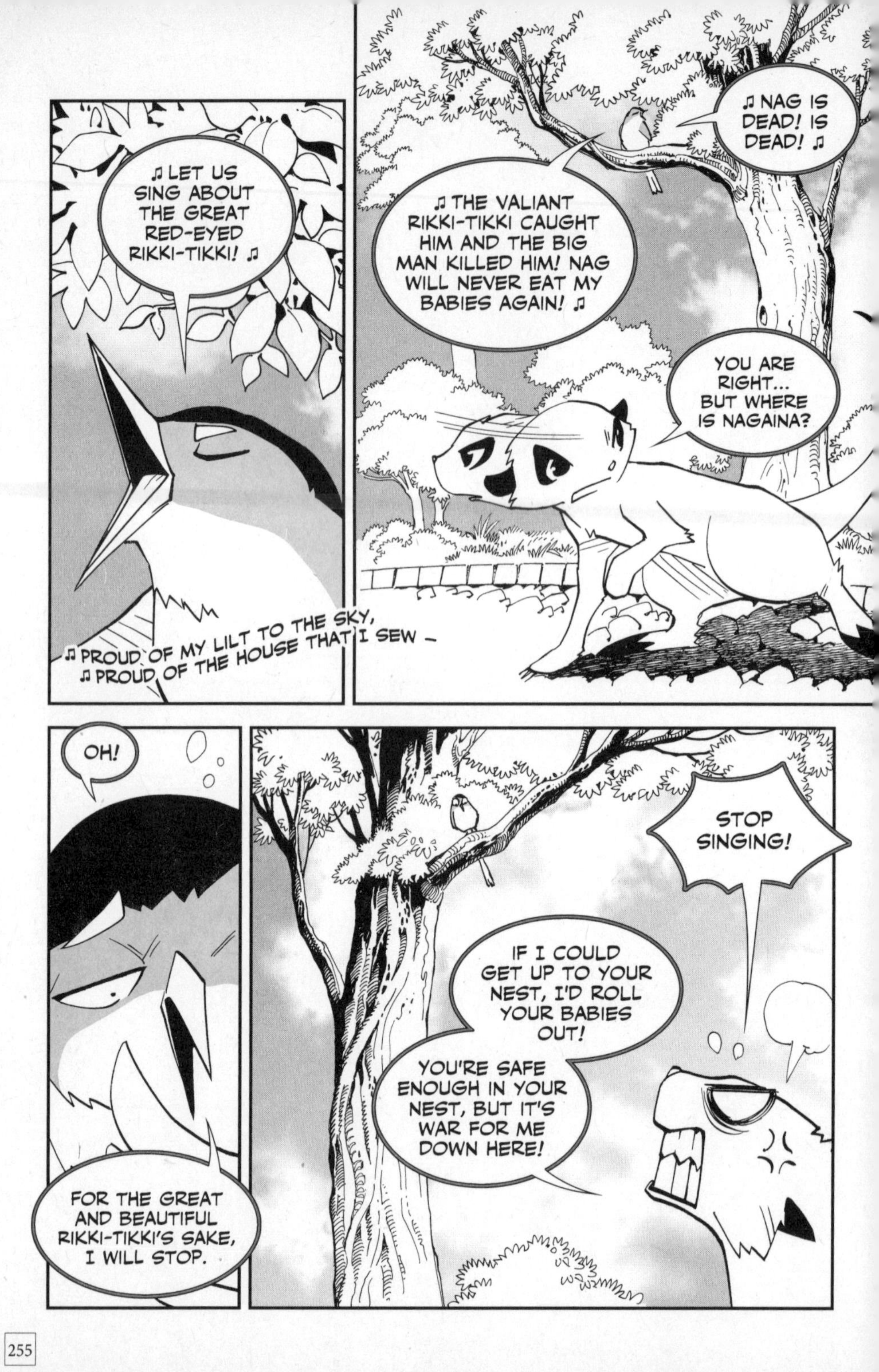
♫ NAG IS DEAD! IS DEAD! ♫
♫ THE VALIANT RIKKI-TIKKI CAUGHT HIM AND THE BIG MAN KILLED HIM! NAG WILL NEVER EAT MY BABIES AGAIN! ♫
YOU ARE RIGHT... BUT WHERE IS NAGAINA?
♫ LET US SING ABOUT THE GREAT RED-EYED RIKKI-TIKKI! ♫
♫ PROUD OF MY LILT TO THE SKY,
♫ PROUD OF THE HOUSE THAT I SEW –
STOP SINGING!
IF I COULD GET UP TO YOUR NEST, I'D ROLL YOUR BABIES OUT!
YOU'RE SAFE ENOUGH IN YOUR NEST, BUT IT'S WAR FOR ME DOWN HERE!
OH!
FOR THE GREAT AND BEAUTIFUL RIKKI-TIKKI'S SAKE, I WILL STOP.

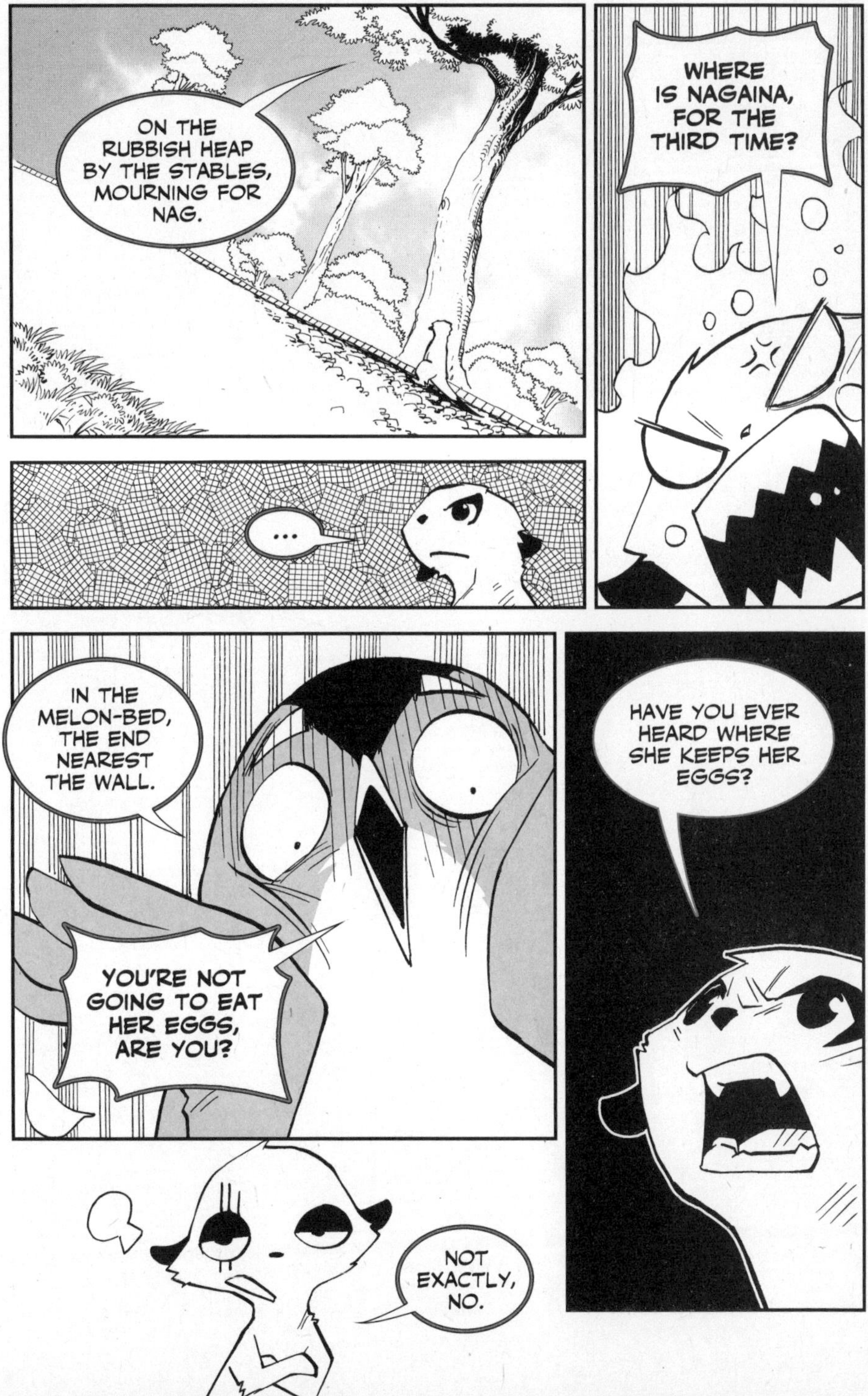
WHERE IS NAGAINA, FOR THE THIRD TIME?
ON THE RUBBISH HEAP BY THE STABLES, MOURNING FOR NAG.
...
HAVE YOU EVER HEARD WHERE SHE KEEPS HER EGGS?
IN THE MELON-BED, THE END NEAREST THE WALL.
YOU'RE NOT GOING TO EAT HER EGGS, ARE YOU?
NOT EXACTLY, NO.

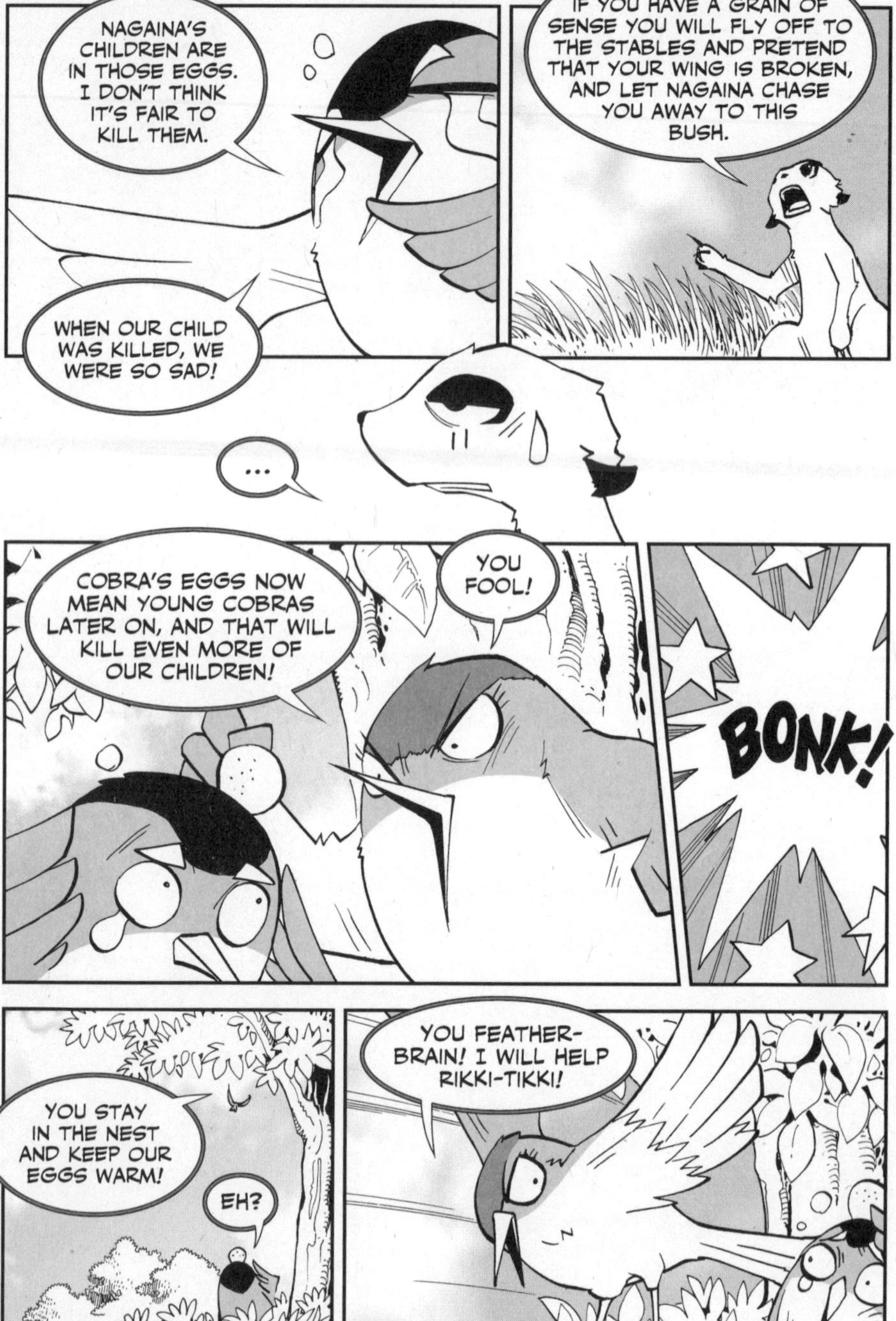
DARZEE, IF YOU HAVE A GRAIN OF SENSE YOU WILL FLY OFF TO THE STABLES AND PRETEND THAT YOUR WING IS BROKEN, AND LET NAGAINA CHASE YOU AWAY TO THIS BUSH.
NAGAINA'S CHILDREN ARE IN THOSE EGGS. I DON'T THINK IT'S FAIR TO KILL THEM.
WHEN OUR CHILD WAS KILLED, WE WERE SO SAD!
...
BONK!
YOU FOOL!
COBRA'S EGGS NOW MEAN YOUNG COBRAS LATER ON, AND THAT WILL KILL EVEN MORE OF OUR CHILDREN!
YOU FEATHER-BRAIN! I WILL HELP RIKKI-TIKKI!
YOU STAY IN THE NEST AND KEEP OUR EGGS WARM!
EH?

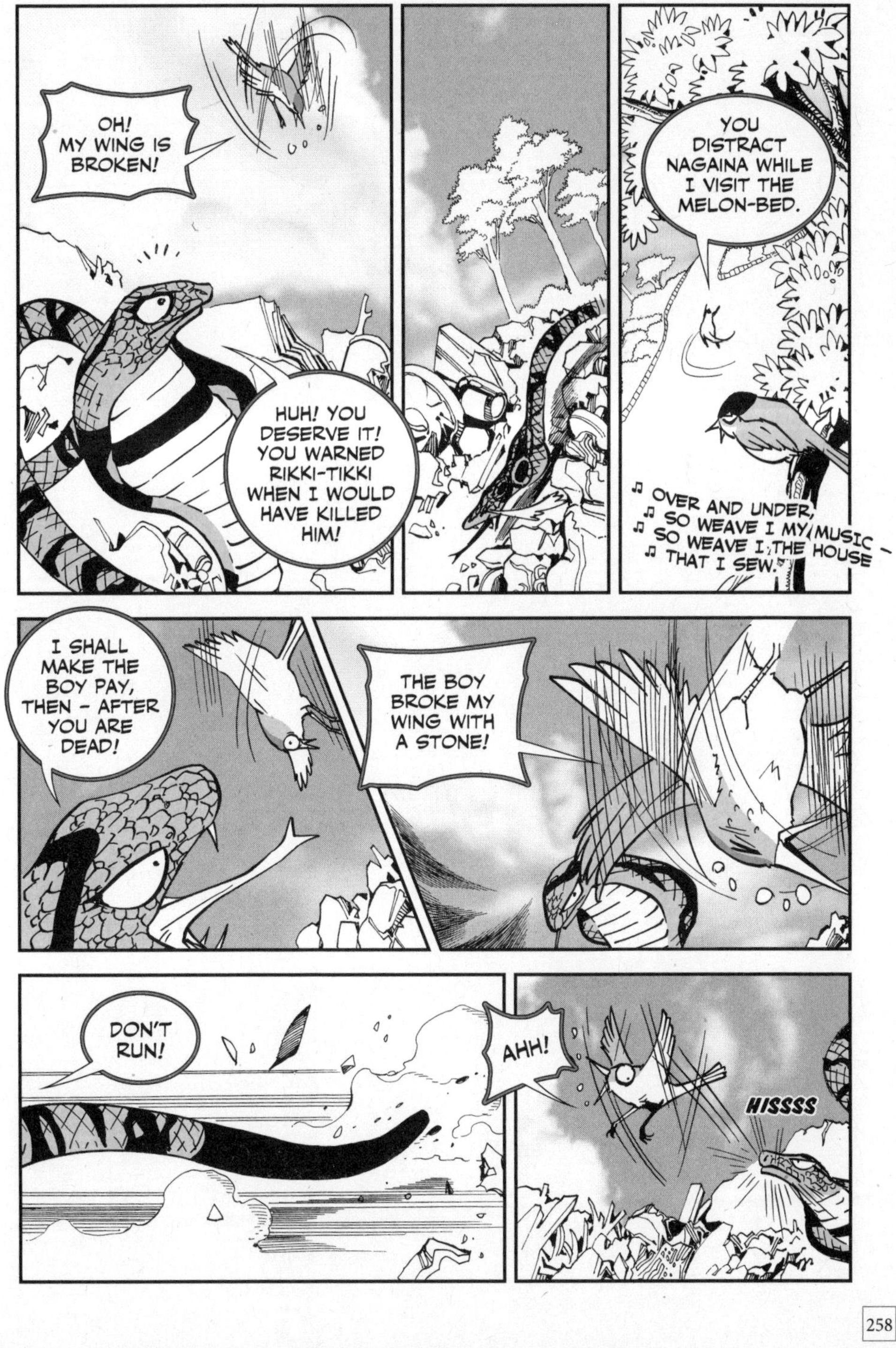
YOU DISTRACT NAGAINA WHILE I VISIT THE MELON-BED.
♫ OVER AND UNDER, ♫ SO WEAVE I MY MUSIC - ♫ SO WEAVE I THE HOUSE ♫ THAT I SEW.
OH! MY WING IS BROKEN!
HUH! YOU DESERVE IT! YOU WARNED RIKKI-TIKKI WHEN I WOULD HAVE KILLED HIM!
THE BOY BROKE MY WING WITH A STONE!
I SHALL MAKE THE BOY PAY, THEN - AFTER YOU ARE DEAD!
AHH!
HISSSS
DON'T RUN!

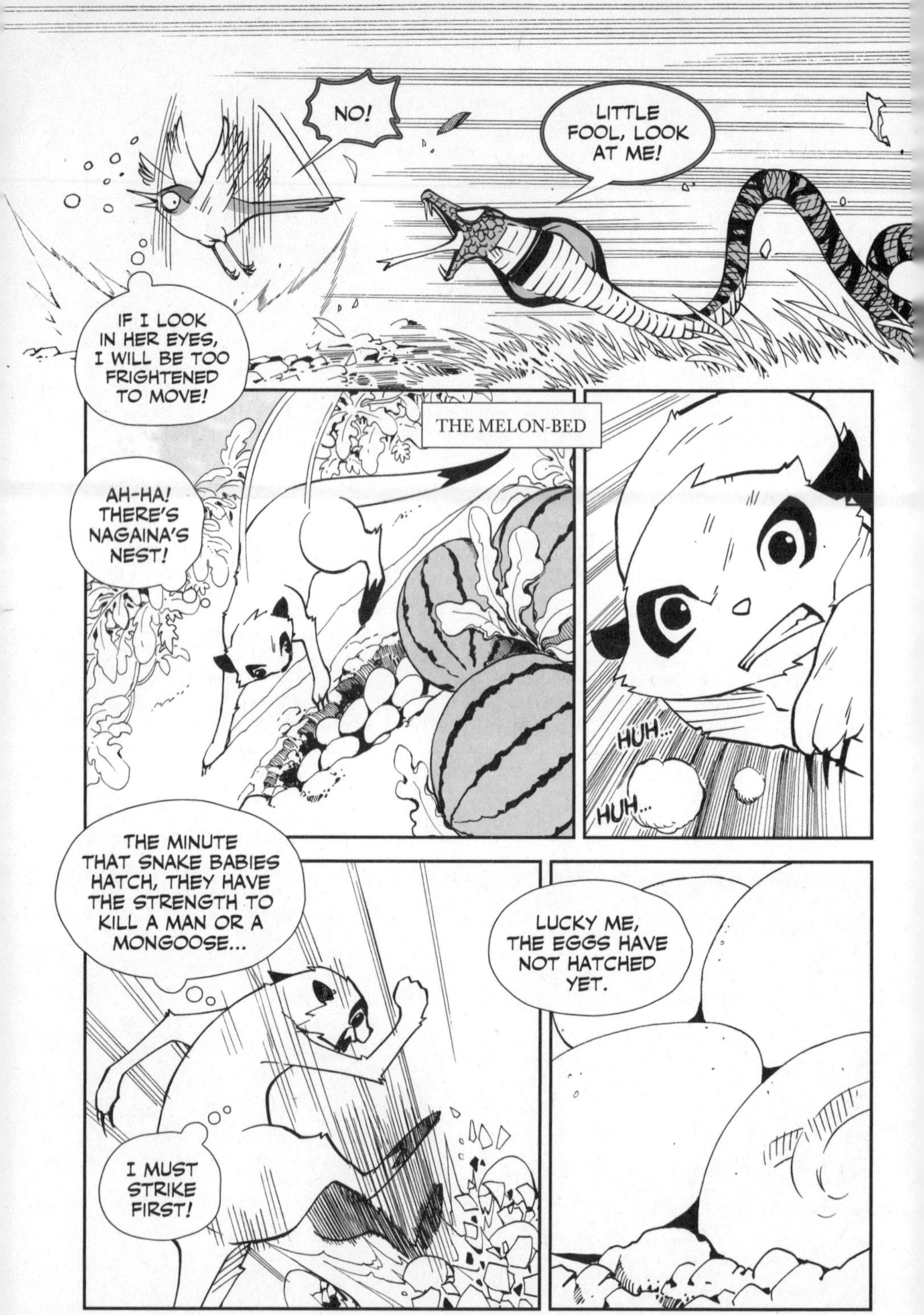

LITTLE FOOL, LOOK AT ME!
NO!
IF I LOOK IN HER EYES, I WILL BE TOO FRIGHTENED TO MOVE!
HUH...
HUH...
THE MELON-BED
AH-HA! THERE'S NAGAINA'S NEST!
LUCKY ME, THE EGGS HAVE NOT HATCHED YET.
THE MINUTE THAT SNAKE BABIES HATCH, THEY HAVE THE STRENGTH TO KILL A MAN OR A MONGOOSE...
I MUST STRIKE FIRST!

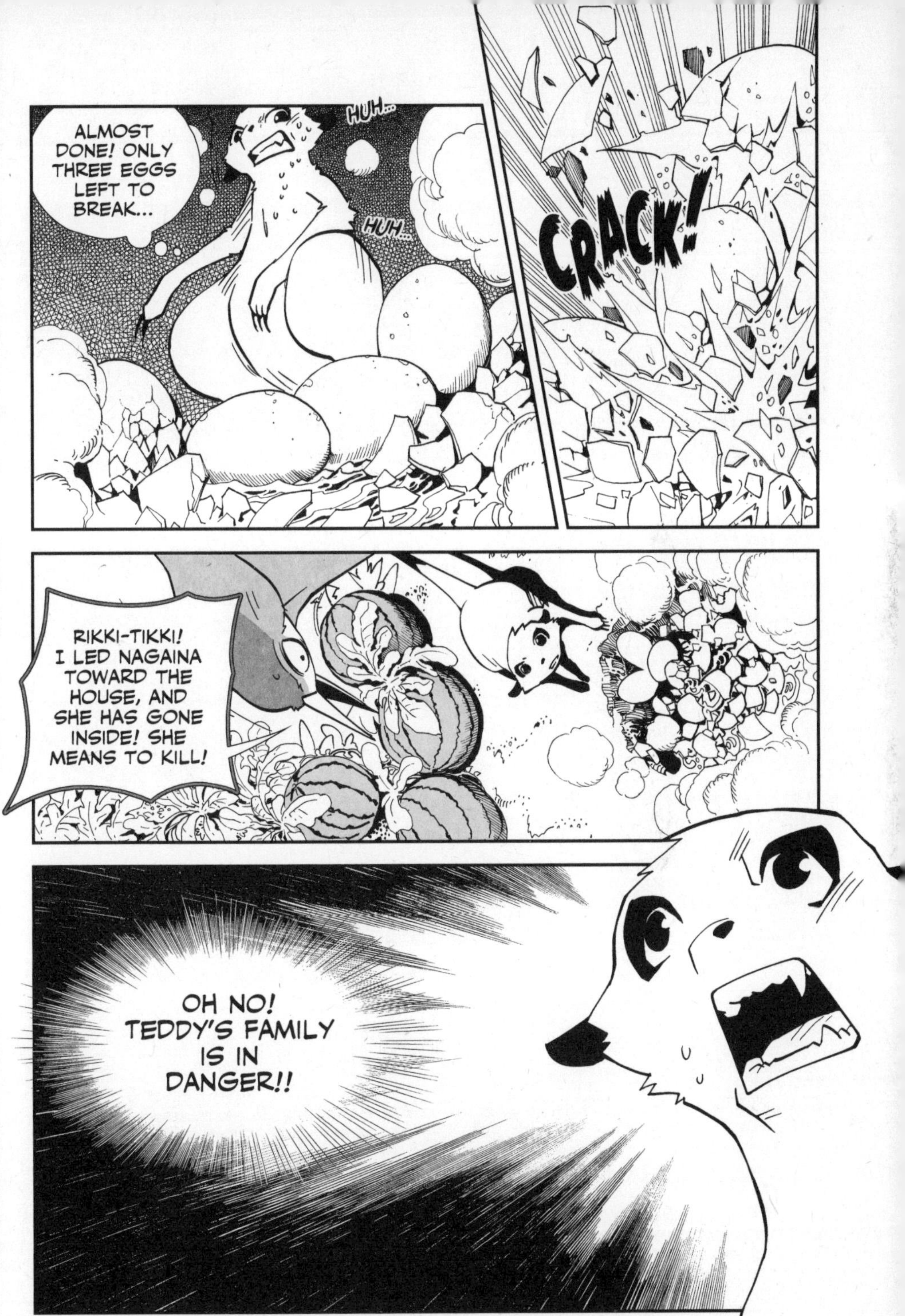
CRACK!
HUH...
ALMOST DONE! ONLY THREE EGGS LEFT TO BREAK...
HUH...
RIKKI-TIKKI! I LED NAGAINA TOWARD THE HOUSE, AND SHE HAS GONE INSIDE! SHE MEANS TO KILL!
OH NO! TEDDY'S FAMILY IS IN DANGER!!

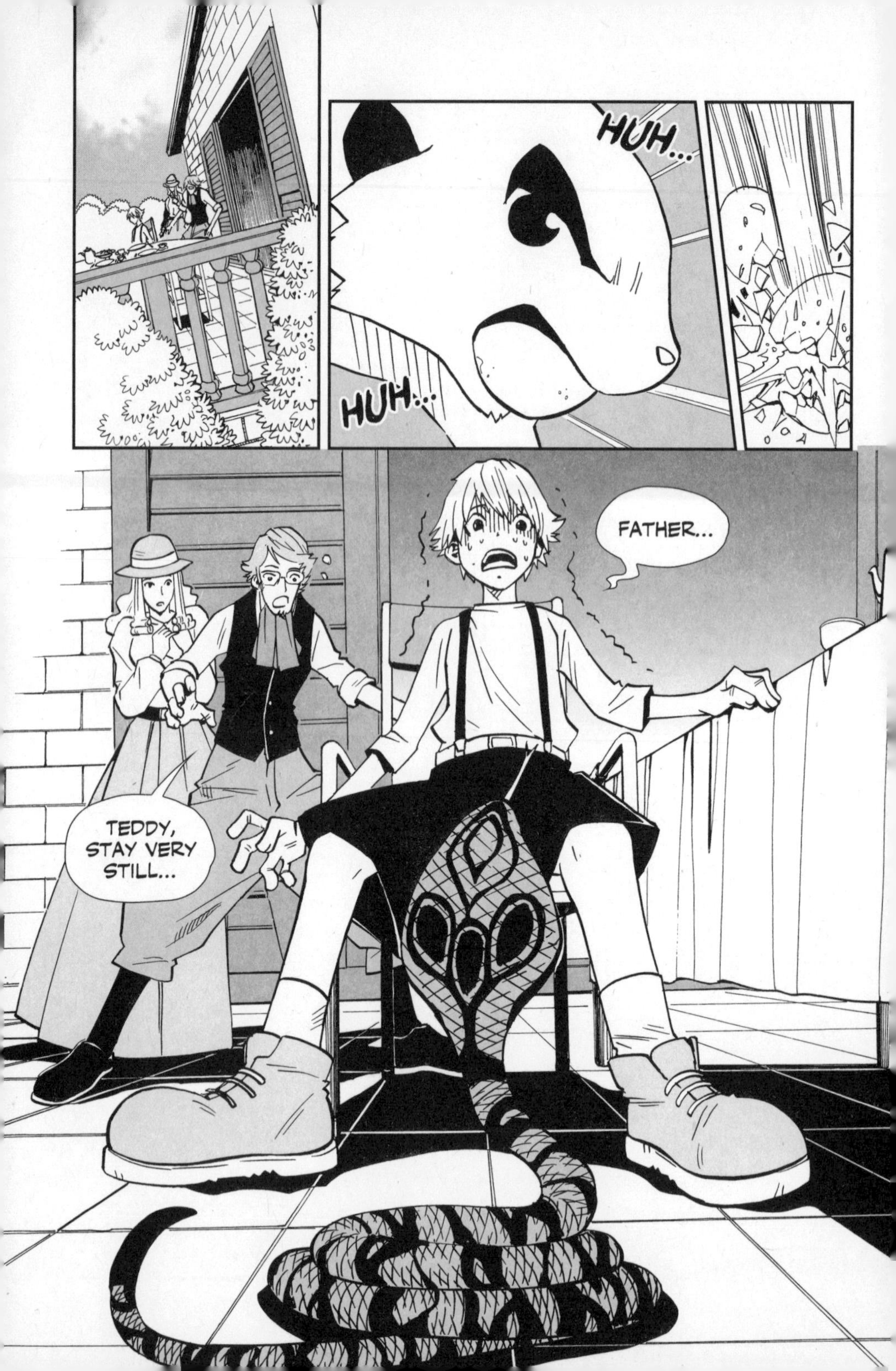
HUH...
HUH...
FATHER...
TEDDY, STAY VERY STILL...

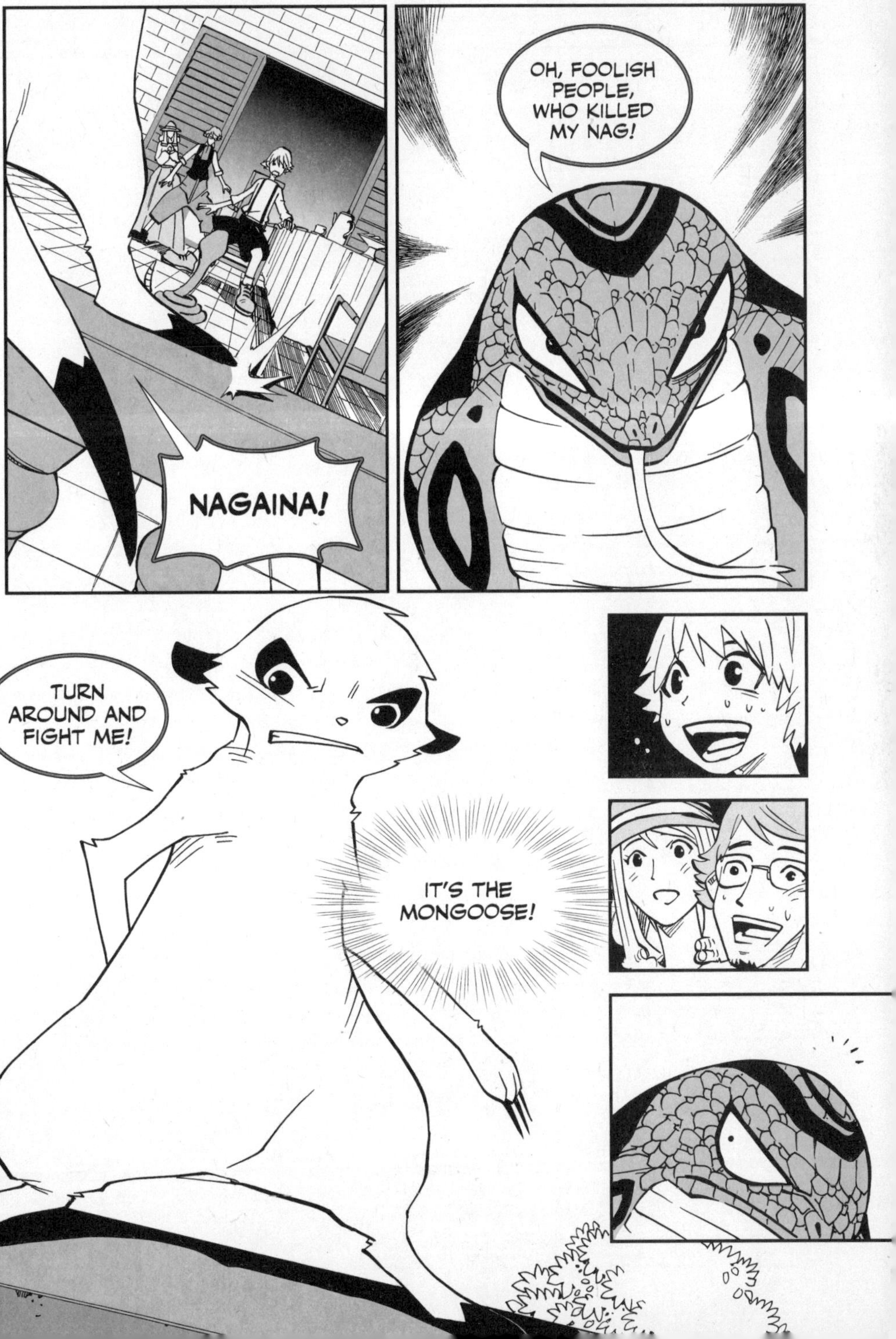
OH, FOOLISH PEOPLE, WHO KILLED MY NAG!
NAGAINA!
TURN AROUND AND FIGHT ME!
IT'S THE MONGOOSE!

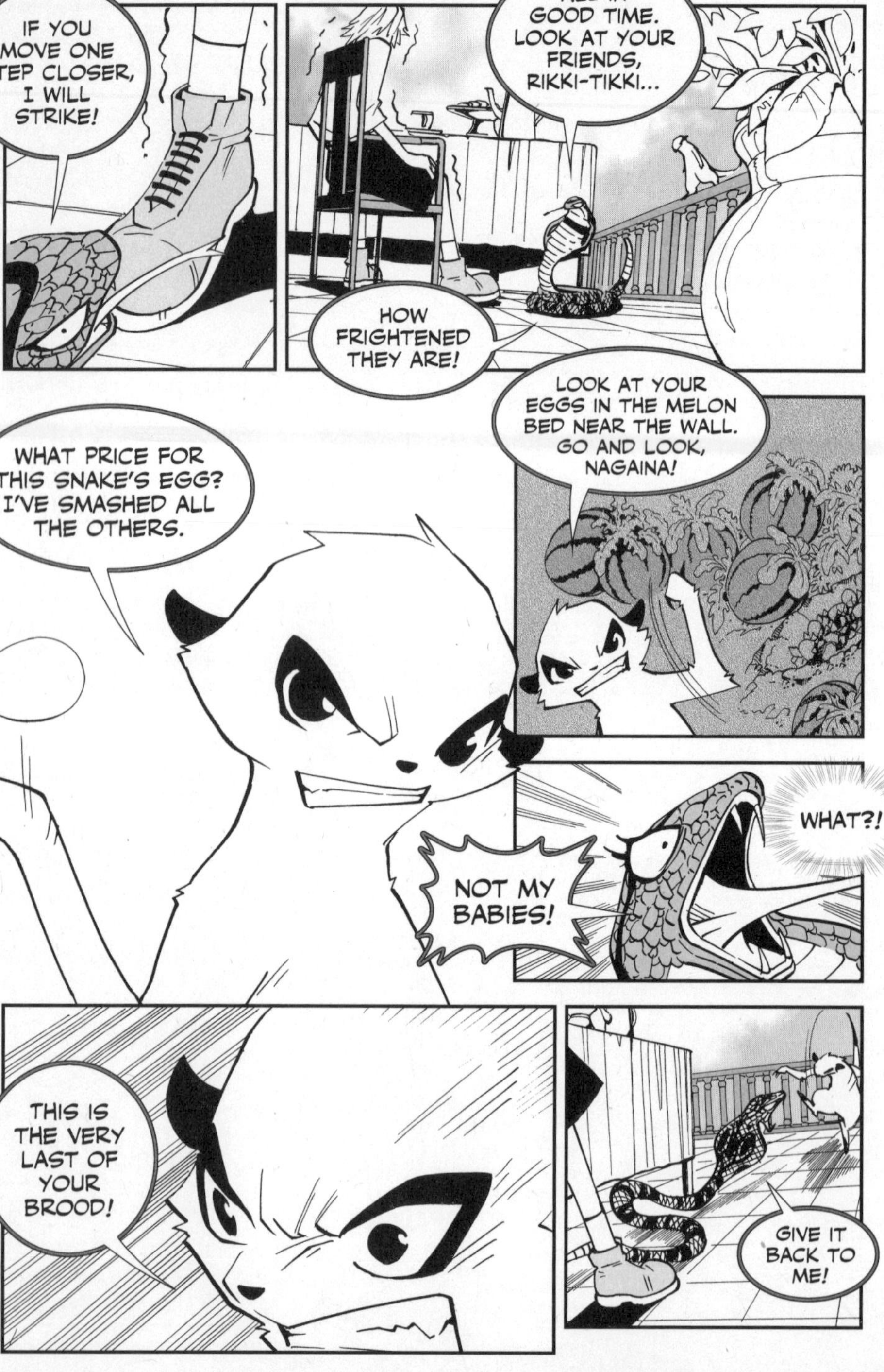
ALL IN GOOD TIME. LOOK AT YOUR FRIENDS, RIKKI-TIKKI...
HOW FRIGHTENED THEY ARE!
IF YOU MOVE ONE STEP CLOSER, I WILL STRIKE!
LOOK AT YOUR EGGS IN THE MELON BED NEAR THE WALL. GO AND LOOK, NAGAINA!
WHAT?!
NOT MY BABIES!
WHAT PRICE FOR THIS SNAKE'S EGG? I'VE SMASHED ALL THE OTHERS.
GIVE IT BACK TO ME!
THIS IS THE VERY LAST OF YOUR BROOD!

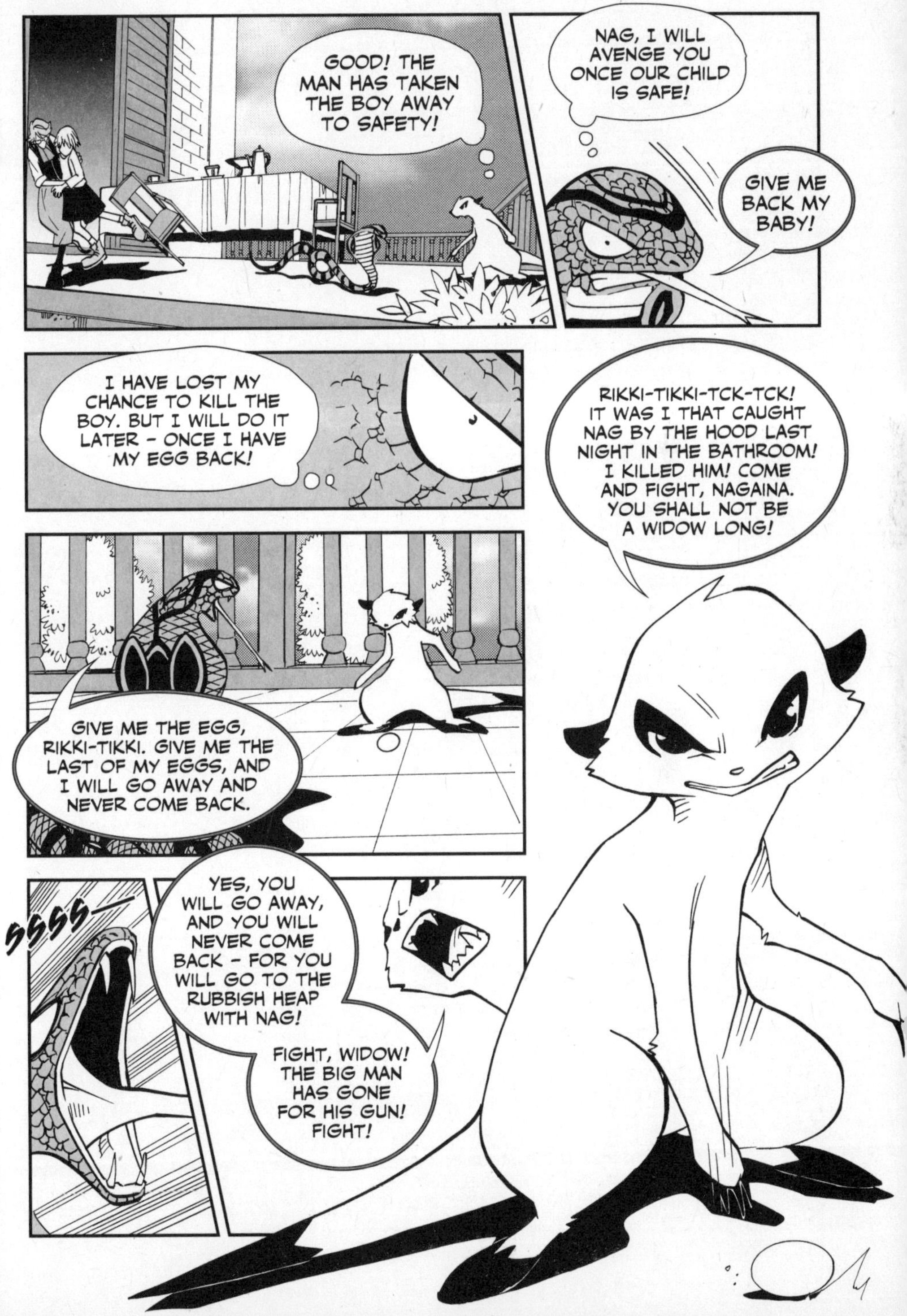
NAG, I WILL AVENGE YOU ONCE OUR CHILD IS SAFE!
GIVE ME BACK MY BABY!
GOOD! THE MAN HAS TAKEN THE BOY AWAY TO SAFETY!
RIKKI-TIKKI-TCK-TCK! IT WAS I THAT CAUGHT NAG BY THE HOOD LAST NIGHT IN THE BATHROOM! I KILLED HIM! COME AND FIGHT, NAGAINA. YOU SHALL NOT BE A WIDOW LONG!
I HAVE LOST MY CHANCE TO KILL THE BOY. BUT I WILL DO IT LATER - ONCE I HAVE MY EGG BACK!
GIVE ME THE EGG, RIKKI-TIKKI. GIVE ME THE LAST OF MY EGGS, AND I WILL GO AWAY AND NEVER COME BACK.
YES, YOU WILL GO AWAY, AND YOU WILL NEVER COME BACK - FOR YOU WILL GO TO THE RUBBISH HEAP WITH NAG!
FIGHT, WIDOW! THE BIG MAN HAS GONE FOR HIS GUN! FIGHT!
SSSS—

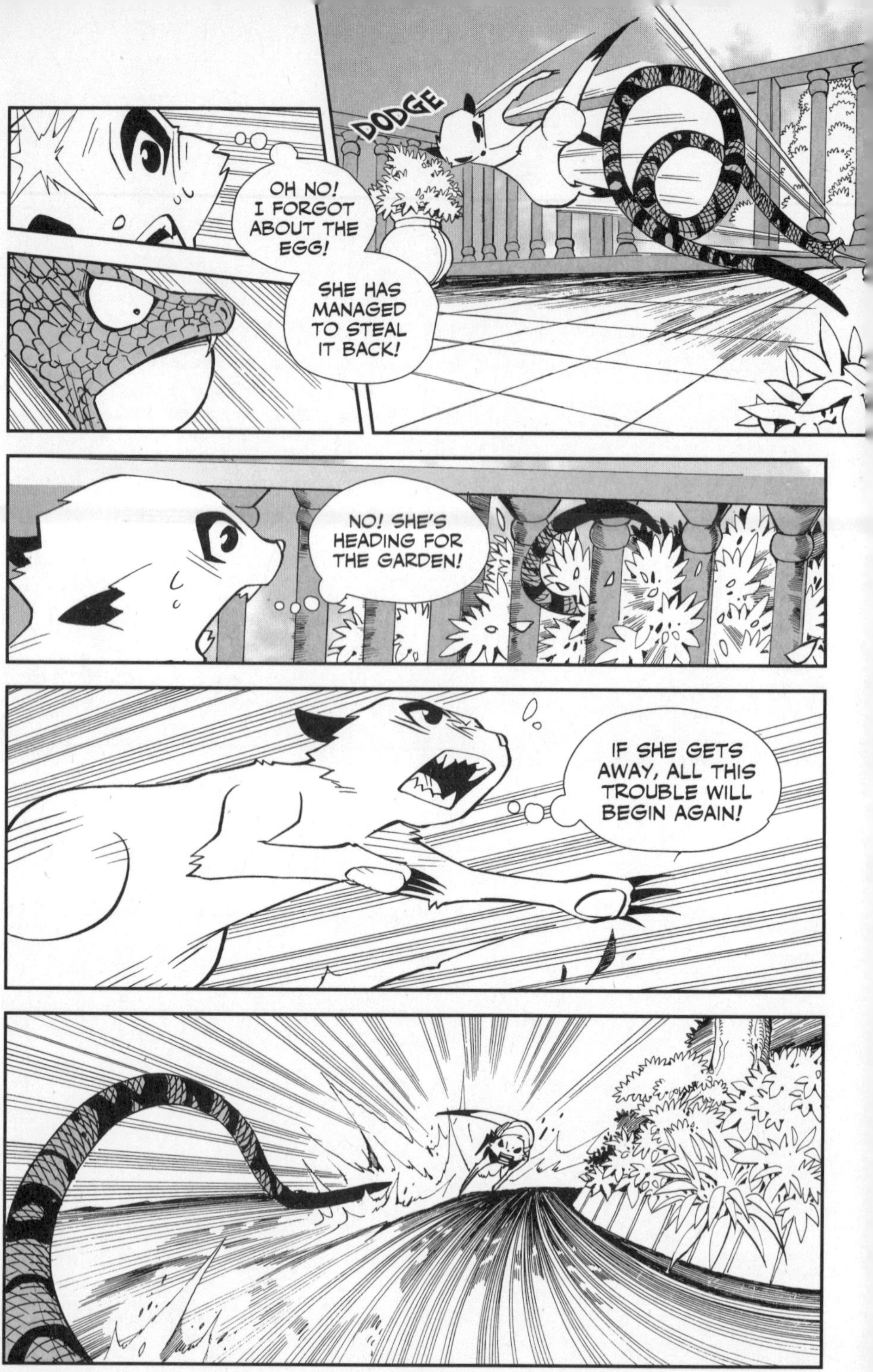
DODGE
OH NO! I FORGOT ABOUT THE EGG!
SHE HAS MANAGED TO STEAL IT BACK!
NO! SHE'S HEADING FOR THE GARDEN!
IF SHE GETS AWAY, ALL THIS TROUBLE WILL BEGIN AGAIN!

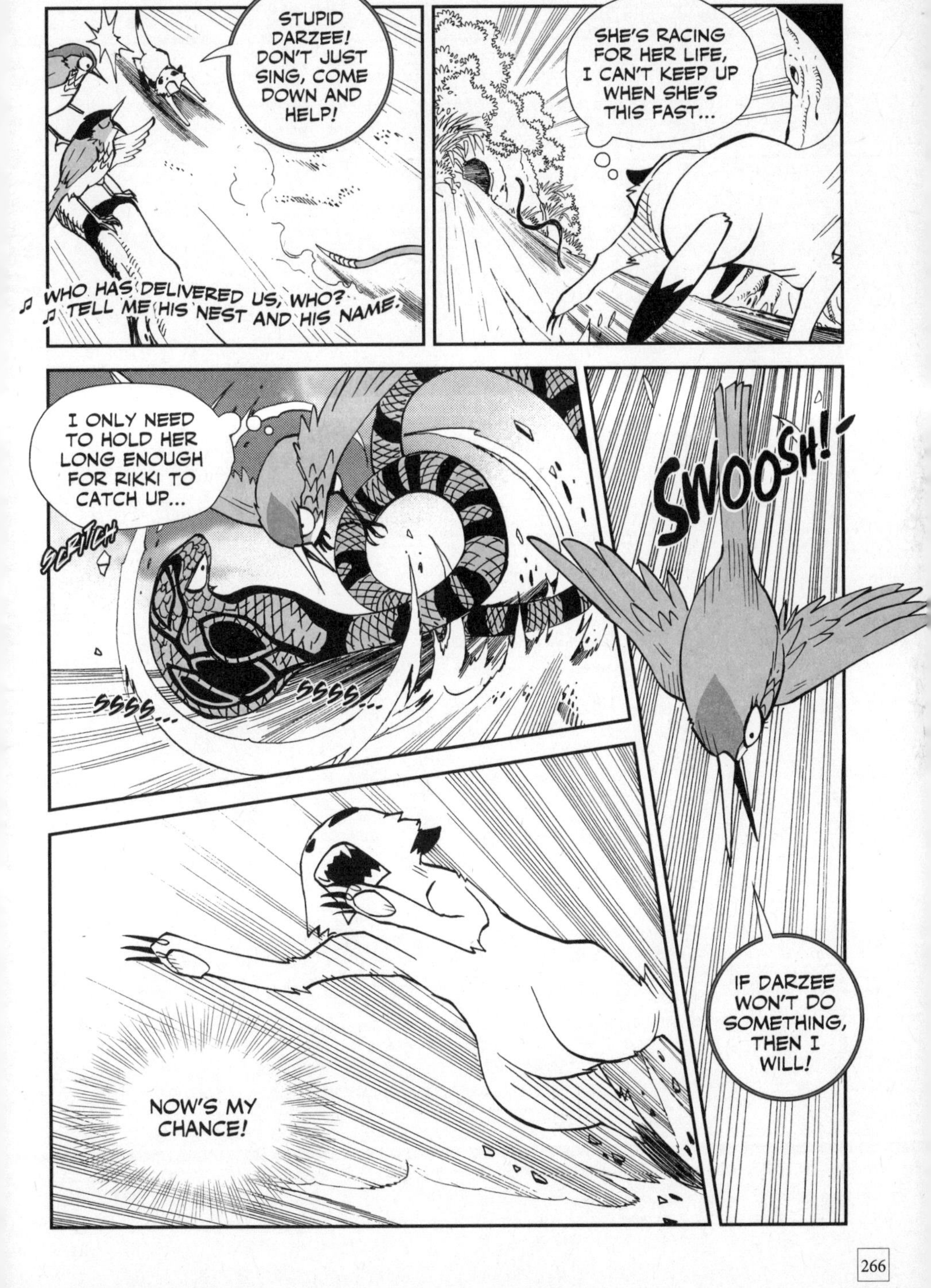
SHE'S RACING FOR HER LIFE, I CAN'T KEEP UP WHEN SHE'S THIS FAST...
STUPID DARZEE! DON'T JUST SING, COME DOWN AND HELP!
♫ WHO HAS DELIVERED US, WHO?
♫ TELL ME HIS NEST AND HIS NAME.
SWOOSH!
IF DARZEE WON'T DO SOMETHING, THEN I WILL!
I ONLY NEED TO HOLD HER LONG ENOUGH FOR RIKKI TO CATCH UP...
SCRITCH
SSSS...
SSSS...
NOW'S MY CHANCE!

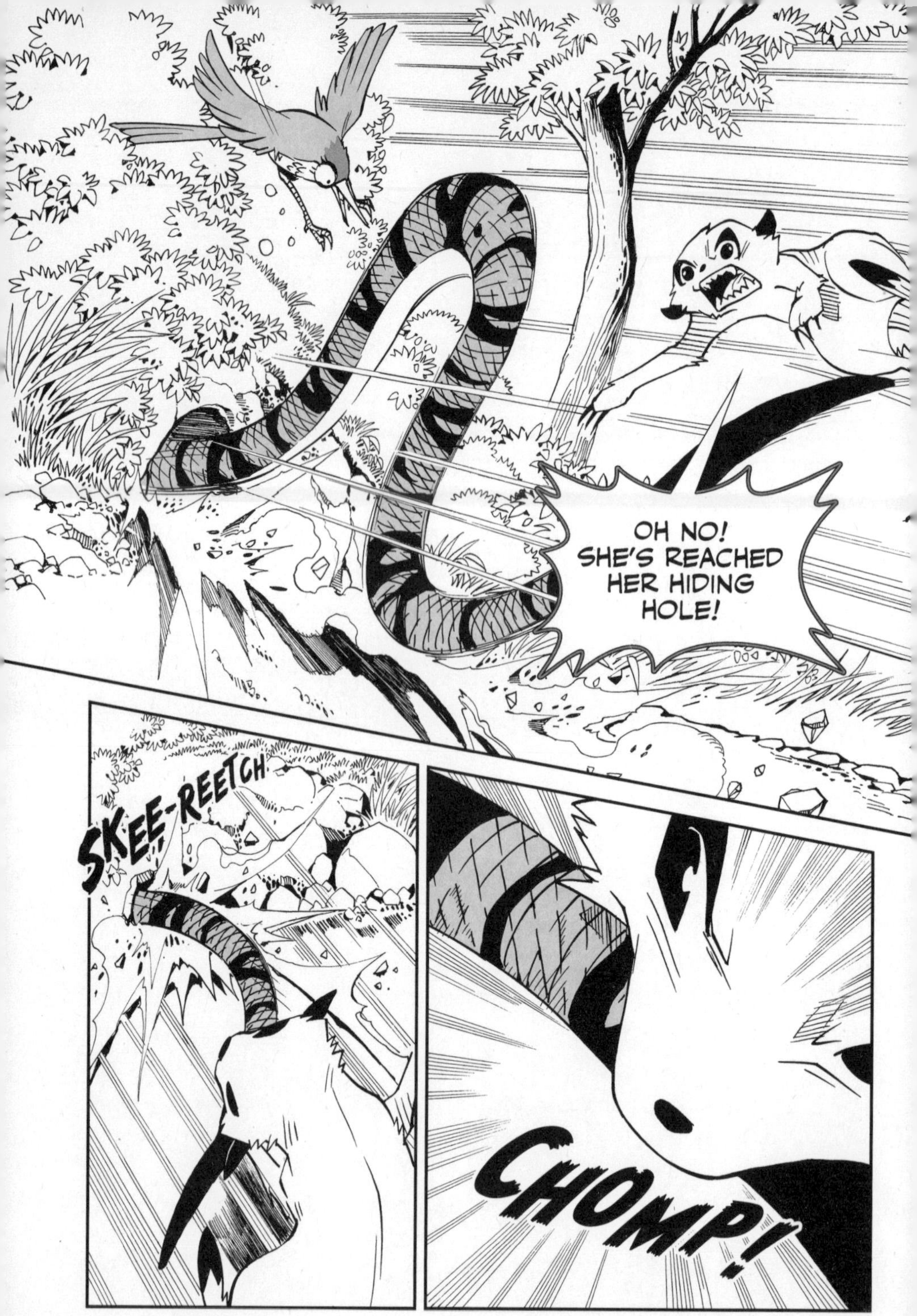
OH NO! SHE'S REACHED HER HIDING HOLE!
CHOMP!
SKEE-REETCH

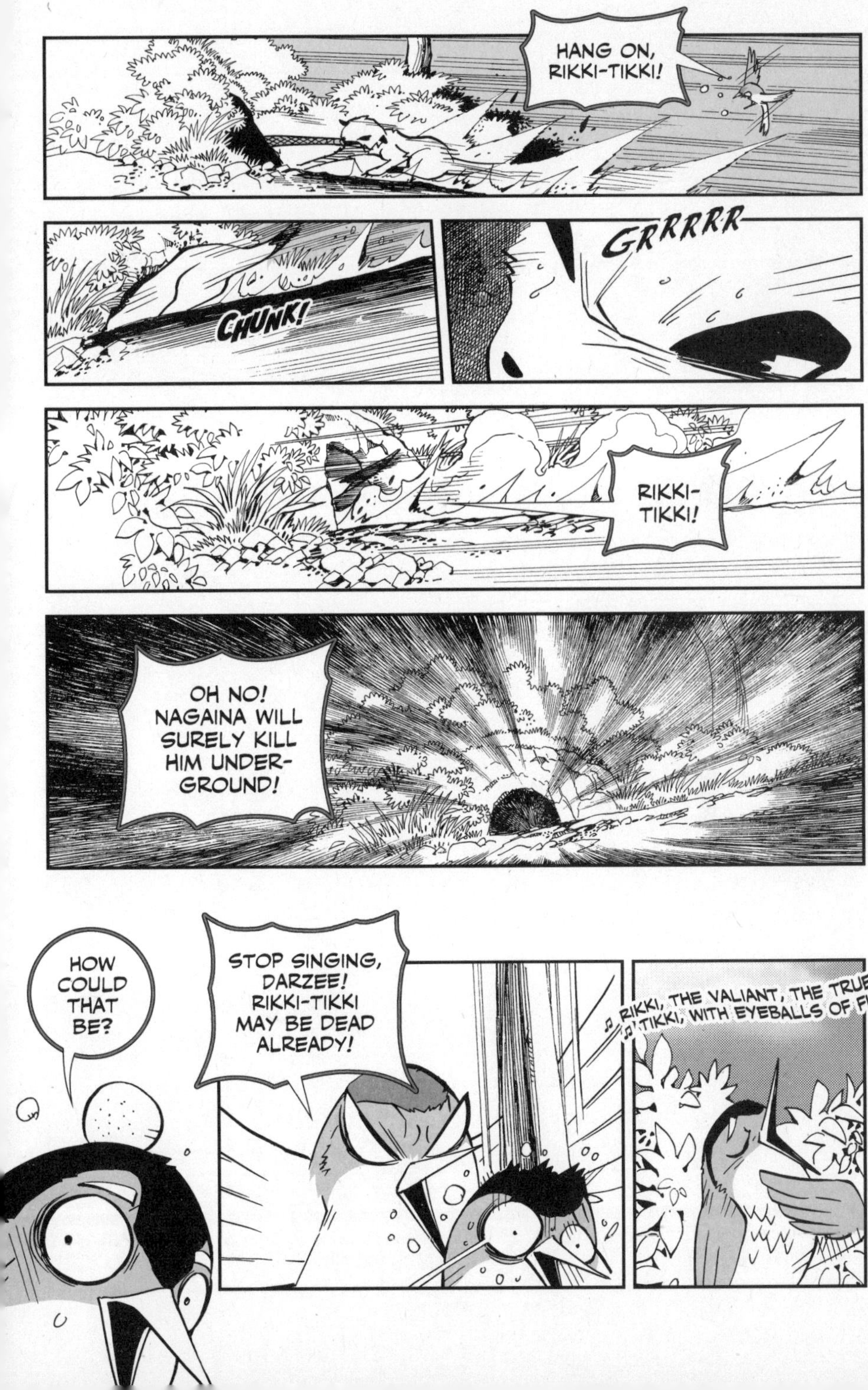
HANG ON, RIKKI-TIKKI!
GRRRRR
CHUNK!
RIKKI-TIKKI!
OH NO! NAGAINA WILL SURELY KILL HIM UNDER-GROUND!
♫ RIKKI, THE VALIANT, THE TRUE,
♫ TIKKI, WITH EYEBALLS OF FLAME.
STOP SINGING, DARZEE! RIKKI-TIKKI MAY BE DEAD ALREADY!
HOW COULD THAT BE?

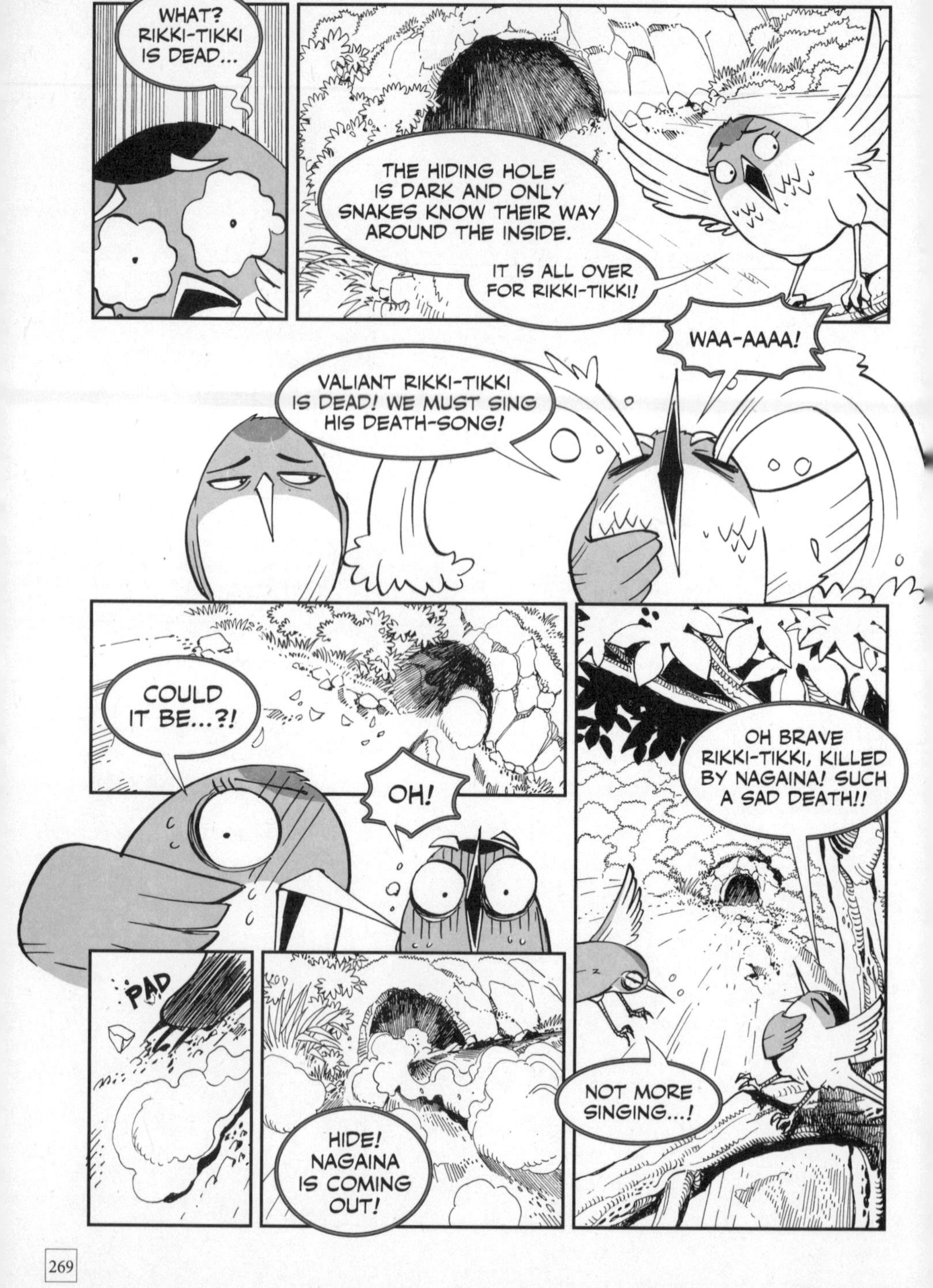
THE HIDING HOLE IS DARK AND ONLY SNAKES KNOW THEIR WAY AROUND THE INSIDE.
IT IS ALL OVER FOR RIKKI-TIKKI!
WHAT? RIKKI-TIKKI IS DEAD...
WAA-AAAA!
VALIANT RIKKI-TIKKI IS DEAD! WE MUST SING HIS DEATH-SONG!
OH BRAVE RIKKI-TIKKI, KILLED BY NAGAINA! SUCH A SAD DEATH!!
NOT MORE SINGING...!
COULD IT BE...?!
OH!
HIDE! NAGAINA IS COMING OUT!
PAD

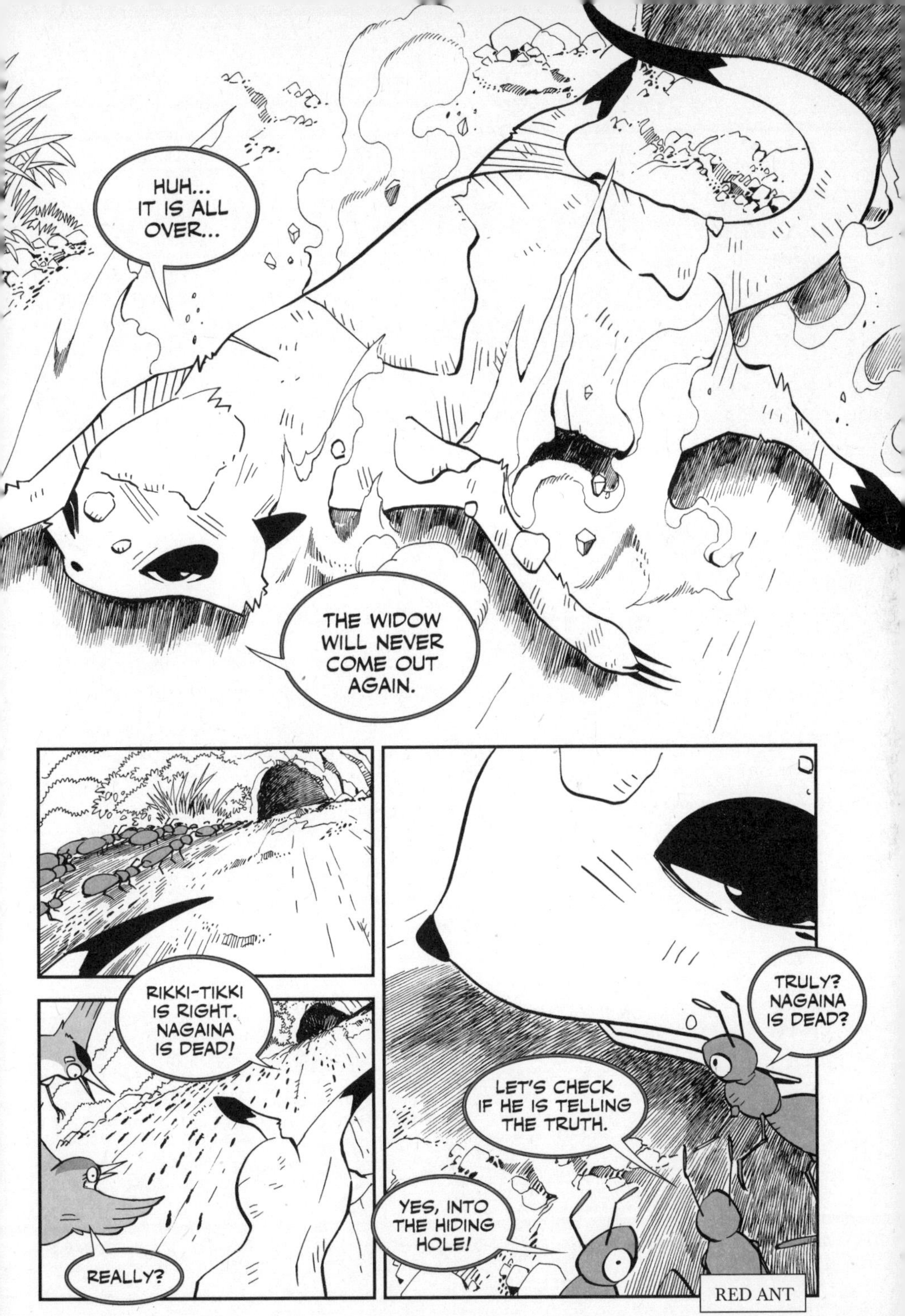
HUH... IT IS ALL OVER...
THE WIDOW WILL NEVER COME OUT AGAIN.
TRULY? NAGAINA IS DEAD?
LET'S CHECK IF HE IS TELLING THE TRUTH.
YES, INTO THE HIDING HOLE!
RED ANT
RIKKI-TIKKI IS RIGHT. NAGAINA IS DEAD!
REALLY?

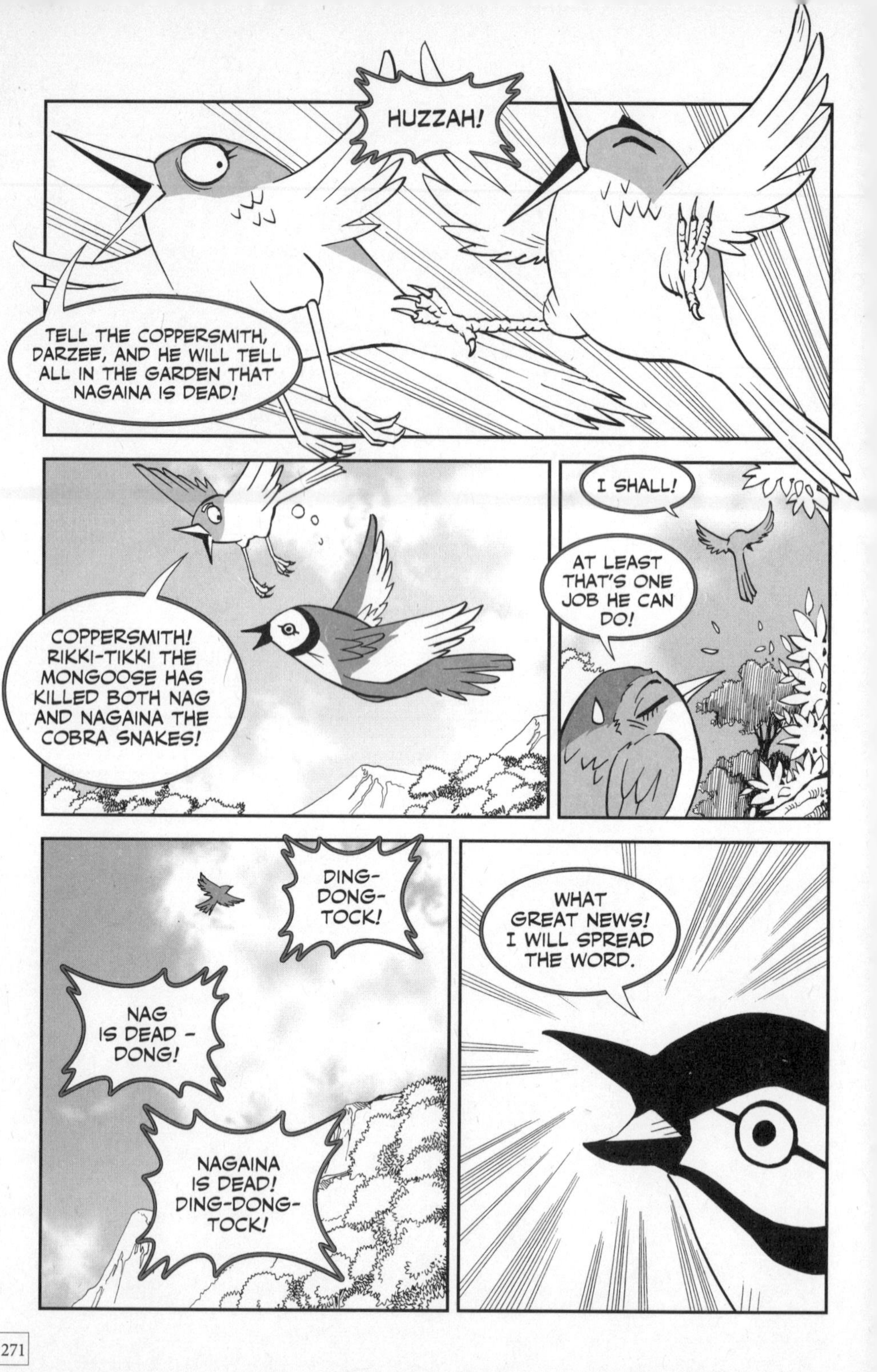
HUZZAH!
TELL THE COPPERSMITH, DARZEE, AND HE WILL TELL ALL IN THE GARDEN THAT NAGAINA IS DEAD!
I SHALL!
AT LEAST THAT'S ONE JOB HE CAN DO!
COPPERSMITH! RIKKI-TIKKI THE MONGOOSE HAS KILLED BOTH NAG AND NAGAINA THE COBRA SNAKES!
WHAT GREAT NEWS! I WILL SPREAD THE WORD.
DING-DONG-TOCK!
NAG IS DEAD - DONG!
NAGAINA IS DEAD! DING-DONG-TOCK!

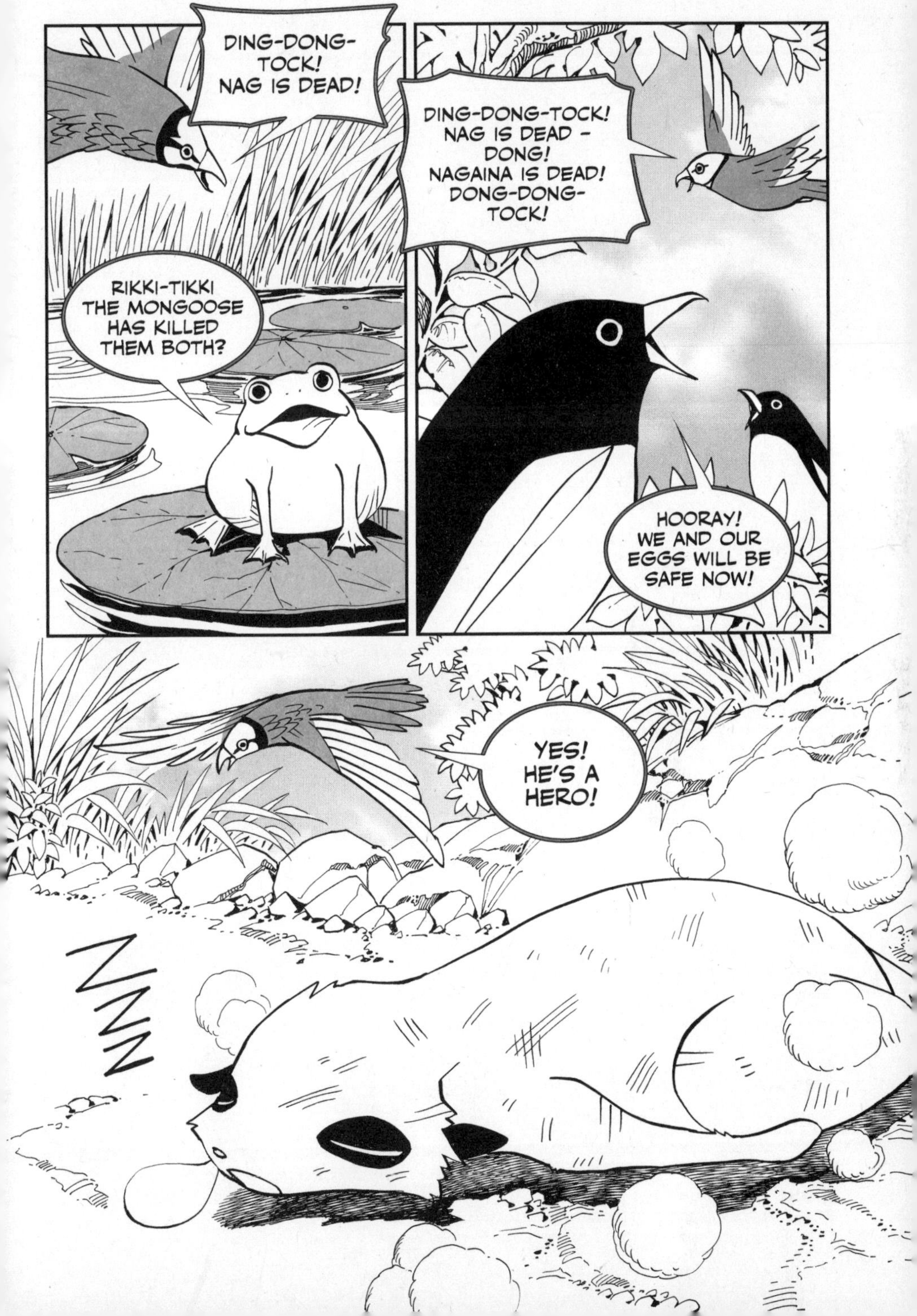
DING-DONG-TOCK! NAG IS DEAD - DONG! NAGAINA IS DEAD! DONG-DONG-TOCK!
HOORAY! WE AND OUR EGGS WILL BE SAFE NOW!
DING-DONG-TOCK! NAG IS DEAD!
RIKKI-TIKKI THE MONGOOSE HAS KILLED THEM BOTH?
YES! HE'S A HERO!

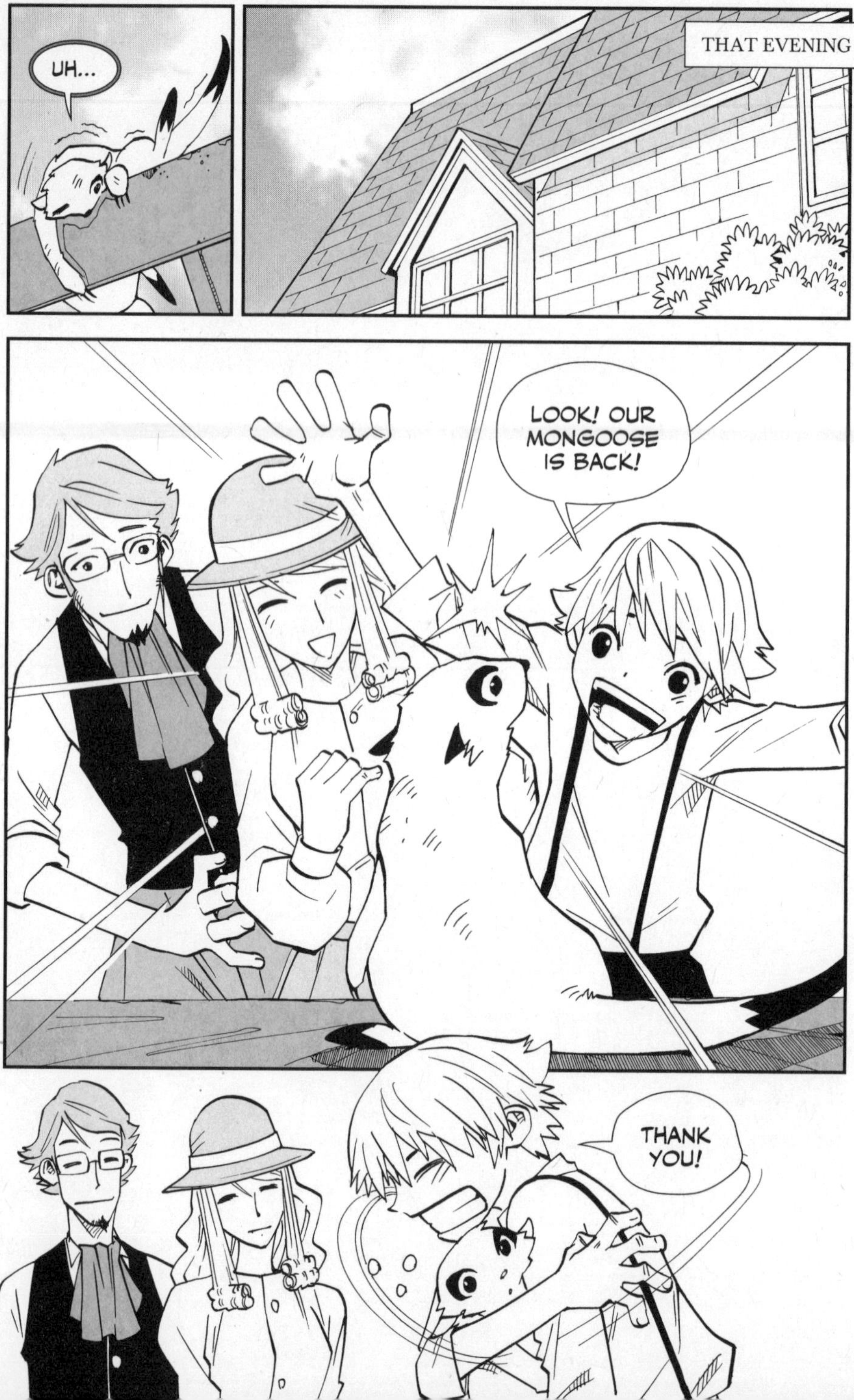
THAT EVENING
UH...
LOOK! OUR MONGOOSE IS BACK!
THANK YOU!

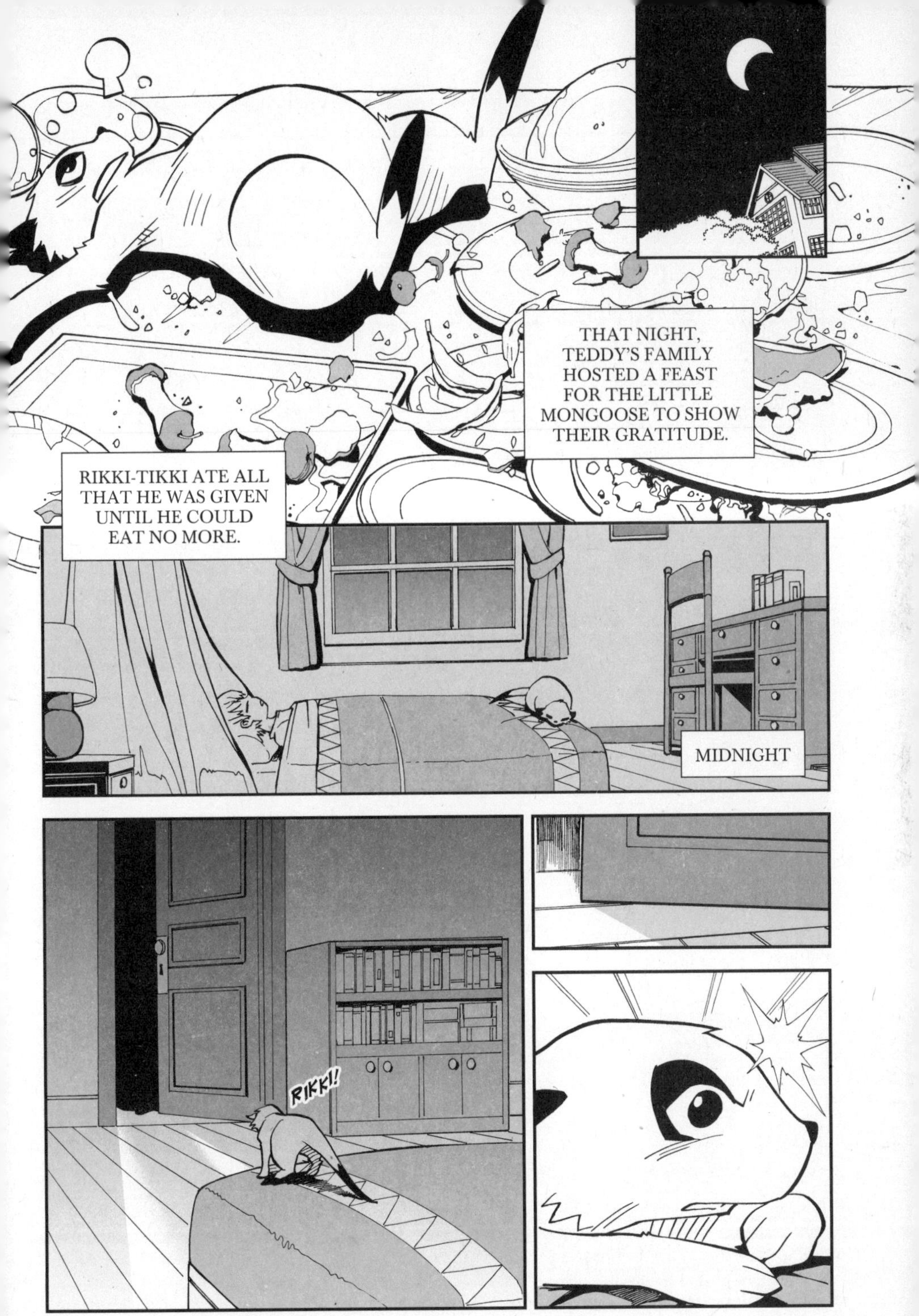
THAT NIGHT, TEDDY'S FAMILY HOSTED A FEAST FOR THE LITTLE MONGOOSE TO SHOW THEIR GRATITUDE.
RIKKI-TIKKI ATE ALL THAT HE WAS GIVEN UNTIL HE COULD EAT NO MORE.
MIDNIGHT
RIKK!

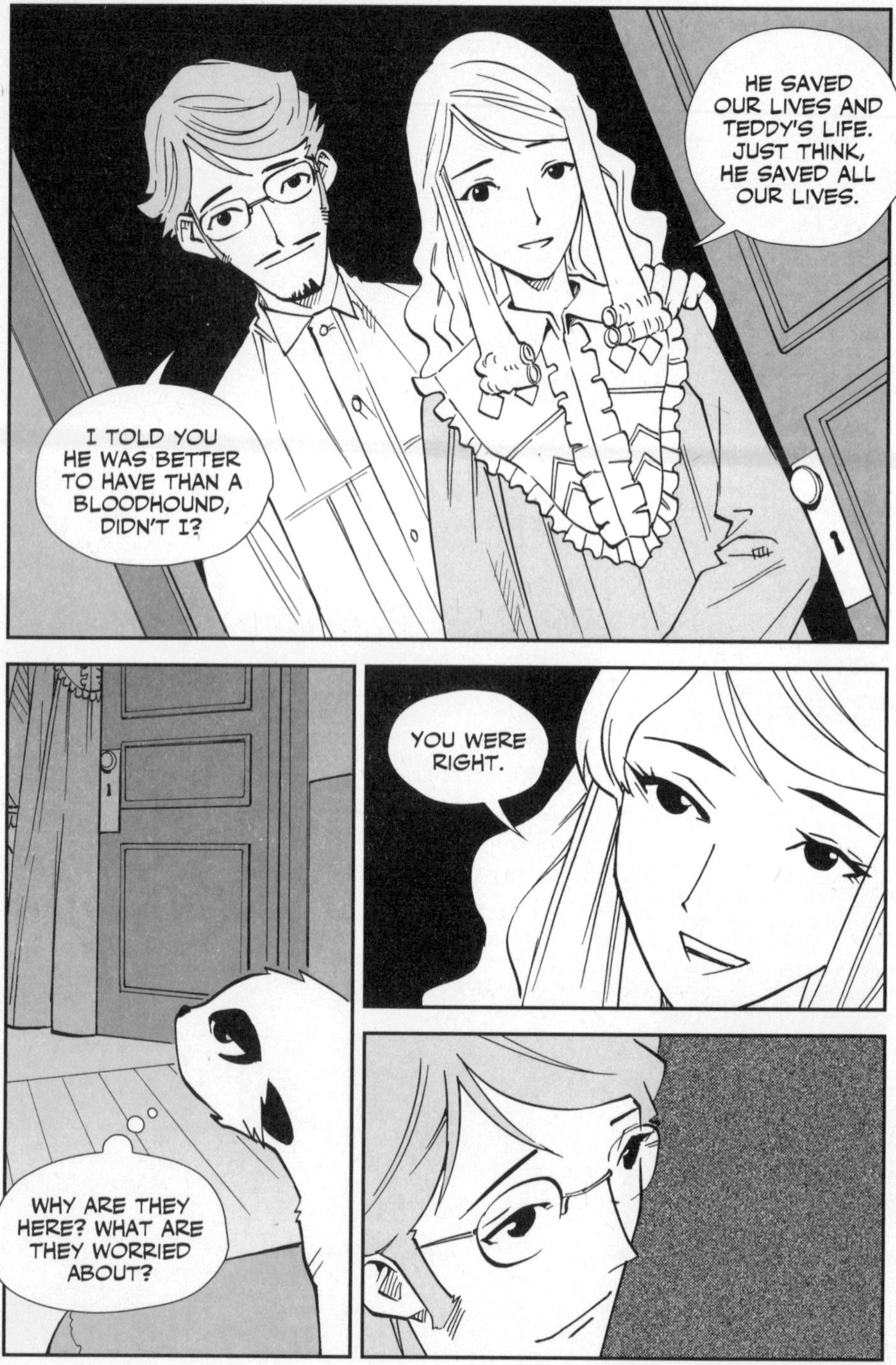
HE SAVED OUR LIVES AND TEDDY'S LIFE. JUST THINK, HE SAVED ALL OUR LIVES.
I TOLD YOU HE WAS BETTER TO HAVE THAN A BLOODHOUND, DIDN'T I?
YOU WERE RIGHT.
WHY ARE THEY HERE? WHAT ARE THEY WORRIED ABOUT?

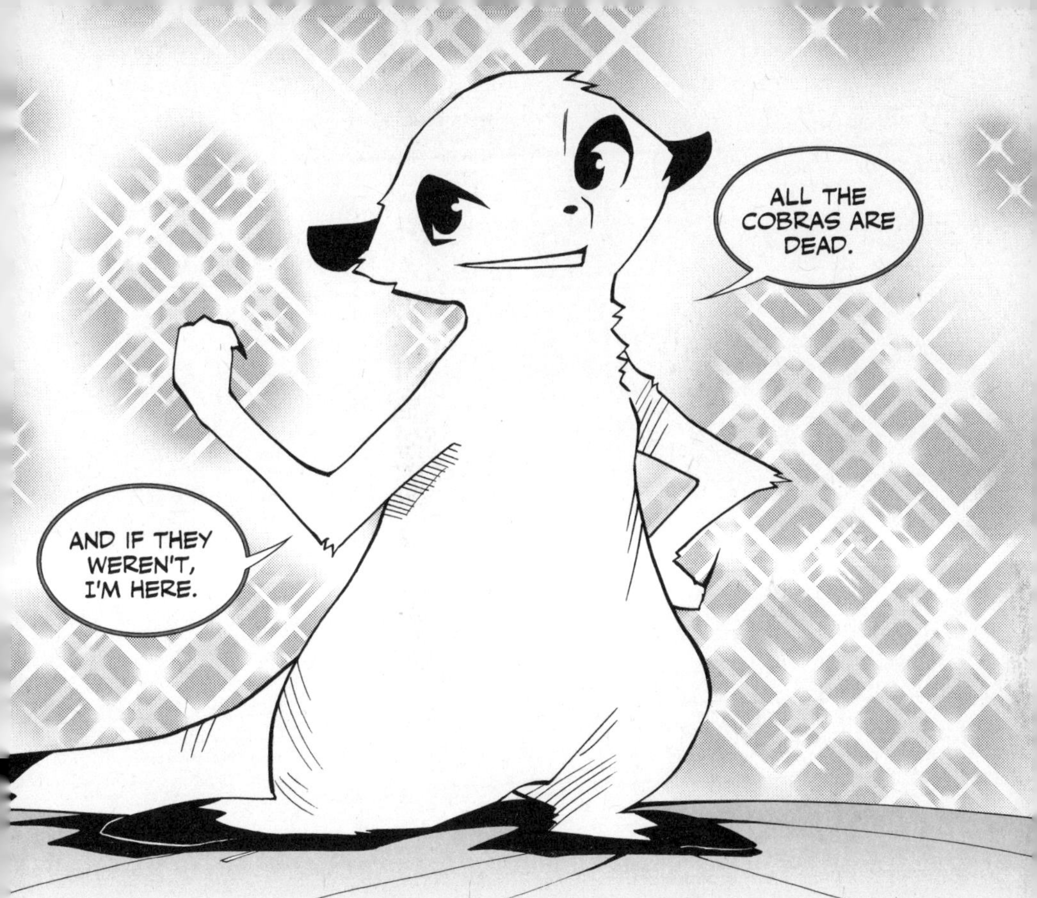
ALL THE COBRAS ARE DEAD.
AND IF THEY WEREN'T, I'M HERE.

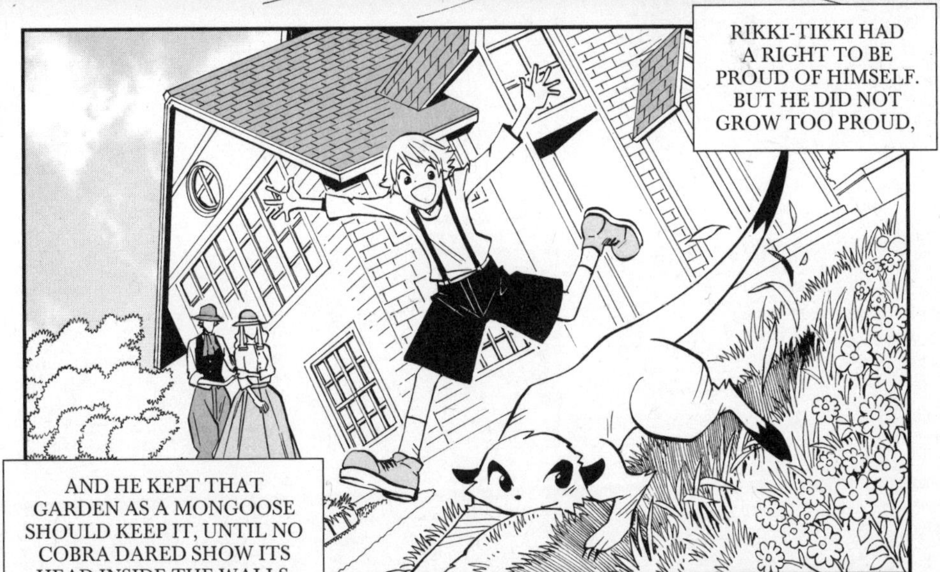
RIKKI-TIKKI HAD A RIGHT TO BE PROUD OF HIMSELF. BUT HE DID NOT GROW TOO PROUD,
AND HE KEPT THAT GARDEN AS A MONGOOSE SHOULD KEEP IT, UNTIL NO COBRA DARED SHOW ITS HEAD INSIDE THE WALLS.

BOOK 5 ~ END

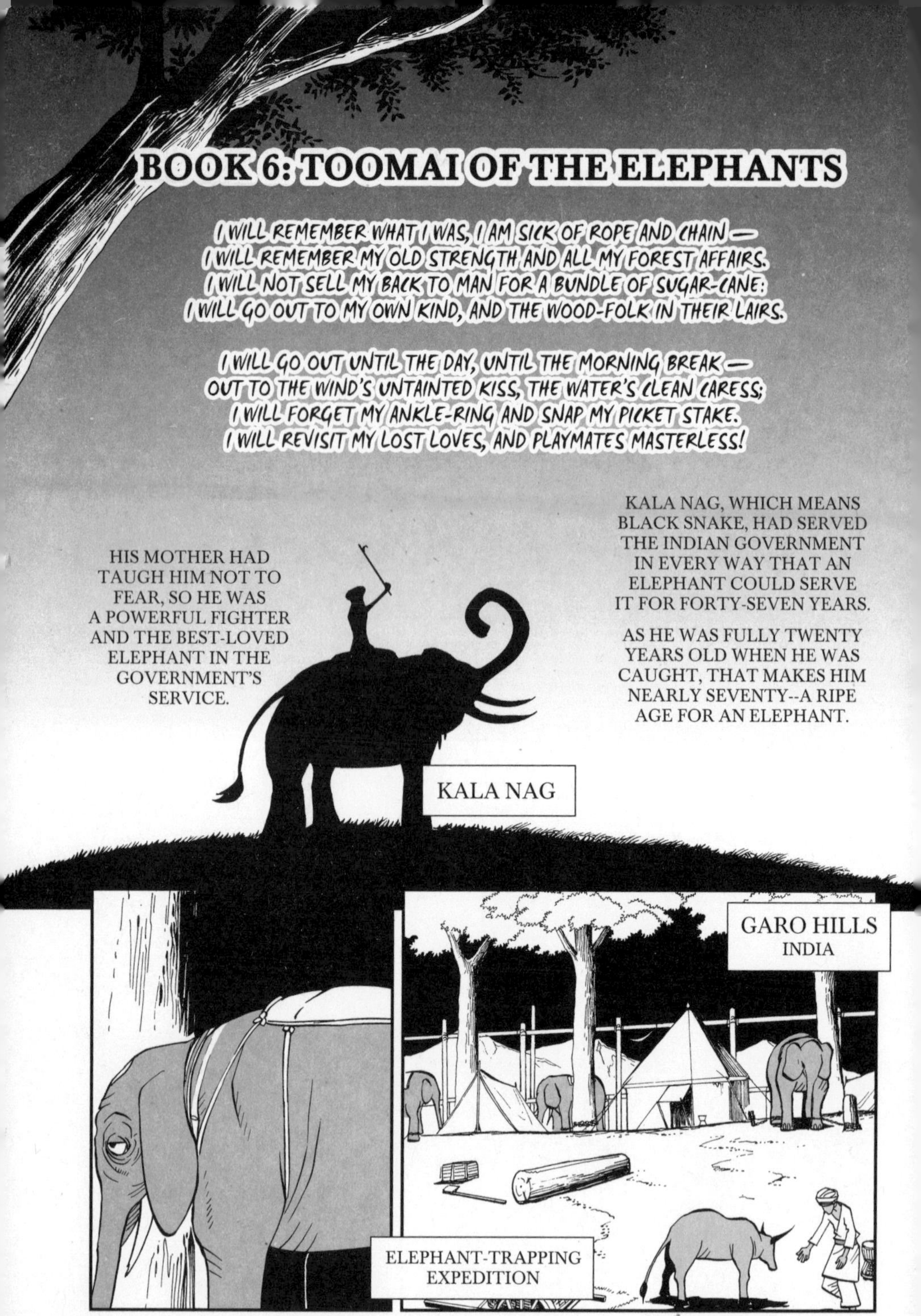
BOOK 6: TOOMAI OF THE ELEPHANTS
I WILL REMEMBER WHAT I WAS, I AM SICK OF ROPE AND CHAIN —
I WILL REMEMBER MY OLD STRENGTH AND ALL MY FOREST AFFAIRS.
I WILL NOT SELL MY BACK TO MAN FOR A BUNDLE OF SUGAR-CANE:
I WILL GO OUT TO MY OWN KIND, AND THE WOOD-FOLK IN THEIR LAIRS.
I WILL GO OUT UNTIL THE DAY, UNTIL THE MORNING BREAK —
OUT TO THE WIND'S UNTAINTED KISS, THE WATER'S CLEAN CARESS;
I WILL FORGET MY ANKLE-RING AND SNAP MY PICKET STAKE.
I WILL REVISIT MY LOST LOVES, AND PLAYMATES MASTERLESS!
KALA NAG, WHICH MEANS BLACK SNAKE, HAD SERVED THE INDIAN GOVERNMENT IN EVERY WAY THAT AN ELEPHANT COULD SERVE IT FOR FORTY-SEVEN YEARS.
AS HE WAS FULLY TWENTY YEARS OLD WHEN HE WAS CAUGHT, THAT MAKES HIM NEARLY SEVENTY--A RIPE AGE FOR AN ELEPHANT.
HIS MOTHER HAD TAUGH HIM NOT TO FEAR, SO HE WAS A POWERFUL FIGHTER AND THE BEST-LOVED ELEPHANT IN THE GOVERNMENT'S SERVICE.
KALA NAG
GARO HILLS
INDIA
ELEPHANT-TRAPPING EXPEDITION

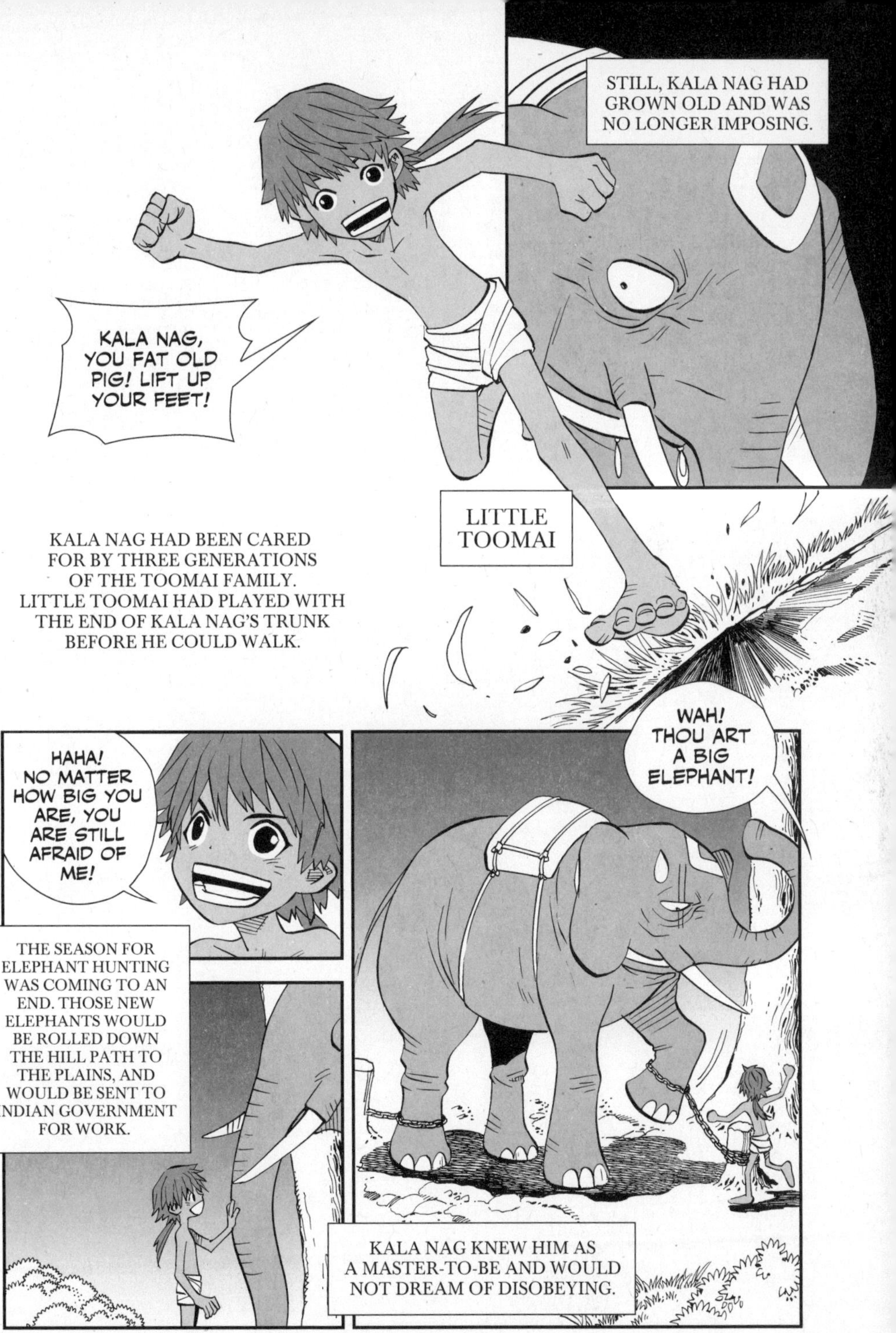
STILL, KALA NAG HAD GROWN OLD AND WAS NO LONGER IMPOSING.
KALA NAG, YOU FAT OLD PIG! LIFT UP YOUR FEET!
LITTLE TOOMAI
KALA NAG HAD BEEN CARED FOR BY THREE GENERATIONS OF THE TOOMAI FAMILY. LITTLE TOOMAI HAD PLAYED WITH THE END OF KALA NAG'S TRUNK BEFORE HE COULD WALK.
WAH! THOU ART A BIG ELEPHANT!
KALA NAG KNEW HIM AS A MASTER-TO-BE AND WOULD NOT DREAM OF DISOBEYING.
HAHA! NO MATTER HOW BIG YOU ARE, YOU ARE STILL AFRAID OF ME!
THE SEASON FOR ELEPHANT HUNTING WAS COMING TO AN END. THOSE NEW ELEPHANTS WOULD BE ROLLED DOWN THE HILL PATH TO THE PLAINS, AND WOULD BE SENT TO INDIAN GOVERNMENT FOR WORK.

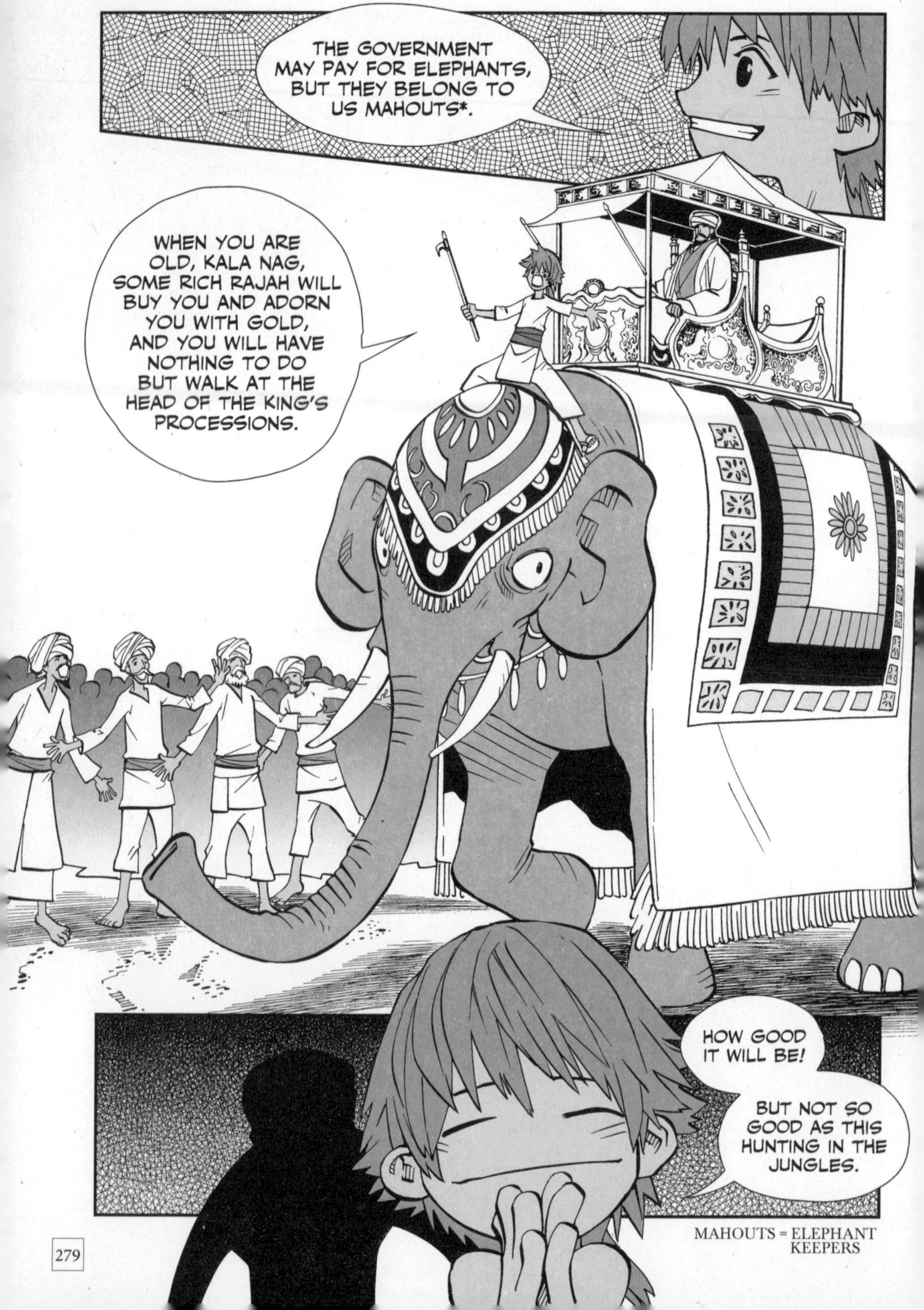
THE GOVERNMENT MAY PAY FOR ELEPHANTS, BUT THEY BELONG TO US MAHOUTS*.
WHEN YOU ARE OLD, KALA NAG, SOME RICH RAJAH WILL BUY YOU AND ADORN YOU WITH GOLD, AND YOU WILL HAVE NOTHING TO DO BUT WALK AT THE HEAD OF THE KING'S PROCESSIONS.
HOW GOOD IT WILL BE!
BUT NOT SO GOOD AS THIS HUNTING IN THE JUNGLES.

MAHOUTS = ELEPHANT KEEPERS

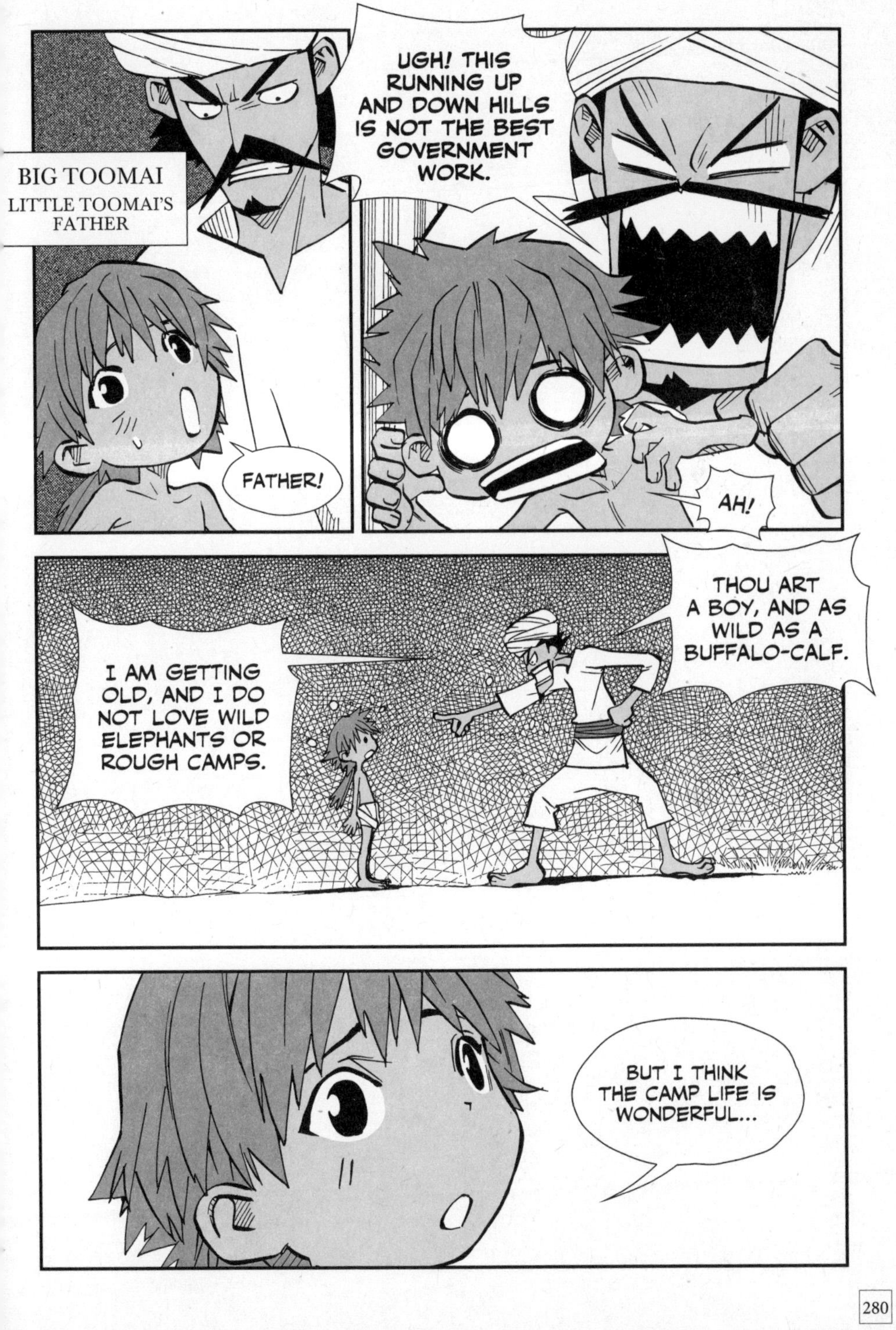
UGH! THIS RUNNING UP AND DOWN HILLS IS NOT THE BEST GOVERNMENT WORK.
AH!
BIG TOOMAI
LITTLE TOOMAI'S FATHER
FATHER!
THOU ART A BOY, AND AS WILD AS A BUFFALO-CALF.
I AM GETTING OLD, AND I DO NOT LOVE WILD ELEPHANTS OR ROUGH CAMPS.
BUT I THINK THE CAMP LIFE IS WONDERFUL...

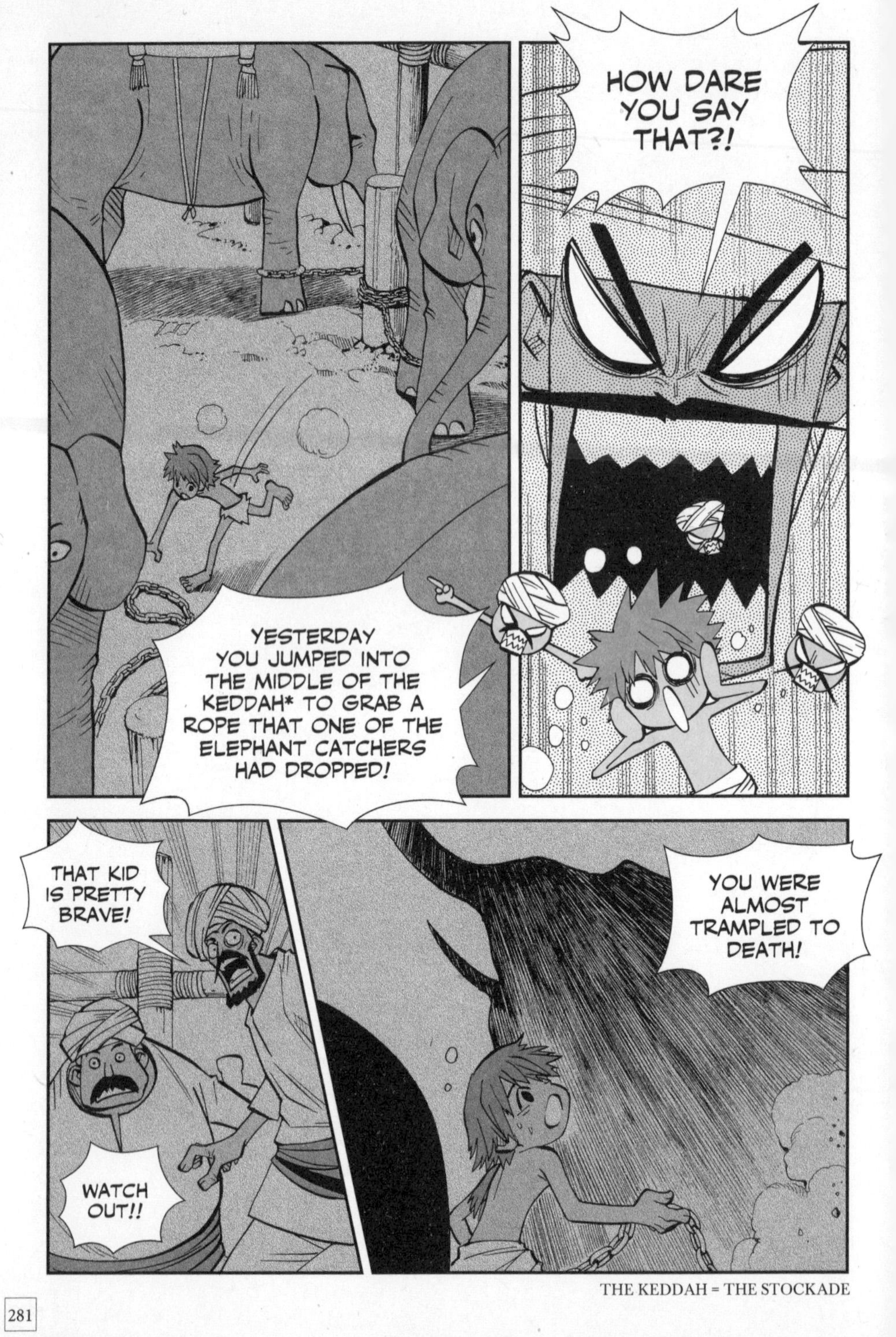
HOW DARE YOU SAY THAT?!
YESTERDAY YOU JUMPED INTO THE MIDDLE OF THE KEDDAH* TO GRAB A ROPE THAT ONE OF THE ELEPHANT CATCHERS HAD DROPPED!
YOU WERE ALMOST TRAMPLED TO DEATH!
THAT KID IS PRETTY BRAVE!
WATCH OUT!!

THE KEDDAH = THE STOCKADE

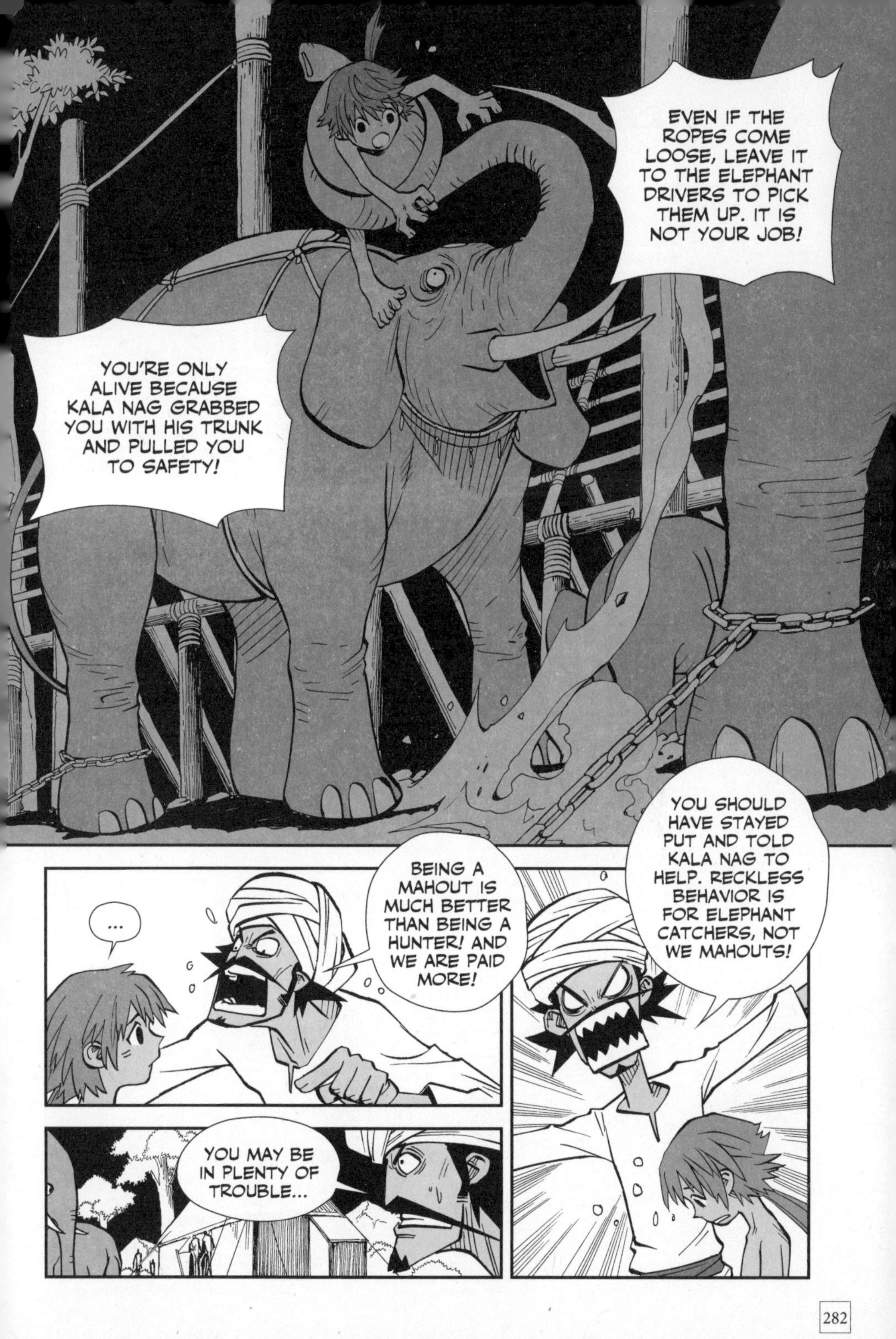
EVEN IF THE ROPES COME LOOSE, LEAVE IT TO THE ELEPHANT DRIVERS TO PICK THEM UP. IT IS NOT YOUR JOB!
YOU'RE ONLY ALIVE BECAUSE KALA NAG GRABBED YOU WITH HIS TRUNK AND PULLED YOU TO SAFETY!
YOU SHOULD HAVE STAYED PUT AND TOLD KALA NAG TO HELP. RECKLESS BEHAVIOR IS FOR ELEPHANT CATCHERS, NOT WE MAHOUTS!
BEING A MAHOUT IS MUCH BETTER THAN BEING A HUNTER! AND WE ARE PAID MORE!
...
YOU MAY BE IN PLENTY OF TROUBLE...

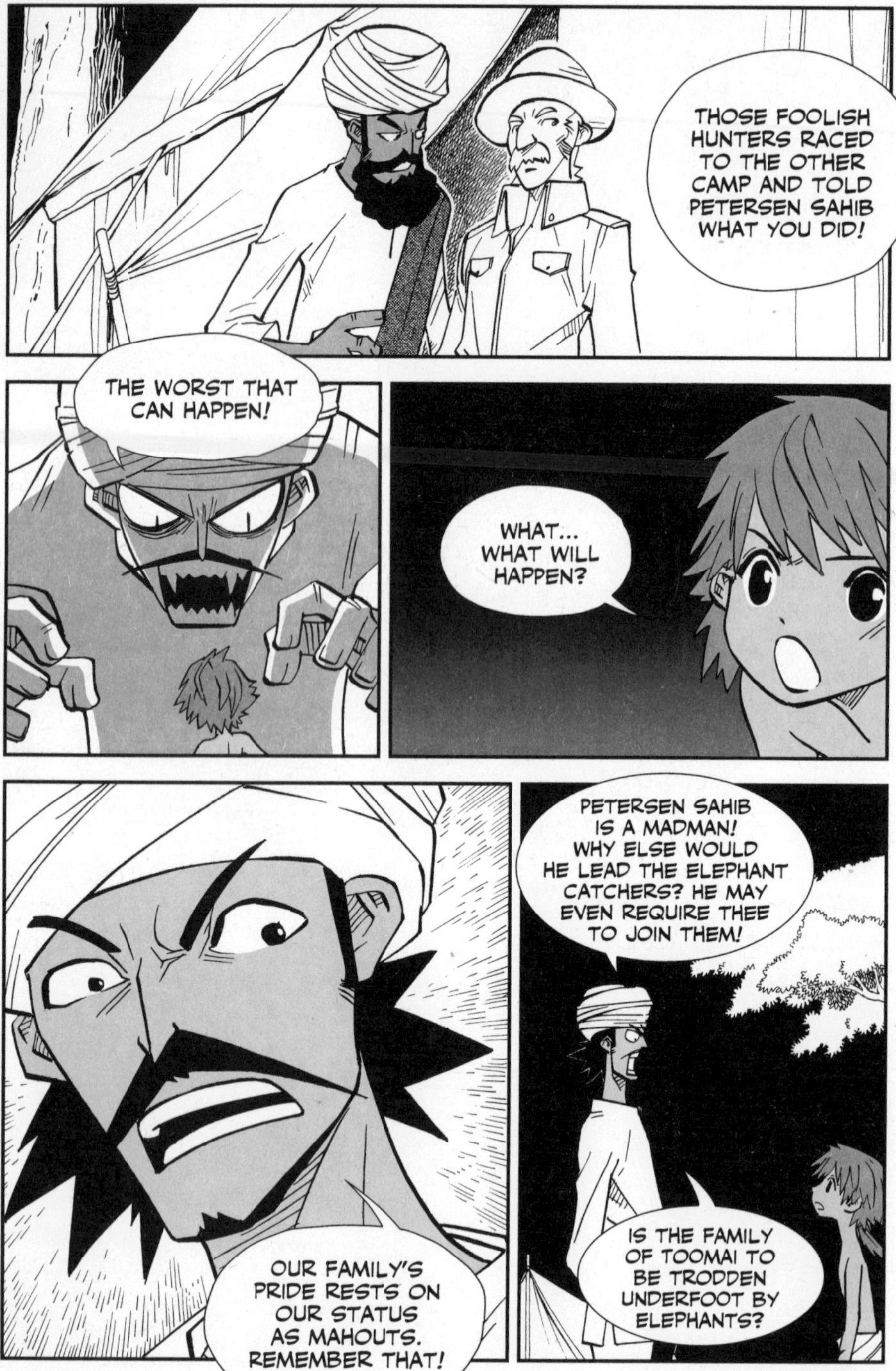
THOSE FOOLISH HUNTERS RACED TO THE OTHER CAMP AND TOLD PETERSEN SAHIB WHAT YOU DID!
WHAT... WHAT WILL HAPPEN?
THE WORST THAT CAN HAPPEN!
PETERSEN SAHIB IS A MADMAN! WHY ELSE WOULD HE LEAD THE ELEPHANT CATCHERS? HE MAY EVEN REQUIRE THEE TO JOIN THEM!
IS THE FAMILY OF TOOMAI TO BE TRODDEN UNDERFOOT BY ELEPHANTS?
OUR FAMILY'S PRIDE RESTS ON OUR STATUS AS MAHOUTS. REMEMBER THAT!

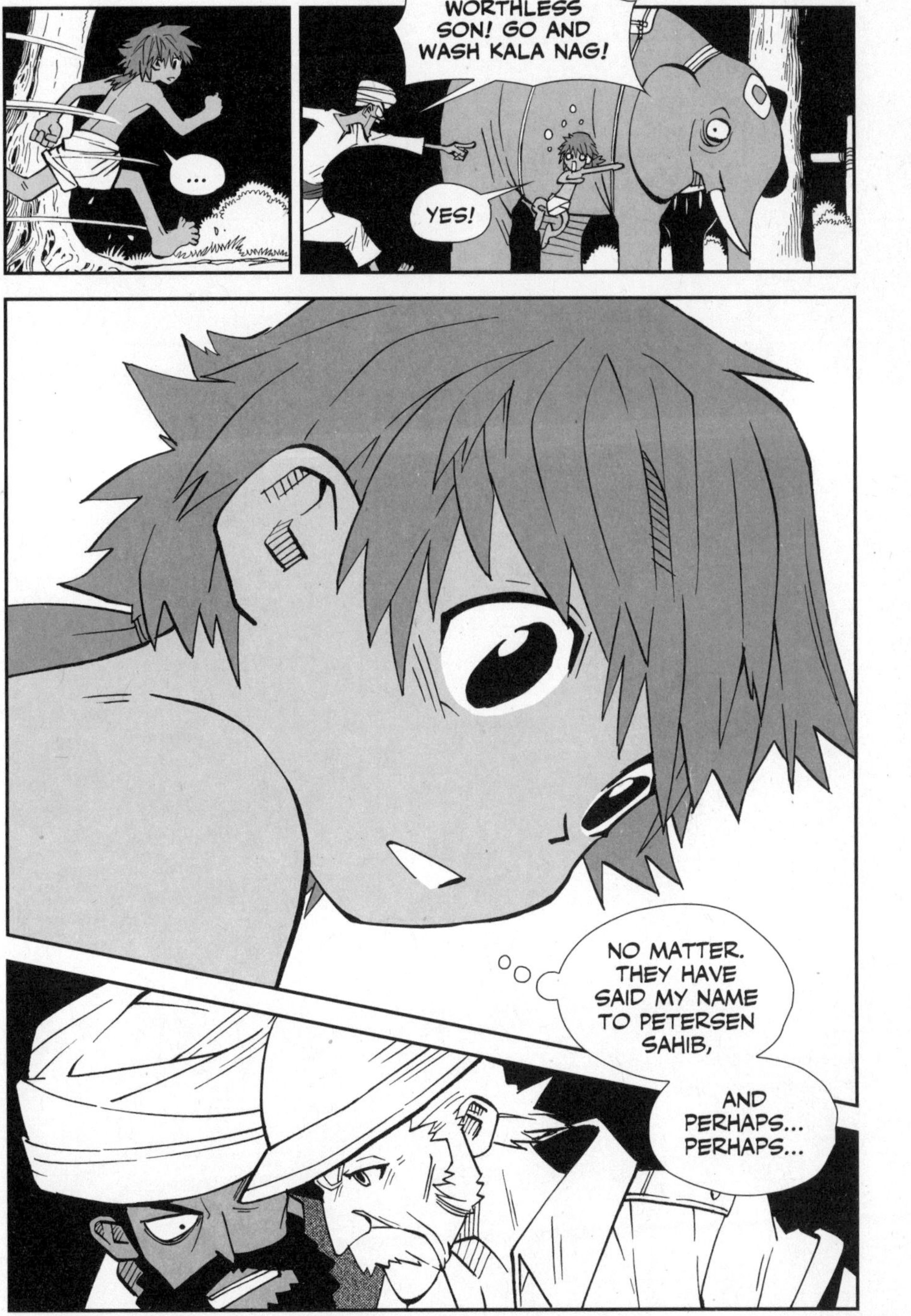
WORTHLESS SON! GO AND WASH KALA NAG!
YES!
...
NO MATTER. THEY HAVE SAID MY NAME TO PETERSEN SAHIB,
AND PERHAPS... PERHAPS...

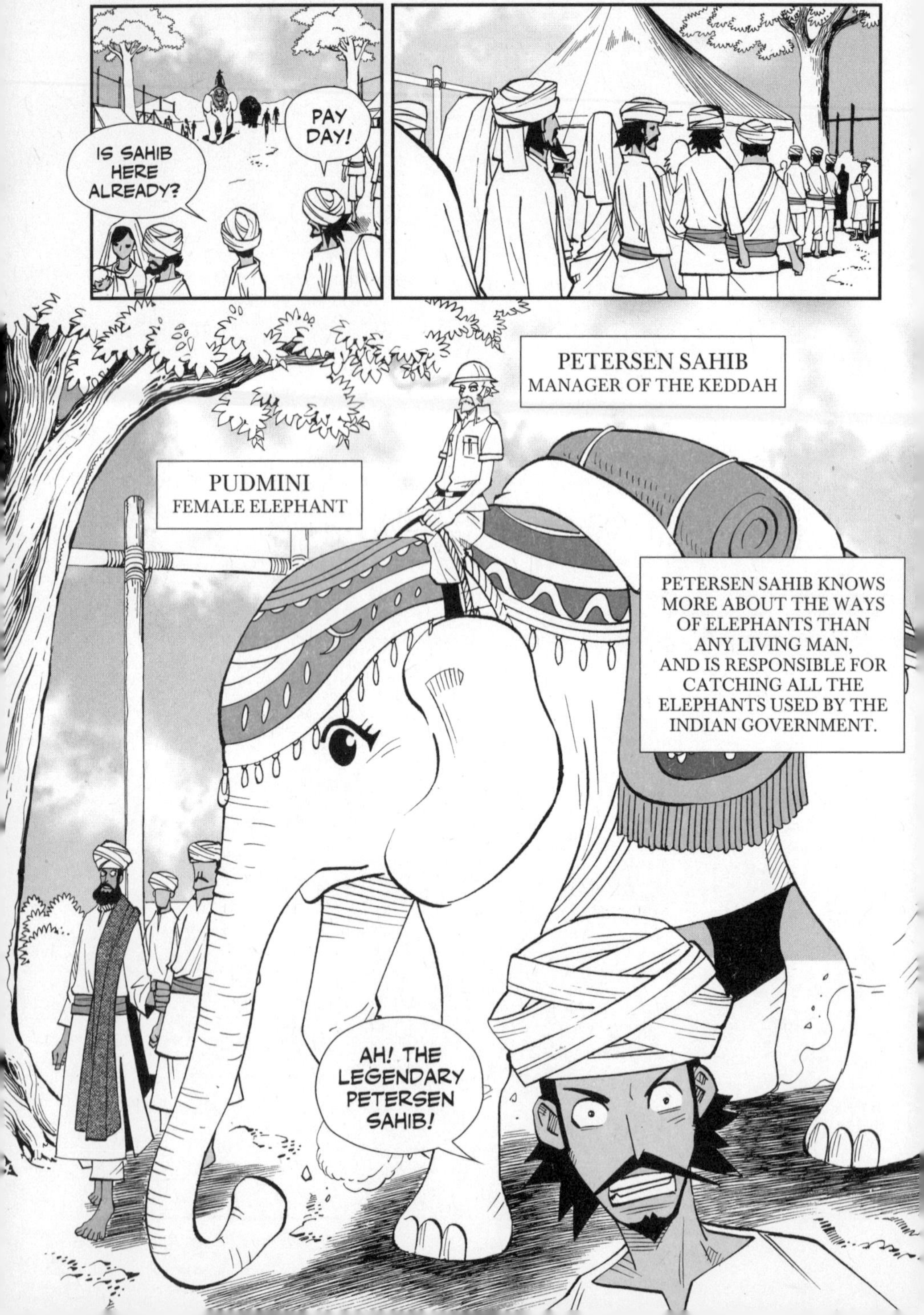
PAY DAY!
IS SAHIB HERE ALREADY?
PETERSEN SAHIB
MANAGER OF THE KEDDAH
PUDMINI
FEMALE ELEPHANT
PETERSEN SAHIB KNOWS MORE ABOUT THE WAYS OF ELEPHANTS THAN ANY LIVING MAN, AND IS RESPONSIBLE FOR CATCHING ALL THE ELEPHANTS USED BY THE INDIAN GOVERNMENT.
AH! THE LEGENDARY PETERSEN SAHIB!

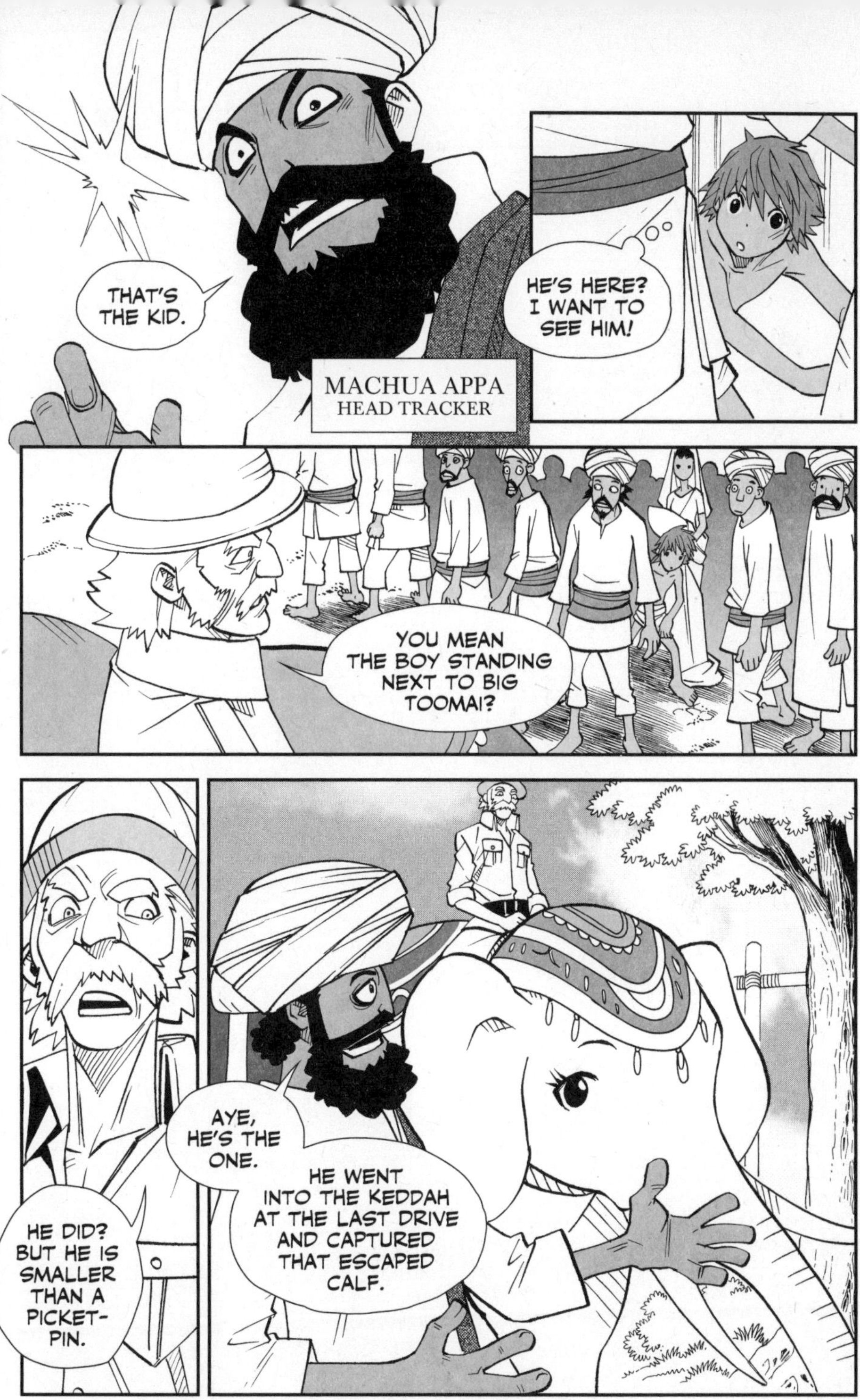

HE'S HERE? I WANT TO SEE HIM!
THAT'S THE KID.
MACHUA APPA
HEAD TRACKER
YOU MEAN THE BOY STANDING NEXT TO BIG TOOMAI?
AYE, HE'S THE ONE.
HE WENT INTO THE KEDDAH AT THE LAST DRIVE AND CAPTURED THAT ESCAPED CALF.
HE DID? BUT HE IS SMALLER THAN A PICKET-PIN.

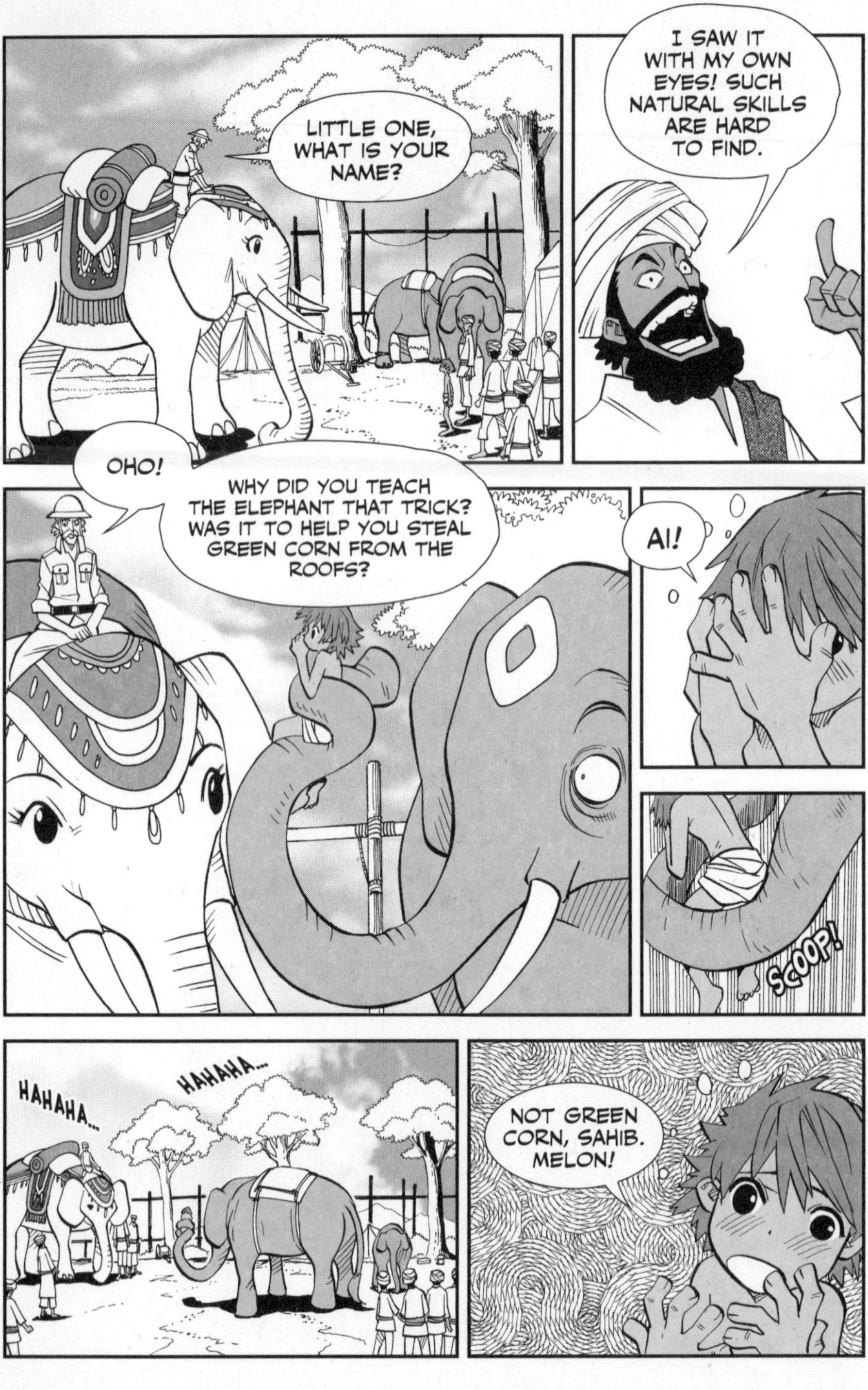
I SAW IT WITH MY OWN EYES! SUCH NATURAL SKILLS ARE HARD TO FIND.
LITTLE ONE, WHAT IS YOUR NAME?
AI!
SCOOP!
OHO!
WHY DID YOU TEACH THE ELEPHANT THAT TRICK? WAS IT TO HELP YOU STEAL GREEN CORN FROM THE ROOFS?
NOT GREEN CORN, SAHIB. MELON!
HAHAHA...
HAHAHA...

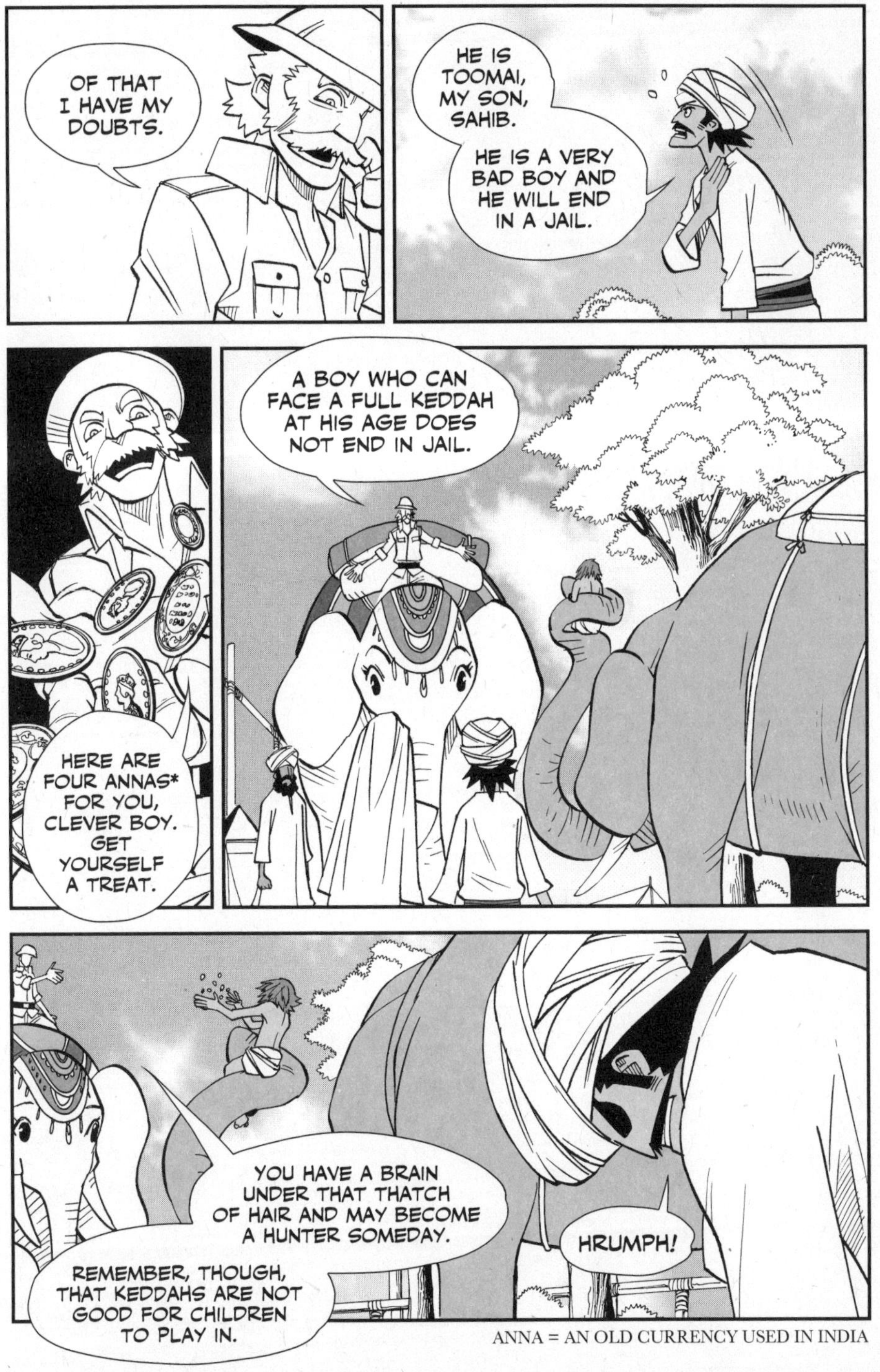
OF THAT I HAVE MY DOUBTS.
HE IS TOOMAI, MY SON, SAHIB.
HE IS A VERY BAD BOY AND HE WILL END IN A JAIL.
HERE ARE FOUR ANNAS* FOR YOU, CLEVER BOY. GET YOURSELF A TREAT.
A BOY WHO CAN FACE A FULL KEDDAH AT HIS AGE DOES NOT END IN JAIL.
YOU HAVE A BRAIN UNDER THAT THATCH OF HAIR AND MAY BECOME A HUNTER SOMEDAY.
REMEMBER, THOUGH, THAT KEDDAHS ARE NOT GOOD FOR CHILDREN TO PLAY IN.
HRUMPH!

ANNA = AN OLD CURRENCY USED IN INDIA

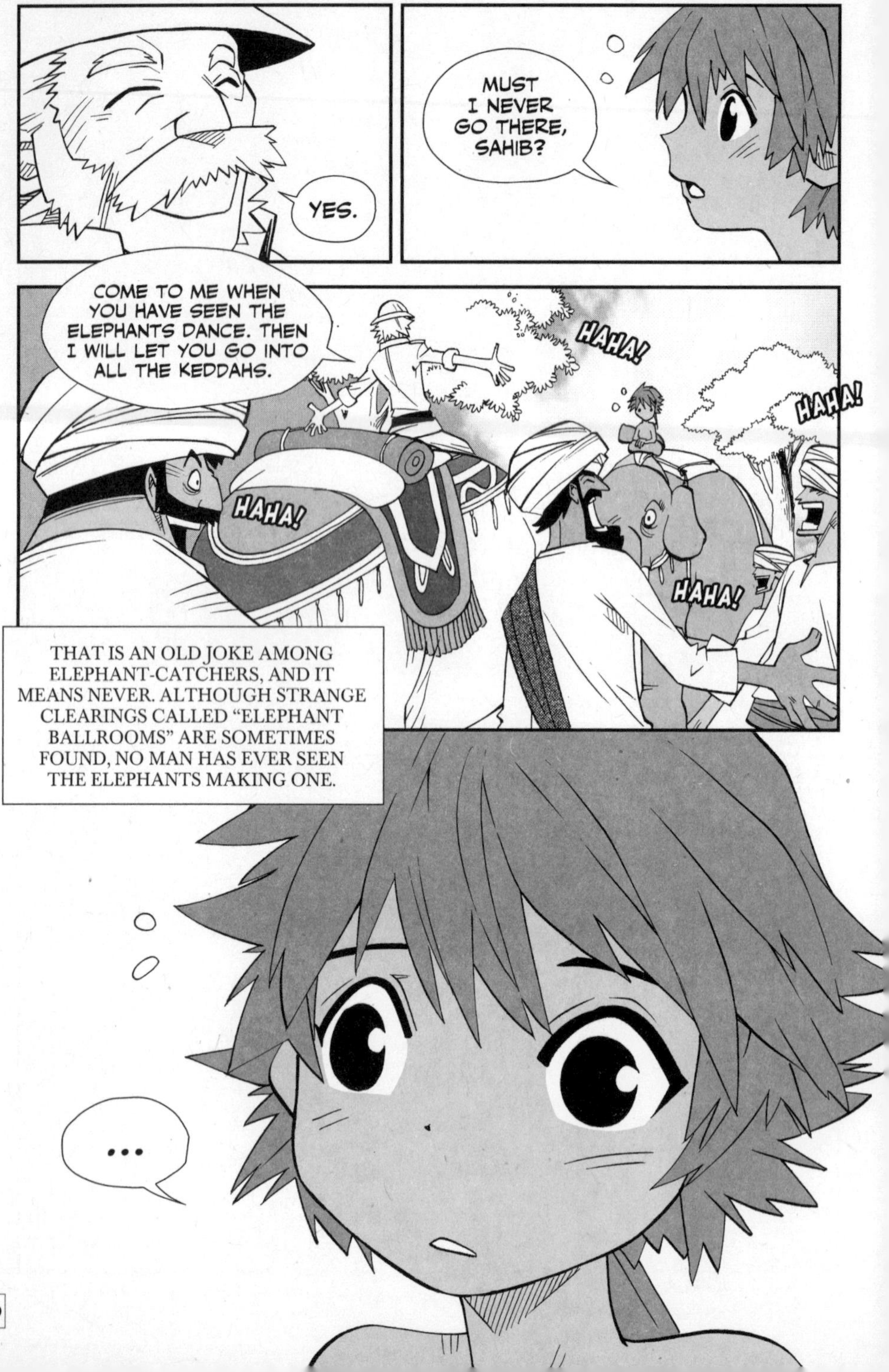
MUST I NEVER GO THERE, SAHIB?
YES.
COME TO ME WHEN YOU HAVE SEEN THE ELEPHANTS DANCE. THEN I WILL LET YOU GO INTO ALL THE KEDDAHS.
HAHA!
HAHA!
HAHA!
HAHA!
THAT IS AN OLD JOKE AMONG ELEPHANT-CATCHERS, AND IT MEANS NEVER. ALTHOUGH STRANGE CLEARINGS CALLED "ELEPHANT BALLROOMS" ARE SOMETIMES FOUND, NO MAN HAS EVER SEEN THE ELEPHANTS MAKING ONE.
...

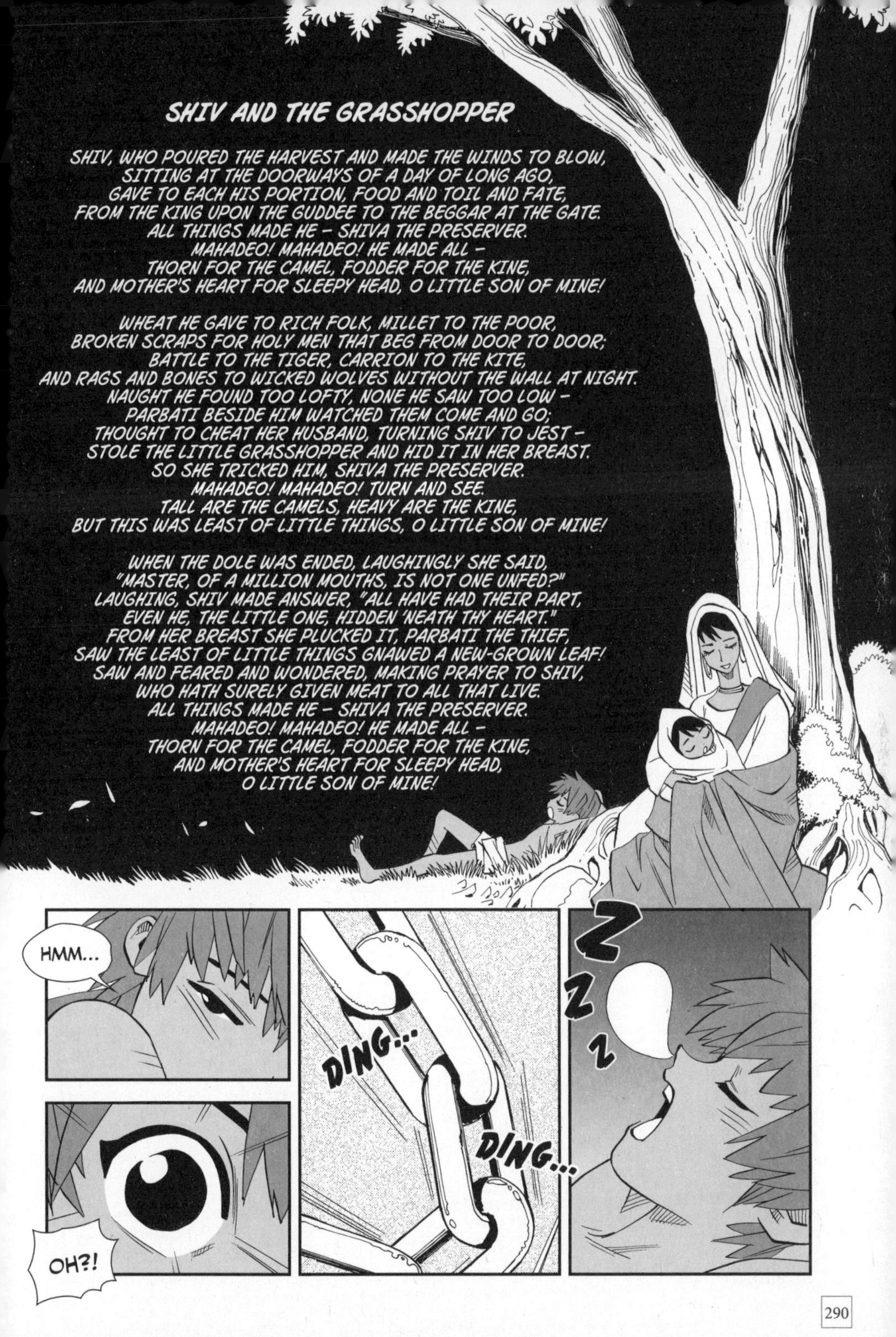
SHIV AND THE GRASSHOPPER
SHIV, WHO POURED THE HARVEST AND MADE THE WINDS TO BLOW,
SITTING AT THE DOORWAYS OF A DAY OF LONG AGO,
GAVE TO EACH HIS PORTION, FOOD AND TOIL AND FATE,
FROM THE KING UPON THE GUDDEE TO THE BEGGAR AT THE GATE.
ALL THINGS MADE HE – SHIVA THE PRESERVER.
MAHADEO! MAHADEO! HE MADE ALL –
THORN FOR THE CAMEL, FODDER FOR THE KINE,
AND MOTHER'S HEART FOR SLEEPY HEAD, O LITTLE SON OF MINE!

WHEAT HE GAVE TO RICH FOLK, MILLET TO THE POOR,
BROKEN SCRAPS FOR HOLY MEN THAT BEG FROM DOOR TO DOOR;
BATTLE TO THE TIGER, CARRION TO THE KITE,
AND RAGS AND BONES TO WICKED WOLVES WITHOUT THE WALL AT NIGHT.
NAUGHT HE FOUND TOO LOFTY, NONE HE SAW TOO LOW –
PARBATI BESIDE HIM WATCHED THEM COME AND GO;
THOUGHT TO CHEAT HER HUSBAND, TURNING SHIV TO JEST –
STOLE THE LITTLE GRASSHOPPER AND HID IT IN HER BREAST.
SO SHE TRICKED HIM, SHIVA THE PRESERVER.
MAHADEO! MAHADEO! TURN AND SEE.
TALL ARE THE CAMELS, HEAVY ARE THE KINE,
BUT THIS WAS LEAST OF LITTLE THINGS, O LITTLE SON OF MINE!

WHEN THE DOLE WAS ENDED, LAUGHINGLY SHE SAID,
"MASTER, OF A MILLION MOUTHS, IS NOT ONE UNFED?"
LAUGHING, SHIV MADE ANSWER, "ALL HAVE HAD THEIR PART,
EVEN HE, THE LITTLE ONE, HIDDEN 'NEATH THY HEART."
FROM HER BREAST SHE PLUCKED IT, PARBATI THE THIEF,
SAW THE LEAST OF LITTLE THINGS GNAWED A NEW-GROWN LEAF!
SAW AND FEARED AND WONDERED, MAKING PRAYER TO SHIV,
WHO HATH SURELY GIVEN MEAT TO ALL THAT LIVE.
ALL THINGS MADE HE – SHIVA THE PRESERVER.
MAHADEO! MAHADEO! HE MADE ALL –
THORN FOR THE CAMEL, FODDER FOR THE KINE,
AND MOTHER'S HEART FOR SLEEPY HEAD,
O LITTLE SON OF MINE!
Z
Z
Z
DING...
DING...
HMM...
OH?!

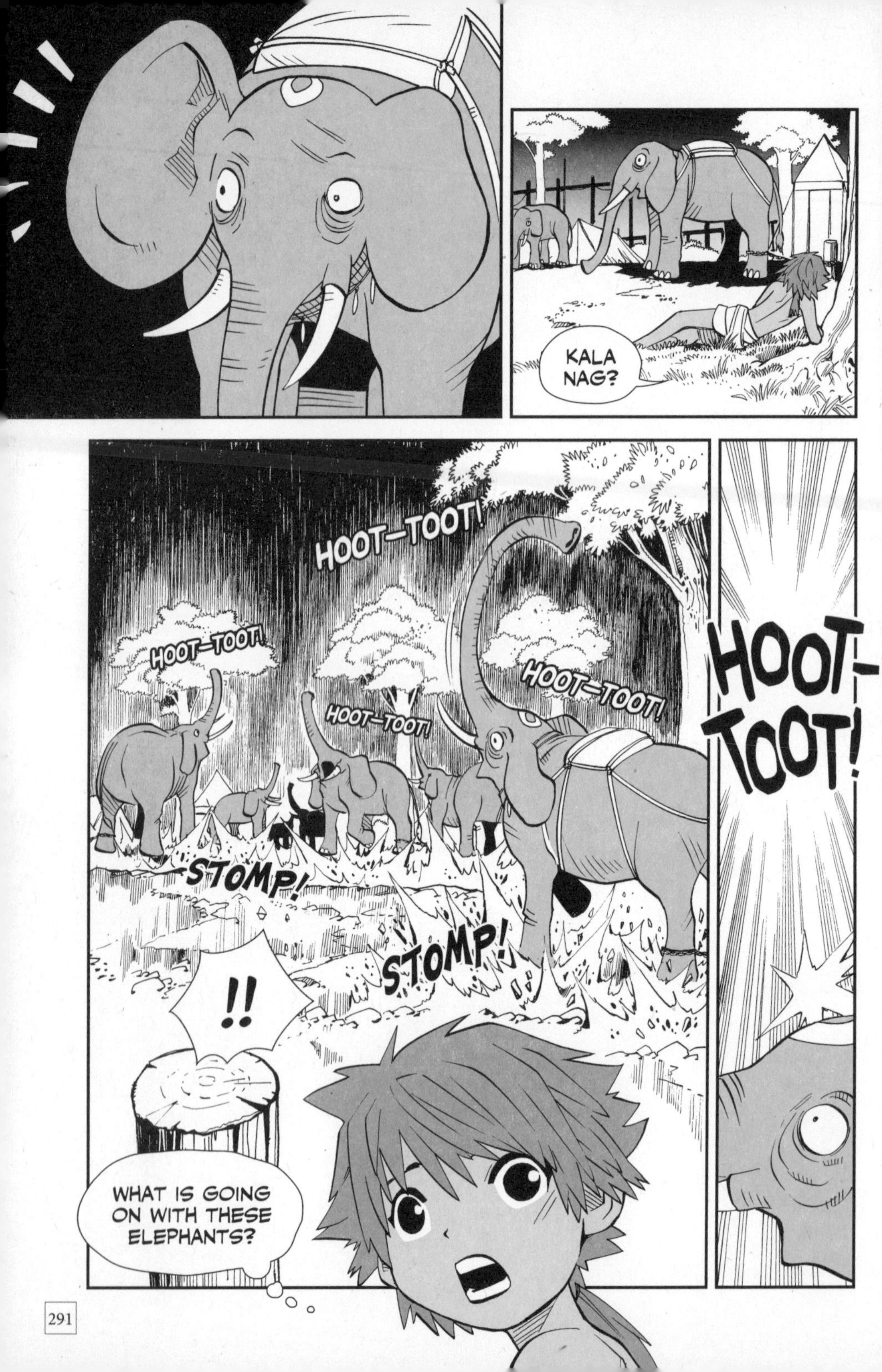
KALA NAG?
HOOT-TOOT!
HOOT-TOOT!
HOOT-TOOT!
HOOT-TOOT!
HOOT-TOOT!
STOMP!
STOMP!
!!
WHAT IS GOING ON WITH THESE ELEPHANTS?

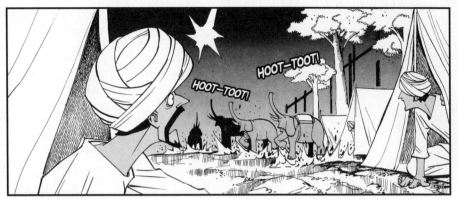

HOOT-TOOT!

HOOT-TOOT!

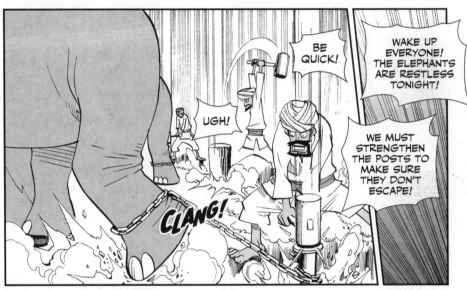

UGH!

BE QUICK!

WAKE UP EVERYONE! THE ELEPHANTS ARE RESTLESS TONIGHT!

WE MUST STRENGTHEN THE POSTS TO MAKE SURE THEY DON'T ESCAPE!

CLANG!

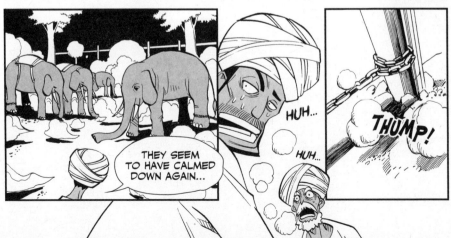

THEY SEEM TO HAVE CALMED DOWN AGAIN...

HUH...

HUH...

THUMP!

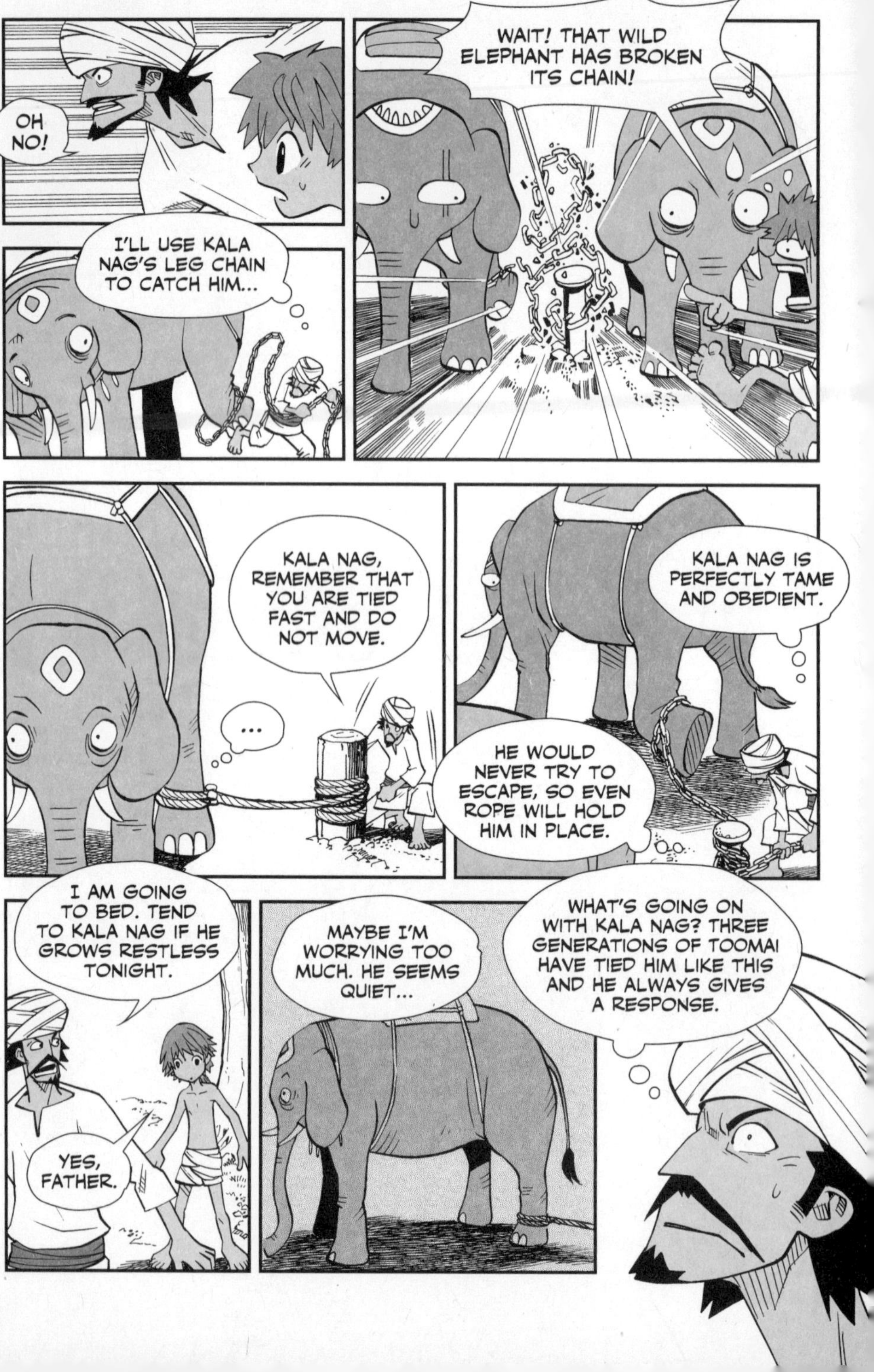
WAIT! THAT WILD ELEPHANT HAS BROKEN ITS CHAIN!
OH NO!
I'LL USE KALA NAG'S LEG CHAIN TO CATCH HIM...
KALA NAG IS PERFECTLY TAME AND OBEDIENT.
HE WOULD NEVER TRY TO ESCAPE, SO EVEN ROPE WILL HOLD HIM IN PLACE.
KALA NAG, REMEMBER THAT YOU ARE TIED FAST AND DO NOT MOVE.
...
WHAT'S GOING ON WITH KALA NAG? THREE GENERATIONS OF TOOMAI HAVE TIED HIM LIKE THIS AND HE ALWAYS GIVES A RESPONSE.
MAYBE I'M WORRYING TOO MUCH. HE SEEMS QUIET...
I AM GOING TO BED. TEND TO KALA NAG IF HE GROWS RESTLESS TONIGHT.
YES, FATHER.

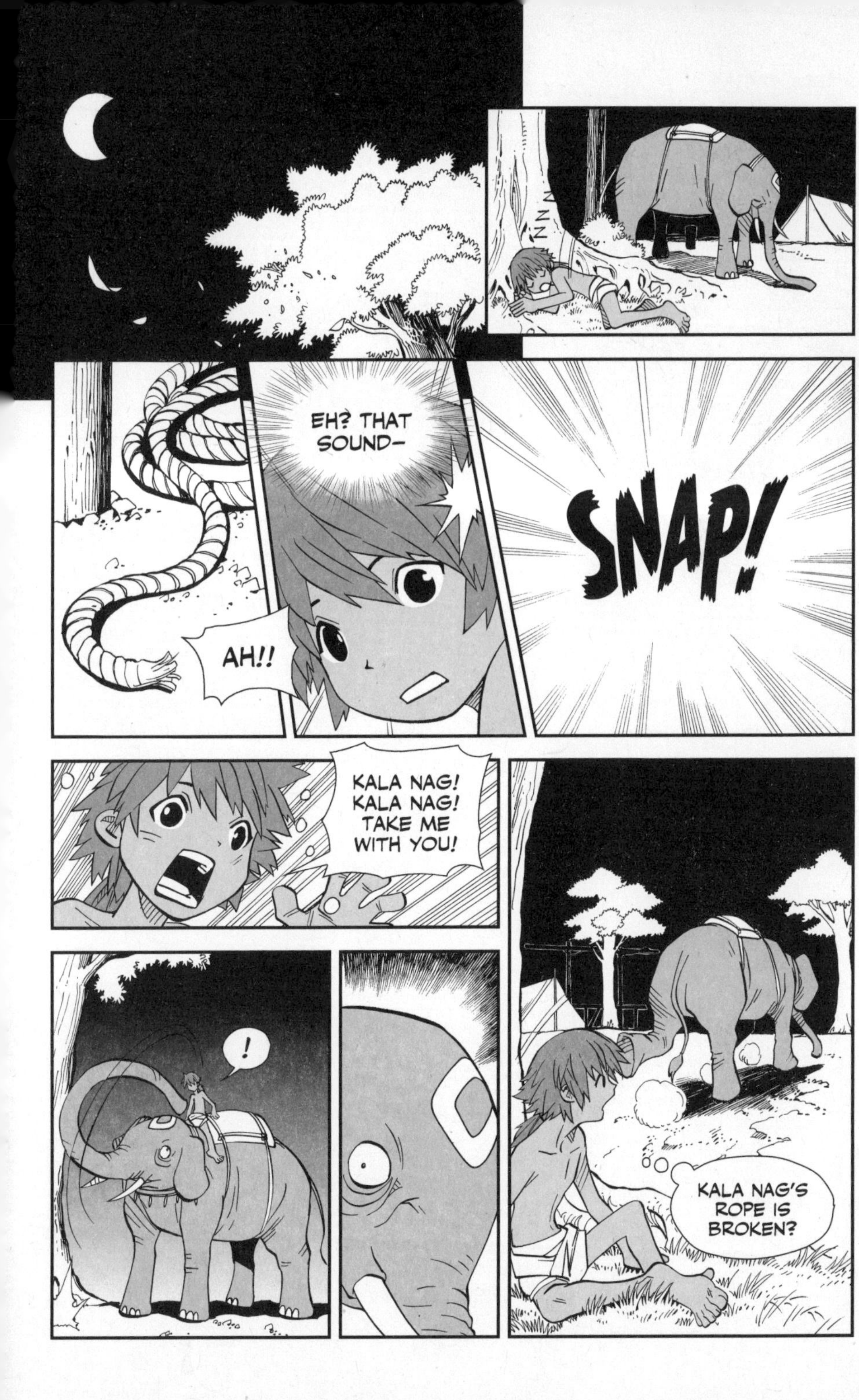
SNAP!
EH? THAT SOUND–
AH!!
KALA NAG'S ROPE IS BROKEN?
KALA NAG! KALA NAG! TAKE ME WITH YOU!
!

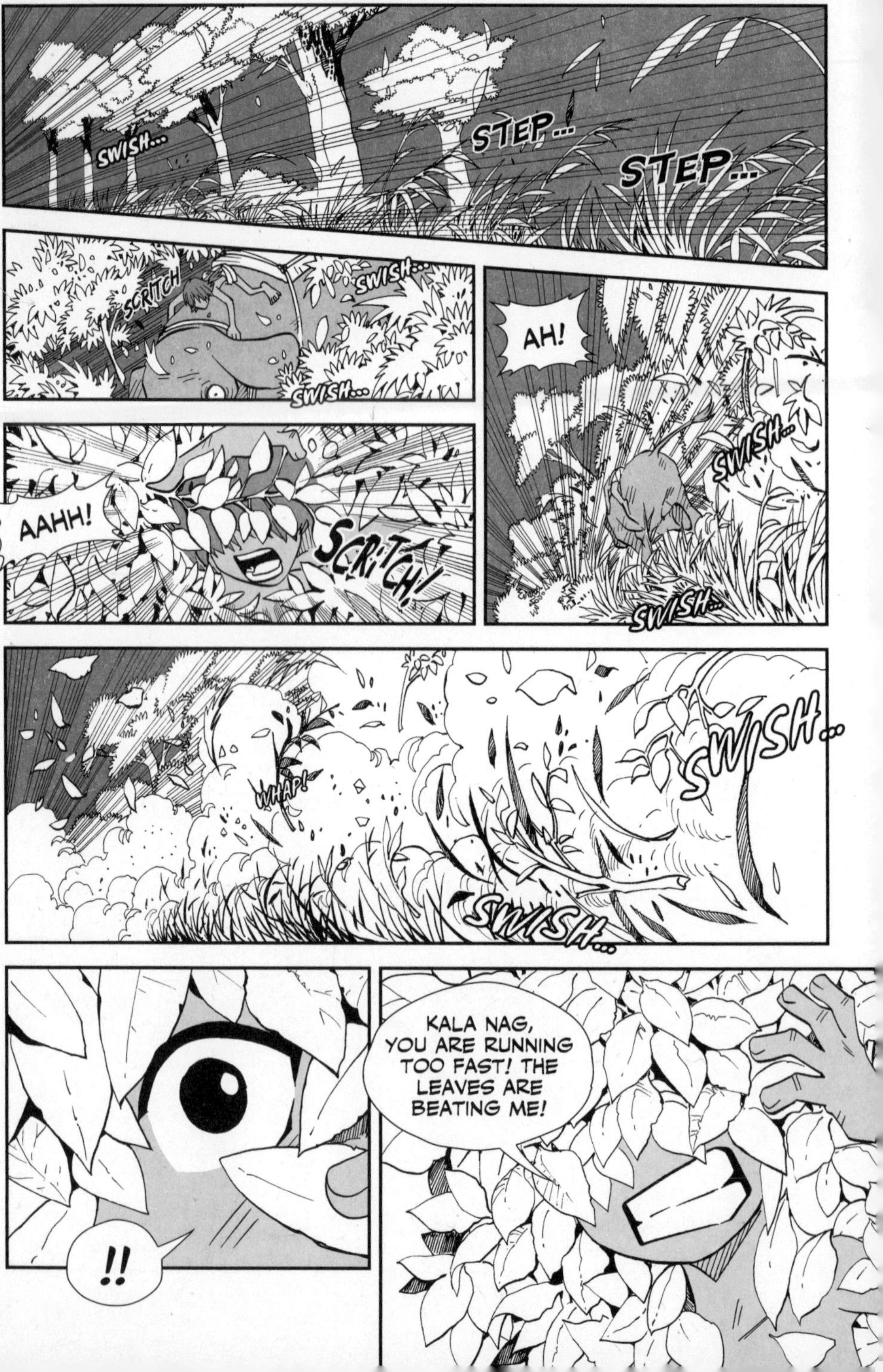
STEP...
STEP...
SWISH...
AH!
SWISH...
SWISH...
SWISH...
SCRITCH
SWISH...
SCRITCH!
AAHH!
SWISH...
WHAP!
SWISH...
KALA NAG, YOU ARE RUNNING TOO FAST! THE LEAVES ARE BEATING ME!
!!

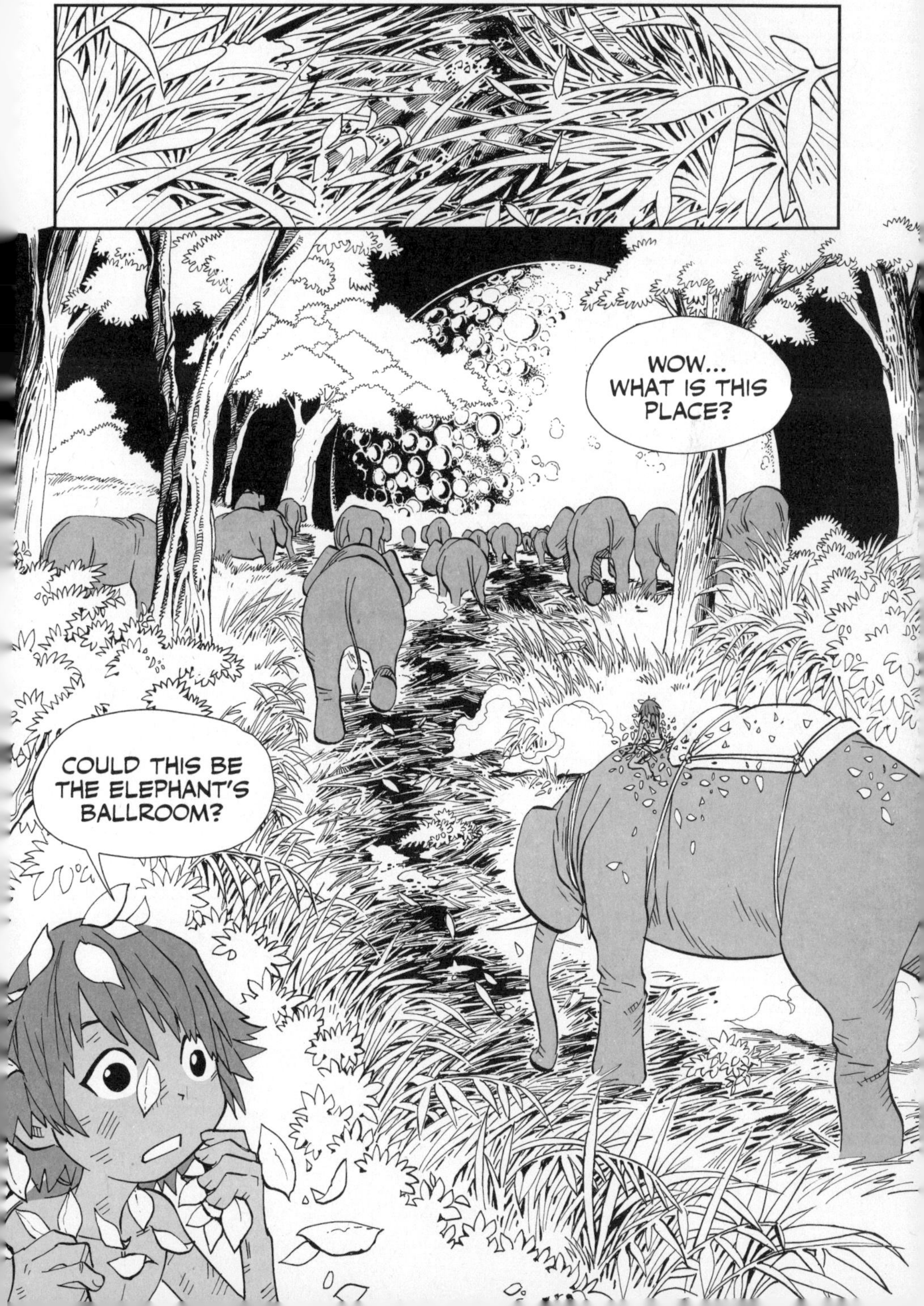
WOW... WHAT IS THIS PLACE?
COULD THIS BE THE ELEPHANT'S BALLROOM?

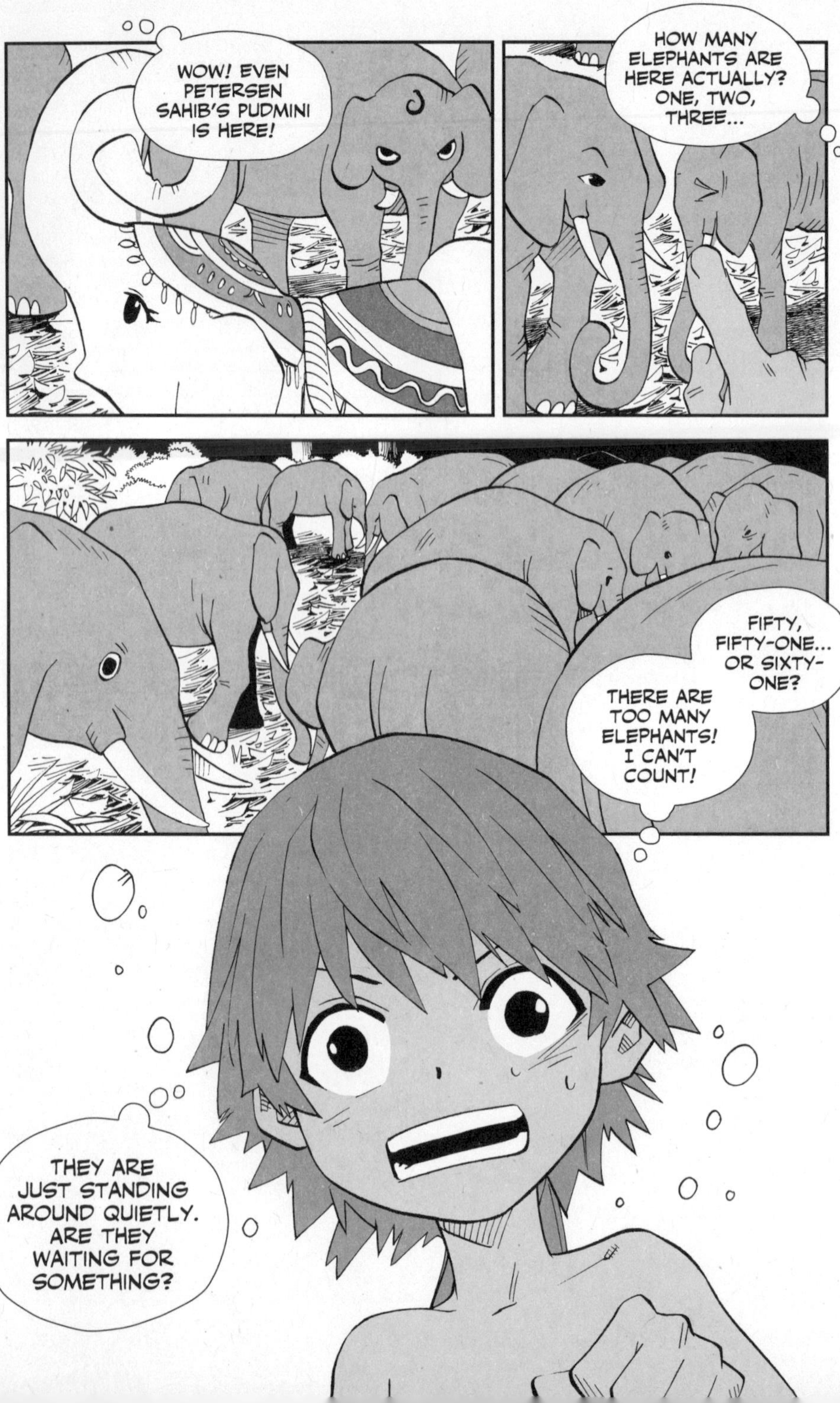
HOW MANY ELEPHANTS ARE HERE ACTUALLY? ONE, TWO, THREE...
WOW! EVEN PETERSEN SAHIB'S PUDMINI IS HERE!
FIFTY, FIFTY-ONE... OR SIXTY-ONE?
THERE ARE TOO MANY ELEPHANTS! I CAN'T COUNT!
THEY ARE JUST STANDING AROUND QUIETLY. ARE THEY WAITING FOR SOMETHING?

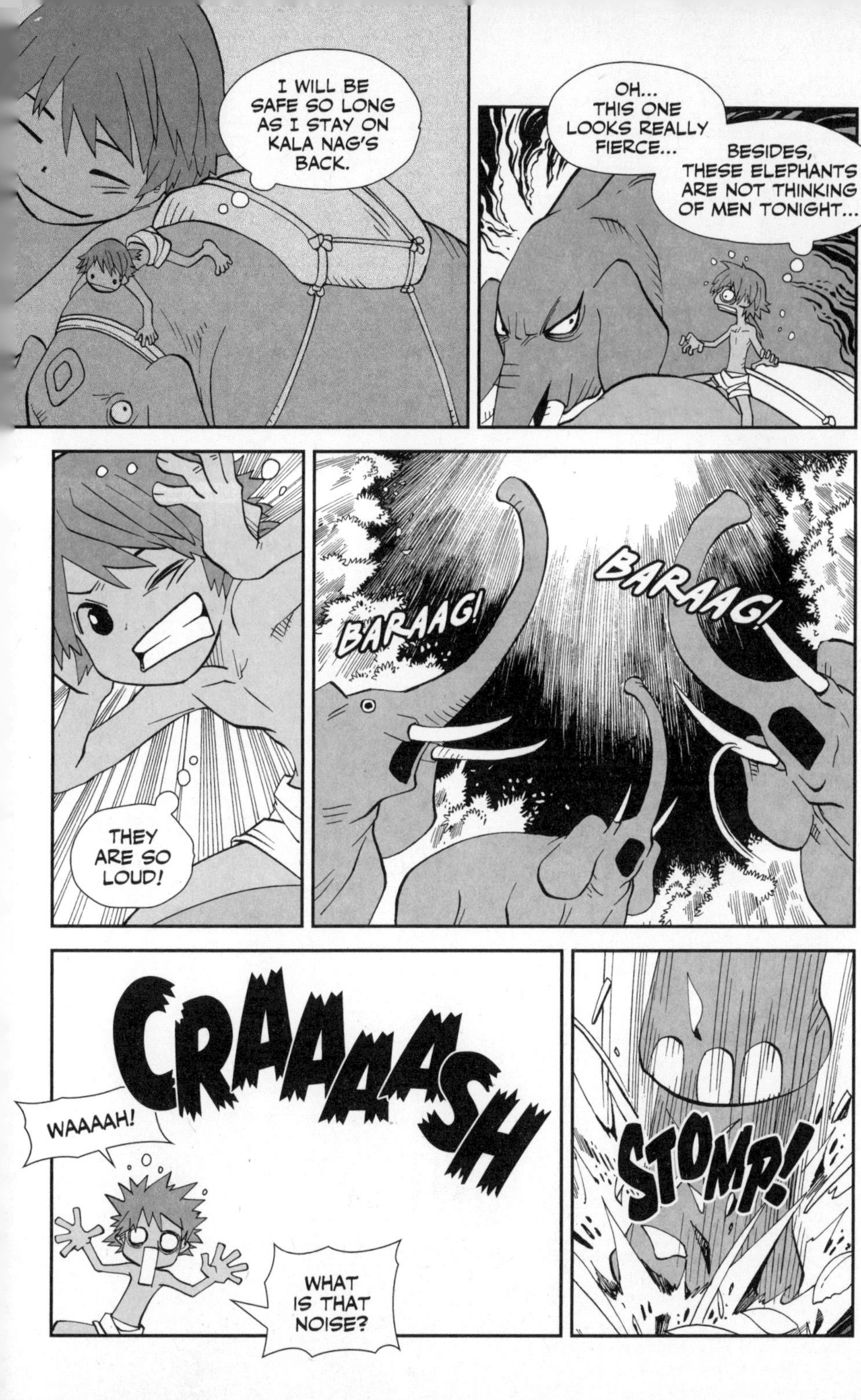
OH... THIS ONE LOOKS REALLY FIERCE...
BESIDES, THESE ELEPHANTS ARE NOT THINKING OF MEN TONIGHT...
I WILL BE SAFE SO LONG AS I STAY ON KALA NAG'S BACK.
BARAAG!
BARAAG!
THEY ARE SO LOUD!
STOMP!
CRAAAASH
WAAAAH!
WHAT IS THAT NOISE?

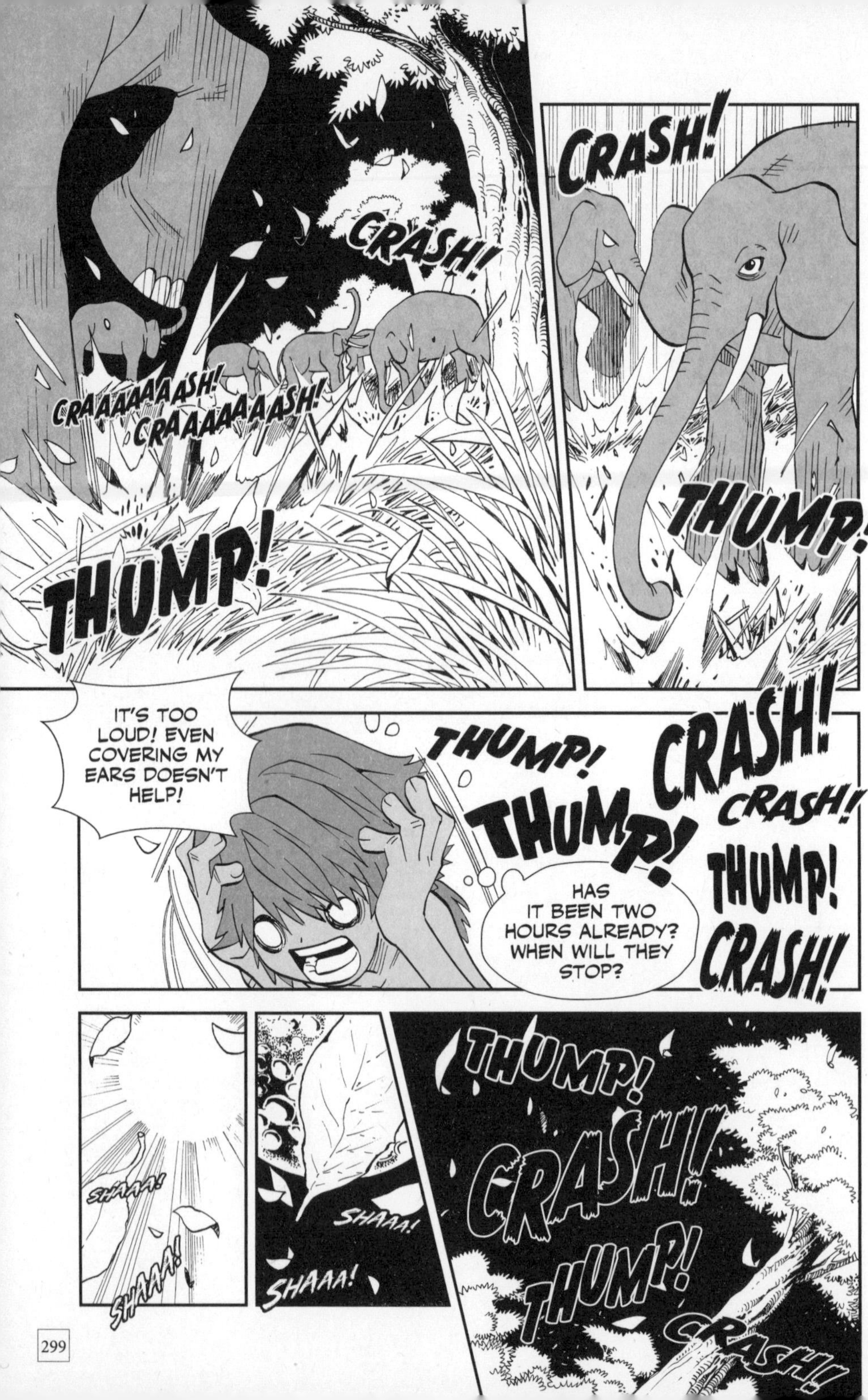
CRASH!
THUMP!
CRASH!
CRAAAAAAASH!
CRAAAAAAASH!
THUMP!
CRASH!
CRASH!
THUMP!
THUMP!
THUMP!
CRASH!
IT'S TOO LOUD! EVEN COVERING MY EARS DOESN'T HELP!
HAS IT BEEN TWO HOURS ALREADY? WHEN WILL THEY STOP?
THUMP!
CRASH!
THUMP!
CRASH!
SHAAA!
SHAAA!
SHAAA!
SHAAA!
SHAAA!

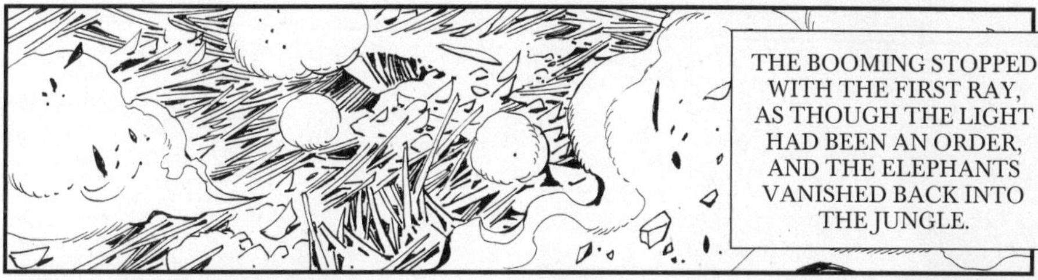
THE BOOMING STOPPED WITH THE FIRST RAY, AS THOUGH THE LIGHT HAD BEEN AN ORDER, AND THE ELEPHANTS VANISHED BACK INTO THE JUNGLE.

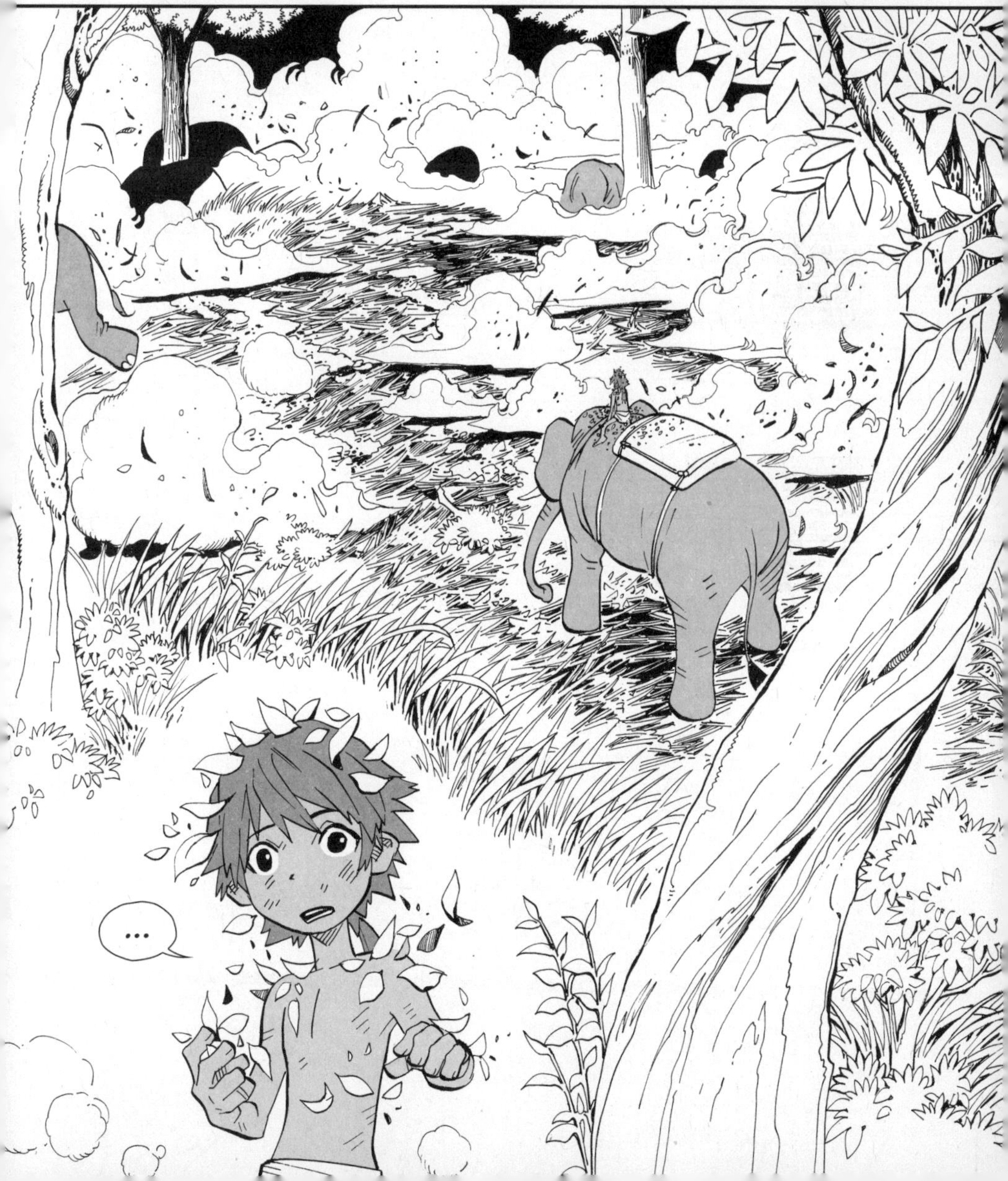
...

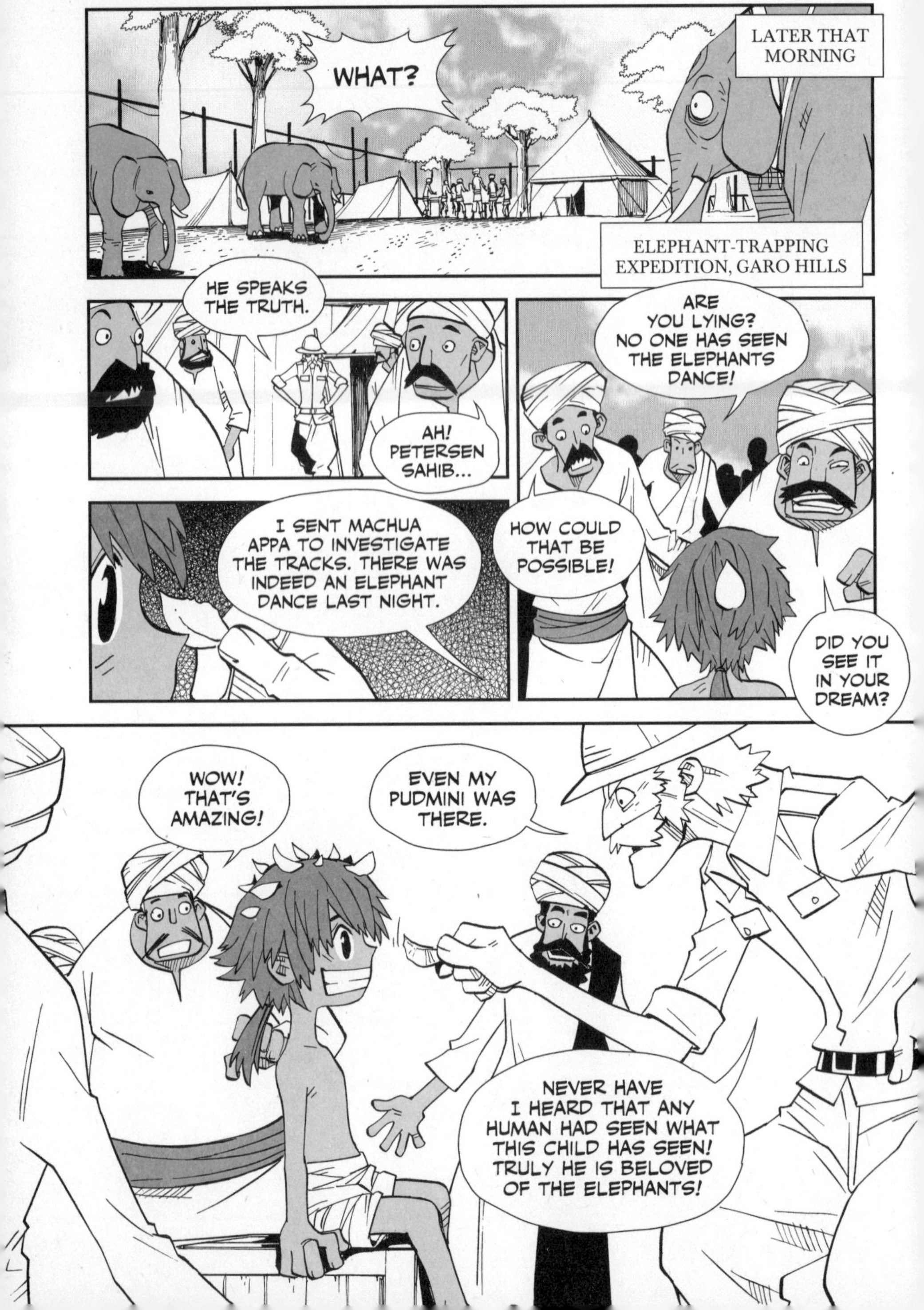
LATER THAT MORNING
WHAT?
ELEPHANT-TRAPPING EXPEDITION, GARO HILLS
ARE YOU LYING? NO ONE HAS SEEN THE ELEPHANTS DANCE!
HOW COULD THAT BE POSSIBLE!
DID YOU SEE IT IN YOUR DREAM?
HE SPEAKS THE TRUTH.
AH! PETERSEN SAHIB...
I SENT MACHUA APPA TO INVESTIGATE THE TRACKS. THERE WAS INDEED AN ELEPHANT DANCE LAST NIGHT.
EVEN MY PUDMINI WAS THERE.
WOW! THAT'S AMAZING!
NEVER HAVE I HEARD THAT ANY HUMAN HAD SEEN WHAT THIS CHILD HAS SEEN! TRULY HE IS BELOVED OF THE ELEPHANTS!

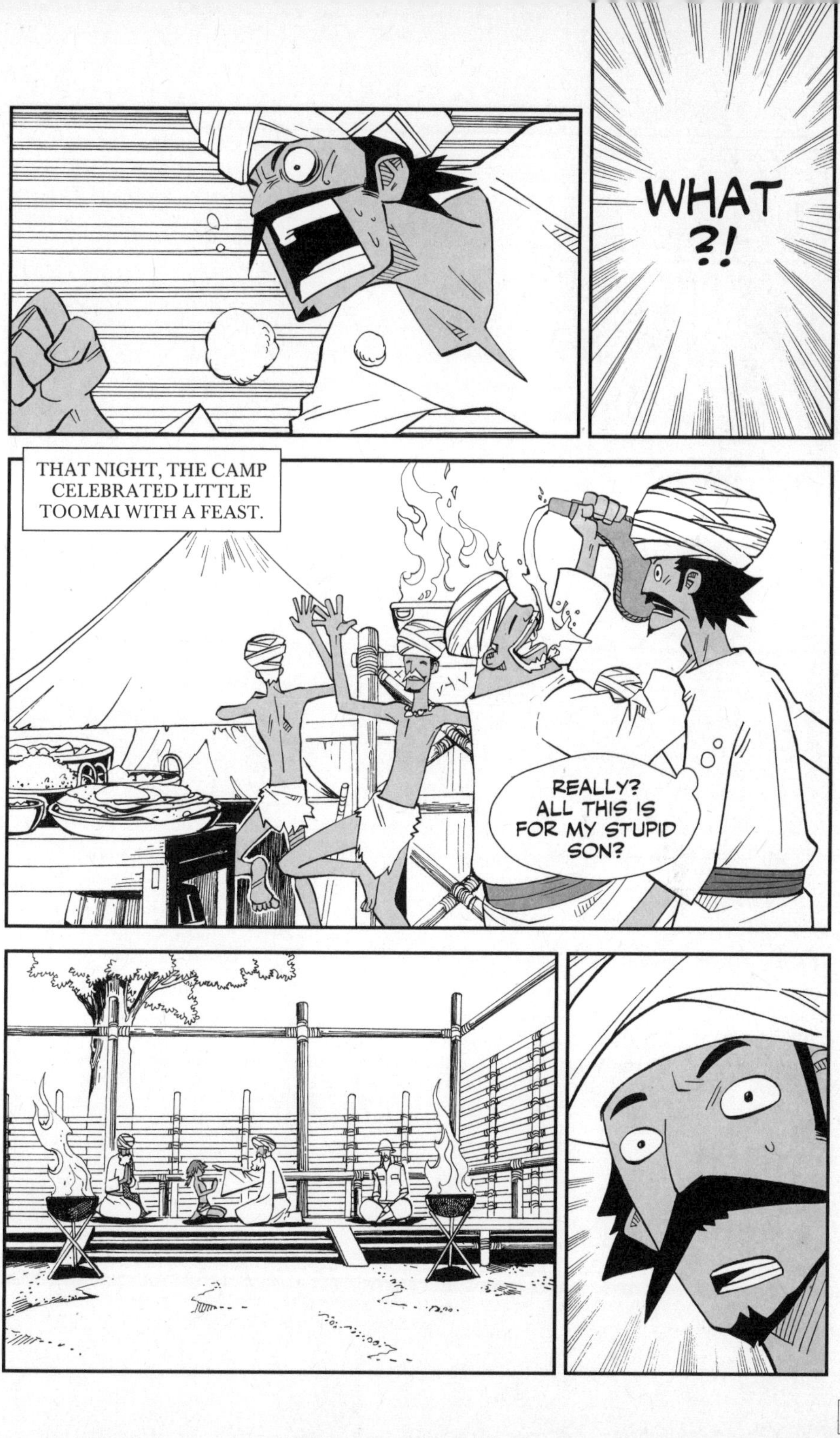
WHAT ?!
THAT NIGHT, THE CAMP CELEBRATED LITTLE TOOMAI WITH A FEAST.
REALLY? ALL THIS IS FOR MY STUPID SON?

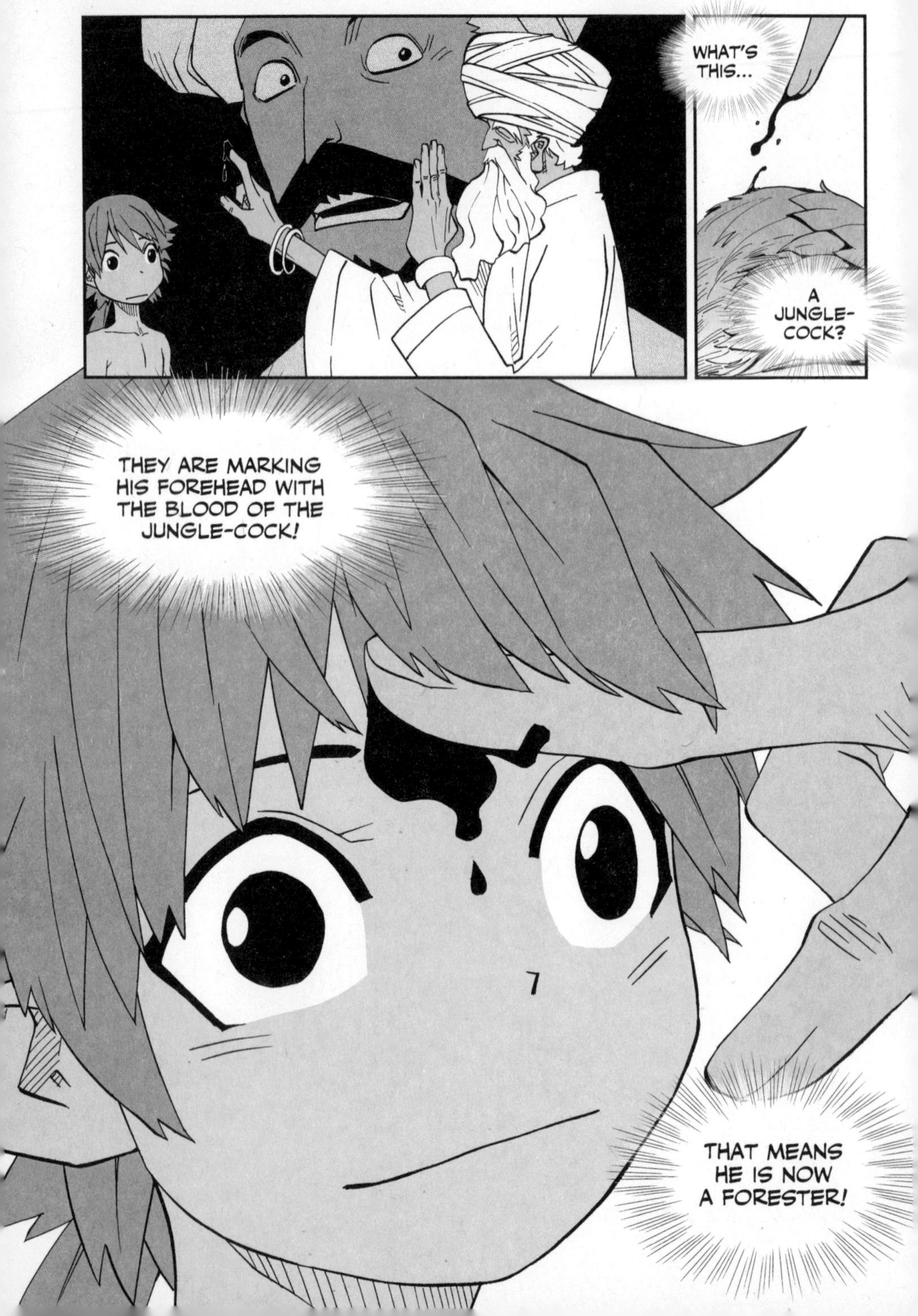
WHAT'S THIS...
A JUNGLE-COCK?
THEY ARE MARKING HIS FOREHEAD WITH THE BLOOD OF THE JUNGLE-COCK!
THAT MEANS HE IS NOW A FORESTER!

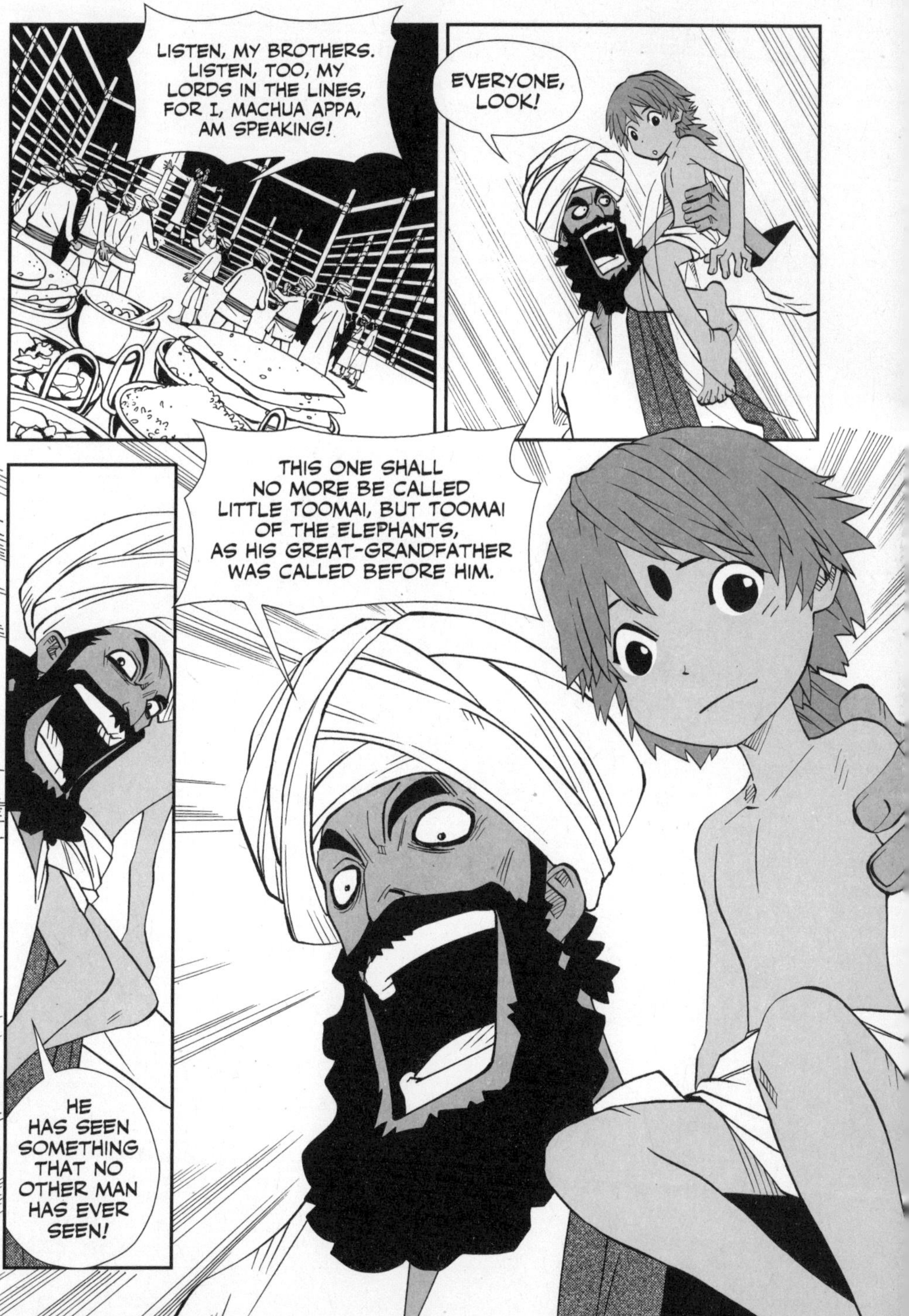
EVERYONE, LOOK!
LISTEN, MY BROTHERS. LISTEN, TOO, MY LORDS IN THE LINES, FOR I, MACHUA APPA, AM SPEAKING!
THIS ONE SHALL NO MORE BE CALLED LITTLE TOOMAI, BUT TOOMAI OF THE ELEPHANTS, AS HIS GREAT-GRANDFATHER WAS CALLED BEFORE HIM.
HE HAS SEEN SOMETHING THAT NO OTHER MAN HAS EVER SEEN!

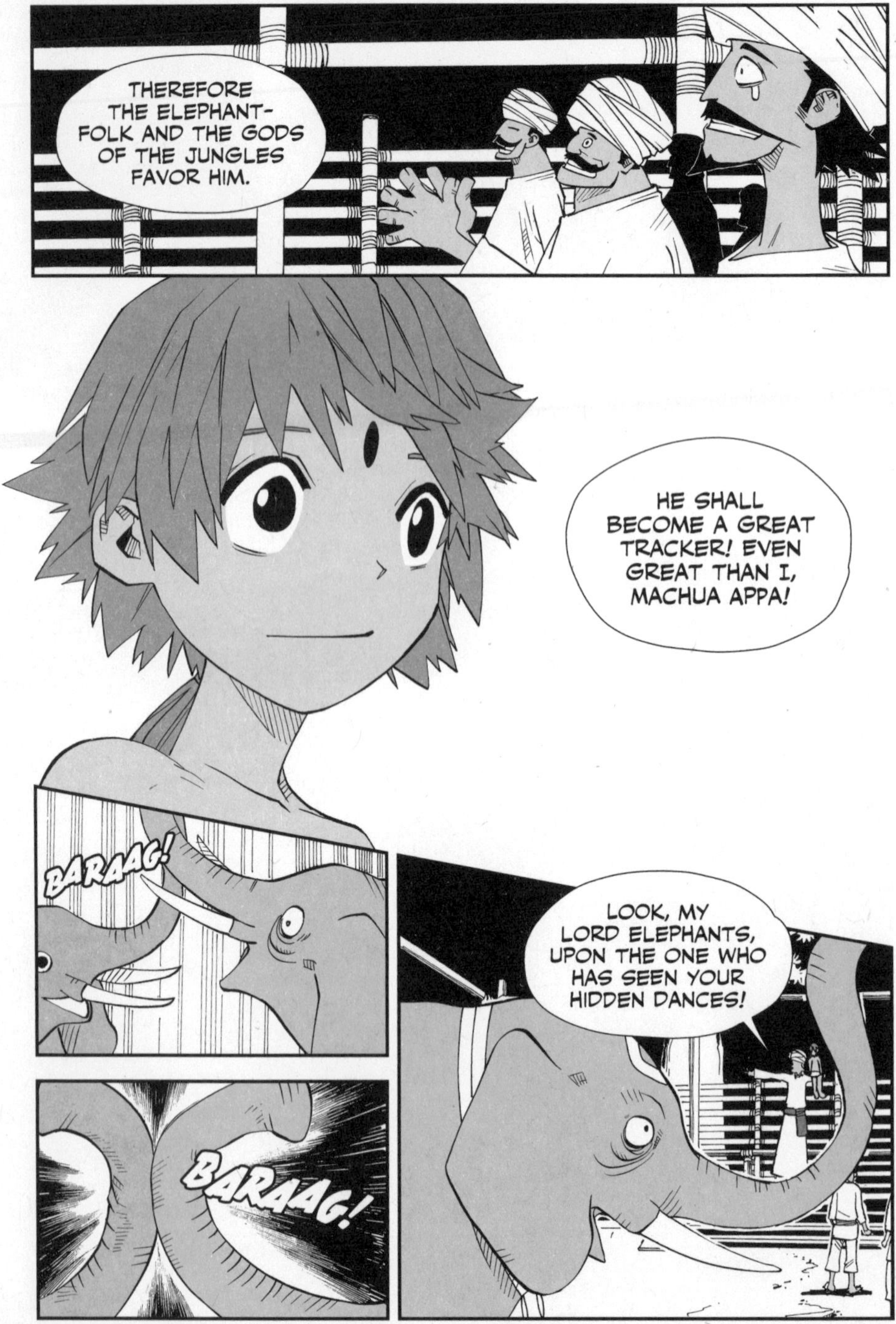
THEREFORE THE ELEPHANT-FOLK AND THE GODS OF THE JUNGLES FAVOR HIM.
HE SHALL BECOME A GREAT TRACKER! EVEN GREAT THAN I, MACHUA APPA!
LOOK, MY LORD ELEPHANTS, UPON THE ONE WHO HAS SEEN YOUR HIDDEN DANCES!
BARAAG!
BARAAG!

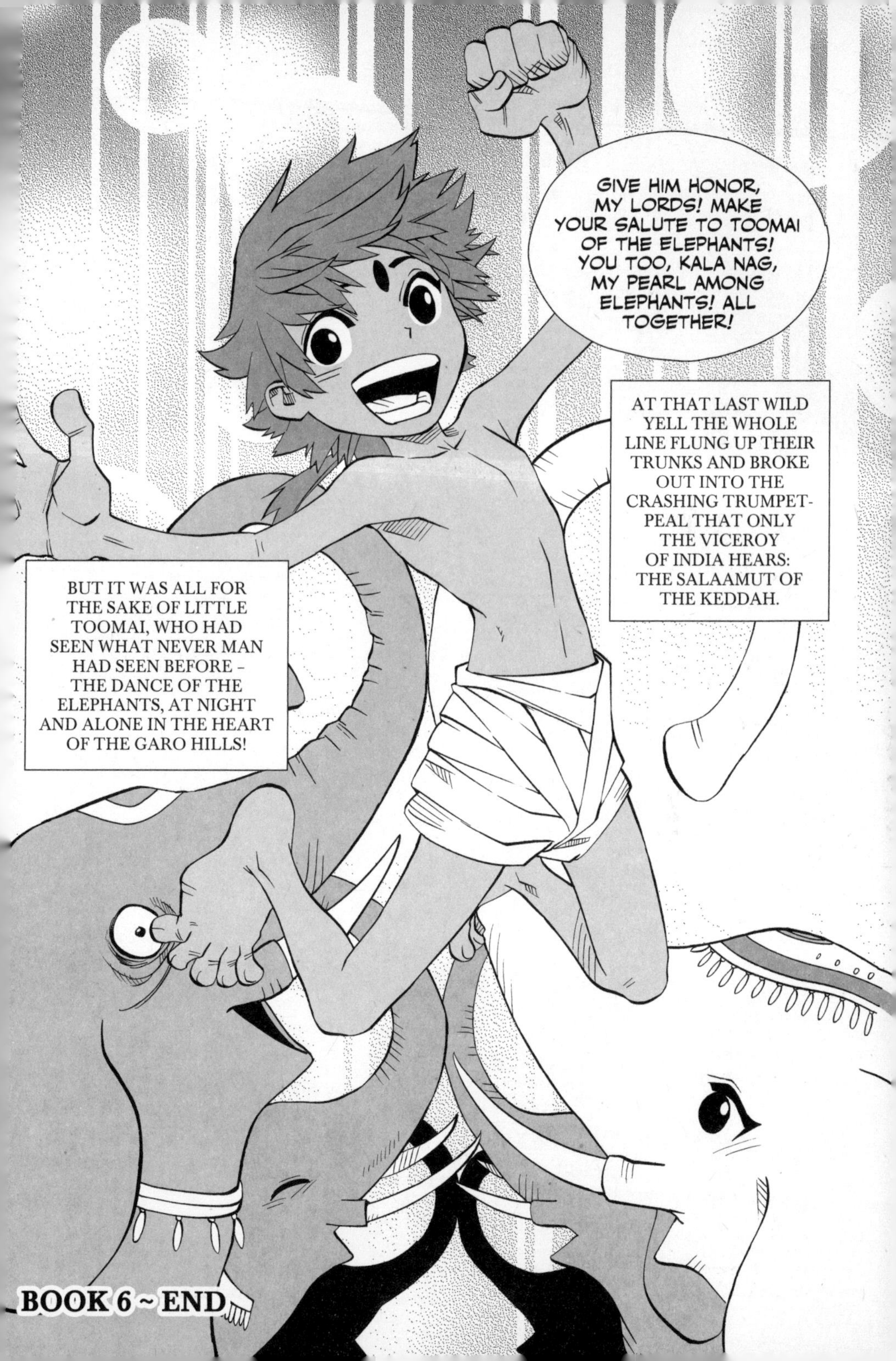
GIVE HIM HONOR, MY LORDS! MAKE YOUR SALUTE TO TOOMAI OF THE ELEPHANTS! YOU TOO, KALA NAG, MY PEARL AMONG ELEPHANTS! ALL TOGETHER!
AT THAT LAST WILD YELL THE WHOLE LINE FLUNG UP THEIR TRUNKS AND BROKE OUT INTO THE CRASHING TRUMPET-PEAL THAT ONLY THE VICEROY OF INDIA HEARS: THE SALAAMUT OF THE KEDDAH.
BUT IT WAS ALL FOR THE SAKE OF LITTLE TOOMAI, WHO HAD SEEN WHAT NEVER MAN HAD SEEN BEFORE – THE DANCE OF THE ELEPHANTS, AT NIGHT AND ALONE IN THE HEART OF THE GARO HILLS!
BOOK 6 ~ END

BOOK 7: HER MAJESTY'S SERVANTS

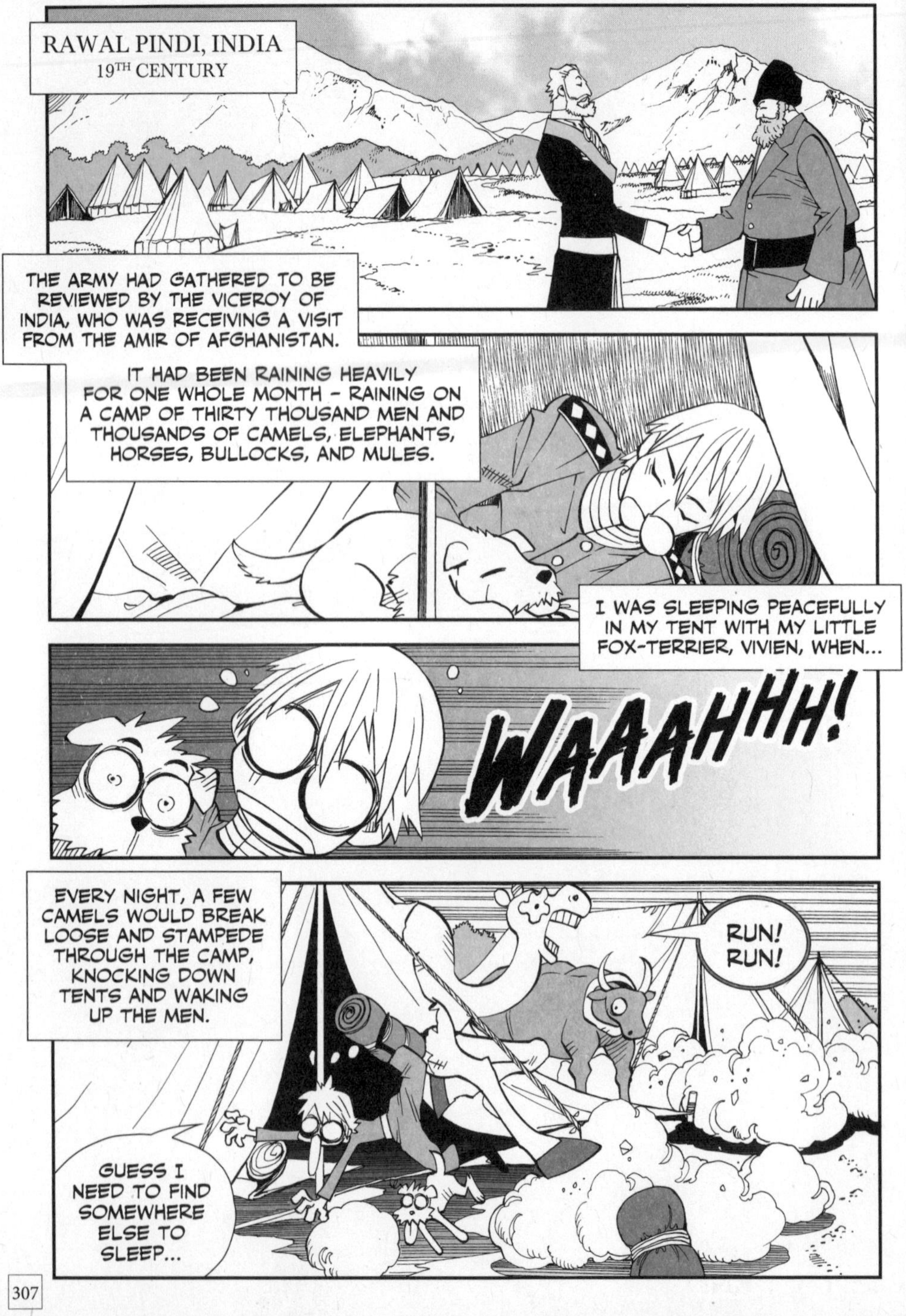
RAWAL PINDI, INDIA
19TH CENTURY
THE ARMY HAD GATHERED TO BE REVIEWED BY THE VICEROY OF INDIA, WHO WAS RECEIVING A VISIT FROM THE AMIR OF AFGHANISTAN.
IT HAD BEEN RAINING HEAVILY FOR ONE WHOLE MONTH – RAINING ON A CAMP OF THIRTY THOUSAND MEN AND THOUSANDS OF CAMELS, ELEPHANTS, HORSES, BULLOCKS, AND MULES.
I WAS SLEEPING PEACEFULLY IN MY TENT WITH MY LITTLE FOX-TERRIER, VIVIEN, WHEN...
WAAAHHH!
EVERY NIGHT, A FEW CAMELS WOULD BREAK LOOSE AND STAMPEDE THROUGH THE CAMP, KNOCKING DOWN TENTS AND WAKING UP THE MEN.
RUN! RUN!
GUESS I NEED TO FIND SOMEWHERE ELSE TO SLEEP...

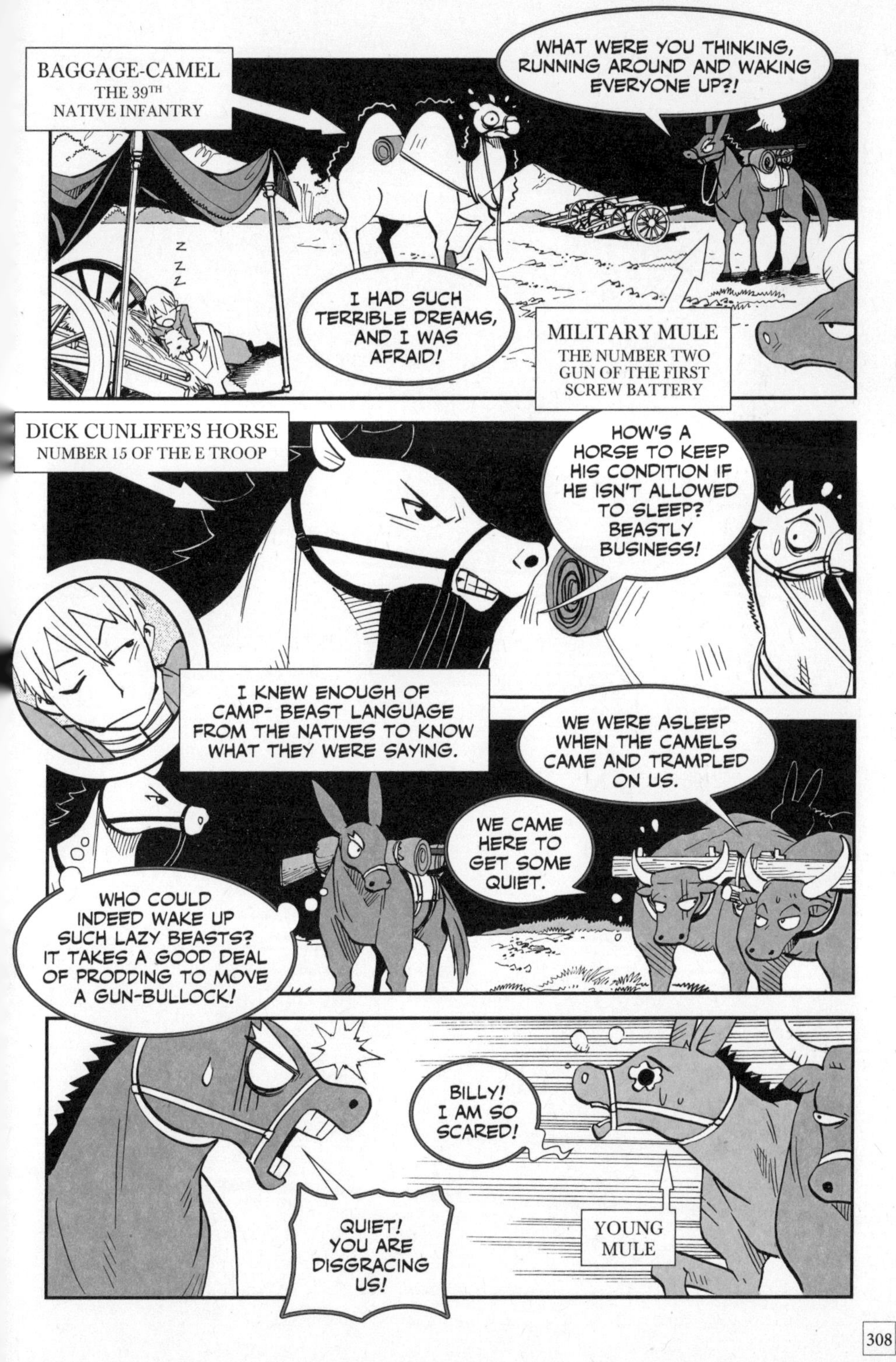
WHAT WERE YOU THINKING, RUNNING AROUND AND WAKING EVERYONE UP?!
BAGGAGE-CAMEL THE 39TH NATIVE INFANTRY
I HAD SUCH TERRIBLE DREAMS, AND I WAS AFRAID!
MILITARY MULE THE NUMBER TWO GUN OF THE FIRST SCREW BATTERY
HOW'S A HORSE TO KEEP HIS CONDITION IF HE ISN'T ALLOWED TO SLEEP? BEASTLY BUSINESS!
DICK CUNLIFFE'S HORSE NUMBER 15 OF THE E TROOP
I KNEW ENOUGH OF CAMP- BEAST LANGUAGE FROM THE NATIVES TO KNOW WHAT THEY WERE SAYING.
WE WERE ASLEEP WHEN THE CAMELS CAME AND TRAMPLED ON US.
WE CAME HERE TO GET SOME QUIET.
WHO COULD INDEED WAKE UP SUCH LAZY BEASTS? IT TAKES A GOOD DEAL OF PRODDING TO MOVE A GUN-BULLOCK!
BILLY! I AM SO SCARED!
YOUNG MULE
QUIET! YOU ARE DISGRACING US!

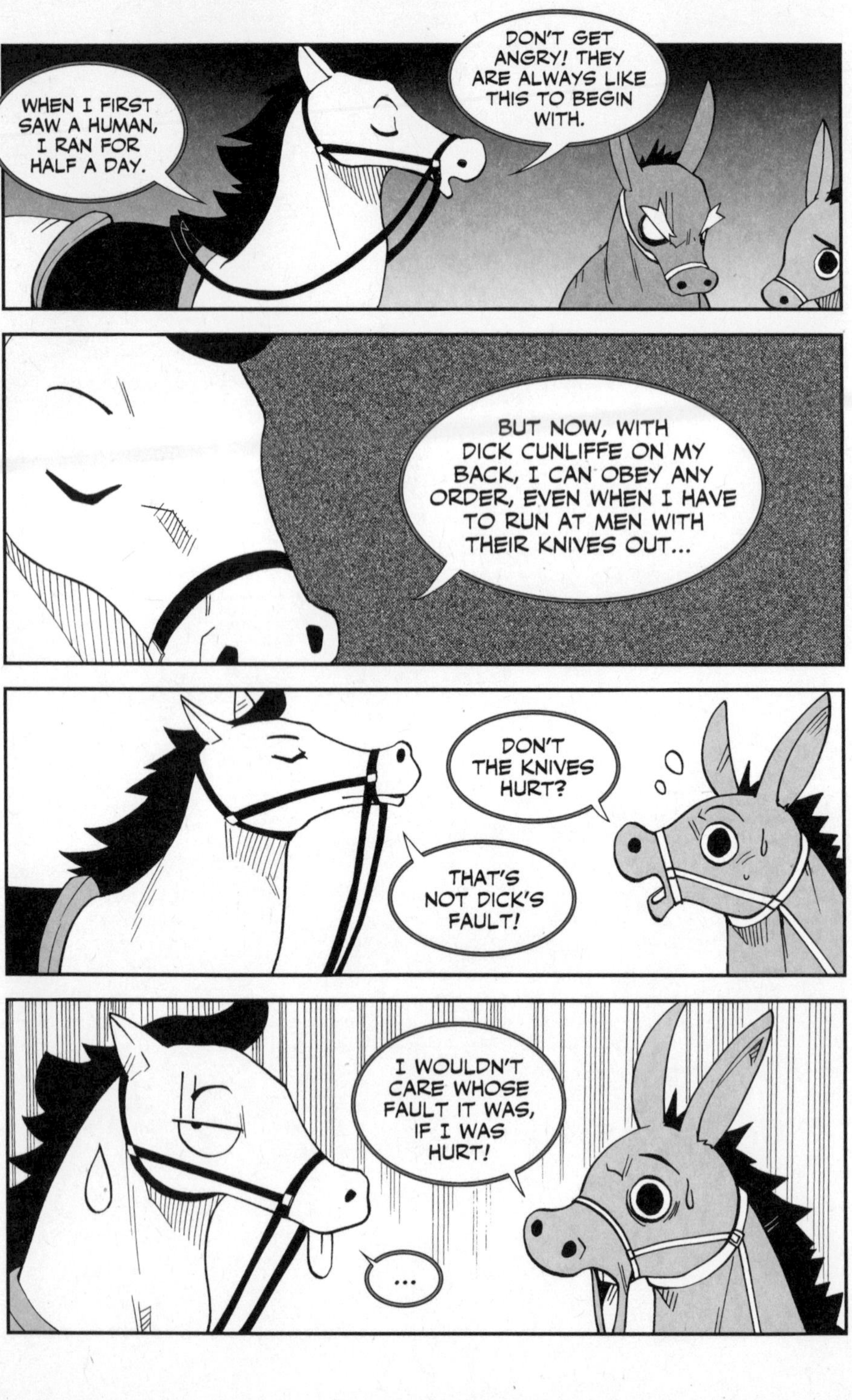
DON'T GET ANGRY! THEY ARE ALWAYS LIKE THIS TO BEGIN WITH.
WHEN I FIRST SAW A HUMAN, I RAN FOR HALF A DAY.
BUT NOW, WITH DICK CUNLIFFE ON MY BACK, I CAN OBEY ANY ORDER, EVEN WHEN I HAVE TO RUN AT MEN WITH THEIR KNIVES OUT...
DON'T THE KNIVES HURT?
THAT'S NOT DICK'S FAULT!
I WOULDN'T CARE WHOSE FAULT IT WAS, IF I WAS HURT!
...

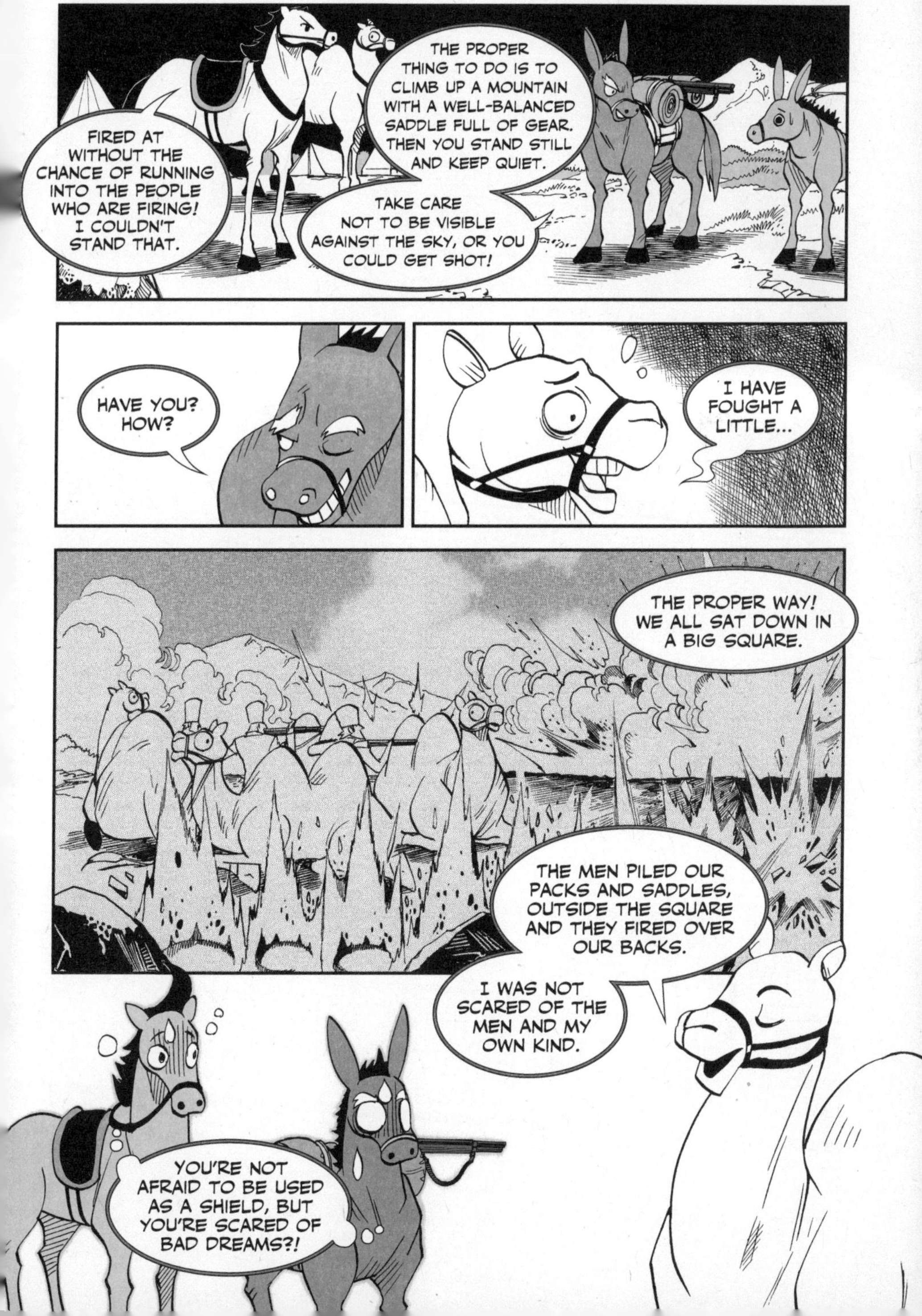
THE PROPER THING TO DO IS TO CLIMB UP A MOUNTAIN WITH A WELL-BALANCED SADDLE FULL OF GEAR. THEN YOU STAND STILL AND KEEP QUIET.
TAKE CARE NOT TO BE VISIBLE AGAINST THE SKY, OR YOU COULD GET SHOT!
FIRED AT WITHOUT THE CHANCE OF RUNNING INTO THE PEOPLE WHO ARE FIRING! I COULDN'T STAND THAT.
I HAVE FOUGHT A LITTLE...
HAVE YOU? HOW?
THE PROPER WAY! WE ALL SAT DOWN IN A BIG SQUARE.
THE MEN PILED OUR PACKS AND SADDLES, OUTSIDE THE SQUARE AND THEY FIRED OVER OUR BACKS.
I WAS NOT SCARED OF THE MEN AND MY OWN KIND.
YOU'RE NOT AFRAID TO BE USED AS A SHIELD, BUT YOU'RE SCARED OF BAD DREAMS?!

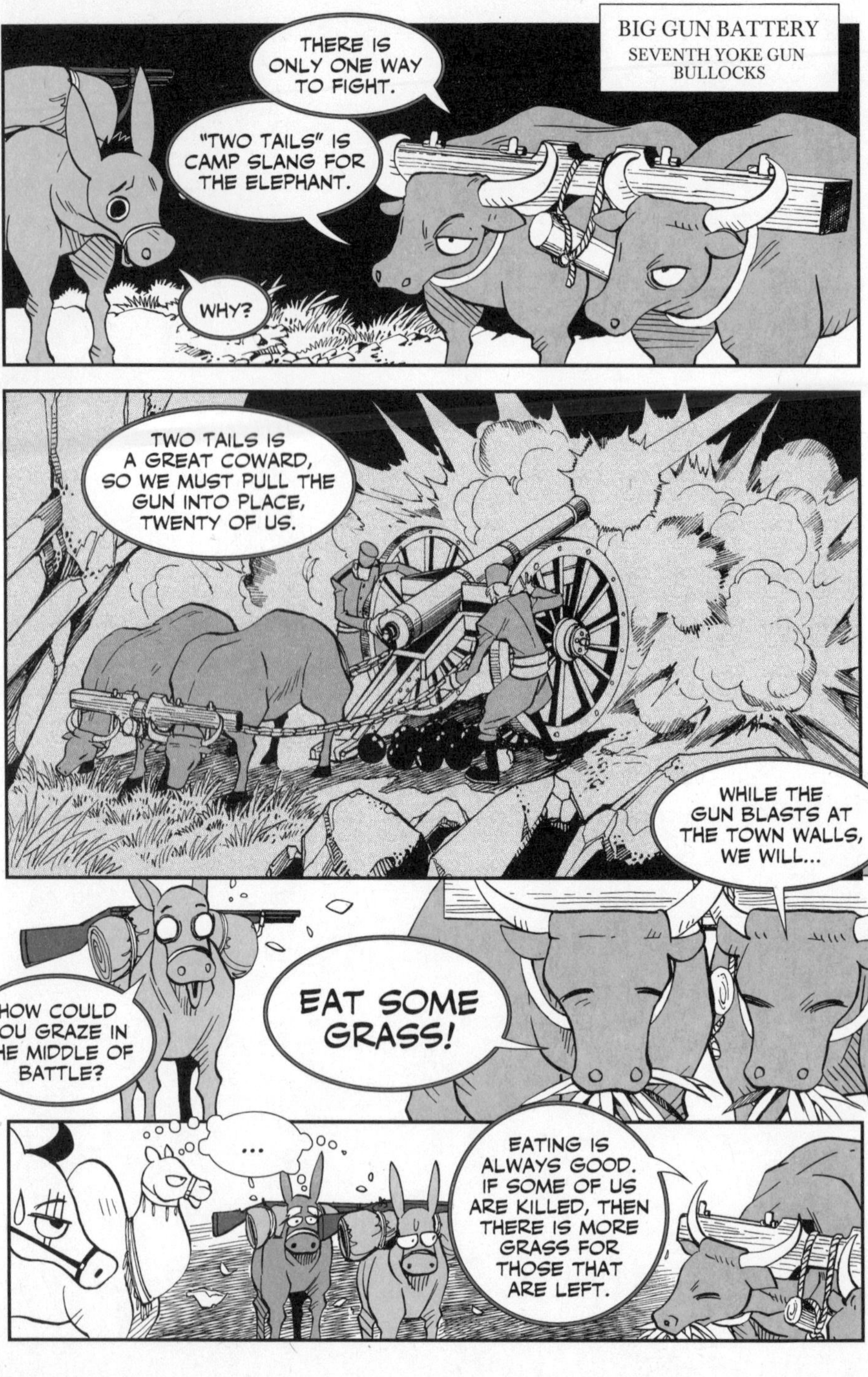
BIG GUN BATTERY
SEVENTH YOKE GUN BULLOCKS
THERE IS ONLY ONE WAY TO FIGHT.
"TWO TAILS" IS CAMP SLANG FOR THE ELEPHANT.
WHY?
TWO TAILS IS A GREAT COWARD, SO WE MUST PULL THE GUN INTO PLACE, TWENTY OF US.
WHILE THE GUN BLASTS AT THE TOWN WALLS, WE WILL...
EAT SOME GRASS!
HOW COULD YOU GRAZE IN THE MIDDLE OF BATTLE?
EATING IS ALWAYS GOOD. IF SOME OF US ARE KILLED, THEN THERE IS MORE GRASS FOR THOSE THAT ARE LEFT.
...

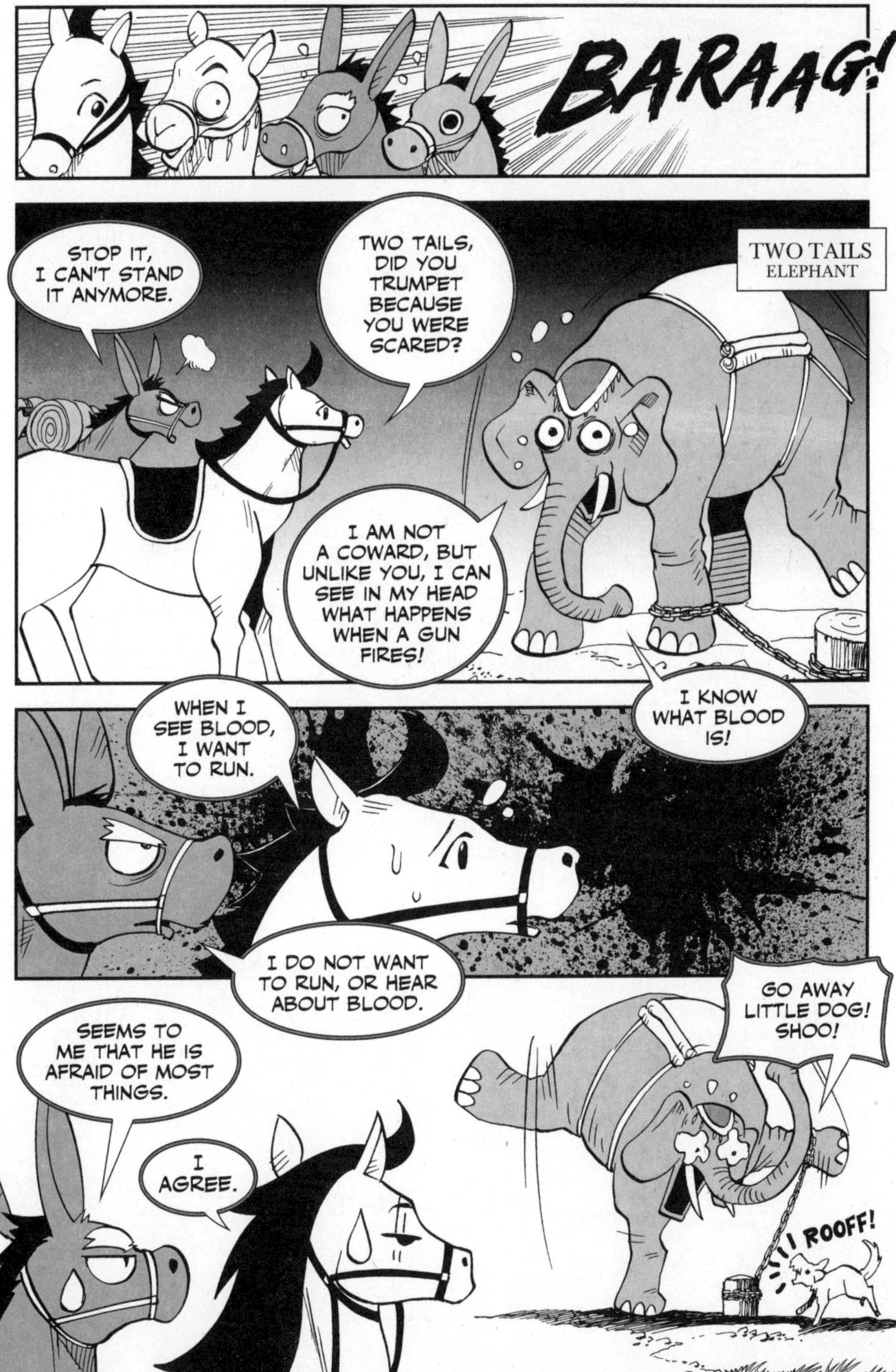
BARAAG!
TWO TAILS
ELEPHANT
TWO TAILS, DID YOU TRUMPET BECAUSE YOU WERE SCARED?
STOP IT, I CAN'T STAND IT ANYMORE.
I AM NOT A COWARD, BUT UNLIKE YOU, I CAN SEE IN MY HEAD WHAT HAPPENS WHEN A GUN FIRES!
I KNOW WHAT BLOOD IS!
WHEN I SEE BLOOD, I WANT TO RUN.
I DO NOT WANT TO RUN, OR HEAR ABOUT BLOOD.
GO AWAY LITTLE DOG! SHOO!
ROOFF!
SEEMS TO ME THAT HE IS AFRAID OF MOST THINGS.
I AGREE.

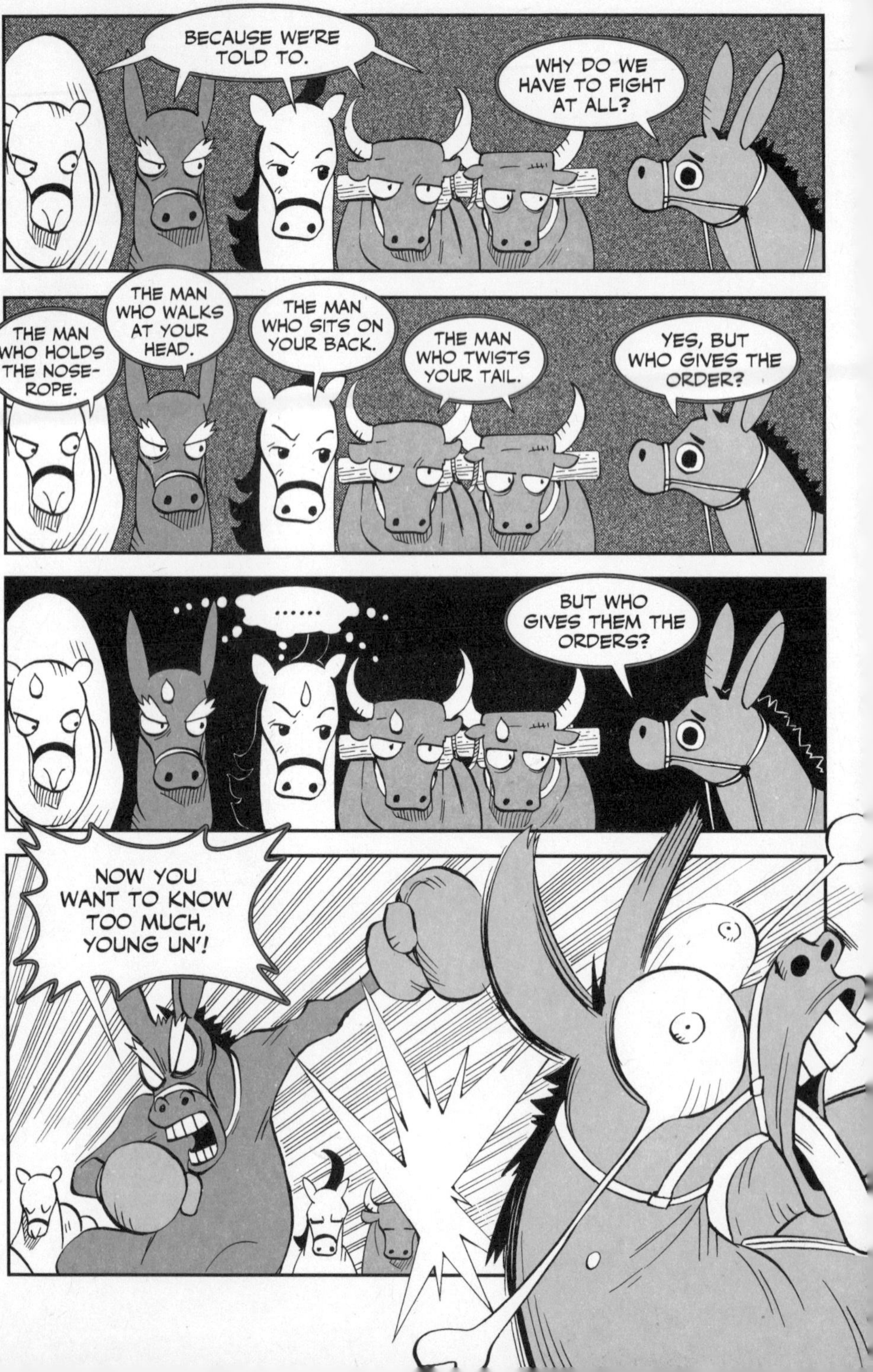
WHY DO WE HAVE TO FIGHT AT ALL?
BECAUSE WE'RE TOLD TO.
YES, BUT WHO GIVES THE ORDER?
THE MAN WHO TWISTS YOUR TAIL.
THE MAN WHO SITS ON YOUR BACK.
THE MAN WHO WALKS AT YOUR HEAD.
THE MAN WHO HOLDS THE NOSE-ROPE.
BUT WHO GIVES THEM THE ORDERS?
......
NOW YOU WANT TO KNOW TOO MUCH, YOUNG UN'!

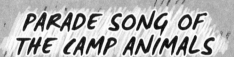

PARADE SONG OF THE CAMP ANIMALS

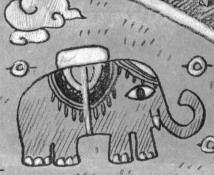

ELEPHANTS OF THE GUN TEAMS
WE LENT TO ALEXANDER THE STRENGTH OF HERCULES,
THE WISDOM OF OUR FOREHEADS, THE CUNNING OF OUR KNEES;
WE BOWED OUR NECKS TO SERVICE: THEY NE'ER WERE LOOSED AGAIN —
MAKE WAY THERE — WAY FOR THE TEN-FOOT TEAMS
OF THE FORTY-POUNDER TRAIN!

  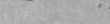

GUN BULLOCKS
THOSE HEROES IN THEIR HARNESSES AVOID A CANNON-BALL,
AND WHAT THEY KNOW OF POWDER UPSETS THEM ONE AND ALL;
THEN WE COME INTO ACTION AND TUG THE GUNS AGAIN —
MAKE WAY THERE — WAY FOR THE TWENTY YOKE
OF THE FORTY-POUNDER TRAIN!

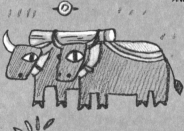

CAVALRY HORSES
BY THE BRAND ON MY SHOULDER, THE FINEST OF TUNES
IS PLAYED BY THE LANCERS, HUSSARS, AND DRAGOONS,
AND IT'S SWEETER THAN "STABLES" OR "WATER" TO ME —
THE CAVALRY CANTER OF "BONNIE DUNDEE"!

THEN FEED US AND BREAK US AND HANDLE AND GROOM,
AND GIVE US GOOD RIDERS AND PLENTY OF ROOM,
AND LAUNCH US IN COLUMN OF SQUADRON AND SEE
THE WAY OF THE WAR-HORSE TO "BONNIE DUNDEE"!

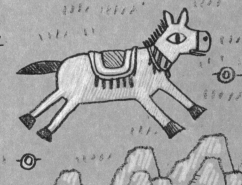

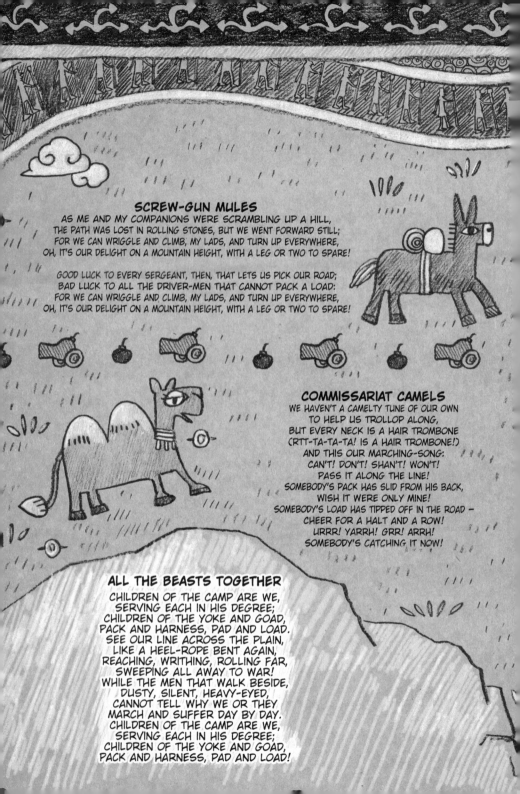

SCREW-GUN MULES

AS ME AND MY COMPANIONS WERE SCRAMBLING UP A HILL,
THE PATH WAS LOST IN ROLLING STONES, BUT WE WENT FORWARD STILL;
FOR WE CAN WRIGGLE AND CLIMB, MY LADS, AND TURN UP EVERYWHERE,
OH, IT'S OUR DELIGHT ON A MOUNTAIN HEIGHT, WITH A LEG OR TWO TO SPARE!

GOOD LUCK TO EVERY SERGEANT, THEN, THAT LETS US PICK OUR ROAD;
BAD LUCK TO ALL THE DRIVER-MEN THAT CANNOT PACK A LOAD:
FOR WE CAN WRIGGLE AND CLIMB, MY LADS, AND TURN UP EVERYWHERE,
OH, IT'S OUR DELIGHT ON A MOUNTAIN HEIGHT, WITH A LEG OR TWO TO SPARE!

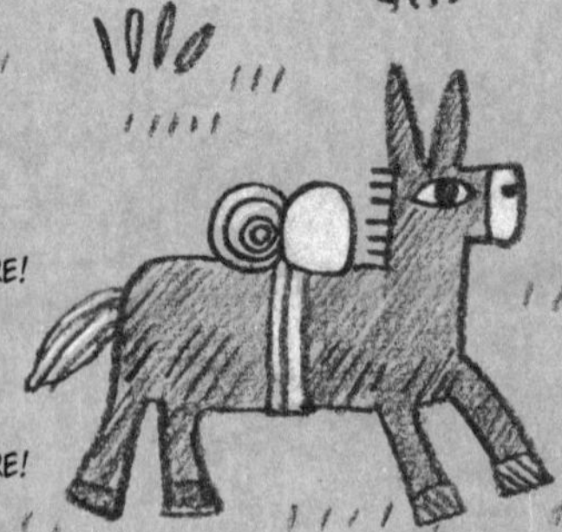

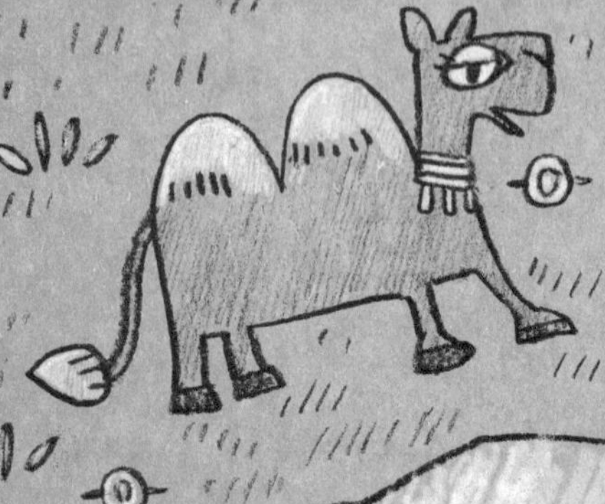

COMMISSARIAT CAMELS

WE HAVEN'T A CAMELTY TUNE OF OUR OWN
TO HELP US TROLLOP ALONG,
BUT EVERY NECK IS A HAIR TROMBONE
(RTT-TA-TA-TA! IS A HAIR TROMBONE!)
AND THIS OUR MARCHING-SONG:
CAN'T! DON'T! SHAN'T! WON'T!
PASS IT ALONG THE LINE!
SOMEBODY'S PACK HAS SLID FROM HIS BACK,
WISH IT WERE ONLY MINE!
SOMEBODY'S LOAD HAS TIPPED OFF IN THE ROAD –
CHEER FOR A HALT AND A ROW!
URRR! YARRH! GRR! ARRH!
SOMEBODY'S CATCHING IT NOW!

ALL THE BEASTS TOGETHER

CHILDREN OF THE CAMP ARE WE,
SERVING EACH IN HIS DEGREE;
CHILDREN OF THE YOKE AND GOAD,
PACK AND HARNESS, PAD AND LOAD.
SEE OUR LINE ACROSS THE PLAIN,
LIKE A HEEL-ROPE BENT AGAIN,
REACHING, WRITHING, ROLLING FAR,
SWEEPING ALL AWAY TO WAR!
WHILE THE MEN THAT WALK BESIDE,
DUSTY, SILENT, HEAVY-EYED,
CANNOT TELL WHY WE OR THEY
MARCH AND SUFFER DAY BY DAY.
CHILDREN OF THE CAMP ARE WE,
SERVING EACH IN HIS DEGREE;
CHILDREN OF THE YOKE AND GOAD,
PACK AND HARNESS, PAD AND LOAD!

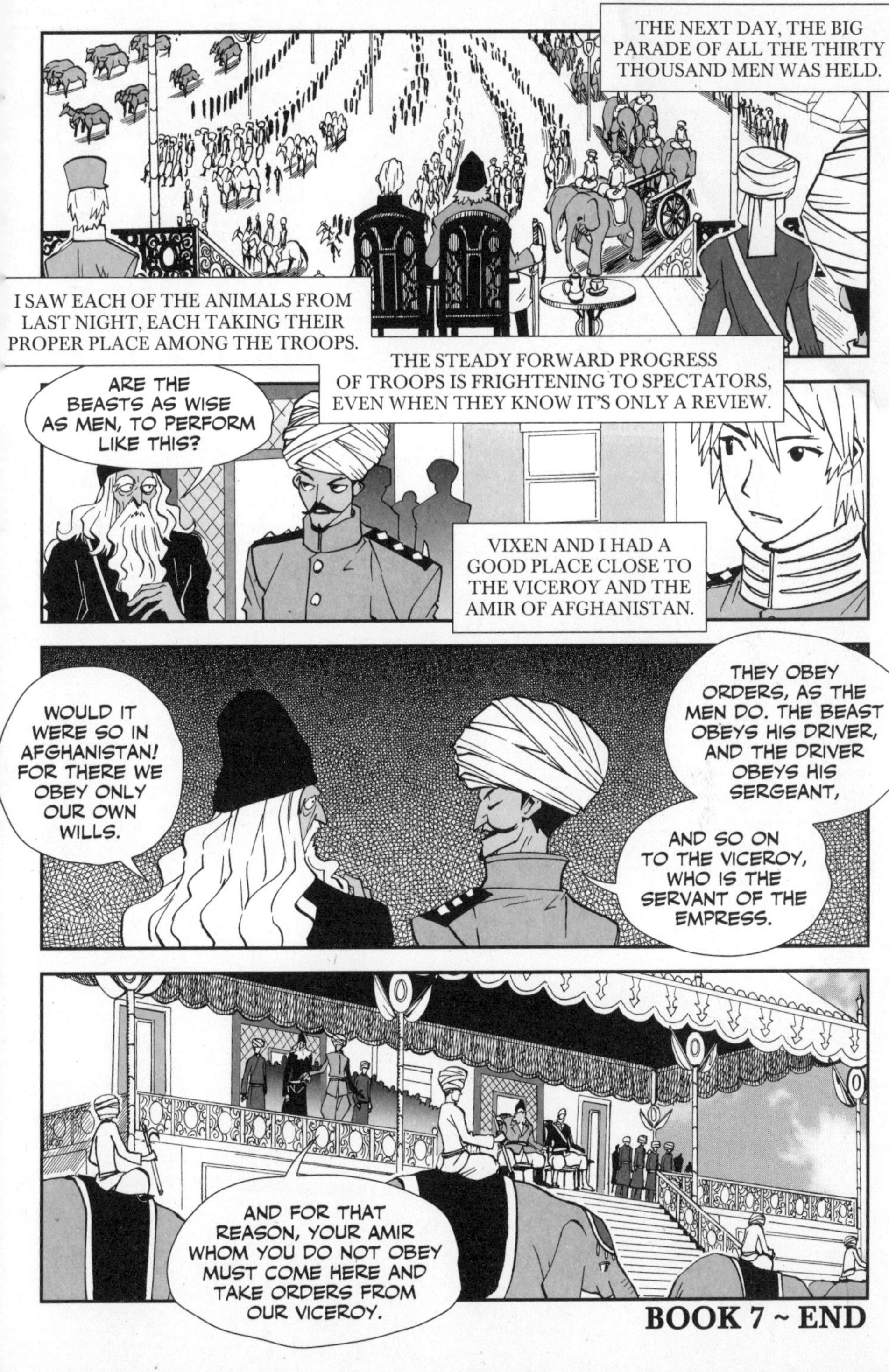
THE NEXT DAY, THE BIG PARADE OF ALL THE THIRTY THOUSAND MEN WAS HELD.
I SAW EACH OF THE ANIMALS FROM LAST NIGHT, EACH TAKING THEIR PROPER PLACE AMONG THE TROOPS.
THE STEADY FORWARD PROGRESS OF TROOPS IS FRIGHTENING TO SPECTATORS, EVEN WHEN THEY KNOW IT'S ONLY A REVIEW.
ARE THE BEASTS AS WISE AS MEN, TO PERFORM LIKE THIS?
VIXEN AND I HAD A GOOD PLACE CLOSE TO THE VICEROY AND THE AMIR OF AFGHANISTAN.
THEY OBEY ORDERS, AS THE MEN DO. THE BEAST OBEYS HIS DRIVER, AND THE DRIVER OBEYS HIS SERGEANT,
AND SO ON TO THE VICEROY, WHO IS THE SERVANT OF THE EMPRESS.
WOULD IT WERE SO IN AFGHANISTAN! FOR THERE WE OBEY ONLY OUR OWN WILLS.
AND FOR THAT REASON, YOUR AMIR WHOM YOU DO NOT OBEY MUST COME HERE AND TAKE ORDERS FROM OUR VICEROY.

BOOK 7 ~ END

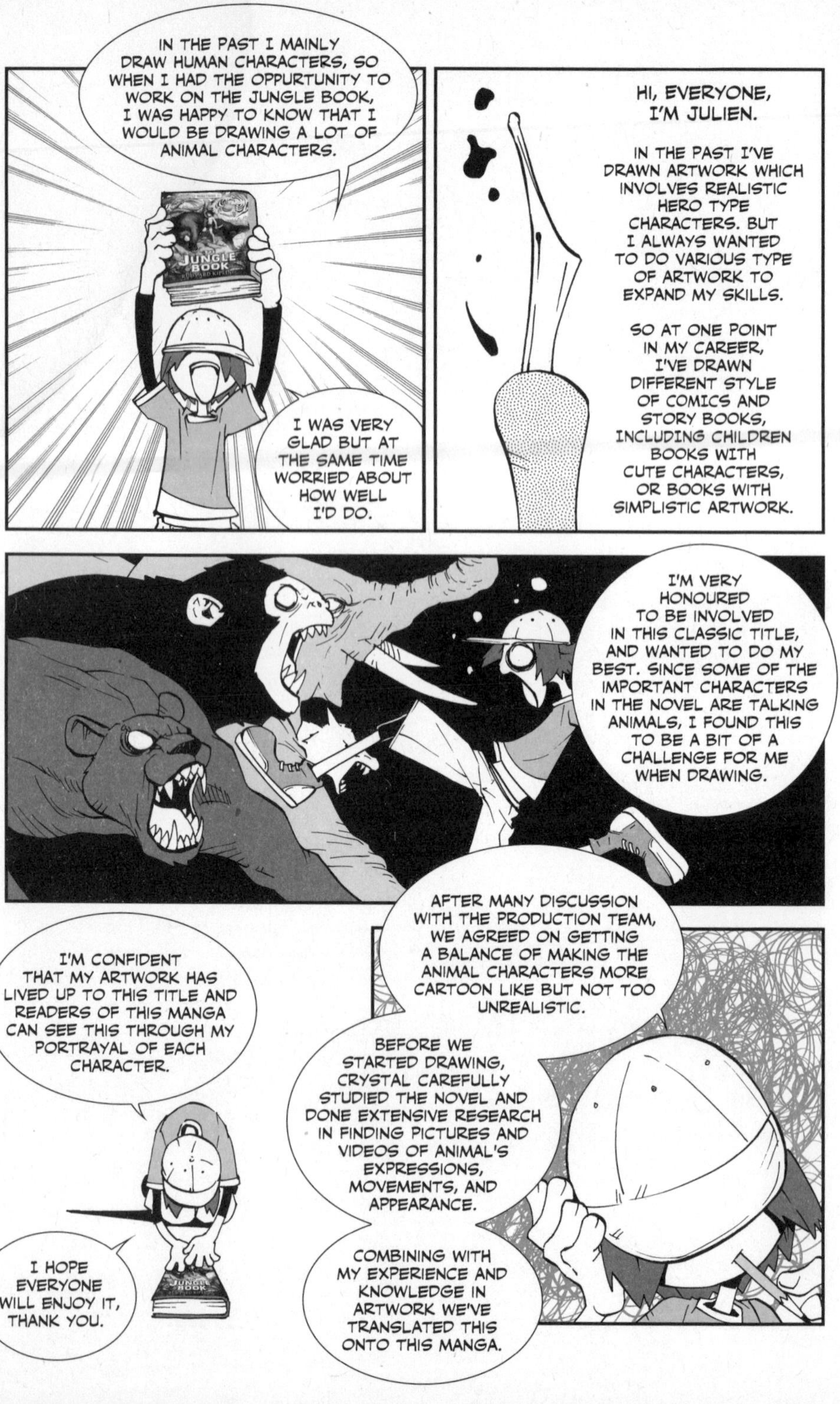
HI, EVERYONE, I'M JULIEN.
IN THE PAST I'VE DRAWN ARTWORK WHICH INVOLVES REALISTIC HERO TYPE CHARACTERS. BUT I ALWAYS WANTED TO DO VARIOUS TYPE OF ARTWORK TO EXPAND MY SKILLS.
SO AT ONE POINT IN MY CAREER, I'VE DRAWN DIFFERENT STYLE OF COMICS AND STORY BOOKS, INCLUDING CHILDREN BOOKS WITH CUTE CHARACTERS, OR BOOKS WITH SIMPLISTIC ARTWORK.
IN THE PAST I MAINLY DRAW HUMAN CHARACTERS, SO WHEN I HAD THE OPPURTUNITY TO WORK ON THE JUNGLE BOOK, I WAS HAPPY TO KNOW THAT I WOULD BE DRAWING A LOT OF ANIMAL CHARACTERS.
I WAS VERY GLAD BUT AT THE SAME TIME WORRIED ABOUT HOW WELL I'D DO.
I'M VERY HONOURED TO BE INVOLVED IN THIS CLASSIC TITLE, AND WANTED TO DO MY BEST. SINCE SOME OF THE IMPORTANT CHARACTERS IN THE NOVEL ARE TALKING ANIMALS, I FOUND THIS TO BE A BIT OF A CHALLENGE FOR ME WHEN DRAWING.
AFTER MANY DISCUSSION WITH THE PRODUCTION TEAM, WE AGREED ON GETTING A BALANCE OF MAKING THE ANIMAL CHARACTERS MORE CARTOON LIKE BUT NOT TOO UNREALISTIC.
BEFORE WE STARTED DRAWING, CRYSTAL CAREFULLY STUDIED THE NOVEL AND DONE EXTENSIVE RESEARCH IN FINDING PICTURES AND VIDEOS OF ANIMAL'S EXPRESSIONS, MOVEMENTS, AND APPEARANCE.
COMBINING WITH MY EXPERIENCE AND KNOWLEDGE IN ARTWORK WE'VE TRANSLATED THIS ONTO THIS MANGA.
I'M CONFIDENT THAT MY ARTWORK HAS LIVED UP TO THIS TITLE AND READERS OF THIS MANGA CAN SEE THIS THROUGH MY PORTRAYAL OF EACH CHARACTER.
I HOPE EVERYONE WILL ENJOY IT, THANK YOU.

INTEGRATING THE POEMS:

When adapting a work like *The Jungle Book*, it is important to preserve the characteristics of the original. *The Jungle Book* is full of poems - there are long poems after every story and shorter poems sprinkled throughout - and we made sure that they were all not only included, but utilized to play up the manga's visuals.

NOW WE'RE GOING TO—NEVER MIND, BROTHER, THY TAIL HANGS DOWN BEHIND!
ALL THE TALK WE EVER HAVE HEARD UTTERED BY BAT OR BEAST OR BIRD— HIDE OR FIN OR SCALE OR FEATHER— JABBER IT QUICKLY AND ALL TOGETHER! EXCELLENT! WONDERFUL! ONCE AGAIN! NOW WE ARE TALKING JUST LIKE MEN! LET'S PRETEND WE ARE ... NEVER MIND, BROTHER, THY TAIL HANGS DOWN BEHIND! THIS IS THE WAY OF THE MONKEY-KIND.
THEN JOIN OUR LEAPING LINES THAT SCUMFISH THROUGH THE PINES, THAT ROCKET BY WHERE, LIGHT AND HIGH, THE WILD GRAPE SWINGS. BY THE RUBBISH IN OUR WAKE, AND THE NOBLE NOISE WE MAKE, BE SURE, BE SURE, WE'RE GOING TO DO SOME SPLENDID THINGS!

The original version of the story "*Kaa's Hunting*" is followed by the poem "*The Road-Song of the Bandar-log*", in which the Bandar-log brag at length about how great and strong they are. For the manga version, I moved the poem into the story itself and had the Bandar-log sing it while Mowgli was their captive, so that Mowgli and the reader discover the true nature of the Bandar-log at the same time! It became the story's 'theme song'.

BOOK 6: TOOMAI OF THE ELEPHANTS
I WILL REMEMBER WHAT I WAS. I AM SICK OF ROPE AND CHAIN — I WILL REMEMBER MY OLD STRENGTH AND ALL MY FOREST AFFAIRS. I WILL NOT SELL MY BACK TO MAN FOR A BUNDLE OF SUGAR-CANE: I WILL GO OUT TO MY OWN KIND, AND THE WOOD-FOLK IN THEIR LAIRS.
I WILL GO OUT UNTIL THE DAY, UNTIL THE MORNING BREAK — OUT TO THE WIND'S UNTAINTED KISS, THE WATER'S CLEAN CARESS: I WILL FORGET MY ANKLE-RING AND SNAP MY PICKET STAKE. I WILL REVISIT MY LOST LOVES, AND PLAYMATES MASTERLESS!
KALA NAG, WHICH MEANS BLACK SNAKE, HAD SERVED THE INDIAN GOVERNMENT IN EVERY WAY THAT AN ELEPHANT COULD SERVE IT FOR FORTY-SEVEN YEARS.
AS HE WAS FULLY TWENTY YEARS OLD WHEN HE WAS CAUGHT, THAT MAKES HIM NEARLY SEVENTY--A RIPE AGE FOR AN ELEPHANT.
HIS MOTHER HAD TAUGH HIM NOT TO FEAR, SO HE WAS A POWERFUL FIGHTER AND THE BEST-LOVED ELEPHANT IN THE GOVERNMENT'S SERVICE.
KALA NAG
GARO HILLS INDIA
ELEPHANT-TRAPPING EXPEDITION

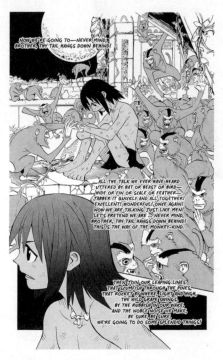

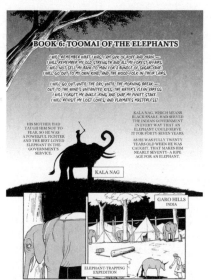

For the most part, I left the shorter poems where they were. In "*Toomai of the Elephants*", both the original story and the manga version lead off with Kala Nag's poem, while the second poem "*Shiv and the Grasshopper*" turns up midway through as a lullaby sung by Toomai's mother. Neither of these poems required more than a page, but the artist and I still had to make sure that there was enough space reserved for them before he started drawing.

Continues on Page 3...

CRYSTAL S. CHAN:
ADAPTING THE JUNGLE BOOK

Unlike the other books in the *Manga Classics* line – and unlike most other works of classic literature - *The Jungle Book* takes place entirely in the world of animals. Moreover, *The Jungle Book* is not a single story but several, only loosely related to one another. Adapting the unusual theme and format of *The Jungle Book* to manga was its own special challenge, and it required me to make some unusual adjustments to the script.

THE BALANCING ACT:

The Jungle Book consists of seven stories, many of which are related to each other only in the sense that they are about animals (although, admittedly, there are three stories about Mowgli). When it came time to decide how many pages I wanted to give to each story, I could have divided the page count equally. Instead, I chose to make four of the stories longer than the others. Is that because those stories had more complex plots? Yes, but that isn't the only reason!

I wanted to be faithful to the original book, but I also wanted to produce an interesting adaptation that everyone could enjoy. To do this, I chose to emphasize the four stories that I felt would really resonate with the readers.

In *"Kaa's Hunting"*, Baloo the sloth bear and Bagheera the black panther are like nothing so much as the parents of a slightly rebellious child. Baloo is the strict parent, while Bagheera is inclined to be more lenient; parents and children alike will be able to identify with this story.

In *"Tiger! Tiger!"*, Mowgli faces discrimination and rejection at the hands of other humans. Even so, he is able to see that not all humans are terrible and he acts accordingly, treating his foster mother kindly and obeying the village rules. His good behavior in the face of adversity is a wonderfully positive message that I was happy to bring to the readers.

In *"The White Seal"*, Kotick the seal wants to find a safe home for the others of his kind, where humans can no longer harm them. No matter how many times he fails, or how many times the other seals mock him, Kotick refuses to give up. Instead, he perseveres until he achieves his goal. We would all do well to learn from such spirit!

In *"Rikki-Tikki-Tavi"*, the child Teddy and his parents rescue the dying mongoose, nursing him back to health and then adopting him into the family. This act of selfless kindness is so beautiful that I wanted to share it with everyone – even if every rescued animal may not repay its new family in such a dramatic fashion!

Also, in the original version of *"Kaa's Hunting"*, we are told why the Bandar-log want to kidnap Mowgli before they do it. On the other hand, for this adaptation I decided to hold off on this revelation until Mowgli had already been kidnapped, in order to keep the readers glued to the page with worry!

NAMES IN THE SCRIPT:

Usually, in a manga script, the characters are referred to by name, but this time I did it differently. Why? I wanted to help the artist visualize the scenes, so I decided to refer to the animal characters only by their species. In my original script for the first thre stories, only Mowgli was ever referred to by name. Baloo became 'the sloth bear', Bagheera became 'the black panther', and so on. This made things easier for the artist, since he could immediately 'see' the characters whenever he drew them rather than having to stop and remember which was which.

Of course, this did not work with *"The White Seal"*, since almost all the characters are seals!

RIKKI-TIKKI AND MY CAT:

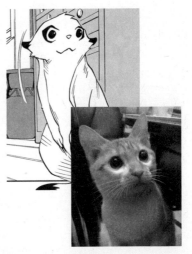

Shortly before I began work on *"Rikki-Tikki-Tavi"*, I found a stray kitten. She was obviously weak and had fleas, but I decided to adopt her anyway. When Teddy and his family saved and adopted the dying mongoose, I couldn't help but feel the similarities. I drew upon many of my experiences with my new cat when writing the script – when Teddy first gave Rikki-Tikki food, when Rikki-Tikki first sniffed at the faces of his new human family – and it really helped me to understand the situation. The resulting story was a lot better thanks to my cat!

I hope you enjoy this version of *The Jungle Book* and find the animal characters to be as lively and interesting as humans. Even though we may not be able to understand the animals like Mowgli does, we can still love them like Teddy does.

If you'd like to share your thoughts with me, please email me at CRYSTAL@MANGACLASSICS.COM

Crystal (Silvermoon) Chan

...Continued from Page 2

THE VISUAL LANGUAGE OF MANGA:

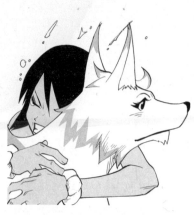

Manga is primarily a visual medium. One of its strengths is the ability to show emotion without needing to use a single word. For example, the original text tells us (in words) that the bond between Mowgli and his wolf foster mother is very strong. When I worked on the adaptation, I wanted every drawing to clearly show their love for one another. In "*Tiger! Tiger!*", when Mowgli and his foster mother see each other after a very long time, I tried to imagine what a similar reunion between a human mother and her child would be like, and then I added the scene where Mowgli jumps forward to hug his mother. Thanks to the manga format, I was able to show their joy and devotion without needing to use a single word.

DESCRIPTIONS OR FORESHADOWING:

Reading *The Jungle Book* is like listening to a storyteller relate to us a tale of events that happened long ago. Reading this manga adaptation is more like watching the events of the story as they happen. I chose to change some of the stories' details in order to make the manga version both subtler and more exciting.

For example, in the original version of "*Mowgli's Brothers*", we are told right away that the 'red flower' Mowgli is going to the village to retrieve is actually fire, a terrifying force that will give him a very human advantage over the animals. For this adaptation, I chose instead to conceal the flame in the pot until the climactic moment. Accordingly, the reader has no idea if this 'red flower' is something capable of defeating Shere Khan - it made the scene much more tense to keep the reader uncertain about whether or not Mowgli will be triumphant.

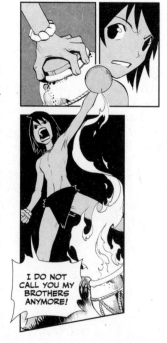

I DO NOT CALL YOU MY BROTHERS ANYMORE!

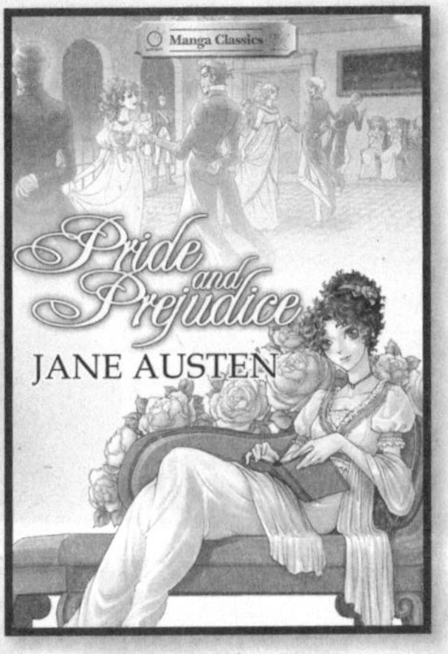
Manga Classics
Pride and Prejudice
JANE AUSTEN

Manga Classics:
Pride and Prejudice
Hard Cover $24.99
ISBN #978-1-927925-17-1
Soft Cover $17.99
ISBN #978-1-927-925-18-8

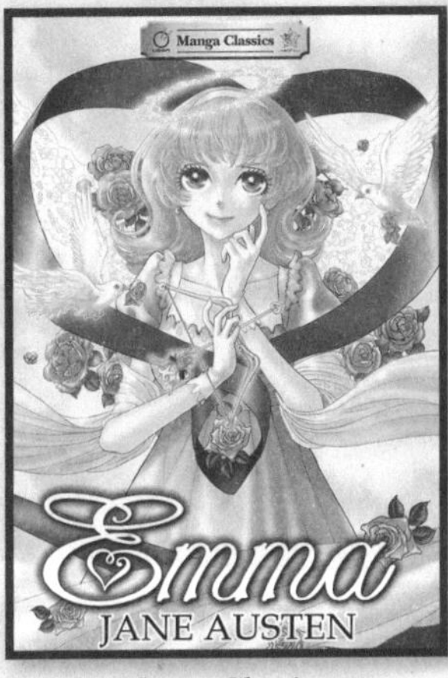
Manga Classics
Emma
JANE AUSTEN

Manga Classics:
Emma
Hard Cover $24.99
ISBN #978-1-927925-36-2
Soft Cover $17.99
ISBN #978-1-927-925-35-5

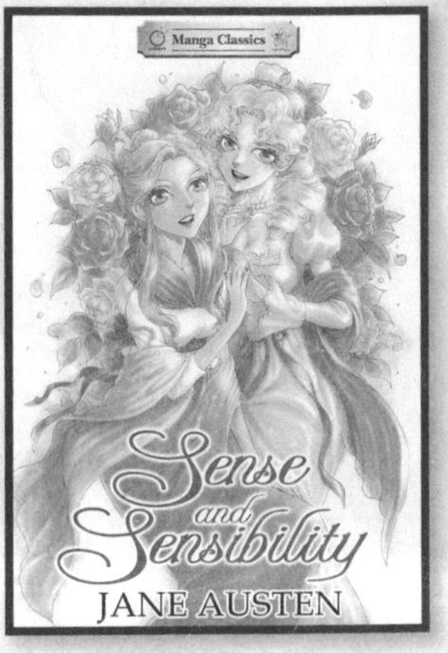
Manga Classics
Sense and Sensibility
JANE AUSTEN

Manga Classics:
Sense and Sensibility
Hard Cover $24.99
ISBN #978-1-927925-62-1
Soft Cover $17.99
ISBN #978-1-927925-63-8

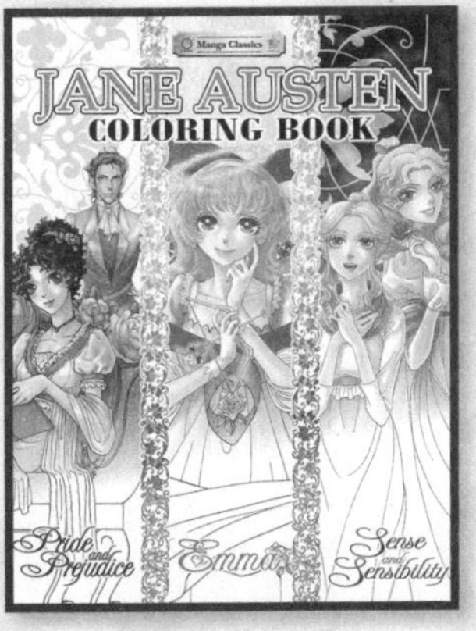
Manga Classics
JANE AUSTEN
COLORING BOOK
Pride and Prejudice
Emma
Sense and Sensibility

Manga Classics:
Jane Austen Coloring Book
Soft Cover $12.99
ISBN #978-1-927925-78-2

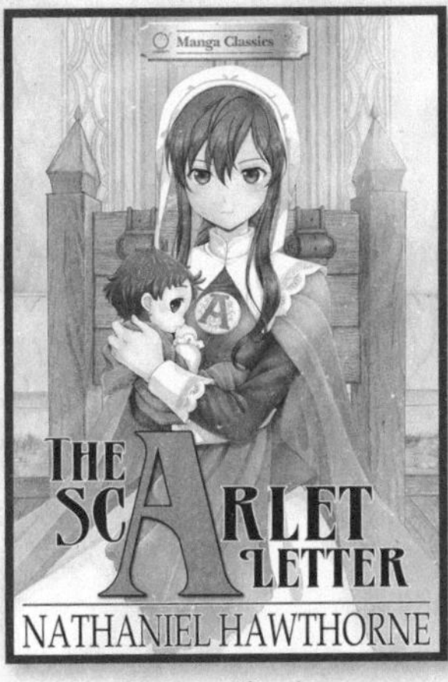
Manga Classics
THE SCARLET LETTER
NATHANIEL HAWTHORNE

Manga Classics:
The Scarlet Letter
Hard Cover $24.99
ISBN #978-1-927925-34-8
Soft Cover $17.99
ISBN #978-1-927925-33-1

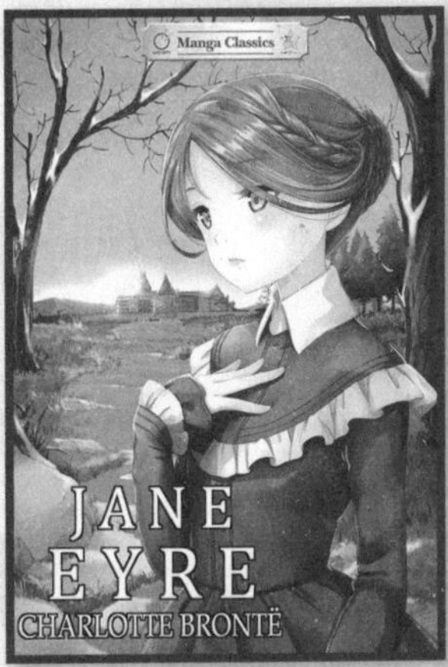
Manga Classics
JANE EYRE
CHARLOTTE BRONTË

Manga Classics:
Jane Eyre
Hard Cover $24.99
ISBN #978-1-927925-64-5
Soft Cover $17.99
ISBN #978-1-9279256-5-2

Check out more MANGA CLASSICS titles !!

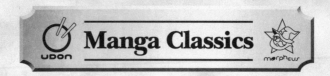

Manga Classics

UDON Entertainment proudly presents: Manga Classics - the finest name in adaptations of beloved classic literature!

UDON is proud to bring you this very special new line of books, adapting classic literature with the same quality and attention to detail as our fantastic graphic novels, art books, and manga releases! UDON's Manga Classics line is the result of an ambitious international partnership with Asian comics and animation studio Morpheus, the aim of which is to bring the highest-quality adaptations of these works to the North American market!

UDON and Morpheus have worked tirelessly to fully realize the rich worlds of these classic works of literature. The artists have extensively researched the settings of these timeless novels in order to give the costumes and architecture a very real sense of weight and accuracy, expertly executed thanks to the studio's animation background. This high-quality work has been coupled with a generous page count of over 300 pages per book, more than double the average comics-format adaptation! This allows for more thorough, accurate, and natural adaptations of the source material, with the artists' vision given as much space as needed to be properly realized. In short, UDON's Manga Classics look and read like great commercial manga while also being faithful adaptations of literary classics!

Intended for a young adult audience, Manga Classics are just as likely to be enjoyed in the reader's free time as in the classroom. The gripping stories and lush artwork easily place them alongside today's best-selling popular manga, with strong and accurate adaptations that are sure to please even the toughest teacher or librarian! UDON's Manga Classics are also the perfect way for adult readers to rediscover their favorite classics - or experience them for the first time!

Now that you have read *The Jungle Book*, look for UDON's Manga Classics adaptations of other classic literature in stores!

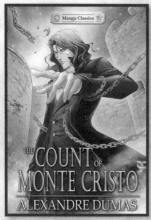

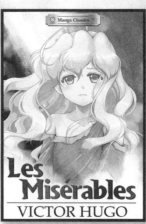

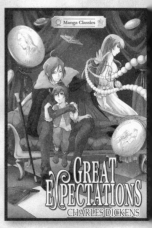

Manga Classics
THE COUNT OF MONTE CRISTO
ALEXANDRE DUMAS

Manga Classics:
The Count of Monte Cristo
Hard Cover $24.99
ISBN #978-1-927925-60-7
Soft Cover $17.99
ISBN #978-1-927925-61-4

Manga Classics
Les Misérables
VICTOR HUGO

Manga Classics:
Les Miserables
Hard Cover $24.99
ISBN #978-1-927925-15-7
Soft Cover $17.99
ISBN #978-1-927925-16-4

Manga Classics
GREAT EXPECTATIONS
CHARLES DICKENS

Manga Classics:
Great Expectations
Hard Cover $24.99
ISBN #978-1-927925-32-4
Soft Cover $17.99
ISBN #978-1-927925-31-7

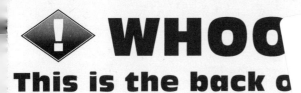 

WHOO

This is the back o

UDON's Manga Classics books follow the Ja___ ___ (___ Manga!) reading order. Traditional manga is read in a ___versed" format starting on the right and heading towards the left. The story begins where English readers expect to find the last page because the spine of the book is on the opposite side. Flip to the other end of the book and start reading your Manga Classics!

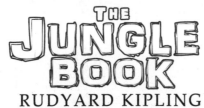

THE JUNGLE BOOK

RUDYARD KIPLING

Art by: Julien Choy
Story Adaptation by: Crystal S. Chan
Lettering: Morpheus Studios
Lettering Assist: Jeannie Lee

UDON STAFF:

UDON Chief: Erik Ko
Manga Classics Group Editor: Stacy King
Senior Editor: Ash Paulsen
Associate Editor: M. Chandler
VP of Sales: John Shableski
Senior Producer: Long Vo
Marketing Manager: Jenny Myung
Production Manager: Janice Leung
Copy Editing Assistant: Michelle Lee
Japanese Liaison: Steven Cummings

MORPHEUS STAFF:

Morpheus Chief: Andy Hung
Production Manager: Yuen Him Tai
Art Assistants: Frances
Man Yiu
Touyu
VIP 96neko
Shougo
Ron
Stoon

AGE: YOUNG ADULT 12+
BISAC CAT: YAF010010 YAF01000 YAF009000 NOVELS/Manga/General
SUBJECT CATEGORIES: Comics, Graphic Novels, Manga,
India, Juvenile Fiction, Animal-Fiction, Jungle-Fiction

Manga Classics: The Jungle Book. Published by UDON Entertainment Inc. 118 Tower Hill Road, C1, PO Box 20008, Richmond Hill, Ontario, L4K 0K0, Canada. Any similarities to persons living or dead are purely coincidental. No portion of this publication may be used or reproduced by any means (digital or print) without written permission from UDON Entertainment Inc. and Morpheus Publishing Limited except for review purposes. All artwork © UDON Entertainment Inc. and Morpheus Publishing Limited. **Printed in Canada**

First Printing April 2017
HARD COVER EDITION ISBN # 978-1-772940-18-3   PAPERBACK EDITION ISBN # 978-1-772940-19-0

www.mangaclassics.com

An UDON Entertainment Production, in association with Morpheus Publishing Limited.
www.udonentertainment.com   www.morpheuspublishing.com